Africa Yearbook

Africa Yearbook

*Politics, Economy and Society South
of the Sahara in 2020*

VOLUME 17

Edited by

Albert Awedoba
Benedikt Kamski
Andreas Mehler
David Sebudubudu

BRILL

LEIDEN | BOSTON

The Library of Congress Cataloging-in-Publication Data is available online at https://catalog.loc.gov
LC record available at https://lccn.loc.gov/2006265660

Typeface for the Latin, Greek, and Cyrillic scripts: "Brill". See and download: brill.com/brill-typeface.

ISSN 1871-2525
ISBN 978-90-04-46025-6 (paperback)
ISBN 978-90-04-50318-2 (e-book)

Copyright 2022 by Koninklijke Brill NV, Leiden, The Netherlands.
Koninklijke Brill NV incorporates the imprints Brill, Brill Nijhoff, Brill Hotei, Brill Schöningh, Brill Fink, Brill mentis, Vandenhoeck & Ruprecht, Böhlau Verlag and V&R Unipress.
All rights reserved. No part of this publication may be reproduced, translated, stored in a retrieval system, or transmitted in any form or by any means, electronic, mechanical, photocopying, recording or otherwise, without prior written permission from the publisher. Requests for re-use and/or translations must be addressed to Koninklijke Brill NV via brill.com or copyright.com.

This book is printed on acid-free paper and produced in a sustainable manner.

Contents

Preface   XI
Abbreviations   XIII
Factual Overview (as of 31 December 2020)   XVI
List of Authors   XX

PART 1

Sub-Saharan Africa   3
    Albert Kanlisi Awedoba, Benedikt Kamski, Andreas Mehler,
    and David Sebudubudu

PART 2

African–European Relations in 2020   21
    Benedikt Erforth and Niels Keijzer

PART 3

West Africa   37
    Albert Kanlisi Awedoba

Benin   50
    Pauline Jarroux and Clarisse Tama Bignon

Burkina Faso   59
    Daniel Eizenga

Cabo Verde   68
    Gerhard Seibert

Côte d'Ivoire   74
    Jesper Bjarnesen

The Gambia   83
    Akpojevbe Omasanjuwa

Ghana 91
   Jennifer C. Boylan

Guinea 105
   Joschka Philipps

Guinea-Bissau 114
   Christoph Kohl

Liberia 121
   Ibrahim Al-bakri Nyei

Mali 130
   Bruce Whitehouse

Mauritania 138
   Helen Olsson and Claes Olsson

Niger 145
   Klaas van Walraven

Nigeria 154
   Heinrich Bergstresser

Senegal 172
   Mamadou Bodian

Sierra Leone 183
   Krijn Peters

Togo 190
   Dirk Kohnert

PART 4

Central Africa 201
   Andreas Mehler

Cameroon 210
   Fanny Pigeaud

Central African Republic   220
    Andreas Mehler

Chad   230
    Ketil Fred Hansen

Congo   239
    Brett L. Carter

Democratic Republic of the Congo   246
    Janosch Kullenberg

Equatorial Guinea   261
    Joseph N. Mangarella

Gabon   266
    Douglas Yates

São Tomé and Príncipe   273
    Gerhard Seibert

PART 5

Eastern Africa   281
    Benedikt Kamski

Burundi   295
    Antea Paviotti and Réginas Ndayiragije

Comoros   306
    Simon Massey

Djibouti   313
    Nicole Hirt

Eritrea   319
    Nicole Hirt

Ethiopia   328
    Jon Abbink

Kenya   342
   Njoki Wamai

Rwanda   354
   Erik Plänitz

Seychelles   365
   Anthoni van Nieuwkerk

Somalia   373
   Jon Abbink

South Sudan   383
   Daniel Large

Sudan   392
   Jean-Nicolas Bach and Clément Deshayes

Tanzania   405
   Kurt Hirschler and Rolf Hofmeier

Uganda   420
   Moses Khisa

PART 6

Southern Africa   433
   David Sebudubudu

Angola   440
   Jon Schubert

Botswana   452
   David Sebudubudu and Dithapelo L. Keorapetse

Eswatini   463
   Marisha Ramdeen

Lesotho   469
   Roger Southall

Madagascar   475
    Richard R. Marcus

Malawi   483
    George Dzimbiri and Lewis Dzimbiri

Mauritius   491
    Roukaya Kasenally

Mozambique   497
    Joseph Hanlon

Namibia   508
    Henning Melber

South Africa   517
    Sanusha Naidu

Zambia   534
    Edalina Rodrigues Sanches

Zimbabwe   543
    Amin Y. Kamete

Preface

In May 2003, the Africa-Europe Group of Interdisciplinary Studies (AEGIS) encouraged some of its member institutions to publish an *Africa Yearbook* with a wider international appeal. Following the first edition in 2004, in 2021 the *Yearbook* entered its 17th year of publication supported by the Arnold-Bergstraesser-Institute in Freiburg (ABI), the Institute of African Affairs in Hamburg (IAA), and the Nordic Africa Institute in Uppsala (NAI). Since 2020, the University of Botswana and the University of Ghana have joined this group and contribute to the success of the project.

The readership includes students, politicians, diplomats, administrators, journalists, teachers, businesspeople, and practitioners in the sphere of development cooperation. The annual overviews of events on the continent are based on scholarly work, and the series provides a cumulative record of domestic politics, foreign affairs, and socioeconomic developments in the states of sub-Saharan Africa. Dynamics in the four sub-regions (West, Central, Eastern, and Southern Africa) during the calendar year under review are summarised in overview articles and chapters that describe continental trends and European–African relations (while linkages with China, the Middle East, the US, and others are also prominently featuring in different contributions).

Naturally, one major focus of the country-specific articles in this year's volume is the impacts of the Covid-19 pandemic – its effects on governance, democratisation, and livelihoods. The public health crisis of 2020 is an unprecedented watershed moment for sustainable development on the continent. We took this as an opportunity to slightly adapt the general approach of the overview chapter on developments in sub-Saharan Africa. While keeping the summarising nature of the country chapters, we have started placing greater emphasis on trends and outlooks in the overview chapter.

In November 2012, the *Yearbook* received the prestigious biennial Conover-Porter Award for outstanding Africa-related reference works from the African Studies Association and the Africana Librarians Council in the USA. Nine years down the road, we are proud to add another year to recording African affairs in what we believe is a solid scholarly contribution towards a better understanding of and more knowledge about SSA countries. Since 2016, Brill has regularly published country-focused chronologies as a compilation of past *Yearbook* chapters – in 2020 on the Central African Republic – which testify to the value of information accumulated over time.

We would like to express our gratitude to all the contributors for dedicating time and effort to the production of the *Yearbook*, especially during these difficult times when many are faced with unusual professional and private challenges. Moreover, the continued commitment to the project of Brill Publishers and the dedicated assistance of Bas van der Mije deserve special mention. The continuous support and encouragement of the partner institutions in AEGIS and universities on the continent is an important driving force behind this yearly endeavour.

The Editors
Accra, Addis Ababa, Freiburg, and Gaborone, July 2021

Abbreviations

ACP	African, Caribbean, and Pacific Group of Countries (Lomé/Cotonou Agreement)
AfCFTA	African Continental Free Trade Area
AfDB	African Development Bank (Tunis)
AGOA	African Growth and Opportunity Act
AI	Amnesty International
APRM	African Peer Review Mechanism
AU	African Union (Addis Ababa)
BCEAO	Banque Centrale des Etats de l'Afrique de l'Ouest (Dakar)
BEAC	Banque des Etats de l'Afrique Centrale (Yaoundé)
CAR	Central African Republic
CBLT	Commission du Bassin du Lac Tchad (N'Djaména)
CEEAC	Communauté Economique des Etats de l'Afrique Centrale (Libreville)= ECCAS
CEMAC	Communauté Economique et Monétaire de l'Afrique Centrale
CEN-SAD	Community of Sahel-Saharan States (Tripoli)
CFAfr	Franc de la Communauté Financière Africaine (BCEAO; BEAC)
COMESA	Common Market for Eastern and Southern Africa (Lusaka)
CPI	consumer price index
CPLP	Comunidade dos Países de Língua Portuguesa
CSO	civil society organisation
DRC	Democratic Republic of the Congo
EAC	East African Community
ECA	Economic Commission for Africa (United Nations; Addis Ababa)
ECCAS	Economic Community of Central African States (Libreville)
ECF	Extended Credit Facility (IMF)
ECOWAS	Economic Community of West African States (Abuja)
EDF	European Development Fund (Brussels)
EIB	European Investment Bank (Luxemburg)
EITI	Extractive Industries Transparency Initiative
EIU	Economist Intelligence Unit
EPA	Economic Partnership Agreement
EU	European Union (Brussels)
FAO	Food and Agricultural Organisation (Rome)
FDI	foreign direct investment
FOCAC	Forum on China-Africa Cooperation
FTA	free-trade area
GDP	Gross Domestic Product

HDI	Human Development Index (UNDP)
HRW	Human Rights Watch
ICC	International Criminal Court
ICGLR	International Conference on the Great Lakes Region
ICJ	International Court of Justice
ICT	information and communications technology
IDA	International Development Association (Washington)
IDP	internally displaced person
IFC	International Finance Corporation (Washington)
IGAD	Intergovernmental Authority on Development (Djibouti)
ILO	International Labour Organisation (Geneva)
IMF	International Monetary Fund (Washington)
IOC	Indian Ocean Commission (Quatre Bornes)
IOM	International Organization for Migration
LNG	liquified natural gas
MoU	memorandum of understanding
NEPAD	New Partnership for Africa's Development
NGO	non-governmental organisation
OAU	Organization of African Unity
OCHA	United Nations Office for the Coordination of Humanitarian Affairs
ODA	official development assistance
OECD	Organisation for Economic Cooperation and Development (Paris)
OIF	L'Organisation Internationale de la Francophonie
OPEC	Organisation of Petroleum Exporting Countries (Vienna)
PPP	Purchasing Power Parity
SACU	Southern African Customs Union (Pretoria)
SADC	Southern African Development Community (Gaborone)
SSA	sub-Saharan Africa
TI	Transparency International
UAE	United Arab Emirates
UEMOA	Union Économique et Monétaire Ouest-Africaine (Ouagadougou)
UN	United Nations (New York)
UNDP	United Nations Development Programme (New York)
UNESCO	United Nations Educational, Scientific and Cultural Organisation (Paris)
UNGA	United Nations General Assembly
UNHCR	United Nations High Commissioner for Refugees (Geneva)
UNHRC	United Nations Human Rights Council
UNICEF	United Nations Children's Fund (New York)
UNSC	United Nations Security Council
UNSG	United Nations secretary general
US	United States

ABBREVIATIONS

USAID	United States Agency for International Development (Washington)
WEF	World Economic Forum
WFP	World Food Programme (Rome)
WHO	World Health Organisation (Geneva)
WTO	World Trade Organisation (Geneva)

Factual Overview (as of 31 December 2020)

West Africa

Country	Area (in sq km)	Population (in m)[a]	Currency	HDI (2020)[b]	Head of State	Prime Minister
Benin	112,622	12,2	CFA Franc	0.545	Patrice Talon	
Burkina Faso	274,122	20.9	CFA Franc	0.452	Roch Marc Christian Kaboré	Christophe Joseph Marie Dabiré
Cape Verde	4,033	0.6	Cape Verdean Escudo	0.665	Jorge Carlos Fonseca	Ulisses Correia e Silva
Côte d'Ivoire	322,462	26,2	CFA Franc	0.538	Alassane Ouattara	Hamed Bakayoko
Gambia	11,295	2.4	Dalasi	0.496	Adama Barrow	
Ghana	238,500	31,1	Cedi	0.611	Nana Akufo-Addo	
Guinea	245,857	12.6	Guinean Franc	0.477	Alpha Condé	Ibrahim Kassory Fofana
Guinea-Bissau	36,125	1.9	CFA Franc	0.480	Umaro Sissoco Embaló	Nuno Gomes Nabiam
Liberia	111,370	5,1	Liberian Dollar	0.480	George Weah	
Mali	1,240,000	20,3	CFA Franc	0.434	Bah N'Daw (on an interim basis)	Moctar Ouane (on an interim basis)
Mauritania	1,030,700	4.6	Ouguiya	0.546	Mohamed Ould Gazouani	Mohamed Ould Bilal
Niger	1,267,000	24,2	CFA Franc	0.394	Mahamadou Issoufou	Brigi Rafini
Nigeria	923,768	206,1	Naira	0.539	Muhammadu Buhari	
Senegal	197,162	16.7	CFA Franc	0.512	Macky Sall	
Sierra Leone	71,740	8	Leone	0.452	Julius Maada Bio	David John Francis
Togo	56,785	8.3	CFA Franc	0.515	Faure Essozimna Gnassingbé	Victoire Tomegah Dogbe

a (Population figures are for mid-2020, according to Stiftung Weltbevölkerung, www.weltbevölkerung.de)
b (Latest data according to UNDP: http://hdr.undp.org/sites/default/files/hdr2020.pdf)

FACTUAL OVERVIEW (AS OF 31 DECEMBER 2020)

Central Africa

Country	Area (in sq km)	Population (in m)	Currency	HDI	Head of State	Prime Minister
Cameroon	475,442	26,6	CFA Franc BEAC	0.563	Paul Biya	Joseph Dion Ngute
Central African Republic	622,984	4.8	CFA Franc BEAC	0.397	Faustin Archange-Touadéra	Firmin Ngrébada
Chad	1,284,000	16.9	CFA Franc BEAC	0.398	Idriss Déby Itno	
Congo	342,000	5.5	CFA Franc BEAC	0.574	Denis Sassou-Nguesso	Clément Mouamba
DR Congo	2,344,855	89,6	Congolese Franc	0.480	Félix Tchisekedi	Sylvestre Ilunga Ilunkamba
Equatorial Guinea	28,051	1.4	CFA Franc BEAC	0.592	Teodoro Obiang Nguema Mbasogo	Francisco Pascual Obama Asue
Gabon	267,667	2.2	CFA Franc BEAC	0.703	Ali Bongo Ondimba	Rose Christiane Ossouka Raponda
São Tomé and Príncipe	1,001	0.2	Dobra	0.625	Evaristo Carvalho	Jorge Lopes Bom Jesus

Eastern Africa

Country	Area (in sq km)	Population (in m)	Currency	HDI	Head of State	Prime Minister
Burundi	26,338	11.9	Burundi Franc	0.433	Évariste Ndayishimiye	Alain Guillaume Bunyoni
Comoros	1.862	0.9	Comoran Franc	0.554	Azali Assoumani	
Djibouti	23,200	1.0	Djiboutian Franc	0.524	Ismail Omar Guelleh	Abdoulkader Kamil Mohamed
Eritrea	124,320	3.5	Nakfa	0.459	Isaias Afewerki	
Ethiopia	1,121,900	114,9	Birr	0.485	Sahle-Work Zewde	Abiy Ahmed Ali
Kenya	569,259	53,5	Kenya Shilling	0.601	Uhuru Kenyatta	
Rwanda	26,338	13	Rwanda Franc	0.543	Paul Kagame	Édouard Ngirente
Seychelles	455	0.1	Seychelles Rupee	0.796	Wavel Ramkalawan	
Somalia (Somaliland)	637,600 137,600	15.9 n.a.	Somali Shilling Somaliland Shilling	n.a. n.a.	Mohamed Abdullahi Mohamed Musa Bihi Abdi	Mohamed Hussein Roble
Sudan	2,505,805	43,8	Sudanese Pound	0.510	Abdel Fattah al-Burhan Abdulrahman (chair of the Sovereignty Council)	Abdalla Handouk
South Sudan	619,745	11.2	South Sudanese Pound	0.433	Salva Kiir Mayardit	
Tanzania	945,087	59,7	Tanzania Shilling	0.529	John Magufuli	Kassim Majaliwa
Uganda	197,000	45,7	Uganda Shilling	0.544	Yoweri Kaguta Museveni	Ruhakana Rugunda

FACTUAL OVERVIEW (AS OF 31 DECEMBER 2020)

Southern Africa

Country	Area (in sq km)	Population (in m)	Currency	HDI	Head of State	Prime Minister
Angola	1,246,700	32,5	Kwanza	0.581	João Manuel Gonçalves Lourenço	
Botswana	581,730	2.3	Pula	0.735	Mokgweetsi Masisi	
Lesotho	30,344	2.1	Lesotho Loti	0.527	King Letsie III	Moeketsi Majoro
Madagascar	592,000	27.7	Malagasy Ariary	0.528	Andry Nirina Rajoelina	Christian Louis Ntsay
Malawi	118,484	19,1	Malawian Kwacha	0.483	Lazarus Chakwera	
Mauritius	2,040	1.3	Mauritian Rupee	0.804	Prithvirajsing Roopun	Pravind Kumar Jugnauth
Mozambique	799,380	31,2	Mozambiquen Métical	0.456	Filipe Nyusi	Carlos Agostinho do Rosário
Namibia	824,269	2.5	Namibian Dollar	0.646	Hage Gottfried Geingob	Saara Kuugongelwa-Amadhila
South Africa	1,219,090	59.6	Rand	0.709	Matamela Cyril Ramaphosa	
Eswatini/ Swaziland	17,364	1.1	Swazi Lilangeni	0.611	King Mswati III	Ambrose Mandvulo Dlamini
Zambia	752,614	18,4	Zambian Kwacha	0.584	Edgar Lungu	
Zimbabwe	390,580	14.9	Zimbabwean Dollar	0.571	Emmerson Dambudzo Mnangagwa	

List of Authors

Jon Abbink
Professor of Politics and Governance in Africa, African Studies Centre, Leiden University, g.j.abbink@asc.leidenuniv.nl

Albert Awedoba
Professor at the Institute of African Studies, University of Ghana and fellow of the Ghana Academy of Arts and Sciences, akawedoba@ug.edu.gh

Jean-Nicolas Bach
PhD in Political Science, independent researcher, jeannicolas.bach@netsanetresearch.org

Heinrich Bergstresser
Media Consultant, Freelance Research Associate of the Institute of African Affairs in Hamburg and Freelance Trainer of Akademie für Internationale Zusammenarbeit (AIZ) within Deutsche Gesellschaft für Internationale Zusammenarbeit GIZ, Germany, heinrich.bergstresser@web.de

Jesper Bjarnesen
Senior Researcher, The Nordic Africa Institute, Uppsala, Sweden, jesper.bjarnesen@nai.uu.se

Mamadou Bodian
PhD in political science, project coordinator at the West Africa Research Centre (WARC), Dakar, Senegal, papexb@gmail.com.

Jennifer C. Boylan
PhD (2016) in Political Science, Managing Editor, Perspectives on Politics, jboylan@apsanet.org

Brett Logan Carter
Assistant Professor, Department of Political Science and International Relations, University of Southern California, blcarter@usc.edu

Clément Deshayes
PhD in Anthropology, Department of Sociology and Anthropology, University Paris 8 Saint Denis, associate researcher at LAVUE and CEDEJ-Khartoum, deshayes.clement@gmail.com

LIST OF AUTHORS

Dr George Lewis Dzimbiri
Lecturer in HRM & Public administration, Malawi University of Business and Applied Sciences, gdzimbiri@poly.ac.mw

Lewis Dzimbiri
Professor of Public Administration, Deputy Vice Chancellor at Lilongwe University of Agriculture and Natural Resources, Malawi, proflewisdzimbiri@gmail.com

Daniel Eizenga
PhD in Political Science, Research Fellow with the Africa Center for Strategic Studies, Washington D.C., daniel.j.eizenga.civ@ndu.edu

Benedikt Erforth (PhD)
Senior Researcher, German Development Institute / Deutsches Institut für Entwicklungspolitik (DIE), Bonn, Germany, benedikt.erforth@die-gdi.de

Joseph Hanlon
Visiting Senior Fellow, Department of International Development, London School of Economics, UK, and Visiting Senior Research Fellow at the Development Policy and Practice Centre of the Open University, UK, j.hanlon@open.ac.uk

Ketil Fred Hansen
PhD in African History, Professor in Social Sciences, University of Stavanger, Norway, ketil.f.hansen@uis.no

Kurt Hirschler
Freelance Political Scientist, Hamburg, Germany, kurt_hirschler@web.de

Nicole Hirt
PhD in Political Science, Research Fellow, Institute of African Affairs, GIGA German Institute of Global and Area Studies, Hamburg, Germany, nicole.hirt@giga-hamburg.de

Rolf Hofmeier
Former Director, Institute of African Affairs, GIGA German Institute of Global and Area Studies, Hamburg, Germany, gr.hofmeier@gmx.de

Pauline Jarroux
PhD in social anthropology, post-doctoral fellow at the Institut des Sciences Sociales du Politique, University of Paris-Nanterre, France, pauline.jarroux@gmail.com

Amin Kamete
Senior Lecturer, Urban Studies, School of Social and Political Sciences, University of Glasgow, Scotland, UK, amini.kamete@glasgow.ac.uk

Benedikt Kamski
PhD in Political Science, senior researcher at the Arnold Bergstraesser Institute, benedikt.kamski@abi.uni-freiburg.de

Roukaya Kasenally
Associate Professor of Media and Political Systems, Department of Social Studies, University of Mauritius and CEO of the African Media Initiative, roukaya@uom.ac.mu

Niels Keijzer
PhD, Senior researcher, German Development Institute / Deutsches Institut für Entwicklungspolitik (DIE), Bonn, Germany, niels.keijzer@die-gdi.de

Dithapelo L. Keorapetse
Member of Parliament of Botswana and former Lecturer in the Department of Political and Administrative Studies, University of Botswana, dkeorapetse@gov.bw

Moses Khisa
Assistant Professor of Political Science and Africana Studies, School of Public and International Affairs, North Carolina State University, USA, and Research Associate at the Centre for Basic Research, Kampala. Also columnist for the Daily Monitor newspaper, Kampala, Uganda, mkhisa@ncsu.edu

Christoph Kohl
Independent researcher, Halle (Saale), Germany, christoph_a_kohl@hotmail.com

Dirk Kohnert
Retired Deputy Director, Institute of African Affairs, GIGA German Institute of Global and Area Studies, Hamburg, Germany, Dirk-k-iak@WEB.de

Janosch Kullenberg
PhD Fellow, Bremen International Graduate School of Social Sciences (BIGSSS), Germany, and Post-Doctoral Researcher at Durham University, UK, janosch.kullenberg@oxon.org

Daniel Large
Associate Professor at the School of Public Policy, Central European University, and Fellow of the Rift Valley Institute, larged@spp.ceu.edu

LIST OF AUTHORS

Joseph N. Mangarella
Guest Researcher, African Studies Centre, Leiden, The Netherlands, joseph.mangarella@gmail.com

Richard R. Marcus
Professor and Director, The Global Studies Institute and the International Studies Program, California State University, Long Beach, USA, richard.marcus@csulb.edu

Simon Massey
Senior Lecturer and Post-Graduate Course Director in the School of Humanities, Coventry University, s.massey@coventry.ac.uk

Andreas Mehler
Director of the Arnold Bergstraesser Institute and Professor of Political Science at the University of Freiburg, andreas.mehler@abi.uni-freiburg.de

Henning Melber
Senior Research Associate of The Nordic Africa Institute and Director emeritus of The Dag Hammarskjöld Foundation, both in Uppsala, Sweden, Henning.Melber@nai.uu.se

Sanusha Naidu
Senior Research Associate, Institute for Global Dialogue, sanusha.naidu@gmail.com

Réginas Ndayiragije
Teaching Assistant and PhD candidate, IOB – Institute of Development Policy, University of Antwerp, Reginas.Ndayiragije@uantwerpen.be

Ibrahim Al-bakri Nyei
PhD in Politics and International Studies; Researcher on the Political Economy, Department of Economics, London Business School. His research areas include decentralisation, local politics, governance and democracy, institutional analysis, and political economy. pericle925@yahoo.com

Helena Olsson
Political Scientist and Staff Member at the Department of Sociology, Uppsala University, Sweden, helena.olsson@soc.uu.se

Claes Olsson
Political Scientist and Editor at Global Publications Foundation, Uppsala, Sweden, claesolsson@globalpublications.org

Akpojevbe Omasanjuwa
Geography Lecturer, University of the Gambia, West Africa, masapele@yahoo.com

Antea Paviotti
FWO PhD fellow, IOB – Institute of Development Policy, University of Antwerp, Belgium, antea.paviotti@uantwerpen.be

Krijn Peters
Associate Professor in Armed Conflict & Post-war Reconstruction, Department of Political & Cultural Studies, Swansea University, UK, k.peters@swansea.ac.uk

Joschka Philipps
Junior Research Group Leader, Africa Multiple Cluster of Excellence, University of Bayreuth, joschka.philipps@uni-bayreuth.de

Fanny Pigeaud
Journalist, France, fanny.pigeaud@gmail.com

Erik Plänitz
PhD. Associated Senior Researcher, Arnold-Bergstraesser-Institut Freiburg, erik.plaenitz@abi.uni-freiburg.de

Marisha Ramdeen
Senior Programme Officer at the African Centre for the Constructive Resolution of Disputes (ACCORD) in Durban, South Africa, Marisha@accord.org.za

Edalina Rodrigues Sanches
Assistant Professor in African Studies at the Department of Political Science and Public Policy and Researcher at the Centre for International Studies at ISCTE-IUL, edalina_sanches@iscte-iul.pt

Jon Schubert
Academic Staff Member, Working Group "Social and Political Anthropology," Dept. of History and Sociology, University of Konstanz, jon.schubert@uni-konstanz.de

David Sebudubudu
Professor of Political Science and Dean of the Faculty of Social Sciences, University of Botswana, sebudubudu@ub.ac.bw

LIST OF AUTHORS

Gerhard Seibert
Research Associate, Center for International Studies (CEI), ISCTE-Instituto Universitário de Lisboa, Portugal, jonschubert@gmx.net

Roger Southall
Emeritus Professor in Sociology at the University of the Witwatersrand, Johannesburg, and Professorial Research Associate in Politics, SOAS, South Africa, Roger.Southall@wits.ac.za

Clarisse Bignon Tama
Lecturer in Anthropology of Education, Head of department in charge of relations with universities and national organizations, University of Parakou, Benin, clartama@yahoo.fr.

Anthoni van Nieuwkerk
PhD in International Relations. Associate Professor and Coordinator of Security Studies at the Wits School of Governance, Johannesburg, South Africa, Anthoni.vannieuwkerk@wits.ac.za

Klaas van Walraven
Researcher, African Studies Centre, Leiden, The Netherlands, walraven@ascleiden.nl

Njoki Wamai
Assistant Professor of Politics and International Relations at the International Relations Department at the United States International University-Africa in Nairobi, Kenya, nwamai@usiu.ac.ke

Bruce Whitehouse
Associate Professor of Anthropology, Lehigh University, USA, bruce.whitehouse@lehigh.edu

Douglas Yates
Professor of Political Science at the American Graduate School in Paris, France, douglas.yates@ags.edu

PART 1

Sub-Saharan Africa

Albert Kanlisi Awedoba, Benedikt Kamski, Andreas Mehler, and David Sebudubudu

Trends

The continent remained dangerously exposed to the *Covid-19* pandemic at the end of the year. While the scale of the first infectious waves during 2020 was relatively low compared with the level of exposure seen, for instance, in Brazil or India, sub-Saharan Africa is likely to experience longer and more severe repercussions. We expect that it will take a comparatively longer time to get the pandemic fully under control in Africa. A lack of crucial data across most sub-regions and limited testing capacities combined with low vaccination rates will determine the return to normality. Hesitant policies and denialism in relation to the health crisis, as well as abusive government approaches, on the other side of the spectrum, could spark a protracted crisis on the continent. In this context, the immediate pandemic-induced effects on African economies will last longer than in Europe.

The closure of borders between African countries in spring and summer 2020 naturally affected intra-continental migration patterns. The number of Africans migrating decreased. Once travel protocols and other policies restricting the movement of people are lifted, this trend will also be reversed. Out-migration (mostly to Europe) will remain constant, responding on the one hand to continuous push factors, but on the other also to reduced labour opportunities and related remittances within Europe.

The slow degradation of democratic standards is likely to continue generally, but results of and reactions to some upcoming elections in key countries will have a strong signalling effects, e.g. in Angola and Sudan in 2022. Constitutional referenda and elections ending a transition like in Mali may have also decisive effects beyond national borders.

The fatigue with peacekeeping missions not only in the West but at the UN more generally will lead to a steady downward trend in deployed troop numbers in big missions. We also expect the chances of new UN missions getting started to be low, even in cases of evident humanitarian emergency as in Ethiopia/Tigray. This in turn means that it will be the AU and regional economic communities that will either take the initiative or decide to remain passive in such cases.

Africa's post-Covid recovery plans present the opportunity to transform economic growth models, foster regional integration, and increase the functionality of markets. The pandemic year 2020 could be an accelerator for digitalisation, increased trade, and diversification. The now operational *African Continental Free*

Trade Area (AfCFTA) provides a blueprint for the expansion of intra-African trade and the empowerment of the private sector. However, the pandemic has also illustrated that the continent needs to strengthen institutions to decrease reliance on outside actors.

Significantly, 2020 has also seen strong public engagement by intellectuals and civil society groups to showcase the long-term effects of colonisation (including racism), not least in former colonial metropoles and slave states – linked to the *Black Lives Matter movement*. We now expect more concrete approaches to adjust memory politics both within Africa and in Europe and the USA. This could translate into tangible successes in the restitution of African cultural objects to the continent. While immediate reparations are less likely, the ongoing debate could also trigger intense discussions as to who is entitled to receive such objects and participate in the decision-making processes, and may even induce confrontations between national policies and local expectations.

Africa in the World Economy

The Covid-19 pandemic was an unprecedented stress test for the economies of sub-Saharan Africa. Interrupted trade flows and value chains, combined with a reduced influx of forex, revealed the vulnerabilities of commodity-driven and debt-investment growth models. Especially affected was the GDP growth of nations that depend on tourism revenues (−11.5%) followed by that of resource intensive (−4.7%) and oil-exporting (−1.5%) economies, according to AfDB data. Average growth across SSA contracted by an estimated 1.9–2.0% and the number of people living in extreme poverty increased by more than 32 m. Significantly, World Bank data illustrate that growth in Southern and Eastern Africa declined by approximately −3.0%, compared with West and Central Africa (combined), where the contraction was only 1.1%. Decreasing economic output was further affected by the need to increasing expenditure on mostly underfunded and already vulnerable health systems across the continent in order to fight the health crisis.

The continent's response to manage the health crisis was slowed down by corruption. Transparency International found that high levels of corruption correlated with delayed and less-effective measures during the first year of the pandemic. Little improvement in the average score of SSA on *TI's Corruption Perceptions Index* can therefore be reported. Seychelles ranked unchanged (27th out of 179 countries in 2020), followed by Botswana, which dropped by one rank to 35th compared with 2019, and Cabo Verde (41st). These top performers could again not disguise the fact that SSA is overall the lowest-scoring region globally; Sudan and Equatorial Guinea scored 16 (out of 100) and ranked slightly better (joint 174th) than Somalia and

South Sudan (joint 179th), which are among the lowest-ranked nations, scoring just 12 points where 0 is 'highly corrupt' and 100 'very clean'.

Just like anywhere else in the world, public debt accelerated significantly due to sky-rocketing public expenditures and the global economic downturn. AfDB's Africa Economic Outlook 2021 estimated that SSA saw a doubling of fiscal deficits, reaching 8.4% of GDP. At the end of the year, the economic effects of the pandemic were already more severe than the 2008–09 financial crisis and the 2014 slump in crude oil prices. Seen in a more positive light, the year also brought an unexpected opportunity for nations in debt distress. In light of massive budget constraints and considerably decreased fiscal revenue following the near standstill of the world economy, the IMF's response to the pandemic was unprecedented. In 2020, the support provided in emergency financing to the continent, grants for debt relief, and other lending mechanisms increased 13-fold compared with the annual average lending rate between 2010 and 2020, mainly through the *IMF's Rapid Credit Facility* (RCF) and the *Catastrophe Containment and Relief Trust* (CCTR). Yet resources allocated to contain the spread of the virus and safeguard public health paralysed spending in other areas; the result of that will be visible in the years to come. At the end of the reviewing period, 6 countries on the continent were in 'debt distress' and 14 of 38 for which sufficient data were available on debt sustainability faced 'high risk'.

Travel bans and global economic growth contraction resulted in a decline in remittances, albeit by less than initially predicted. The World Bank estimated a decline of 12.5% in 2020 for SSA, mainly the result of a 28% drop in inflows to Nigeria. Significantly, leaving aside Nigeria, overall remittances to SSA actually increased slightly, by 2.3%. Yet the lower inflow of cash-based remittances also had a noticeable impact on parallel markets in countries with tight currency controls. At the same time, digital payment solutions and the fintech sector experienced an unexpected upswing, with increasing international transfers of cryptocurrencies. With Nigeria leading the way, South Africa and Kenya were second and third in SSA in terms of trading volumes of cryptocurrencies in 2020. Automated teller machines (ATM) for selling and buying Bitcoin, the oldest and most widely known cryptocurrency, can be found in eight African countries, including Ghana, Zimbabwe, Botswana, Uganda, and Djibouti.

The pandemic fast-tracked important milestones for the digital transformation of several sectors on the continent, first and foremost the health sector. However, the 'Network Readiness Report' published by the Portulans Institute (until 2019 by the World Economic Forum) noted that overall access to and usage of ICT continues to be imbalanced between the sub-regions and compared with the rest of the world. While only Mauritius ranked in the upper half (61st out of 134 countries) on the *Network Readiness Index* (NRI) for 2020, the next-best performers were South

Africa (76th) and Kenya (82nd), with the DRC (133rd) and Chad (134th) at the bottom of the ranking. Overall internet penetration in SSA remains low despite notable growth among mobile users in particular. In 2020, MTN and Vodacom in South Africa were the only operators in SSA providing 5G networks in selected cities. The number of mobile internet users is expected to grow from 272 m in 2019 to 475 m in 2025, of which one-third will be in Nigeria and Ethiopia, according to GSMA, a global lobby organisation for mobile network operators.

Following global trends, Jumia, Africa's largest e-commerce platform, based in Nigeria, reportedly increased its customer base to 6.8 m users – illustrating also a change in consumer habits among mainly urban buyers. Yet in many countries, e-commerce remained limited due to weak mobile payment systems and poor delivery infrastructure. Major investments in ICT infrastructure and cross-boundary payment options will be crucial for broader digitalisation and intra-regional trade.

In this regard, positive news came from the *AU's Programme for Infrastructure Development in Africa* (PIDA), which entered the transition from its first priority action plan (PIDA PAP-1), which supported the implementation of over 400 projects on the continent, to PAP-2, the second phase scheduled to run from 2021 to 2030. PIDA is the common continental strategic framework for regional infrastructure development under the *AU's Agenda 2063*. The planning and implementation of cross-border infrastructure projects is complex and involves various actors. The *AU Development Agency* (AUDA-NEPAD) plays a central role in coordinating the different steps of the project preparation cycle. However, the pandemic diminished the available resources of the organisation due to unpaid contributions of member states. PIDA PAP-2 will focus on the promotion of an *Integrated Corridor Approach* (ICA). Amani Abou-Zeid, AUC commissioner for infrastructure and energy, stressed the importance of climate-resilient infrastructure and digitalisation, including employment-oriented and gender-sensitive aspects, in the planning and implementation of PAP-2.

Trading under the AfCFTA, a flagship project of the AU's Agenda 2063, was delayed by six month and scheduled to start on 1 January 2021. Hopes remain high that the quick ratification process of the AfCFTA could soon boost a single continental market. However, negotiations to adopt the protocols under Phase II, covering competition policy, investment, and intellectual property rights, were still ongoing, as were those on the expected e-commerce protocol under Phase III. Despite impressive sustained political momentum, the implementation of the AfCFTA remains full of complex challenges. At the national level, countries need to build the necessary capacity to reduce regulations on the importing and exporting of goods and find ways to efficiently coordinate transboundary bureaucratic procedures. It will be a long process before a preferential trade arrangement such as the AfCFTA can deliver its full benefits. One crucial factor for success will be the timely and coordinated development of transport and logistics infrastructure.

Infrastructure financing remained a central challenge. The main creditors to African governments, China Development Bank and China Exim Bank, are likely to further align financing commitments to the strategic pillars of the *Belt and Road Initiative* (BRI). The next *Forum on China–Africa Cooperation* (FOCAC), scheduled to take place in 2021, could be an indicator for post-pandemic investments. However, budget restrictions and lost revenue in 2020 could also increase foreign takeovers of distressed companies, especially in the oil and mining sectors. Both China and Russia increased their economic foothold on the continent during the year. For instance, following the first-ever Russia–Africa summit in 2019, Russian state-owned companies Rosatom (nuclear industry), Rosneft (energy and mining), and Rosoboronexport (defence industry) signed MoUs and cooperation agreements in several countries. Africa became one of Russia's foreign policy priorities, and the new US Strategy for Africa announced in 2018 by the Trump administration was aimed at countering not only China, especially its BRI, but also Moscow's growing influence on the continent. Russia successfully launched new security relationships and investment deals with countries across all sub-regions. The ongoing power competition between China and the United States will continue to shape US Africa policy under incoming president Joe Biden. With an end to the 'America First' foreign policy, China and Russia could indeed play a central role in shaping future trajectories of US–Africa relations. As a strategic response to the BRI, the Trump administration launched the 'Prosper Africa' plan in November 2020 to accelerate trade and investment. In the future, US support for the AfCFTA is likely to increase, given the expiration of the African Growth and Opportunity Act in 2025. The AfCFTA could then become a central game-changer, first and foremost for intra-African trade dynamics but equally for global trade relations. However, the path to market liberalisation and the removal of trade barriers remains relatively far from reality.

The AU and the APRM

The theme of the year was 'Silencing the Guns'. Adopted in 2016 as part of the Lusaka Road Map, the AU's objective was to end conflicts on the continent, prevent genocide, and ensure peace and security in Africa by 2020. However, the global public health emergency tied up considerable financial and human resources and delayed several initiatives of Agenda 2063.

The year started off in the usual fashion with the meeting of the African heads of state and government in February in Addis Ababa. During the *33rd ordinary summit of the AU*, South Africa took over the AU chairship from Egypt. The ambitious priorities laid out by President Cyril Ramaphosa – resolving conflicts in the spirit of the annual theme and supporting economic integration through the operationalisation of the AfCFTA – were quickly pushed into the background with the rapid spread of confirmed Covid-19 cases across the continent. Nevertheless, the AU made great strides to live up to its purpose and eventually stood at the forefront of continental efforts to fight the Covid-19 pandemic through its *Africa Centres for Disease Control and Prevention* (Africa CDC) and *Africa Task Force for Coronavirus* (AFTCOR). The so-called AU Bureau, representing all sub-regions of the continent, also became a more political entity in addition to its mainly administrative tasks. Strategies for future economic recovery plans and rapid responses to the health crisis dominated the agenda, and the establishment of the *African Vaccine Acquisition Task Team* (AVATT) and the *African Medical Supplies Platform* are evidence of that. Special envoys appointed by the AU played a central role in negotiating debt relief and financial assistance for AU member states. In March, the AUC, led by chairperson Moussa Faki Mahamat, established the '*AU Covid-19 Response Fund*'.

While in absolute numbers of infections Africa was still an outlier at the end of the year and reported fatalities lower than anticipated, economic recovery will require a continental approach to get back to pre-pandemic growth trajectories. Indispensable for this is a well-functioning and adequately funded union. However, the AU's quest for more budgetary self-sufficiency and less dependency on donor contributions stalled in 2020. The 2020 budget, adopted during an extraordinary summit in July 2019 in Niger, was $ 30 m less than in 2019, with $ 157.2 m allocated for the AU's operational expenses, $ 216.9 m for programme implementation, and $ 273.1 m for peace support operations. Contributions by AU member states continued to be a point of contestation, in terms of both the commitment and the amount paid by individual states. A disproportionate number of states were in arrears with their payments, due on 1 January, affecting both the total budget and the operating budget, with the latter fully funded by member states.

The AU took strong action against South Sudan and suspended the country in June for defaulting on contributions for more than two years. Mali was suspended from all activities of the AU following a military coup in August, but sanctions were lifted in October by the *AU Peace and Security Council* (PSC). The AU responded swiftly to the overthrow of President Ibrahim Boubacar Keïta and stepped up its diplomatic game with the appointment of three special envoys to Ethiopia tasked with supporting mediation to end the military actions in its northern Tigray Region. Yet the call by the AU for dialogue was met with critique from Ethiopia, which stressed its national sovereignty and principles of non-interference. On a more promising note, the AU assumed a key role in 2020 in the tripartite negotiations between Ethiopia, Sudan, and Egypt after unsuccessful previous efforts spearheaded by the US government and the World Bank were aborted. African-led arbitration under the slogan 'African solutions to Africa's problems' helped to de-escalate tensions over the *Grand Ethiopian Renaissance Dam* (GERD), albeit only briefly. Ethiopia started the first filling of the reservoir in June without a legally binding agreement and consensus over downstream water allocation. A looming border dispute between Sudan and Ethiopia in al-Fashaga further accentuated the situation between Khartoum and Addis Ababa. Notably, the PSC still lacks a strategy for transboundary water dispute resolution, although this would be in the interest of many of its members. The 2015 legal framework accepted by all parties governs negotiations. However, the positions of upstream Ethiopia and downstream Egypt remain entrenched. The enduring deadlock over the river use and Ethiopia's determination to go ahead without legally binding agreements have already led to a reconfiguration of political dynamics in the Blue Nile Basin. Significantly, the *League of Arab States* (Arab League) sided with its members Egypt and Sudan in June 2020, calling upon Ethiopia to honour the 2015 Declaration of Principles.

AU ministers of foreign affairs elected ten new countries to sit on the 15-member PSC in February. Egypt; Cameroon and Chad; Malawi and Mozambique; and Ghana, Benin, and Senegal were nominated for the opening seats for northern (two seats), central (three seats), southern (three seats), and western (four seats) Africa respectively. For East Africa, four candidates, Sudan, Ethiopia, Djibouti, and Somalia, entered the race for two opening seats. Somalia has never been a member of the PSC since it became operational in 2004; the country withdrew from the election at the last minute, paving the way for Djibouti's re-election together with Ethiopia after Sudan received the fewest votes in the third round.

The continent was not spared from new conflicts and crises requiring mediation and eventually intervention. With the upcoming elections in Somalia in sight, the deployment of the *AU Mission in Somalia* (AMISOM) was extended until 2021 in May. The 2019 AU-mediated peace agreement in the Central African Republic suffered a set-back with the outbreak of fighting in the run-up to the December presidential and parliamentary polls. In Sudan, the AU could build on visible achievements with troops still present in the joint AU-UN mission in Darfur, including the 2020 *Juba Peace Agreement* in October 2020, yet much more support is needed to guarantee a peaceful transition. Intercommunal violence peaked in the Sahel and the AU opted for military action in support of the G5 Sahel Joint Forces, including AU-member states Niger, Burkina Faso, Chad, Mauritania, and coup-ridden Mali. The Anglophone crisis in Cameroon and the Cabo Delgado province of Mozambique are additional trouble spots likely to make it onto the PSC's agenda soon.

At the end of the year, preparations for the upcoming selection of a new AUC were already underway. Moussa Faki, AUC chairperson since 2017, announced that he would stand for re-election for another four-year term (2021–24). No other candidate entered the race for the elections, scheduled to take place during the 34th Ordinary Session of the assembly in February 2021. One result of the AU institutional reform process adopted in 2018 was the merger of the economic affairs and infrastructure and energy departments, as well as a new department combining political affairs and peace and security. This will reduce the number of future commissioners standing for elections to six. Moreover, the new principles of gender parity and equal representation of all regions in the new AUC leadership clearly shaped the nomination list of candidates for deputy chairperson, as no other candidate declared an intention to contest the incumbent. Faki's leadership style is not undisputed and he has been the subject of allegations of cronyism brought forward by the AU Staff Association in March. Allegations of corruption and nepotism within the AU overshadow the uncontested race despite visible achievements in the reform process.

The accession of Zimbabwe and the Seychelles to the APRM during the *29th Summit of the African Peer Review Forum of Heads of State and Government* in February increased the number of AU member countries to 40. In 2020, the APRM focused mainly on the responses of member states to the pandemic and health governance. For instance, a targeted review took place in Sierra Leone in November. Nigeria also announced its readiness to undergo a second peer review, while Kenya started disseminating the results of its second country review to the counties. A Government Experience Exchange Programme, jointly implemented by the APRM, UNDP, and the government of UAE, was announced during the virtual Africa Futures Forum in December.

The APRM, a specialised AU agency since 2003, went through a challenging year. The leadership of the APRM, including Edward Maloka, director-general of the secretariat based in Johannesburg, South Africa, and the APRM's director of corporate services, Mamathimolane Makara, faced serious accusations of corruption and bad governance in a letter written by an employee. Corruption was described as an endemic problem of the organisation. For an organisation designed to improve peer learning in the field of governance, this could seriously damage legitimacy. While an AU commission of inquiry and internal investigations are an important sign and illustrate the seriousness of the claims made, the handling of this affair will likely set the tone for other ongoing investigations on alleged mismanagement and nepotism within the African Union. All this comes at a time when the APRM faces enormous challenges in light of the unprecedented magnitude of governance responses required to address the public health crisis and socioeconomic effects of the pandemic. In June, the APRM presented its preliminary findings on Africa's governance response to Covid-19, including recommendations for the AU member states for post-pandemic recovery. In this regard, the *African Risk Capacity (ARC) Agency* is regarded as a central entity for better preparedness and continental disaster risk management capacities, yet thus far only 34 AU member states have signed the ARC Establishment Treaty.

Democracy and Elections

Despite the promises democracy holds for the citizenry, the sustenance of it has continued to elude many countries. Varying indices attested to a bleak future for democracy.

The *2020 World Press Freedom Index* reported that press freedom in SSA continued to be particularly frail, and that the future of journalism in Africa was 'under threat from all sides'. Most countries in SSA fared badly in terms of the Index. Benin and Tanzania were among those that experienced a major decline in terms of the 2020 Index (based on 2019 data) as they resorted to legislative hurdles to present a challenging environment for journalists.

In terms of the *2020 EIU Democracy Index*, democracy was evidently retarded owing to the stringent regulations introduced across countries to contain the Covid-19 pandemic, with close to 70% of 167 countries assessed recording a decrease in their aggregate score during the year. The democracy deficit was quite apparent in SSA. Most countries in the region occupied the lower end of the index, and SSA's score declined from 4.26 in 2019 to 4.16 (on a 0–10 scale) in 2020. Out of 44 countries reviewed in SSA, Mauritius was the only one that sustained its classification as a 'full democracy', 6, 13, and 24 countries were regarded as 'flawed', 'hybrid regimes', and 'authoritarian regimes', respectively. Mauritius secured an overall score of 8.14, a global rank of 20th, and a regional rank of 1st, while the DRC had a score of 1.13 and a global and regional rank of 166th and 44th, respectively. It was also noted that stringent measures to curb the spread of Covid-19 contributed to a low score for the region, as they disrupted the enjoyment of civil liberties. In some countries, these gave rise to their non-observance, sparking protests. In other countries, it was evident that Covid-19 responses were being used to silence the opposition. The index suggests that the majority of people in SSA live under an authoritarian regime.

The *2021 Freedom House* report suggested that overall the state of democracy in 2020 continued to deteriorate around the world, for the 15th year in a row, especially in 'struggling democracies and authoritarian states'. The Covid-19 pandemic aided and provided impetus towards the deterioration of democracy, as countries applied stringent rules and regulations meant to control the pandemic, with adverse implications for freedoms. The report cautioned that 'as a lethal pandemic, economic and physical insecurity, and violent conflict ravaged the world in 2020, democracy's defenders sustained heavy new losses in their struggle against authoritarian foes, shifting the international balance in favour of tyranny. Incumbent leaders increasingly used force to crush opponents and settle scores, sometimes in the name of public health, while beleaguered activists – lacking effective international support – faced heavy jail sentences, torture, or murder in many settings.' This presents a dim picture of the state of democracy in the world.

In SSA, only 16% of the 49 countries assessed in 2020 were regarded as 'free', while 43% and 41% were considered 'partly free' and 'not free', respectively. Malawi and Sudan were among the few that registered an improvement, while Burkina Faso, Cameroon, Central African Republic, Côte d'Ivoire, Ethiopia, Guinea, Mali, Mozambique, Rwanda, and Tanzania were among those that evidently deteriorated, with violation of freedoms registered, according to Freedom House.

Despite the Covid-19 pandemic, elections were held in a number of countries in SSA, albeit under imperfect conditions because most of those that held elections were either considered 'hybrid regimes' or 'authoritarian regimes' by the EIU Democracy Index in 2020. Burkina Faso, Burundi, CAR, Côte d'Ivoire, Ghana, Guinea, Malawi, Niger, Seychelles, Tanzania, and Togo held presidential elections while Chad, Mali, Cameroon, Comoros, and Liberia conducted parliamentary elections. Some countries held both presidential and parliamentary elections while others decided to defer them. In almost all these countries, elections attracted controversy.

Malawi was able to offer a fully different scenario. With election results from 2019 annulled by the Constitutional Court a re-run was necessary that was won by opposition candidate Lazarus Chakwera defeating incumbent Peter Mutharika by a margin of 59% to 40%. This was the single most important event representing democratic progress on the continent. Still, election results also showed a regionally split country, with the Southern region of the country behind Mutharika, Central and Northern backing Chakwera.

Seychelles was the other positive story, with opposition candidate Wavel Ramkalawan winning over incumbent Danny Faure with close to 55% of the votes. This was the first peaceful transfer of power via elections in the island republic. Faure attended Ramkalawan's victory speech in which the latter professed reconciliation.

Unconstitutional Rule: Coups or Constitutional Crisis

Mali's military coup removed the country's elected civilian leadership and was the clearest case of unconstitutional rule, leading to a temporary suspension of the country from the AU. The coup on 18 August began as a mutiny and was preceded by popular protests against the president and the government. Subsequently, high-ranking officials including President Keïta (popularly known by his initials IBK) and Prime Minister Boubou Cissé were arrested, and IBK declared that he was stepping down and dissolving the government. In the night, five senior officers took to the media and made it clear that this was a full coup (the last had occurred in 2012). In September, the junta agreed to limit a transitional period to 18 months. They installed a government of technocrats. The coup was unanimously condemned by the AU, UNSC, and ECOWAS. Mali was sanctioned by ECOWAS and excluded from the OIF. The coup clearly complicated the search for legitimacy not only of state authorities, but also for several military missions in the country.

Guinea was potentially another case in point, where president Alpha Condé (82 years old), standing a third time, was credited with winning close to 60% of the vote in the first round. This was made possible only by a prior controversial referendum that abolished a two-term limit. Guinea was therefore a further example of the 'third term debate' in which incumbents manipulated the political game to cling to power. This was particularly ironic given the past of Condé as long-term opponent of autocracy in the 1990s. Main challenger Cellou Diallo had declared himself the winner based on early results and after the announcement of Condé's win called for protest action, in which at least 12 people were killed. No less controversial was the re-election of Alassane Ouattara (78 years old) in *Côte d'Ivoire* with an incredible score of 95% of the votes. Ouattara had originally imposed Prime Minister Amadou Gon Coulibaly as the candidate of the ruling party. When Coulibaly died on 8 July, the president reversed his repeatedly announced conviction that he would stand only for two terms by referring to the fact that the current constitution had been in force only since 2016 and hence would allow him to stand again. At least 30 people died preceding the elections and all competitors pressed for a government of transition afterwards. As in the case of Guinea, it is relevant to recall the past of Ouattara as a long-term opponent who more than once accused his predecessors of being 'badly elected'. In his own case, he had acceded to power after a coup in 2011 meant to correct official election results confirmed by a constitutional court at the mercy of then president Laurent Gbagbo. Ouattara definitely did not look any more republican-spirited than Gbagbo.

Armed Conflict; Peace and Security

The topography of *violent conflict* in 2020 looked mostly familiar, but one new serious confrontation with growing numbers of casualties started in November, with armed conflict between the federal government of Ethiopia and the regional government led by the *Tigray People's Liberation Front* (TPLF) of the northern regional state of Tigray. This war had its origins in old rivalries between components within the ruling party, which itself was an outgrowth of a rebel alliance. The TPLF had refused to join a new united government party earlier and conducted regional elections in September despite the federal government's decision to postpone regional and general polls. Ethiopia's premier Abiy Ahmed Ali had received the Nobel Peace Prize back in 2019 for manufacturing a peace agreement with archenemy Eritrea. This in turn had raised suspicions among Tigrayan elites that had been in a dominant position prior to Abiy's rise to power. Narratives diverge as to what triggered full escalation, but the humanitarian disaster was plain to see. What has been labelled a 'law enforcement operation' by the federal administration quickly became extremely costly; in one early massacre, 600 civilians were killed. An internationalisation of the conflict looks possible as the Eritrean army took part in military operations of the Ethiopian national defence forces and the TPLF shelled Eritrea's capital Asmara on 14 November. Eritrean armed forces were accused of atrocities in an alleged massacre in Axum a little later, as they took the opportunity to control now vast stretches of land in the east (as did Amhara militias in the western part of Tigray). The UAE also intervened on the government side by providing drones from their military bases in Assab (Eritrea). The battle of Mekelle (26–28 November), in Tigray's regional capital, looked at first like a decisive blow to the Tigray Defense Forces, troops loyal to the TPLF, which lost its stronghold, but fighters regrouped in the mountainous area. More than 1 m people were internally displaced at year's end, with about 50,000 having fled to Sudan. Relations between Sudan and Ethiopia, already tense, soured further when four Sudanese soldiers were killed at the joint border.

While the AU and IGAD were immediately active in starting mediation initiatives, the wider international community looked helpless with the Ethiopian government reluctant to agree on any form of outside interference. Addis Ababa vehemently declined mediation attempts, arguing that the conflict was an 'internal affair'.

Nor were new major international missions launched in Cabo Delgado (Mozambique), where Islamist militias continued their attacks, resulting in more than 500,000 IDPs, or in the western part of Cameroon, where about 1,500 people were killed, mostly civilians. It appeared as if the era of big UN missions was over, with both troop-sending nations and receiving countries hesitant to engage in new and apparently endless adventures. At face value, 'strong' states were also (over-)confident of winning over their contestants.

Still, seven out of thirteen UN peace operations were conducted in Africa, and four of them were also the major ones, namely in Mali, DRC, CAR, and South Sudan, followed by the one in Abyey (Sudan) and a quite small mission in Western Sahara. The hybrid UN-AU mission UNAMID in Darfur (Sudan) was formally ended on 31 December. A UNSC resolution justifying the termination of the mission stressed the commitment of the government of Sudan 'to assume full responsibility for the protection of its civilian citizens, [and] to comply strictly with all international standards for the protection of civilians, including proactive monitoring and anticipation, increased army and judicial police deployment, and community protection'. The drawdown of the mission was expected to end by July 2021.

An end to the mission was far out of sight in CAR. With a new episode of full civil war starting in December in close connection with general elections held on 27 December (first round), the services of the *Mission des Nations Unies en RCA* (MINUSCA) were in high demand, while not exempt from criticism. The 13,200-strong mission (uniformed personnel) had failed to make substantial progress in disarming rebel forces and therefore also in protecting civilians. The refugee and IDP figures (690,000 and 729,000 respectively) were telling enough. Potentially of even greater importance is that the peace agreement of 2019 was not worth the paper it was written on. Individual signatories to the agreement openly violated it frequently during the year, and at year's end, a new rebel coalition was formed. Realistic options for ending the cycle of peace negotiations and violations of agreements – though never openly discussed – could include federation or separation in two, three, or four entities – though this would admittedly also come with armed struggles for dominance in those territories.

In neighbouring DRC, what was once the largest UN mission, *MONUSCO*, was further reduced to 14,900 personnel. The decentralised conflict with confrontations in many provinces, often on small scale but never fully managed, meant that the mission could only operate by isolating hotbeds of violence from each other and from cross-border dynamics (from Uganda, Rwanda, and Burundi), allowing the creation of one 'island of peace' after the other. With over 6,000 casualties, DRC was this year again far from a peaceful place. Some 948,000 refugees in neighbouring countries and a mind-blowing 5.2 m IDPs were officially registered.

The *UN mission in South Sudan* (UNMISS) came close in size to MONUSCO, with some 14,200 armed personnel. Some progress was recorded on the peace process. Indeed, 2020 saw the formation of a transitional government under the aegis of President Salva Kiir with his arch-rival Riek Machar as first vice-president. This process should culminate in elections in 2022, but still over 2200 people lost their lives in violent encounters in 2020.

The MINUSMA mission in Mali (13,700 strong) also looked indispensable to guarantee some sort of stability in this Sahelian country. However, increasingly the intervention of the UN, but also related operations from within the region by the G5 Sahel Joint Forces (Chad, Niger, Mali, Mauritania) working in close cooperation with the French Operation Barkhane and the EU, were scrutinised for their ineffectiveness at combating what was called terrorism in the Sahel. The mission received a serious set-back when the Malian army launched a coup in August.

MINUSMA had no role in Burkina Faso, where nearly as many casualties were counted (more than 2,200 in comparison with about 2,700 in Mali). The entire Sahelian region from Mali in the west to Lake Chad was embroiled in a combination of conflicts that had religious, political, and economic underpinnings in diverse local configurations. By pure numbers, the confrontations between the Nigerian government and the Boko Haram insurgency were among the most significant, claiming over 7,000 lives. Northern Cameroon and Chad were not exempt from the consequences of this confrontation.

The AU continued to sponsor *AMISOM*, the largest peacekeeping mission in Africa, though reducing to some 19,000 personnel. The UNSC extended the mission for a final period of nine months in May, with a clear request for improved security in preparation for national elections; a gradual hand-over to Somali forces by 2021 was planned. Still, over 2,000 people were killed and the confrontation in neighbouring Ethiopia, in which the Somali government was reportedly implicated, did not augur well.

Epidemics and Disasters

Covid-19 blighted the world in 2020; in terms of numbers of infected and deaths, Africa fared relatively better than other regions. The relatively low infection rates raised initial optimism that Africa would weather the Covid-19 storm, but by year's end the pandemic had wrought havoc on economies and lives. The triple disasters of floods, locusts, and Covid-19 afflicted some parts of Africa more than others. Devastating rains and the attendant floods and landslides with humanitarian consequences added to the pandemic calamities.

South Africa seemed the worst hit by the Covid pandemic, while some countries exhibited a cavalier attitude. By 14 February, Covid-19 had arrived in Africa, with Egypt reporting the first case, and Nigeria followed suit by the end of the month. Within three months, the virus had spread throughout the continent. Lesotho, which had until then remained Covid-free, reported a case on 13 May. By 26 May, most African countries were experiencing community transmission, despite evidence of under-reporting. New strains of the virus were found in December in South Africa and Nigeria, including the Lineage B.1.1.7 variant reported in the UK in September. By year's end, South Africa had hit a million cases and nearly 29,000 deaths.

On 18 November, the WHO finally declared the *Ebola outbreak*, which had lingered on from 2018, over. That was 42 days after the DRC Ministry of Health had declared the 11th outbreak of Ebola in the country on 1 June, following four deaths in Equateur Province between 18 May and 30 May. Additional cases were confirmed in western DRC.

This year has been labelled 'a year of record climate disasters in Africa'. The *UN OCHA* estimated that millions were affected by floods across East, West, and Central Africa, thus precipitating a humanitarian crisis. Heavy rains and massive flooding and landslides were reported between March and May in Rwanda, Kenya, Somalia, Burundi, Ethiopia, Uganda, DRC, Djibouti, and Tanzania. At least 700,000 were affected and deaths reportedly numbered over 430. The *UN's Central Emergency Response Fund* (CERF) allocated over $ 44 m to provide life-saving assistance to those affected by the flooding in eight countries. OCHA reported that about 20% of arable land in Somalia and parts of Sudan was inundated, which usually means that crops would be destroyed. While heavy rains and floods may not be news in Africa, they are getting worse by the year due to climate changes, and the 2020 situation is remarkable for the Covid-19 coincidence.

Overall, the year's *flood victims* numbered, according to OCHA, 1.6 m in Somalia and nearly 1.1 m in Ethiopia. In Kenya, OCHA estimated 350,000 affected. Over 100,000 were displaced and 194 lives were lost, while the Ethiopian rains affected over 200,000 and killed 8. Flooding in Uganda displaced 5,000 and caused 6 deaths. In South Sudan, heavy rains and the flooding of the White Nile spelled disaster for communities in an already impoverished country. Over 600,000 people were displaced (OCHA estimated over 850,000). The floods affected four counties in six states where rivers overflowed their banks and dykes. Jonglei and Lakes were the worst hit. Affected people were left at the mercy of malaria, diarrhoea, and water-borne diseases.

In the case of Sudan, the *floods* were reported to have been even worse than the devastating 1946 and 1988 flood disasters. All but one of the country's 18 states were affected. North Darfur, Sennar, West Ordofan, and Kassala were the worst off; 99 lives were lost, more than 100,000 houses and infrastructural facilities were destroyed, and about 875,000 people were affected. Sudan declared a three-month state of emergency due to the disaster at the end of August. In Sudan, millions were exposed to water- and vector-borne diseases, and by the end of September, over 1.5 m malaria cases had been reported, thus taking malaria to epidemic levels in 15 out of 18 states. Outbreaks of chikungunya and viral haemorrhagic fever were also reported.

Central Burkina Faso (particularly the regions of Centre, including the area of the capital Ouagadougou, and Centre-Nord) experienced severe floods in September. The country declared a nationwide state of emergency on 9 September after days of heavy rains caused floods leading to at least 13 deaths and 19 injured. Affected families sought shelter with relatives and host communities. Burkina Faso's Ministry of Finance allocated CFAfr 5 bn ($ 9.1 m) to assist in rehabilitating flood victims, and the Ministry of Territorial Administration was instructed to house the affected in public buildings.

Other West African countries including Togo, Ivory Coast, Nigeria, and Ghana also experienced flooding throughout August–September. The August rains displaced about 120,000 in Chad – at least 32,000 in N'Djamena alone. Ten lives were lost. Niger reported more than 88,000 flood victims in eight regions – Agadez, Diffa, Dosso, Maradi, Niamey, Tahoua, Tillaberi, and Zinder – with 33 deaths. Over 515,000 Nigériens were affected, according to OCHA.

Forest fires in Africa were becoming more intense and destructive than even those devastating the Amazon rainforest. Satellite imaging using the VIIRS (Visible Infrared Imaging Radiometer Suite) showed fires spreading across Angola and DRC on 25 June. Many of these fires were due to agricultural activities in the farming areas, where slash-and-burn practices persist. Hertzogville, in the Free State province, South Africa, experienced huge fires that destroyed fields and killed several hundred animals. The fire was suspected to have been started when tyres were set alight, possibly by community members protesting about lack of water provision. However, many urban fires due to arson and faulty electrical wiring also caused considerable damage. The Ghana National Fire Service recorded nearly 6,000 fire outbreaks, a 4.9% increase on the 2019 statistic. The Nigerian Zamfara State Fire Service recorded 767 fire outbreaks, the highest in the state's annals. Lagos suffered several outbreaks: Balogun Market was gutted twice, and Mile 12 seemed to suffer a worse fate. Lives were lost and property and livelihoods were affected.

No serious *earthquakes* were reported for Africa in 2020 and none of the ten most serious earth tremor events took place in Africa. However, tremors were reported in Accra, Ghana, and in Kenya and Tanzania. On 13 March, an earthquake measuring 4.9 magnitude struck parts of Tanzania and coastal Kenya. On 12 August, parts of Kenya and Tanzania again experienced earth tremors. Accra experienced three earth tremors occurring in rapid succession on 24 June; no injuries or serious damage to property were reported, but several residents were worried enough to abandon their houses. Worrying activity was reported at Mount Nyiragongo, near Goma, a city close the DRC–Rwanda border. On 13 October, it was reported that the lava lake had risen to dangerous levels and eruption in the immediate future could not be ruled out. The prediction was fulfilled in 2021 with the eruption of 22 May that killed 15 and resulted in more than 200,000 evacuations.

The *desert locust* menace of 2019 did not abate for East Africa and especially the Horn of Africa. An assessment carried out by the Ethiopian government, the FAO, and others estimated that about 1 m Ethiopians would require emergency food assistance due to the desert locust invasion. Overall, impacts on food security could be substantial across East Africa, especially Ethiopia, Somalia, and Kenya, which experienced the worst invasion of locusts in decades. The International Federation of Red Cross and Red Crescent Societies (IFRC) issued an appeal to upscale funding to mitigate the negative impacts on livelihoods in April 2020. Intensified control efforts coordinated by the FAO showed an impact in the first half of the year and led to the reduction of locust populations in some affected areas of East Africa. However, the FAO's 'Desert Locust Bulletin', issued by the Desert Locust Information Service (DLIS), warned in December 2020 that eastern Ethiopia and central Somalia were seeing increased breeding, which led to the development of large numbers of hopper bands. DLIS forecast that northern Kenya could be severely affected by swarms invading from Ethiopia and central Somaliland, a regional threat potential further exacerbated by increased breeding activities along the Red Sea (i.e. Eritrea and Sudan, as well as Saudi Arabia and Yemen).

The *Famine Early Warning Systems Network* (Fews NET) reported severe food shortages resulting from drought in Southern Africa. The year's maize production level was expected to be lower than the average of the last five years.

The *IOM* estimated that more than 414 people died en route from West Africa to the Canary Islands, which represented a more than 100% increase on 2019 cases. On 25 December, Tunisian authorities reported that at least 20 migrants of sub-Saharan origin had died when their boat capsized in the Mediterranean off the coast of Tunisia; six were rescued and at least 20 or more people were missing. Even worse was the late October disaster off Senegalese coasts where a boat about carrying over 200 refugees bound for Europe exploded and sank; 140 lives were lost and 59 were rescued. On the night of 25–26 October, another boat carrying between 60 and 70 sank five kilometres off the coast of Dakar; only 39 people were saved.

PART 2

African–European Relations in 2020

Benedikt Erforth and Niels Keijzer

The year 2020 proved to be a pivotal year for Europe and Africa, but by no means as anticipated. The EU had already built up serious ambitions by prioritising future relations with Africa on the European Council's strategic agenda, and Commission president Ursula von der Leyen confirmed this direction in her political manifesto.

As one of the main priorities for von der Leyen's first 100 days in office, the European Commission published its proposals for the EU's future partnership with Africa on 9 March, two days before the WHO declared the coronavirus outbreak a pandemic and after the first border closures had been introduced within the EU. The Commission tabled its proposals a few days after its annual 'College to College' with the AU Commission on 29 February. While not including a strong emphasis on public health, the agenda, with its five partnership areas, was detailed and sufficiently comprehensive to offer a future cooperation agenda. The EU stuck to it as the year progressed, while the AU did not reciprocate the enthusiasm – a potential spoiler that could only have been overcome by way of organising a formal dialogue.

Yet this dialogue, in preparation for the AU–EU summit scheduled for 28–29 October in Brussels, failed to gain pace and deliver, leading to the postponement of first a preparatory meeting of foreign ministers and subsequently the summit altogether. It appeared that the three-year summit rhythm hindered rather than helped the partnership dialogue.

A similar postponement was deemed not possible in the negotiations for a successor agreement to the Cotonou Agreement between the EU and the ACP states. The Cotonou Agreement has often been heralded as the most ambitious north–south partnership agreement in existence. Its successor's claims to fame may include being the first to be largely agreed using online conferencing websites. A political deal was struck on 3 December, at a time when it became clear that the EU would successfully conclude its Multi-Annual Financial Framework (MFF) for the period 2021–27 – thus securing development assistance resources for cooperation with the ACP states during the same period.

Adding to the end-of-year drama was the last-minute cancellation of an AU–EU leaders' meeting planned for 9 December. The meeting had been convened at the initiative of European Council president Charles Michel and was cancelled the night before at the initiative of the AU Commission, as conveyed in a letter by the chair of the AU and president of the Republic of South Africa Cyril Ramaphosa. The cancelled meeting indicated the difficulty of orchestrating high-level exchanges in the absence of a clear goal and agenda, and the risks that the EU's attempt to take the lead in proposing such an agenda entailed. Towards the end of the year, EU high representative Josep Borrell appeared to recognise that the year had been lost in this regard, declaring that 2021 would become Europe's 'Africa Year'. Africa's half-hearted reactions to the EU's initiatives revealed a certain lethargy in the relations between the two regions. For the EU–Africa partnership to become more appealing, it needs to prioritise function over form.

Covid-19

As news of a new virus started to emerge from the Chinese province of Wuhan, few pundits grasped the magnitude of the crisis that soon would engulf the entire globe. By spring, both the scale of the pandemic and its human, social, and economic toll had become the grim facts of a new reality. After an initial period of paralysis and inward-looking crisis response, the EU and its Member States began to craft a *global response to Covid-19*. In a joint communication drafted by the European Commission and the European External Action Service, the EU called for a 'fast, massive and coordinated global response', which should combine the efforts of all EU institutions, Member States, and financial institutions in order to mobilise 'a critical mass that few others can match'.

This initial declaration was soon to be followed by a publicity-friendly global pledging event and the Coronavirus Global Response Summit. In its relations with partner countries, the EU's response was informed by geopolitical considerations, its normative aspirations and self-understanding as the world's largest development partner, and the acknowledgement that 'as long as Covid-19 exists somewhere in the world, no one is safe'. European leaders began to consider a global response not only as an ethical issue but as a 'question of stability around the world'. Particularly during the early phase of the pandemic, European leaders expected the crisis to 'get out of control very rapidly' and take on catastrophic dimensions in Africa. As we now know, Covid-19 on average had a more important immediate health-related effect on Europe than on Africa. When it became clear that Europe could not avoid exposure to a second wave of the pandemic, the global dimension of the response lost its spot in the limelight of public attention. Discussion of the EU's recovery support to Africa became a more contained debate within the development community.

Some African leaders urged the G20 and the EU to provide debt relief and additional aid packages, such as Ethiopia's Abiy Ahmed in his call for a $ 150 bn *African crisis response*. Others argued that new response mechanisms were needed. These should be built up independently of an EU which itself continued to be shaken by the crisis.

As part of the efforts to halt the spread of Covid-19, the EU and its Member States mobilised over € 38 bn by the end of 2020 under a common framework, called Team Europe. Team Europe had been set up as a rapid reaction to the raging pandemic.

Over the course of the year, it turned into a broader reflection and inspiration for reform of the EU's engagement with the world in general, and with Africa in particular. A substantial part of the allocations under Team Europe resulted from a redirection of existing funds. The largest share of these commitments was allocated to the European Neighbourhood (€ 10.5 bn) and sub-Saharan Africa (€ 6.2 bn). Approximately 50% of the total commitments had been spent by the end of 2020.

The *Africa Centres for Disease Control and Prevention* (CDC) emerged as an early and preferred actor in joint African-European efforts to tackle the crisis. On 7 December, this partnership was formalised when the Africa CDC and the European Centre for Disease Prevention (ECDC) launched a new four-year project 'to strengthen the capacity of Africa CDC to prepare for and respond to public health threats in Africa'.

By the end of 2020, a comparatively small share of Covid-19 cases and fatalities had been registered across the African continent (February 2021 figures showed 3.7 m cases, 99,840 deaths). Some of this was due to lower testing capacities, but mainly it was thanks to African governments implementing swift and strict lockdown policies at an early stage of the pandemic. The fragility of many African health and social security systems, as well as the economic downturn and its severe effects on African exports, are likely to be at the heart of joint recovery efforts in the years to come.

Green and Digital Transition

Despite, or because of, the crisis mode in 2020, the digital and green transformations received additional momentum. On the digital front, the European Commission published communications on 'Shaping Europe's Digital Future' and on a 'European Strategy for Data', a 'White Paper on Artificial Intelligence', a proposal for a European Data Governance Act, and as a last deed before the winter break, a proposal for a Digital Services Act. All transmit the EU's aspirations to global leadership and digitally enabled, sustainable growth.

In her opening statement at the AU–EU Commission to Commission meeting on 27 February, President von der Leyen insisted that the world is facing a dual challenge: climate change and an accelerated digital transformation. The harnessing of these two structural transformations requires a strong partnership between Africans and Europeans.

This new partnership with Africa should be strengthened through various different initiatives that, broadly speaking, fall under the *Digital 4 Development framework* (D4D) label, which emerged in 2017 as a staff working paper and constituted the basis of the recent efforts to mainstream digital technologies in the EU's international cooperation policy.

Notwithstanding such high-flying political ambitions, the EU was still missing a discernible strategic agenda with Africa that would facilitate coherent policy-making in the digital realm. For instance, in their assessment of the EU's external cooperation for development in the field of digitalisation in sub-Saharan Africa, two evaluators, the Data Pop Alliance and Analysis for Economic Decisions (ADE), found that 'no apparent patterns are evident, potentially indicating the lack of a coherent approach to reaping the cumulative effect of projects pertaining to D4D'.

A similar story unfolded with regard to the *European Green Deal*, praised as an epochal project and the start of a new, more sustainable post-Covid-19 era. Its goal is to reach climate neutrality by 2050. Yet, just like much of the digital transition, the EU Green Deal had largely remained a European project. Given the global scope of climate change and the digital transformation, the partnership dimension with Africa continued to be under-represented. Discrepancies between African and European partners persisted as to how to reach the climate goals and how to implement a green transition of the global economy. Throughout 2020, the discourse on the green transition was dominated by tropes that framed the coronavirus pandemic as a once-in-a-lifetime opportunity to foster the much-needed change. Whether this promise will be kept depends much on the design and implementation of the economic recovery that is expected to take off in 2021.

Peace and Security

The EU maintained ten *Common Security and Defence Policy (CSDP) missions* across Africa and along the continent's shores, half of which were civilian and the other half military missions. As such, the EU and its Member States remained among the most active external security actors on the continent. Besides France's significant and continuous presence in the Sahel region through Operation Barkhane, the EU itself upheld its military and civilian deployments in the Sahel region and the Horn of Africa.

The Covid-19 pandemic not only led to a mobilisation of European military staff across Europe but also affected the nature and processes of European security deployments abroad. For instance, European military personnel were among the EU's first responders and in charge of numerous repatriation and evacuation missions. Beyond the crisis response, a global pandemic also affected defence spending and was likely to cause a deterioration in an already fragile global geopolitical environment. This thinking motivated the April Foreign Affairs Council, which underscored the need for deployed EU personnel to maintain their presence abroad, notably in regions and countries that were affected by instability. At the same time, high representative/vice-president (HR/VP) Borrell announced that the non-essential staff and activities – including specific visits and training sessions – of some missions might be temporarily reduced. Operations such as Atalanta, however, would continue at full capacity. CSDP missions began to incorporate public health alongside their other objectives. This could be witnessed in Mali, where the EU capacity-building mission provided training for Malian authorities in the fight against the pandemic and donated essential medical equipment.

With the launch of *two new missions*, the civilian EU Advisory Mission in the Central African Republic (EUAM RCA) and the naval operation EUNAVFOR MED IRINI, the EU sought to bolster its engagement in the world, the global pandemic notwithstanding. The EU civilian mission in CAR reached full operational capability in July. The mission's objective is to provide strategic advice to the CAR Ministry of Interior and Public Security and to the internal security forces to help the state's authority to be extended over the entire territory in accordance with principles of the rule of law and human rights. Following the international Berlin conference on Libya in January, the EU committed to supporting the political process aimed at putting an end to the ongoing conflict. Operation IRINI seeks to translate these commitments into practice by enforcing the UNSC arms embargo on Libya. In addition, the mission is charged with preventing illicit petrol export, the training of the Libyan coastguard and navy, and the disruption of human smuggling and trafficking networks.

The security situation in the Sahel remained extremely volatile in 2020. After weeks of unrest starting in June, Malian military forces orchestrated a coup in August, demonstrating both the fragility of the country's social fabric and the limited achievements over the past seven years. The mutiny prompted the EU to *temporarily suspend its training and capacity-building missions in Mali* (*EUTM Mali and EUCAP Sahel Mali*). This came after the European Council had previously agreed upon an extension of the mandates until May 2024. Following the coup, Brussels announced that it would prioritise supporting the mediation efforts of ECOWAS.

While the Sahel remained a place of instability, it was above all developments in Ethiopia that caught the public eye and mobilised the international community. In November, violent conflict erupted in *Ethiopia's Tigray Region* after Prime Minister Abiy Ahmed ordered a military offensive against the ruling faction in the northern region. He accused the Tigray People's Liberation Front of attacking a government military base. Soon afterwards, first reports about human rights violations emerged and the violent conflict began to count thousands of deaths and over 2 m displaced people.

In reaction to the crisis, Brussels initially offered muted condemnations in the direction of the warring parties. The tone, however, soon changed. Against the backdrop of the political void caused by the US election, which slowed down the country's ability to decisively act on the international stage, the EU's mediation efforts took centre stage. The EU's reaction was made after a foreign ministers' meeting on 29 November, when HR/VP Borrell expressed deep concern over the ethnically-targeted violence, allegations of atrocities, and human rights abuses. In what the online magazine 'POLITICO Europe' called the elevated mediation role of the EU, both HR/VP Borrell and Commissioner Lenarčič offered the support of the EU in contributing to a de-escalation of the crisis and a return to dialogue and securing the rule of law throughout Ethiopia. The EU's commitment to stability in the region translated into direct calls to grant international aid organisations access to conflict zones and more direct support to the activities of IGAD and the AU to resolve the situation.

At the same time, the European Commission considered postponing a € 90 m budget support disbursement planned for the end of the year as a means of obtaining 'political leverage' over the question of limited humanitarian access. This stirred ill feelings in Addis Ababa. The Ethiopian government rejected 'any suggestion that the security crackdown was illegitimate or that it should be financially punished'. On Twitter, Prime Minister Ahmed put it bluntly: 'My message to friends of #Ethiopia is that we may be poor but we are not a country that will negotiate our sovereignty. Threatening Ethiopia for coins will not work.'

Given the absence of progress, in the end the EU had no choice but to follow through with its decision to postpone the disbursement. Other funding lines, for instance to NGOs, remained unaffected. This situation was not alien to the Ethiopian context, where the EU and its Member States had already faced a similar dilemma in 2006, when they rerouted planned budget support disbursements through the 'Protection of Basic Services Scheme'.

The end of the current budget cycle also affected Africa–EU security cooperation at a structural level. In order to respond to what the EU describes as a challenging global environment, the EU created a new € 5 bn fund, the so-called *European Peace Facility (EPF)*. The EPF is a single instrument with the purpose of financing all Common Foreign and Security Policy (CFSP) actions in the military and defence areas. Its adoption in the form of an extra-budgetary instrument effectively put an end to the African Peace Facility (APF), which was set up to support peace and security on the African continent yet was mainly used to finance African peace and security operations. The new instrument is global in nature and for the first time in the EU's history allows for the provision of military equipment to partner countries. While the APF maintained the AU as its main interlocutor, the new instrument is open to international and regional organisations as well as individual partner countries – effectively curbing the AU's influence on African peace and security operations.

Reforming AU–EU Relations

As noted in the introduction, 2020 was to be a year of change in AU–EU relations. This most certainly happened, but not in a way that was in line with the EU's ambitions and plans. After the December 2017 AU–EU summit in Abidjan, the next summit was to take place this year and would once again be hosted in Brussels. In preparation for the summit and seeking an update to the long-term cooperation strategy, the European Commission published a proposal on 9 March titled 'Towards a Comprehensive Strategy with Africa'.

The wording of the title followed the framing in President von der Leyen's manifesto, as well as the European Council's strategic agenda adopted in the summer of 2019. The 19-page document presented a total of five thematic areas for cooperation as envisaged by the EU. A press release on the Commission's first 100 days in office referred to the Commission's Africa strategy proposals as representing 'a new positive agenda with Africa ranging from climate change to digitalisation, jobs and skills to migration'. Although published after Italy had gone into its first lockdown, there was no reference to Covid-19 in the document and while it covered many other topics, public health was not prominently visible among them.

On 30 June, European ministers for foreign affairs adopted a political statement welcoming the communication as a basis for developing a joint strategy with Africa, though adding specific comments and proposals in relation to Covid-19. Even then, the communication failed to initiate a dialogue with the AU towards the adoption of a new, shared cooperation agenda. Instead, discussions were absorbed in preparations and negotiations for the AU–EU ministerial meeting, the October summit, and potential side events. Rather than facilitating strengthened cooperation, the meeting structure thus proved an obstacle to improving the relationship. The decision to postpone the October summit to an undefined point in the future, as well as a failed attempt by Council president Charles Michel to organise a 'mini-summit' on 9 December, showed that the EU struggles to strengthen its 'continent-to-continent' partnership with Africa.

African Continental Free Trade Area

As one of the principal flagships of the AU's Agenda 2063, the African Continental Free Trade Area (AfCFTA) endured heavy weather soon after clearing the port as a result of the pandemic. With the agreement establishing the AfCFTA ratified in May 2019, the road was opened to creating the world's largest free trade area. While preparatory discussions continued and the AfCFTA's secretary-general was sworn in by March, the formal launch of the AfCFTA was postponed to 2021. *Negotiations on tariff schedules and rules of origin proved difficult*, and the fact that they had to take place virtually caused further delays.

Hence, like the EU-driven efforts to renew its partnership with the AU, the AfCFTA had already been deemed challenging at the start of 2020 and witnessed further set-backs due to the global pandemic. Yet unlike the EU's efforts, where the lack of progress led to a drop in political engagement among the top leadership, the AfCFTA very much remains a driving project for pan-African cooperation. The interest of the EU and several of its Member States in increasing their support to operationalise and implement the free trade area will thus provide a key entry point to continue a technical-level dialogue on the path to the desired future partnership.

West Africa

Relations with West Africa continued to be governed by the 2014–20 EDF and the Regional Indicative Programme for West Africa. With the expiration of the EDF, the Regional Indicative Programme, too, ceased to exist as a self-standing extra-budgetary funding line. Over the course of its existence, € 1.07 bn had been made available.

General elections were held in Ghana on 7 December 2020, leading to the re-election of incumbent president Nana Akufo-Addo. While Akufo-Addo secured a clear majority in the first round, the results of the parliamentary elections were less clear-cut, resulting in a hung parliament. The EU's *election observation mission* (EU OM) to Ghana was the only one organised by the EU in West Africa in 2020. Aside from observations on the misuse of state resources and unregulated political finance, the EU OM attested to a highly confrontational yet fair, efficient, and transparent election.

As in other African regions, the EU's engagement in West Africa was largely dominated by the Covid-19 pandemic and ways of handling the socioeconomic fallout. In December, the EU mobilised additional funding in support of the response to the pandemic in three West African countries: Benin, Liberia, and Sierra Leone. By far the largest share went to Benin (€ 46.6 m) in the form of budget support. Payments to Sierra Leone (€ 15 m) and Liberia (€ 8.7 m) were also disbursed as budget support. This followed earlier decisions to make available an additional € 112 m to Senegal (jointly disbursed with € 100 m stemming from the German emergency Covid-19 support programme) and € 86.5 m to Ghana as part of the Team Europe global Covid-19 response. In each of the cases, the EU insisted on the immediate nature of the disbursement as the major added value.

East Africa

Four East African countries were scheduled to hold general elections in 2020: Burundi, Tanzania, Ethiopia, and Somalia; the latter two postponed their elections to 2021 due to the coronavirus pandemic. Neither Burundi nor Tanzania were visited by an EU election observation mission. This was a particularly relevant decision regarding Tanzania, which had been visited by EU observation missions in the 2015, 2010, and 2000 elections. Instead, on 2 November the EU issued a short statement observing that the elections were 'well organised and peaceful in many parts of the country', while noting with regret the social media disruption, 'claims of opposition candidates' that there had been no level playing field, and the limited possibilities for electoral observation.

Finally, the EU first provided € 42 m early in the year and in July added another € 15 m to support a broad humanitarian-development approach to assisting the region in fighting its severe *desert locust outbreak*. Explaining its response to the natural disaster, the EU interestingly referred to its European Green Deal and the fact that it has sustainability at its heart. It is to be hoped that the support given will, in addition to meeting the immediate needs, also contribute to longer-term food security and resilience in the region.

Central Africa

Similarly to its relations with West Africa, the EU viewed its partnership with Central Africa mainly through the prism of the 11th EDF and the Regional Indicative Programme, with a focus on political integration, cooperation towards peace and security, economic integration, and the sustainable management of resources and biodiversity.

Cameroon remained the only country in the region to have signed an EPA with the EU, whereas Congo still traded with the EU under the Generalised Scheme of Preferences and Gabon's classification as an upper-middle-income country rendered it ineligible for the scheme. Only an EPA would allow both countries free access to the European market. All other countries in the region, due to their classification as least-developed countries (LDCs), enjoyed free access to the European market under the 'Everything but Arms' scheme of the EU's General System of Preferences.

In March, the EU signed a € 15.5 m financing agreement in support of the general elections in CAR that were scheduled for late 2020. Elections took place in a highly volatile context and against the backdrop of a continuing UN peacekeeping mission (MINUSCA), militant activity, and fears of a spreading pandemic.

As part of the EU's broader efforts to contain the spread of the coronavirus and to mitigate the pandemic's socioeconomic effects, the EU stepped up its support to CAR by increasing budget support and funds dedicated to reforming the security sector, and allocating additional funding for basic healthcare and civil protection programmes through the *Bêkou Trust Fund*.

Southern Africa

Six Southern African countries, all members of the SADC, remained the only regional sub-group with a full EPA with the EU. In February, senior officials met their European counterparts on the Trade and Development Committee on 19–20 February in Brussels. Among the topics on the agenda was Angola's request to join the EPA, for which next steps were discussed. Meanwhile, three meetings took place in 2020 between the EU and the 'Eastern and Southern African' grouping – consisting of Comoros, Madagascar, Mauritius, Seychelles, and Zimbabwe – in order to 'deepen' the interim EPA agreed in 2007.

It was clear that the EU and *South Africa* had very different expectations of their cooperation in 2020, the year when South Africa took charge of the AU presidency. Moreover, bilateral relations between the two parties witnessed some challenges during this first pandemic year. In the same year that it was seeking close cooperation to further a comprehensive EU strategy with Africa, the European Commission lobbied against South Africa's planned copyright reform. It did so after considerable pressure from Europe's significant cultural sector, which feared that the new law would set a standard for the rest of the continent. The South African government subsequently put the legislation on hold in June, citing constitutional challenges.

In April, the EU adopted a political statement simply titled 'Council Conclusions on Mozambique', in which it reiterated its commitment to supporting the peace agreement concluded in August 2019. The statement expressed the EU's readiness to determine options for effective assistance, while acknowledging the complex and regional nature of the situation. Several months later, in September, the *Mozambican government requested EU assistance* in dealing with the crisis in the north of the country, where it faced repeated attacks by rebels linked to Islamic State. In October, the EU responded and offered to provide logistics for training and technical training in selected areas, as well as humanitarian assistance that included medical services.

Brexit and Its External Implications

Overshadowed by the Covid-19 pandemic, 2020 also witnessed the first exit of a country from the EU since its inception in 1951 (in its original incarnation as the European Coal and Steel Community). On 31 January, the UK officially left the bloc, a move that affected not only the EU's internal policies but also its external relations. Formally, *relations between Africa and the UK* stayed the same in many regards throughout 2020, given that the UK remained a member of the EU Customs Union and Single Market until the end of the year.

Yet this did not prevent the EU and the UK from developing grand visions for future strategic partnerships with Africa. Early on, the UK announced that it wanted to boost trade and investment links with Africa, not least to strengthen the UK's global reach and to counter Chinese investments in the region. Ahead of the *UK–Africa investment summit* on 20 January, the UK committed £ 397 m to new programmes and endorsed new partnerships between the continent and the City of London.

Perceptions in Africa were mixed regarding a future preferential relationship. Many Africans considered Britain's influence a relic from a colonial past, mixed with a feeling of neglect that was only further cemented by Brexit. Still, there was some hope that a post-Brexit relationship with the UK might become more equitable and respectful and allow for more investment and trade relations with fewer strings attached. The UK–Africa investment summit, as well as the appointment of James Duddridge as the minister for Africa at the Foreign, Commonwealth and Development Office, endorsed this vision of a renewed relationship.

Facing economic fallout in light of the Covid-19 crisis, African governments reaffirmed the need for debt relief and economic stimulus. By April, the UK's commitments to the global fight against the coronavirus amounted to £ 744 m, which could be read as an affirmation of 'Global Britain'. Later that year, the same government steered away from its initial course, by merging the Department for International Development with the Foreign Office and announcing a cut to the UK's aid target from 0.7% to 0.5% of gross national income, resulting in a reduction of £ 4.5 bn relative to 2019. A more lasting and mutually beneficial relationship was likely to be based on investment and trade.

For countries like South Africa, which maintained close ties with the EU and the UK, 2020 was first and foremost a year of uncertainty. Already in 2017, the Southern African Customs Union and Mozambique (SACUM) had struck a deal with the UK on a new bilateral economic partnership agreement, essentially replicating the existing EPA between the EU and SACUM. Despite this insurance, SACUM countries were anxious for their top trading partners to reach a deal to avoid additional frictions and different sets of standards in their trade relations.

The UK's exit from the Union also altered the EU's representation in multilateral institutions, affecting for instance its voting power in multilateral development banks like the European Bank for Reconstruction and Development (EBRD), and required a reorganisation of troop contingents of European military operations. While these processes enjoyed a grace period throughout 2020, they fully came into effect on 31 December.

Post-Cotonou

In addition to being the first woman in charge of European development policy, Jutta Urpilainen was the first commissioner to hold this position under the function title 'International Partnerships'. With a name change like that, it went without saying that the successful conclusion of negotiations with the ACP group over a successor to the 2000 Cotonou Agreement was a key element of her political mandate. Since they began in September 2018 under the Juncker Commission, negotiations had advanced at snail's pace, in part because the stalled EU budget negotiations meant that the ACP 'partnership returns' were not yet known. Other reasons included the departure of the UK, whose European Economic Community (EEC) accession in 1973 had stimulated the creation of the ACP group, and a simple lack of enthusiasm and support for the partnership beyond the ACP-EU inner circle.

The commissioner started her race against the clock directly after the Christmas break and sought to accelerate the pace of negotiations, yet the start of the pandemic soon necessitated a fundamental change in approach. Due to the slow progress in preceding years, it was not possible to have a new agreement in place before the Cotonou Agreement expired on 28 February, which is why Cotonou was extended until the end of December. Yet *negotiations were interrupted* altogether after the start of the pandemic and only resumed in June, using an online conference tool to bring together the EU negotiators and their ACP counterparts. The late July political agreement on the next EU budget in the European Council was a key moment in keeping the negotiations going; yet these negotiations remained challenging for several more months. Particularly, the Commission was faced with a balancing act in seeking to conclude a text that was acceptable to both the ACP states and EU Member States, which were strongly divided on several contentious issues, notably migration and sexual and reproductive health and rights.

On 3 December, a short meeting between the chief negotiators resulted in the conclusion of a *political deal on a new cooperation agreement* that would govern relations for a period of at least 20 years, with the possibility for review and extension towards the end of that period. The future agreement would guide political, economic, and development cooperation between the EU and the ACP states concerned, in the form of a common foundation agreement and separate regional partnerships catering to the African, Caribbean, and Pacific members of the group. This political deal marked the beginning of another long process, consisting of reaching an agreement, initialling the agreement and subsequent steps towards ratification. For this reason, the Cotonou Agreement was extended a second time until the end of November 2021.

EU Multi-Annual Financial Framework (MFF)

Like the post-Cotonou talks, negotiations also continued in 2020 towards fundamental reform in the funding structure of the EU's cooperation with Africa. Rather than a multitude of EU funding regulations and the EDF existing outside of the EU budget, though aligned to much of its rules, the EU proposed in 2018 to govern its spending through a single instrument. This instrument would bring various policy objectives in relation to Africa under a single legal roof. Its long name *'Neighbourhood, Development and International Cooperation Instrument (NDICI)'* was revealing of its component parts. Moreover, it captured updated political framing reflecting the EU's desired global role, with the legislative proposal referring to 'projecting European values'.

The multitude of associated policy communities complicated the negotiations in the 'trilogue' between the Commission, the Council representing the Member States, and two leading committees in the European Parliament mandated with foreign and development policy. There was already considerable resistance to the proposal in the run-up to the negotiations in 2019, particularly among those Member States that wished to keep the Neighbourhood Policy institutionally separate, but also among others who preferred to keep the EDF as a separate instrument. A European budget summit convened by President Michel on 20 February, discussing on the basis of a 'negotiation box' shared on Valentine's Day, was broadly considered a missed opportunity. That the decision to incorporate the EDF into the budget was taken out of the negotiation brackets was barely noticed in the process.

In May, after the pandemic had radically changed the socioeconomic landscape in Europe in a matter of weeks, the Commission decided to replace its 2018 MFF proposal. Key in the new proposal was the so-called 'Next Generation EU', a new element authorising the Commission to borrow funds for exceptional expenditure and for loans to Member States to help them recover from and respond to the pandemic. The marathon European Council negotiating meeting from 17 to 21 July resulted in a political deal on the new MFF, including its Next Generation EU. And apparently with little fanfare, or in the slipstream of that fundamental innovation in the EU's budget, the decision to include the EDF in the budget passed too. Even the amounts for the NDICI were agreed, along with its regional distribution in view of the Member States' favoured regions. As with the post-Cotonou negotiations, the European Council unblocked the negotiations over the instrument, which after many subsequent negotiation hours resulted in a political deal on 12 December. The resulting agreement, to be detailed and adopted in 2021, represented a fundamental reform of the EU's budgetary framework for its relations with Africa, and one that might not have been realised had there been no pandemic. The realisation that the pandemic was perhaps not even halfway over by the end of the year, however, should prompt further thinking about more fundamental changes to Africa–EU relations in the years to come.

PART 3

West Africa

Albert Kanlisi Awedoba

The year began with uncertainties about the Covid-19 pandemic as some West African countries were among the first in sub-Saharan Africa to report cases. Some popular perceptions that West Africa and the rest of African would weather the Covid-19 storm proved to be incorrect as Covid-19 wrought havoc on economies and lives. Then there were those who expected Africa to take the brunt of the pandemic. Nevertheless, the worst fears were not realised, as some countries and their economies exhibited resilience, and the infection and death rates were comparatively low. During the year, several countries held presidential elections resulting in a return to power of sitting presidents, but in one case a military coup led to a change of government and compelled ECOWAS intervention.

The Covid-19 Pandemic and West Africa

The *first case of Covid-19* in West Africa was reported on 27 February in Lagos, Nigeria. By early August, numbers of West African Covid-19 infections were estimated at 131,680, representing 13.6% of African cases. The fatality rate was a relatively low 1.5% compared with the African and global rates of 2.1% and 3.8% respectively, while the recovery rate stood at 69%, compared with the continent's recovery rate of 65%. By comparison, therefore, West Africa seemed to have fared better. Previous experiences with the Ebola and SARS epidemics seemed to have better prepared some West African countries for the Covid-19 pandemic than others. Nevertheless, Covid-19 seemed total in its impact on many aspects of life and sectors of West African societies and economies. Political life, economic and business activity, religious programmes, education, recreation, and social life were all affected, though to different degrees depending on the country. In response to the pandemic, lockdowns were instituted and land, sea, and air borders were closed for various periods of time. Many West African governments sought to support their healthcare sectors as well as small and medium-sized businesses and provided relief to vulnerable sectors and communities. Donor partners provided financial support, but internally, some countries were able financially to mobilise support through voluntary donations, as in the case of Ghana.

Government interventions aimed at limiting the spread of Covid-19 by educating communities on the pandemic and insisting on health protocols – social distancing, wearing of nose and facial masks, staying at home where possible, and contact tracing and quarantining of infection cases. Public places were fumigated, including marketplaces, schools, and hospitals. The provision of necessary equipment such as ventilators and personal protective equipment (PPE) for health personnel was a challenge for many governments. Official travel was reduced to the minimum. Meetings were to be held online, and where physical congress was necessary the meeting should not exceed a specified number attending. The public was advised to remain at home, except where necessary.

Covid-19 proved to be no respecter of person, and not even heads of state were spared; in Ghana's case, a former president, Jerry John Rawlings, fell prey to the pandemic on 11 November. Many notable West Africans contracted Covid-19 and recovered. The exact tally of affected persons, those who succumbed, and Covid survivors remained uncertain, as many West African countries lacked the capacity to conduct widespread community testing, while some of the affected themselves were asymptomatic and did not present any of the known and recognised symptoms or, if they did, did not report to health facilities due to the stigma associated with the pandemic in some societies. There was clear evidence of stigma in parts of Ghana in the early days of the pandemic.

Due to the pandemic, about 66% of 352 points of entry within the ECOWAS zone had to close, though 26% were open to the transport of goods or returning nationals. With the first signs of Covid-19 in March–April, *12 countries officially closed their borders*. Benin, Côte d'Ivoire, and Senegal were said to have opted for humanitarian corridors enabling essential crossings overland. The pressure to reopen or lift the lockdowns was considerable, however, and compelled most West African countries to reopen some of their borders sooner than health specialists would have wished. By October, most countries had reopened for international flights, though many land borders remained closed for a while longer.

The *lockdowns* came at considerable cost. Human lives were lost due to the deployment of the forces to ensure urban communities maintained the lockdowns. In the early days of the pandemic, Nigerian security forces deployed to maintain lockdowns ended up being rather responsible for the killing of 18 people, not to mention many human rights abuses. A few suicides were also reported.

The West African Economy in the Covid-19 Era

West African economies were projected to suffer *negative growth of −2.0%* in 2020, six percentage points below the projected pre-pandemic growth rate. Real output was expected to drop by about 4.3% in worst-case scenarios. This would be due to government spending on social interventions to support the health, economy, and vulnerable sectors. There was a reduction in tax inflows and internal revenue mobilisation, as well as decline in production and productivity levels, loss of revenue from regular exports like minerals and petro-chemicals for countries like Ghana and Nigeria, and decline in tourism, external remittances, and more. On 20 April, the price of West Texas Intermediate crude oil slumped, falling to $ 37.63 per barrel. Nigeria's high-quality crude oil dropped to about $ 19 per barrel from $ 55–60, and although the price improved towards the end of the year, it did not attain the expected levels. A number of West African countries fell into recession and attracted relief measures and donations. Nigeria's economy fell into lasting recession, with a 5–6% GDP decline considered unprecedented in more than three decades. Unemployment soared, and by December, the number of beneficiaries under Nigeria's national social investment programme rose to one million. Côte d'Ivoire's economic growth of 7.5% in 2019 dropped to 1.8%.

West African economies with the most notable improvement in the 2020 *Doing Business* report included Togo and Nigeria. Togo, ranking 97th globally and 7th in sub-Saharan Africa, was one of the economies that made remarkable improvement in the year. Nigeria conducted reforms that impacted six indicators, including making the enforcement of contracts easier. After Togo, Côte d'Ivoire ranked 110th, followed by Ghana and Senegal, ranking 118th and 123rd respectively. Nigeria and Niger were ranked 131st and 132nd respectively. Many West African countries featured low down in the rankings – Guinea-Bissau and Liberia scored 43.2 each and were ranked 174th and 175th respectively.

Despite the impact of Covid-19 on global economies, *remittances* continued to flow into West African countries; the region received $ 27 bn for the year. Nigeria, the largest recipient in sub-Saharan Africa in absolute terms, received nearly 64% of this total ($ 17.2 bn), while The Gambia (15.6%) and Cabo Verde (13.9%) received the most remittances per GDP. Though remittances to the sub-region dropped by 19.3% due to Covid-19, for 5 of the 15 countries the data suggest that they increased. Remittances to Ghana shot up by 5% to $ 3.6 bn; those for The Gambia increased by 5% too. Remittances received in Nigeria fell by 27.7%, according to World Bank estimates. Mali received $ 1 bn, while Senegal grossed $ 2.6 bn.

In October, ECOWAS announced the official virtual launch of EU support for the 'West African Response on Cybersecurity and Fight against Cybercrime' (OCWAR-C) project, to deal with *money laundering and the financing of terrorism, cybersecurity and cybercrime, and organised crime*, including trafficking. Not surprisingly, some Western countries such as the UK – popular study-abroad destinations – were accused of turning a blind eye to Nigerian political elites, and to some extent their Ghanaian counterparts, laundering dirty money through university fees. A paper published by the Carnegie Endowment for International Peace by a West Africa expert and non-resident scholar affirmed this. Ghana had been on the EU blacklist for failing to put in place measures to fight money laundering. Media reports indicated that British authorities had intercepted £ 26 m being carried in suitcases to the UK from Ghana.

Some West African countries did well in the rankings of the Global Cybersecurity Index (GCI) of the International Telecommunication Union (ITU); Ghana ranked 3rd in Africa, behind Mauritius and Tanzania, with a score of 86.69%, representing major progress since the previous ratings in 2017 and 2018 of 32.6% and 43.7% respectively. A key intervention was the revision of the National Cybersecurity Policy and Strategy, and the passage of the Cybersecurity Act 2020 (Act 1,038). Nigeria ranked 4th in Africa and 58th in the world. Internet penetration in Cabo Verde stood at 57% in January 2020.

Governance and Politics

Despite the ravages of Covid-19, several West African countries went to the polls to elect heads of state and members of parliament. Questions were asked about the wisdom of countries holding mass elections under Covid-19 conditions. There were fears that vigorous political campaigns and the elections themselves would lead to spikes in Covid-19 infections.

Burkina Faso went to the polls on 22 November to elect a president and members of the national assembly; Roch Marc Christian Kaboré was elected in the first round with nearly 58% of the vote. *Guinea* elected its national assembly in February and held presidential elections on 18 October (the latter had been postponed from January/February 2019). The outcome was disputed, but nevertheless, on 24 October, the national electoral commission declared the sitting president, Alpha Condé, elected with 59.5% of the vote. *Ghana* elected its president and members of parliament on 7 December. The sitting president, Nana Akufo-Addo, was declared winner with a narrow margin; in the parliamentary elections there was heightened drama – the president's New Patriotic Party and the main opposition were tied, with a difference of one seat between them. The opposition National Democratic Congress contested the results as declared by the Electoral Commission and, after street protests, decided to send the issue to the supreme court. Prior to the elections, the decision of the Electoral Commission to re-register eligible voters divided the country.

Côte d'Ivoire chose 31 October for its presidential elections. Alassane Ouattara was re-elected president with 95% of the vote, though the opposition boycotted the elections. In the case of *Togo*, the presidential elections were held on 22 February and the incumbent Faure Gnassingbé was re-elected for his fourth term with 71% of the vote. *Senegal* should have held local elections within the year but postponed them.

Parliamentary elections were held in *Mali* on 29 March, with a second round on 19 April. They had initially been scheduled to be held on 25 November and 16 December 2018 but were moved to April 2019 and then to June 2019, before being postponed until 2020 by the Council of Ministers. Then, on 18 August, a *military coup* ousted Mali's civilian government. A group of army officers arrested President Ibrahim Boubacar Keïta and his prime minister, Boubou Cissé, without bloodshed. It made nonsense of the parliamentary elections held earlier in the year. In Mali's case, discontent within the military ranks and anger about the government's inability to deal with insurgence within the country, among other factors, had boiled over. The public seemed to welcome the coup, but it prompted the diplomatic intervention of ECOWAS heads of state, leading to the formation of an interim government.

Niger held its national assembly and presidential elections on 27 December. No presidential candidate won outright; a run-off was to be held on 21 February 2021. The incumbent president did not seek re-election, choosing instead to throw his weight behind his favourite candidate.

On another note, while for official communication purposes, English, French, and Portuguese are the dominant language media for West Africa, especially for government administration, business, and parliament, on 7 March, *Mauritania* decided that its parliamentary debates would no longer be translated into French and MPs were encouraged to use Arabic and the three 'national' languages of Poular, Soninké, and Wolof. French would, however, remain the working language of administration.

Human Development Indicators

In terms of world rankings for human development, West African countries did not perform well on some of the SDGs. The best performance was from Cabo Verde, ranked 126th in the world out of 189 countries assessed. It was categorised as a 'medium' human development country, with life expectancy at birth of 73 years, 12.7 expected years of schooling, and a mean of 6.3 years of schooling. Its gross national income (GNI) per capita of $ 7,019 (PPP) was the highest in the region. Ghana came next, at 138th in the global rankings. Mauritania, Benin, Nigeria, Côte d'Ivoire, Togo, and Senegal were ranked 157th, 158th, 161st, 162nd, 167th, and 168th respectively. The lowest-ranked countries were Burkina Faso, Sierra Leone, Mali, and Niger. The last of these, Niger, had a life expectancy at birth of 62.4 years, 6.5 expected years of schooling, a mean of 2.1 years of education, and GNI per capita of $ 1,201 (PPP).

Personal and economic freedoms: Cabo Verde was ranked 44th in the world with a score of 7.75 (on a scale of 1 to 10, where 10 represents considerable freedom), according to the Fraser Institute's Human Freedom Index for 2020. Cabo Verde ranked top in sub-Saharan Africa, with a personal freedom score of 8.09 and an economic freedom score of 7.4. Ghana and Benin were ranked 72nd and 90th in the world respectively, and 6th and 9th in sub-Saharan Africa. Nigeria ranked 131st and 29th in the world and in sub-Saharan Africa, respectively, with a score of 6.05.

Guinea and Mauritania were ranked 146th and 150th respectively. Mauritania still had not come to terms with domestic slavery, despite the efforts of the anti-slavery movement. Not only did the state agencies and courts fail to deal with perpetrators of the crime, even in the face of incontrovertible evidence, but there was collusion. In one case, there was tampering with a witness. Niger and Mali ranked 176th and 137th in the world respectively.

On press freedoms, the West African Freedom of Expression Monitor recorded 56 violations in the April–June period, 27 between July and September, and 48 in October–December. Most countries were found culpable, although to varying extents. Nigeria accounted for 16 violations, including the killing of at least 12 protesters in the Lekki Tollgate massacre. Guinea had six violations, including the massacre of 21 opposition supporters protesting the results of the country's presidential elections. Guinea also severed internet connections and shut down media houses. In the case of Côte d'Ivoire, six violations were reported.

In the run-up to the year's national elections when the stakes were deemed high, a number of journalists lost their lives, not to mention damage to filming and recording equipment and the verbal and physical insults dished out. Eleven countries featured in the reports on West Africa. Laws were put in place aimed at restricting press reportage considered unfavourable to the authorities; notably, President Julius Maada Bio officially assented to a new law that repealed criminal libel in Sierra Leone. In Mali, on 10 June, Netblocks, monitors of internet shutdowns, announced that the internet and social media had been censored. Several offices of the Office de Radio-Television du Mali (ORTM) were ransacked and equipment was looted.

Against the backdrop of Nigerian state and federal media harassment, the justice minister and attorney-general of the federation proclaimed on 1 November the federal government's determination to see to the 'proper' investigation of crimes against journalists. This seemed in order, given the many cases brought against journalists and media organisations that reported on governmental and official malpractice, especially that bordering on corruption. Prior to that, on 7 August, the president signed the Companies and Allied Matters Act (CAMA) into law; however, serious concerns were raised, namely that the act would enable the authorities to clamp down on NGOs and the media.

Ghana's Right to Information (RTI) law passed in 2019 came into effect this year. For critics, not only does it not go far enough but it has many restrictions, particularly when it comes to accessing information from the presidency and some government institutions. The Centre for Law and Democracy remarked that 'The regime of exceptions in the bill leaves much to be desired'. Concerns were voiced that certain provisions in the law might serve as 'a backdoor exception to grant the state broad discretion to decide when information is deemed to be confidential'.

On 24 June, the Mauritanian parliament passed a law against disinformation. The West African media was awash with misinformation and disinformation, which negates press freedoms and fuels media attacks; in the run-up to the 2020 elections, a newspaper was used to peddle misinformation about the Ghanaian president receiving a bribe in his office. The pictures used turned out to be Photoshopped and fake. The media outlet involved realised it had been abused and apologised to the president.

The EIU 2020 *Democracy Index* highlights did not suggest that West Africa had performed any better this year than previous years. The lockdowns constrained anti-government expression while enabling governments to ascribe extra powers to themselves. In Ghana, for example, the parliament passed the Imposition of Restrictions Act, which empowered the president to impose restrictions on citizens during the Covid-19 emergency.

Cabo Verde and Ghana ranked 32nd and 59th and were categorised as flawed democracies, while Senegal, Liberia, and Senegal were deemed to be hybrid democracies, ranking 86th, 90th, and 99th respectively. Niger, Guinea, Togo, and Guinea-Bissau, ranking 125th, 133rd, 141st, and 147th respectively, fell low down within the 'authoritarian regimes' category. For functioning of government, Guinea-Bissau and Mali were classified as without any. The government of Ibrahim Boubacar Keïta in the latter country was unstable and unable to contain the rebels and jihadists. Due to the military coup that deposed the civilian government and Mali's loss of territory to jihadist control, the country dropped 11 places from its previous standing and ended up downgraded from a hybrid to an authoritarian regime. Togo fell by 15 places from the previous year's standing, sinking lower within the ranks of authoritarian regimes. Burkina Faso, which, like Mali, faced a jihadist insurgency and did not have full control of its territory, was also downgraded from a hybrid to an authoritarian regime.

The Institute for Economics and Peace (IEP) report for 2020 assessed countries for their state of peace across three domains: the level of societal safety and security, the extent of ongoing domestic and international conflict, and the degree of militarisation. Some West African countries appeared to do well. Five West African states, Ghana, Sierra Leone, Senegal, Liberia, and The Gambia, were categorised as *highly peaceful*. Seven, nearly half of the total, were classified as in a state of 'medium' peace. Three others, namely Nigeria, Mali, and Niger (ranked 147th, 144th, and 138th respectively), were in a state of *'low' peace*. Ghana ranked 2nd in sub-Saharan Africa and 43rd on the global index – news warmly received by the Ghanaian media. Sierra Leone and Senegal ranked 46th and 47th respectively on the global index. The Gambia ranked 60th. Several West African countries did not do nearly so well, thanks to the activity of jihadists and insurrectionists. Burkina Faso ranked 122nd and Niger came in 138th; Mali and Nigeria ranked 144th and 147th respectively.

The Gambia experienced considerable youth unemployment – over 40% – and recorded increased police brutality and clashes with anti-government protesters. A deterioration in peacefulness was expected. *Benin* was said to have experienced the largest deterioration in peace, as it fell by 34 places in the ranking to 106th. The exclusion of former president Boni Yayi and opposition politicians from the 2019 elections resulted in sporadic clashes that continued into 2020. *Niger* also suffered a deterioration in peace – the fourth-largest deterioration on the index – falling 11 places to 138th in the overall ranking. It experienced cross-border armed robberies and violent crime. It ranked 16th for entrenched criminality in Africa in the 2019 Africa Organised Crime Index.

The World Happiness Report 2020's ten happiest African cities/countries included three from West Africa: Niamey/Niger (ranked 100th in the world) was 2nd, Freetown/Sierra Leone (125th) was 8th and Accra/Ghana (129th) was 9th. Of the least happy cities/countries in Africa, two were found in West Africa, namely Kumasi/Ghana (175th in the world) and Monrovia/Liberia (173rd), ranked 6th and 8th respectively.

Within the year, heightened *terrorist activity* in West Africa and the Sahel region was described as 'unprecedented'. The head of Nigeria's Sunni Muslims, the Sultan of Sokoto, is reported to have grieved on two occasions – 26 November and 2 December – about the worsening security situation in Nigeria; he remarked that nowhere was safe and that the north had become the worst place to live in Nigeria. To help contain the canker, the ECOWAS heads of state summit 'adopted a 2020–2024 action plan to eradicate terrorism in the sub-region'. The death of 13 French soldiers in a helicopter crash and several reversals in the fight against the jihadist terrorists reaffirmed French and Sahel country leaders' resolve to intensify the military campaign against jihadists in the West African Sahel. A one-day summit of the presidents of Burkina Faso, Chad, Mali, Mauritania, and Niger, as well as those of France and Spain, in Nouakchott, Mauritania, took stock and agreed a more aggressive strategy in the Sahel. The leaders stressed the need to intensify the fight on all fronts and to commit national and international forces to the struggle. However, in early January, 1,200 Chadian troops – part of the Multinational Joint Task Force (MNJTF) – withdrew from the Lake Chad area in the state of Borno in north-east Nigeria.

The litany of reversals and defeats and jihadist atrocities was unimaginable for countries like Nigeria, Niger, and Mali. Given its size and the theatre of conflict, Nigeria stands out. On 24 March, at least 47 soldiers were killed in an ambush in Borno, prompting the military to respond with aerial bombardments. On 9 June, 80 villagers in Gubio were massacred and on 28 November, Boko Haram killed dozens of rice farmers in Zabarmari, near Maiduguri.

But the army too had its successes, even if they tended to be overstated. On 11 January, officials disclosed that within the past few weeks no fewer than 100 bandits in the states of Zamfara and Katsina had been killed by joint forces comprising military personnel, special police units, and the state security service (SSS) in 'Operation Hadarin Daji'; furthermore, several ringleaders had been arrested. In multiple air strikes on 22–23 May, at least 200 bandits lost their lives. On 5 February, a police operation in the Birnin Gwari local government area led to the killing of some 250 alleged terrorists. On 5 June, a combined ground and air operation in the Kachia local government area resulted in the killing of 70 bandits.

The army in some cases was also implicated in *attacks on civilian populations* suspected of harbouring terrorist sympathies. Information from Armed Conflict Location and Event Data Project (ACLED) sources showed that in Burkina Faso, Human Rights Watch had reported the army arrest and execution of 31 men in the town of Djibo on 9 April. Four weeks later, the Mentao refugee camp was raided by security forces; about 32 people were reportedly wounded in the event, and the refugees were told to leave within 72 hours or be killed. Other atrocities attributed to armed forces were reported about the same time in Burkina Faso, where jihadists and insurrectionists had caused considerable displacement of communities. In Niger, security forces reportedly executed or were responsible for the disappearance of 102 Tuareg and Fulani pastoralists. In Mali, the UN's peacekeeping mission MINUSMA documented 101 summary executions of Fulani in the regions of Mopti and Ségou. In Nigeria, on 11 October, the presidency had to disband the infamous FSARS and SARS – the Federal Special Anti-Robbery Squad, and on 13 October, the inspector-general of police replaced them with a new team – Special Weapons and Tactics (SWAT). This was after the FSARS had been persistently accused of crimes against civilians, culminating in the #EndSARS campaign and widespread protests.

The Gulf of Guinea saw increased piracy activity within the year; International Maritime Bureau (IMB) statistics indicated a 40% increase in piracy and kidnappings in the Gulf, and of the 85 seafarer kidnappings and ransom demands in the year, 80 were in the Gulf of Guinea; 14 attacks occurred off the coasts of Nigeria, Benin, Gabon, Equatorial Guinea, and Ghana. On 17 July, eight pirates armed with machine guns boarded a tanker 196 nautical miles south-west of Bayelsa, Nigeria, and, after holding 19 crew hostage, stole valuables and escaped with 13 kidnapped crew.

Religious and ethnic violence: Conflicts continued to rage in the Sahelian fringe of West Africa, implicating Mali, Niger, Burkina Faso, and northern Nigeria. Countries such as Mauritania could not feel secure even if no active terrorist activity took place on their soil. Mauritania's foreign minister, in a report to the UN and the G5, referred to growing security threats from Islamic State in the Grand Sahara and went on to remark on a 'diabolical alliance of terrorist and drug trafficking groups, with violence spreading every day to new territories'. Jihad-motivated conflicts seemed to be complicated by ethnic issues and brigandry, and the two can be confused. The spate of highway robberies in non-Sahelian countries such as Ghana seem to be more an example of brigandry than of a quest for ethnic or religious assertion.

On 10 August in Nigeria, a young musician was sentenced to death by a Sharia court for blasphemy against the Prophet in a song circulated via social media, and a minor, in an argument with a friend, was given a ten-year prison sentence with manual labour for blasphemy. Both judgments were appealed, though the outcomes remained unknown. Between January and August, Kano state courts reportedly passed death sentences for offences ranging from rape to murder; nine people, including a woman, were sentenced to death. These were rights violations for which the administration of Sharia law in northern Nigeria was responsible within the year. Kano State gained notoriety in this regard, for its harsh verdicts.

Accountability, Contentment, and Migration

It is estimated that over 7.6 m international migrants resided in the ECOWAS subregion as of mid-year 2020 (according to the UN Department of Economic and Social Affairs). It is suggested that the number is an underestimation. About 34% (2.6 m) were believed to be in Côte d'Ivoire and 17% (1.3 m) in Nigeria. People continued to move away from home in response to levels of internal insecurity and in search of better opportunities and jobs. About two out of three ECOWAS migrants resided in another ECOWAS country. The shares of West African migrants residing in North America and Europe were 10% and 19% respectively, by mid-year. For Sahel countries like Burkina Faso, security was to be sought in neighbouring countries such as Côte d'Ivoire, even in the midst of the Covid-19 pandemic. Mauritania hosted approximately 62,000 refugees at its Mbera refugee camp, near the Malian border.

The picture gleaned from the year's Transparency International Corruption Perceptions Index shows that Cabo Verde remained the top performer in West Africa in *fighting corruption* and was ranked 3rd in sub-Saharan Africa, with a score of 58 and a global ranking of 41st. The score of Nigeria, ranked 149th, declined marginally from 26 to 25. Despite the hue and cry over vote buying in the run-up to its 2020 elections, Ghana improved, with a score of 43 and ranked 75th, as opposed to 80th last year. The Gambia maintained last year's score of 37 but declined in the rankings from 96th to 102nd.

There is evidence that countries take these rankings seriously. *Mauritania* set up a bipartisan anti-corruption investigations commission in January to investigate the awarding of government contracts. The commission's report implicated senior state officials in fraudulent deals; prime minister Ismael Bedde Cheikh Sidiya and his entire government resigned on the day the report was handed to the prosecutors.

In *Nigeria*'s case, the authorities responsible for preventing and controlling corruption were often themselves implicated in the corruption. A number of these were prosecuted and assets confiscated. On 25 February, after a trial lasting four years, the former national publicity secretary was convicted of money laundering in connection with a $ 2.1 bn arms procurement deal and sentenced to seven years' imprisonment.

The island of Jersey, the US, and Nigeria signed a trilateral agreement to repatriate confiscated loot amounting to $ 308 m which had been traced back to the former Nigerian military dictator Sani Abacha. The amount was eventually transferred in early May.

As reflected in international reports, West African countries continued to lag behind the rest of the world on several parameters, including happiness, democracy norms, press and personal freedoms, gender empowerment, and transparency and accountability.

International and Sub-regional Diplomacy

The pandemic reduced diplomatic travel considerably within the year, but it did not minimise diplomatic dealings. Meetings and summits adopted a virtual mode. Heads of state were still able to show up at their counterparts' inaugurations. In early August, the Ghanaian parliament approved the agreement between the government and the AU for the establishment of the African Continental Free Trade Area (AfCFTA) Secretariat in Accra. The commencement date of the operation of the secretariat had to be rescheduled from 1 July due to the pandemic and the closure of borders in many African countries.

In December, Nigeria finally agreed to reopen its borders with neighbouring West African countries – a relief to ECOWAS countries. Conflicts between Ghanaian petty traders and their Nigerian counterparts trading in Ghana were of diplomatic concern. The Ghana Union of Traders Association (GUTA) was intransigent over Nigerian traders' right to operate in the retail trade sector and locked some Nigerian shops. When a video of the forcible closure of shops belonging to Nigerians went viral, the Nigerian foreign affairs minister expressed his government's 'dismay'. The Nigerian government vowed to take 'urgent steps' i.e. retaliatory action. The fracas was compounded by a businessman's illegal demolition of property belonging to the Nigerian mission in Ghana. He claimed that the plot on which the Nigerian property was situated belonged to him. The Ghanaian authorities were concerned, and quickly brought closure to the issue.

The Nigerian president expressed displeasure at sitting presidents violating their constitutions by going for unconstitutional third terms. His comments were made at a summit of ECOWAS leaders in Niamey, Niger. His concerns were about developments in Côte d'Ivoire and Guinea, but they did not change anything. ECOWAS maintained a united front in the face of the military coup staged in Mali on 18 August. Mali was suspended from all ECOWAS decision-making bodies, financial and commercial exchanges with Mali were stopped, and ECOWAS members closed their borders with Mali. These sanctions were lifted after Mali had complied with ECOWAS demands and a civilian-headed transitional government was instituted with an agreement to hold democratic elections in 18 months.

Gender Empowerment

On the Global Gender Gap Index 2020 rankings, West African countries ranked between 52nd and 142nd on the overall global index. Cabo Verde ranked 52nd with a score of 0.725, which was above the sub-Saharan overall score of 0.680. Liberia and Senegal ranked 96th and 99th respectively, scoring higher than the sub-Saharan mark. However, the rest of West Africa fell below the sub-Saharan average. Mali, Togo, Mauritania, and Côte d'Ivoire ranked 139th, 140th, 141st, and 142nd respectively out of a total of 153 countries compared. For economic participation and opportunity, West African countries performed relatively well. Benin ranked top while Guinea and Cabo Verde ranked 10th and 15th respectively. Benin was deemed to have closed 84.7% of the gender gap, while Côte d'Ivoire managed 54.5%. Cape Verde, Mali, Nigeria, and Sierra Leone were adjudged the most improved for the year. For educational attainment, performance was low, as most West African countries ranked between 104th (Cabo Verde) and 145th (Nigeria). Ghana, Burkina Faso, Liberia, and Mali were reported to have reduced their educational attainment gender gap by between 1.5 and 4.7 percentage points. Senegal ranked 32rd for political empowerment. Côte d'Ivoire, Benin, Gambia, and Nigeria were close to the bottom of the ranking table. Few women made it into parliaments and key decision-making bodies in West Africa.

On 15 October in Nigeria, the Kwara state governor affirmed an existing federal bill that addressed violations including rape, domestic violence, and female genital mutilation (FGM). This needs to be placed in the context of the fact that Kwara had an FGM prevalence rate of 46% for the year, while the state of Ondo in the south-west was reported to have a 77% prevalence rate, one of the highest in Nigeria. Imo, Ekiti, Ebonyi, Kaduna, and Osun all had high prevalence rates of between 62% and 40%.

Natural Hazards

West African countries experienced natural hazards within the year, of which *erratic rainfall and devastating floods* were noteworthy, but also bouts of dry weather. Much of West Africa, from south-eastern Senegal and Guinea across eastern Mali, Burkina Faso, Niger, and northern Nigeria, was reported to have experienced early-season dryness and drier-than-average conditions. This was compensated for by wetter weather later. Heavy rainfall in August–September led to flooding in many areas throughout Niger, Mali, Nigeria, Chad, Cameroon, Senegal, Burkina Faso, Guinea, Guinea-Bissau, Mauritania, Côte d'Ivoire, Ghana, Gambia, Benin, and Cabo Verde. Fatalities, material damage, destruction of livelihoods, and population displacements were reported. The impact of the rains was considered severer than last year, and the toll in human catastrophe was estimated to have almost doubled.

In Ghana, on 6 August, Operation Thunderbolt 2020 was launched to prepare communities along the White Volta for the imminent flooding resulting from the spillage of the Bagre Dam in Burkina Faso. Communities in the area were also advised to move to higher ground. Benin experienced exceptional rainfall in the year. In September, the Niger overflowed its banks in the northern parts of Benin, affecting more than 8,000 households in Malanville; Niamey was also affected by floods. In June, despite the various initiatives undertaken in previous years to stem the floods, Cotonou did not escape. The paving of roads, contrary to expectations, rather exacerbated flooding in the city.

Mauritania was confronted with a desert locust menace. Between 26 and 31 January, large-scale testing using drones was conducted as part of coordinated efforts to minimise the damage to food crops.

Benin

Pauline Jarroux and Clarisse Tama Bignon

The year 2020 marked 60 years of Benin's independence, which was celebrated modestly as compared with the 50th anniversary, without the traditional parade of security and defence forces, and without foreign guests. Though Benin, like other countries, had to deal with the Covid-19 pandemic, the low-key celebrations also symbolised the relatively morose political atmosphere, resulting from the recent controversial elections.

On the socioeconomic front, the government's efforts and the country's continued growth contrasted with strong inequalities running through the territories and the population.

Domestic Politics

The 2020 *local elections* were one of the most important moments in the country. They took place on 17 May, one year after the controversial legislative elections marked by strong post-election violence, and against the background of the Covid-19 pandemic. The first controversies – which began several weeks before the elections – related to the application files' admissibility, as far as the new provisions enacted in the wake of the 2019 electoral code were concerned. To be allowed to compete, each political party had to present candidates in each of the 546 districts (subdivisions of the communes, i.e. the municipalities) of the country. As a result, only political parties with a nationwide presence were able to participate, especially since alliances were now prohibited; in March, only eight political parties received provisional certificates from the Commission Électorale Nationale Autonome (CENA), out of the 34 parties and alliances which had competed during the 2015 municipal elections. But on 30 March, after further examination, the CENA rejected the files of three political parties – the Mouvement des Élites Engagées pour l'Émancipation du Bénin (MOELE-BENIN), the Force Cauris pour le Développement du Bénin (FCDB), and the Parti pour l'Engagement et la Relève – due to incomplete documentation. The Mouvement Populaire de Libération, another party claiming to be in the opposition, had been excluded from the beginning of the process. The decision rekindled opposition protests, some of which had already called for a boycott of the elections because of the new application rules and the Covid-19 pandemic. A few months after it had been called upon by opponent and businessman Sébastien Ajavon, in April the African Court of Human and People's Rights (ACHPR) issued a non-binding order on provisional measures to suspend the municipal elections. In his claim, Ajavon had insisted on the irregularity of the last legislative elections and on the impossibility of his party, the Union Sociale Libérale, participating in the electoral process because of the absence of a certificate of conformity. Though the court requested that the municipal elections be suspended before a decision on the merits of the case, as Ajavon had wished for, it nevertheless did not favour suspending some of the laws recently voted for by the national assembly, as he had demanded. Soon afterwards, the Beninese government announced the withdrawal of its declaration under Article 34 of the protocol on the establishment of the ACHPR, thereby closing off the possibility of Beninese citizens and NGOs being able to refer cases to the institution. Despite these contestations, the electioneer campaign – mainly conducted in the media – took place from 1 to 15 May, and voting went off in a mostly calm atmosphere. Only five parties finally competed: the two main parties of the presidential camp, the Union Progressiste (UP) and the Bloc Républicain (BR), and three others, including the Union Démocratique pour un Bénin Nouveau (UDBN), and the Parti du Renouveau Démocratique (PRD). The last one, the Force Cauris pour un Bénin Émergent (FCBE), was the only one associated with the opposition but was nevertheless divided, with some of the factions sympathetic to the president. The turnout rate was reported as just over 49%, higher than for the last legislative elections (27%) but lower than the 2015 municipal elections figure (more than 57%). Agence France Presse (AFP) noted that participation was even lower (around 10% or less) in opposition strongholds, such as the district of Cadjehoun in Cotonou and in the city of Tchaourou.

At the beginning of June, the 77 mayors took office. Confirming the dominance *of the parties of the presidential camp* in the Beninese political landscape, 70 mayors were affiliated to either the UP or the BR and only seven to the FCBE (in the municipalities of Bembèrèkè, Copargo, Savè, Kandi, Parakou, Bantè, and Sinendé). The other two parties did not get any elected councillors, although the PRD came out ahead in Porto Novo and Sèmè-Podji. Indeed, they were not able to reach the 10% national representation threshold – one of the new provisions of the 2019 electoral code which was still hotly debated in the country. The FCBE, the party of former president Thomas Boni Yayi, thus maintained its position as the main opposition party, despite the loss a few weeks later of Parakou, one of the seven municipalities it had won and also the third-largest city and the gateway to the northern part of the country. In fact, in July, the supreme court overturned the victory of a newly elected FCBE councillor deemed ineligible because of judicial precedents. This decision cost the party its absolute majority in the municipal council, and consequently the position of mayor. In mid-August, a new councillor affiliated to the BR was appointed. The FCBE had already faced a crisis some time before, when Boni Yayi announced his withdrawal from the party he had founded. He teamed up with Éric Houndete – a former vice-president of the national assembly – in the creation of a new political party, Les Démocrates, whose statutes were filed in July. Houndete presented the initiative as a response to 'the need to create a new opposition party' in the face of 'denial of rights', as reported by the 'Jeune Afrique' journal. The statement shared by many observers of an authoritarian drift of political power took on a new dimension with regard to the results of the municipal elections, in view of the presidential elections of 2021.

Indeed, according to the 2019 constitutional reforms, candidates for the *positions of president and vice-president of the Republic* must be sponsored by 10% of all MPs and mayors, i.e. by 16 elected officials out of 160 (83 MPs and 77 mayors), to validate their candidacy. As the 83 MPs elected in 2019 would *a priori* be sympathetic to the ruling power, the couple of opposition mayors alone should not be sufficient to ensure the opposition candidates' participation. If the situation was worrying at the international level, especially for human rights NGOs such as Open Society Initiative for West Africa, it was also denounced at the national level; several civil society organisations and associations mobilised in September behind the 'Let me choose in 2021' banner to request removal of the sponsorship requirements. Criticism also came from Beninese intellectuals and lawyers, such as Joël Aïvo, the former dean of the University of Abomey-Calavi faculty of law and political science, or Jean-Nazaire Tama, professor of law at the University of Parakou and author of a 'manifesto' calling for an end to the sponsorship system. Appeals were also lodged with the constitutional court, which will issue its opinion in 2021.

In November, the president began the first part of his *national tour* known as the 'accountability tour'. On the road linking Savè to Parakou, to populations known to support former president Boni Yayi and where violence notably took place following the 2019 legislative elections, the president delivered speeches aimed at forgiveness and reconciliation while touting his record as head of state. The tour was also a campaign tour for the upcoming presidential elections. The president used the opportunity to backtrack on his promise of a single term of office, made during the 2016 electoral campaign; in January 2021, he announced his candidacy to the Beninese people.

The year 2020 was also marked by *important trials*. While for some they marked the end of impunity for the country's leaders and highly placed civil servants, they also fuelled accusations of political manipulation of the justice system, in particular in the proceedings of the Court de Répression des Infractions Économiques et du Terrorisme (CRIET). A highly anticipated trial in the country was that of the former minister of finance, Komi Koutché, as well as his co-defendants, in a case of embezzlement of public funds and abuse of office within the Fonds National de la Microfinance, of which he had been the general manager between 2008 and 2013. In April, the CRIET sentenced Mr Koutché, exiled for three years in the US, to 20 years' imprisonment and a fine of CFAfr 500 m (about $ 909,000), in addition to the payment, jointly with the others found guilty, of more than CFAfr 20 bn (approximately $ 36.4 m) in damages. The CRIET also looked into the fate of Léhady Soglo, son of former president Nicéphore Soglo. This opposition figure, exiled in France since 2017, was tried for financial malpractice when mayor of Cotonou, a post from which he was dismissed in 2017 after a rapid procedure. He was convicted in late June on the charge of abuse of office and sentenced *in absentia* to ten years' imprisonment in addition to a fine and the payment of damages to the Beninese state amounting to CFAfr 267 m (about $ 486,000). The businessman and former mayor of Ouidah Séverin Adjovi was convicted on the same day by the same institution of tax fraud, money laundering, and swindling. International arrest warrants have been issued against the individuals in question, who have announced that they would appeal against the decisions. On the other hand, the young journalist Ignace Sossou was released from prison in June after his sentence was reduced on appeal to 12 months' detention, six of which were suspended. At the end of 2019, he had been found guilty of harassment for having reported the public prosecutor Mario Metonou's criticisms of the country's authorities. Journalists and human rights groups and NGOs such as Amnesty International and Reporters Without Borders took the opportunity of Sossou's appeal decision to draw attention to the growing threats to freedom of the press and of speech in Benin.

While another businessman, the wealthy Kikissagbé Godonou Bernard, alias KGB, was also sentenced to a heavy fine and five years in prison for organised fraud, other emblematic cases were still pending. Particularly notable among them was the case of the disappearance, in 2010, of the agent of the Ministry of Economy and Finance and opposition activist *Pierre Urbain Dangnivo*. August 2020 marked the tenth anniversary of what has gradually become a 'state affair', due to the strong politicisation of the case and its multiple reversals. In January 2020, the constitutional court required a judgment within a reasonable time; in fact, the trial has been postponed several times since 2015, and the two accused persons have been in custody for nearly ten years.

Finally, the year has also been marked by the passing of several *political figures*. Among them were the king of Savalou, who died at the beginning of the year, and Kpɔtozounmè Dê Hakpon III, on the throne of Porto Novo for 23 years, who passed away in February. In November, Abiola Félix Iroko, the renowned historian who was much appreciated in Benin for his work on kings among other subjects, also passed on.

Foreign Affairs

At the very beginning of the year, President Patrice Talon went to Washington for a four-day working visit, during which he met successively with representatives of the IMF and the World Bank to discuss the various reforms undertaken. He also met with the US secretary of state Mike Pompeo to discuss issues relating to democracy and regional security, as reported by the press. The second notable *presidential trip* took place at the end of the year: Patrice Talon went to the investiture ceremony of Alassane Ouattara, re-elected for a third term as President of Côte d'Ivoire, together with several other African heads of state, as well as France's former president Nicolas Sarkozy. For the rest of the year, diplomatic activity was rather sedentary, particularly because of the global pandemic.

In addition, Beninese authorities restructured the country's *diplomatic map*, for essentially budgetary reasons. Out of the 30 or so representations (embassies and consulates) of Benin in the world, 17 were closed at the end of July following the recommendations of a council of ministers held a few months earlier. Only two representations remained in Africa – in Nigeria and Morocco – and in the Americas – the US and Brazil. In the Middle East and Asia, Beninese representation remained in China, Saudi Arabia, and the UAE. In Europe, Benin maintained its representation only in Paris, Moscow, and the Vatican. In addition to the closure of the Brussels and Geneva embassies – European and international institutions' headquarters – it was also more directly the country's representations to regional and international organisations that were scrapped, notably those to the AU, the UN, the OIF, and UNESCO. In the face of criticism and concerns, Beninese authorities offered reassurances that the country's diplomatic activity would be maintained through non-resident ambassadors and missions reorganised along regional lines.

Under consideration by the French parliament since July 2020, the law on the *restitution of looted works* to Benin and Senegal was finally promulgated on 24 December. This applied to 26 cultural objects constituting the 'Treasure of Behanzin', looted during the sack of the Abomey palace by French colonisers in 1892. The restitution project was welcomed in Benin, but was also criticised, particularly regarding the scope of the objects concerned. Indeed, other works deemed more important had also been the subject of requests that remained unanswered, notably the statue of Gou, god of war and iron, commissioned by the king of Abomey and made around 1860. Exhibited at the Louvre, the statue is considered by some to be one of the finest works of pre-colonial African art and therefore of particular importance to Beninese art and heritage specialists.

On 29 September, the Office Français de Protection des Réfugiés et Apatrides (OFPRA), an agency supervised by the Interior Ministry, removed Benin from the *list of 'safe countries of origin'* for at least 12 months. According to the agency's website, the safety of a country is assessed 'with regard to the guarantees of protection that the authorities of these countries offer against persecution and ill-treatment, as well as the sanctions that they provide for in the event of proven violation of individual rights'. Demanded for several months by French associations working with migrants such as Forum Réfugiés-Cosi, this decision was based on 'the situation of public and political freedoms in the country', Jean-François Monteils, president of OFPRA, told AFP. This removal could thus increase the admissibility rate of asylum applications from Beninese nationals submitted to France. The publication, a few weeks earlier, of the 2020 World Happiness Record for 2017–19 offered a different picture of the country. In this report, published by the UN Sustainable Development Solutions Network, Benin displayed the highest improvement rate in wellbeing since the previous period 2008–12 and ranked third among African countries, after Mauritius and Côte d'Ivoire.

In the same vein, in its decision on the merits of Sébastien Ajavon's claim, on 4 December the ACHPR issued a very critical ruling against the Beninese political authorities, listing numerous grounds for *violations of fundamental rights and obligations*, such as the right to participation in one's country's public affairs and the principle of independence of the justice system. The court also found that the 2019 constitutional revision had been adopted in violation of the principle of national consensus and should therefore be repealed. While the court demanded – among other things – the abrogation of the text before any election was held, the government spokesperson declared that this decision bordered on 'heresy', recalling that the revision had been voted for 'unanimously by the people's representatives', as reported on Radio France International. At the end of the year, the political opposition, meeting on the occasion of the 30th anniversary of the promulgation of the Beninese constitution, echoed the ACHPR's decision and demanded a return to the spirit of the constitution of 11 December 1990.

On another note, the long-awaited reopening of the *Nigeria–Benin land border* occurred on 16 December. The closure, decided on August 2019 by the Abuja authorities in order to combat illegal cross-border trafficking, had heavily impacted the Beninese economy and negatively affected a large part of the population. ECOWAS had organised several high-level meetings to try to find a way out of a situation that called into question the principles of the AfCFTA, whose agreement had just been signed by Benin and Nigeria. Nevertheless, the reopening appeared to be partial: certain goods, such as rice or poultry, were still banned from circulation, and trucks and vehicles registered in Nigeria in particular were still not allowed to pass through the Sèmè-Kraké border post.

Socioeconomic Development

The country's economic, health, and social plans were significantly affected by the *Covid-19 crisis*. After the discovery of the first cases in March, the initial restrictive measures taken included, in addition to the generic rules of social distancing, the systematic quarantining of incoming travellers, the suspension of government officials' missions abroad, and the postponement of burials. The decision not to close schools and universities was much commented on in the country, and led the Fédération nationale des associations de parents d'élèves et étudiants du Bénin (Fenapeb) to refer the matter to the three ministers concerned, without success. Under popular pressure, the decision was finally taken on 22 and 23 March to close places of worship as well as schools, high schools, and universities. The government also announced the implementation of a sanitary cordon around the municipalities most exposed to the risk of propagation, such as Cotonou, Porto Novo, Sèmè-Podji, Zè, and Adjarra. On 24 March, when students of the University of Abomey-Calavi mobilised to press for the suspension of lectures, it soon escalated into clashes with the police in which a young student was shot. Unlike some of his African counterparts, President Talon ruled out the possibility of a lockdown. In a televised address, he explained that the country did not have the 'means' of rich countries to take such a decision, which could also cause 'chaos' in a context where the majority of workers lived on non-salaried income. At the same time, and notably with the support of various regional and international actors, Benin deployed special measures in various sectors. Healthcare-wise, the country committed to developing the capacity of its healthcare facilities in each of the 12 departments. On the economic front, a CFAfr 74 bn (approximately $ 134.5 m) 'support and response plan for the productive sector' was announced in June. While most of the package was reserved for the formal businesses sector – a fact that drew criticism – nearly CFAfr 5 bn (about $ 9 m) was set aside to support artisans and small trades, particularly in the informal sector. Two other allocations were more specific to citizens, including the poorest. On the education front, primary, secondary, and high schools reopened in May, and important measures were taken to ensure pedagogical continuity in higher education. In May, an e-learning platform was launched supported by telephone companies. This unprecedented experiment in Benin encountered numerous difficulties: in addition to connectivity problems, the unequal access to electronic and computer equipment was also an issue, despite the investment of the Ministry of Digital Affairs in the creation of multimedia centres throughout the country.

Although the number of Covid cases remained limited compared with other countries (at the end of December, 44 deaths had been reported among almost 3,200 confirmed cases), the pandemic had significant *economic repercussions*. Growth in 2020 remained positive at around 2%, but was down sharply from 7% in 2019, due to the health crisis and the consequences of the closure of the Nigeria borders. The price increase of agri-food products in the vast majority of WAEMU member states has been particularly significant in Benin, with an average annual inflation rate of 3%. Benin was nevertheless able to count on an excellent 2019/20 cotton harvest, confirming its position as the continent's leading seed cotton producer. More generally, despite budgetary pressure, Benin continued to enjoy the trust of international financial organisations. In February, the World Bank's Doing Business report ranked Benin 149th out of 190 countries, up four places from 2019. In April, the IMF, satisfied with Benin's performance criteria and macro-structural indicators, announced an increase in its financial support to the country. Shortly afterwards, in July, the World Bank classified Benin for the first time in the list of middle-income countries, due to the increase in annual per capita income. While this decision was an opportunity for Patrice Talon to highlight the reforms implemented, it was also used by several trade unions to demand better working conditions and wages for the country's many precarious workers.

More broadly, Benin's HDI progress for the year 2019 (which placed the country in 158th position out of 189 countries, an improvement of five places compared with 2018) hid an increase in the coefficient of inequality in the country, which is measured by health indices, decent living standards, and *access to knowledge*. It is worth mentioning here the setting up, at the beginning of the year, of the Conseil National de l'Éducation (CNE), aimed at coordinating the sector, participating in future-oriented reflection on education, and assessing the projects and reforms to be implemented. First created in 2003, the CNE was overhauled following the observation of its limited effectiveness during recent years. The CNE's new president, Ahonagnon Noël Gbaguidi, professor of private law and former holder of the UNESCO Chair in Human Rights and Democracy at the University of Abomey-Calavi, will be responsible, along with the other 28 members, for monitoring the transformation of the education system.

Education was precisely one of the areas associated with serious *gender inequality* in the country. The UNDP's HDI for 2019 pointed out that only 18.3% of women aged 25 and over have achieved a secondary education, compared with nearly 34% of men. In a broader perspective, the WEF's 2020 Global Gender Gap Report ranked Benin 119th out of 153 countries (nine places lower than in the 2006 survey), while revealing its complex structure of gender inequalities. As far as the gender gap in the economic sector was concerned (based on indicators such as women's participation in economic life, wage equity, etc.), Benin rated first out of 153 countries, although some missing data, such as the proportion of women in management positions in companies, would certainly have helped to refine the ranking. On the other hand, the country fell to 134th place on 'political empowerment'. The last municipal elections provided a meaningful illustration: of the country's 77 newly elected mayors, only four were women, in Kandi, Kétou, Adja Ouèrè, and Toffo. In Benin as in many countries, women were more numerous in the ranks of councillors and deputy mayors (as in Cotonou, Porto Novo, Abomey-Calavi, etc.). Women were proportionally more numerous in the government. At the end of 2020, out of 24 ministers, five were women, in higher education and scientific research, trade and industry, civil service and labour, social affairs and microfinance, and digital affairs.

The launch of the 2020 Human Development Report in Cotonou at the end of December was also an opportunity to look into the impact of human activities on global warming, and especially the recurring problem of *flooding* in the country, which faced exceptional rainfall in 2020. In September, in the north of the country, the Niger River overflowed its banks, affecting more than 8,000 households in Malanville, after having caused deadly floods in Niamey. In June, Cotonou had been affected, despite the various initiatives that had been undertaken in the past few years. The recent paving of the roads of the economic capital was intended to facilitate the evacuation of run-off water. Paradoxically however, this work has had the opposite effect in some areas, particularly those located beneath the roads. April 2020 marked the beginning of a rainwater sanitation programme (the Programme d'assainissement pluvial de Cotonou) supported by the government and financed by the AFD, which aimed to build drainage channels and retention basins throughout the city. At the same time, other donors (such as the World Bank, the AfDB and the Banque Ouest Africaine de Développement) were committed to financing the building of other basins in the city.

Burkina Faso

Daniel Eizenga

In Burkina Faso, 2020 presented yet another tumultuous year.[1] The first person to officially die of Covid-19 in sub-Saharan Africa fell victim to the pandemic in Ouagadougou. President Roch Marc Christian Kaboré and his political party faced down electoral challengers in joint presidential and legislative elections in November. Insecurity worsened in areas already hard hit by militant Islamist insurgencies, which showed worrying signs of spreading to new regions of the country. The mounting challenges presented by the insecurity propelled ever greater international coordination among neighbouring countries and international supporters. In September, disastrous flooding as a result of unseasonably heavy rains exacerbated the already challenging humanitarian situation facing the country. By the end of the year, nearly one in 20 citizens had been displaced from their homes.

---

[1] The views expressed in this chapter are those of the author and are not an official policy or position of the Africa Center for Strategic Studies.

Domestic Politics

Burkina Faso organised presidential and legislative elections on 22 November. Incumbent president Roch Marc Christian Kaboré won the contest in the first round with nearly 58% of the vote. His party, the Mouvement du Peuple pour le Progrès (MPP), won 56 seats in the legislature, increasing their representation by one seat but still short of a majority in the 127-seat national assembly. The Congrès pour la Démocratie et le Progrès (CDP), the former ruling party, obtained the second-largest number of seats with 20, an increase of two from the previous elections organised in 2015. The CDP's presidential candidate, Eddie Komboïgo, took second place with 15.5% of the vote. The presidential candidate of the Union pour le Progrès et le Changement (UPC), Zéphirin Diabré, who also served as minority leader in parliament, claimed the third spot with just over 12% of the vote. No other candidate won more than 4% of the vote.

The UPC, which had previously been the largest opposition party in parliament, lost 21 seats in the national assembly, bringing its total down to 12. The UPC's electoral losses benefited the Nouveau Temps pour la Démocratie (NTD), which jumped from three to 13 parliamentarians. Overall, seven new political parties gained representation within the national assembly. Since no party obtained a majority, however, the MPP once again needed to build a coalition in parliament to support its legislative agenda. This proved straightforward with the gains made by the NTD, whose leader, Vincent Dabilgou, served as Kaboré's transportation minister and remained a supporter of Kaboré and his party during and after the electoral cycle.

Electoral controversies centred on the administration of the elections, including debates over the electoral list and voter registration. This was in part because the diaspora gained the ability to vote in national elections for the first time in the country's history. Burkinabè citizens in the diaspora were able to register at embassies until 26 January. This issue became a political foil in Côte d'Ivoire, where some 1.2 m to 2 m potential Burkinabè voters reside. Despite this, only a few thousand registered to vote, as many lacked proper identification. Among the diaspora, many did not have an up-to-date national identity card or passport and thus could not register.

The most significant controversy surrounding the elections related to the implications of rapidly deteriorating security in the Est and Centre-Nord regions of the country. In the context of worsening insecurity, the legislature voted to establish a parliamentary team to lead an investigation in the areas experiencing lethal violence and evaluate the viability of organising elections. On 8 July, the team submitted a report recommending that the legislative elections be postponed for one year; two days later, the ruling and opposition parties agreed to reject the proposed postponement. Instead, on 25 August, the Burkinabè parliament endorsed a bill to modify the electoral code to stipulate that if exceptional circumstances, such as insecurity, prevented the organisation of elections in certain districts, the results of the election would be validated by those polling stations that were able to open on election day. According to the minister of the territorial administration, Siméon Sawadogo, the bill struck a compromise between the government and the opposition, despite some critics challenging the bill as a threat to democracy. Ultimately, insecurity prevented voter registration in nearly 20% of electoral districts. A total of 1,619 out of 9,299 electoral districts were not included in the electoral list registration process carried out from 3 January to 17 July, according to the Independent National Electoral Commission. This represented a total of up to 417,000 lost votes, or roughly 7% of the country's registered voters.

Violent events associated with militant Islamist insurgencies wrought havoc on communities in 2020, causing more fatalities and destruction than in any previous year. According to the Armed Conflict Location and Event Data Project, 1,625 fatalities were associated with militant Islamist violence, marking a 27% increase in fatalities since 2019. The worsening insecurity was heavily concentrated in the regions of Nord, Sahel, Est, and Centre-Nord. The eastern regions experienced a 75% increase in violent events in 2020 compared with 2019.

This violence took many forms, at times targeting villagers indiscriminately, causing them to flee from their homes, while at other times targeting strategic resources or individuals. In one example on 7 August, at least 20 people were killed during an armed attack against the Namoungou village in the Est region when unidentified armed men on motorbikes, presumably militant Islamists, opened fire at a cattle market.

The governor of the region, Colonel Saidou Sanou, urged civilians to remain vigilant and collaborate with the army. However, collaboration with the armed forces remained a challenge, as credible accounts emerged of human rights abuses committed by the military in the north of the country. On 10 June, Amnesty International released a report alleging human rights abuses by security forces in Burkina Faso between February and April 2020. It noted extrajudicial killings, and disappearances of civilians, notably of displaced people, by security forces acting under the cover of anti-terrorist activity. On 8 July, HRW released a report stating that 180 bodies had been uncovered in mass graves around the town of Djibo, claiming that the Burkinabè security forces had targeted and killed ethnic Fulani individuals extrajudicially. Residents of the town buried the bodies between March and April. Such atrocities committed by government authorities contributed to an overall acceleration of violence in the wider Sahel region.

In an example of militant Islamist group violence in Djibo, armed men targeted a prominent cleric who had spoken out against the jihadists. On 11 August, presumed jihadists kidnapped the grand imam of Djibo, Souaibou Cissé. Djibo had been at the epicentre of terrorist violence since 2016, and the imam was one of the local authorities who had refused to abandon the town. He was abducted on his way back from Ouagadougou by an armed group that stopped the public bus on which he was travelling to check the identities of the passengers. The armed men allowed all others to proceed, suggesting that they were specifically looking for the imam. Cissé had openly spoken out against the ideology of jihadist groups in the area, advocating for tolerance and peace. On 15 August, Cissé was found dead. President Kaboré condemned the assassination, stating that the murder of this religious dignitary, head of the Muslim community in the province of Soum, was indicative of the extremist and inhuman nature of its perpetrators. No group claimed responsibility for the assassination.

Insecurity contributed also to the internal displacement of nearly 1 m citizens, the vast majority of whom fled their homes in 2020. Internal displacement in the wider Sahel region has quadrupled over the last two years, largely driven by IDPs in Burkina Faso. At the beginning of 2019, there were 490,000 IDPs in the entire Sahel region; by the end of 2020 there were nearly 2 m, and more than half were Burkinabè, according to the UNHCR. The wave of displacements grew as the year progressed and violence persisted. On 5 October, 25 people were killed by a presumed militant Islamist group in the town of Pissila, in the Sanmatenga province of the Centre-Nord region. The attack targeted an IDP convoy returning people to their home villages. These events contributed to the UNHCR's assessment that Burkina Faso was now the site of the world's fastest-growing displacement and protection crisis, with more than one in every 20 inhabitants displaced by surging violence.

The worsening security conditions, the inability of the government to hold elections in all electoral districts, and limitations on citizens' freedom of movement have all contributed to a trend of diminishing civil liberties and political rights in recent years. Freedom House's annual rankings reflect that trend, though the country maintained its rating as 'partly free', with 2020's score dropping slightly from 56/100 to 54/100. In 2019, the score dropped four points from 60/100 the previous year.

Foreign Affairs

The ongoing insecurity driven by militant Islamist insurgencies left significant impacts on Burkina Faso's foreign relations. Burkina Faso continued its participation in the Sahel G5, participating in multiple joint operations targeting militant Islamist groups in the Liptako-Gourma region where the borders of Mali, Burkina Faso, and Niger meet. Despite the efforts of the joint force, the degree to which insecurity had already worsened by the start of the year raised alarm among the G5's foreign partners, particularly France, which also maintains a counter-terrorism force in the region of more than 5,100 deployed soldiers.

On 13 January, Emmanuel Macron received the presidents of the G5 Sahel at the southern French city of Pau to clarify their positions on the situation. This summit was organised in response to the increased insecurity and growing anti-French sentiment. Since 2016, violent attacks had increased fivefold, with Burkina Faso displaying the most alarming deterioration in security. During the summit, topics discussed included an increase in aid from the rest of the international community; the search for solutions to the Libyan crisis, which contributes to instability in the wider region; and the elaboration of a new framework for stabilising the region. The summit's conclusion offered little actual clarity other than a declaration that signalled the G5's desire for a continued French presence in the region, and willingness to work collectively to reinforce military cooperation. A follow-up summit was held on 30 June in Mauritania with the objective of reinforcing the collaboration between French military forces and the G5 Sahel member countries.

In an example of the anti-French sentiment that had been growing in the region and the frustration of citizens with their governments' inability to address the drivers of insecurity, leaders of Burkinabè civil society organised a counter-G5 summit in the southern city of Pô (pronounced similarly to the French city, Pau) on 13 January to coincide with the French summit. Burkinabè civil society and political leaders met to demonstrate their opposition to the French presence in the region. Representatives from neighbouring countries also attended the event. Participants criticised the cooperation between France and the G5 Sahel, which they characterised as defined by paternalism, deception, and blackmail. They called on Sahelian states to preserve their national sovereignty by assuming responsibility for their own defence, as well as the reorganisation of Sahelian armies to better address the methods and underlying political causes of violence.

The armed forces expanded their engagement and collaboration with the Ivoirian military to combat terrorism and a growing insurgent threat in south-western Burkina Faso. While this area has not seen the degree of violence present in northern and eastern regions, militant Islamist fighters increasingly launched attacks on Burkinabè communities using an Ivoirian national park near their shared border as a rear base. The two countries organised a joint operation in May, named Comoé after the national park, that resulted in the arrest of 38 suspects and the deaths of eight others. It also led to the destruction of a terrorist base, with arms, ammunition, and other materiel being seized.

On 10 June, jihadist fighters carried out a reprisal attack against a military base in the north-east of Côte d'Ivoire, killing at least ten soldiers. This retaliation by jihadists occurred in the same area as joint operation Comoé. The jihadist fighters in the area are reportedly part of Katiba Macina, a jihadist group led by the Malian preacher Amadou Koufa. The leader of this contingent is believed to be Dramane Sibidé or 'Hamza', a Fulani fighter who was sent by Koufa to establish a recruiting network in Côte d'Ivoire. The successful attack on Ivoirian forces underscored the capabilities and organisation of this nascent contingent of Katiba Macina insurgents.

On 26 February, the Burkinabè president received two representatives from the EU: the European commissioner of crisis management, Janez Lenarčič, and the European commissioner on international agreements, Jutta Urpilainen. After their meetings, the Burkinabè minister of foreign affairs, Alpha Barry, announced € 11 m in EU aid to help Burkina Faso to manage the humanitarian and security crises. The two commissioners also visited internally displaced sites in the Centre-Nord region and asked national decision-makers to address the causes of the crisis, not only humanitarian needs. Since 2014, the EU has provided more than € 1 bn in humanitarian and developmental aid to Burkina Faso.

Two westerners kidnapped in 2018 in Burkina Faso were freed 13 March. Canadian Édith Blais and her Italian friend, Luca Tacchetto, were found by MINUSMA near the city of Kidal in Mali. Although they were kidnapped at the same time, they were separated for months and were relocated at least twice by the kidnappers. Men with connections to militant Islamist groups in the region took Blais and Tacchetto hostage while they were driving from Ouagadougou to Bobo-Dioulasso as tourists.

Socioeconomic Developments

The Covid-19 pandemic hit Burkina Faso early and relatively hard. The government suspended public gatherings after the first two cases of coronavirus were detected on 9 March in Ouagadougou. The two patients were a couple who had recently returned from France. The cases made the country the eighth on the continent to report coronavirus infections, after Cameroon, Senegal, South Africa, Nigeria, Algeria, Togo, and Egypt. The first Covid-19 death reported in Africa occurred in Burkina Faso, during the evening between 17 and 18 March. The victim, Rose Marie Compaoré, was a member of parliament and the second vice-president of the national assembly. She was 62 years old. By 19 March, the number of people who had tested positive had risen to 33, with 31 positive cases in Ouagadougou, one in Houndé, and one in Bobo-Dioulasso. Covid-19 hit government ministers particularly hard, with five testing positive, including the minister of education, Stanislas Ouaro, and the minister of foreign affairs, Alpha Barry, by the end of March. Authorities successfully isolated the first cases and established a surveillance system through an official prevention plan, but an initial lack of means (with only 400 coronavirus test kits and three health facilities in the country able to carry out tests) quickly revealed that the government had limited ability to manage the disease.

Officials reacted quickly, however, implementing shutdowns and quarantines in major urban areas, imposing a curfew across the country, closing airports in

Ouagadougou and Bobo-Dioulasso, and closing land borders to all but commercial traffic. Effective 27 April, wearing a face mask became obligatory throughout the country. Some precautions were lifted gradually during the pandemic. On 4 May, officials lifted the city quarantine orders and by 3 June, the curfew was no longer in effect except in provinces under a state of emergency due to insecurity. Airports returned to normal operations on 1 August, though all land borders remained closed except to commercial traffic throughout the rest of the year.

As the pandemic wore on, humanitarian assistance groups, such as the Alliance Technique d'Assistance au Développement, warned about the impact of the spread of Covid-19 in rural areas experiencing humanitarian crisis. Rural populations in Burkina Faso were particularly vulnerable because of the number of displaced persons, and experts feared a potential health crisis would complicate the situation further. Armed attacks in the region also slowed the humanitarian response, including the delivery of personal protection equipment (PPE) to displaced people and other rural populations.

On 24 October, the Burkinabè government announced a $ 15.6 m. package from the Arab Bank for Economic Development in Africa for prevention of and fight against Covid-19. The loan is aimed to strengthen the health system. The funds were used to acquire new equipment for laboratories and operating rooms in university and regional hospital centres. Additionally, they will help support the process of tracing and controlling the spread of coronavirus. According to the African Centers for Disease Control and Prevention, more than 15,000 cases of coronavirus had been detected, resulting in more than 150 deaths by the end of the year.

In September, authorities declared a state of natural disaster after days of unseasonably heavy rains. The resulting floods killed at least 13 people and injured 50. Along with other damages, the floods swept away a makeshift bridge in the southwest of the country, cutting off the village of Marabagasso from the city of Bobo-Dioulasso, 70 km away. Burkina Faso's Ministry of Finance allocated $ 9.1 m for an aid package announced by Minister of Cultural Affairs Abdoul Karim Sango, to help the flood victims. According to official government numbers, at least 71,000 Burkinabè were affected by the flooding. Multiple cities sustained damage in the floods, which destroyed at least 1,700 residences. The aid will be used to rebuild houses, purchase sanitation kits, and ensure health assistance to victims. A separate report estimated the need for $ 16 m in aid to manage the damages.

An AfDB report released in 2020 found that a sub-project for sanitation in the outlying districts of Ouagadougou, which had been implemented in 2013, reduced the number of victims of flooding from 45,000 in 2009 to fewer than 9,000 in 2019. The $ 39.8 m project was funded by a grant from the AfDB's African Development Fund. The project objective was to facilitate the evacuation of rainwater and improve solid waste management in Ouagadougou. It constructed canals and increased the volume of the retention basin. The flooding in 2020 underscored the importance of such projects, as climate scientists predict an increasing chance of flooding in the region due to the effects of climate change.

On 19 October, the UN emergency food relief agency WFP warned that unless access is urgently granted to humanitarian organisations, thousands in the central Sahel will be pushed further into destitution, sounding the alarm that catastrophic levels of hunger could hit Burkinabè communities. Increasing violence jeopardised the delivery of food items by humanitarian organisations, which are often the target of non-state armed groups. Among the goals established for the Sahel, WFP identified the need to build resilience through rehabilitating community assets, improving degraded land, feeding students, and community-based nutrition activities to prevent and treat malnutrition.

Burkinabè minister of water and sanitation Niouga Ambroise Ouédraogo officially launched the Priority Action Program for Drinking Water in Bobo-Dioulasso in October. This programme is sponsored by a € 20 m loan from the Agence Française de Développement (AFD). The funds will be used to strengthen raw water production in the rural commune of Nasso and transfer treated water to a site in Bolomakoté. The government aims to build a new water pumping station, a pipe, and a reservoir and estimated that the construction would take two years. Thanks to the project, the National Office for Water and Sanitation (ONEA) will reduce prolonged water cuts and increase the rate of water supply in Bobo-Dioulasso over the next 15 years.

On 8 December, the national anti-corruption network, known as REN-LAC (Le Réseau national de lutte anti-corruption), organised a forum on transparency and accountability in the management of mineral resources during the 15th edition of its national anti-corruption day. REN-LAC denounced cases of tax evasion and demanded that Kaboré's government reinforce its management strategy for the mining sector, which represents more than 11% of GDP and supports nearly 40,000 jobs. The country's subsoil is rich in gold, copper, and zinc and their production represents more than 70% of national exports.

On 11 December, the town of Banfora in the region of Cascades hosted the annual independence day celebration. The military and civilian parade marked the commemorative ceremony under the 2020 theme, 'National cohesion and patriotic commitment for sustainable development in Burkina Faso in a context of insecurity and Covid-19'. Around 3,500 people took part in the parade. The number of defence and security forces was lower than in past years due to the security operations underway as part of the country's fight against terrorism. Marking 60 years of independence, President Kaboré called on the government and the people to assume their share of responsibility to make social cohesion and patriotism concrete realities across political, administrative, economic, and social divides.

The Association of Journalists of Burkina (AJB), representatives of civil society organisations, the government, and family members gathered for an annual demonstration to pay tribute to the journalist Norbert Zongo and his companions, who were assassinated 22 years ago on 13 December. President of the AJB Guézouma Sanogo recalled the events of 1998 and denounced the silencing of Zongo, who was investigating the mysterious death of François Compaoré's driver. In the ongoing legal case, the judiciary authorised the extradition of Compaoré, who is former president Blaise Compaoré's brother, from France. In March 2020, the French government signed an extradition decree for Compaoré, though his legal representative indicated that they would continue to fight the decision.

Cabo Verde

Gerhard Seibert

The pandemic prompted a severe set-back in the country's important tourism sector, which dropped drastically by 75% in terms of tourist arrivals. In addition to the crisis provoked by the pandemic, in the second half of the year the controversial extradition proceedings against the arrested Colombian businessman Alex Saab, the special envoy of Venezuela's President Nicolás Maduro wanted by the US for money laundering, dominated the local debate. In the municipal elections of 25 October, the ruling Movimento para a Democracia (MpD) lost the capital Praia and three other municipalities to the opposition Partido Africano da Independência de Cabo Verde (PAICV) but remained the dominant party at the local level, controlling 14 of the country's 22 municipalities.

Domestic Politics

On 8 January 2020, Prime Minister Ulisses Correia e Silva *reshuffled his government* by replacing the minister of tourism and transport and of the maritime economy, José da Silva Gonçalves, who had requested his own dismissal for personal reasons. Paulo Veiga, hitherto secretary of state for maritime economy, took over the maritime economy portfolio while Carlos Jorge Santos, previously local administrator of the Portuguese Oásis Atlântico hotel group, was appointed minister of tourism and transport. In addition, Rui Figueiredo Soares, since 2016 the MpD's parliamentary leader in the national assembly, was appointed deputy minister to the prime minister and minister of regional integration.

On 9 February, *Correia e Silva was re-elected unopposed* as leader of the MpD, a post he had occupied since 2013, by 99% of the votes cast in direct party elections. Only 58.4% of the registered 31,541 party members participated in the voting, less than the 65% turnout in the previous MpD leadership elections in 2017. At the MpD's 12th national convention in Praia on 6–7 March, Filomena Delgado, a former minister of education, was elected secretary-general by the 300 participating delegates. In his opening address, Correia e Silva claimed that with the political results of governance achieved in the current legislature, his party was committed to rule at least until 2026.

In *response to the pandemic*, on 10 March the government approved a National Contingency Plan for the Prevention and Control of Covid-19. Eight days later, Cabo Verde Airlines suspended all of its operations, flights to a few international destinations having already been interrupted since 27 February. On 20 March, the national health authorities reported the first case of coronavirus infection, in Boa Vista. Three days later, this person became the country's first Covid-19 fatality. On 2 April, President Jorge Fonseca declared a nationwide state of emergency to contain the coronavirus outbreak. On 27 April, the emergency was lifted in six islands without cases of infections, but maintained in São Vicente until 3 May, in Boa Vista until 14 May, and in Santiago until 29 May. On 1 March, the government decreed a moratorium until 31 December on all credit payments to ease the financial hardships caused by the pandemic. On 30 July, the national assembly approved a revised budget of 75 bn escudos (CVE; equivalent to € 680.1 m), with revenue of CVE 871 m (€ 7.9 m) – 13% less than in the initial budget due to the crisis. On 12 October, the government reopened the country's international airports and sea ports. Between 20 March and 31 December, the local health authorities reported 11,793 Covid-19 cases and 112 deaths.

On 12 June, the *Colombian businessman Alex Saab, special envoy of Venezuela's President Nicolás Maduro, was detained by the local authorities* during a refuelling stop-over at Sal airport in a San Marino-registered private jet on a business trip on behalf of the Venezuelan government to Iran, due to an international arrest warrant issued by the USA. The US authorities, who have no extradition treaty with Cabo Verde, accused Saab of money laundering of $ 350 m in US banks to maintain Maduro's underground financial network and with intent to undermine US-imposed sanctions, and demanded his extradition to have him tried in a US court. The Maduro government claimed that Saab's alleged diplomatic immunity rendered his detention illegal and demanded his immediate release. On 31 July, the court of appeal in Mindelo decided in favour of Saab's extradition to the USA, whereupon his international defence team, including the widely known Spanish lawyer Baltasar Garzón, lodged an appeal with the supreme court. On 19 October, the latter decided to return the case for review to the court of appeal in Mindelo. On 30 November, the ECOWAS Court of Justice in Abuja ordered the Cabo Verdean authorities to transfer Saab from prison to house arrest while awaiting the court verdict. However, Cabo Verde did not comply with the order, as it repudiated the court's jurisdiction. In an attempt to grant Saab diplomatic status, on 24 December Venezuela's government appointed him as its deputy permanent representative to the AU in Addis Ababa.

In the *local elections held on 25 October*, surprisingly, the ruling MpD lost the capital Praia to the opposition PAICV. Altogether the MpD won 14 municipalities, while the PAICV captured the remaining eight, six more than in 2016. In addition to Praia, the MpD lost another four of the 18 municipalities won in 2016 to the PAICV (Ribeira Grande, São Domingos, Tarrafal de Santiago, and São Filipe) but captured a new one (Ribeira Brava), held by independents since 2016. In addition to the five municipalities taken from the MpD, the PAICV also won in Boa Vista, hitherto ruled by independents. The voter turnout was 52.2%, despite the pandemic only the third lowest in the country's history.

Foreign Affairs

The pandemic significantly reduced diplomatic travelling to and from the archipelago. On 10 February, health minister Arlindo do Rosário received the local Chinese ambassador Du Xiaocong to discuss the evolution of the outbreak of the coronavirus pandemic in China in general and Wuhan in particular, where 13 Cabo Verdean students were staying. Another issue on the meeting's agenda was the safe return of Cabo Verdean students from other provinces and that of Chinese residents in the archipelago, who had spent the Chinese New Year at home. On behalf of the government, Rosário recognised the Chinese authorities' enormous efforts to contain the spread of the disease. On 12 March, foreign and defence minister Luís Filipe Tavares and Ambassador Du Xiaocong signed an agreement on the *concession of Chinese military assistance* worth $ 5 m for five years, including the supply of military hardware and training.

On 17 February, Tavares received Luxembourg's ministers of economy, cooperation, and humanitarian affairs, Franz Fayot; of environment, climate, and sustainable development, Carole Dieschbourg; and of energy and spatial planning, Claude Turmes. The local delegation comprised the ministers of agriculture and environment, Gilberto Silva, and of industry, trade, and energy, Alexandre Monteiro; and the national director of political, economic, and cultural affairs, Ambassador Júlio

Morais. The two delegations discussed *Luxembourg's 5th Indicative Cooperation Programme (PIC) for Cabo Verde* for the period 2021–25. On 26 June, finance minister Olavo Correia signed agreements worth € 1.63 m with Luxembourg's *chargé d'affaires* in Praia, Angèle da Cruz, on financial aid for the fight against the pandemic, including € 495,000 to finance the deployment of a 33-member Cuban medical team in the archipelago. On 9 July, ministers Tavares and Fayot, via videoconference, signed the PIC Development, Climate and Energy (2021–25) worth € 78 m.

On 30 April in Moscow, Tavares and *Russia's foreign minister Sergey Lavrov* signed a bilateral agreement on mutual visa waivers between the two countries. On 28 June, the minister of tourism and transport, Carlos Santos, received the local Russian ambassador Vladimir Sokolenko to discuss a new bilateral agreement on aviation and the promotion of Cabo Verde as a tourist destination, as well as the possibility of Russian private investments in the archipelago's tourism and transport sectors.

On 3 August, *Guinea-Bissau opened an embassy in Praia*, where hitherto it had only had a general consulate. During the inauguration ceremony, Fernando Elísio Freire, the minister of state, declared that in turn Cabo Verde would soon open its embassy in Bissau. He said that it was necessary for the two countries to strengthen their bilateral relations because in addition to a common official language, historical ties, and common interests, they both belonged to the same inter-state organisations, namely ECOWAS, AU, and CPLP. Finally, on 16 December, Correia e Silva announced the inauguration of his country's first embassy in Bissau for early 2021. He said the embassy would also provide services to the 40,000 Cabo Verdean migrants and their descendants living in Guinea-Bissau.

Socioeconomic Developments

On 3 January, the *state acquired 27.44% of the shares in Caixa Económica de Cabo Verde* (CECV), owned by the Macau-based GeoCapital before 2018. The central bank, Banco de Cabo Verde, had initially approved the acquisition of the stake by International Holding Cabo Verde (IHCV), but in 2019 disagreements with the government regarding CECV's future prompted the withdrawal of that investor. Finance minister Olavo Correia declared that the government's objective with the deal was to guarantee both the bank's shareholder stability and the stability of the national financial system. He said that the government retained its right and interest to sell the stake to a sound and experienced private investor. The Instituto Nacional de Previdência Social remained the CECV's major stakeholder with 47.21% of shares, while the other stakeholders were Correios de Cabo Verde, with 15.14%, and private investors and employees, who held 10.21% of the shares.

On 21 February, the stock exchange Bolsa de Valores de Cabo Verde announced that the sale of 7.65% of the shares in *Cabo Verde Airlines* (CVA) to 44 investors from the migrant communities in the US and 13 other countries had generated CVE 108,765,050 (€ 986,216) for the state. On 22 March, Correia e Silva declared that the scheduled sale of the remaining 39% of CVA owned by the state to institutional investors would be delayed, since, due to the crisis, the airline was expected to become a recipient of economic support. On 27 July, the government approved a guarantee for a loan from the International Investment Bank (IIB) amounting to € 10.2 m for CVA. On 31 July, finance minister Olavo Correia affirmed that without state intervention the airline would disappear, but guaranteed that the government's support would be proportional to the size of the state's stake in the company. On 3 November, the government guaranteed another loan of CVE 218 m (ca. € 2 m) from IIB for CVA to pay the salaries of its 300 employees in arrears and delayed debt service payments. The same day, the executive authorised another guarantee for an emergency loan of CVE 100 m (€ 906,865) from CECV for CVA – also to pay salaries in arrears.

On 29 May, in *litigation between Unitel T+ and CV Telecom* over access to the terminal of the submarine cable of the West Africa Cable System (WACS) in Praia, the regulator Agência Reguladora Multissectorial da Economia' (ARME) decided in favour of the former. CV Telecom had tried to deny Unitel T+ access to the WACS, arguing that the company, owned by Angolan businesswoman Isabel dos Santos, daughter of former Angolan president Eduardo do Santos, did not belong to the consortium of investors of the WACS. CV Telecom rejected the verdict and announced its intention to appeal at court.

On 8 June, the *national assembly adopted the law on the Zona Económica Marítima in São Vicente (ZEEMSV)*, which created a special regime for the organisation, development, and functioning of an integrated economic zone of sea-related enterprises and services in São Vicente and the neighbouring islands of Santo Antão, São Nicolau, and Santa Luzia. By 2035, the ZEEMSV, whose viability study had been supported by China, was expected to become a regional maritime logistics platform for the transhipment of cargo and containers and the processing, marketing, and distribution of products from the sea, and a prestigious international tourist destination. Under the law, parties making private investments of above € 2.5 m were entitled to receive special incentives from the state, depending on the amount invested, socioeconomic impact, job creation, and relevance to the implementation of the free trade zone.

On 15 December, finance minister Correia signed an agreement with the Spanish real estate businessman Enrique Bañuelos de Castro, the representative of IHCV in Praia, *on the implementation of the tourism project Little África Maio*. The project, aimed at the touristic development of Maio Island with an extension to neighbouring Santiago, was for an estimated € 500 m, the biggest private investment ever made in Cabo Verde. The project, which included the construction of the country's fifth international airport in Maio, was expected to create more than 2,000 direct local jobs during the three-phase construction period and more than 4,000 jobs after its complete implementation. The government classified the investment as of enormous national interest in the context of the national development strategy.

As expected, the *pandemic severely hit the important tourism sector*, which represents about 25% of Cabo Verde's GDP. The number of foreign tourists dropped by 74.7%, from 819,308 in 2019 to 207,125, of whom 189,110 arrived in the first quarter of the year. Hotel accommodation was preferred by 87.4% of the tourists, while hostels, guest houses, and tourist villages were chosen by 4.9%, 4.3%, and 2.2% of the visitors respectively. As in previous years, Sal Island was the major destination with 40.2% of tourists, while Boa Vista and Santiago followed with 28.1% and 16.0% of the total, respectively. The UK was again the main country of origin with 19.4% of all tourists, followed by Cabo Verde (12.4%), France (11.8%), Germany (11.0%), Netherlands/Belgium (10.3%), Portugal (6.3%), and Italy (2.3%).

Côte d'Ivoire

Jesper Bjarnesen

Côte d'Ivoire went through another turbulent election year in 2020, cementing an unfortunate trend, which began with the presidential elections in 2000 and continued in 2010, of controversy, political polarisation, and widespread election-related violence recurring at a ten-year interval. The global Covid-19 pandemic placed additional burdens on the Ivorian population, as national lockdowns and global recession affected local livelihoods and overall economic growth significantly. Despite a turbulent political year, however, the government responded with a series of measures to alleviate the effects of the pandemic, and most macroeconomic indicators were already showing signs of some recovery by year's end.

Domestic Politics

The long build-up to the 2020 presidential elections intensified in the first months of the year. Debates and negotiations between the ruling party and the main opposition continued around the composition of the Independent Electoral Commission, following a 2019 vote to proceed with minor reforms and a consolidation of its mandate. Despite continued disagreements, however, the main opposition parties signalled their intention to participate in the elections for the first time since the controversial elections of 2010, which cost more than 3,000 lives in election-related violence.

On 5 March, President Alassane Ouattara officially declared that he would *not present his candidacy* in the 31 October vote but would 'transfer power to a younger generation'. With this statement, Ouattara finally laid to rest speculation that he was considering an unconstitutional third-term bid, having previously insisted that the 2016 constitutional reform allowed him two additional presidential mandates. The announcement was met with relief and praise from all sides of the political spectrum, with opposition leader Pascal Affi N'Guessan expressing a 'feeling of respect' for Ouattara's decision not to run for a third term.

Ouattara's prime minister and close political ally for more than 30 years, *Amadou Gon Coulibaly, was launched as the official ruling-party candidate* on 12 March. In light of the fallout between Ouattara and vice-president Daniel Kablan Duncan, as well as the heated rivalry with former rebel leader turned prime minister Guillaume Soro, Gon Coulibaly was an obvious choice for Ouattara. Gon Coulibaly's candidacy signalled a consolidation of Ouattara's political agenda and a bolstering of the ruling Rally of Houphouëtists for Democracy and Peace (RHDP) despite the splintering of the coalition between Ouattara and Henri Konan Bédié's Democratic Party of Côte d'Ivoire (PDCI). Gon Coulibaly, in other words, entered the presidential race as the clear frontrunner.

Following the sentencing *in absentia* of Guillaume Soro to 20 years in prison in December 2019, the rivalry between Ouattara and his former prime minister, whom many had seen as Ouattara's likely successor, had reached a point of no return, and Soro proceeded to launch his legal battle to overturn the verdict from exile in Paris, while also mobilising his supporters around the Générations et peuples solidaires (GPS) movement via social media. Soro also filed a complaint to the African Court on Human and Peoples' Rights (AfCHPR), the court siding with the claimant and against the Ivorian state on 22 April and ordering the suspension of the arrest warrant issued against Soro. On 29 April, in response to the ruling, government spokesperson Sidi Touré announced Côte d'Ivoire's decision to *withdraw* its acceptance of the AfCHPR's jurisdiction over complaints by individuals and NGOs. The announcement was met with condemnation from civil society and human rights groups, such as the Ivorian Human Rights Observatory (OIDH), as well as from the political opposition. Guillaume Soro's legal representation stated on Twitter that the decision to withdraw from the AfCHPR 'joins a series of political manoeuvres aimed at removing his candidature from the presidential election, at the cost of a serious politicisation of the judiciary'.

The ruling party faced another challenge from exile from former president Laurent Gbabgo, under house arrest in Brussels while awaiting the appeal of his

2019 acquittal by the International Criminal Court in The Hague. With the presidential poll approaching, Gbagbo became increasingly involved in the newly forged opposition alliance between his Ivorian Popular Front (FPI) and the PDCI of his former rival, ex-president Henri Konan Bédié. By mid-year, Côte d'Ivoire's domestic political agenda was dominated by the build-up to the presidential elections, which were promising to see the ruling party introduce a new figurehead but seasoned politician, Amadou Gon Coulibaly, to confront the challenge of three veterans in Ivorian politics: former presidents Laurent Gbagbo and Henri Konan Bédié, and former rebel leader turned prime minister Guillaume Soro. Symptomatically, the leader of Laurent Gbagbo's FPI, Pascal Affi N'Guessan, who was likely to become the FPI's official candidate in the absence of Gbagbo, was receiving far less attention than his illustrious patron.

On 10 June, Côte d'Ivoire sustained its first jihadist attack since the 2016 attack on the coastal town of Grand Bassam, which claimed 19 lives. The Ivorian security forces initiated a joint anti-jihadist mission with the armed forces of neighbouring Burkina Faso, named Operation Comoé, following the detection of jihadist operatives in the Comoé National Park on the border between the two countries. Having established their presence in mid-May, the Ivorian forces came under attack on 10 June, with jihadists attacking a military base in Kafolo in the north-east, near the border with Burkina Faso. The attack claimed the lives of ten Ivorian soldiers and confirmed the growing threat of the Sahelian security crisis expanding southwards into Côte d'Ivoire. On 22 June, defence minister Hamed Bakayoko announced the capture of the leader of the group responsible for the attacks, without offering any details regarding the identity of the captive or the composition or affiliation of the group.

On 8 July, less than four months before the 31 October elections, *prime minister Amadou Gon Coulibaly passed away* following heart failure as he was leaving a cabinet meeting. In addition to the many expressions of shock and condolences, the sudden death of the frontrunner sparked immediate speculation around whether or not Alassane Ouattara would be willing and able to appoint another candidate to represent the RHDP; whether the elections would be postponed; or whether the incumbent would go back on his pledge to leave the presidential race to a new generation. Given the president's dominance in all major legislative bodies, this decision was viewed as primarily a personal choice for Ouattara rather than a procedural one. On 13 July, *Vice-President Duncan resigned*, citing personal reasons. It was speculated that his main reason for leaving the government was his disappointment with not having been considered by the president as a potential successor, and his gradual marginalisation within Ouattara's inner circle since the splintering of the ruling alliance in 2018, which led to Duncan's former PDCI patron, Henri Konan Bédié, leaving the coalition and expelling anyone who chose to remain in government from the party. On 30 July, *Defence Minister Hamed Bakayoko was appointed prime minister*. Bakayoko was, like his predecessor, a long-standing ally of Alassane Ouattara within the Rally of Republicans (RDR) party long before it merged with the RHDP in 2018. He was widely seen as the obvious choice, given the untimely death of Amadou Gon Coulibaly, and as another loyal supporter of the Ouattara throughout his presidency.

On 6 August, during the celebration of Côte d'Ivoire's 60 years of independence from France, Ouattara announced that, in light of the unprecedented circumstances, he had decided to answer the call of the Ivorian people and *stand for re-election*. He later insisted that this decision was a 'real personal sacrifice', and that he had been genuine when he declared that he was stepping down in March. Ouattara's candidacy further united the historically divided Ivorian opposition, with all major opposition figures condemning Ouattara's decision to stand in the elections as a 'constitutional coup d'état' and filing a complaint with the Independent Electoral Commission to have Ouattara's candidacy declared unconstitutional. Unsurprisingly, the complaint was rejected in early September, a decision that was celebrated by RHDP supporters and met with frustration and public protests by the opposition. Throughout the month of August, public protests had been escalating in traditional opposition strongholds such as Divo, Daoukro, Bonoua, and Gagnoa in the centre-west, as well as in opposition-friendly neighbourhoods in the country's financial capital of Abidjan, leading to clashes with police and security forces and attacks against perceived supporters of the incumbent, with at least five people reported killed in the confrontations. The dramatic scenes fuelled widespread concerns that the elections would mirror the violent elections in 2000 and 2010. Given that the main political figures, Ouattara, Bédié, Gbagbo, and Soro, had been at the centre of these earlier devastating confrontations, many observers noted that Ivorian politics, in this sense, seemed to be repeating history.

Escalating confrontations across opposition-dominated regions of the country led the government to issue a ban on public gatherings in mid-August – a ban that was eventually extended until late November, but was generally poorly respected. On 14 September, the Constitutional Council published the full list of eligible candidates. Out of 44 officially registered candidates, only four were deemed eligible: Alassane Ouattara, FPI president Pascal Affi N'Guessan, PDCI president Henri Konan Bédié, and Kouadio Konan Bertin, a former member of Bédié's PDCI running as an independent. The most notable candidates to be rejected by the Constitutional Council were Laurent Gbagbo and Guillaume Soro, both declared ineligible due to the criminal verdicts against them in the Ivorian courts. Although there were rumours that Gbagbo's name had been registered by his supporters as a statement rather than a serious bid, his presence on the initial list of candidates was a clear illustration of the deep-seated division within the FPI, with one faction loyal to the former president and another supporting the official head of the party, Pascal Affi N'Guessan. Other prominent candidates who were rejected included former foreign ministers Marcel Amon Tanoh (independent) and Albert Mabri Toikeusse (UDPCI), both estranged former allies of the incumbent, as well as Mamadou Koulibaly (LIDER, Liberté et Démocratie pour la République), formerly the president of the national assembly under Laurent Gbagbo's presidency. The reason for the three rejections was cited as technical shortcomings in the registration of their candidacies.

Following the publication of the list of eligible candidates, notable opposition figures such as Henri Konan Bédié, Guillaume Soro, and Laurent Gbagbo took to social and traditional media, calling for 'civil disobedience' to put pressure on the authorities to reject Ouattara's candidacy, postpone the elections, and reconfigure the central electoral bodies. During October, public mobilisation intensified across the country, with opposition leader Affi N'Guessan's hometown residence set ablaze by protesters on 18 October and several people killed in clashes. With no concessions from the government in sight, the two main opposition candidates, Affi N'Guessan and Bédié, announced their decision to boycott what they perceived as the 'unlawful' electoral contest.

Instead, the opposition called for an '*active boycott*', encouraging their supporters not only to abstain from voting but also to 'prevent all operations relating to the vote' in their districts. On 31 October, Côte d'Ivoire went to the polls in a tense atmosphere, with violent incidents reported in opposition strongholds prior to and during election day. The 54% turnout was unequally divided, with RHDP strongholds in the north and in parts of Abidjan seeing significantly higher turnout than opposition strongholds, where many voters abided by the 'active boycott', at least in response to the call to abstain from voting. Election observers reported significant incidents in opposition-dominated districts, with 23% of polling stations nationwide unable to commence operations due to threats or attacks. The government later officially recognised that 20 people had been killed in election-related violence on election day, and an additional 31 in the days after. A joint Electoral Institute for Sustainable Democracy in Africa (EISA) and Carter Center election observation mission concluded that 'the overall context and process of the presidential election did not allow for a genuinely competitive election', given the level of voter intimidation and violence, the absence of the main opposition parties, and persistent irregularities in the voter registration process.

On 2 November, before the official results were announced later on the same day, Bédié and Affi N'Guessan announced their intention to form a '*National Transitional Council*', doubling down on their claim that Ouattara's likely victory constituted an 'electoral coup d'état'. A few hours later, the official provisional results were announced by the electoral commission, with *the incumbent sweeping 94% of the popular vote* and the only remaining opposing candidate, Kouadio Konan Bertin, receiving a mere 2%. Bédié and Affi N'Guessan received around 1% of the vote each, despite boycotting the election. The announcement led to further confrontations between security forces and protesters in cities across the country. The results were ratified on 9 November by the Constitutional Council.

On 6 November, FPI president *Pascal Affi N'Guessan and three of his aides were arrested*, accused of plotting sedition on the basis of the stated intention to form a parallel government following the presidential elections. Although Bédié had led the initiative to set up a National Transitional Council, he was not detained by the authorities, but his residence was tightly guarded by security forces following the 2 November announcement. Eleven opposition party members were arrested in front of Bédié's residence on 3 November for suspected involvement in the attempt to establish a parallel governing structure, with most suspects released within a week. Affi N'Guessan was released on 30 December along with the two other remaining detainees, pending further investigations.

On 11 November, with clashes continuing in Abidjan and across the centre-west, *Alassane Ouattara and Henri Konan Bédié met publicly* for the first time in more than two years, urging an end to confrontations in a joint press conference and vowing to engage in a continued dialogue in order to normalise the political climate in the country. The veritable siege of Bédié's residence was lifted earlier on the same day. This initiative seemed to calm the atmosphere in most places, although the political class remained deeply polarised. At least 87 people were estimated to have been killed in election-related violence during the second half of the year, and more than 17,000 were displaced, according to UNHCR.

On 14 December, Alassane Ouattara was officially sworn in for a third presidential term. In his address to the public, he vowed to make national reconciliation his main priority and announced the creation of a new ministry for reconciliation in the immediate future. He also stated that he had charged Prime Minister Bakayoko with the task of continuing the dialogue with the political opposition, which still perceived the electoral result as illegitimate, ahead of the parliamentary and legislative elections scheduled for March 2021.

Foreign Affairs

Côte d'Ivoire's foreign affairs were equally dominated by the dramatic events surrounding the presidential elections. In March, French president Emmanuel Macron welcomed Ouattara's announcement that he would not run in the elections, calling it a 'historic decision' and celebrating Côte d'Ivoire as an exemplar, presumably among (West) African democracies. The most vocal reactions came from the Ivorian political class, while the international community generally reacted without as much surprise and relief, remaining notably muted on the controversy.

In early September, Alassane Ouattara carried out a scheduled state visit to France, sharing a working dinner with President Macron. Following Ouattara's decision to run for a third presidential term, France had been notably silent on the constitutionality of the incumbent's candidacy, and the silence continued as no official press conference or statement was issued in connection with the visit. The lack of an official reaction provoked stern responses from the Ivorian opposition, with Guillaume Soro stating in an open letter to the French president that by commenting on Ouattara's initial announcement that he would not present his presidency, Macron had already taken a stand in Ivorian politics, which made his silence about Ouattara's about-face a complicit one. Pascal Affi N'Guessan added in an open letter of his own that 'your silence is interpreted diversely in my country … Your pronouncement [parole], to the contrary, is keenly awaited.'

On 18 September, the high representative on behalf of the EU issued a statement in reaction to the escalating violence in the build-up to the October vote. The statement did not address the constitutionality of Ouattara's third-term bid but urged all sides to 'pursue dialogue', a call that was echoed by UNSG António Guterres on 23 October in the face of continued pre-electoral violence.

Following the declaration of Alassane Ouattara's electoral victory on 2 November, international reactions were restrained once more, with most commentaries focusing on the need for an end to election-related violence and a commitment on both sides to national reconciliation. Ouattara was sworn in for his third term on 14 December in the presence of the heads of state of most of the ECOWAS member states, including Macky Sall (Senegal), Roch Marc Christian Kaboré (Burkina Faso), acting ECOWAS president Nana Akufo-Addo (Ghana), and Mahamadou Issoufou (Niger). The attendees also included Ethiopian president Sahle-Work Zewde, president of Mauritania Mohamed Ould Ghazouani, and the president of the AU Commission, Moussa Faki Mahamat. France was officially represented by foreign minister Jean-Yves Le Drian, with former presidents Goodluck Jonathan of Nigeria, Ernest Bai Koroma of Sierra Leone, and Nicolas Sarkozy of France also in attendance.

In addition to the international attention to the Ivorian presidential elections, the effects of the global Covid-19 pandemic also led to targeted interventions. The EU and the UNDP, in collaboration with the Magic System and Didier Drogba Foundations, among other local and European partners, initiated a 'Solidarity Caravane' bringing hygiene and nutrition kits to 11,000 vulnerable families. The EU also pledged targeted economic relief packages to the Ivorian health and livelihoods sectors to assist in Covid-19 response and recovery.

Socioeconomic Developments

The global Covid-19 pandemic effectively brought Côte d'Ivoire's impressive overall economic growth over the past eight years to a halt, with the growth rate plummeting from an average of more than 7% per year since 2012, and 7.5% in 2019, to 1.8%

in 2020. A survey of 800 households conducted by the World Bank in April 2020 found that 71% had experienced a decrease in income and were unable to meet their basic living expenses. By the end of the year, 137 Covid-related deaths were officially registered and a total of roughly 22,500 cases. Although a tragic loss of human lives, these direct effects of the pandemic were relatively minor compared with infection and mortality rates in other parts of the world. The secondary effects, on the contrary, were severe, with nationwide school closures imposed in March as well as a slight increase in the national unemployment rate – from 3.32% in 2019 to 3.42% in 2020, with the youth unemployment rate reaching 5.2%, significantly higher than the national average.

Among the main sectors of the economy impacted by the pandemic was the private sector, mainly due to the disruption of global value chains, employee absence, temporary closures, and slowing global demand. Households relying on income from informal and service activities were particularly affected. The decreased global demand severely affected the Ivorian export sector, with export agriculture decreasing by 2.2%, following years of sustained expansion, forestry exports reducing by 16.5%, mining exports by 4.8%, and petroleum products by 26.9%.

Despite significant drops in world market prices for *cocoa*, of which Côte d'Ivoire maintained its position as the world's leading producer at approximately 40% of global produce, the government maintained the buying price of the 2018/19 season in order to relieve local producers of the economic impact of the global recession. The 2020 harvest, completed in late March, showed an increase from 1,656 m tonnes in 2019 to 1,780 m tonnes. Domestic *cashew production reached 900,000 tons* in 2020, up from 634,641 tonnes in 2019, illustrating the general trend that global demand, rather than local production capacities, was at the heart of the secondary effects of the pandemic. Côte d'Ivoire's *crude oil production* fell dramatically from around 48,000 barrels per day in the first quarter to around 35,000 barrels per day in the fourth quarter. Compared with an average of around 49,000 barrels per day in 2019, this marked a significant decline in production.

Despite the global pandemic, a World Bank report published mid-year ventured some optimism, commending the country's progress over the past decade, which included a low fiscal deficit of 2.3% of GDP, achievements estimated to keep the Ivorian economy from falling into recession during the pandemic. The national debt in relation to GDP did rise significantly, however, from 41.22% in 2019 to 45.71% in 2020. Although socioeconomic inequality persisted, the share of the population living below the poverty line continued its downward trend, according to the World Bank, falling steadily from 46.3% in 2015 to 39.4% in 2020. These improvements were mainly restricted to urban areas, with rural poverty levels rising by 2.4% over the same five-year period.

Other key indicators showed a similar resilience to the effects of the pandemic, as Côte d'Ivoire continued the trend of gradual but slight improvement in its global HDI ranking, from 165th in 2019 to 162nd in 2020. Similarly, the overall public health indicators registered a slight improvement in the average life expectancy rate, from around 57 years in 2019 to about 58 years in 2020, which was still significantly lower than the continental average of 64 years. As an illustration of its international standing, Côte d'Ivoire also maintained its ranking as 110th on the World Bank's Doing Business ranking, out of 190 countries ranked, and improved its ranking in TI's Corruption Perceptions Index from 106th to 104th, out of 176 countries ranked.

In response to the Covid-19 pandemic, the government supported the healthcare sector with a CFAfr 95 bn (approximately € 145 m) relief package, intended to increase capacity and fund the tracking, tracing, and quarantining of infection cases and the purchase of medical equipment. The government also passed an economic response package of approximately € 2.6 bn for 2020/21, including dedicated support funds to the private sector and vulnerable households and measures to promote the quick recovery of the economy. Regulatory and fiscal measures were temporarily put in place to ease the burden for households and enterprises. The four emergency funds were operational by mid-year, with the informal sector fund delivering CFAfr 3.18 bn (approximately € 4.8 m) to more than 13,000 beneficiaries and cash transfers to vulnerable populations reaching more than 100,000 households.

To meet the challenge of school closures, which were mandated from March in order to limit the spread of the virus, the government turned to online technology. On 6 April, the Ministry of National Education, Technical Education and Vocational Training introduced free online courses, providing students with access to educational materials through special websites, and through Facebook and YouTube. From 9 April, lessons were broadcast on television and radio on weekdays in order to include students without access to online resources.

In addition to the measures implemented in response to the Covid-19 pandemic, January 2020 marked the rollout of the ambitious *universal health coverage* (couverture maladie universelle/CMU), approved by parliament in 2014 and trialled through a three-year pilot phase, monitored by the National Health Insurance Fund (Caisse nationale d'assurance maladie/CNAM). The rollout OF CMU, mandatory for anyone residing in the country, was expected to include two pillars: basic general coverage (régime général de base/RGB) for most users, involving a monthly subscription of CFAfr 1,000 (approximately € 1.50), and medical assistance coverage (régime d'assistance médicale/RAM) without payment intended for the most vulnerable parts of the population who had so far generally been without access to the public healthcare system. The rollout marked the culmination of a € 1.3 bn investment in public health infrastructure, including the renovation of existing health facilities throughout the country and recruitment to prepare to accommodate at least 70% of the population within the new healthcare plan.

The Gambia

Akpojevbe Omasanjuwa

President Adama Barrow's reneging on his promise to relinquish office at the end of a three-year transitional mandate sparked the 16 December 2019 demonstration staged by the 'Three Year Jotna' (TYJ) movement. Despite the ensuing protests in early 2020 over the president's decision, the country remained characteristically calm. With the 2021 presidential election at hand, and the dissolution of the coalition that brought Adama Barrow to power, there were new arrangements to form future alliances. The outbreak of Covid-19 in March caused changes in the budgetary allocations approved by the House of Assembly (HA). Funds were channelled from low-priority areas to augment the health sector, while the Foreign Ministry played a pivotal role in coordinating foreign assistance and procuring materials to address the problems presented by Covid-19. Meanwhile, the people anxiously awaited the benefits that the post-Jammeh era had in store.

Domestic Politics

The anti-establishment demonstration staged by TYJ on 16 December 2019, calling for a three-year instead of five-year presidential term, continued in 2020.

On 16 January, in continuation of the 2019 agitation for the return of Yahya Jammeh from exile, supporters of the Alliance for Patriotic Reorientation and Construction (APRC) demonstrated in Sukuta. Also in January, anti-APRC demonstrators gathered in the vicinity of the Kanifing Municipal Council (KMC) building, demanding justice for the atrocities committed during Jammeh's administration. The TYJ request for another permit, which was initially declined, received approval following the intervention of civil society organisations and religious leaders. Inadequate crowd control coupled with the presence of paramilitary personnel turned the protest violent, as protesters intended to storm the state house at Banjul. One hundred and thirty-seven people were arrested and arraigned before a magistrate, besides 50 others who sustained injuries. Subsequently, TYJ was proscribed, with stern warnings for any person or establishment that associated with the movement. The Human Rights Commission expressed concerns over the crackdown, while the Gambia Press Union condemned the temporary closure of some media houses. The arrestees were later granted bail and suspended radio licences were restored, while three journalists charged with incitement to violence were released on bail on 28 January.

In July, the Independent Electoral Commission (IEC), fixed 4 December 2021 as the presidential election date. The announcement pricked the minds of analysts, as the electoral prospects of the main opposition leader, Ousaino Darboe, a former vice-president, remained contentious. The crux of the matter remained his eligibility to contest the upcoming election. He and 18 others were imprisoned for staging an unauthorised protest in 2016. Although he later received a pardon, this was contentious, as the 1997 constitution differentiates between 'ordinary' and 'free' pardons. After regaining his freedom, in January he lost his bid to overturn the conviction at both the supreme court and the ECOWAS Court of Human Rights; this was after a court ruling upheld an adverse finding against him by a Tax Evasion Commission in 2012. His dismissal from office as vice-president was another issue of contention, as it could impede his running for president. On his part, Darboe claimed that save insanity, death, or the United Democratic Party's (UDP) decision, nothing could bar him from contesting.

The Gambia Unity Party and All People's Party were registered, bringing the total number of registered political parties to 15, with some probably defunct. Carpet-crossing among party loyalists and talks of possible alliances were rampant. The chairperson of the Gambia Democratic Congress, along with another member, defected to the National People's Party (NPP) launched by President Adama Barrow in December 2019, while the Gambia Action Party expelled its leader over a scandalous video on social media. Having lost the leadership of the People's Progressive Party (PPP) to Papa Njie in December 2018 at a party congress election, Bakary Darboe launched the Gambia For All Party on 8 February 2020. Papa Njie later defected to the NPP and received an ambassadorial appointment. Meanwhile, media outlets published a swiftly rebutted report corroborating rumours of coalition arrangements between the APRC and the NPP – a strategy intended to enable Adama Barrow to contest the 2021 election.

To usher in a third republic, a controversial draft constitution, costing D 116 m (dalasis), was presented to the national assembly (NA) for ratification. The NA voted 31:23 in favour, falling short of the two-thirds majority of the 58 members needed for approval. The Christian Council expressed reservations over the elevation of Sharia in the constitution, which could lead the country to take after an Islamic state. Another snag was the allegation of plagiarism levelled against members of the Constitution Review Commission. The draft literally consisted of plagiarised sections of the 2010 Kenyan constitution. During the debate, under the cloak of enforcing the social distancing regulations, some journalists were barred from covering the proceedings. Observers, however, interpreted it as stifling dissenting voices over the draft constitution, as press personnel had had unrestricted access to the assembly since March when social distancing regulations were introduced.

The disintegration of the coalition that brought President Adama Barrow to office resulted in some public officers, perceived as supporters of Ousaino Darboe, being relieved of their appointments. In October, the central bank governor declined redeployment to the Trades and Employment Ministry as minister, a move perceived as politically motivated. The bank governor questioned the legality of the redeployment, as the Central Bank Act entitles him to a non-transferable term of five years; besides, he may only be removed by an adverse finding of an independent tribunal. Similarly, the director of the Social Security and Housing Corporation declined to become the deputy executive secretary at the Senegalo-Gambian permanent secretariat in Dakar, Senegal, after being relieved of his position.

A diplomatic passport scandal raged in May when it came to public attention that some prominent but undeserving citizens had been issued the document clandestinely. Fourteen people were charged at the close of investigations.

Socioeconomic Developments

The Freedom House world index 2020 ranked The Gambia 46th/100 ('partly free'), while on the Transparency International Corruption Perceptions Index 2020 the country scored 37% and ranked 102th/180, with a score change of +3 since 2012. Part of the nationwide forlorn cries against graft in President Barrow's administration were allegations against Roads Authority officials for receiving kickbacks from contractors. Insinuations were widespread of impropriety in the execution of Banjul road and sewage projects, the Sir Kairaba Jawara International Conference Centre

(KJICC) landscaping, the Senegambia Bridge, and the 122-kilometre Lamin Koto Passimas road projects. The works minister reacted by branding the accusations fabrications designed to undermine the implementation of projects by his ministry.

The Fisheries Ministry permanent secretary (PS) proceeded on administrative leave, pending the outcome of investigations. He was heard on audio negotiating a D 100 m kickback with officials of a foreign company that violated regulations regulating fishing in Gambian waters.

In reaction to allegations of financial impropriety rocking the Barrow administration, the director-general of the Foods, Safety and Quality Authority was, in April, transferred to the Ministry of Energy as PS Number 3, a fallout of unilaterally dismissing 30 staff who had signed a petition reproaching her for corruption and maladministration.

At the NA in April, the health minister elicited public admiration for exposing the sensational level of corruption in Covid-19 fund allocation to frontline health workers.

The appointment of Sheriff Muhamed Hydara as president of the Supreme Islamic Council engendered disagreement among its members and the *Majmuatul Rawdatul Majalis*. At the launch of the Islamic Foundation and Conference, the khalifa-general of Bansang town, who was also the chief justice, enjoined religious leaders to coexist and respect each other's differences. Also, a revered cleric, Imam Momodou Ceesay, arrived from overseas to douse tension as part of his efforts in dispute resolution.

Land disputes necessitating police intervention occurred at Farato and Jarra during the rainy season. Chieftaincy disputes rocked Beakanya, Niamina, and Sambang. Beakanya community in Kombo South has grappled with Alkaloship (chieftaincy) crises for years, prompting the intercession of the local government minister, while the KMC mediated in chieftaincy-related disputes in Tallinding and Latrikunda Yiringanya Kebba Mbye of Touba Mourit village was appointed district chief of Niamina to replace the ailing Sulayman Keita of Dankuku village.

The justice minister who inaugurated the Truth, Reconciliation and Reparation Commission (TRRC) and was acclaimed for filing a case at the ICJ accusing Myanmar of genocide against the Rohingya Muslims resigned in June to take up a UN appointment.

The chief of defence staff, Lieutenant General Masaneh Kinteh was replaced by Major General Yankuba Drammeh in March and the governor of North Bank Division left office due to non-renewal of contract.

Community opinion leaders who passed away included the imam of Pipeline Mosque Momodou Njie, Alhagie Mpakary Conteh (Gambissara), Michael Cleary (Irish bishop), Willy Carr (Methodist clergy), Andrew Da Costa (newspaper boss), Imam Alasan Gigo (Kuntaya), Gibril Kujabi, Habib Mbye (Drug Squad), Ali Mboge

(Banjul elder), Imam Biran Joof (Serrekunda), Biri Biri (sportsman), Lamin Dibba (ex-local government minister) and Lamin Darboe (deputy governor, Central River Region/CRR).

Natural disasters, ranging from flash floods to fire outbreak to windstorms, now becoming perennial, afflicted more than 60,000 people. Basse, Latrikunda Sabiji, the main market of Brikama, and a compound in Bundum were gutted by fire. The Ahmadiyya Muslim Jamat supported some victims of a fire disaster with food and cash. At Niamina (Touba Mourit), a flood disaster in September displaced families, and livestock were lost. To enhance infrastructural and rural development, Brikama Area Council inaugurated the new Nema Kunku market while the KMC mayor commissioned a D 14 m market project at Latrikunda Sabiji.

In June, Iman Baba Leigh was openly chastised for advising government to protect the rights of the gay community. In response, the cleric apologised for being misunderstood, as he had no powers to forbid or enforce gay and lesbian rights – only god does. The Gambia Criminal Code (Amendment Act) 2014 stipulates a maximum sentence of life imprisonment for the offence of 'aggravated homosexuality and other penalties for certain homosexual acts'.

The Janneh Commission probing the financial activities of former president Yahya Jammeh recommended that M.A. Kharafi and Sons Company Limited should refund $ 2,367,426 to government. Kharafi challenged the order before the court of appeal. In June, the court held that a commission is not a court, and therefore its report is neither a judgment nor an order capable of being executed.

The TRRC submitted an interim report in January and continued sitting in 2020.

Sixteen NA members voted against a loan agreement reached by their colleagues in November. With barely two years to the expiration of their tenure, their approval of a sum of D 54 m in loans to facilitate building their houses sparked public debate.

Yankuba Touray's refusal to cooperate with the TRRC's probe into the murder of ex-finance minister Koro Ceesay in 1995 necessitated his prosecution. During his high court trial, his lawyer asked the court to invoke the immunity clause of paragraph 13 of the 1997 constitution shielding him from prosecution, as a member of the 1994–96 ruling junta. The protracted trial came up for hearing at various times in 2020 and was referred to the supreme court, which ruled on 27 January 2021 that Touray was not entitled to immunity from prosecution. Consequently, his trial resumed in the high court.

In another incident, Madi Jobarteh, the country representative of the Westminster Foundation for Democracy, was arrested in June for allegedly spreading false information after he accused the government of failing to act and investigate the killings of certain Gambian citizens. The charges were dropped through civil society interventions.

In December the appeal court, on a legal technicality, freed all eight soldiers convicted in May 2019 by a military tribunal for committing treason in 2017. The state had failed to obtain a written statement from the attorney-general before commencing the court martial.

The Covid-19 pandemic impacted budgetary allocations adversely, as resources were diverted to the health sector from other sources. Besides, a supplementary budget received the approval of the NA to reinforce tourism, agriculture, health, and infrastructure. The revision yielded D 500 m lodged in a dedicated central bank account with stringent internal audit oversight to facilitate country-wide food distribution. Workers in the tourism and aviation industries received palliative support for a period of three months, while local government employees received assistance for six months. Licence fees on behalf of the hotel industry were paid to the Tourism Board and the municipalities. While only workers in essential services were reporting for duty, overseas travel for public officers remained suspended. Emergency measures were invoked to prohibit price hikes and hoarding. Non-essential businesses and designated public arenas were closed, with curfew imposed. The revenue authority gave businesses two months' grace to file returns and effect payments, while the central bank relaxed regulatory measures to boost liquidity to support essential sectors.

The Gambia ranked 155th out of 190 on Doing Business 2020 country rankings. The reduction of the corporate income tax and turnover tax rates and elimination of the constraint of needing to obtain a company seal eased the setting up of businesses. $ 21.3 m in assistance was received from the IMF Rapid Credit Facility. The World Bank provided a grant of $ 10 m for purchase of medical equipment and an additional $ 13.5 m for social safety net programmes and the education sector, while the AfDB provided $ 14 m to strengthen the health sector. Emergency measures interrupted school timetables, and hence final-year junior and senior secondary school students wrote their exams outside schedule.

Members of the Gambia Teachers' Union (GTU) affiliated to the Catholic Education Secretariat (CES) went on strike demanding the refund of savings and loan repayments deducted from their salaries by CES. The deductions had not been remitted to the requisite accounts since September 2019. The situation involved an insurance company with which some teachers were registered, the Gambia Trade Union (GTU), the Cooperative Credit Union (GTUCCU), and other unions. In March, the strike was called off after the GTU confirmed receipt of D 7.2 m from the central bank.

Protracted climate change impact on agriculture escalated rural poverty. However, the revitalisation of 23-years-dormant cotton production was noteworthy; as a result, during the farming season over 100 farmers registered with the Cotton Producers Marketing Cooperative. In defiance of regulations and for better terms, farmers still engaged in cross-border sales of groundnuts, an unabated colonial legacy.

Nevertheless, they received 310 metric tons of certified seeds and over 100,000 tons of fertilisers from IFAD and other sources. Additionally, 150 households benefited from the enhancement of small ruminant production and fattening schemes, with more than 135,000 animals vaccinated, besides an enlightenment campaign on foot and mouth diseases. Two slaughterhouses were rehabilitated to meet food safety and zoo sanitary standards, while the Department of Water Resources handed 14 fishing boats equipped with outboard engines to fishing communities.

In January, the Small Ruminant Production Enhancement Project launched a nationwide project to enhance the production of small ruminants. A loan project partly funded by the Inter-American Development Bank (IDB) was designed to target 39 districts harbouring 30,000 households, by reducing the importation of livestock.

The Covid-19 outbreak in March precipitated an exodus of tourists from the country, causing an abrupt shutdown of the tourist industry. The FTI Group, Europe's fourth-largest tour operator, shut down operations in The Gambia. Seasonal and most regular hotel workers were laid off, while the airport remained dormant. The government funded hoteliers with D 900 m in palliative support, out of which D 5 m went to artists adversely affected by the lockdown. In addition, 6,400 vendors received palliative support from the Tourism Board. By June, the Business Environment Reform Programme was established, and the Essential Commodities Regulatory Powers Measures were designed to stabilise prices and prohibit re-export and hoarding of essential commodities.

As a prelude to hosting the Organisation of Islamic Cooperation (OIC) conference in 2022, $ 50 m in funding was secured for the construction of 50 km of urban roads. The KJICC was officially inaugurated. The construction of the governor's residence and office complex at Kerewan, the rehabilitation of the burned-out Brikama and Basse markets, and market construction works at Farrafenni and Soma were concurrently executed. Projects nearing completion included the Kalleng–Bushtown Road, and North Bank rural roads in Sabah-Sanjal, Saloum, and other locations in CRR, totalling 105 kilometres; 75% of roads in the Upper River Region and the Banjul rehabilitation projects were completed. The Soma–Basse Highway, Old Cape Road Bridge, sections of Kombo Coastal Highway, and Pakalinding–Mansakonko Highway were upgraded with part of the D 300 m budgetary allocation for road maintenance.

The generating capacity of the National Electricity and Water Corporation (NAWEC) was 71 MW, satisfying peak load need of 65–70 MW in Greater Banjul Area. Fifty-five years after independence, the district of Kiang received electricity, part of the rural electrification scheme.

Revenue and grants for the first nine months increased by 16% from D 12.3 bn (14% of GDP) in January to D 14.2 bn in September 2019 (15% of GDP). Expenditure increased by 13% in the same period. Current expenditure increased by 30%.

Interest payments on loans increased from D 2.2 bn to D 2.5 bn, due to debt restructuring negotiations with external creditors.

The public debt stock was D 67.6 bn in September; domestic debt constituted D 32.1 bn while external debt was D 35.5 bn. Net foreign assets increased to D 21.3 bn at the end of September from D 14.1 bn in September 2019, while net domestic assets grew by 5.4% and domestic credit increased by 4.3 % to D 32.1 bn within the period.

The consumer price index declined by 2.4 %, from 7.6% in September 2019 to 5.2% in September 2020. Food inflation declined from 7.2% to 6.6% within the period. Non-food inflation dropped to 3.7% over the year, from 8.3% in September 2019.

The dalasi appreciated against the pound sterling by 0.2% but depreciated against other major currencies (December 2019–September 2020). Imports amounted to $ 336.4 m, an increase from $ 275.5 m in the same period in 2019. Exports decreased to $ 52.1 m in the second period from $ 70.1 m in the corresponding period of 2019. Net workers' remittances improved by 56%, from $ 122.7 m to $ 191.9 m.

Foreign Relations

The Foreign Ministry synchronised foreign assistance and procurement of Covid-19 medical materials. Consequently, financial obligations associated with the ministry increased. Travel restrictions necessitated the cancellation of most international engagements, although in September, President Barrow attended the ECOWAS summit meeting in Niamey, Niger. In October he was in Nigeria as a follow-up to an earlier visit by the defence and foreign ministers regarding the terms of a Memorandum of Understanding within the context of Gambia's security sector reform, linked to Nigeria's military presence in The Gambia. Also in October, he proceeded to Guinea-Bissau on another state visit.

The NA majority leader attended a meeting of the ECOWAS Parliament Joint Committee on Trade, Customs and Free Movement in Cotonou, Benin. The Turkish president was in The Gambia in January; during his visit, regional and international security issues were discussed. The EU, UN, and AU sustained their support for the security sector reforms and the TRRC, while ECOWAS extended the mandate of ECOMIG (ECOWAS Mission in The Gambia) forces in the country.

Ghana

Jennifer C. Boylan

The economic outlook for Ghana in 2020 was initially strikingly positive. In January, a number of credit agencies had raised Ghana's rating, economic growth was projected at 6%, and, despite the election year, there was a strong belief that debt would remain below the 5% legal threshold. Once the Covid-19 pandemic hit, the two largest cities went through a military-enforced lockdown, schools closed and social gatherings were banned for much of the year, and the typically large and vibrant election campaign rallies went largely online. Nana Akufo-Addo was re-elected as president, again defeating former president John Mahama, but 63 New Patriotic Party (NPP) parliamentarians lost their seats and Ghana now had a hung parliament for the first time. Former president J.J. Rawlings died at age 73 after a short illness. The special prosecutor abdicated his position in 2020, while the auditor-general was compelled to take his accumulated leave. Though greatly diminished, Ghana's positive economic growth stood out in comparison with that of its peers. The country was also credited for activating oil savings to help buoy its economic outlook.

Domestic Politics

On 28 March, Akufo-Addo famously declared 'We know how to bring the economy back to life. What we do not know is how to bring people back to life', in announcing the pandemic-related lockdown of Ghana's two largest cities.

Ghana's first two cases of Covid-19 were recorded on 12 March. A day before, Akufo-Addo had announced $ 100 m to battle the virus via funding of infrastructure, personal protective equipment (PPE), and education, up from the $ 6.5 m originally proposed. Next, on 16 March, a number of measures were implemented to slow the spread of the virus, including shutting down schools, banning public gatherings, and barring foreigners from travelling to Ghana from countries with more than 200 cases. Schooling was moved online, with the accompanying limitations of technical/monetary internet access issues, power outages, lack of access to computers or smartphones, and lack of support for students with disabilities.

On 10 March, the Bank of Ghana made all mobile money transfers below 100 cedi (GH₵) free to help discourage the spread of the virus. The existing national emergency short code, 112, was transformed to the official Covid-19 helpline, which also provided free access to Covid-19 information on the Ministry of Health website.

A lockdown of Accra and Kumasi, two cities with a combined population of 7 m, began on 30 March. It was enforced by armed police and members of the military, and some described the atmosphere as that of a war zone. Indeed, an encounter with the military enforcing the lockdown resulted in the death of a man from Ashaiman on 5 April.

On 21 March, the Imposition of Restrictions Act was passed by parliament and signed by the president. This act empowered the president to impose restrictions on citizens during an emergency or disaster. Critics of the act pointed out that it was redundant, overlapping with the Emergency Powers Act (1994), and greatly extended state power by eliminating Emergency Powers Act safeguards, such as enabling parliament to override the emergency declaration and providing detained persons with special protections.

Finance minister Ken Ofori-Atta, who also chairs the UN ECA, requested IMF funding in March and led calls for large financial institutions to be flexible and supportive of African nations in their handling of the crisis. In mid-April, Ghana was awarded a $ 1 bn loan from the IMF under the Rapid Credit Facility (RCF), a $ 315 m loan and a debt moratorium from the World Bank in June, and a $ 69 m grant from the AfDB in July.

On 19 April, three weeks after the start of the lockdown, Ghana became the first African country to lift its coronavirus lockdown. Schools remained closed and large gatherings were still banned, but non-essential businesses reopened. Akufo-Addo cited the country's ability to track infected individuals, enhanced testing and treatment capabilities, and concern for the poor as reasons to lift the lockdown.

However, within ten days, the Ghana Medical Association raised the alarm over rising health worker infections due to poor supply of personal protective equipment (PPE). By mid-year, nine health workers had died, including the rector of the Ghana College of Physicians and Surgeons.

On 26 April, Ghana reported 1,550 cases and 11 deaths. By 9 July, the country was said to have conducted more than 300,000 tests, resulting in 23,000 cases, and 129 deaths were reported. By 26 August, 44,000 were infected, with 270 total deaths. By December, Ghana saw at least 50,000 Covid-19 infections, resulting in a minimum of 300 deaths. Throughout the year, Ghana was credited with one of the highest testing rates in Africa (1,265 tests per million in April). The country also utilised 'enhanced contact tracing' whereby 34,000 travellers arriving in Ghana before 22 March were identified and both they and those close to them were tested. By 19 April, 1.27% of this sample were found to be positive.

The state utilised pooled testing, where multiple samples were combined and tested and, where the test was positive, individual samples would be tested. While Ghana was heralded for its strong testing capacity, including the use of drones to transport samples, the concern was raised that if all test results were being reported, the double-counting of individuals who had taken multiple tests might be decreasing the country's overall Covid-19 positivity rate.

A financial analyst at Renaissance Capital reported that Ghana spent five times more on interest payments than on healthcare. Beginning on 5 April, for six months frontline health workers received a 50% monthly basic salary increase, an insurance package, a separate daily allowance during the contact-tracing period, and an exemption from tax payments on their wages. On 14 May, finance minister Ofori-Atta announced a GH₵ 600 m stimulus for manufacturing, pharmaceutical, and tourism companies, which included reorienting domestic production towards the manufacture of PPE. Millions of locally produced gowns, scrubs, and face masks were distributed to hospitals throughout the year.

On 26 April, Akufo-Addo announced that 88 new district hospitals and six new regional hospitals would be built within a year, as well as three infectious disease centres and eventually a Ghana Center for Disease Control. In his announcement, the president referenced a recent cerebrospinal meningitis (CSM) outbreak of over 409 cases across five regions, which claimed 40 lives in 2020.

On 10 May, Akufo-Addo publicised that a single fish factory worker at Tema Port had infected all 533 other people working at the facility. On 29 May, Tullow Oil announced that 58 workers at one of their oil production facilities at the Jubilee Oil Field had tested positive for Covid-19 and had to be brought ashore for isolation and treatment.

On 19 May, the $ 200 m Coronavirus Alleviation Program (CAP) was launched to support a variety of programmes addressing the pandemic, including writing off electricity and water bills for the very poor and subsidising bills for all others, establishing or renovating regional or district hospitals across the country, and distributing food packages and hot meals to over 400,000 families when the lockdown was first imposed. The CAP Business Support Scheme (CAPBuSS) directed GH₵ 1 bn towards micro and soft loans for small and medium-sized enterprises, including 110,000 enterprises owned by women.

In mid-June, schools were reopened and public gatherings could again take place, but with a maximum capacity of 100 people. However, the government also made wearing of face masks in public mandatory across the country. Ghana reopened its airport to international flight passengers on 1 September. These passengers would have to present a negative Covid-19 test result and would be charged for a quick antigen test at the airport.

In July, parliament approved Ofori-Atta's request to temporarily suspend the Fiscal Responsibility Act, which required a fiscal deficit of less than 5% of GDP. On 23 July, the mid-year budget was revised from a deficit of 4.7% of GDP to 11.4%.

On 18 November, the GH₵ 100 bn Covid-19 Alleviation and Revitalization of Enterprise Support (CARES) initiative was formally launched in Accra. The first 'Stabilisation' phase included pandemic response initiatives to be taken during the second half of 2021, while the second medium-term 'Revitalization' phase would last from 2021 until 2023.

In other pandemic news, on 11 April the University of Ghana announced that its West African Centre for Cell Biology of Infectious Pathogens (WACCBIP) and the Noguchi Memorial Institute for Medical Research (NMIMR) had successfully sequenced Covid-19 genomes, and then made their work open access online.

Joseph Hammond, a 95-year-old Second World War veteran, was inspired by Captain Tom Moore of the UK to walk two miles a day in Accra to raise about $ 50,000 over the course of a week for PPE for frontline workers and veterans. On 22 June, Hammond received a Commonwealth Points of Life award from Queen Elizabeth II.

On 22 September, the already established Greater Accra Metropolitan Area Sanitation and Water Project (GAMA-SWP), funded by World Bank, received an additional $ 125 m in funding for 120 km of new water pipes and 10,000 new household connections.

A number of government functionaries and members of parliament were diagnosed with Covid-19 over the year, including the health minister in June and finance minister Ofori-Atta in December. The member of parliament from Tema West, Carlos Ahenkorah, had to resign from his post as deputy minister of trade and industry in early July after he admitted to breaking Covid-19 protocols soon after testing positive. Education minister Matthew Opoku-Prempeh tested positive in late June, and by early July it was also reported that many Ministry of Education employees had tested positive for Covid-19. The metro chief executive (MCE) of

Sekondi-Takoradi Metropolitan Assembly reportedly died of complications due to a Covid-19 infection on 12 June.

The pandemic also inspired new coronavirus-themed Ghana textile print (GTP) wax-print fabrics, including a fabric depicting Akufo-Addo's round glasses as a reference to his many appearances throughout the lockdown, including seven addresses to the nation from 30 March to 19 April.

On 15 April, makeshift homes in Old Fadama, the largest slum in Accra, were demolished to allow for the dredging of the Korle Lagoon. The demolition affected over 1,000 residents, some of whom the Accra Metropolitan Assembly (AMA) temporarily housed in tents. Amnesty International condemned the demolition, though the government said it had the consent of community leaders.

On 17 July, the Ghana Railway Development Authority (GRDA) carried out a demolition exercise of makeshift homes put up alongside the Tema–Mpakadan Railway Project in Tema. GRDA claimed that the encroachments were delaying the project and that a 120 km/hour train would require a 50-metre buffer on each side. Criticisms included the bad timing during the pandemic and that officials moved in at 3 AM when residents were asleep.

Innovations for Poverty Action (IPA) carried out its 'RECOVR' (Research for Effective Covid-19 Responses) household survey of the effects of the pandemic from 6 to 26 May. It found that 10% of respondents' households had someone who had delayed or skipped a healthcare appointment since mid-March and that over 40% of respondents had had to limit meal sizes or skip meals in the past week, among other findings.

On 30 June, a $ 2.97 m National Adaptation Plan (NAP) was announced through which the government would explore institutional resilience strategies in the face of both climate change and Covid-19. The funding was provided by the Green Climate Fund of the UN Environment Programme (UNEP).

The Minerals Income Investment Fund was established in 2018 to monetise state royalties from gold and created an offshore company, Agyapa Royalties Limited, to help in this process. In August 2020, a plan presented to parliament established an agreement between the government of Ghana, the fund, and Agyapa Royalties Limited, whereby the fund would retain majority shareholder status, while 49% of shares would be sold to investors. The Act quickly passed through the NPP-controlled parliament on 14 August, under a 'Certificate of Emergency'.

On 15 October, independent special prosecutor Martin Amidu completed a review of the Agyapa plan and forwarded a highly critical 67-page report to Akufo-Addo and Ofori-Atta. On 2 November, Amidu made the report public. While Ofori-Atta argued that the plan was a good way to raise cash, Amidu identified conflicts of interest, including the use of Databank Financial Services, which Ofori-Atta co-founded, as a transaction advisor and several breaches of the law. The deal was also criticised by industry exports for undervaluing Ghana's future gold royalties, while others noted that establishing the company through a British tax haven would make it difficult to properly identify future shareholders once shares were floated. In early November, Akufo-Addo instructed Ofori-Atta to send the bill back to parliament 'in the interest of transparency and accountability' and said that the matter would be revisited after the December elections.

On 16 November, Martin Amidu resigned. In a letter to Akufo-Addo, he made it clear that his resignation was due to the administration's interference in the independence of his office. Akufo-Addo had originally asked Amidu to delay releasing the Agyapa report and to heed Ofori-Atta's advice about the deal. In the letter, Amidu claimed that his office was under-resourced and that the president had downplayed and politicised the seriousness of the corruption risks raised regarding the Agyapa deal.

On 29 June, auditor-general Daniel Domelevo was placed on involuntary leave by the president. On 26 October, nine CSOs filed a writ at the supreme court challenging the leave directive. The Center for Democratic Development (CDD) issued a statement highlighting an ongoing power struggle in which the Audit Service Board was trying to restrict the independence of the auditor-general's office. Further, Domelevo had previously charged the senior minister, Yaw Osafo-Maafo, and four other finance ministry officials with a breach of the Public Procurement Act (PPA); the legal hearing of the case was ongoing at the time of Domelevo's leave.

The Right to Information (RTI) Act, passed in May 2019, officially came into effect at the start of 2020. On 19 August, a seven-member RTI governing board was inaugurated by Akufo-Addo in a short ceremony at Jubilee House.

In September, it was reported that a suspicious and lucrative contract to test for Covid-19 at Kotoka Airport (travellers were charged $150 a test) had been awarded to a company – Frontier Healthcare Services Limited (FHSL) – which had only been incorporated in Ghana on 21 July. Furthermore, FHSL is owned by Healthcare Solution Services Limited (HSSL), which was incorporated in Ghana on 3 June. HSSL is itself owned by the Peters Family Company Limited, incorporated in tax haven Dominica, in which Benedict Peters, a Nigerian oil tycoon and close friend of Akufo-Addo's, is reportedly a major shareholder. Peters had been on a self-imposed exile in Ghana since 2018 while he fought allegations from Nigeria's Economic and Financial Crimes Commission (EFCC).

Over 500 excavators seized from illegal Galamsey miners were found to be missing from an Inter-Ministerial Committee on Illegal Mining (IMCIM) storage facility in February. Six suspects were initially arrested, but with no further movement on the issue by October, various members of the National Democratic Congress (NDC) began publicly declaring that the NPP were behind the missing equipment.

The Homeland Study Group Foundation (HSGF) had been working towards greater autonomy for the Volta Region and, at times, campaigning for parts of the

Northern and Volta regions to split from Ghana to form a new country. A break-off group within this movement, the Western Togoland Restoration Front (WTRF), erected roadblocks and embarked on violent attacks in September; weapons and police vehicles were seized at two police stations, and two vehicles were set on fire at a bus depot in Ho. After the attacks, 60 members of the HSGF were arrested, despite the leader of the group issuing a statement decrying the actions of the WTRF. All 60 were later released by Ghana's courts. On 29 October, a member of the WTRF died while in police custody. The cause of death was not released.

The Togoland independence issue was most recently aggravated by the creation of Oti Region carved out of Volta Region, and then further with the deployment of the military to border towns in Volta Region during the new voter registration process. On 29 June, former president Jerry John Rawlings condemned the deployment of the military to Volta and Oti. The NDC similarly claimed that these moves were an attempt to disenfranchise voters with dual Ghana/Togo citizenship, while the NPP claimed that it was preventing Togolese nationals from illegally voting in Ghana's election. After the WTRF's violent attacks in September, the military was again deployed to Volta on election day.

On 12 November, at the age of 73, Jerry John Rawlings died at Korle-Bu University Hospital a week after admission. He was survived by his wife, Nana Konadu Agyeman-Rawlings, and three children. Even though Rawlings had supported Akufo-Addo in 2016, there was some expectation that his death would encourage sympathy votes for the NDC. Both the NPP and NDC temporarily suspended their presidential campaigns in honour of Rawlings.

The NDC's deep distrust of the Electoral Commission (EC) had been brewing ever since the previous EC chairperson (Charlotte Osei) and two deputies were removed from office by Akufo-Addo in 2018. The new Akufo-Addo-appointed chairperson, Jean Adukwei Mensa, was formerly the head of the Institute of Economic Affairs (IEA) and considered an NPP agent by members of the NDC. The distrust deepened when the EC announced that it would pursue a new voter register ahead of the December 2020 elections and would limit the forms of identification necessary for registration to the National Identification Authority (NIA) Card ('Ghana Card'), a passport, or, in the absence of a valid form of identification, two registered voters verifying an unregistered person's identity.

Other concerns with the compilation of a new voter register included whether a new register was technically necessary, the high cost of establishing it, and the worrying prospect of having to continually re-register citizens every few years. These concerns were raised prior to the coronavirus pandemic and when the EC continued to pursue the new register in spite of both the objections and the pandemic, the new register became even more politicised.

The NDC challenged the legality of a new voter registration and the EC's decision to limit the acceptable forms of ID in the supreme court. On 22 June, several

CSOs submitted *amicus curiae* briefs related to the case but, ultimately, the supreme court dismissed the majority of NDC challenges on 25 June and permitted the registration process to continue as planned. The re-registration exercise took place from the end of June through to 28 July across all 33,367 polling stations. Over 16 m registrants were given instant voter ID cards during this process. The NIA Ghana Card registration process was suspended in March, but resumed from 10 to 18 June.

Some violence occurred during the voter registration exercise, including five serious injuries at the EC district office in the Pru West constituency, a stabbing of a 28-year-old in Bono Region on 13 July, and a gunshot death during the mop-up registration phase in Dormaa West constituency on 8 August. On 20 July, cabinet minister and MP for Awutu Senya East Hawa Koomson claimed that she had fired warning shots after feeling threatened at a registration exercise in Central Region. Koomson had gone to the registration site after hearing reports that the NDC was busing non-residents into the area to register illegally.

A pre-election survey conducted by the Center for Democratic Development (CDD-Ghana) from September to October found that 80% of respondents were in favour of stationing armed security personnel at polling stations. A significant portion of respondents also expressed serious concerns about the integrity of the vote count.

At the beginning of the year, before the pandemic was declared, corruption and economic growth were the two top political issues. Leading up to the election, it was generally understood that Akufo-Addo had done little to address corruption but that, on this score, Mahama did not have any better record. Akufo-Addo's 2016 campaign promise to build a factory in each of the 260 districts had also not been met (a maximum of 90 were built). However, though not without its critics, Akufo-Addo's handling of the pandemic was generally applauded.

Some noted that the pandemic also allowed the NPP administration creative opportunities to dispense patronage ahead of the election; indeed, some believe that relief efforts were distributed in a partisan manner. For the NDC, Mahama tried to energise his campaign by picking the first female running mate for a major party ticket. Jane Naana Opoku-Agyemang was a former education minister and the first woman to be vice-chancellor of a public university in Ghana. Mahama also announced a number of NPP measures that he would undo if elected to office and challenged Akufo-Addo to a presidential debate several times ahead of the election, though one never materialised; no such debate has taken place since 2012.

The 7 December elections were the third time Mahama and Akufo-Addo had faced one another at the ballot box. Twelve candidates competed for the presidency in a race which saw the re-election of Akufo-Addo with 51.59% of the vote. Mahama accused Akufo-Addo of mobilising the military both during voter registration and on election day to sway the outcome of the vote – allegations which the Akufo-Addo administration denied.

Despite a 2020 Election Peace Pact signed by Mahama and Akufo-Addo on 4 December, more than 60 incidents of violence took place on election day. Across the otherwise peaceful 38,000 polling stations, six of these violent events involved gunfire, resulting in five deaths.

In the lead-up to the election, polls showed that Akufo-Addo's popularity did not necessarily extend to other members of the NPP. A shake-up of a NPP majority hold in parliament was expected, but the NPP's loss of its 63-seat majority, and the resulting hung parliament, was unprecedented. The number of women parliamentarians increased by one, from 36 to 37 seats of the 275-seat legislature.

A controversial Plant Variety Protection Bill was passed in parliament on 4 November. First introduced as the Plant Breeders' Bill in 2013, the legislative instrument was designed to encourage the development of new disease- and drought-resistant seeds that would improve agricultural yields of staple produce/crops. The bills were strongly opposed by the Peasant Farmers Association of Ghana (PFAG), which claimed that they paved the way for large corporations to engage in commercial plant-breeding at the expense of smallholder farmer rights. Supporters say that the law would spur scientific innovation and help to address food security issues.

On 20 March, Ghana's parliament decriminalised cannabis use for health and industrial purposes via the Narcotics Control Commission Bill 2019. Through this bill, the existing Narcotics Control Board (NACOB) was empowered to oversee the industrial use of cannabis and other narcotics.

Further consideration of the Public University Bill, first introduced in parliament in April 2019, was officially tabled in October amid a widespread backlash. The bill would allow the government of the day to appoint the chancellor and a majority of council members of public universities as well as giving it the right to dissolve the council during times of emergency. Mahama vowed to repeal the bill if elected president, while the dean of the University of Ghana School of Law, Raymond Atuguba, threatened to resign in order to take legal action against the bill if it were to pass.

On 12 March, Ghana's government banned an LGBT+ conference scheduled to take place in Accra in July. The conference would have been the first of its kind in West Africa.

On 24 June, three small earthquakes/tremors struck Accra just before 11 PM. Accra had experienced eight such tremors since January 2018, and Ghana is the most seismically active country in West Africa.

In January, the Ghana Football Association fired all coaches of the men's and women's senior national teams and youth teams. The move was unexpected and no reason was given for the decision.

Foreign Affairs

The coronavirus outbreak strained the relationship between Ghana and China when Guangzhou, the Chinese city with the largest African community, imposed restrictions on African nationals regardless of travel history. After videos of African nationals facing sanctions at local establishments went viral, Ghana's ambassador in Beijing joined other African ambassadors and the AU in exerting pressure on China to lift the restrictions. The Chinese ambassador to Ghana was also called upon to explain the disturbing videos to the Akufo-Addo administration. The Chinese Ministry of Foreign Affairs announced a lifting of the restrictions on 13 April.

On 6 April, Ofori-Atta singled out African debt to China ($ 145 bn) as needing relief, in comments which were then raised at a press briefing with the Chinese Foreign Ministry the following day. China opted to work with individual governments on debt relief and other relief measures, including state-owned enterprise Jiangxi International Economic and Technical Corporation Co, a transport company, providing 10,000 masks to Ghana's Ministry of Roads and Highways.

On 13 April, 100 South African nationals were permitted to be repatriated to South Africa, despite the Covid-19 lockdowns in both countries. After the South African and Ghanaian governments had agreed on the issue, the South African ambassador to Ghana escorted the South African nationals to Kotoka International Airport.

In December 2019, the WAEMU, consisting of Francophone nations, announced that it would convert the CFA franc into the 'eco', which would be a first step towards generating an ECOWAS currency for the whole region. At the time, Akufo-Addo announced support for the WAEMU's plans. However, on 16 January, Ghana signed a joint statement by Anglophone ECOWAS countries (Nigeria, Sierra Leone, Liberia, and Gambia) and Guinea which condemned the plan as an appropriation of the planned ECOWAS eco currency and as a usurpation of Nigeria's role as currency leader. Furthermore, rumours circulating about France's covert influence on the WAEMU placed Ghana in an awkward position, given Akufo-Addo's close relationship with France.

The president's travel was very limited during 2020, due to the coronavirus pandemic. Akufo-Addo left Ghana on 21 February for a 12-day trip to Norway, the UK, Switzerland, and Belgium. Then, in the first week of March, the president suspended all foreign travel for public officials.

On 14 December, Akufo-Addo witnessed the inauguration of President Ouattara of Côte d'Ivoire, and the following day the inauguration of President Condé of Guinea, before then travelling to the UK. The trip was explained as part of Akufo-Addo's duties as the new chairperson of ECOWAS, a position to which he was elected on 9 October.

On 6 February, Ghanaian police raided a compound rented by Eliminating Barriers for the Liberation of Africa (EBLA). The organisation was accused of creating more than 200 social media accounts with the goal of inflaming divisions in America in the lead-up to the 2020 US elections. Ahead of the raid, Ghana's Cyber Security Unit found the group engaging in 'organised radicalism' with significant funding from Russia. Sixteen Ghanaians worked at the compound and may not have been aware that they were working as trolls with funding from Russia.

On 13 April, the US Securities and Exchange Commission charged an employee at Goldman Sachs Group, Asante Berko, with arranging more than $ 200,000 in bribes funnelled through a Turkish energy company and a Ghanaian intermediary to various Ghana government officials. The bribes were intended to help secure a client's power plant project.

Implemented through the Legal Resources Center (LRC), on 23 October USAID launched a new education mechanism in support of justice sector reform in Ghana, whereby individuals from 40 districts across seven regions were educated about Ghana's case tracking system (CTS).

After a pilot programme in 2019, 17 November was the graduation day for the US Department of State's Academy for Women Entrepreneurs (AWE) in Accra: 78 Ghanaian women entrepreneurs have completed the programme since 2019.

Chipper Cash, a mobile-based peer-to-peer payment service founded in San Francisco by Ghanaian Maijid Moujaled and Ugandan Ham Serunjogi, raised $ 13.8 m in a first funding round in June and another $ 30 m in a second round in November. The service is currently operating in seven African countries, including Ghana.

The 'international feature film' category at the 2020 US-based Oscar Awards included a first-ever submission from Ghana, with the 2018 film 'Azali'. The film used the Dagbanli language throughout, a northern language less commonly used in major films.

On 17 November, Google Arts & Culture partnered with their first ever Ghanaian partner, the Nubuke Foundation, to virtually showcase 270 artworks and nine online exhibits portraying contemporary Ghanaian art.

Socioeconomic Developments

At the beginning of the year, economic growth was predicted to dip slightly from 7% to 6%, in part because of decreased oil industry growth, the general underperformance of which contributed to Tullow Oil's chief executive resigning. Economic growth had also been somewhat held back by rising inflation, debt servicing costs, and the decreasing strength of the cedi against the dollar. But early in 2020, the cedi was the best-performing currency in the world, gaining 6.6% from January to mid-February, and Ghana's $ 3 bn Eurobond sale in early February was well sought after by investors. Investors credited Ghana's fiscal discipline and commitment to reform, including the aggressive banking reforms in 2017 which investors saw as now paying off. Moody's Investor Services changed Ghana's outlook from stable to positive in January.

Once the pandemic hit, the rosy predictions for 2020 turned to negative economic growth estimates and cancellation of financial agencies' improved credit ratings for Ghana. Ghana's credit rating was downgraded from B to B– after the government increased expenditure to curb the impact of Covid-19, something which the Akufo-Addo administration criticised as a hasty 'punishment' for one-off expenditures and temporary economic adjustments required to protect the economy and save lives.

However, Ghana was also credited for maintaining oil savings and investments in the cocoa and gold industries, which it could utilise to help pay for the state's response to the pandemic. By June, the IMF revised its previous negative economic growth projections to 1% in 2020 and 4% in 2021. However, the deficit accumulated during the response to the pandemic was now projected to be anywhere from 11% to 16% or higher, stimulating continued concerns about Ghana's debt accumulation. Food prices were 14.4% higher in April than a year prior. And by November, domestic inflation had risen to double digits, with food prices still rising.

Ghana continued to bail out the financial sector in 2020, beyond the $ 2.8 bn cost estimate that Ofori-Atta had announced in November 2019. This included $ 863 m in payments in February to compensate depositors with accounts in defunct finance institutions for losses.

Once the pandemic hit, crashing oil prices caused delays in Aker Energy's plans for the major offshore Pecan oil project. By June, Aker Energy announced a shift from a centralised FPSO (floating production, storage, and offloading vessel) for the entire Pecan field to one FPSO in the south with another to be added in the north after a few years. However, a new date for the final investment decision (FID) was not announced.

Ghana is the second-largest gold producer in Africa and tenth-largest in the world. By September, the price of gold had increased 28% since January. Total gold production increased by 3% on 2019 levels, mostly as a result of increased production at Damang Gold Mine in Western Region. Galiano Gold reported production of 249,904 ounces from the Asanko Gold Mine, beyond the 225,000–245,000 ounces projected for the year.

Prior to the pandemic, the 2019/20 cocoa growing season had already been hit hard by dry, hot winds, resulted in a projected 800,000-ton output, falling short of the 875,000 tons forecast in late January. However, in August, Ghana's Cocobod projected 900,000 tons of cocoa for the 2020/21 growing season. Cocobod then secured $ 1.3 bn in syndicated loans from 28 banks to fund the projected 900,000-ton purchases by late September. Also, the first effects of the efforts of ChocPec, the informal name given to Côte d'Ivoire and Ghana's cocoa price-setting initiative, began with the October start of the growing season. This included a living income differential

(LID), whereby cocoa bean buyers are charged a premium so that farmers are paid more. In September, the largest shea butter processing facility in Africa opened in Tema, helping to advance the shea supply chain in the region.

BACE API, a facial recognition software developed by four software engineers in Ghana in 2018, won the UK Royal Academy of Engineering's 2020 Africa Prize for Engineering Innovation, and $ 32,000 in prize money. The company had developed a more diverse facial recognition database to more accurately address identity fraud and cybercrime issues affecting Ghanaian banks.

Ghana start-up mPharma raised $ 17 m in its May funding round and appointed Helena Foulkes, former president of CVS (the largest pharmacy retail chain in the US), to its board; mPharma provides prescription drug inventory management to improve pharmaceutical supply chain efficiency.

Three Ghanaian companies were selected to participate in the first Africa Artificial Intelligence Accelerator, hosted in Ghana. Born out of a partnership with Ghana Tech Lab, Deutsche Gesellschaft für Internationale Zusammenarbeit (GIZ), and IBM, the five-month structured accelerator pairs 11 companies with technical mentors to feasibly produce proposed artificial intelligence (AI) projects. The three Ghanaian companies work on diagnosing skin diseases (Diagnosify), tracking and preventing road traffic accidents (Kwanso), and personal finance management (Xpendly).

In July, USAID awarded $ 15 m to support the new Center for Applied Research and Innovation in Supply Chain – Africa (CARISCA) at Kwame Nkrumah University of Science and Technology (KNUST), in partnership with Arizona State University. The Covid-19 pandemic greatly distorted supply chains worldwide, and particularly agriculture and healthcare supply chains in sub-Saharan Africa. The 2018 AfCTA provides new opportunities for regional manufacturing growth, with trade commencing 1 January 2021. Accra serves as the secretariat of the AfCTA and the office was commissioned and handed over to the AU by Akufo-Addo on 17 August.

In July, Radisson Hotels announced a new site in Accra in addition to five other African nations. On 12 June, the Year of Return committee, in partnership with the Diaspora African Forum, organised a memorial service for George Floyd, the black man murdered by a white police officer in the US. The minister of tourism, Barbara Oteng Gyasi, spoke at the event and Akufo-Addo sent a package of kente products to the Floyd family in the US. Then, on 13 June, Economic Fighters League (EFL) demonstrators gathered at Black Star Square in a peaceful Black Lives Matter solidarity vigil for Floyd, which abruptly ended when armed police officers rushed to the scene, fired shots in the air, and arrested leader Ernesto Yeboah for allegedly failing to notify authorities about the vigil. Yeboah denied the charges and claimed that authorities had been notified.

Building on the Year of Return and Beyond the Return tourism initiatives, in November the Wakanda City of Return project was launched in Cape Coast. The city of Cape Coast partnered with the African Diaspora Development Institute

(ADDI) and two local companies to build the modern smart city. Construction is to start in August 2021 and will include a five-star hotel, health resort, entertainment centres, and continental corporate headquarters for ADDI. Similarly, Ghana's government worked with local chiefs to earmark 500 acres of land near Accra for members of the African diaspora; it also waived survey and land registration fees.

At an unveiling ceremony on 3 August, Akufo-Addo announced the first Volkswagen vehicle to be assembled at a new VW assembly plant in Ghana, the manufacturer's fifth on the continent. Separately, plans were also broadcast to create an Automobile Industry Development Support Centre, to connect vehicle assemblers and manufactures in Ghana and ensure industry compliance standards are met.

Guinea

Joschka Philipps

The year was marked by the re-election of President Alpha Condé after the adoption of a new constitution, and the strengthening of the ruling party RPG (Rassemblement du Peuple de Guinée). The elections were highly controversial and accompanied by large-scale protests and severe political violence. A double ballot on 22 March combined the hitherto delayed legislative elections and a constitutional referendum. Boycotted by the main opposition parties, it gave the RPG a majority of votes (55%) and allowed President Condé, first elected in 2010, to run for a third mandate. On 18 October, Condé won the presidential elections by 59.5%; his main opponent Cellou Dalein Diallo (Union des Forces Démocratiques de Guinée, UFDG) was credited with 33.5% of the votes cast, though the outcome remains contested by the opposition and drew severe criticism from international observers. Over the year, clashes between security forces and anti-government protesters, especially from the FNDC movement (Front National pour la Défense de la Constitution), resulted in dozens of fatalities and hundreds of injuries and arrests. Economically, the alleged corruption scandal surrounding minister Zénab Nabaya Dramé and the mining deal signed over the Simandou iron ore deposits, promising $ 15 bn of foreign investment, point to an ever more contested political economy in which significant economic gains in the mining sector failed to benefit the general

Guinean population. The coronavirus pandemic, while adding significantly to the socioeconomic precariousness of most Guineans, did not significantly reduce economic growth. Guinea's GDP grew by 5.2% in 2020, compared with 5.6% in 2019, based on the continued increase in mining activities.

Domestic Politics

Guinea's election year 2020 saw a radicalisation of the political conflict between the RPG-led government under President Alpha Condé on the one hand, and the political opposition led by the UFDG and the socio-political movement FNDC on the other. Rumours had permeated political debates for the better part of President Condé's second term since 2015 that he would seek a third mandate by changing the constitution.

Since October 2019, tensions had become aggravated. On 18 December 2019, the 81-year-old Condé released the text for the proposed *new constitution*, which would be decided upon through a constitutional referendum. Condé claimed that the old constitution, dating from 2010, lacked legitimacy because it had been adopted under the National Transitional Council (CNT) and had not been submitted to a referendum; therefore, it was not 'legally constitutional'. He also defended the new constitution as 'modern' insofar as it would codify gender equality, prohibit female circumcision and underage marriage, and make the country's natural resources a common good, with mining resources to be dedicated in part to local community development. Most importantly, however, adopting the new constitution, which further expands the powers of the executive, would legally set Condé's count of presidential mandates back to zero and allow Condé to run for president for a third time, although the maximum number of presidential terms is still two in the new constitution.

In January 2020, the opposition's indignation about what they considered a 'constitutional coup d'état' inspired *mass protests* in Conakry, Labé, Pita, Dalaba, Mamou, and Boké. While largely peaceful, the demonstrations also featured outbreaks of violence. Police headquarters were ransacked and official buildings attacked, 12 protesters were injured in clashes with security forces, and in Kankan, the stronghold of the ruling RPG, protesters also clashed with civilian government supporters.

The constitutional referendum and the legislative elections took place in a *double ballot* initially scheduled for 1 March. The opposition boycotted the vote, first because the referendum was authorised only by the president of the national assembly, an ally of President Condé, and not by parliament as required by the constitution, and second because of the flawed electoral register. Indeed, both ECOWAS and the OIF (Organisation Internationale de la Francophonie) counted about

2.5 m 'problematic voters', 98% of whom did not have any documents to identify themselves, including duplicates, deceased people, and undeclared voters, who the opposition claimed were exclusively registered in strongholds of the ruling party. On the eve of the referendum, President Condé succumbed to international pressure concerning the electoral register by delaying the vote, first by two weeks and then by another week, while charging the CENI (Commission Électorale Nationale Indépendante) to modify the electoral register, which it supposedly did on 17 March, as well as giving a 20% pay rise to all military personnel on 16 March.

In the near absence of international observers and in parallel to the emergence of the coronavirus in Guinea, the double ballot finally took place on 22 March. With an official turnout of 58.27%, the new constitution was approved by 89.76% of votes. In the same vein, the RPG won 79 of the 114 seats in the national assembly, gaining a two-thirds majority in parliament that protects the ruling party from any legislative deadlock.

On polling day, demonstrators and militants attacked and blocked polling sites, burned voting material, and ransacked various public offices. With the exception of the ruling party's stronghold of Upper Guinea, the unrest was countrywide. In Conakry, at least ten protesters died in clashes with government forces; in N'Zérékoré, the regional capital of Forested Guinea, the vote reignited an amalgam of political, religious, and ethnic conflicts between Muslim Konianké (associated with the ruling RPG) and mostly Christian Guerzé. After the vote, churches and mosques were set alight and an estimated 32 people, including an imam, were killed. As local authorities buried the bodies of victims in a secret mass grave on 25 March, the true number of fatalities remains unknown.

Surprisingly, the *'new constitution'* that was published on 14 April differed considerably from the constitution that Guineans had voted on. It now contained 156 articles, whereas the original version, published in the official gazette after the constitutional referendum on 22 March, had contained 157 articles. Several articles (42, 43, 47, 76, 77, 83, 84, and 106) had been significantly modified in the meantime, some of them fundamentally altering institutional responsibilities. Equally surprisingly, the constitutional court did not express any reservations about the mysterious correction of the constitution and remained silent about the questionable legal value of the document published on 14 April as the new constitution. Following its approval by the court, Alpha Condé remained silent as to whether he would actually run as one of the *presidential candidates*. On 6 August, his RPG party officially asked for his candidacy; on 11 August, he announced the official election date of 18 October, and on 2 September, Condé confirmed he would run, sparking uproar among the opposition, which promised new protests. However, a split emerged within the opposition on 9 September, mainly between the FNDC coalition, which sought to boycott the elections, and Cellou Dalein Diallo's UFDG, the main opposition party, which decided to participate.

The *election campaign* of Alpha Condé, in turn, consisted of explicitly ethnically divisive and war-mongering rhetoric. Speaking in Malinké to crowds in his strongholds of Kankan and Siguiri, for instance, the RPG candidate argued: 'This election is not just an election, it is as if we were at war' and 'If you vote for a Malinké candidate who is not from the RPG, you vote for Cellou Dalein Diallo'. Alluding to his previous legislative victory in March, Condé also assured the inhabitants of Upper Guinea of the region's electrification: 'In the next five years, there will be no elections. We have a majority in parliament, which means that our projects will pass. Upper Guinea will have electricity as well as [Forested Guinea].'

Condé's rhetoric pointed to his uncertainty as to whether the *Upper Guinea* region would still unitedly vote for him. Indeed, besides the trans-ethnic opposition movement that had formed through political and civil society organisations within the FNDC, even the capital city of Upper Guinea, Kankan, had since June 2020 become a key site of recurrent protests over the lack of electricity, akin to Boké and Kamsar in Maritime Guinea. Kankan's youth in particular had started the 'Mouvement Citoyen pour l'Électrification de la Haute-Guinée' to demand the construction of a hydroelectric dam to provide stable electricity. Their frequent demonstrations led to 22 arrests among members on 21 July, and demonstrators repeatedly argued that they would not be persuaded by the government's electoral promises. Yet the movement's leaders unexpectedly announced a 'definitive halt' to the demonstrations on 5 September, which triggered various suspicions of corruption by the government and its allies.

The election campaigns were marred by *conflict*. Cellou Dalein Diallo and the UFDG, for instance, were violently prevented by RPG youth crowds from entering Kankan for a planned rally on 11 October, allegedly with no intervention by security forces. Prime Minister Kassory Fofana's attempt to hold an RPG rally in Dalaba (Middle Guinea) on 29 September was met with resistance by opposition groups. As Fofana's visit and the conflict in Dalaba cost yet another demonstrator's life, a debate ensued about the number of deaths caused by security forces since October 2019, when the political conflict over Condé's third mandate first turned violent. The FNDC published a list according to which 92 people had been killed during crackdowns, while Guinea's security minister Albert Damantang Camara admitted that there had been 42 deaths, without attributing them exclusively to security forces. Amnesty International reported at least 50 victims of police violence between October 2019 and July 2020. Amnesty furthermore highlighted ten unconstitutional bans on demonstrations and condemned the unconstitutional involvement of military personnel in crackdowns, while urging the government to end impunity for its security forces. This critique of impunity in Guinea also concerns the still-pending trial against the perpetrators of the 28 September 2009 massacre in Conakry, which took the lives of an estimated 150 demonstrators protesting against the then-ruling military junta CNND (Conseil National pour la Démocratie et le Développement). In January 2020, minister of justice Mamadou Lamine Fofana assured the UNHRC in Geneva that the trial would take place in June 2020, but this once more failed to become a reality.

On 18 October, the *presidential elections* finally took place. Though the voting itself took place in an atmosphere of relative calm, unrest began a day later, when Cellou Dalein Diallo claimed his victory before the official results were out. His team, Diallo argued, had made its own nationwide count of the official tally sheets (PV, procès verbaux), according to which he had won the first round of the elections with 53.84% of the tally as against 39.4% for Alpha Condé. The CENI disputed these claims and on 24 October presented its official provisional figures, according to which Alpha Condé had won 59.5% of the votes cast, while opposition leader Diallo was credited with 33.5%. These figures were disputed the next day by the vice-president of the CENI, a commissioner of the opposition, Mamadou Bano Sow. He highlighted various anomalies that hinted at electoral fraud, including the impossibly high voter turnout of around 100% in five prefectures of Upper Guinea (including the prefecture of Faranah, with 100.14%), and 'soviet scores' of over 95% for President Condé in the Kankan region. Nonetheless, on 7 November, Guinea's supreme court validated the CENI's provisional results and confirmed Alpha Condé as elected.

In the meantime, Guinea had already descended into a spiral of *post-electoral violence*. In Conakry, the opposition strongholds along the Route Le Prince in the Ratoma commune were virtually under siege for more than two weeks; estimates of fatalities ranged between 21 and 46, including four deaths among security forces, and the government confirmed that over 240 people had been arrested. Following his auto-proclamation, Cellou Dalein Diallo's offices were ransacked by state forces, while Diallo himself was put under house arrest from 20 October to 30 October. The military was highly present across the capital city in what seemed like an attempt to purge the city of anti-government resistance. While Alpha Condé boasted 'The mayhem is over [...]. Whoever it is, when you pull your dick out, we're going to cut it off' (in Sosso to a crowd in Kaloum, Conakry), Amnesty International and the US Department of State reported widespread human rights violations, including arbitrary arrests, killings, and torture, which lasted well into December.

In parallel, community-based violence rocked the prefecture of Macenta in the N'Zérékoré region in late December 2020. There were clashes between the Toma (a Christian ethnic group of Forested Guinea) and the Manian (a Malinké-related Muslim group), resulting in the deaths of 12 people. The violence resulted from disagreements over the respective groups' autochthonous status and the role of Macenta's patriarch.

Foreign Affairs

On the international level, the 2020 Guinean elections attracted strong *international criticism* from ECOWAS, the AU, the UN, the EU, and several individual governments. With regard to the double ballot in March, the French foreign ministry condemned, among other aspects, the 'non-inclusive and non-consensual nature of these elections [which] did not allow the holding of credible elections'. Ultimately, however, international criticism proved inconsequential, not least because the coronavirus pandemic attracted the bulk of international political attention in 2020. Particularly significant in this regard was ECOWAS's decision in October 2020, shortly before the presidential elections, to cancel a high-level visit to Guinea in order to mediate in the controversy over the electoral register. The mission would have been led by three political heavyweights: ECOWAS president and former Nigérien head of state Mahamadou Issoufou, Ivoirian president Alassane Ouattara, and Nigerian president Muhammadu Buhari, who a month earlier had already called on West African leaders to respect constitutional term limits to preserve peace in the region. Officially, ECOWAS's cancellation was due to travelling risks posed by the coronavirus. However, insiders remarked that Alpha Condé's determination to hold the referendum at all costs had rendered an ECOWAS-led mediation challenging, if not futile. After the presidential elections, various international election observer missions retreated and later expressed their criticism in view of the results. The US, France, and the EU expressed doubts about the credibility of the presidential election result, though ultimately and grudgingly congratulating Alpha Condé on his electoral victory. UNSG António Guterres condemned the violence over the vote dispute.

As to the coup d'état in neighbouring *Mali* in August 2020, Alpha Condé shared the ECOWAS position and condemned the coup while asking for the release of former president Ibrahim Boubacar Keïta and his staff. With almost 1,000 Guinean peacekeepers serving in Mali, Guinea remains one of the largest troop contributors to MINUSMA, the UN Multidimensional Integrated Stabilization Mission in Mali.

Socioeconomic Developments

The first case of the *coronavirus* in Guinea was recorded on 13 March, when a Belgian EU official was hospitalised and tested positive in Conakry. Nine days before the highly contested constitutional referendum, the Guinean government put in place containment measures, including the prohibition of gatherings of more than 100 people (later reduced to no more than 20 people), the closure of Conakry Gbessia International Airport (on 23 March), and ultimately a state of emergency on 26 March, officially closing all borders and blocking traffic between Conakry and the interior of the country.

The coronavirus, in contrast to the previous Ebola epidemic that killed 2,536 people in Guinea in 2013–16, was initially seen as a 'rich people's' virus. Early *deaths as a result of the virus* in April included those of well-known political figures who were exposed to international travel and to infected people. Among them were Salifou Kébé, president of the CENI; Sékou Kourouma, secretary-general of the government; Louncény Fofana, the second vice-president of the national assembly; and Victor Traoré, former director of Interpol Guinea. Rumours as to whether the coronavirus was part of a political plot accordingly circulated in Guinea as elsewhere. Yet the virus quickly affected poorer populations as well. One hotspot was the main prison in Conakry, the Maison Centrale. On 12 May, authorities confirmed that out of 130 tests, 58 people were infected, and reported three deaths linked to the virus. The Maison Centrale is the most overcrowded prison in the country, with a capacity of 300 but currently housing 1,500 inmates. Over the course of 2020, 13,722 cases of Covid-19 were recorded in Guinea, with 81 deaths. Guinea began vaccinating against the coronavirus on 30 December, using the Russian Sputnik v vaccine.

Among the general population, the coronavirus aggravated *food insecurity*, which had already loomed large before the crisis. A UN survey in October found that 73% of Guinean household members had reduced their expenditure as a result of the Covid-19 crisis and the resulting loss of income, and half had had to reduce the number of meals or amount of food they ate. The closure of land and air borders impacted prices for both food and manufactured goods, as major importers were prevented from leaving the country. Moreover, arbitrary arrests and corruption accompanied the enforcement of containment measures and added to a general sense of tension and fear, notably in the context of political tensions. The closure of mosques, notably during Ramadan, caused confusion and doubt; for many Guinean Muslims, the epidemic was god's doing.

Roadblocks and restrictions for taxi drivers further added to the socioeconomic precariousness of local working populations and sparked violent anti-government *protests*, especially on 12 May in Coyah and Dubreka, two cities adjacent to Conakry's suburbs. Six deaths and numerous injuries were recorded during clashes with security forces; the central police station of Coyah and the neighbouring police and gendarmerie stations of Manéah were vandalised. On the same day, young people protested against repeated electricity shortages in Kamsar, a port city for the bauxite mining industry in Maritime Guinea, burning down the home of the mayor and blocking the trains of two main mining companies, CBG and GAC. One demonstrator was shot dead by state forces. In general, the health crisis overlapped with and amplified both the existing socioeconomic crisis and the political grievances in Guinea.

The *macroeconomic effects* of the pandemic on GDP growth initially seemed disastrous. Ultimately, however, the Guinean economy grew by 5.2% in 2020, only a slight decrease from 5.6% in 2019. This is mainly due to the continuing mining boom. As the world's major bauxite supplier since 2017, Guinea's mining sector saw an increase of 18.4% in mining activity in 2020, while growth rates outside the mining sector were relatively low (2.5% in 2020, down from 5.1% in 2019). This trend is likely to continue, within and beyond the bauxite mining sector. Over the year, Guinea's Simandou iron ore mine in the country's south-east benefited from an unexpected and significant rise in global commodity prices for iron ore. Due to China's continued demand for steel and supply disruptions in Brazil, various stakeholders sought to accelerate the necessary infrastructure development for iron ore export via the port at Matakong in the prefecture of Forécariah, notably the Singaporian-Chinese-Guinean consortium SMB-Winning (which controls blocks 1 and 2) and Rio Tinto (which owns 45.05% of blocks 3 and 4, with China's Chinalco holding 39.95% and the Guinean government 15%). On 4 June, the SMB-Winning consortium and the Guinean government signed a basic agreement for a period of 25 years for the exploitation of the iron ore deposits of blocks 1 and 2 of Simandou. The 650 km railroad from Simandou to Matakong and the port project are estimated to require investment of about $ 15 bn.

Inflation rose only slightly to 10.4% in 2020, from 9.5% in 2019, with the central bank seeking to decrease the difference between official and parallel exchange rates. Guinea's budget deficit stood at 3.1% of GDP in 2020, compared with 0.5% in 2019, an increase caused by reduced tax revenues and the government's increased spending to mitigate the effects of the pandemic. As to the latter, the IMF's Rapid Credit Facility contributed $ 148 m to Guinea to address fiscal financing needs in June. Overall, the 2020 Ease of Doing Business report (based on data from 2019) downgraded Guinea from a score of 51.51 in the previous year to 49.4, and from rank 152 to rank 156 out of 190 economies. As had previous reports, it highlighted taxation as the country's lowest-performing indicator (rank 183 out of 190). To improve the taxation rate and transparency, on 14 September the Guinean government launched a new eTax tool to facilitate the declaration and remote payment of taxes on the internet.

In November 2020, an *alleged corruption scandal* over 200 bn Guinean francs (roughly $ 20 m) made headlines in Guinea. Zénab Nabaya Dramé, the current minister of technical education and vocational training, was accused in an article by Guinéenews investigative journalist Youssouf Boundou Sylla and other news media of embezzling the said amount while serving in different government positions, including as a director of financial affairs at the Ministry of Agriculture and the Ministry of Health. Dramé in turn filed a defamation complaint against the managers of three media outlets, Guinéenews, Guinee7, and Inquisiteur, which she lost.

Dramé had been Alpha Condé's deputy election campaign manager for the presidential elections.

Finally, Guinea's position on various socio-political indices slightly worsened in reports for 2020 (based on data from 2019). The 2020 World Press Freedom Index ranked Guinea 110th of 180 countries, three positions lower than in the previous year. The 2020 Freedom House report considered Guinea 'partly free', noting a slight decrease in political rights and civil liberties from 43 to 40 points out of 100. The 2020 Human Development Report situates Guinea at rank 178 out of 189 (the 2019 position was 179) and among the lowest-performing countries (group 5) on the gender development index.

Guinea-Bissau

Christoph Kohl

Former prime minister Umaro Sissoco Embaló won the 2019 presidential elections. His victory produced yet another political crisis, as the results were challenged by the majority party Partido Africano da Independência da Guiné e Cabo Verde (PAIGC) and its candidate, party leader Domingos Simões Pereira. Eventually, Embaló unilaterally declared himself president, assisted by the armed forces. He appointed Nuno Gomes Nabiam (Assembleia do Povo Unido – Partido Democrático da Guiné-Bissau, APU-PDGB) as the new prime minister. The legitimate prime minister, Aristides Gomes (PAIGC), and some of his allies were persecuted. Autocratic tendencies and political tensions increased considerably. The global Covid-19 pandemic hit the country's impoverished population, its ailing health sector, and the economy.

Domestic Politics

According to the definitive results released by the Comissão Nacional de Eleições (CNE) on 17 January, Embaló, candidate of the Movimento para a Alternância

Democrática (MADEM-G15), won the *run-off presidential elections of 29 December 2019* with 53.55% of the votes, leaving behind Pereira with 46.45%. Pereira and the PAIGC disputed the results, speaking of *irregularities and manipulation*, and went to Guinea-Bissau's supreme court. Local narratives accused Senegal of providing Embaló with money to buy votes. Embaló threatened both the parliament and the supreme court, saying that he and his followers would even go to war if his victory was not accepted; Gomes condemned Embaló's statements. On 15 February, the court demanded that the CNE check the vote tally sheets; the CNE confirmed the results on 25 February, yet without reviewing individual polling station results as demanded by the court. The PAIGC upheld its objections.

On 27 February, *Embaló swore himself in as president* without the presence of the government, the coalition parties, or representatives of the international community. He bypassed both a final ruling by the supreme court that did not recognise Embaló's victory and constitutional provisions that required the parliament to approve the swearing-in. The army, however, was present in significant numbers during the ceremony at the hotel where the swearing-in took place. Subsequently, Prime Minister Gomes and the PAIGC described the events as a *coup d'état*. On 28 February, Embaló dismissed Gomes while troops invaded the prime minister's office, the parliament, the court, the public radio and TV stations, and Bissau's town hall. Embaló appointed Nabiam as the new prime minister. Although the parliament, with its PAIGC majority, did not recognise Embaló's take-over, it declared a vacancy and appointed speaker of parliament Cipriano Cassamá (PAIGC) as acting state-president.

Political opponents of Embaló's rule were increasingly intimidated, while respect for *human rights deteriorated* and the *separation of powers was put into question*. Two days after his appointment as interim state-president, on 1 March, Cassamá stepped down after having received threats. Following Nabiam's appointment as prime minister, several journalists were assaulted and the private Radio Capital headquarters destroyed. Covid-19 pandemic restrictions were thenceforth used as pretext to suppress public demonstrations by opposition circles. On 5 March, the army invaded the residences of several of Gomes' previous cabinet members; meanwhile, Gomes' house was invaded again on 11 March by armed troops. The same day, Embaló ordered the ECOWAS Mission in Guinea-Bissau (ECOMIB) to terminate its protection of the residences of Gomes, Pereira, and the judges of the supreme court. Consequently, Gomes sought refuge at UNIOGBIS (United Nations Integrated Peacebuilding Office in Guinea-Bissau) in Bissau. Gomes' justice minister, Ruth Monteiro, fled to a diplomatic mission in Bissau, citing security concerns. Several former cabinet members were prohibited from leaving the country, having been accused of corruption and other crimes, according to reports on 1 April. PAIGC leader Pereira managed to leave for Portugal.

On 23 April, Nabiam submitted his *government's programme* to the parliament to be debated in May. Due to the shifting alignments of some deputies, it was uncertain whether the programme would receive majority approval. The day before, Embaló had threatened to dissolve the parliament if the request for debate was rejected, threatening in the process to slash parliamentarians' salaries. Without disclosing further details, including the names of its members, on 11 May Embaló announced the creation of a *constitutional reform* committee. This was because in past years the inconsistent constitution has been repeatedly held responsible for political instability, as it allowed for conflicting interpretations of the competences of the president and the parliament. Yet critics interpreted Embaló's move as an attempt to secure more power and competences for the president.

Pressure on the legislature and the judiciary was upheld. On 22 May, a parliamentarian of Nabiam's APU-PDGB was abducted by the police, but he was later freed. He had refused to support the government but instead continued to vote with the party's coalition. Eventually, Nabiam obtained a majority in an extraordinary parliament session on 29 June after five PAIGC parliamentarians resisted their party's decision to boycott the assembly; critics assumed bribery. Attorney-general Fernando Gomes – appointed by Embaló on 30 April – subpoenaed seven of the eleven supreme court judges, it was reported on 26 June. On 17 June, they had accused the court's vice-president, Rui Nené (the court's president, Paulo Sanhá, had been absent for a long time for medical reasons), of preventing the bench for months from dealing with the PAIGC's presidential election suit. On 7 July, Embaló announced the technical supervision of social media – interpreted as an attempt to transform the country into a police state. The *Liga Guineense dos Direitos Humanos* (LGDH) accused Embaló on 12 October of the 'implementation of terror' in Guinea-Bissau. Previously, the self-declared president had argued that the LGDH was selective in its reports of human rights violations, criticising the new administration and the new president. Embaló had repeatedly declared that it was he who governed the country ('Boss is boss. I decide, they obey!') and that *he stood above both the judiciary and the legislature* – ignoring the fact that the constitution does not grant him any executive powers and that the government is responsible to the parliament. On many occasions Embaló held cabinet meetings, thus sidelining the prime minister, who is constitutionally head of government. On 13 October, it became known that former prime minister Aristides Gomes had been prohibited from leaving the country due to three legal cases (dating from 2006, 2019, and 2020) against him, as confirmed by the attorney-general. Gomes spoke of 'political persecution', arguing that the attorney-general did not have any evidence. Attorney-general Fernando Gomes issued an international arrest warrant against Pereira on 18 December; he was accused of embezzling IMF funds during his tenure as prime minister (2014–15). On 17 December, Embaló threatened again to dissolve the parliament if the state budget for 2021 was not approved. Simultaneously, on 17 December he announced his resolve to '*discipline and moralise society*' by freezing the salaries of parliamentarians who did not participate in the plenary discussion. Thenceforth, the salaries would be deposited in individual commercial bank accounts.

Foreign Affairs

The *international community* was divided on Guinea-Bissau and *only hesitantly recognised Embaló's victory*. In March, Embaló toured Niger, Nigeria, and Senegal to win international recognition. In January, he was received as elected president in both Portugal and Cape Verde. On 9 March, ECOWAS cancelled a mediation mission of legal experts to Guinea-Bissau: after they had sought to meet the deposed prime minister Gomes, Embaló criticised the mission harshly. Eventually, ECOWAS recognised Embaló's victory on 23 April – despite the outstanding final ruling of the divided supreme court. The Comunidade dos Países de Língua Portuguesa (CPLP) followed suit on 24 April, while the EU lay low. ECOWAS handled Embaló with kid gloves: the 22 May deadline set by ECOWAS for Embaló to appoint a government based on the 2019 legislative elections results passed without consequences. Portugal was quick to normalise the relationship with its former colony: a visit by Prime Minister Nabiam to Portugal in July and a working visit of Portugal's foreign minister in September enhanced the legitimacy of the regime in power. Portugal's recognition was reinforced by Embaló's official visit to Lisbon on 8–9 October, although a state visit to Guinea-Bissau by Portuguese prime minister António Costa planned for December had to be cancelled.

On 28 February, the UNSC renewed the mandate of *UNIOGBIS* for a last time until 31 December. After 21 years, the UN mission was terminated in the midst of a profound political crisis. Despite the closure, the Bissau UN mission continued to grant refuge to former prime minister Gomes.

In mid-March, Nabiam demanded the withdrawal of *ECOMIB* by later that month. ECOMIB had been deployed to the country since 2012; its mandate was redefined in 2015 due to a politico-institutional crisis, when the focus shifted to stabilisation, pacification, and protection of institutions and personalities. ECOMIB's mandate officially ended on 10 September.

International narco-trafficking reintensified. Following reports, notable individuals, including some senior military personnel who were known to be involved in narco-trafficking, joined Embaló's presidential self-proclamation ceremony. Indeed, the new administration quickly created precedents that seemed to confirm the worst fears: in March, the head of the judicial police (criminal investigation department), Filomena Mendes Lopes, who had been responsible for the confiscation of about 2.6 tons of cocaine in 2019, was dismissed. She should have been replaced by Mário Iala, then working at the attorney's office. Iala had been accused in 2019 by then justice minister Ruth Monteiro of trying to thwart one of the operations that led to the confiscation of 789 kg of cocaine. However, due to widespread criticism, Iala's nomination was withdrawn. Instead, Teresa Silva was appointed new director of the judicial police. Silva, previously vice-attorney-general, was known to be close to Embaló. Another individual accused by Monteiro of thwarting drug trafficking investigations, Herculano Sá, was also regarded as an ally of the new administration. He was tasked with coordinating the crime department within the attorney's office. In early April, Braima Seidi Bá, who had been subject to an international arrest warrant and was sentenced to 16 years imprisonment by a court in Canchungo one week earlier, returned to Bissau. Bá allegedly maintained links to former general chief of staff António Indjai, accused of being involved in narco-trafficking. Reportedly, Bá stayed at the residence of the director of the state-owned enterprise Empresa Nacional de Pesquisa e Exploração Petrolíferas (Petroguin), Danielson 'Nick' Francisco Gomes Ié. Ié had been nominated director of Petroguin on 31 March. His appointment was rejected by the Partido para a Renovação Social (PRS), which supported the Embaló administration. The PRS claimed that Ié was strongly connected to organised crime, including narco-trafficking.

A report by the Global Initiative Against Transnational Organized Crime (GI-TOC) that was released in May said that Guinea-Bissau was once again becoming a narco-state. GI-TOC linked Bá to a Bissau-Guinean/Colombian/Mexican/Malian cocaine network. On 14 October, the court of appeal drastically reduced the penalties against leading drug traffickers. A document released by the IMF criticised the justice sector for *fundamental deficiencies in fighting corruption and drug trafficking*, lamenting a lack of transparency, lack of resources, lengthy and costly procedures, and the dependence of judges, as well corruption within the judiciary.

Child trafficking remained a problem in Guinea-Bissau. Portuguese authorities arrested a man of Bissau-Guinean nationality at Lisbon airport on 20 September, suspected of intending to traffic a five-year-old child to Belgium, using forged documents.

Guinea unilaterally closed its borders to Guinea-Bissau from 27 September; presidential elections were held in the neighbouring country on 18 October. Guinea-Bissau is home to a large Guinean migrant community, many of them ethnic Fulani who are active in transnational trade and are supporters of the opposition candidate. After facing difficulties voting in the Guinean consulate in Bissau, many of them tried to return home to vote.

Freedom House's 2020 *Freedom in the World* index classified Guinea-Bissau as 'partially free' (ranked 46th compared with 42nd the year before).

Socioeconomic Developments

The global *Covid-19 pandemic* also hit Guinea-Bissau. On 18 March, self-proclaimed president Embaló ordered the closure of all land, sea, and air borders and all commercial sites. Further measures followed on 26 March, limiting the circulation of people and vehicles and imposing a night curfew. Schools were closed from March until October. A state of emergency was first imposed on 28 March. In mid-April, the IMF approved immediate debt service relief, through its Catastrophe Containment and Relief Trust, to 19 African countries, including Guinea-Bissau. On 26 April, the first official Covid-19 death was reported. In late April, Nabiam and several government officials tested positive. The real number of people infected and fatalities were most likely much higher than officially reported, also because about 60% of the population do not have access to healthcare centres within 5 km. Whereas the curfew was lifted on 25 June, other emergency measures were extended, including limitations on assembly. The Portuguese airline TAP resumed its flights to Lisbon on 5 September; they had been suspended since March. Air Maroc resumed its flights to Bissau on 30 October. Real GDP growth data released in November projected a decrease of 1.7% in 2020 and a growth of 4% in 2021. In December, joblessness stood at 11.6%, with young people in particular the worst affected. In December, the AfDB approved a $ 9.8 m grant aimed at supporting the national control project Programa de Apoio de Urgência para a Luta contra o Virus de Covid-19 (PALPC) to reduce the spread of the virus and to boost the resilience of both the ailing health sector and vulnerable communities.

On 16 December, the parliament approved the *state budget for 2021*. The budget obtained a majority of 54 votes. The vast majority of the PAIGC and two coalition partners boycotted the vote, as they did not recognise the Nabiam government. The budget of about € 386 m did not consider investments, ignoring the private sector, which was suffering from the pandemic. Instead, it introduced five new taxes that also affected the disadvantaged strata of the population. The leading trade union – União Nacional dos Trabalhadores da Guiné (UNTG) – announced that it would turn 2021 into a 'year of strikes' should the budget be approved.

Corruption remained an issue. According to Transparency International's 2020 Corruption Perceptions Index, Guinea-Bissau ranked 165th out of 179 countries based on 2019 data. The president of the court of audit, former prime minister Dionísio Cabi, accused the supreme court in mid-February of obstructing an audit, as it refused to allow the court of audit to check the provenance and use of funds. On 26 August, Cabi said that the level of corruption in the public service was a cause for concern and that it was urgent to take steps to fight the 'financial disorder'. During its audits of public institutions over the past years, the court had discovered spending without justification worth € 18.5 m. Cabi endorsed an employment ban in the public sector for individuals connected to corruption cases.

The development of the country's *infrastructure and connection* continued. The Senegalese transport company Dakar Dem Dikk announced on 23 January the inauguration of a direct bus service to Bissau. Guinea-Bissau would also profit from Senegalese plans to rehabilitate its National Road 4, which links the Trans-Gambia

Highway with Mpack at the Senegalese–Bissau-Guinean border, it was reported in March. Many imports are processed through Senegal and The Gambia. In November, it became known that the UAE would fully pay for the construction of a new € 600 m international airport in Nhacra, about 30 km from the capital Bissau.

As one of the poorest countries in the world, Guinea-Bissau also remained dependent on international *financial cooperation*. According to World Bank data for April on publicly guaranteed external debt service, Guinea-Bissau had one bilateral and five multilateral creditors and thus belonged to those countries with the lowest number of external creditors. On 18 December, the AfDB board of directors approved the Lusophone Compact Guarantee Programme (LCGP). The programme, with a maximum risk exposure of up to € 400 m, was designed for non-sovereign operations in the continent's five lusophone countries – including Equatorial Guinea and Guinea-Bissau. Portugal would act as the guarantor. The programme would allow for bank projects to be covered for up to the full maturity of the loan and up to 85% of the bank loan principal amount.

Guinea-Bissau remained heavily dependent on *foreign aid and international cooperation*. The US Department of Agriculture announced in February that it would launch a six-year project in Guinea-Bissau, Senegal, and The Gambia to enhance the value chain of cashew kernels – the country's main cash crop. Only about 5–6% of the kernels were processed locally. A total of $ 38 m was to be invested. In March, IFAD announced its support for a new project aimed at reducing poverty, increasing productivity and incomes, and improving the food and nutrition security of at least 287,000 small-scale farmers in Guinea-Bissau. A US project worth $ 65.7 m was envisaged to promote the diversification of crops, following media coverage in March. While Guinea-Bissau had signed fisheries agreements with the EU, Senegal, and China, the minister of fisheries, Malam Sambú, declared in August his intention to sign a separate contract with Portugal.

Liberia

Ibrahim Al-bakri Nyei

Political and socioeconomic developments in Liberia, in 2020, were dominated and severely affected by the outbreak of the coronavirus disease (Covid-19). Liberia's rapid and proactive response may well have saved the country from mass community transmission. Long before the first case was recorded in Africa, Liberia was among the first countries in the world to institute epidemic control measures. Early in February, Liberia instituted a thorough virus control protocol (hand washing, temperature checks, and contact tracing) at its international airport for travellers coming from abroad. On 16 March, the country recorded its first official case of the virus in a government official. With experience from dealing with the Ebola virus disease epidemic (EVD, 2014–16), the Liberian government reactivated emergency response measures, and communities quickly adapted to new rules and went on high alert. This saved the country from widespread community transmission of the virus throughout the year; but due to the spread of the virus in other parts of the world, particularly Europe and America, and mutual border closures that affected the movement of goods and people in the sub-region, the fallout from the outbreak of Covid-19 weighed heavily on political and social development in the country. Production slumped, and workers in many sectors suffered lay-offs. The greatest blow to the government was its defeat in the senatorial election held in December, when the ruling party lost in 12 of the 15 senate elections. Alongside the senatorial election, Liberians finally voted on proposed changes to the country's constitution after years of debate on constitutional reform. The opposition called for a boycott of the referendum or a 'no' vote on all items while the government supported a 'yes' vote on all items, but no item was passed in the referendum.

Domestic Politics

The outbreak of Covid-19 was the first major crisis to confront the George Weah government. Previous crises of economic governance had been met with short-term interventions that minimised their effects, but Covid-19 presented the first major leadership test, since its impacts were multifaceted. Despite it being a health epidemic, the outbreak impacted political and socioeconomic development and posed major challenges to the government in dealing with the fallout. But before the outbreak of the virus, the government was already facing waves of opposition protests due to declining economic standards and allegations of corruption against key allies of the president. On 6 January, opposition pressure group the Council of Patriots (COP) staged another mass protest at the seat of the government – the second in less than a year. This protest was violently disrupted by security forces, and the COP leader, radio talk-show host Henry Costa, was charged with forging an immigration document during his return to the country ahead of the protest. He fled arrest and returned to the United States, where he was based. The COP, which is aligned with the opposition Collaborating Political Parties (a coalition that comprises the former ruling Unity Party, the Liberty Party, the Alternative National Congress, and the All Liberia Party), reported in August that its attempts to obtain an official registration document had been rebuffed by the Liberia Business Registry.

On 16 March, a senior government official who had returned from Geneva was diagnosed with the novel Covid-19 – the first case to be officially reported in the country. The government responded by imposing a state of emergency and declaring a curfew in Monrovia and surrounding counties and by restricting the movement of people to and from these areas. The military was deployed alongside the police to enforce these public-health-related regulations. But their intervention saw an increase in harassment of citizens, as they deployed excessive force to enforce the measures. The press and local civil society organisations also accused the government of using the public health enforcement measures to harass opposition figures and suppress dissent. In response to these allegations, the solicitor-general reminded them that 'Liberia is technically at war', and so all rights, including freedom of speech, were suspended under the state of emergency and anyone spreading 'fake news' would be arrested. This became pertinent when a COP executive, Manipekai Dumoe, was arrested for sedition after he questioned the government's

Covid-19 relief programme and suggested in a Facebook post that the citizens should be given guns instead of rice.

On 22 July, the government ended the state of emergency and lifted most of the restrictions. Citizens largely complied with the health protocols, thanks to their experience in dealing with an even more deadly viral epidemic just four years earlier.

As a result of the state of emergency, the planned special senatorial election for half of the senate's 30 seats and the constitutional referendum were postponed from October to December due to logistical challenges posed by the spread of the epidemic and the containment measures. The National Elections Commission (NEC) also suggested that there were financial constraints to holding the elections, in addition to the Covid-19-related constraints. This decision to postpone the election was resisted by members of the opposition, who insisted that the polls be held in line with the constitution and warned of a potential constitutional crisis should the government fail to hold the elections before January 2021, when the tenure of the sitting 15 senators was due to end.

The president reorganised the electoral commission in April after the tenure of some of its members ended. Those appointed in this reorganisation were mainly members and supporters of his party, a move condemned by the opposition and civil society organisations. They accused the president of departing from a precedent in which appointment of commissioners took place in consultation with opposition parties and civil society organisations. Despite the criticism, the president did not back down. However, his initial pick for the position of chairperson was rejected by the senate due to the failure of the nominee (who was Nigerian-born with no Liberian ancestry) to prove his Liberian citizenship.

Ahead of the senatorial election, opposition parties organised themselves into various alliances to mobilise and strengthen their bases against the ruling party. In August, the Collaborating Political Parties (CPP) received certification from the NEC to operate as an alliance. Another group of seven opposition parties, including the True Whig Party (Africa's oldest and longest-ruling political party, which ruled Liberia from 1869 to 1871 and again from 1876 to 1980), received its certificate from the NEC to operate as the Rainbow Alliance. These alliances led the parties to pool resources and strategies in fighting the ruling coalition, which was already experiencing its own internal problems due to a long-running feud between the president and his vice-president, who are members of separate parties within the ruling Coalition for Democratic Change (CDC).

The outcome of the senatorial election and the constitutional referendum showed an increase in support for the opposition and a corresponding decrease in support for the ruling party. The ruling party won in three of the fifteen counties – Grand Gedeh, Maryland, and Sinoe, all in the south-east. In Nimba County, the second most populous county, a candidate supported by the ruling party in a rather loose alliance won in a very tight race with the CPP. The leading opposition CPP won in six counties, including Montserrado, Bong, and Lofa, while smaller parties and independent candidates won the remaining four counties. The greatest blow to the ruling party was in its defeats in vote-rich regions, particularly Montserrado County, which accounts for one-third of the national vote. Montserrado, in which the national capital Monrovia is located, has been a heartland of Weah's Congress for Democratic Change, while Bong County, which the ruling party also lost to the CPP, is the traditional heartland of vice-president Jewel Howard-Taylor and her National Patriotic Party. Their defeat in these counties by the CPP undoubtedly makes their position untenable and is a bad signal for their future and the stability of the ruling coalition. The vice-president declined to support the candidate of the ruling party in her home region of Bong even though the president personally campaigned there. Her low profile during the election and failure to support the ruling party's candidate confirmed how deep the rift between her and the president had become. Following the election, factional fighting in the ruling party deepened as grassroot activists called on the leadership to resign and further pressed President Weah to implement rapid reforms and reshuffle his cabinet, whom they blamed for poor performance and corruption. The cabinet and the party leadership remained intact up to the end of the year as the rift widened.

The senatorial elections were held alongside a constitutional referendum. Liberians began discussions on constitutional reform in 2012, when former president Ellen Johnson Sirleaf established a Constitution Review Committee to hold consultations on the 1986 constitution and make recommendations for reform where necessary. At the end of the review process, in 2015, the committee's proposals were forwarded to the legislature for approval. However, the approval was obtained only in 2019 and a referendum held in December 2020 as provided by law. The eight propositions presented to voters were: (1) to amend Article 28 of the constitution to provide for the inalienability of the citizenship of natural-born citizens of Liberia and allow for dual citizenship for natural-born Liberians; (2) to amend Article 83(a) of the constitution to change the date for general elections from October (the rainy season) to November (the dry season); (3) to amend Article 83(c) of the constitution to reduce the time frame for resolution of complaints emanating from general elections from 30 days to 15 days; (4) to amend Article 50 of the constitution so that the term of the president is reduced from six years to five years; (5) to amend Article 45 of the constitution so that the term of senators is reduced from nine years to seven years; (6) to amend Article 47 of the constitution to provide for election of a president pro tempore for a term of five years; (7) to amend Article 48 of the constitution so that the term of the members of the House of Representatives is reduced from six years to five years; and (8) to amend Article 49 of the constitution so that the terms of the speaker, deputy speaker, and other officers of the House of Representatives are reduced from six years to five years.

The propositions on dual citizenship and reduction in presidential tenure were the most contentious during the referendum campaign. Many Liberians oppose dual citizenship because they believe it might benefit only people of Liberian ancestry based in the diaspora, who might have divided loyalty. On the issue of presidential tenure, the opposition contended that it might provide justification for President Weah to launch a third-term bid with arguments that his initial six years would not count under the new constitution. Weah's party debunked this assertion and offered reassurance that he had no intention of seeking a third term. The ruling party supported a 'yes' vote on all items, while the opposition and civil society organisations called for a postponement of the referendum due to the lack of public knowledge and voter education on the final items. After the government rejected this proposal, the opposition called for a massive boycott or, where necessary, a 'no' vote on all items. The returns from the referendum showed that none of the eight proposed changes passed the two-thirds threshold required for amendment. It is unclear whether voters responded to the call from the opposition to boycott the referendum or declined to participate due to lack of knowledge on the propositions.

Other politicians seem to have identified entry points in the last year to remake themselves through new parties. The NEC announced that it had received several applications from potential parties. In December, the NEC certified the newly formed People's Liberation Party (PLP), which comprises former executives who had lost internal factional battles in existing parties. For instance, the chairperson of the PLP, Wilmot Paye, is the immediate past chairman of the Unity Party. Paye was removed from that position in July after nearly three years of internal squabbles and blame-trading over the party's defeat in the 2017 presidential election. His removal paved the way for the election of a Liberian businessman with no known political experience, Amin Modad, as chairperson. The PLP only added to a flood of smaller political parties seeking to establish themselves in a terrain that is gradually lurching towards a two-party democracy dominated by the CDC and the CPP.

Foreign Affairs

Liberia maintained peaceful relations with its neighbours and the wider international community. Its strategy of economic and aid diplomacy, with foreign engagements focused on wooing more investments and development aid to the country, was severely undermined by the outbreak of the Covid-19 pandemic. The president and his envoys could not go on their usual year-round diplomatic 'charm offensives' due to restrictions meant to stop the spread of the virus. However, engagements continued remotely, and Liberia's traditional development partners supported the country throughout the year, particularly with resources meant to fight the spread of the epidemic.

Despite the stalling of diplomatic engagements, 17 ambassadors from friendly countries presented letters of credence in Liberia. The country maintained 23 resident foreign ambassadors, 19 non-resident ambassadors, and 15 honorary consuls-general. Liberia also maintained foreign missions on all continents except for Oceania, where the government announced it was exploring the possibility of establishing a mission. The country had 26 diplomatic missions, including two consulates-general spread across Africa, Europe, Asia, the Americas, and the Middle East.

Liberia remained a member of major international organisations. The country hosted 29 heads of international organisations, including the UN and some of its specialised agencies resident in Monrovia. Liberians held leading positions in the Mano River Union, where the secretary-general is a Liberian, and in ECOWAS, where a Liberian sits as one of the leading commissioners. At the AU, however, its status and influence diminished in 2020 due to a failure to pay its dues or access contribution, which had climbed to about $ 1.5 m. Member countries indebted to the AU are usually denied certain rights, including voting on crucial issues and speaking at the assembly of heads of state. As a result, Liberia had low-profile participation at the 2020 assembly of heads of state in January, with both the president and the minister of foreign affairs conspicuously absent. However, the country restored those rights when it made payments to the organisation in September. It is unclear why Liberia has demonstrated waning interest in the AU over the last few years. This lack of interest was shown by the absence of a permanent representative to the AU for nearly three years. Liberia's ambassador to Ethiopia doubles as the country's permanent representative to the AU, but since the end of 2018, the post has been vacant. On the other hand, the AU mission that included a military attaché closed in 2018, the same year that the UN peacekeeping mission closed. While there has been no diplomatic row between Liberia and the AU, these developments suggest declining interest in the AU as a strategic focus for the country's foreign policy and international development engagements.

Socioeconomic Developments

The Liberian economy had not fully recovered from the fallout from the Ebola epidemic of 2014–16 when the Covid-19 pandemic struck. In 2018, the UN Mission in Liberia (UNMIL) closed, and the withdrawal of the thousands of peacekeepers inflicted another blow on the Liberian economy, mainly in the housing and service sectors. Structural reforms were underway to cushion the economic effect of these events before the outbreak of Covid-19. Before 2020, Liberia was implementing an IMF facility meant to stabilise government finances. The pandemic derailed progress made on recovery and sank the country into deeper economic crisis. Although the country did not suffer mass community transmission, as had been the case with the EVD, it did not escape the recession caused by the pandemic. Prospects for growth were frustrated by the outbreak of the pandemic, which led the economy to further contract by 3% in 2020.

Liberian workers were hit by the pandemic as companies began laying off workers. The government immediately negotiated a policy that ensured redundant workers got their due benefits, and that conditions of lay-off followed due process. As a result of this intervention by the government, some companies avoided mass lay-offs but kept some employees under a category dubbed 'non-essential staff'. These staff, while given leave of absence from work, still received a proportion (about 50%) of their monthly salaries. At the Firestone plantation, the largest private sector employer, 20% of workers were declared non-essential, while Golden Veroleum Liberia, a palm plantation company, and Bea Mountain, a mining company, each declared 10% of workers redundant. By May, most companies had already begun to implement this policy. The government similarly gave leave of absence to some civil servants under the 'non-essential staff' category, but unlike those in the private sector, these workers received their full salaries throughout while remaining at home. This was the government's own strategy to reduce crowding at workplaces, a strategy previously deployed during the EVD pandemic, and it proved effective at minimising the risks of transmitting the virus.

However, in August Firestone announced it was still laying off more than 350 workers due to 'unsustainable business'. This situation also affected smaller rubber farmers who sold harvested natural rubber to the company. The company extended a previous moratorium on the purchase of rubber from independent farmers due to the pandemic, and this forced thousands of them into very precarious financial situations. Similarly, MNG Gold, which operates in Bong County, laid off 250 Liberian miners and 62 expatriate workers in the same month. MNG did not cite Covid-19 as reason for the lay-offs but said rather that the miners' contracts had ended when they closed one of their pits. But closures in other sectors meant that these workers would struggle to find new jobs.

The government's Covid-19 response measures implemented during the state of emergency included daytime curfews which affected many businesses, the self-employed, and people in the informal sector whose subsistence depended on daily labour wages or sales. The government designed a relief package valued at $ 25 m that distributed food to vulnerable households. An additional $ 2 m was approved to support market women and petty traders in the informal sector.

Despite the shock caused by the pandemic, the government of President George Weah remained primarily focused on road connectivity as its 'flagship' infrastructural development project. The success of this programme is likely to open up the country and speed up productivity in sectors such as agriculture, tourism, and manufacturing, particularly in rural areas that remain disconnected from major economic centres. By the end of the year, the government had completed the surfacing of 66 km of primary roads, while construction works were ongoing on an additional 365 km.

Liberia's major challenges were perhaps in political governance and fighting corruption. Despite President Weah's promise to fight corruption, Liberians remained sceptical of his commitment, and the institutions charged with supporting the fight against corruption suffered a legitimacy crisis. For instance, the Liberian Bar Association refused to cooperate with the chairman of the Liberia Anti-Corruption Commission after it was uncovered that he had falsified citizenship documents – his citizenship came under question after he was nominated to head the NEC. The Corruption Perceptions Index for 2020 published by Transparency International reported that Liberia scored a dismal 28 out of 100 points (the same as in 2019).

Some high-profile corruption cases were heard in the courts, with wins and losses for the government. In March, a criminal court found former defence minister Brownie Samukai and two other former officials of the Ministry of Defence guilty of theft of property and misuse of public money involving the pensions of members of the Armed Forces of Liberia, and they were ordered to refund $ 1,147,656.35. The officials appealed the ruling at the supreme court, and based on this appeal, Samukai was allowed to contest the special senatorial election in Lofa County, which he subsequently won. However, in August the same judge acquitted former officials of the Central Bank of Liberia (including its former governor) in the landmark case of 16 bn Liberian dollars (LRD) in missing banknotes.

The fallout from the LRD 16 bn case continued to haunt the Liberian economy. There have been occasional periods of inflation, declining value in the local currency, and acute cash shortage experienced mostly in July and December for each year since 2017. Ordinary Liberians felt the pinch of the economic crisis during the Christmas season when they could not easily access cash from the banks due to an acute shortage of both US and Liberian dollars. The year-long monetary crisis peaked in the third quarter of the year, at which time banks had run out of cash, particularly the local currency, and began rationing daily withdrawal. This crisis was worse than previous cash shortage crises, as it came at a time many Liberians had lost their jobs and were relying on remittances which they could not easily access. Rises in prices (inflation rose to 12% by year's end) resulting from the pandemic also meant that Liberians received little value from their savings. The central bank attributed the cash shortage crisis to the pandemic and to the ongoing reforms at the bank that were supported by the IMF and the USAID. The reforms were recommended in 2019 after an audit into the missing billions uncovered several procedural lapses in the operations of the bank. The legislature had also refused to approve the printing of additional LRD 17 bn which the bank had previously requested in response to the 2019 cash shortage crisis. As in previous cash shortage crises, the government partly blamed citizens and local businesses for not trusting the banks and largely keeping their savings at home or in informal saving clubs, thus leaving the banking system with only about 10% of local currency in circulation. Some members of the legislature proposed criminalising cash hoarding as a policy response to the situation.

While the pandemic affected overall socioeconomic and political development, governance and political development indicators showed that the state of governance did not change much in 2020 compared with the immediate pre-pandemic years. The Freedom in the World 2021 report (published by Freedom House) categorised Liberia as 'partly free' in 2020 – Liberia has been in this category for at least five years now. As noted above, the state of corruption – as perceived by citizens – remained the same according to TI. But the EIU's Democracy Index pointed to a backsliding in democratic culture. While the index categorised Liberia as a 'hybrid regime', the rating of the overall state of democracy slightly declined, from 5.45 in 2019 to 5.32 in 2020 on the index's 0–10 scale.

These indices are instructive and come very close to explaining local realities. Liberia's public institutions suffered severely in 2020, partly due to Covid-19 and partly due to pre-existing economic challenges. These unfortunate developments gravely affected the capacity of the government to deliver basic services. The government's inability to respond to the basic needs of citizens led to numerous demonstrations in communities regarding access to electricity, water, and policing. The most prominent of these took place from 21 to 23 August, when citizens took to the streets to demand action from the government on the rise in cases of rape and other forms of sexual and gender-based violence, which peaked during the pandemic. The Ministry of Gender, Children and Social Protection had received reports of about 1,000 cases of rape and other gender-based violence. The demonstrators demanded answers from the government and petitioned for the speedy prosecution of rape cases. In response, the government organised a national conference on sexual and gender-based violence in September at which the president declared rape a national emergency, promised to appoint a special prosecutor for rape cases, and announced an additional $ 2 m in funding for the Ministry of Gender, Children and Social Protection.

The EIU Democracy Index showed that the government's capacity to function ('functioning of government' indicator) declined from 3.07 in 2019 to 2.71 in 2020. The call for governance reform continues to ring in Liberia, and the UN has centred 'governance and transparency' in its Country Development Framework (2020–2024). Certainly, Liberia's post-pandemic recovery and long-term stability will depend on crucial reforms to its public institutions.

Mali

Bruce Whitehouse

Mali experienced unprecedented levels of violence and upheaval throughout 2020. The government of President Ibrahim Boubacar Keïta struggled to cope with the combined challenges of escalating insecurity in Mali's northern and central regions, the global Covid-19 pandemic, and intensifying political dissent in southern cities. In August, a group of military officers overthrew Keïta and established a ruling junta. While announcing its intention to guide the country to multi-party elections, the junta also consolidated its power and established a tight grip over the new, ostensibly civilian-led transitional government. Economic recession and other consequences of the pandemic made life more precarious for many Malian residents.

Domestic Politics

According to ACLED (Armed Conflict Location & Event Data Project) data, 2020 was Mali's deadliest year on record, due to *political violence* associated with ongoing terrorist activity and insurgent and counter-insurgent operations; 2,835 people were reported killed in this violence throughout the year, a 52% increase over 2019. Nearly 1,000 of these fatalities were civilians, most of them killed by government security forces targeting suspected insurgent members and supporters. UN investigators accused Malian security forces of carrying out hundreds of extrajudicial killings as well as acts of torture and arbitrary arrest. While episodes of fatal violence occurred in every region of the country, the vast majority took place in the central Mopti region. Violence also continued between ethnic Dogon and Fulani communities, especially in the Mopti region, inflamed by local resource conflicts and by the struggle between government security forces and jihadi groups in the area.

The *jihadi insurgent coalition known as Jama'a Nusrat al-Islam wa-l-Muslimin* (JNIM), or Group to Support Islam and Muslims, stepped up its operations against the Malian military, UN peacekeepers, and French troops deployed to the region for the Barkhane counter-terrorism mission. In addition to launching ambushes and roadside bomb attacks against these forces' patrols and convoys, jihadi insurgents assaulted fortified bases of the Malian army, police, and gendarmerie and on two occasions captured prominent civilians, most notably opposition party leader and former presidential candidate Soumaïla Cissé, whom JNIM abducted in March from the town of Niafunké where he was campaigning ahead of legislative elections. Cissé was freed along with three European hostages in a prisoner exchange with the Malian government in October. JNIM declared its willingness to negotiate with the government on the condition that all foreign troops depart, and in March, President Keïta revealed that his government had initiated talks with senior jihadi leaders Iyad ag Ghaly and Amadou Koufa. Fighting continued undiminished, however. Abdalmalek Droukdel, emir of JNIM sub-group al-Qaida in the Islamic Maghreb (AQIM), was killed during a raid by French special forces in June; AQIM announced his successor, Abu 'Ubayda Yusuf al-'Annabi, in November. JNIM fighters skirmished repeatedly with fighters loyal to the Islamic State in the Greater Sahara (ISGS) as these organisations fought over territory in the inland Niger Delta area and the volatile frontier zone where Mali borders Niger and Burkina Faso.

Mali was also affected by the *global Covid-19 pandemic*. Beginning in March, cases of the coronavirus were detected in Bamako and in regional capitals, but the country lacked the health infrastructure to provide critical care to infected patients. President Keïta's government closed the borders, ordered a nationwide curfew, and closed many schools and workplaces in an attempt to slow the spread of the virus. Despite the pandemic and the abduction of Soumaïla Cissé, *new legislative elections* that had been repeatedly postponed since 2018 were conducted throughout the country, with the first round in March and the run-off round in April. Opposition parties contested the official results, according to which Keïta's party won several hotly disputed seats in the 145-member national assembly. Foreign observers estimated turnout to be unusually low due to the pandemic and the continuing threat of political violence.

Exacerbated by economic hardship imposed by public health restrictions on schools and businesses, political unrest grew in many urban areas throughout southern and western Mali as *political opposition to President Keïta's rule* mounted. Then in the third year of his second five-year term of office, Keïta was increasingly perceived as aloof and unable to take the necessary steps to halt the country's decline. Beginning in May, unruly demonstrations and rioting inflamed the cities of Bamako, Kati, Kayes, and Sikasso. Brutal police tactics, government efforts to tamp down dissent, and renewed allegations of official corruption heightened public hostility to the Keïta regime. In June, an Islamic civil society group led by influential cleric Mahmoud Dicko joined forces with a coalition of opposition parties known as the Mouvement du 5 juin – Rassemblement des forces patriotiques (June 5 Movement – Rally of Patriotic Forces) or M5-RFP. Together they called on the president to resign and organised massive street rallies that drew tens of thousands of people in Bamako. Keïta resisted this pressure, however, and talks mediated by former Nigerian president Goodluck Jonathan failed to resolve the political stand-off between his government and the opposition.

On 11 July, elements of the Malian security forces used live ammunition to quell demonstrations by unarmed protesters in Bamako, leaving 14 dead and over 40 wounded, according to the UN, which called for those responsible for the shooting to be prosecuted. Keïta tried to demonstrate his resolve by ordering the arrest of two opposition leaders, but his opponents intensified their civil disobedience campaign throughout July and early August. Amid increasing political tension, *a military coup* ousted Mali's civilian government for the fourth time in the 50 years since the country's independence. On 18 August, a group of army officers arrested Keïta and his prime minister, Boubou Cissé, without bloodshed. Jubilant crowds in Bamako celebrated their ouster. A military junta official took power after Keïta announced his resignation on national television that evening. In September, the 76-year-old Keïta was flown to the UAE for treatment for a mild stroke after ECOWAS agreed to guarantee his return to Mali. He returned several weeks later to Bamako, where he remained under house arrest with members of his family.

As the international community condemned the coup, the junta announced a *transitional government* and a plan to organise new elections and return Mali to civilian rule within 18 months. In September, Bah N'Daw, a retired army colonel and former defence minister, was named the transitional president, and former finance minister Moctar Ouane was named transitional prime minister. A new cabinet was announced the following month, and in December a 121-member transitional governing council was established in place of the national assembly, which the junta had dissolved upon taking power. Although many civilians were named to these bodies, active-duty military officers dominated the transitional apparatus, demonstrating the junta's intent to continue to manage affairs of state. The junta's senior figure, Colonel Assimi Goïta, became vice-president but was viewed by many as Mali's 'shadow president'. Another junta leader, Colonel Malick Diaw, was elected to preside over the transitional governing council; 13 of 20 newly appointed regional governors were also military personnel. Mahmoud Dicko and leaders of the M5-RFP coalition, whose supporters had thronged to the street protests leading up to the August coup, complained that the new government was ignoring its demands. Security forces arrested four prominent public figures in December without charge amid rumours that the men were suspected of attempting to destabilise the transitional government.

A number of Mali's *senior statesmen died* in the later months of the year. Former president Moussa Traoré, who had ruled the country from 1968 to 1991, died in September at age 83. Amadou Toumani Touré, who had ruled from 1991 to 1992 and again from 2002 to 2012, died in November at the age of 72 after going to Turkey for medical treatment following complications from heart surgery in Bamako. Opposition leader Soumaïla Cissé died in December at the age of 71, of Covid-19; he had been freed only weeks earlier following more than six months in JNIM custody in northern Mali.

Foreign Affairs

The Malian government's relations with foreign governments and international organisations were dominated by its continued efforts to contain growing insecurity in the northern and central regions and by the military coup in August. The *UN*, through its diplomacy and its ongoing MINUSMA (UN Multidimensional Integrated Stabilization Mission in Mali) deployment, played a lead role in organising the international response to events on the ground in Mali. At an October donors conference, the organisation received pledges amounting to $ 1.7 bn for humanitarian aid needed in Mali and neighbouring *Burkina Faso* and *Niger*, all of which had been severely affected by jihadi insurgent violence. MINUSMA was bolstered by the arrival of 250 troops from the *UK* as part of a projected three-year British deployment. *Germany* also extended its forces' participation in the mission through to May 2021 and increased its contingent to 450 troops. By year's end, MINUSMA had over 15,000 uniformed personnel in Mali.

Military assistance came from various multilateral sources. In March, the *EU* budgeted € 133.7 m to support the EUTM (EU Training Mission in Mali) military training mission, then in its seventh year, for another four years, but it temporarily suspended funding following the coup in August. The EU also launched a multinational force, *Task Force Takuba*, combining special operations detachments from various EU member states under French command with the mission of assisting Mali's security forces in the fight against terrorism. The governments of *Belgium*, *Denmark*, *Estonia*, *Greece*, *The Netherlands*, *Portugal*, and *Sweden* all committed troops to this task force, which did not deploy to the region before the end of the year.

At a summit of the *G5 Sahel* group of five Sahelian states meeting in July, member governments vowed to devote more resources to the fight against jihadi insurgents in the region. The *AU* announced plans, at a February summit, to deploy 3,000 troops to help stabilise the Sahel alongside forces from the G5 Sahel and ECOWAS. This multinational force failed to materialise, however, due in part to the coup in Bamako. ECOWAS, which had sponsored Goodluck Jonathan's unsuccessful mediation between President Keïta and the political opposition in June, imposed sanctions on Mali after the 18 August coup. It lifted them in October following the formation of Mali's new transitional government. ECOWAS held meetings with Malian leaders in Bamako and in *Ghana* to encourage a smooth return to civilian rule. Malian transitional authorities also received a delegation from *Mauritania* following the coup and discussed security concerns, while an envoy from *Algeria* arrived in September to secure authorities' commitment to the Algerian-mediated 2015 peace accord between the Malian government and Tuareg rebel groups.

Mali's relations with *France* remained both significant and highly contested. France expanded the size of its *Operation Barkhane* military mission to combat terrorism in the Sahel region by some 10% to over 5,100 troops. This mission remained unpopular with many Malians, however, who saw it as a neocolonial imposition rather than as support of their democratically elected government. Demonstrators in Bamako called for the departure of all French forces from Mali. President Emmanuel Macron of France invited the five presidents of the G5 Sahel countries to talks in the French town of Pau in February, a meeting rescheduled from December 2019 following the deaths of 13 French soldiers in a helicopter crash during operations in Mali. Amid growing doubts about France's military presence in the region, the six leaders reaffirmed their shared commitment to fighting jihadi insurgents. Yet in subsequent months, the governments of France and Mali publicly diverged on the issue of whether to negotiate with jihadi leaders: while both President Keïta and the post-coup transitional government voiced support for talks, French officials maintained consistently that no negotiation was possible with 'terrorist' groups.

The *US* played a diminished role in Mali. In January, President Donald Trump's envoy to the UN argued that peacekeeping missions were unsuitable for countering terrorist threats in the region and called for MINUSMA to be reduced in size, a call that was swiftly criticised by other permanent members of the UNSC. After the August coup in Bamako, the US announced the suspension of its military aid to Mali until new elections were held, but it continued sending humanitarian and development assistance to the country. *Russia* pursued closer military cooperation through the sale of helicopter gunships to equip the Malian air force, with the first pair being delivered in January. The *UAE* sent six tonnes of medical supplies in May to strengthen the Malian government's capacity to stop the spread of Covid-19.

Socioeconomic Developments

Economic activity in Mali suffered due to political instability, violence, and the Covid-19 pandemic. Economic growth was predicted to fall sharply, from 5% in 2019 to 2.5% in 2020. In response to this downturn, the *Paris Club* of creditors suspended Mali's debt service payments from May through to the end of the year. The IMF approved a disbursement of $ 200 m in May under the Rapid Credit Facility to help Mali meet urgent balance-of-payments and fiscal needs stemming from the Covid-19 pandemic and approved a second six-month tranche of debt service relief in November. Commercial activity plummeted following the August coup and subsequent international sanctions. The Malian government, after raising CFAfr 31 bn (€ 45 m) in a one-year bond issue in May, was unable to issue bonds in September due to sanctions imposed by ECOWAS. In September, the ratings agency Moody's downgraded Mali's bond rating from 'speculative' to 'highly speculative' due to heightened political and economic risk in the country.

In the *agricultural sector*, Mali's cotton production declined by 75%, from 704,000 tonnes during the 2019/20 harvest to a projected 147,000 tonnes for the 2020/21 harvest. This dramatic drop was caused in large part by lower global demand for cotton amid the pandemic's economic recession. As Mali's state-owned cotton company ended a popular fertiliser subsidy and slashed its payment to cotton producers from CFAfr 275/kg in 2019 to CFAfr 200/kg in 2020, Malian farmers devoted less land to cotton cultivation. By contrast, cereal harvests were only slightly below the previous year's totals, due to generally favourable rains. In the central Segou region, the state authority responsible for large-scale irrigation, known as the Office du Niger, received a € 6.5 m investment from the French and Malian governments to develop its hydraulic infrastructure. Growing insecurity and jihadi presence in this region, however, threatened to reduce the future production of cereals, especially rice.

In the *mining sector*, Mali saw record gold production in 2020, with 65.2 tonnes of industrial production and a further 6 tonnes of artisanal production. Gold mining was slightly disrupted by labour unrest at the Syama mine in November. After a report issued by the Malian government's auditor-general highlighted some $ 108 m of gold mining revenue lost in 2019 due to financial irregularities, President Bah N'Daw pledged to crack down on corruption in the industry. The prospects for lithium production in southern Mali increased, with the Morila mine transitioning from gold to lithium and a new lithium mine set to begin operations near the town of Bougouni in 2021.

The *energy sector* saw less investment than previous years, with two new solar energy plants constructed in Bamako to power the largest public university and hospital facilities, funded by the Malian Ministry of Energy and Water in cooperation with the Lithuanian Ministry of the Environment. In *transport*, work to refurbish the 1,300-km railway line from Bamako to Dakar, Senegal, stalled due to lack of funding, despite stated support for the project by the governments of Mali and Senegal.

Continued *labour unrest* disrupted many areas of activity. Strikes by public school teachers, concerned about heightened risks from the Covid-19 pandemic, were one factor behind the 2019/20 academic year ending in June with only two full months of instruction. The Union Nationale des Travailleurs du Mali (National Union of Malian Workers) launched two five-day national strikes in November and December to press for higher worker compensation. The second of these strikes deprived the Malian state of an estimated CFAfr 7 bn of revenue.

Already rendered precarious by insecurity, *humanitarian conditions* throughout the country worsened as the global and national economies contracted. Many Malian households reliant on remittances from family members working abroad found that funding source reduced or cut off altogether due to the global economic recession. Emergency pandemic relief came from multiple sources, including the World Bank, which approved $ 25 m in relief funding in April. The Malian government announced an aid package in April worth CFAfr 500 bn (€ 762 m) to provide emergency relief; this package included funds for food distribution, water and energy subsidies, and tax rebates to Malian companies. In May, the government organised the distribution of 56 tonnes of cereals to feed vulnerable citizens. Facing a spike in new Covid-19 infections in December, Mali's government ordered a two-week shutdown of restaurants, bars, and shops in Malian cities and towns. By year's end, over 7,000 cases were recorded in Mali, with 278 deaths from the virus. An estimated 333,000 Malians had also been internally displaced due to conflict, and 6.8 m Malians needed humanitarian assistance, more than twice the previous year's estimate. Heavy rains also caused flooding that resulted in the destruction of houses and a proliferation of malaria cases in many communities in the north of the country.

Gender issues rose in national prominence following the arrest of Sidiki Diabaté, one of Mali's most popular musicians, in October after an ex-girlfriend posted photos on social media showing physical injuries she claimed he had inflicted on her. His arrest and the scandal it provoked prompted a wave of public discussion about gender-based violence, formerly a taboo topic, and spurred activists to lobby for legislation against this form of violence. Diabaté was released on bail in December. That same month, four NGOs filed suit against the Malian government in the ECOWAS Court of Justice, claiming that Mali's failure to criminalise female genital mutilation violated its responsibility to protect its female citizens against abuse and its obligations under various international conventions, including the Protocol to the African Charter on Human and Peoples' Rights on the Rights of Women in Africa (also known as the Maputo Protocol) and the Convention on the Elimination of all Forms of Discrimination Against Women (CEDAW). This lawsuit raised the possibility of breaking the silence on female genital mutilation, a practice to which an estimated nine out of ten Malian girls are subjected but which, like gender-based violence, is seldom openly discussed in Mali.

The lingering problem of *descent-based slavery* in Malian society similarly drew attention after a mob beat four activists to death in the western region of Kayes in September. Three other people were hospitalised, and 11 alleged attackers were arrested. The activists had been campaigning to end the marginalisation of people whose ancestors were formerly enslaved. The four men's deaths drew international condemnation and brought new scrutiny to a subject that had long been taboo in Mali. Alioune Tine, the UN's independent expert on the situation of human rights in Mali, called for a thorough investigation into the killings and accused the Malian state of failing to protect its citizens' fundamental rights.

Mauritania

Helen Olsson and Claes Olsson

After an unexpected dispute between President Mohamed Ould Ghazouani and his predecessor, Mohamed Ould Abdel Aziz, at the end of 2019 when Aziz signalled his intention to remain in the leadership of the ruling party, Union Pour la République (UPR), Ghazouani strengthened his position and undertook a major shake-up in order to isolate from political power officials close to the former president. Investigations under the auspices of a parliamentary committee that scrutinised Aziz's time in power consolidated Ghazouani's position, while Aziz's unpopularity unified political forces behind a judicial process that could, if not get him imprisoned, at least block him from returning to power.

Like the rest of the world, Mauritania faced the shock of the Covid-19 pandemic, which, together with sinking prices of export products, the lack of rainfall, and the threat of terrorism, created major challenges in both political and economic terms.

Domestic Politics

The political system in Mauritania was shaken by the *anti-corruption investigation* of former president Aziz. The national assembly announced the creation of a nine-member Commission d'Enquête Parlementaire (CEP) in January 2020, tasked with investigating suspect government contracts that were concluded during Aziz's time in office. The commission was composed of both opposition and ruling party representatives. The sale of state-owned property, the handling of oil revenues, and the activities of the Fuzhou Hong Dong Yuan Yang Fishing Company ('Poly Hong Dong') were included in the investigation.

The 900-page CEP report was released in July and formally handed to the prosecutors on 5 August. It revealed that senior state officials had disbursed hundreds of millions of dollars in illegal concessions, sale of public land, property allocations through partnerships, fake companies, and tax evasion. Among the ministers mentioned in the commission report were prime minister Ismael Bedde Cheikh Sidiya, petroleum minister Mohamed Ould Abdel Vettah, fisheries minister Nanci Ould Chrougha, and former prime minister Yahya Ould Hademine.

Prime Minister Sidiya and his entire government resigned on the same day the CEP report was handed to the prosecutors. On 6 August, President Ghazouani appointed a veteran government official, Mohamed Ould Bilal, as prime minister. Bilal had served as a cabinet minister under the former president Sidi Ould Cheikh Abdallahi (2007–08), who was ousted in the coup d'état orchestrated by Aziz. The *government reshuffle* on 9 August reduced the number of ministries to 22 after merging the basic and secondary education sectors into one ministry, and integrating investment and industrial development into the Ministry of Economy and Industry. Eighteen former ministers were reappointed.

The new ministers were minister of justice Mohamed Mahmoud Ould Cheikh Abdoullah Ould Boya, who had served as an Islamic affairs minister in the 2003–05 period under President Maaouya Ould Sidi Ahmed Taya and who until the appointment was Mauritania's ambassador to Oman; minister of economy and productive sectors promotion M. Ousmane Mamoudou Kane; minister of social affairs Naha Mint Haroun Ould Cheikh Sidiya; and minister of oil, energy, and mining Abdessalam Mohamed Saleh.

After initially being reluctant to cooperate with investigators, former president Aziz eventually agreed. This compliance contrasted with his attitude during the ten years he was in office, when calls from the opposition to investigate corruption were frequently ignored. Aziz was taken into custody on 17 August and released on conditional bail after a week, but he was banned from leaving the capital and placed under surveillance. As Aziz had lost much of the support of key military leaders since 2019, they refused to support him for a third mandate and rather persuaded him to hand over power peacefully. Ghazouani and the ruling UPR still need to take into consideration that Aziz might continue with efforts to worm his way back into power using his networks among those disenchanted with the current regime, including factions within the military and members of his ethnic group, the Oulad Bou Sbaa.

Mauritania placed 134th on the *TI corruption rankings*, a three-point improvement. On the Freedom House index 2020, Mauritania's status improved from 'not free' to 'partly free', with a score of 34/100 compared with 32/100 in 2019. An essential factor was the relatively credible presidential elections and the successful inauguration of President Ghazouani in August 2019, which marked the country's first peaceful and democratic transfer of power since independence in 1960.

As an additional sign of a *new political climate*, several opponents of former president Aziz returned in March, including one of the country's most powerful businesspeople, Mohamed Ould Bouamatou, as well as former senator Mohamed Ould Ghadda, poet Mohamed Yahya Ould Mssaïdef, and journalist Babah Sidi Abdallah.

Despite visible progress in the struggle against corruption and for a more inclusive political climate, the deep-seated social issues that confounded Aziz also continued to confront Ghazouani – most of all, racial polarisation and its attendant discrimination, including slavery. Human rights organisations expressed their concern that there was not enough progress in overhauling a number of repressive laws frequently used by the authorities to censor and persecute critics, including journalists. In February, 14 people were arrested during an inaugural meeting of the Alliance pour la Refondation de l'État Mauritanien (AREM), an organisation promoting good governance. Those arrested and released in February included journalist and member of l'Autorité de régulation de la publicité Eby Ould Zeidane; Aminetou Mint El Moctar, who heads women's rights organisation Association des Femmes Chefs de Famille; and Mekfoula Mint Brahim, president of Pour une Mauritanie Verte et Démocratique, a human rights organisation founded in 2009, leading women's empowerment projects in rural areas.

The long-lasting failure to eradicate *slavery*, despite its having been officially abolished in 1981 and criminalised in 2015, came into focus when the country joined the UNHRC in February. Anti-slavery activists, among them the former (2019) presidential candidate Biram Dah Abeid from l'Initiative pour la résurgence du mouvement Abolitionniste (IRA Mauritania), called on the other council members to put pressure on Mauritania to finally end the practice. According to the 2018 *Global Slavery Index*, more than 2% of the population – or 90,000 in total – live as slaves or under slave-like conditions. The IRA reported at the beginning of the year that 'an 8-year-old boy who ran away and told police he was enslaved had been detained in the same cell as his alleged master for several days, pressured to change his story and then sent back home after a local court hearing'. According to the HRW report, 'no slave owners or traffickers were held in prison, and ten appeals cases remained pending at the three anti-slavery courts'.

On 24 June, the parliament adopted the Law on Combating Manipulation of Information ('La loi contre la manipulation de l'information'). The objective of the law was to prevent disinformation 'especially during periods of elections and during health crises' ('en particulier pendant les crises sanitaires et les périodes électorales').

To bring the national *counter-trafficking legislation* into line with the UN Palermo Protocol to Prevent, Suppress and Punish Trafficking in Persons Especially Women and Children, which Mauritania ratified in 2005, on 7 July the parliament adopted a new law against trafficking in people, and it also endorsed the reform of the law against the smuggling of migrants. Despite these steps and previous agreements with Spain on implementing strict controls, Mauritania continued to be a major transit point for African migrants attempting to reach Europe, with the city of Nouadhibou, opposite the Canary Islands, being a key departure hub.

Despite *increasing tension* in the neighbouring Sahel region, no jihadist attacks have taken place on Mauritanian soil since 2011. In January, President Ghazouani emphasised the importance of 'the anchoring of the values of tolerance and acceptance of the other to deconstruct and destroy the religious foundations of terrorist action' ('l'ancrage des valeurs de tolérance et d'acceptation de l'autre pour déstructurer et détruire les fondements religieux de l'action des terroristes'). Ghazouani referred to long-term positive effects of the dialogue organised in 2010 between the main ulama (Muslim scholars) and around 70 jailed jihadists, when the clerics convinced some 50 of them to repent and to preach to young people that jihad was not the right way. The young people were also offered vocational training. However, since the security situation had deteriorated in the other Sahel countries, the risk of armed groups exploiting poverty as well as religious and ethnic divisions to recruit fighters and stoke more violence remained high.

Foreign Affairs

Security cooperation within the five-nation regional counter-terrorism force, the G5 Sahel, had high priority on the foreign policy agenda. In mid-January, President Ghazouani participated in the G5 meeting in the French city of Pau together with Mali's Ibrahim Boubacar Keïta, Burkina Faso's Roch Marc Christian Kaboré, Niger's Mahamadou Issoufou, and Chad's Idriss Deby, as well as French president Emmanuel Macron. The meeting was initially scheduled for mid-December 2019 but was postponed after devastating attacks in which 71 Nigérien troops and 89 Nigerian troops were killed. In February, Mauritania took over the rotating presidency of the G5 Sahel.

Especially challenging for Mauritania's security was the deteriorating security situation in neighbouring Mali. In June, at least 24 Malian soldiers were killed in an ambush of an army patrol in the Segou region, and on 4 September at least ten Malian soldiers were killed in an attack by Islamic extremists in Guire, both areas near the Mauritanian border. In April, the European Commission pledged € 194 m in additional support to G5 Sahel, which nevertheless continued to suffer from insufficient long-term funding.

On 5 June, foreign minister Ismail Ould Cheikh Ahmed reported to the UN that G5 was facing a growing security threat from jihadist groups, including Islamic State in the Grand Sahara (ISGS), and this constituted not only a local but a global problem that demanded an international response, since the security situation was deteriorating due to a 'diabolical alliance of terrorist and drug trafficking groups, with violence spreading every day to new territories'.

Beside G5 cooperation, security cooperation with the US also continued, despite signals that US military interest in the Sahel could be waning and the US might switch from a strategy of weakening the extremist groups in the region to merely containing them. In mid-February, the US-led Flintstock exercise took place in Mauritania and Senegal, with troops of 34 nations assembled as part of the US-led annual *counter-terrorism* exercise in West Africa.

Relations with the Arab countries remained good. In late February, President Ghazouani and Algerian president Abdelmadjid Tebboune visited Saudi Arabia. A high-level Moroccan delegation visited Riyadh during the same period. A resolution of the Libyan crisis was among the topics discussed. On 2 February, President Ghazouani made an official visit to the UAE, where he met Crown Prince Sheikh Mohamed bin Zayed Al Nahyan. The UAE pledged a $ 2 bn soft loan for investment projects. On 15 August, Mauritania announced its support for the UAE in signing an accord with Israel to agree to normalise relations 'in the appreciation of their positions in accordance with their national interests, the interests of the Arabs and Muslims and their just causes' ('l'appréciation de leurs positions conformément à leurs intérêts nationaux, aux intérêts des arabes et des musulmans et à leurs justes causes'). The foreign ministry also declared that Mauritania was confident that 'all measures and guarantees will be implemented to restore the rights of the Palestinians and establish their independent state with El Quds Acharif [Jerusalem] as its capital' ('toutes les mesures et garanties seront prises pour restaurer les droits des Palestiniens et établir leur État indépendant avec comme capitale El Qods Acharif'). No information about a possible resumption of Mauritania–Israel diplomatic relations was given.

While 2020 marked the 50-year anniversary of the formation of a common front between Morocco, Algeria, and Mauritania to accelerate the decolonisation of the Spanish Sahara/Western Sahara, the round-table negotiations on the long-lasting Western Sahara conflict, involving Morocco, the Polisario Front, Algeria, and Mauritania, were suspended for several months because of the increased tension in October/November in the area of Guerguerat, close to the Mauritanian border, when around 200 Moroccan truck drivers were stranded on the Mauritanian side of the border. Government spokesperson Sidi Ould Salem told journalists on

11 November that Mauritania was 'not party to this dispute but was directly affected by it due to its geographical location'. Foreign minister Ismail Ould Cheikh Ahmed discussed the conflict situation with UNSG António Guterres. The minister was quoted by the BBC on 12 November as telling Guterres that his country had been carrying out 'intense' mediating efforts. According to a Moroccan official statement on 13 November, King Mohammed VI of Morocco expressed his interest in meeting President Ghazouani in Morocco and in visiting Mauritania, which would be the first visit of its kind since 2001. Since 1979, Mauritania had recognised the Polisario Front as the sole representative of Western Sahara, but the US recognition of Morocco's sovereignty over Western Sahara on 10 December generated significant political attention.

At the beginning of the year, President Ghazouani announced that Mauritania would soon implement the *free trade agreement* with ECOWAS. No date was set. Mauritania has had an associate-membership agreement with ECOWAS since 2017.

The good relations between China and Mauritania continued, including extensive cooperation in the fields of agriculture, mining, fishery, health, and especially infrastructure. At the beginning of February, Mauritania announced it was to build a new fishing port with an $ 87 m loan from China. The EU and Mauritania agreed on 7 July to a one-year extension of the current extended *Fisheries Partnership Agreement*. Negotiations for a new agreement and protocol continued, but the initially scheduled negotiation process was suspended due to the Covid-19 pandemic. The EU fleet was authorised to fish up to around 287,000 tonnes per year, for shrimp, demersal fish, tuna, and small pelagics. In addition to the fees paid by the European fleet, the EU contributed € 61.6 m per year, including € 4 m allocated to support research and fisheries governance.

Socioeconomic Developments

The operational environment in Mauritania remained generally poor, despite government initiatives to facilitate foreign investment. Major constraints to business included limited access to credit, costly financing, high bank collateral, a weak tax policy, politically motivated tax audits, and inadequate infrastructure, particularly the often erratic electricity supply. Mauritania's *HDI ranking* (2020 Human Development Report) was 157 – the same as for 2019 – representing low human development on the threshold to medium human development. Mauritania continued to host approximately 62,000 refugees at the Mbera refugee camp, close to the Malian border.

The IMF expected *real GDP* to contract by 3.2% (compared with + 5.9% in 2019) in the context of the weak global macroeconomic environment and the *Covid-19 pandemic*, affecting commodity price trends and leading to a slowdown in FDI as well as delays in investment decisions concerning the country's offshore gas field projects. The CPI increase was estimated to be 3.9%. To support domestic demand during the Covid-19 pandemic, the interest rate was cut from 6.5% to 5.0% in March. On 23 April, the IMF approved a disbursement of about $ 130 m for health services and social protection programmes. On 2 September, the fifth review under the three-year ECF arrangement (2017–20) was completed, with total access of about $ 164 m and an additional $ 28.7 m to address needs stemming from the Covid-19 pandemic.

The *mining sector*, which is focused primarily on the extraction of iron ore and other metal ores, e.g. gold, generated around a third of the state's revenues and was therefore strongly affected by significant fluctuations in world market prices. Non-metallic resources (namely, construction materials, phosphate, industrial minerals) were inadequately exploited. A three-year project – 'Promoting the non-metallic resource sector in Mauritania' – was launched in April, financed by the German Ministry for Economic Cooperation and Development.

Mauritania's health ministry confirmed the first Covid-19 case on 13 March, and the country imposed travel restrictions and closed schools soon afterwards. The second wave hit Mauritania in December and forced the authorities to impose a curfew on 13 December, since the first series of restrictions, including the closure of schools and universities, were found to be inadequate. The appearance of a second wave was linked to the cooling of temperatures, but also to a relaxation in vigilance on the part of the population, which, after the first wave, gathered at ceremonies or sporting events, without people wearing masks or respecting social distancing. At the end of the year the total number of confirmed Covid-19 cases was 15,893, with 14,008 recoveries and 396 deaths.

Desert locusts were a serious threat to food security. A large-scale test of drones was conducted from 26 to 31 January. This was part of the coordinated efforts to minimise the damage inflicted by locusts, described by the FAO as the world's most dangerous migratory pest.

The parliament decided on 7 March that parliamentary debates would no longer be translated into French, and MPs were encouraged to express themselves in Arabic and the three 'national' languages, Poular, Soninké, and Wolof. French remained the working language of the administration and MPs continued to use it within parliament. It was also present at all levels of education. Mauritania has been a member of the 'Organisation internationale de la Francophonie' since 1980 and French is spoken by about 12% of the population.

On 16 December 2020, UNESCO added 'couscous' to the intangible world heritage list. The petition to have it listed had been a cross-Maghreb initiative, submitted by Mauritania, Tunisia, Algeria, and Morocco.

Niger

Klaas van Walraven

The political scene was dominated by the elections scheduled for December. As President Issoufou promised to respect the constitutional term limit, they held the potential for a peaceful political transition – the first in the country's history. However, Issoufou had groomed his right-hand man, interior minister Mohamed Bazoum, to succeed him, and the constitutional court declared main opposition leader Hama Amadou ineligible. Thus, although opposition parties managed to establish an electoral alliance, the prospect for real change remained limited. The battle for the presidency was fought in conjunction with legislative polls and was preceded by municipal and regional elections. At year's end, provisional results showed a head start for Bazoum, though he fell short of the 50% benchmark required to avoid a run-off the following year. The ruling Parti Nigérien pour la Démocratie et le Socialisme (PNDS) scored a good 48% of the votes for the national assembly. Issues that dominated electoral debates included the results of a government audit that uncovered embezzlement in defence procurement contracts. The security situation remained precarious. In the south-east Boko Haram forces staged erratic attacks, and in the north-west jihadist forces wreaked havoc in the border regions with Mali and Burkina Faso. Western NGO staff were murdered while on an outing in the Kouré national park famous for its giraffes. France declared all of

Niger a 'red zone', save the capital Niamey. This compounded the downturn caused by the Covid-19 pandemic, which depressed oil prices and turned growth forecasts negative. Food security was precarious as a result of the cereal shortfall the preceding year. Rains were abundant and augured well for the next harvest, though torrential rains and flooding destroyed crops in several localities.

Domestic Politics

On 13 October, *President Mahamadou Issoufou* confirmed that he would respect the constitutional two-term limit and step down in April 2021. Notwithstanding his authoritarian reflexes, this earned the 68-year-old the praise of the international community. The presidential elections, scheduled for 27 December, were heralded as 'historic', despite the advantage that Bazoum and his ruling PNDS, much criticised for graft, reaped from their incumbency. The electoral commission moved the timetable for legislative and presidential polls forward to December (from February 2021). As municipal and regional elections were held on 13 December, this was seen as a means to increase government opportunities to mobilise voters. Some parties deemed the commission, which included representatives of the opposition, to be partial to the government majority. One bone of contention was the new biometric *voter register*, whose reliability was questioned by opposition voices but confirmed by ECOWAS and OIF. With 76% of adult Nigériens on the rolls, it counted 7.4 m eligible voters (5,000 names were removed). The election campaign formally opened on 6 December.

Mohamed Bazoum started canvassing earlier, his 'proximity tours' drawing criticism from other candidates. On 29 June, he stepped down as interior minister (he was succeeded by Alkache Alhada). While Bazoum benefited from the support of the president, his own support base was more limited than Issoufou's. An excellent orator and networker, he represented the eastern Tesker Region and hailed from a minority Arabic-speaking community. With his light complexion, the 60-year-old Bazoum had to guard against rivals playing the race card and was forced to deny rumours of being Libyan-born. His *limited support base* forced Bazoum to tap into strongholds of party stalwarts such as the president's Tahoua Region and Agadez, the fief of Prime Minister Rafini. In Zinder, Bazoum faced competition from long-time opposition leader Mahamane Ousmane. He also made trips to western cities such as Dosso (disputed between the PNDS and the opposition), Niamey (an opposition stronghold), and Tillabéri, which previously eluded the government. As Issoufou's successor, Bazoum emphasised a message of continuity, boasting of the government's investment in infrastructural development and promising to reduce poverty further. It was hoped that his programme, named 'Renaissance III', would resonate with the rural electorate. The government's fledgling security record formed Bazoum's weak point.

Scoring a 'knock-out' first round was difficult, although the government managed to neutralise *principal opposition politician* Hama Amadou, leader of the Mouvement Démocratique Nigérien (Moden), strong in Niger's western regions. Amadou, who served part of a prison sentence that never seemed free of political motives, was pardoned on 30 March in the context of anti-Covid measures. Amadou had been nominated as a candidate the previous year, despite the revision in the electoral code barring candidatures of people with court convictions of one year or more, and launched his campaign at the Moden congress (19 September). However, the party was divided over his leadership, with the interim chair, Noma Oumarou, disputing the supremacy of Amadou, known for his inflammatory style. On 7 November Amadou held a mass rally in Niamey, but on the 13th the constitutional court rejected his candidature. As Moden's leader declined to issue advice to voters, the party's political bureau gave a belated instruction on 22 December to cast the presidential vote for a non-Moden candidate, the 70-year-old Mahamane Ousmane, whose political machine was recast in April as the Renouveau Démocratique et Républicain (RDE).

The constitutional court also rejected 11 other candidatures (usually on the grounds of non-payment of the required deposit). Thirty *candidacies* were approved, including those of old tycoons such as Mahamane Ousmane, Seini Oumarou, and Yacouba Idrissa. Oumarou, leader of the Mouvement National pour la Société de Développement (MNSD), pursued a middle-way strategy between the PNDS and Moden, marked by moderation, though others favoured an opposition profile. These divisions did not help to stem the MNSD's decline. Mahamane Ousmane was influential in Zinder, the country's second city, and could take some of the Kanuri vote in the east. Yacouba Idrissa, leader of the Mouvement Patriotique Nigérien (MPN) and with a fief in Maradi, hoped to repeat his performance in the elections of 2016. A *new presidential contender* was Salou Djibo, the four-star general who toppled Mamadou Tandja in 2010 and headed the transition government before handing over to Issoufou. Like some of his rivals, he aimed to pursue a third way between the PNDS and the embattled Moden. The upshot remained a *divided opposition*, which formed a broad alliance of parties, the Coalition pour l'alternance politique (Cap 21), for the presidential run-off.

The results of the *local elections* augured well for the PNDS, which took just short of 1,800 council seats out of a total of more than 4,000. All other parties trailed behind, with the MNSD scoring 358 and Moden 268. The legislative and *presidential polls* passed off peacefully, although there were accusations of PNDS vote-purchasing. On 30 December, partial results showed that Bazoum was well ahead of his rivals. A statement by the electoral commission was expected in the new year.

A government audit of *defence procurement contracts* caused outrage, although its definitive conclusions, announced on 23 June, cut the total of embezzled funds by half. Some $ 50 m was reportedly unaccounted for as a result of over-invoicing, non-delivery of goods, and Western and East European firms working through front companies and Nigérien businesspeople with friends in high places. This pointed to the extent of *corruption* in well-connected circles, which included the president's son. The army's casualties in the war with jihadist groups fuelled the popular outcry, which did not lessen with reports about arrangements by which suspects could avoid prosecution.

The escalation of hostilities in the north-west in late 2019 continued into the new year. On 9 January, 89 soldiers perished in an assault by jihadists on a garrison at Chinagodrar, not far from Bani Bangou and near the border with Mali. On 12 January, the *chief of staff was dismissed* (he was replaced by Brigadier General Salifou Modi, formerly military attaché in Germany), as well as the chief of land staff and the secretary-general of the defence ministry. The government reported that besides its own troops, 77 jihadists had been killed. A group presenting itself as a wing of Islamic State claimed that 100 members of government forces had died. The authorities in Tillabéri Region introduced new security measures, banning the use of motorbikes (often used by insurgents) and closing markets where jihadists procured food. Village mayors withdrew to the safety of the city of Tillabéri. Insurgents were reported to be roaming freely in remote areas, levying 'taxes' on the local population, subjecting villagers to propaganda, and abducting or killing targeted individuals. In response, Niger and its allies decided to concentrate forces on the region intersected by the borders with Mali and Burkina Faso. The government also *reversed its strategy* of relying on its own capacities. It rejected the formation of local militias (which had created havoc in the neighbouring countries) and asked for French military back-up to push the insurgents back across the border.

On 6 February, insurgents on motorbikes killed four people in the village of Molia, in Tillabéri Region. That same month, security forces were attacked in Tamou, near the W National Park on the border with Burkina Faso, while on 12 March at Ayorou nine perished in an attack on national guards (Islamic State claimed that 25 had been killed or wounded). Niger alerted French forces, which dispatched a jet fighter and drones. The assailants were reportedly killed. While army troops, together with Malian and French forces, undertook joint operations, on 22 March insurgents attacked Tamou again, allegedly killing six soldiers in an unconfirmed ambush. A brief lull in attacks was followed by a triple strike in Tillabéri Region on 8 May in which *insurgents killed 20 inhabitants* of three hamlets, many adolescents. Shops were looted and cattle taken. Days before, the relay antennas of mobile phone companies had been destroyed. Villagers fled into the bush. The army dispatched troops, food aid was promised, and Bazoum visited the scene. On 2 June, a coordinated attack took place on a camp housing Malian refugees at Intikane, on the border with Mali but adjacent to the central Tahoua Region. Some 50 insurgents on motorbikes killed three local leaders (a standard tactic by then), sabotaging the water supply, destroying communication equipment, and kidnapping a guard. Refugees moved inland to Tilemsès. On 24 June, insurgents kidnapped ten aid workers distributing food in a village of Tillabéri Region. After this, the south-west of the country became quieter, possibly because of better coordination between Niger's forces and its allies. However, on 4 December insurgents killed two forestry workers at Tapoa in the W National Park, while two soldiers went missing. On 21 December, an army patrol was ambushed at Taroum, north of Ouallam. Attackers appeared with motorbikes and vehicles and killed at least seven of the military and wounded others. Eleven insurgents were allegedly killed.

In the course of the year, the International Crisis Group (ICG) issued a report criticising strategy in Niger's western regions, which was held to focus excessively on counter-terrorism measures and not enough on local competition over resources fuelling intercommunal conflicts. Both HRW and AI claimed in June that between February and April, soldiers had killed nearly 200 inhabitants of villages in the joint border zone of Niger, Mali, and Burkina. The government denied reports of *extrajudicial killings* in Inates as baseless. Niger's human rights commission investigated claims by AI that 102 civilians had gone missing in the course of military operations in March and April. One NGO reported six mass graves, and the UN repeated the allegations. The responsibility of the army command could not be established. Typically, the fallout of the *Kouré park murders* was greater. On 9 August, six French aid workers, and their guide and driver, both Nigérien, were killed while on a tourist outing. The murders took place in the park famous for West Africa's last giraffes, east of Niamey and far from the border with Mali. It was frequented by Western people during the weekend. Men on motorbikes suspected to be part of Islamic State laid an ambush and shot their victims, including women. One woman who tried to escape had her throat cut. French President Macron called his Nigérien counterpart, and the following day troops supported by French planes launched an operation to track down the killers. A suspect was arrested. The Conseil national de sécurité, including the defence and interior ministers, went into emergency session with President Issoufou. This could not prevent a French decision to reclassify Niger in its entirety (the capital excepted) a 'red zone', which was likely to impact negatively on the economy.

Attacks by *Boko Haram forces* in the south-east continued throughout the year. On 7 March, insurgents with numerous vehicles attacked an army post at Chétima Wango. Eight soldiers were killed; three went missing. Several clashes took place with army contingents, and jet fighters intervened, allegedly killing most insurgents. Heavily armed insurgents, again travelling in a convoy of vehicles, were engaged by army troops in Diffa Region on the night of 15–16 March – attacks were facilitated by the low waters of the Komadougou River (the frontier with Nigeria) at this time of year. The military pursued the insurgents to the shores of Lake Chad, reportedly capturing suspects. On 3 May, an army camp was attacked outside Diffa, the regional capital. Two soldiers were killed, three wounded. This was followed by another attack on 9 May. In retaliation, troops of the regional anti-insurgency force (in this case involving the Nigérien and Nigerian militaries) launched an operation south of Diffa on 11 May. Twenty-five jihadists were reportedly taken out, and another 50 within Nigeria. Equipment, weaponry, and ammunition were confiscated, fuel dumps and shelters destroyed. This could not prevent another attack on an Nigérien army base on 18 May – this time 20 km north-east of Diffa. Twelve soldiers were killed, ten wounded, while seven insurgents were reportedly 'neutralised'. HRW claimed on 12 June that at least two had been summarily executed with the help of tanks running over them. This was denied by the authorities.

On 26 September, the government declared a state of emergency in Diffa Region (as well as in Tahoua and Tillabéri), but the day after, insurgents attacked a Red Cross post at Toumour, west of Bosso on Lake Chad. A *new low was reached* in an attack – again on *Toumour* – on 12 December, a day before local elections were supposed to be held (they were suspended). The attackers had swum across the Komadougou and arrived on foot. More than 30 villagers were murdered during a three-hour operation and up to 1,000 homes were burned, as well as the central market. The authorities announced three days of mourning, but people continued to live in fear, also because Boko Haram was known to have sympathisers in Diffa.

In an unrelated incident, clashes took place between rival drug runner groups at the Salvador Pass, in the far north on the border with Libya, on 18–19 June.

The country's strong political culture compensated somewhat for the decline in recent years in its democratic governance. On 15 March, *protesters took to the streets* in Niamey to express their anger over the defence procurement scandal. At least one person was killed in altercations with the police, who arrested a dozen people including civil society spokespeople Moussa Tchangari, Nouhou Arzika, and Mounkaila Halidou (they were released in September). Samira Sabou, an influential blogger, was detained on charges of defamation on 10 June after reporting on the possible involvement of President Issoufou's son in the embezzlement of funds. She was acquitted on 28 July. Earlier in March, journalist Kaka Goni was arrested for reporting on Covid infections. As in Sabou's case, the authorities used a new cybercrime law to intimidate reporters. In early July, Ali Soumana, another journalist, was detained for two days after reporting that the government would allow suspects in the procurement scandal to reimburse funds to avoid prosecution. Against this background, the opposition criticised a new wire-tapping law on 29 May.

Former president Tandja died on 24 November after years of chronic illness. The 82-year-old former army officer had been toppled in 2010 after attempting to stay in power upon expiry of two presidential terms; his death symbolised the declining political influence of the military establishment.

Foreign Affairs

External relations were dominated by security issues. The *G5 Sahel* force, in which Niger participated with Chad, Burkina, Mali, and Mauritania, remained hampered by poor funding. The limited capacity of its headquarters in Mauritania to handle the inflow of funds and donors reneging on pledges complicated its functioning. The summit in Pau in southern *France*, rescheduled from December the previous year, took place on 13 January. While the French aimed to neutralise criticism about supposed neocolonial interference, relations with Niger remained close, buttressed by the close ties between presidents Issoufou and Macron. The Pau summit also resulted in a decision to focus joint military efforts on the three-frontiers region of Niger, Burkina, and Mali. G5 contingents, the French Barkhane force, and national militaries would now operate under a single integrated command. The force commander, in post since July the previous year was Niger's General Oumarou Namata Gazama. France promised the dispatch of 600 additional reinforcements. An ordinary G5 Sahel summit was convened in Nouakchott, Mauritania, on 25 February, in which French foreign minister Le Drian took part as well as a delegation from the AU, which pledged the deployment of no less than 3,000 troops to the Sahel region (observers were sceptical about its practicality). On 30 June, the G5 again convened in Nouakchott to take stock of the more aggressive approach and the actions taken in Niger's frontier region with Mali and Burkina.

Niger's *ties with Nigeria* were marked especially by the latter's decision, the previous year, to close its common border in an effort to protect domestic producers (notably of rice) against imports. In March, the restrictions were beefed up, making travel by Nigériens impossible (though trans-border traffic across the two countries' highly porous border could not really be prevented). Niger's Maradi Region, known for its agricultural exports to Nigeria, including the cities of Kano and Katsina, was badly hit. Niger mobilised ECOWAS to help resolve the issue, leading to several high-level talks that finally resulted in Nigeria's announcement on 16 December that it would reopen the border.

Socioeconomic Developments

Food security became seriously impaired. It was estimated that up to August around 2 m people would require assistance (a 70% increase compared with 2019). The situation was compounded by the numerous refugees and IDPs on Niger's territory, in both the south-east and the west. Tragically, 5 children and 15 women died in a stampede in the course of the distribution of money and food to refugees in Diffa (17 February). *Pastoralism* and livestock trade were hampered by the closure of the border with Nigeria as well as by the insecurity in the Lake Chad region and the border zones with Burkina and Mali. By contrast, *rains* were abundant, auguring well for the *cereal harvest* except where torrential rains and floods destroyed fields.

Flooding led to the loss of lives and the destruction of homes and livelihoods. Various regions were affected, including Agadez, Tahoua, Tillabéri, and Dosso. Rains led to record water levels in the Niger River, with several villages and parts of the capital hit after the collapse of embankments. By September, the number of casualties had risen to over 60, with well over 300,000 people affected by the destruction; 34,000 homes were destroyed, as well as granaries, mosques, schools, water supplies, and more than 5,700 hectares of cultivated fields.

Growth forecasts were reduced from over 5% to a negative 2.8% as the fallout of the Covid pandemic began to make itself felt. It was feared that infrastructural development would suffer delays, depressing FDI. Plummeting oil prices and the closure of the Nigerian border further negatively affected growth. In January, The IMF finalised its fifth review linked to the current three-year ECF, releasing another $ 19.5 m. In order to dampen the effects of the Covid-induced recession, the institution also approved six months of debt relief ($ 7.7 m), while on 15 April the G20 finance ministers agreed to freeze debt service obligations for IDA countries.

It was feared that the pandemic would have a detrimental effect on the struggle against *poverty*. Job and income losses and higher food prices could push up to 270,000 Nigériens under the poverty datum line, according to the World Bank, thus increasing the proportion of poor to 42.1% of the population. This reversed the trend of the preceding decade, when the poverty rate dropped from 48% in 2011 to 40.8% in 2019. In the same period, the growth in security spending cut *spending on health* by half to just 4.5% of the government budget.

At the end of February, a first batch of tubes for the *Niger–Benin oil pipeline* was delivered by the China National Petroleum Company, responsible for the exploitation of Niger's crude. With China badly hit by the Covid pandemic, further deliveries were discontinued. Similar delays were expected for the Kandadji Dam, though the World Bank approved additional IDA funding worth $ 150 m aimed at improving access to energy and water resources for more than 300,000 people living in the Niger River basin.

The government took stern measures against the spread of Covid. Its technical experience in crisis management was put to use to draw up a quick response plan, which Prime Minister Rafini presented to donors on 25 March. Pledges were made to the tune of $ 212 m to finance responses to the outbreak, train hospital staff, and hire additional personnel. Treatment would be free of charge. Credit support and tax relief were granted where businesses were hit by quarantine measures in the capital and a night curfew imposed on 29 March. Lockdowns were lifted in mid-May; there had been protests against them in Niamey on 17–21 April, notably against the ban on collective prayers. In the following months, mosques, churches, and schools progressively reopened. Initially there were fears that Nigérien migrants from West

Africa's coastal states would boost figures upon return for the planting season. But infection rates (at least, those reflecting registered cases) remained within bounds and mainly concentrated in the capital. By July, there were just over 1,000 confirmed cases, with 68 recorded deaths, including that of labour minister Mohamed Ben Omar (3 May). Cases rose to over 3,000 by year's end, with 91 deaths. New measures were imposed. In the context of special Covid-related programmes, the IMF awarded Niger an additional $ 114.5 m by way of rapid credit facilities.

The plight of *refugees and IDPs* did not improve. After the attack on Chinagodrar on 9 January, 5,000 people fled to Bani Bangou and Ouallam (which already counted well over 7,000 Malian refugees), while up to 1,000 Nigériens, including many unaccompanied children, crossed over into Mali. Around 6,000 Nigériens were now living in Mali and another 11,000 displaced further inland in Niger. The Tillabéri and Tahoua regions counted around 80,000 IDPs in addition to well over 50,000 Malian refugees. UN figures in October reported more than 260,000 people uprooted in Diffa's south-east (IDPs as well as refugees, of whom 120,000 were from Nigeria). Niger harboured almost 450,000 refugees within its borders, who hailed from Nigeria, Mali, and Burkina Faso. Ongoing deportations of seasonal workers (Nigériens and others) from Algeria did not help. Between January and April, around 8,000 people, including children, ended up in tents at Assamakka, in the desert on the Algerian border, and Arlit, Niger's uranium city. In March, the government intercepted people on the Libyan border and sent them back. The IOM provided humanitarian assistance. It also launched an emergency healthcare programme for 14,000 IDPs in the Tillabéri and Diffa regions (25 August). The EU provided € 22.5 m in *humanitarian aid* to vulnerable people affected by conflict and food shortages.

Hydrologist Fadji Zaouna Maïna became *Niger's first NASA scientist*. She was congratulated by President Issoufou on her appointment to a climate project.

Nigeria

Heinrich Bergstresser

Throughout the year, Nigeria faced enormous security and political challenges, exacerbated by the Covid-19 pandemic and the protests against the Special Anti-Robbery Squad (SARS). The political and socioeconomic situation was characterised by the country's economic downturn, the worst for three decades, by the ongoing Islamist insurgency in the North East, by the precarious situation in the north-central states (which, *inter alia*, involved nomadic herders pitched against settled farmers), by the widespread, apparently organised, banditry in parts of the North West, and by a persistently high crime rate in almost all the federal states and the Federal Capital Territory Abuja. Some 12,000 people, most of them civilians, lost their lives. Moreover, election and by-election re-runs – out-of-cycle gubernatorial elections at the federal and state levels respectively – posed major challenges to the electoral commission.

Domestic Politics

President Muhammadu Buhari and his government got off to a good start when, on 14 January, the supreme court controversially nullified the election of Emeka Ihedioha of the People's Democratic Party (PDP) as state governor in Imo. In his place, the court unanimously declared the candidate of the ruling All Progressives Congress (APC) Hope Uzodinma as the rightful winner of last year's gubernatorial election and upheld all petitions except one, a judgment which reinforced the APC's power at state level. Soon afterwards, however, on 13 February, the party suffered a set-back when the supreme court annulled the election of Davis Lyon, the apparent winner of the gubernatorial election in Bayelsa, hours before his inauguration; the verdict was passed on the grounds that his deputy had presented a false certificate to the *Independent National Electoral Commission* (INEC) in the run-up to the election, which had taken place in November 2019 outside the statutory election cycle. Consequently, the former senator and PDP runner-up Duoye Diri was named governor, a decision which triggered violent protests and was followed by a dusk-to-dawn curfew for several days. A few days later, the APC filed a new application seeking a review and reversal of the court's judgment. On 27 February, however, the supreme court reprimanded the plaintiff's lawyers as having dishonoured the judiciary and ordered each of them to pay a fine of 10 m naira. On 3 March, a controversial verdict in Imo State was overturned, with one out of seven judges dissenting.

The Bayelsa saga continued later in the year. On 17 August, in a surprising move, the state's election petitions tribunal annulled the *gubernatorial election* based on the fact that one of the 74 registered parties had been unlawfully excluded, and ordered fresh elections to be held within 90 days. After more legal wrangling, this verdict was eventually voided by the two highest courts in the land, on 2 October and 18 November respectively, as a result of the appellant's failure to observe the time limit, and similar appeals were also dismissed.

Finally, two further gubernatorial elections outside the statutory election cycle took place in the states of Edo (19 September) and Ondo (10 October), in which the PDP's candidate Godwin Obaseki and the APC's Rotimi Akeredolu both triumphed.

Apart from the gubernatorial elections, INEC and the courts ordered parliamentary re-runs and by-elections in various states at both federal and state levels throughout the year.

The *Federal Special Anti-Robbery Squad* (FSARS) and the better-known state counterparts SARS, members of the 370,000 strong *police force*, had long been involved in perpetrating gross civil rights violations, extortion, arbitrary arrests, and extrajudicial killings. Ostensibly fighting organised crime, including cybercrime, these squads frequently targeted youths, who reacted with a tough #EndSARS campaign culminating in widespread protests in the southern states. In this regard, a protracted legislature process finally came to an end when, on 16 September, the long-overdue Police Reform Bill 2020 was signed by the president and came into force. This bill notwithstanding, the pent-up anger and animosity felt for an incompetent government and a weak president was not alleviated.

Despite several directives from the inspector-general of police, Muhammed Abubakar Adamu, in which SARS and other special squads were forbidden to undertake routine street patrols, traffic checks, and other stop-and-search operations dressed as civilians, they were nevertheless involved in killing innocent citizens in the states of Delta and Lagos in early October. These incidents provoked yet more protests in various southern states and in Abuja, and demands for the *dissolution of SARS* grew stronger by the day. On 10 October, one Jimoh Isiaka was shot dead in Ogbomosho in Oyo State, apparently by police. He was one of the first victims, and dozens more were to follow. The following day, the police, directed by the presidency, announced that FSARS and SARS would be disbanded, and on 13 October, the inspector-general of police replaced them with a new team, Special Weapons and Tactics (SWAT).

Nevertheless, within days the protests gained further momentum, and between 19 and 23 October the violence culminated in the deaths of demonstrators, police officers, and both violent and peaceful protesters. Although Lagos and Edo were the most violent hot spots, all southern states, the capital Abuja, and Kaduna and Kano in the north were also affected. Interestingly, in the north there were occasional clashes between anti- and pro-SARS demonstrators.

However, although the *military took over* from the rather helpless and overwhelmed police force, the disorder intensified, with further deaths and casualties; the situation was exacerbated by the fact that law-breakers infiltrated various groups of protesters. On 19 October, Lagos was literally locked down, with police stations attacked and facilities such as the old Lagos High Court, the toll gate at the Ikoyi–Lekki bridge, and television stations set ablaze while shopping malls were looted. Moreover, after former Lagos state governor, influential local politician, and possible APC presidential candidate from the south Bola Tinubu was implicitly denounced by the federal government as a brain behind the protests, he went into hiding. He apparently realised that this subtle attack had made him a target for the protesters and in fact endangered his life. Edo State fared no better, with protesters and hoodlums taking over the streets of the capital Benin City and even breaking into two prisons; close to 2,000 inmates escaped.

The next day, on 22 October, President Buhari spoke to the nation but failed to address the *precarious security situation of ordinary citizens*. When, from 23 October, curfews in the respective states were successively relaxed, the destruction was assessed and the physical damage estimated at billions of naira. However, the psychological impact triggered by the deaths of dozens of civilians and several police officers, some even decapitated, was much worse. The widely publicised prosecution of police officers in Lagos on 23 October for murder, abuses, and other misdeeds actually worsened the impact; others were dismissed, demoted, or reprimanded shortly thereafter. The charges somehow served as a cover-up for the government's irresponsibility and for the heavy-handed involvement of the military.

Shortly thereafter, on 26 October, the *national broadcasting commission* imposed a fine of 2 m to 3 m naira on Channels TV, Arise TV, and AIT for having violated transmission codes by showing footage from unverified and unauthorised sources of the shootings by soldiers in Lekki. The commission even maintained that the stations' coverage of the protests had heightened the tension in the country. However, the protests and their aftermath were also covered by international stations such as BBC, CNN, and Deutsche Welle, which have a large Nigerian audience. Both the Nigerian and the international stations focused on the role of the military, an emphasis which prompted sharp criticism from President Buhari, who on 8 December rather disingenuously said that he was disgusted with the international media.

Shortly before, the ICC had announced that it was conducting a preliminary enquiry into the *#EndSARS* protests and their ramifications. In addition, some states in the south and south-west, such as Lagos, announced that they were setting up panels aimed at investigating the impact of the protests and the role of the security forces. This action prompted hundreds of petitions concerning the crimes committed and the various acts of brutality.

Earlier in the year, the *Covid-19 pandemic took centre stage*. The first confirmed case was made public on 28 February when an Italian expatriate fell ill shortly after he had returned to Lagos from northern Italy, where the pandemic had erupted. The health authorities in Lagos and neighbouring Ogun, where the patient had been working, swiftly identified close to 30 people with whom he had been in contact, and quarantined them. Over the next two weeks the government took no further action although several other countries had already issued international travel restrictions. Only on 19 March did the Ministry of Education order a nationwide closure of schools, and Arik Air, one of the leading national airlines, suspended its services to all West African destinations. Soon afterwards, on 21 March, the federal government banned all but emergency and essential international flights, although domestic flights were allowed to continue.

While the official number of infections was still within the medium two-digit range, the first death from the virus was reported in Abuja on 23 March. The victim had returned from Britain shortly before. Within days, however, the spread of Covid-19 gained momentum, and on 30 March, a presidential order went into force, enjoining a two-week lockdown in the hot spots – Abuja and the states of Lagos and Ogun. This order also aimed at empowering the national health authorities, in particular the Nigeria Centre for Disease Control despite its limited capacity, to conduct some form of contact tracing and testing. This *first lockdown was extended* by another two weeks on 14 April. Soon afterwards, on 22 April, the 36 state governors unanimously banned all inter-state movement for two weeks and, in addition, prohibited the treatment of infected people in another state.

In the early days of the first lockdown in Abuja, Lagos, and Ogun, however, security forces wrongly enforced the provision, killing 18 people; this number was higher than the number of Covid-19 fatalities. In the following weeks, similar incidents took place in other parts of the country.

At this point in time, if not earlier, the state of Kano, with its ancient capital of the same name, emerged as a new epicentre of the pandemic, a situation which was scandalously denied by the state governor. His denial notwithstanding, the spike eventually triggered the presidency to impose an immediate two-week lockdown on 27 April along with a *nationwide dusk-to-dawn curfew*; the curfew was extended on 18 May.

On 1 June, against the backdrop of some 10,000 officially infected and close to 300 deaths, the federal government and state governors approved a relaxation of some restrictions on places such as churches, mosques, hotels, and banks. Barely three weeks later, the number of cases exceeded 20,000 and deaths passed the 500 mark, indicating the continued spread of the virus. Thus, the partial lockdown had to be extended for another four weeks on 29 June, although the *ban on inter-state travel was withdrawn* and schools were reopened for graduating students; furthermore, it was announced that domestic flights would resume on 8 July in Abuja and Lagos. Gradually, other airports opened and the first international flight, operated by Middle East Airlines, landed in Lagos on 5 September. Three months later, Nigeria's economic hub experienced another Covid-19 spike, and on 18 December, the Lagos governor Babajide Sanwo-Olu ordered the closure of all schools in the state until further notice and imposed restrictions on all places of worship.

Towards year's end, the number of people infected with Covid-19 approached the 90,000 mark, with more than 1,200 fatalities. In all probability, however, these figures did not reflect the real situation, given the *low rates of testing and poor data collection*. The exceptionally high number of infected health workers – over 1,000 – and the inability to deliver urgently needed oxygen cylinders revealed the vulnerability of the run-down and underfunded public health sector. In December alone, 20 physicians fell victim to the virus within just one week.

The virus did not leave the wealthy and the power elite unaffected. Several high-ranking people such as ministers, governors, clergy of both faiths, and businesspeople contracted the virus, although few were seriously ill. Nevertheless, quite a number passed away. The most prominent victim was the president's powerful chief of staff, Abba Kyari, who on 17 April fell victim to Covid-19 during the first phase of the pandemic. Most probably he had been infected during his trip to Europe the previous month. Back in Nigeria, he apparently became a super-spreader, who, within a ten-day timeline, extensively toured the country.

Moreover, and not surprisingly, the top echelons of the security services were not spared. Major General Olubunmi Irefin, general officer commanding (GOC) of 6 Division in Port Harcourt, died on 10 December and the Cross River commissioner of police, Abdulkadir Jimoh, on 18 December.

President Buhari used his executive powers to appoint and remove chairpersons and board members of the numerous *state agencies and federal parastatals*. On 28 February, he appointed the acting head of the federal civil service, Folasade

Yemi-Esan, as substantive head. On 2 May, the director-general of the national emergency management agency, Mustapha Maihaja, was dismissed and replaced by retired Air Vice Marshal Muhammadu Alhaji Muhammed. Shortly thereafter, on 12 May, the ageing Ibrahim Gambari, a seasoned diplomat who had served military as well civilian regimes and the UN, emerged as the president's chief of staff. Eventually, after internal wrangling, intrigues, and an orchestrated delay of about one year, Buhari agreed to have eight supreme court nominees sworn in on 6 November, putting an end to an extended and significant shortage of judges.

Despite INEC's overall weak performance under the leadership of Mahmood Yakubu, on 9 December President Buhari retained him as chairperson for a second and final five-year term of office. Much earlier, on 26 June Yakubu Pam took over the helm of the Christian pilgrim commission, while on 28 August, amid controversy, Nasiru Kwarra was appointed as the new chairperson of the National Population Commission. On 20 October, Aisha Dahiru-Umar became the new director-general of the National Pension Commission, which administers some $ 30 bn.

These appointments were controversial. Buhari hails from Katsina State in the north, and most of the higher positions in state agencies and federal parastatals were given to northern personnel. This policy of *extreme patronage in favour of elites from the crisis-ridden north* further sharpened the north–south divide and reinforced growing suspicion in the south.

Despite the *worsening security situation* and several set-backs in the fight against Islamist insurgents and the increasing banditry in several parts of central and northwest Nigeria, President Buhari retained the four service chiefs, Gabriel Olonisakin (defence), Tukur Buratai (army), Ibok-Ete Ekwe Ibas (navy), and Sadique Abubakar (air force), even though they had been due for retirement much earlier. However, the military could not conceal internal wrangling, visible in a number of courts martial and secular court cases, and in the low morale of non-commissioned officers; an increasing number of applications were made to leave the armed forces and the number of fatalities among combatants increased, as did desertions. The armed forces had a mediocre track record at best, and it was no surprise that demands for the replacement of the service chiefs grew stronger among politicians and the clergy and in civil society.

On 14 and 16 January, the national industrial court ordered the reinstatement of two lieutenant colonels – Thomas Arigbe and Abdulfatai Mohammed. In addition, the army was ordered to pay them their full entitlements up to their reinstatement as well as compensation of several hundred thousand naira. The court maintained that the compulsory retirements were wrongful and unconstitutional since the conduct of the plaintiffs had never been queried nor had they previously been indicted. On 5 February, the court rendered a similar verdict in favour of an intelligence officer, one Colonel Mohammed Auwal Suleman. However, at year's end the army had not yet complied with any of these judgments.

On 27 March, Major General Olusegun Adeniyi, theatre commander of Operation Lafiya Dole in the North East zone, was removed and replaced by GOC of 1 Division Farouq Yahaya, of the same rank. Yahaya's position was taken by Major General Usman Mohammed. On 25 November, however, the army announced the promotion of more than 421 of its top officers, among them 39 brigadier generals and 97 colonels, to new ranks.

Major General Adeniyi caused some controversy in a video which went viral on social media. In it, he complained that Islamic insurgents were out-gunning troops and that poor intelligence caused unnecessary deaths among soldiers. Together with his aide, Tokunbo Obanla, who had posted the video, he was eventually court-martialled and, on 1 December, found guilty of violating social media guidelines. Adeniyi was demoted for at least three years and his aide was sentenced to four weeks' imprisonment with hard labour.

Earlier, on 17 June, a *general court martial* eventually found Major General Hakeem Oladipo Otiki, former GOC of 8 Division, guilty of having stolen 260 m naira from the military. The court proceedings had begun the previous year. He was dishonourably dismissed and demoted by one rank. This was one of the rare cases in which an officer of the upper echelons was held responsible for his wrong-doings.

At the start of the year, the *debate over the reliability of state police* gained momentum, particularly in the six states of the ethnic Yoruba-dominated southern zone, South West. At the beginning of the year, a new regional security outfit, Àmòtékùn (meaning 'leopard' in the Yoruba language), received official approval. Such security outfits, however, were known to have operated in several federal states for quite some time, forming a grey area of outfits such as the Kaduna State Vigilante Service, the Taraba Marshals, and the Anambra Vigilante Services, to mention a few. This also applied to the 'security vote', opaque regular federal payments of some $ 600 m per annum to the governors aimed at reinforcing their capacity to fight crime. Most of the funds, however, were stashed away by the recipients.

The six governors of the region met with vice-president Yemi Osinbajo and attorney-general Abubakar Malami on 23 January, and in a follow-up meeting on 13 February, with the inspector-general of police and the local police commissioners. At these meetings, the Àmòtékùn undertaking was confirmed but the original idea of founding a regional security unit was abandoned in favour of a structure organised on a state-by-state basis. By early March, all six state assemblies had passed the bill establishing the new security force.

The *precarious security situation in the crisis-ridden North East, North West, and North Central* continued, and Nigeria retained its third place in the list of those countries most affected by terrorism, close behind Afghanistan and Iraq. As in previous years, security forces, in particular the military, frequently engaged with Islamist insurgents and bandits. However, the year started badly for the military when, in early January, some 1,200 Chadian troops – part of the Multinational Joint

Task Force (MNJTF) – withdrew from the Lake Chad area in Borno State in the North East zone.

Shortly afterwards, on 26 February, a corporal ran amok and shot dead four of his colleagues; he then committed suicide. This gruesome incident once again implied that there are *widespread psychological problems within the army*, an issue which the armed forces have tried to ignore for years.

Against this backdrop, at least 47 soldiers were killed in an ambush in a forest in Borno State on 24 March – a serious set-back to which the military responded with aerial bombardments. To the surprise of observers and journalists, the chief of army staff, Tukur Buratai, relocated to Borno on 10 April to oversee and coordinate the counter-insurgency war in person. Hardly had he announced a successful two-month campaign, claiming that more than 1,000 insurgents had been eliminated by the end of May, than his troops suffered further shock defeats. On 27 June, an ambush on the Maiduguri–Damboa highway cost the lives of at least nine soldiers, and shortly thereafter, on 7 July, no fewer than 37 combatants were killed on the same road. In another attack on this notorious route, Colonel Dahiru Bako and some of his subordinates fell victim to a deadly ambush on 20 September. The colonel's death in combat and further deadly assaults on 26 September and 21 November, respectively, indicated that *the insurgency in the states of Borno, Yobe, and Adamawa was far from over*. The assault in September claimed the lives of 15 security personnel, including police, soldiers, and civilian joint task force members on their way to Baga, while the November attack left six soldiers dead near Monguno.

To some extent, the high death toll among combatants in Borno veiled the *high number of civilian fatalities* in the state. On 9 June, for example, some 80 villagers of Foduma Kolomaiya in the Gubio local government area were massacred, an event which caught international attention; the same was true of the massacre on 28 November in Zabarmari in the Jere local government area, close to Maiduguri, in which dozens of rice farmers fell victim to Boko Haram attackers, despite the fact that troops were stationed in the area. Not surprisingly, the commanding officer was immediately removed. Evidently, this assault was an act of revenge and a gruesome warning to anyone reporting insurgents to the security forces.

Towards year's end, on 26 November and 2 December, the nominal spiritual head of Nigeria's Sunni Muslims, the Sultan of Sokoto, Muhammad Sa'ad Abubakar III, twice aired his grievances about the worsening security situation in the country. Moreover, he even acknowledged that nowhere was safe and that *the north had become the worst place to live in Nigeria*. This unusual confession painfully matched reality in his home region – North West – as well as in North Central and, of course, in the North East zone, where the Islamist insurgency continues.

Soon thereafter, in his Christmas message, Catholic bishop Matthew Hassan Kukah of Sokoto Diocese used the occasion to sharply criticise Buhari's poor security performance and *unparalleled nepotism and policy of northern hegemony*.

Nevertheless, several *notorious gangs* were put out of action and hundreds of perpetrators arrested or killed. On 11 January, officials disclosed that within the past few weeks no fewer than 100 bandits in the states of Zamfara and Katsina had been killed by joint forces, comprising military personnel, special police units, and the state security service (SSS), as part of Operation Hadarin Daji; furthermore, several ringleaders had been arrested. In multiple airstrikes on 22–23 May, conducted during another campaign in the area, at least 200 bandits lost their lives.

Kaduna State was another trouble spot; on 5 February, a combat operation in the besieged Birnin Gwari local government area, undertaken by police forces, led to the death of some 250 alleged terrorists. On 5 June, in a combined ground and air operation in the Kachia local government area, some 70 bandits were killed.

These sophisticated campaigns notwithstanding, the number of attacks, counter-attacks, and atrocities in the North West zone increased, with victims among both civilians and security services, indicating that the new strategy would most probably end in another standstill. Given the fact that both sides have mobilised huge financial resources, ostensibly based on the formula 'the war nourishes the war', some analysts even argue that both sides of the divide see all the campaigns and operations in the north as a kind of broader business model.

In the Shiroro local government area in Niger State, for example, 29 security officials were ambushed and killed on 25 March. Over the course of the year, the 200-km dual-carriageway connecting Abuja and the city of Kaduna gradually became notorious, with bandits robbing, kidnapping, and killing scores of innocent civilians as well as members of the security forces. Two attacks in the Sabon Birni local government area in Sokoto State on 24 and 27 May, by more than 100 armed men on motorcycles – the bandits' preferred means of transport – killed more than 50 people as they celebrated Eid-al-Fitr.

Scores of students at the government science secondary school in Kankara, Katsina State, abducted on 11 December by dozens of armed men on motorcycles, were more fortunate: in an opaque deal with the state governor, the students were eventually released unharmed on 17 December. However, this incident triggered another controversy as to whether a ransom had been paid, an accusation denied by the state government. In the past however, the *government has paid ransoms and even swapped arrested bandits for kidnappees.*

Much earlier, sometime in April, the UNHCR had reported that the ongoing violence had forced some 23,000 Nigerians in the area to take refuge in the Niger Republic, which brought the number of refugees from the North West zone alone to more than 60,000 in one year, heralding another serious refugee crisis.

Organised crime persisted unabated and the lucrative business of kidnappings, bank raids, and killings was rife in almost all the federal states and in Abuja – an indication that the generally precarious security situation had deteriorated even further. People from almost all walks of life fell victim to murderers, robbers, and kidnappers. Police officers, for example, were often targeted in bank raids such as the one which took place on 4 June in the Yagba East local government area in Kogi State, where eight officers, including a civilian woman, lost their lives. Moreover, *secret cult activities and cult violence*, increasingly related to organised crime, even spread to Europe, where groups such as 'Black Axe' and 'Vikings' were running formidable criminal networks. In October, for example, Italian police arrested more than 70 Vikings members, including its leader Emmanuel Okenwa, aka 'Boogye'.

Even more alarming was the rise in the *killing of kidnappees after ransom had been paid*. On 12 April, 15-year-old Abubakar Sadiq, son of a medical doctor at the university teaching hospital in Bauchi, the capital of the state of the same name, was abducted and murdered after a ransom of 4.5 m naira had been paid. A similar incident took place on 30 May in Jigawa State, where a businessman, Yusuf Maifata, died in the kidnappers' custody despite the payment of a ransom of 5 m naira. Security personnel were not exempted from such double-dealing; for example, on 12 September, one Sadiq Bindawa, an SSS official serving at the headquarters in Abuja, was kidnapped in Katsina State. After receiving a 5 m naira ransom, the perpetrators were ambushed by security operatives; some of the kidnappers died in the shoot-out, but those who escaped made it back to their hideout and murdered the hostage in cold blood. Abdullahi Bello, an official in a clinic attached to the Federal University of Dutse in Jigawa State, was luckier; after a few days in captivity and a ransom payment of 1 m naira, he was released unharmed on 26 October.

As in previous years, the government's *anti-corruption campaign* yielded only mixed results despite some noteworthy achievements. For instance, on 3 February, the island of Jersey, the US, and Nigeria signed a trilateral agreement to repatriate confiscated loot amounting to $ 308 m, which was traced back to the former military dictator Sani Abacha in the 1990s. The amount was eventually transferred in early May. Against this backdrop, the supreme court, on 7 February, finally declined a request by the late Abacha's family members to unfreeze Abacha's and family members' foreign accounts overseas. In a similar case, the Irish government agreed to return € 5.5 m stashed away by Abacha.

In one of the rare cases in which a high-ranking politician was brought to justice, on 7 February the supreme court confirmed the appeal court's verdict of 12 years' imprisonment passed on the former Taraba state governor, Jolly Nyame, for corruption. On 25 February, after a four-year trial, the former PDP national publicity secretary, Olise Metuh, was convicted on a seven-count charge for *money laundering* in connection with a $ 2.1 bn arms procurement scandal; he was sentenced to seven years' imprisonment. Metuh was the last prominent figure convicted while the then-chairperson of the Economic Financial Crime Commission (EFCC), Ibrahim Magu, was in office. Months later, on 6 July, Magu himself was targeted, investigated by a presidential panel for corruption and subordination, and temporarily detained. He was replaced by Mohammed Umar, an assistant police commissioner, in an acting capacity on 8 July.

The seemingly *unending $ 1.3. bn Malabu oil deal saga*, however, saw a further twist when the former attorney-general Bello Adoke was granted bail by a federal high court on 10 February. He had been accused of multiple corruption charges in connection with the deal back in 2011, extradited from Dubai in 2019, and then detained. Another prominent figure in the Malabu saga, former oil minister Dan Etete, who was on the run, was again in focus when on 29 May, at the request of the Nigerian government, his luxury private jet was impounded in Canada; the seizure in Nigeria's favour was eventually confirmed by a local judge on 4 August.

Last but not least, on 16 July, the Lagos federal high court sentenced a former executive director of the Nigerian maritime administration and safety agency, Captain Ezekiel Agba, to a seven-year jail term for laundering money to the tune of 1.5 bn naira. In addition, on 3 December, Abdulrasheed Maina, former chairperson of the Pension Reform Taskforce Team, was extradited from the capital of Niger, Niamey, charged with having used his company to launder 2 bn naira.

The *dethronement of the Emir of Kano*, Muhammadu Sanusi II, was not without drama. A sophisticated network led by governor Abdullahi Ganduje accused the emir of embezzlement and insubordination; in this network, established the previous year, intrigue and malice apparently played an important role. Following a resolution by the Kano state executive council on 9 March, Sanusi II was deposed, temporarily detained, and succeeded by Aminu Ado Bayero, son of Sanusi's predecessor, his major rival for the throne in 2014.

The precarious security situation in the country, exacerbated by the Covid-19 pandemic and the SARS protests, as well as by the federal and state governments' wilful abuse of press freedom, had various consequences for *human and civil rights*. Over much of the year, journalists and activists were molested and several of them arrested. The following list is nowhere near complete.

On 13 February, for example, the publisher of CrossRiverWatch, Agba Jalingo, was released on harsh bail conditions after more than five months in detention. It was his third request for bail. He was facing trial for treason over his report that the Cross River state governor, Ben Ayade, had diverted 500 m naira of public funds. The case of the activist Ibrahim Wala, popularly called I.G. Wala, accused of inciting public disorder, reached the appeal court on 20 March; the court overturned the seven-year prison term to which he had been sentenced the previous year and reduced it to two years.

More was to come when, on 27 May, after one month in the custody of the SSS, Kufre Carter, a radio broadcaster with XL 109.6 FM in Akwa Ibom State, was granted bail and released. He had been charged after criticising the state commissioner of health for his handling of the Covid-19 pandemic in the state. One of the worst cases involved Benjamin Ekom of the Nasarawa State Council of Nigeria Union of Journalists, who was gunned down in the Nasarawa-Eggon local government in Nasarawa State on 3 August.

Other activists, such as Gabriel Ogbonna, a lawyer and social media activist in Abia State, were also targeted. Ogbonna was detained for four months by the SSS before being released on 28 August. He was arraigned for alleged *cybercrime* and for publishing false and threatening messages against the state governor, Okezie Ikpeazu. Although he was granted bail shortly after his arrest in April and released, the SSS rearrested him the same day.

On 7 August, the president signed the Companies and Allied Matters Act (CAMA) into law, an act which gave rise to serious concerns in civil society; it was widely believed that the act would enable authorities to clamp down on NGOs and the media whenever it suited them. Against this backdrop, the statement issued by the justice minister and attorney-general of the federation, Abubakar Malami, on 1 November, claiming that the federal government was determined to see that *crimes against journalists* and other members of the public would be properly investigated, did little to assuage public concern.

Over the course of the year, Kano State and its capital of the same name became a focal point of harsh verdicts, mirroring a deteriorating social and political climate. On 10 August, Yahaya Aminu Sharif, a young musician, was sentenced to death by a Sharia court for *blasphemy against the Prophet* in a song circulated via social media. In a similar case, on the same day, the same court sentenced a minor, one Umar Farouk, to a ten-year prison term with manual labour. He was convicted of blasphemy after an argument with a friend. Both judgments were appealed. At the end of the year, the court's decisions were pending

Between January and August, both Sharia and secular courts in Kano State passed further death sentences for offences ranging from rape to murder; nine people, including a woman, were sentenced to death.

Despite the death sentences passed in Kano State and elsewhere, some good news on human and civil rights was reported. On 15 October, for example. The Kwara state governor, Abdul Razaq, approved the Violation Against Persons (Prohibition) Bill, which *inter alia* addresses rape, domestic violence, and genital mutilation. Thus, Kwara State transposed a federal law which was passed in 2015 into state law. However, two days earlier, the federal minister for women's affairs, Pauline Tallen, acknowledged that of the 36 federal states, 11, including Kano, had yet to put the national Child's Rights Act – passed in 2003 – on the books.

Last but not least, the trial against the leader of the *Islamic Movement of Nigeria*, also known as Muslim Brethren or Shiites, Sheikh Ibrahim el-Zakzaky, continued in Kaduna High Court. However, on 21 February, with no verdict in sight, the court acquitted the last batch of 100 members, who along with their leader had been detained in connection with a deadly clash with the military in December 2015 in Zaria.

Foreign Affairs

Over the course of the year, Nigeria's foreign policy was shaped largely by its protracted domestic security crises and the Covid-19 pandemic. Although hundreds of British citizens were evacuated in April and May, the relationship with the UK was to a large extent determined by legal and economic issues. Faced with the imminent reality of Brexit, President Buhari and his delegation attended the UK–Africa investment summit in London on 20 January. As well as signing commercial deals worth £ 324 m, he held private meetings with the prime minister, Boris Johnson, and with the Prince of Wales.

The most controversial issue was still the long-running saga involving a dispute between a British Virgin Islands engineering and project management company, Process and Industrial Developments Limited (P&ID), and the Nigerian government over an alleged gas sham involving $ 9.6 bn back in 2010. In 2020, the case was being heard in both Britain and the United States and took a new twist. Initially, an arbitration court in Britain had awarded the $ 9.6 bn to P&ID, to be paid by Nigeria for breach of contract. However, Nigeria appealed, and in late April, a New York court ruling offered the Nigerian government the opportunity to prove its claim that the arbitration award was obtained by fraud. Nigeria was now able to subpoena ten US banks for information on companies and individuals – including Nigerian government officials – allegedly connected to the sham. In addition, on 10 September, the British court ordered P&ID to make an interim payment of £ 1.5 m to the Nigerian government, a payment which was intended to cover the legal costs of Nigeria's successful application earlier in the year for the additional time it needed to challenge the arbitration award. Furthermore, Nigeria ruled out any compromise settlement of the kind former president Goodluck Jonathan had agreed upon in 2015; the case was still in court at year's end.

In November, the James Ibori saga took a further twist when it was reported that the £ 60 m loot in Britain, which could be traced back to the former Delta state governor, would soon be repatriated; the governor had spent several years in a British prison for fraud and money laundering.

Over the course of the year, relations with the US were once again dominated by *legal and crime issues* and cooled down somewhat.

With effect from 21 February, US president Donald Trump banned the issuance of US immigration visas to Nigerians; Nigerians make up the largest African diaspora in the US. Hardly had the US president disclosed his decision than US ambassador Mary Beth Leonard modified it, maintaining that the ban was not permanent and was subject to concerns such as over information-sharing. In addition, it did not apply to Nigerian residents in the US.

On 16 June, however, the US administration published a statement referring to the arrest of six Nigerian nationals, including one Richard Uzor, for an alleged $ 6.3 m internet fraud. The case of the young billionaire Obinwanne Okeke, arrested the previous year, took a new twist when, on 18 June, the respondent pleaded guilty in connection with cybercrime to the tune of $ 11 m. However, the court in Norfolk, Virginia, postponed the verdict initially scheduled for October to February of the following year.

Barely two weeks later, on 3 July, one Ramon Olorunwa Abbas, known by his huge number of Instagram followers as Ray Hushpuppi, appeared in a Chicago court accused of a multimillion-dollar fraud and of money laundering. Following an investigation by the FBI, he and his partner Olalekan Jacob Ponle, aka Mr Woodberry, had been arrested in Dubai and expelled to the US. The Nigerians, however, denied any wrong-doing, claiming that they were kidnapped by the US authorities.

Against the backdrop of an apparently ever larger number of Nigerian delinquents in the US, it was reported that over the years, about half of all deported Nigerians had a record of criminal convictions.

These awkward affairs notwithstanding, *cooperation on security issues and the fight against Islamist terrorism continued*. On 9 November, the Nigerian air force disclosed that the long-awaited delivery of the first batch of the Super Tucano A-29 planes was apparently in the offing. Soon afterwards, the office of the Nigerian national security advisor co-chaired a US-led international (virtual) meeting of 82 countries on the challenges of global terrorism. And on 11 December, the US handed over equipment to the Nigeria navy to help with maritime issues in the region.

However, the efforts of the US administration to discredit the chairperson of the AfDB, Akinwumi Adesina, for misconduct and abuse of office finally came to nothing. At the beginning of the year, the US, as a major shareholder, enforced a controversial inspection by the bank's ethical board. But in April, Adesina was cleared of any wrong-doing, a decision which did not go down well with the US representative, who demanded an independent panel review. In July, the panel announced that the ethical board had rightly cleared the chairperson of all allegations. To the great displeasure of the US, Adesina was re-elected on 27 August.

In a similar case concerning Ngozi Okonjo-Iweala, the US administration failed to prevent the former Nigerian finance minister and one-time director of the World Bank from emerging as the sole WTO director-general candidate. Initially, President Buhari shared this negative stance, but he gave in when the AU and almost all of the WTO member states held on to the candidate.

The relationship with China was shaped mainly by economic issues; nevertheless, Covid-19 also had an impact when, on 13 April, Africans in Guangzhou were allegedly tested by force, quarantined, and ill-treated after more than 100 were found to be infected. Since Nigerian citizens were the largest group, the government responded immediately; its sharp protest calmed the rhetoric, and the matter of maltreatment was amicably resolved.

A fortnight earlier, on 30 March, the China Harbour Engineering Company, one of the shareholders of the Lekki Deep Sea Port Project, invested more than $ 220 m in the project. On 8 August, it became apparent that the Nigerian National Petroleum Corporation (NNPC) had reached an agreement with the China National Offshore Oil Company (CNOOC) and Nigeria's South Atlantic Petroleum (SAPETROL) in which all outstanding financial issues concerning the development of oil mining lease 130 were resolved. This contentious issue had arisen after a tax dispute over the CNOOC's acquisition of the lease from SAPETROL, worth some $ 2.3 bn.

Against this backdrop, there was rising public concern about the amount of loans from China. Over the course of the year, it turned out that as of 30 September, Nigeria owed China $ 3.2 bn, some 10% of total foreign debts.

Nigeria's relationships with other African countries were affected by the *lasting closure of the land borders*, by incidents in Ghana, and by legal issues with South Africa. At the beginning of the year, Nigeria's government claimed that the closure of its borders in August of the previous year had improved the country's security, had reduced the smuggling of agricultural produce, and would be maintained until further notice. However, on 16 December President Buhari ordered the immediate reopening of four of its main border crossings: Seme in South West, Illela and Maigatari in North West, and Mfum in South South geopolitical zone.

On 19 June, some of the buildings housing the Nigerian High Commission in Accra were attacked by armed men with a bulldozer, destroying some of the apartments under construction. Shortly before, Ghanaian media had reported that a local businessman had accused the High Commission of encroaching on his land, an accusation that was denied by the high commissioner, who maintained that Nigeria had recently acquired the land quite legitimately. The Ghanaian authorities apologised, increased security at the affected facilities, and vowed a thorough investigation. Not long after, it was reported that 39 Nigerians had been arrested and detained several weeks earlier after allegedly entering Ghana illegally at Aflao, the border crossing with Togo. However, on 1 July the chairperson of the Nigerians in Diaspora Commission, Abike Dabiri-Erewa, eventually facilitated their release.

In August, Shoprite, the South African supermarket chain with branches all over Africa, announced that it would end its operation in Nigeria within the foreseeable future. On 7 September, however, Lagos Federal High Court restrained Shoprite from transferring its assets until a final decision was taken. This was another blow to Shoprite since, earlier in May, the court of appeal had upheld the 2018 verdict of a lower court which awarded the local company AIC Limited $ 10 m against Shoprite for breach of contract.

On 2 October, Nigeria ratified the Doha Amendment of the Kyoto Protocol on climate change. Soon after, on 11 November, the Federal Executive Council also ratified the AfCTA, which was to come into effect on 1 January 2021.

In contrast with previous years, President Buhari reduced his travel schedule, a consequence of both the pandemic and his age. However, he attended the 33rd ordinary AU summit in Addis Ababa (9–10 February), and on 18 September he addressed the UNGA in person. On 6 March, Nigeria was re-elected to chair the UN Special Committee on Peacekeeping Operations. Moreover, the extraordinary virtual ECOWAS summit on 23 April appointed Buhari as coordinator of the Covid-19 response and eradication process.

Socioeconomic Development

Oil and gas prices were reasonably strong at the start of the of year, with Nigeria's high-quality crude oil priced at around $ 55–$ 60 per barrel. But the price plummeted in the second quarter, closing as low as $ 19 per barrel in April; this was triggered by the Covid-19 pandemic and once again highlighted the volatility of international energy markets. In early June, prices steadily recovered, and, despite a temporary decline, Nigeria's crude oil price was listed slightly above the $ 50 mark at year's end, heralding a further modest increase. Shortly before, in May, Nigeria Liquified Natural Gas signed a $ 7 bn contract with an international consortium to build Train-7 of the plant at Bonny Island.

Foreign reserves dropped from $ 38.1 bn at the start of the year to $ 35.4 bn at year's end. VAT was increased from 5% to 7.5%, with effect from 1 February. Meanwhile, the exchange rate on the parallel market remained quite stable, at some 360 naira to $ 1, although the central bank kept its own exchange rate at 306 naira to $ 1. However, no sooner had the pandemic hit the economy than the central bank devalued the official rate twice, to 360 naira and then 379 naira. Consequently, the rate on the parallel market successively fell and eventually listed at 460 naira to $ 1 towards year's end, while inflation continued to rise from some 12% in January to 15% in December.

As of 31 December, the *total debt* of the federal government, the 36 federal states, and the Federal Capital Territory (FCT) Abuja stood at $ 86.4 bn, of which $ 33.3 bn was external debt and $ 53 bn domestic debt. The states' share of all domestic debts was some $ 11 bn, while their external debts stood at $ 4.8 bn. Against the backdrop of 2.1 tr naira debt service for the current year, the Debt Management Office, on 12 May, released new external and domestic borrowing guidelines with a particular emphasis on state government and FCT external borrowing. The guidelines stipulated that any proposal for the next fiscal year must be submitted to the finance minister not later than four months before the start of that year, and that the resolution passed by the state assembly must be duly signed by the house clerk. Furthermore, the total loans, including that proposed in the new resolution, should not exceed 250% of the total revenue of the preceding year. As far as the FCT was concerned, the proposal needed the approval of the executive committee and had to be signed by the secretary and the minister in charge of the FCT.

The beginning of the pandemic heralded a *deep and lasting recession* and a decline in GDP of 5 to 6% for the current year – a decline unprecedented in more than three decades. On 28 April, the IMF approved a $ 3.4 bn loan to address the adverse economic impact of the pandemic. Shortly before, on 14 April, the EU had donated € 50 m to support Nigeria's efforts against the virus.

Nevertheless, the economic downturn forced the federal government to review the 2020 budget of 10.6 tr naira ($ 34.6 bn) based on a crude oil benchmark of $ 57 per barrel and a production capacity of 2.2 m barrels per day (b/d). By June, both houses of the national assembly had passed the revised budget of 10.5 tr naira, which was signed by the president on 13 July. Although the total amount did not differ much from the original budget, key indicators such as the crude oil benchmark and oil production, as well as the exchange rate and deficit spending, were significantly modified. The benchmark was reduced to $ 28 per barrel and production capacity to slightly less than a quite unrealistic 2 m b/d. Meanwhile, the official naira rate was reduced to 360 to $ 1 and the budget deficit increased to 5.5 tr naira.

On New Year's Eve, President Buhari signed into force the *2021 federal budget* of 13.6 tr naira ($ 36 bn) based on a crude oil benchmark of $ 40, a production capacity of 1.8 m b/d and an exchange rate of 379 naira to $ 1. The budget deficit was put at 5.2 tr naira, equivalent to about 4% of GDP; debt services increased to 3.3 tr naira. The pricey subsidy of petrol and kerosene was abandoned, a follow-up to the higher fuel price which heralded further regulation in the years to come.

Against the backdrop of the naira's depreciation and a predicted drop of 14% in the $ 24 bn in *diaspora remittances*, the Nigerian central bank published new policies granting unfettered access to any form of remittances to banks and to international money transfer operators. The decision took effect on 4 December.

Over the course of the year, the pandemic and its ramifications took their toll. The rate of unemployment, particularly among young people (ages 15–34), surged, and by December the federal government doubled the number of N-Power beneficiaries under the National Social Investment Programme to one million. Earlier in August, however, some five million candidates had applied.

Notwithstanding the extent of the crises, Nigeria remained one of the most *lucrative telecommunications markets* in the world. By mid-year, the government disclosed that the number of mobile phone subscribers had risen to more than 190 m, with 80% of them actively using the internet. In addition, broadband penetration was 43%. Earlier, on 10 January, Nigeria withdrew a $ 2 bn disputed tax evasion claim against Africa's largest telecom and internet provider, MTN of South Africa, thereby ending a 16-month legal battle. Shortly thereafter, MTN announced investment plans to the tune of $ 1.6 bn to consolidate and strengthen its operations in Nigeria's huge market. Not surprisingly, on 28 January Google Nigeria launched its first *Google Developer Space* in Lagos.

Predictably, the Covid-19 pandemic largely overshadowed other relevant health issues such as HIV/AIDS and vesicovaginal fistula. In May, the United Nations Population Fund reported that Nigeria had close to 150,000 cases of this fistula, with about 12,000 new cases every year, mostly triggered by underage girls giving birth. In November, the Joint UN Programme on HIV/AIDS (UNAIDS) announced that some 45,000 Nigerians infected with HIV/AIDS had died in 2019.

Senegal

Mamadou Bodian

Domestic politics was dominated by issues related to the Covid-19 pandemic outbreak, and the national dialogue culminating in a cabinet reshuffle on 29 October. The government took measures to stop the disease's spread within national borders and to strengthen the capacity of health systems. Increased economic hardship resulting from the pandemic spurred a wave of migrants from Senegal to the Canary Islands across the hostile sea, furthering a controversy over the alleged mismanagement of migration policy. In foreign policy matters, Senegal pursued an active policy while prioritising cooperation with African states and foreign countries, and international institutions. Economically, the growth sustained over several years suddenly slowed down from 6% to 1.3% due to the Covid-19 pandemic, which put Senegal in the top ten countries most affected by unemployment globally (with 48% of the population unemployed).

Domestic Politics

At the onset of the pandemic in February, the government took measures to stop the disease's spread within national borders and strengthen the capacity of health systems. The measures included production of test results within 24 hours, transforming hotels into quarantine units, and provision of advanced and low-cost ventilators. To calm the political and social climate and mobilise the nation in the fight against Covid-19, President Macky Sall held consultations with leaders of political parties, unions, and various heads of state institutions throughout March. On 23 March, he declared a state of emergency, along with a curfew and (semi-)lockdown measures, and suspended international commercial flights. These measures were extended in April for one month, and then again until 2 June. This proactive approach resulted in Senegal being ranked second out of 36 countries on 'Foreign Policy' magazine's Covid-19 Global Response Index, despite a fragile health system and relatively limited resources. In April, the government launched a food aid distribution campaign to support 1 m vulnerable households affected by Covid-19, but in September controversy erupted over the alleged mismanagement of the Covid-19 food relief package involving the minister of community development and social equity. In June, the impact on the economy of the restrictive measures sparked demonstrations in Dakar and several cities across the country, forcing the government to lift the state of emergency at the end of June. However, land and sea borders remained closed until 15 July.

The resumption of international flights was accompanied by a new health protocol that required a laboratory-certified negative Covid-19 test result less than a week old for anyone wishing to enter Senegal. On 16 September, with Covid-19 cases declining, the minister of transport authorised the lifting of safety measures. Despite calls for a ban on popular religious ceremonies, the government did not take action. On 6 October, the Sufi Mouride order's holy city of Touba hosted the annual pilgrimage, which typically attracts 4–5 m pilgrims from across the country and worldwide. On 13 October, after a spike in cases, the government reintroduced restrictive measures, including requiring a negative Covid-19 test result obtained less than seven days prior to entering the country through its airports.

Political life this year resumed with the reopening of the '*national dialogue*' that Macky Sall launched on 28 May 2019. These consultations involved political and civil society actors and aimed to address the political crisis that followed Sall's disputed victory in the controversial elections of February 2019. Other political and socioeconomic problems fell within the agenda of the political dialogue. The dialogue process is led by a National Dialogue Steering Committee composed of six commissions. The committee chairpersons' conference met on 24 January, and on 5 February the national dialogue validated its terms of reference and appointed the executive officers of its six committees. Since mid-March, work has been halted because of the pandemic and disagreements over the electoral roll audit. In August, the national dialogue's political commission discussions resumed, and a progress report was submitted to Macky Sall. The consensuses reached included those on the electoral file audit by independent experts, the evaluation of the electoral process, and election of mayors by direct universal suffrage. Initially scheduled for June 2019, after two postponements (in December 2019 and March 2020) the local elections, which are supposed to be held by the end of March 2021, could be postponed for the third time.

On 29 October, Macky Sall dissolved his cabinet, 18 months after being re-elected to a second term, and on 1 November he appointed a new government. The new cabinet was in line with the openness and consensus-building resulting from the national dialogue. Idrissa Seck, former prime minister under President Abdoulaye Wade and unsuccessful opposition candidate in the 2019 elections, became the president of the Economic, Social and Environmental Council (CESE), the third most crucial institution after the national assembly. The appointment of the new government was also aimed at responding to the challenges posed by the Covid-19 pandemic and making the changes necessary to accelerate Senegal's re-emergence.

Increased economic hardship resulting from the pandemic accelerated irregular migration by sea to the Canary Islands, which caused approximately 400 deaths. Between 7 and 25 October, the Senegalese navy, supported by the Spanish civil guard, intercepted five canoes bound for Europe and rescued a total of 388 people. On 30 October, an estimated 150 migrants were thought to have died after a wooden boat they were travelling in was shipwrecked off Senegal's coast. The accident put additional pressure on the new government, furthering a controversy over the alleged mismanagement of migration policy. This migration crisis has been linked to the recent scandal around fishing licences granted to European and Chinese companies. On 4 February, violent clashes between fishers from Guet Ndar (in Saint-Louis, a city located on the north-west coast of Senegal) and the security forces caused damage to property and the arrest of 31 people on the side of the demonstrators and 17 injured among the security forces. It all started with a demonstration by fishers to demand the fishing licences they should have received in January to operate in the Mauritanian maritime zone.

From the beginning of the year onwards, there were many restrictions on freedom despite constitutional guarantees. In January, the Audiovisual Regulatory Council (Conseil National de Régulation de l'Audiovisuel; CNRA) suspended the signal of the private television station Sen TV for seven days because the channel refused to comply with the law prohibiting the broadcasting of advertisements relating to cosmetic products that cause skin depigmentation. On 10 January, activists from the protest movement 'Ño lank, ño bañ' – which brings together several political and civil society organisations including Y'en a Marre and FRAPP-France Dégage – organised a protest march against the increase in the price of electricity, which came into effect in December 2019. In June, more than 200 people were arrested following violent night-time demonstrations that broke out in Dakar and several cities across the country to protest the government's restrictive state of emergency measures in response to the Covid-19 pandemic. Civil society activist Guy Marius Sagna, who had been released in early March after 95 days in pretrial detention related to an unauthorised demonstration against electricity price increases in November 2019, spent a day in police custody in August while seeking permission to protest. On 27 June, the Place de l'Europe on Senegal's Goree Island, which was the centre of the African slave trade between the fifteenth and nineteenth centuries, was renamed the Place of Freedom and Human Dignity, following the police murder of George Floyd in the US and as part of a movement to rename public places and symbols of Senegal's colonial past.

Criminality continued to be a concern, but the Senegal customs authorities and other security forces were determined to fight domestic and transnational organised crime. A 39-year-old man was arrested on 10 November after threatening to kill his father in Touba. Investigations were opened into his presumed involvement with terrorist groups after his father revealed that he had lived in North Africa for some years. The presumed jihadist's stay in Libya allowed him to become familiar with several armed terrorist groups, including Islamic State, the Muslim Brotherhood, and al-Qaida. He was transferred to Dakar, where he confessed to investigators that a Libyan allegedly offered him money to attack Senegal. On 28 January, customs authorities at the Port Autonome de Dakar discovered 120 kg of cocaine worth CFAfr 9.6 bn in the ventilation system of the ship 'Grande Nigeria'. This seizure came more than six months after more than 700 kg had been captured from the same ship. Detained in Dakar's port since June, the ship is at the heart of a scandal that has put its owner, the Italian company Grimaldi, in an awkward position. On 3 February, the Mobile Brigade No. 2 of the Dakar-Extérieur Customs subdivision seized 1,900 forged banknotes in $ 100 denominations.

Until recently, rape was classified as a misdemeanour and not a crime under Senegalese law. In January, however, Macky Sall signed an executive order criminalising rape in response to a mass demonstration in May 2019 following the murder of a 23-year-old girl in an attempted rape.

There were a significant number of deaths of public figures in all spheres (political, sports, financial, cultural, and media), some of which were related to Covid-19. On 31 March, former president of OM (Olympique de Marseille), Pape Diouf, passed away in Dakar aged 68. On 26 July, the founder of the independent press group Sud Communication, Babacar Touré, died at 69. Senegalese soccer player Papa Bouba Diop died on 29 November in Lens, France, of motor neurone disease. He was known for having scored the first goal of the 2002 World Cup, for Senegal against France (1–0), in Seoul, South Korea. The eminent Senegalese historian and politician Iba Der Thiam died on 31 October 2020 at 83. A member of UNESCO's scientific committee, he played a leading role in the organisation's General History of Africa project and later oversaw the production of Senegal's General History.

Foreign Policy

Bilateral relations between Senegal and Mauritania have undergone a dramatic transformation since Mohamed Ould Cheikh El-Ghazouani came to power. On 17 and 18 February, Macky Sall made an official visit to Mauritania and signed several cooperation agreements with his Mauritanian counterpart, including an amendment to the maritime fishing protocol linking the two countries. During the Council of Ministers meeting of 19 February, President Sall welcomed the president of the Republic of Mauritania's measures favouring Senegalese fishers, particularly the upward revision of the number of fishing licences and the abolition of the payment of the fee of € 15 per ton of fish landed. On 10 March, the president of Guinea-Bissau, Umaro Sissoco Embaló, paid a 48-hour friendship visit to Dakar. Stating that the new administration of Guinea-Bissau had much to learn from Senegal, he expressed the wish that Senegal would speak on behalf of Guinea-Bissau to the IMF. On 24 September, President Sall attended the celebration of the National Day of the Republic of Guinea-Bissau.

The historical and geographical ties between Senegal and The Gambia have taken a new turn over the last two years. On 12 March 2020, Dakar hosted the 2nd Senegal – Gambia Presidential Council under the joint chairship of Macky Sall and his Gambian counterpart, Adama Barrow. They affirmed their cooperation in the fight against the illicit traffic of wood and insecurity at their border. Mali is Senegal's most significant economic partner and the primary destination for the country's exports. On 1 September, approximately 3,050 tons of ammonium nitrate were transported to Mali from Senegal. Following the deadly explosion in Beirut of that chemical, killing at least 190 people, President Sall called for the immediate withdrawal of the stockpile stored in Dakar's port. The transportation of the chemical had been delayed due to political upheaval and the subsequent military coup in Mali, but the shipment eventually reached its final destination.

Senegal maintained cordial and mutually beneficial relations with *other African countries*. On 2 October, Burkina Faso's president, Roch Marc Christian Kaboré, arrived in Dakar for a private visit. On 28 December, Macky Sall visited Ouagadougou to participate in President Kaboré's inauguration ceremony following his re-election. On 8 July, Sall presented his heartfelt condolences to Alassane Ouattara following the death of Ivorian prime minister Amadou Gon Coulibaly. He also participated in the ceremony of posthumous tributes to prime Minister Coulibaly on 14 July. On 14 December, President Sall visited Abidjan to participate in President Ouattara's inauguration ceremony, following his re-election. On 9 June, Sall sent his condolences to Burundi following the death of President Pierre Nkurunziza. Macky Sall arrived in Abuja (Nigeria) on 15 October for a two-day friendship and working visit and had a meeting with President Muhammadu Buhari during a dinner also attended by the president of Guinea-Bissau, Umaro Sissoco Embaló.

Senegal maintained close and multiform *relations with France*, and meetings between the two countries' political leaders were frequent. On 23 January, Senegalese foreign minister Amadou Ba met in Paris with French minister of Europe and foreign affairs Jean-Yves Le Drian. Regional security issues discussed including establishing an international coalition for the Sahel, announced at the 13 January Pau Summit, and strengthening the regional fight against terrorism. On 15 July, the French government considered a bill that would allow the transfer of cultural objects taken during the colonial era to their countries of origin. French president Emmanuel Macron had announced the decision to return these objects in 2018. This followed a report by two academics, Bénédicte Savoy (Collège de France) and Felwine Sarr (Gaston Berger University in Saint-Louis, Senegal), who identified 90,000 African works in French museums. From 25 to 28 August, Macky Sall was in Paris for bilateral discussions with the French president. He also met with the international private sector to discuss the post-Covid-19 economic recovery. President Sall revisited France from 11 to 13 November as part of the Paris Peace Forum and was welcomed by Emmanuel Macron. On the sidelines of the forum, he received in audience the managing director of the IMF, Kristalina Georgieva, who reiterated her commitment to supporting the economic policy of President Sall aimed at promoting youth employment.

Senegal also maintained cordial relations with other *Western democracies*. On 22 November, Spanish foreign minister Arancha González Laya met with Macky Sall in Dakar to discuss migration and border cooperation between Spain, the EU, and Senegal. Although friendship and cooperative relations have always prevailed between Switzerland and Senegal, a diplomatic incident occurred this year. On 16 July, the Swiss ambassador to Senegal, Marion Weichelt Krupski, was summoned to the Ministry of Foreign Affairs and Senegalese Abroad to explain unacceptable remarks made by her husband in an article published in the Swiss press; he had been critical of the behaviour of two young Cameroonians hosted by the ambassador as part of a schools programme and had drawn negative conclusions about the 'African elite of tomorrow'. Relations between Senegal and the EU are mainly based on political dialogue, trade relations, and development cooperation, though tensions arise from time to time. On 15 July, Senegal reopened its airports to international flights, but it applied a tit-for-tat approach to the EU, which had refused to include Senegal in the list of 15 countries whose nationals were deemed safe to enter Europe. On 13 November, Senegal and the EU approved a new fisheries agreement, following negotiations that had been ongoing since July 2019. This agreement will allow French, Spanish, and Portuguese vessels to fish over

10,000 tons of tuna and 1,750 tons of black hake per year in Senegal's waters for a financial compensation of € 15 m (CFAfr 10 bn) over a five-year period. According to the EU delegation in Dakar, these quotas do not interfere with Senegalese artisanal fishing. This statement coincided with numerous accusations concerning overfishing due to the issuance of fishing licences to foreign companies.

Senegal enjoyed good bilateral relations with the US. On 9 January, receiving the credentials of Senegal's new ambassador to the US, Mansour Elimane Kane, the Trump administration reiterated its willingness to work to strengthen cooperation between the two countries. On 14 February, US secretary of state Mike Pompeo visited Dakar to begin an African tour. This included a business forum, a bilateral meeting with President Sall, and the signing of five agreements. On 28 February, the multinational anti-terrorism exercise Flintlock 2020 was held for two weeks, simultaneously in Senegal and Mauritania. The exercise was attended by 11 countries. On 20 November, Macky Sall received General Stephen Townsend, head of the US Africa Command (AFRICOM). The long tradition of cooperation in the areas of peace and security, intelligence, and training, among others, were on the agenda of the discussions. Canadian prime minister Justin Trudeau arrived in Senegal on 11 February for an official visit. The visit was a test case of Trudeau's commitment to women's empowerment and human rights, given the conservative nature of Senegalese society regarding protections for women's rights.

Relations with the BRICS countries were essentially motivated by the pursuit of Senegal's strategic interests. On 6 January, Macky Sall strongly condemned the armed robbery on the premises of West Africa Agriculture (WAA), a Chinese groundnut collection and processing unit based in Sanghil in Kaolack (central Senegal), by assailants who allegedly stole an estimated CFAfr 20 m. On 19 February, at the Council of Ministers meeting, Macky Sall reassured Senegalese living in China, and particularly in Wuhan, that all health and social measures had been taken by the Senegalese diplomatic and consular services, in relation with the Chinese authorities, to monitor their health situation and the processing of their repatriation. On 17 June, President Sall participated, via videoconference, in the Extraordinary China–Africa Summit on Solidarity against Covid-19. During the meeting, Chinese president Xi Jinping announced the cancellation of interest-free loans due at the end of the year from the African countries involved in the Forum on China–Africa Cooperation (FOCAC) in Beijing.

Senegal has a special relationship with *the Arab and Muslim world* due to cultural proximity. This is the case with Turkey, which is partnering with Senegal in the diligent realisation of significant development infrastructures, including the completion of the Blaise Diagne International Airport in Diass. On 27 January, Turkish president Recep Tayyip Erdogan arrived in Dakar, the last stop on his African tour. This visit was part of the multifaceted cooperative relations between the two countries. The two heads of state had a bilateral meeting before presiding over the economic forum's opening ceremony, which brought together representatives of the Senegalese and Turkish private sectors. Macky Sall expressed the hope that Senegalese peanuts would be marketed in Turkey after successful entry into the Asian and European markets. On 11 September, Sall received the Turkish foreign minister, who was on a working visit. On 11 March, the new 'ambassador extraordinary and plenipotentiary' of Senegal to Oman, Alioune Cissé Dème, presented his credentials to Sultan Haitham Ben Tariq. On 20 October, President Sall received the Saudi minister of foreign affairs, Prince Faisal bin Farhan, bearing a message from His Majesty King Salman. The kingdom wanted to improve economic and trade relations between the two countries.

Senegal is distinguished by its dynamic presence on *regional and international bodies*. President Sall participated in the extraordinary session of the ECOWAS Conference of Heads of State and Government held by videoconference on 23 April. Member states discussed the evolution of the situation and the impact of Covid-19 on the ECOWAS region. Before this extraordinary summit, ECOWAS ministers of finance and central bank governors held an extraordinary meeting by videoconference on 21 April on the same subject. To address Covid-19 in the region, ECOWAS immediately made financial support available to complement international partners' assistance in purchasing essential medical supplies. On 23 July, Macky Sall visited Bamako as part of an ECOWAS mission to resolve the political crisis in Mali. On 27 July and 20 August, he also participated by videoconference in the ECOWAS extraordinary summit on the situation in Mali. On 7 September, President Sall arrived in Niamey for the opening of the 57th Ordinary Session of ECOWAS, during which the member states discussed economic issues and the consequences of the pandemic for the economy.

On 13 January in Dakar, President Sall chaired the eighth ministerial meeting of the Committee of Ten Heads of State and Government of the AU (C10) on the reform of the UNSC. Established in 2005, the C10 defends the Common African Position (CAP) resulting from the Sirte Declaration (Libya) on granting the African continent two permanent seats and two additional non-permanent seats on the UNSC. President Sall said that since Africa has the largest membership in the UN – with 54 member states – and given that African issues are at the top of the UNSC agenda, these issues cannot be addressed without African participation. The secretary-general of La Francophonie, Louise Mushikiwabo, appointed the vice-president of the national assembly, Cheikh Tidiane Gadio, as a special envoy to monitor the situation in Mali. This appointment is in line with the resolution adopted on 25 August by the 111th extraordinary session of the Permanent Council of La Francophonie (CPF) to support restoring democratic institutions in Mali and finding sustainable and credible solutions to the crisis. In close coordination with international partners, primarily ECOWAS and the AU, the special envoy will support La Francophonie's secretary-general in the civil transition process. The 9th World

Water Forum took place in Dakar, from 22 to 27 March, under the title of 'Water Security for Peace and Development'. The fourth Africa Anti-Corruption Day was celebrated on 11 July, under the theme 'Fighting Corruption through Effective and Efficient Judicial Systems'. The day is celebrated under the auspices of African Governance Architecture (AGA) with technical support from the AU Advisory Board on Corruption.

Economic Development

Senegal's economic growth had remained above 6% annually since 2014, but the Covid-19 pandemic considerably changed the country's economic outlook. Growth decreased significantly to an estimated 1.3%, down from 6% in 2019. Sectors such as tourism, hotels, restaurants, transportation, trade, culture, construction, and public works, among others, were severely affected. The country experienced a 3% decline in overall investment, resulting not only from reduced public investment and FDI but also reduced remittances from the diaspora (which accounted for more than 10% of Senegal's GDP) due to the pandemic, with a significant impact on host countries, including France, Spain, Italy, and the US.

In early March, Senegal's government responded with an Economic and Social Resiliency Programme (PRES) with five pillars of action to strengthen the Senegalese health system and support households, the diaspora, companies, and their employees. This CFAfr 1,000 bn national response fund was financed by the state, the private sector, and voluntary donations. Data compiled by Devex indicated that Senegal received over $ 880 m in direct donor support. For instance, on 29 May the board of directors of the AfDB approved a loan of € 88 m to Senegal, whereas the EU and Germany mobilised € 112 m from the EU and € 100 m from Germany's global emergency programme for Covid-19, as part of the overall 'Team Europe' envelope intended to support their partners' efforts to face the coronavirus crisis.

The Covid-19 response plan led to an increase in the country's indebtedness. On 6 August, Moody's maintained Senegal's 'Ba3' rating with a negative outlook. In June, the agency placed Senegal under surveillance after it adhered to the Debt Service Suspension Initiative (DSSI) launched by the G20 countries. Between 9 and 18 September, an IMF staff team held a virtual mission under Corinne Deléchat's leadership to assess Senegal's macroeconomic situation and update its projections and goals. On 29 September, Macky Sall enacted and presented the Covid-19 economic revival plan, 'Programme d'Actions Prioritaires 2 Ajusté et Accéléré' (PAP2a). The plan involved a total investment of CFAfr 500 bn by 2023. Among the key sectors in the plan, special attention was paid to health, aiming to accelerate the construction and rehabilitation of health infrastructures and the hiring and training of health professionals to tackle the pandemic more effectively. PAP2a also aimed to increase the financing of agricultural investment by 50% to accelerate food sovereignty. Other investments included those in the hotel industry, tourism, and digital economic transformation. The plan aimed to bring GDP growth to 5.2%.

Although Senegal is a small natural gas producer, it expected oil and gas production to increase following significant offshore discoveries in 2015 that have made the country attractive to oil exploration companies. On 27 July, the British company Cairn Energy sold its entire stake (40%) in several oilfields off Senegal's coast (the Rufisque Offshore, Sangomar Offshore, and Sangomar Deep Offshore contract area) to the most prominent Russian oil company Lukoil for up to $ 400 m. The firm intended to return at least $ 250 m to shareholders as part of a special dividend after sale completion. The project's final investment decision was taken in January, with plans to begin drilling in 2023 and with a designed production level of 5 m tons of oil a year (for 500 m barrels of oil in total).

Senegal made significant progress in improving its transportation infrastructure. On 28 August, the government signed a CFAfr 17.6 bn (€ 26.9 m) financing contract with the French Public Investment Bank (BPI) for the pre-operation of the Regional Express Train (TER) that will connect Dakar's cities and the new International Blaise Diagne International Airport in Diamniadio (55 km). Senegalese criticised the controversial contract that would enable the TER Operating and Maintenance Company (SETER) to set up the services necessary for the proper operation of the TER and protested the loss of their land.

Senegal's agricultural sector has performed poorly in recent decades but offers enormous investment potential. On 9 January, Senegal and the AfDB signed an agreement to finance the Southern Agro-Industrial Processing Zone Project (PZTA-Sud or 'Agropole Sud'), one of the flagship projects of the Emerging Senegal Plan (PSE) for 2035. The project provides for expanding the growth drivers from two (telecommunications and services) to six – with the four new ones being agriculture and agri-food, housing, mining, and tourism – in Casamance (the regions of Kolda, Sédhiou, and Ziguinchor). The AfDB will provide € 43.1 m, slightly more than half of the € 80.29 m provided for this initiative's overall financing. The Islamic Development Bank had already made € 27.85 m available to the Agropole Sud project, which is expected to create 14,500 direct jobs and 35,000 indirect jobs.

Senegal is making substantial improvements in its water supply. On 10 September, the Senegalese minister of water and sanitation, Serigne Mbaye Thiam, announced the project's final phase to build a seawater desalination plant at Les Mamelles in the district of Ouakam (in Dakar). The plant's construction began in January 2018 and is scheduled to be completed in 2021. Financed by the Japan International Cooperation Agency (JICA) to the tune of CFAfr 135 bn ($ 240 m), the plant will have a capacity of 50,000 m^3/day, extendable to 100,000 m^3/day, and will therefore increase the production capacity of drinking water in Dakar.

Despite the various bodies set up to fight corruption, Senegal struggled to curb this scourge. In early October, Greenpeace denounced the Senegalese government's non-transparent process for issuing fishing licences to Chinese vessels. Also, two

Senegalese fishing associations – the Association for the Promotion and Accountability of Actors in Maritime Artisanal Fishing (APRAPAM) and the Senegalese Association of Fishing Companies and Ship Owners (GAIPES) – wrote to Macky Sall denouncing the issuance of fishing licences to 52 foreign vessels, mainly Chinese. On 16 September, President Sall approved, in a Council of Ministers meeting, the National Strategy to Fight Corruption in Senegal for the period 2020–24. OFNAC launched the process of developing the National Strategy to Fight Corruption in late October 2017.

The social front underwent a relative calming because of the ban on gatherings following the Covid-19 outbreak. On 28 August, the Union of Justice Workers (SYTJUST) finally accepted the agreement negotiated with the minister of justice, thus putting an end to more than three months of strikes that negatively impacted the entire Senegalese judicial system. The two parties agreed on specific points, including the management of professional career paths for justice workers. The Covid-19 pandemic undermined gains in terms of welfare and improved access to essential services and employment opportunities. Listed in the top ten countries most affected by unemployment globally, Senegal ranks third (with 48% of the population unemployed) in the 2020 report of the ILO.

Sierra Leone

Krijn Peters

Up to the end of March, Sierra Leone was on track for another year of solid economic growth, but then the Covid-19 pandemic struck, making the economic forecasts less rosy. Fortunately, the country experienced just one, and a rather minor, Covid 'wave', taking place during the second quarter of the year. The country recorded around 80 Covid deaths for the whole year. Swift action and decisive planning – partly informed by the country's experiences when confronted with an Ebola epidemic just a few years ago – were instrumental to achieving this relatively positive outcome. Nevertheless, the impact on the economy required the country to apply for emergency aid funds and grants. On the political front, few events or changes took place, with President Julius Maada Bio approaching the halfway point of his five-year term by year's end.

Domestic Politics

Early in January, at the request of the government of Liberia, the Sierra Leone police briefly detained Henry Costa, the chairperson of the Council of Patriots, a Liberian youth activist group. According to Abdurahman Swarray, the Sierra Leone information minister: 'there was a call from our counterparts in Liberia to investigate him and we did the due diligence'. Costa was subsequently released. On 10 January, President Bio of the ruling Sierra Leone People's Party (SLPP) announced that four government officials, including labour minister Alpha Timbo, had been suspended from office due to an ongoing corruption investigation by the Anti-Corruption Commission (ACC). The alleged corrupt practices related to large quantities of rice donated by China. On 16 July, high court judge Cosmotina Jarrett discharged Timbo on the basis of lack of evidence by the ACC. Timbo was subsequently reinstated by the president and took up his position as labour minister again. Emily Gogra – one of the four others who were accused and then acquitted – was reinstated as well. Gogra was the former deputy in the Ministry of Education when Alpha Timbo was minister of education. On 1 May, Sylvia Blyden was arrested and detained, together with a small number of opposition activists. Blyden, now a prominent activist and journalist, was previously the minister of social welfare, gender, and children affairs under the former All People's Congress (APC) government. She was a close ally of former APC president Ernest Koroma, who was the country's fourth president and in charge between September 2007 and April 2018. On 8 May, in an address to the country to give an update on the coronavirus situation, President Bio took aim at the APC, accusing them of '*acts of terrorism* targeting state officials and public buildings'. This statement followed the attack on a health clinic and police station on 6 May by angry fishermen in Tombo, a town at the south-eastern tip of the Freetown peninsula. The attack was in response to the government limiting the number of fishing boats allowed to leave port, in an effort to curb the spread of the virus.

On 10 May, the president temporarily suspended Abu Abu Koroma, the minister of Northern Province. The one-month suspension was for 'unacceptable conduct and public remarks', following his threat to shoot at youths who did not follow the rules and regulations in Makeni, the capital of Northern Province and hometown of former APC president Koroma. On 17 and 18 July, again in Makeni, *riots broke out* following an attempt by the government to relocate an unused generator plant to Lungi International Airport, in advance of the airport's reopening. The Energy Ministry released a statement clarifying that this would be a temporary measure until faulty equipment at the airport had been repaired, while promising that Makeni would continue to receive electricity from the nearby Bumbuna hydroelectric plant. As a result of heavy-handed police tactics, including the use of live bullets and tear-gas, 12 people were injured and six were killed when protesters attacked the ruling SLPP's offices in the town, traditionally the political base of the main opposition party. A further 50 people were arrested and taken to Freetown. The independent Human Rights Commission of Sierra Leone released its report on the riots and the police actions on 18 August, noting that the right to live and the right to freedom of movement had been violated by the security forces.

On 6 August, President Bio made a statement during the presentation of the 2019 annual report of the ACC. *Fighting corruption* had been a key commitment of the government and it seemed to be paying off, according to the president, since Sierra Leone had scored above the sub-Saharan average for the first time on the Transparency International Corruption Perceptions Index in 2019. The country also performed better than previously in the Millennium Challenge Corporation Control of Corruption Indicator. Free and independent journalism plays a vital role in bringing corrupt practices to the surface. On 28 October, the president provided a statement on the occasion of the *repeal of Part v of the Public Order Act*. This covered a 55-year-old criminal seditious libel law, which in the words of the president 'criminalised journalism'. According to 'The Global Expression Report 2019/2020: The State of Freedom of Expression around the World', Sierra Leone ranked among the top five countries in Africa for facilitating and supporting freedom of expression. In his remarks, the president pointed out that Part v of the Public Order Act contravened Article 19 of the Universal Declaration of Human Rights and Article 19(3) of the International Convention on Civil and Political Rights, to both of which the country is a signatory. The president also referred to a meeting two days earlier, with the leadership of the Independent Medica Commission and the Ministry of Information and Communications, to discuss ways to support the 42 registered television stations, the 165 registered radio stations, and the 130 registered newspapers in the country. Following an investigation launched in 2019 into alleged corrupt practices by former president Koroma, anti-corruption investigators interviewed Koroma on 23 November. This followed the release of a report in March that found that tens of millions of dollars remain unaccounted for from the time of Koroma's presidency.

On 19 November, the president formally launched the *National Disaster Management Agency*. In his speech, he reminded the audience of the August 2017 mudslide that happened on the outskirts of Freetown, which killed hundreds of people. The new agency, in the words of the president, would help to 'anticipate, understand, manage, recover from, and minimise the impact of disasters on lives and livelihoods, without forestalling the long-term prospects for national development'; 13% of the country's area is prone to disasters and more than 35% of the country's population lives in areas vulnerable to disasters. The capital Freetown suffers from yearly flooding during the peak of the rainy season, which nearly always claims human lives.

This year, only a small number of cabinet positions changed hands. On 7 May, David Maurice Panda-Noah replaced Edward Soluku as minister of internal affairs. On 6 July, Priscilla Schwartz was replaced as attorney-general and minister of justice by Anthony Yiehwoe Brewah. Three weeks later, on 27 July, Musa Timothy Kabba replaced Foday Rado Yokie as minister of mines and mineral resources, while Evelyn Daphne Blackie was replaced by Ann Marie Baby Harding as deputy minister.

Foreign Affairs

On 3 February, President Bio gave an address at the Investing in African Mining Indaba in Cape Town, South Africa. This is the world's largest mining investment conference and the largest mining event in Africa. The title of his address was: 'Sierra Leone: Optimising Growth and Investment in the Mining Sector in an Age of Technology', and the president explained how his government had introduced fiscal reforms and was reviewing land and regulatory issues relevant to the sector. The importance of appropriate infrastructure and technology and future mining labour force was also highlighted in his speech. The president also attended the 33rd AU Heads of State and Government summit, which took place on 9 and 10 February in Addis Ababa, where he delivered a keynote address at the high-level panel discussion on reducing inequality. While acknowledging the challenges Sierra Leone still faces – it ranks 153rd out of 157 in Oxfam's Commitment to Reducing Inequality Index – he also highlighted the government's heavy investment in *free quality education*, to which 21% of the government's annual budget is allocated. During the same summit, President Bio provided remarks on the 21st report on the AU's Committee of Ten (C-10) on UN reforms. The president is the coordinator of the C-10, which is tasked with looking into reforms to the UN and opportunities to advance the Common African Position, including two permanent and two non-permanent seats for the continent on the UNSC. Due to the advancement of the coronavirus pandemic, increasingly, international summits moved from face-to-face events to virtual online ones. On 23 April, President Bio addressed the extraordinary session of the ECOWAS Authority of Heads of State and Government, in a videoconference. The key issues highlighted in his address, and in the videoconference as a whole, were to do with the coronavirus and how the disease was impacting the West African region. On 27 July, at a videoconference for another extraordinary session of the ECOWAS Authority of Heads of State and Government on the political crisis in Mali, the president reiterated the importance of maintaining peace and order in Mali, for the country itself and the region. Another statement by the president was made at commemoration of the 75th anniversary of the UN on 21 September, in which he expressed his country's commitment to achieving the 2030 agenda for sustainable development and contributing to *global peace, security, and mitigating climate change.*

Following a three-week undercover operation, on 24 June the Senegalese police announced the arrest in Dakar of two Sierra Leoneans involved in running a human trafficking network. In addition, nearly 80 young women from Sierra Leone were arrested who were about to be trafficked to the Middle East. The women, who had travelled from Sierra Leone via Guinea to Senegal, had paid around $ 700 each to the traffickers for this first leg of their journey.

Socioeconomic Developments

The Covid-19 pandemic had a significant effect on Sierra Leone. The country had only just recovered from the 2014–16 Ebola virus outbreak – the worst Ebola outbreak in history – which claimed around 4,000 lives in Sierra Leone. However, Sierra Leone's experiences with the Ebola epidemic may have put it in a slightly better position than many other sub-Saharan countries. Firm and rapid decisions and actions were taken right from the start, even before the first Covid-19 case was confirmed within the country. The government reactivated its Emergency Operations Centre, which had been established during the Ebola outbreak, with the minister of defence acting as interim coordinator and with most of its members having gained experience in fighting Ebola. Later, the centre was rebranded the *National Covid-19 Emergency Response Centre* (NACOVERC). The NACOVERC structure was copied at district level, and 16 district coordinators were appointed to oversee sub-national responses.

On 21 March, President Bio suspended all international flights into and out of the country until further notice. Following a four-month closure, the airport resumed welcoming international flights in July. On 25 March, in a television statement, Bio announced a year-long state of emergency, while simultaneously inviting members of the opposition parties to collaborate with the government in its efforts to fight the pandemic. A series of measures were announced as well. The number of people permitted at public gatherings was set at a maximum of 100. Schools, universities, and places of worship were closed. The preparations for a Covid-19 Health Response Plan were initiated with two scenarios: a 'no confirmed cases' scenario (prevention) and a 'confirmed cases' scenario (containment). Additionally, the government prepared a *Quick Action Economic Response*, focusing on five components: building and maintaining an adequate stock of essential commodities at stable prices; providing support to the hardest-hit businesses; providing safety nets for the most vulnerable through cash transfers and food assistance; supporting labour-based public works; and providing assistance for the production and processing of local food items to keep businesses in operation and to forestall shortages of locally produced commodities. In the 25 March broadcast, President Bio stated: 'this is not a lockdown and nobody must use this as an excuse to hoard goods, hike prices, or engage in acts of lawlessness'. However, one week later, on 1 April, *a three-day lockdown* was announced. This followed the recording of a second Covid-19 case. On 9 April, a 14-day 9 PM-to-6 AM curfew was imposed. A second three-day lockdown was announced starting on 3 May. The wearing of face masks in public places became mandatory on 1 June. In addition, and very much in line with Ebola-related measures, treatment centres were established for the management of positive patients and isolation centres were allocated for primary contacts of positive patients as a way of containing the spread of the virus.

Reduced international trade and restrictive measures at home started to have an effect on the country's economy, and it soon became clear that without *external help* the negative impact on lives and livelihoods would be considerable. Early in April, the World Bank made available a $ 7.5 m IDA grant to Sierra Leone to help the country in its efforts to deal with the Covid-19 epidemic. This was part of a World Bank fast-track package worth $ 14 bn to help around 20 African countries with their Covid emergency response projects. On 3 April, the IMF executive board completed the second review of the country's performance under the programme supported by an ECF. The review found the country to have performed satisfactorily, paving the way for the disbursement of a further $ 21 m. Including this latest disbursement, just over $ 63 m had been disbursed under the programme. On 3 June, the IMF approved, under its Rapid Credit Facility (RCF) arrangements, the disbursement of $ 143 m to support the government in its effort to mitigate the impact of the Covid epidemic. Early in June, the World Bank launched the new 2021–2026 Country Partnership Framework, focusing on supporting a more robust health system, economic diversification, job creation, and investments in human capital. In June, the World Bank approved a $ 50 m grant to support the country's Free Education Project. The money was to be used by the government to support Covid-19 response activities such as facilitating remote learning. The Free Education Project will pay for the construction of just over 500 fully furnished classrooms, via performance-based grants to primary schools. A further $ 100 m in IDA grants was awarded in the same month to strengthen governance, given the many coronavirus-related challenges currently faced. Another grant was awarded by the AfDB on 24 July, providing Sierra Leone with direct budget support worth UA 18 m (Units of Aid, the official currency for AfDB projects; UA 1 = approximately $ 1.40), to further bolster the country's Covid-19 response. The grant was part of a multi-country grant to Sierra Leone, The Gambia, and Liberia, worth in total slightly over $ 53 m.

At the start of May, a total of 124 Covid cases and seven Covid deaths were reported. The government had by now switched to the full implementation of the above-mentioned Quick Action Economic Response Programme and – for the health sector – a Covid-19 Preparedness and Response Plan. By early June, Sierra Leone had recorded 1,000 Covid cases. Between late May and early June, the country experienced its highest number of average daily Covid cases – measured on a one-week rolling basis – namely, 33 cases. This number then started to decline, and by mid-August the one-week rolling average dropped below ten Covid cases, with several subsequent months having less than a handful of cases. However, right at the tail end of 2020, in the latter weeks of December, average case numbers started to increase again, triggering fears that this might be the start of a second wave. Over the whole year, Sierra Leone recorded a total of 79 Covid deaths, which all happened during the first few months of the pandemic in the country; 3 July was the last date on which the country recorded a Covid-related death.

In a report released by the World Bank in July, it was forecast that the country's economy would see its annual growth reduced by between 2% and 3%, resulting *in growth of between 1.5 and 2%* – down from 5.1% in 2019. Given the country's 2.1% annual growth in its population, this growth would in effect be a per capita negative growth. Furthermore, inflation and current and fiscal account deficits were all likely to increase. A short-term measure proposed by the report was to support the public health sector and increase direct cash transfers to the most vulnerable. Longer term, diversifying the economy – reducing its reliance on revenue from the mineral extraction sector – and improving transparency and debt management would result in a healthier economic outlook. Importance was put on inclusive growth, with access to education for girls particularly highlighted as a way to achieve this in the longer term. To support the diversification of the economy, a $ 40 m IDA grant was awarded in July to support small and medium-sized enterprises, as long as these were operating outside the mining productive sectors. This was part of the Sierra Leone Economic Diversification Project, which, among other things, is aimed at capacity-building for the private sector and public institutions. Another IDA grant – worth $ 30 m – was released in support of the Smallholder Commercialisation and Agribusiness Development Project. A key focus for this project is to reduce rural isolation for highly productive agricultural areas by improving roads and building bridges, particularly focusing on feeder roads. On 23 December, the Bank of Sierra Leone lifted a year-long restriction on foreign-currency transactions, which was put in place the previous year to curb inflation. The restriction prohibited holding or exporting more than $ 10,000 or the equivalent of that amount in any other foreign currency. The restriction was put in place to protect the local currency, the leone.

Togo

Dirk Kohnert

In February, the president again won the disputed presidential elections and thus consolidated his power, assisted by the loyal army and security services. The outbreak of the Covid-19 epidemic in Togo in March and the subsequent economic recession may have contributed to limiting popular protest against the Gnassingbé regime. The human rights record of the government improved, but remains poor. Yet the international community, in the interests of regional stability, pursued a 'laissez faire' approach. The economy dropped into recession due to the worldwide negative economic effects of the coronavirus crisis. The Democracy Index of the Economic Intelligence Unit, London, still rated Togo as an 'authoritarian regime'.

Domestic Politics

Togo's contested presidential elections dominated the domestic political scene in Togo right from the start of the year. The government had fixed the date for the elections only shortly before, on 6 December 2019, for 22 February 2020. Thus, it paved the way for a fourth, and perhaps eventually a fifth, five-year mandate for Faure Gnassingbé in 2020 and 2025 respectively. Altogether, ten candidates had been accepted for the presidential elections by the constitutional court, as released on 17 January – notably the incumbent Faure Gnassingbé; the leader of the biggest opposition party, Alliance nationale pour le changement (ANC), Jean-Pierre Fabre; and Agbéyomé Kodjo from the Mouvement Patriotique pour la Démocratie et le Développement (MPDD). The latter had been prime minister already under the late Eyadéma Gnassingbé. Capitalising on the disunity of the opposition, Kodjo, backed by some of the parties of the opposition C14 coalition as well as by the retired archbishop of Lomé, Monseigneur Philippe Kpodzro, contested the leadership of the opposition by Jean-Pierre Fabre. Consequently, a new opposition political movement – Dynamique Mgr Kpodzro (DMK), an association of opposition parties and civil society organisations – was formed by supporters of Archbishop Kpodzro to back Kodjo for the presidentials on 22 February.

The electoral campaign started on 6 February, two weeks ahead of the polls, and ended 24 hours before the opening of the polling stations. About 10,000 troops were deployed to secure the elections, a prospect which, according to activists of the opposition, amounted to intimidation.

The election was monitored by 315 international election observers, mainly from the UN, the African Union (AU), and ECOWAS. In addition, each candidate was allowed to send representatives to the almost 9,400 polling stations. But on 17 January, the government cancelled the election observer credentials of the largest independent civil society organisation, Concertation Nationale de la Société Civile, as well as those of the Catholic Church monitors. In addition, the National Democratic Institute (NDI) in Washington, DC, had its accreditation retired and one of its staff members expelled from Togo without warning. On election day, internet access was restricted and social networks, as well as critical media websites, were blocked.

The new electoral code of May 2019 and the endorsement of diaspora votes by parliament on 5 November 2019 made it possible for Togolese from the diaspora (estimated at 2 m people) to vote, for the first time in the country's history. However, implementation provisions ensured that hardly any opposition voters had the opportunity to register to vote at any of the embassies. All told, just 348 citizens from the diaspora participated.

According to the National Election Commission (CENI), there were 3,738,786 registered voters, of whom 2,769,286 went to the polls, according to the preliminary results. The CENI counted 983,413 blank and invalid votes. According to the official final results confirmed on 3 March by the one-sided constitutional court, incumbent president Faure Gnassingbé won the elections with 70.78 % or 1,760,309 votes in the first round, as against 19.46 % or 483,926 votes for his closest contender, Agbéyomé Kodjo. Former opposition leader Jean-Pierre Fabre of the ANC ended far behind in third place with 4.68 % or 116,336 votes. The suspiciously high voter turnout of 76.62%, 15 percentage points above the 2015 figure, suggested a growing interest among the general public in multi-party elections despite the biased organisation of the electoral process.

Kodjo, supported by the opposition, immediately declared the preliminary election results a forgery and maintained that he had gained the majority of votes. Kodjo's appeal against the results to the constitutional court was dismissed. On the contrary, AU and ECOWAS observers congratulated the Togolese people for the good conduct and peaceful course of the elections. In March, the immunity of Kodjo was lifted by the parliament because he still maintained his victory. Shortly afterwards, on 21 April, he was questioned by the police and arrested for failing to appear before the country's intelligence and security police after proclaiming himself 'elected president' of Togo.

Togo's Catholic bishops condemned the arrest of the opposition leader, a move that inspired continuing post-election tensions in the country. However, the outbreak of the Covid-19 epidemic in Togo in March 2020, with 3,604 confirmed cases and 68 deaths by 29 December, and the subsequent economic recession – mostly due to external shocks – may have mitigated the popular protest against the Gnassingbé regime.

Because DMK was perceived as a potential threat to the ruling powers, it was targeted by the security services. Some of its leading members, including the lawyer and human rights activist Brigitte Kafui Adjamagbo-Johnson, in 2010 the first woman to stand in a presidential election in Togo, and Gérard Yaovi Djossou, were imprisoned because of an alleged attack on the internal security of the state on 27 and 30 November. They were released provisionally on 17 December after almost three weeks of detention. Prior to this, on 21 April, around 16 DMK members who had protested against the arrest of the opposition politician Agbéyomé Kodjo on the same day were arrested and later found guilty of 'rebellion' and 'complicity in the rebellion' and sentenced to one year in prison, eight months of which were suspended. They were released on 25 August.

Because of the Covid-19 pandemic, various civic rights provisions were suspended. In an attempt to control the spread of the Covid-19 virus in Togo, all borders were closed and a lockdown applied to the cities of Lomé, Tsévié, Kpalimé, and Sokodé on 20 March for two weeks. On 16 March, the government announced a fund of 2 bn CFA (Communauté Financière Africaine) francs (CFAfr) to fight the pandemic.

On 28 September, a new prime minister, Victoire Tomegah Dogbé (aged 61), was nominated. She was the first woman to hold the office. An economist by training, Dogbé had been minister of grass-roots development, handicrafts, youth, and youth employment, as well as cabinet director in President Gnassingbé's government since 2010. She appointed a new government with a record 30% of the 33 ministerial positions given to women, including Essozimna Marguerite Gnakade as defence minister – the first time a woman has held that portfolio.

On 19 October, the president reorganised his team of close collaborators. The 'Kitchen Cabinet' of a new guard of young and dynamic councillors, including a liaison officer of the army, was formed to assist the prime minister. It included the following new councillors: Sandra Ablamba Johnson, promoted to the rank of a minister as the new secretary-general of the Presidency; Kouessan Joseph Yovodévi, new director of communication at the presidency; Komlan Adjitowou, head of the military cabinet and formerly deputy chief of staff of the Togolese Armed Forces (FAT), raised to the rank of general in 2018; and Djibril Mohaman Awalou, appointed national coordinator for the management of the response to Covid-19. The latter is a university professor and chief director of the army health service. The new 'Kitchen Cabinet' was meant to complement the president's old guard of special advisors, such as the notorious French lawyer Charles Debbasch, Barry Moussa Barqué, and Koffi Sama. In October, Carlos Lopes, a Bissau-Guinean development economist and former executive secretary of the United Nations Economic Commission for Africa, also joined Faure Gnassingbé's crew of retired senior advisors of international standing, which included the likes of Tony Blair, Dominique Strauss-Khan, and Lionel Zinsou.

Simmering unrest within the security services alarmed the government as well as the general public. On 4 May, Colonel Bitala Madjoulba, commander of the 1st Rapid Intervention Battalion (BIR), was murdered – shot in his office with his own revolver. The fact that this crime concerned a senior officer responsible for the protection of senior state officials turned this assassination into a state affair. Only one day after the assassination, Faure Gnassingbé nominated Lieutenant Colonel Atafai Tchangani to replace him. The latter had been head of a section at the Special Military School of Saint-Cyr, the foremost French military academy, and commander of the UN operations in Côte d'Ivoire, UNOCI Battalion. The Commission of Inquiry set up by the government in May, headed by the minister of security and civil protection, Brigadier General Yark Damehame, did not discover those responsible for the assassination.

On 3 October, President Gnassingbé made several crucial appointments by decree within the FAT. Brigadier General Komlan Adjitowou was appointed chief of staff of the president of the republic. Colonel Kassawa Kolémaga, previously director of operations of the FAT and former head of the National Intelligence Agency (ANR), was promoted to chief of staff of the army. Colonel Tassounti Djato, until then commander of the Niamtougou Hunting Base (BCN, 350 personnel) in Niamtougou, the capital of Doufelgou Prefecture in Kara Region, the homeland and fief of the Gnassingbé family, was appointed chief of staff of the air force. Finally, at the end of December, General Dadja Maganawé became the new strongman of the Togolese army, nominated as chief of staff. It is noteworthy that while the general chief of staff of the FAT is Brigadier General Félix Abalo Kadanga, the Ministry of Defence remains in the hands of Faure Gnassingbé, a measure aimed at forestalling coup attempts.

The continuing violation of human rights in Togo remained a special concern of the international community. According to a report by Amnesty International, presented at the UNHCR (from 2 to 27 March), the human rights situation in Togo sharply deteriorated due to growing political and social tensions related to the prospects of the head of state running for fourth and fifth terms and the contested 2019 constitutional reforms. Furthermore, Togo still ranked among the most corrupt states worldwide (ranked 130th of 180 countries). Finally, the high level of illicit financial flows (IFF), which strongly correlates with money laundering, attracted the concern of the international donor community. These IFFs came mainly from three sources: commercial tax evasion, trafficking of bills in international trade, and abusive transfer prices set by transnational corporations that shift profits out of the countries where they operate and into tax havens, thus selling themselves goods and services at artificially high prices. Examples of other IFFs are criminal activities such as drug dealing, illegal transactions on weapons, smuggling, active corruption, and the collusion of corrupt civil servants. IFFs represented almost 500% of Togo's tax revenues, ranking Togo second in the world.

Increasing encroachment on internet media freedoms took various forms, ranging from subtly increasing regulatory powers over social media to country-wide internet shutdowns. In June, the Haute Autorité de l'Audiovisuel et de la Communication (HAAC) suspended the bi-monthly 'Panorama' for violating the professional rules of journalism and commenting unfavourably on the head of state in May. On 25 March, the HAAC withdrew the licence of the newspaper 'La Nouvelle' for publishing 'unverified information' and incitement of ethnic and religious hatred. On 4 November, the editor of the opposition journal 'L'Alternative', Ferdinand Ayité, as well as the journal itself were condemned and each fined CFAfr 2 m for defamation in the 'Pétrolegate-affaire', because Ayité had accused the head of the committee responsible for monitoring petroleum product price fluctuations, Fabrice Adjakly, of being responsible for the diversion of CFAfr 500 bn. On 29 December, Carlos Kétohou from the 'L'Indépendant Express' was arrested. Also, government interference with internet and mobile phone companies was of special concern in the context of participatory development approaches espoused by international donor agencies, given the growing reliance on digital information and communication technologies.

Togo's overall status in Freedom House's 2020 Freedom in the World rating remained 'partly free' as in the previous two years. In the Economist Intelligence Unit's Democracy Index 2019 (the most recent available), Togo was upgraded from 130th to 126th out of 167 countries. As in the previous year, the EIU classified Togo as an 'authoritarian regime'.

Foreign Affairs

On 17 January the five heads of state of Congo-Brazzaville, Uganda, Senegal, The Gambia, and Togo met in Lomé for a summit against drug trafficking. Trafficking in fake drugs is said to kill about 900,000 Africans every year, among them 120,000 children under five. Thus, more Africans die from fake drugs than of malaria.

On 26 February, the US government released a remarkably frank criticism of the conduct of the 2020 presidential elections in Togo. In particular, it disapproved of the meagre efforts of independent election observation, notably the decision of the CENI to revoke the accreditation of the NDI in Washington, DC, and the expulsion of its observers three days before the election.

Because of the economic burden of the Covid-19 pandemic, the heads of state of the WAEMU/UEMOA declared a temporary suspension of the WAEMU growth and stability pact. As a result, member countries were allowed to raise their overall fiscal deficit temporarily.

On 24 April, the government announced the completion of the application process for the country's membership of the African Trade Insurance Agency (ATI), thus becoming the eighth African sovereign shareholder of currently 18 member countries. The move had been backed by the EIB and reflects a trend that has seen a record number of West African countries join Africa's multilateral guarantee agency – including Ghana, Niger, and Nigeria, all of which have completed the process for membership in the last nine months. This trend is expected to continue as countries seek support to ensure investment and trade flows on the continent to manage the economic fallout from the coronavirus.

The intimidation of the opposition continued on all fronts and by all means. According to a survey conducted by 'Le Monde' (Paris) and the 'Guardian' (London), published on 3 August, the government in Lomé had spied on members of the opposition DMK, using the highly sophisticated Israeli Pegasus software to monitor mobile phone and internet activity.

In advance of the ECOWAS announcement on 9 September of a gradual withdrawal of its intervention force in Guinea-Bissau, a first batch consisting of 130 men – mainly from the Togolese Special Forces – left Bissau on August 27.

On 4 November, Lomé prepared to ratify a convention with neighbouring Benin on the creation of the Mono Basin Authority (ABM), regulating the status of the Mono River bordering the two countries. On 1 December, the national assembly adopted a bill authorising the Togolese state to ratify the agreement establishing the African Intellectual Property Organization (OAPI), headquartered in Yaoundé, which embraced 17 mostly francophone African states. The agreement, adopted in

December 2015 in Bamako, would allow Togo to better protect intellectual property rights – the inventions and creations of its citizens – and to fight effectively against counterfeiting.

The EU and its member states, notably France and Germany, continued to aid Togo. The EU announced on 15 January its budget support of more than CFAfr 10.5 bn (€ 16 m) for the 'consolidation of the State, phase 3 (CCET 3)'. Germany's KfW provided € 5 m on 18 May to reinforce the decentralisation process.

In August, France extended its support to Togo and Ghana for anti-jihadist aerial surveillance. Moreover, on 16 November, Paris supported the Togolese navy in combating piracy in the Gulf of Guinea with Sillinger sea hunters of the same type already intended for the Libyan coastguard.

In November, Lomé was involved in mediation efforts in the Malian crisis precipitated by the August coup staged by the Malian Armed Forces, which led to President Ibrahim Boubacar Keïta being forced to resign and his government being dissolved. Lomé's partisan mediation role was aimed at 'saving' the junta. On 13 November, the transitional president in Bamako, Bah N'Daw, visited Lomé for negotiations. But behind the scenes, contacts had already been made in the greatest secrecy the day after the putsch, which included an exchange of visits in private jets and clandestine meetings.

In November 2019, the Nigerian multinational Dangote Industries and the Togolese government had agreed to develop and transform the Togolese phosphate and cement industry. In January 2020, the first contract for a 2.5 m tpa (tons per annum) cement grinding plant with vertical roller mill (VRM) crushers from the Cimenterie de Côte Ouest-Africaine (CimCo) was awarded to the Intercem Group (Cimfaso & Cimasso in Burkina Faso and CimIvoire in Côte d'Ivoire) by the CimMetal Group. The start of production was scheduled for the first quarter of 2021. The new facility, named Cimco SA, will be strategically situated at the port of Lomé and is destined to become the country's largest grinding plant by capacity. HeidelbergCement announced an expansion of its Togolese subsidiary, Cimtogo, spending more than $ 30 m in the process, which will create 30% more direct jobs in addition to the nearly 4,000 direct and indirect jobs already provided in Togo. Heidelberg already has a grinding station in Kara and an integrated clinker plant in Tabligbo.

Socioeconomic Development

In April, the World Bank and the IMF provided considerable additional support for Togo to counteract the economic impact of the Covid-19 crisis. On 3 April, the IMF authorised an immediate disbursement of $ 131.1 m to Togo in line with the completion of the sixth and final review of the country's economic performance under the programme supported by the ECF agreement. The disbursement was four times greater than what was initially planned ($ 35 m), due to the human and economic implications of Covid-19.

Before the Covid-19 pandemic, the prospects for Togo's economy had been encouraging, with growth expected to reach 5.3% in 2020 and 5.5% in 2021, on the back of good performance in agriculture and sound monetary management. However, under the Covid-19 shock, Togo was likely to record a loss of growth of between 4.6% and 6.8 % in 2020. In the worst-case scenario, the fiscal deficit, initially forecast at 1.5% of GDP in 2020, would rise to 6.4% due to the increase in health expenditure and the fall in tax revenues caused by the fall in the general level of economic activity. The current account deficit was expected to follow a similar trajectory. Forecast at 3.2% of GDP, it was projected to worsen to 5.7% or possibly 7% of GDP in 2020 under the effect of lower exports and declining migrant remittances and FDI in the main economic sectors.

On 18 December, the parliament voted on the financial law for 2021. According to the provisions, the 2021 budget will be balanced in allocations with expenses at CFAfr 1,521.6 bn, or $ 2.84 bn. The budget deficit of CFAfr 280.8 bn represents 6.1% of GDP and would be 'entirely financed by the surplus balance of treasury operations', according to finance minister Sani Yaya. The budget allocated CFAfr 445.1 bn ($ 831.83 m) to the social sectors, up 10.8%. Agriculture will benefit from CFAfr 65.7 bn, while CFAfr 77.9 bn will be reserved for the health sector, i.e. 10%. Education was allocated CFAfr 195.5 bn, or 25.1% of the 2021 budget.

The Covid-19 pandemic had a discernible effect on the level of social exclusion too, notably of people employed in the informal sector. Roughly 62% of jobs were at risk, 49% in the services sector and 13% in the industrial sector. To counteract the negative effects on the poor and vulnerable, the African Financer of Micro-Projects (Financière Africaine de Micro-Projets, FINAM), the first public limited company for microfinance, embarked on the digitalisation of its services by creating the application Finam Mobile in response to the Covid crisis. The app allows people to manage their account at home, including making deposits and withdrawals, starting on 11 September. It launched the first iteration of its '1,000 micro-projects' campaign to combat youth unemployment. The target groups can benefit without prior deposits: with simple guarantees from members of FINAM, they can obtain loans of up to CFAfr 600,000 for the realisation of their micro-projects.

In addition, through its National Agency of Volunteers in Togo (Agence Nationale de Volontariat au Togo, ANVT) the government tried to counteract un- and underemployment, though with limited success. Since 2011, more than 43,000 candidates have registered. Overall, 8,989 people – 4,610 women and 4,348 men, including 31 disabled people – were targeted in 2020.

The coronavirus crisis accelerated the establishment of a universal solidarity income scheme by the National Solidarity and Economic Fund in April called 'Novissi' (meaning 'brotherhood' and 'living together' in the Ewe language). The stipends were paid twice a month and were mainly intended for people living on daily earnings, without social security and affected by the decline in activity. Novissi was a 100% digital scheme that reached nearly 570,000 of the affected poor between 8 April and 6 June 2020, the date of the lifting of curfews in Grand Lomé and the prefecture of Tchaoudjo in Centrale Region. The programme was extended to the rural canton of Soudou in Kara Region in north-eastern Togo when the circulation of the coronavirus forced a drastic reduction in activities. Those entitled were to receive directly, through mobile enrolment, a state grant of at least 30% of the minimum wage. Based on programme data, 65% of the beneficiaries were women. The cash transfer programme was expected to last three months at a cost of CFAfr 36 bn ($ 61 m; 1.1% of GDP). The Novissi scheme was revised in late June, with eligibility limited to workers in specific districts recording a high Covid-19 contagion rate. In total so far, 1.4 m individuals have registered and close to 600,000 have received a Novissi payment, at a total cost of CFAfr 11.4 bn ($ 19 m; 0.3% of GDP).

Cotton production for the 2019/20 season gave a poor yield of 116,000 tons, against the forecast of 150,000 tons, according to the New Cotton Company of Togo (NSCT).

In February, ECOWAS, including Togo, agreed to adopt a regional standard on imported gasoline and diesel fuels of 50 parts per million (ppm) starting in January 2021, with local refineries given until January 2025 to comply. In December 2016, Togo and four neighbouring countries (Nigeria, Ghana, Benin, Côte d'Ivoire) had already agreed in principle to ban imports of 'dirty' fuels from Europe. The average 'unofficial' imported diesel tested was 152 higher in sulphur than the level of EU sulphur standards, while for gasoline the levels were 40 times higher than the standard. The WHO ranked these as among the top global health risks associated with heart disease, lung cancer, and respiratory problems.

Togo continued to be a 'safe' haven for money laundering. On 20 September, CENOZO, an investigative reporting unit in West Africa revealed suspicious transactions aimed at financing terrorist networks in the frontier zone in the north of Togo. Cinkassé, Dapaong, and other localities bordering Burkina Faso were classified as a 'red zone' where the presence of jihadists had been noticed by the population.

PART 4

Central Africa

Andreas Mehler

While the overall political situation in the notoriously unstable DRC – the biggest country of the sub-region – was somewhat consolidated, this was not the case for popular security. With the CAR entering a new cycle of violence and Cameroon plus Chad equally embroiled in violent conflict, the sub-region looked particularly unsafe. Covid-19 had effects on both the regional and the world economy, which in turn hit mostly the oil-producing countries in Central Africa. The future of the Central African franc as a common currency within CEMAC remained unclear, and CEMAC itself did not make important headlines.

Democracy and Elections

Central Africans in their large majority continued to live in autocracies with national rulers who refused to be held accountable by republican institutions, the media, and the broader public. All Central African countries, with the exception of the tiny island republic of São Tomé and Príncipe, employed some level of repression, with the restrictions on civil liberties and political freedom meant to guarantee continuity, possibly of family rule. National elections were held only in Cameroon (national assembly) and in the CAR, but past or future elections oriented political life in all countries.

In the CAR, the first round of presidential and legislative elections was organised under particularly difficult circumstances at the end of the year. Tensions built up over months after former dictator and coup-maker François Bozizé was allowed to enter the country in January. President Touadéra lost popular support and faced a somewhat better-united opposition. However, it was much more the combined effect of Bozizé's intrigues following his disqualification by the constitutional court from standing in elections and new alliances of rebel groups that brought the country to the brink of a new civil war – instead of just the absence of peace in about a dozen former hotspots of violence, which has now been a familiar condition over many years. The second round of elections was held only in 2021.

Cameroon's history of meaningless elections continued, with partially boycotted legislative elections that permitted the entry of even more MPs from the ruling party to the national assembly. The innovation of regional elections did not alter the political game one iota, given that regional councillors were indirectly elected by municipal councillors and traditional chiefs, most of them again loyalists of President Biya.

Chad's parliamentary elections had already been pending for five years, but were again postponed to April 2021. Thus, they would coincide with presidential elections in 2021 which were forecast to be won again by warlord-president Idriss Déby Itno. *Congo*'s president Sassou Nguesso also prepared for another win in 2021 elections.

DRC's new president, Félix Tchisekedi, moved carefully to consolidate his own rule, sidelining some supporters of his predecessor, Joseph Kabila. It was too early to conclude that democracy would have a chance to be established, even to minimal standards.

Family rule and dynastic politics were instead features of nearly all countries in the region, but most visibly in Gabon, Chad, Congo, and Equatorial Guinea. *Gabon*'s Ali Bongo clearly positioned his son Noureddin as his eventual successor, after naming him general coordinator of presidential affairs and sidelining two of his own half-brothers. In *Equatorial Guinea*, President Teodoro Obiang Nguema Mbasogo watched over the struggles between his sons Teodorín and Gabriel Lima, who were both obviously ambitious to succeed their father. In *Chad*, Idriss Déby filled further government positions with close relatives, as well as relatives of his influential wife, Hinda Déby. *Congo*'s Sassou Nguesso fully supported the further ascent of his son Denis Christel, although the latter was implicated in the highly mediatised 'bien mal acquis' trial around embezzled money invested in France (as was Teodorín Obiang Nguema, son of Equatorial Guinea's president), while one of his nephews still appeared as a potential challenger to the 'dauphin'. Franck Biya, son of president Paul Biya and his first wife Jeanne-Irène, returned to *Cameroon* in March, having spent the past few years abroad. Although he was much more discreet than others listed here, this was enough to raise speculations about Franck Biya's ambitions to succeed his elderly father (aged 87). It was obvious that all of these heads of state had reasonable motivations, such as unconditional loyalty and dynastic plans, when promoting their own kin to important positions, which at the same time entailed very apparent risks, including a disastrous effect on popular legitimacy and rising tensions within their families. *São Tomé and Príncipe* (STP) saw continued leadership struggles within one of the key political parties. However, the small island republic was the only country in the region that upheld democratic standards and guaranteed basic human rights.

Standard *ratings of democracy* in Central Africa, such as the Freedom House index, classified Cameroon, CAR, and Equatorial Guinea as 'not free' with slightly worsening indicator figures, while Gabon and Congo remained unchanged. In comparison, DRC showed a slight improvement (though still 'not free') while STP was the only country regarded as 'free', with unchanged indicator data. This situation contrasted with other African sub-regions, where many hybrid regimes ('partly free' according to Freedom House) could be found, but overall the trend of steady deterioration of democratic standards was not particular to Central Africa.

Instability, War, and Peace

The topography of violence did not change significantly. The Armed Conflict Location and Event Data Project (ACLED) noted 5,778 fatalities for DRC, over 2,000 more than in the previous year. Nearly 1,600 fatalities were recorded in Cameroon, up by 350 compared with the previous year. The two most severe individual battles took place in the Lake Chad area between Boko Haram fighters and Chadian security forces, claiming several hundreds of lives (see below). Such figures only partially represent the plight of populations that in some places were massively displaced or suffered from hunger and disease as a result. The 2019 peace agreement for CAR has proven meaningless, with the latest formation of a new rebel alliance in December – made up of signatories of the peace agreement – which subsequently tried to conquer the capital, Bangui.

DRC's different conflict arenas saw an overall marked increase in casualties, though local situations were diverse. North Kivu Province saw more attacks by the Allied Democratic Forces (ADF), but also by the Forces démocratique de libération du Rwanda (FDLR) and a number of ethnically oriented militias. ADF and FDLR were originally linked to contestation in neighbouring Uganda and Rwanda, though they were now mainly operating in DRC. In South Kivu, some militias were related to the lingering conflict in Burundi. Such groups added to the complex situation, with cross-border dynamics on the one hand fuelling local intercommunal violence on the other. The UN peacekeeping mission in DRC, MONUSCO, just as in previous years, did not prove effective in stopping the ongoing violence. Civilians as well as park rangers were among the victims of violent acts. Ituri Province remained a hotbed of violence despite intense peace negotiations. In Tanganyika Province, Bantu and Twa communities clashed over land rights. Elsewhere, security was mixed, with Haut-Katanga, Lualaba, and Congo Central provinces also reporting new acts of violence, while Kasai Central, Kwilu, Mai-Ndombe, and Sankuru remained largely stable.

Boko Haram represented a real threat to security in Chad. The number of violent attacks increased, including a series of attacks on soldiers in the Lake Chad area that killed about one hundred of them and triggered a major counter-attack in late March which was directly supervised by President Déby. According to official sources, more than 1,000 Boko Haram fighters were killed. In addition, the army fought rebels, and clashes between nomadic herders and farmers again escalated in the northern Tibesti Mountains

Dozens of attacks by Boko Haram in northern *Cameroon,* killing mostly low numbers of civilians, and counter-attacks by the national army made a large area bordering Chad and northern Nigeria very unsafe. The civil war around secession in the two Anglophone regions became fully entrenched and even more difficult to resolve, with a growing number of armed groups. Only some of them had a political agenda, while others were acting like bandits, surviving on the backs of the local population by kidnapping – sometimes prominent – individuals (such as Archbishop Emeritus Christian Tumi) and asking for ransom. Grave human rights violations were recorded on both sides. These included a massacre of civilians by the army in Ngarbuh, triggering numerous reactions on social media just as much as a massacre attributed to separatists in Kumba. Educational facilities were particularly targeted. The government was unable or unwilling to offer a political solution to a steadily degrading situation for the local population.

In this environment, the number of *refugees and IDPs* unsurprisingly remained high throughout the sub-region. More than 690,000 refugees from CAR were registered, most of them in the neighbouring countries of Cameroon (323,524), DRC (206,036), and Chad (114,445), according to the UNHCR. DRC received some 520,000 refugees, with Rwanda the second most important source, but also saw 948,007 of its inhabitants taking refuge elsewhere; about 45% went to Uganda, with Burundi, Tanzania, and Rwanda the next most important destinations. In Chad, refugees from CAR represented less than a quarter of the total refugee population of 504,584, while a stronger proportion came from Sudan. Cameroon and Nigeria saw refugee movements from both sides of the border into the neighbouring country. On the one hand, about 118,000 Nigerians, mostly fleeing from Boko Haram attacks, temporarily resided in Cameroon. On the other hand, some 67,000 Anglophones from Cameroon took shelter across the border in Nigeria. In some countries, IDPs had become even more important. The CAR's number of IDPs grew to 729,005 in the second half of the year. This meant that, again, more than a quarter of CAR's population was on the run. CAR was not alone in experiencing such drama: in August, 363,807 displaced people were counted in Lake Chad Province in Chad, more than half of the provincial population. While no concrete figures on Anglophone IDPs could be procured, around 322,000 IDPs were recorded in Cameroon's Far North Province (around 8% of the local population). According to the UNHCR, there were 5.2 m IDPs in the DRC, a slight increase from last year.

Humanitarian help for those affected was the most common international reaction; most sanctions against perpetrators of war crimes remained in force. New initiatives were rare: the 50th meeting of the UN Standing Advisory Committee on Security Questions in Central Africa (UNSAC), initially scheduled for late May in Malabo, could be held only virtually on 2–4 December due to the Covid-19 pandemic. The head of the UN Regional Office for Central Africa (UNOCA), François Louncény Fall (from Senegal), later gave a sobering report to the UNSC at a briefing and pointed to similarities between the Sahel region and Central Africa in reference to the Boko Haram rebellion, as well as the need to closely coordinate with his counterpart working on the Great Lakes region.

Human Rights and Transnational Justice

The Covid-19 pandemic was a pretext for many governments to *restrict civil liberties and political rights*, but most of the severe crimes against humanity were related to violent intra-state conflict. Cameroon saw widespread human rights abuses committed by both armed rebels and government forces in the Anglophone west (South West and North West regions) and in Far North. Security forces were accused of extrajudicial executions and mass killings. They also arrested about 500 opposition supporters on 22 September, one day after opposition leader Maurice Kamto was placed under house arrest (lifted only on 8 December). Two individual events received strong media coverage. The aforementioned massacre of 21 civilians in Ngarbuh, a village in North West Region, was attributed to an alliance of security forces with armed Mbororo and renegade 'Amba boys' on 14 February, though this was also contested. On 24 October, unidentified gunmen attacked a school in Kumba (South West) and killed seven children – this was in turn attributed to separatist fighters. These spectacular attacks made headlines internationally while daily violations of human rights received scant attention. Reporters sans Frontières (RSF) saw a general deterioration of working conditions for journalists, with Cameroon losing five ranks in their World Press Freedom Index over two years. The suspicious death of a journalist in custody in 2019 and the lengthy judicial procedure against former television and radio director Amadou Vamoulké were among the many rights violations pinpointed by RSF.

In the CAR – like in previous years – it was mostly armed groups, now formally at peace with the government, which committed serious human rights abuses. However, the government also behaved more and more dictatorially. RSF pointed to disinformation campaigns by the government. Leading journalists and bloggers were targeted with hate messages, defamation, and attacks on social media. In a special report, AI analysed the so-called 'Bangassou trial' at the Special Criminal Court that led to the first conviction for crimes under international law in the CAR. Five Anti-balaka leaders were found guilty of war crimes and crimes against humanity in which 72 people had been killed, including 62 civilians and 10 UN peacekeepers (back in 2017). AI lauded the trial as a first step in the fight against impunity, but criticised shortcomings in the legal aid system for victims and witnesses, slow procedures, and limited cooperation by state authorities. In July, the ICC announced a trial date for two Anti-balaka leaders in its custody. Amnesty International also followed up on the environmental damage caused by four Chinese mining firms operating at Ouham River; the firms had stopped their operations upon massive criticism by law-makers and NGOs, but had not engaged in restoring the river.

In a special report, HRW exposed the cooperation between some commanders of DRC's state security forces and warlord *Guidon* Shimiray Mwissa, whose fighters had forcibly recruited young men and boys and imposed forced labour and taxes on the population in stretches of land under their control. Earlier, HRW pointed to large-scale kidnappings around the Virunga National Park, a UNESCO World Heritage Site. Authorities in the DRC used state of emergency measures imposed due to the Covid-19 pandemic to curb protests. They also only selectively prosecuted high-level corruption. Key politician Vital Kamerhe was sentenced to 20 years in prison for embezzlement of money, while other blatant cases were not even investigated.

On 14 February, authorities in *Equatorial Guinea* released the human rights defender Joaquín Elo Ayeto from the notorious Black Beach prison, where he had been imprisoned for almost a year. Radio Asonga, formally a private radio station, owned by the president's son Teodorín Obiang Nguema, saw a popular programme suspended and four journalists fired after they had criticised the rough handling by military forces in imposing adherence to anti-Covid-19 measures.

In *Chad*, more than a dozen newspapers were suspended under a new press law. Journalists were often arbitrarily arrested, some for weeks or even months. In one instance, the police fired tear-gas into a radio station's courtyard and arrested 30 journalists. As a response, the 'Day without Radio' strike was launched. Additionally, a Covid-19-related state of emergency was declared by President Déby in April, which, *inter alia*, restricted free movement. The violent attack on Boma by alleged Boko Haram fighters killed some 98 soldiers in this village close to Lake Chad. In revenge, the government officially killed 1,000 militiamen and held a human rights defender incommunicado, AI reported.

In *Congo*, authorities closed borders in response to the pandemic in March and took other measures which included a curfew maintained until September. A main TV anchorperson was taken off the air after asking questions that embarrassed a government minister over Congo's response to the pandemic in April.

In *Gabon*, the government declared a state of emergency after a first Covid-19 case was detected. This resulted in a full lockdown, including a 12-hour curfew that lasted over a month. Freedom House reported that in some parts of the country people were unable to access essential commodities. On the positive side, the government passed a law in June decriminalising homosexuality – which cancelled a recent revision of the Penal Code only one year earlier criminalising homosexual relations between consenting adults, with a potential penalty of imprisonment up to six months and a fine of up to CFAfr 5 m.

Socioeconomic Developments

The reported number of *infections and deaths related to the pandemic* was probably fully unreliable. According to OCHA, the entire region counted 74,778 cases and 1,481 deaths by the end of the year, unevenly distributed over the countries, with Cameroon reporting the highest number (26,848 cases; 313 deaths), followed by DRC with 17,849 cases but comparatively more deaths (591). The 'World Malaria Report 2020' issued by the WHO pointed to the risk that 'early lockdown measures in many malaria endemic countries may have protected people from Covid-19, but they have also affected people's access to health care and other services'. This might have specifically applied to Central Africa, where DRC alone accounts for 12% of malaria cases recorded globally. The WHO expected that excess malaria mortality would be larger than direct Covid-19 mortality.

In January 2021, the IMF noted that the Covid-19 pandemic had led to a sharp *deterioration of fiscal and external balances* for the CEMAC countries in 2020, attributed mostly to the related oil price shock. The IMF saw the crisis as mostly under control but expected long-lasting effects. IMF experts forecast a 3% recession for 2020 and a 5.5% increase to the current account deficit for the entire region. The IMF appreciated the revision of budgets and diverse assistance policies for particularly affected sectors, helping to mitigate the economic fallout of the crisis. Both governments and BEAC, which eased its monetary policy, were positively judged. The IMF itself made available emergency funding to some countries, but also used the opportunity to repeat the key recommendation to diversify state income, making public purses less dependent on oil income. Furthermore, the AfDB projected a sharp drop in the GDP growth rate from the originally envisaged 3.5% (pre-Covid-19) – contrasting slightly with the 3.3% originally expected by the IMF. The AfDB also pointed to factors like a 'decline in international trade, a slump in oil prices, a drop in investment, financial resources and tourism revenues, and pressure on health and social systems', with the slowdown of the economy in China, the United States, and Europe – the region's major partners – responsible for a drop in exports from Central Africa. The AfDB, however, did not fail to point to domestic instability as a further risk factor. In a 'best-case scenario', the AfDB now calculated on a recession of –2.5%. The IMF's World Economic Outlook (published in April 2021) reported neither growth nor strong decline in GDP for the CAR and DRC, with rates slightly lower than zero. In comparison, Congo (–7.8%), Equatorial Guinea (–5.8%), and Cameroon (–2.8%) were clearly suffering from the crisis, while the calculations for Chad (–0.9%) and Gabon (–1.8%) were less dramatic.

Though noting some minor improvements in individual sectors in some of the sub-region's countries, the World Bank's Doing Business report ranked all countries in Central Africa at the bottom of their Ease of Doing Business list, with Cameroon rated best but only at rank 167 out of 190 countries, followed by Gabon (169th), STP (170th), Equatorial Guinea (178th), Congo (180th), Chad (182nd), DRC (183rd), and CAR (184th). Similarly, the Transparency International Corruption Perceptions Index drew a more or less stable picture of low-ranking countries, with Equatorial Guinea, DRC, and Congo at the bottom, unchangedly identified as 'very corrupt' (ranked 174th, 170th, and 165th). Better rated were Chad (160th, +1), Cameroon

(149th), CAR (146th, +1), and Gabon (124th, –1). Only STP was perceived as relatively incorrupt (41st, +1).

Sub-regional Organisations

The major CEEAC reform decided on in late 2019 had to be implemented. The 17th Assembly of Heads of State and Government was held virtually on 31 July and was able to choose the seven members of the newly formed CEEAC Commission, with Gilberto Da Piedade Verissimo (Angola) as president. The vice-president position was assigned to Francisca Tatchouop Belobe of Equatorial Guinea, with five further commissioner positions for representatives of Cameroon, Chad, Congo, DRC, and Rwanda. Verissimo thereafter met with secretary-general Ahmad Allam-Mi (Chad) and gradually gained some prominence in sub-regional initiatives, not least with regard to the security crisis in the CAR. A first official trip by Verissimo was to his home country, Angola. At the opening of a Commission retreat on 13 October, he urged his fellow commissioners to speed up the operationalisation of new CEEAC institutions, with the aim of creating 'an invigorated, dynamic, innovative and ambitious organization, capable of fully assuming its regional missions and contributing to the achievement of the integration and development objectives of the African continent'. An extraordinary summit of heads of state was held as a videoconference on 26 December and was fully devoted to the new episode of civil war in the CAR. Most prominently, the heads of state called on CAR citizens to vote in general elections the next day and appealed to the UNSC to scrap the arms embargo on the CAR to allow its government to procure the necessary military means to fight the rebellion. For the elections, CEEAC had also organised an election observer mission lead by former Burundian president Sylvestre Ntibantunganya.

Inside CEMAC, trouble was brewing. Yaya Dillo Djérou, the representative of Chad on the CEMAC Commission, was suspended in July upon an official request linked to first lady Hinda Déby Itno. The former warlord had fallen into disgrace for openly criticising the influence in government affairs of the charity Fondation Tchadienne Grand Cœur, which is presided over by the first lady – who immediately took juridical action for defamation. The episode highlighted the limited autonomy of the CEMAC Commission, as well as the mixing of domestic and regional affairs. CEMAC chairperson Daniel Ona Ondo held a meeting in Paris on 17/18 November to attract public and private investment into infrastructure projects within CEMAC, apparently attracting no firm commitments at the occasion. No conference of heads of state was organised this year.

The CBLT launched a Civil Society Organisation Platform in December in the context of its Regional Strategy for the Stabilization, Recovery and Resilience of the Boko Haram-affected Areas of the Lake Chad Basin Region (RSS), in the hope of addressing the root causes of the crisis and enhancing resilience. The Lake Chad Basin Commission (LCBC) formally spearheaded the RSS. Affected communities were invited to share experiences and existing good practice. NGOs and community-based organisations were given a significant role in the definition and implementation of multi-sectoral Territorial Action Plans (TAPs) and advocacy, *inter alia*.

Cameroon

Fanny Pigeaud

Cameroon was still engaged in a war against separatist groups in its two Anglophone regions, where each belligerent party committed massacres, thereby putting the authorities in a difficult position vis-à-vis their international partners. In spite of the deteriorating security situation, regional and local elections were held by the government, all of which were carried by the presidential party. Hundreds of people were arrested at demonstrations organised by the opposition in the context of these elections. Though the Covid-19 pandemic only moderately impacted the country's health situation, the damage inflicted on the economy was much more serious.

Domestic Politics

Despite the continuation of hostilities in its two Anglophone regions, the Northwest and the Southwest, Cameroon held three elections in the course of the year, beginning with the *parliamentary and municipal elections* on 9 February. However, voting had to be cancelled in ten constituencies of the Northwest and one constituency of the Southwest due to armed separatist groups that threatened the local inhabitants with reprisals if they cast their ballots. As a consequence, the authorities held parliamentary by-elections on 22 March; these were also accompanied by acts of violence, notably in the Northwest, where separatists attacked a convoy of the national electoral commission, Elections Cameroon (Elecam), that was transporting a member of parliament. A number of soldiers and two Elecam officials sustained bullet wounds. This dual parliamentary/municipal election was also marked by the non-participation of the opposition party Mouvement pour la Renaissance du Cameroun (MRC), led by Maurice Kamto, former minister-delegate to the minister of justice, who had finished second in the presidential election of 2018. Very present in the media, the MRC announced at the very last moment, on the official closing date for submitting candidacies, that it would boycott these elections. In his justification of this withdrawal, which surprised everyone, Maurice Kamto invoked the conflict in the Anglophone regions and the failure to revise the electoral code, which put the ruling party at an advantage.

In the end, the Rassemblement Démocratique du Peuple Camerounais (RDPC), as the presidential party, carried both elections with an overwhelming majority, winning 316 municipalities out of a total of 360. Only four were won by the Social Democratic Front (SDF), once the foremost opposition party. The RDPC also retained the absolute majority in the national assembly, with 152 seats out of 180, four seats more than in the 2013 election. The remaining 28 seats were shared by seven other parties. The Union Nationale pour la Démocractie et le Progrès (UNDP), part of the presidential majority led by the former prime minister and current minister of state for tourism Bello Bouba Maigari, obtained seven seats in two regions (Adamawa and North). The SDF was only able to send five deputies to the national assembly, compared with 18 in the preceding legislative period. The recently founded Parti Camerounais pour la Réconciliation Nationale (PCRN) of Cabral Libii made it into parliament, also with five seats. The Union Démocratique du Cameron (UDC), whose national leader Adamou Ndam Njoya, for three decades one of the leading opponents to President Paul Biya, died on 7 March, was able to send four deputies to the assembly, while the Front pour le Salut National du Cameroun (FSNC) picked up three seats. The Mouvement pour la Défense de la République (MDR) and the Union des Mouvements Socialistes (UMS) each obtained two seats. While many observers reported that the number of voters at the polling stations was low, the official turnout was given as 45.98%.

The third and final election took place on 6 December, this being the first time in the country's history that *regional elections* had been held, as stipulated by the constitution adopted in 1996. A total of 24,000 electors – municipal councillors and traditional chiefs – elected 900 regional councillors, 90 for each region. There was little suspense, as the municipal councillors, who elect the majority of the representatives in these new regional assemblies, mostly belonged to the RDPC. In both Anglophone regions, moreover, the RDPC was the only party to put forward candidates, enabling it to secure yet another overwhelming majority of seats in nine regions out of ten. The only region in which it failed to do so was Adamawa, which was carried by its ally the UNDP.

A few months earlier, the MRC had called for demonstrations against the holding of these regional elections, while renewing its appeal for a revision of electoral law, a prior resolution of the conflict in the Anglophone regions, and Biya's departure from power. The SDF also chose not to participate in this election. Even though the authorities announced that the calls for demonstrations were tantamount to 'calls for insurrection' and fell under anti-terrorism laws, the MRC decided to organise a *series of marches* that took place on 22 September in Douala (the economic capital), Yaoundé (the political capital), and a number of cities of the West region, including Bafoussam and Nkongsamba, where it is popular. Security forces were deployed in large numbers to prevent any possibility of mobilisation in Yaoundé and quickly put an end to an attempted demonstration by a few hundred people, firing tear-gas and using water cannon to disperse the crowd. On this day, *at least 500 people were arrested* throughout the country, mostly militants of the MRC. Eight journalists were also apprehended and held for a few hours. Many of those arrested at these protest events (at least 160, according to human rights organisations) were still being held in December, some having been sentenced to fixed prison terms by civil courts, others having been referred to military courts, among other things for 'attempted revolt', 'rebellion', and 'aggravated riotous assembly'. Two MRC officials, treasurer Alain Fogue Tedom and party spokesperson Bibou Nissack, were among those detained. As for Maurice Kamto, he became the target of special measures as early as 20 September: dozens of police officers and gendarmes set up checkpoints around his residence in Yaoundé, which remained in place for several weeks. Tantamount to a house arrest, these surveillance measures were not lifted until 8 December, just after the election.

Meanwhile, the *war in the Anglophone regions* continued to wreak havoc. As in previous years, it pitted the security forces against various armed groups, of which some voiced political demands while others lapsed into large-scale banditry, abducting people for ransom and carrying out targeted assassinations. Atrocities were committed on both sides. Public opinion was particularly moved by *two massacres*, the first of which occurred on 14 February in Ngarbuh, a neighbourhood of the town of Ntumbaw in the Northwest: the army killed 21 civilians, including a pregnant woman and ten children, all of whom were burned to death. The authorities initially denied the facts and laid the blame on separatist groups. But in mid-April, following an official investigation, they finally acknowledged the implication of several soldiers, who were said to have set houses on fire after an exchange of gunfire. The government blamed 'uncontrolled' elements within the army, claiming that they had disobeyed orders and killed ten children and three women (far fewer than various NGOs reported) with the help of auxiliary personnel. The three soldiers were also accused of having 'tried to conceal the facts by laying fires' and of having falsified their reports on the operation. Two soldiers and one gendarme were arrested and charged with murder, arson, destruction, violence against a pregnant woman, and disobeying orders. Their trial began on December 17 before the military court of Yaoundé. A total of 17 members of the auxiliary force, as well as one former separatist fighter, were also indicted for having participated in the massacre alongside the soldiers, but remained free.

The second bloody incident to rock the country occurred on 24 October. Just before the end of classes, a commando consisting of at least nine armed men on motorcycles carried out an attack on the Mother Francisca International Bilingual Academy, a private school in the city of Kumba (Southwest region), killing eight children between the ages of nine and twelve, most of them shot at point-blank range. No one claimed responsibility for the attack, but the government accused separatist fighters of having perpetrated the massacre. In addition to the children killed as a result of gunshot wounds, an OCHA report referred to children who had been 'cut down by machetes'. About 15 others were said to have been injured. While many inhabitants of Kumba also blamed an armed separatist group, they were astonished at how easily the separatists had been able to carry out the attack. Some 30 civil society organisations published an open letter deploring the fact that the government, at the beginning of the year, had urged students and teachers of both Anglophone regions to return to school without affording them adequate protection. According to human rights organisations, the education boycott imposed by armed separatist groups since 2017 in the Anglophone regions had deprived some 700,000 children of schooling. Though by far the deadliest, the attack in Kumba was not the only operation conducted against an educational facility: separatist fighters attacked other schools, assaulting and abducting students, as well as teachers who did not obey their orders to shut down schools. On 3 November, 11 teachers were thus abducted from a Presbyterian school in Kumbo, in the Northwest, by a group of heavily armed men, before being released two days later under the pressure of the local population.

Throughout the year, as the army conducted violent 'combing' operations and made numerous arbitrary arrests, the *separatists committed other serious violations of human rights*. In August, a video recorded in Muyuka, in the Southwest, showed three suspected separatist fighters beating a young woman whose hands were tied behind her back, accusing her of collaborating with the army before beheading her. Armed groups also abducted traditional chiefs, as for instance in mid-December, when one such group kidnapped four chiefs in Buea, killing at least one of them. On 5 November, another group abducted the famous cardinal and archbishop emeritus of Douala, 90-year-old Christian Tumi, as well as 11 other people, including the traditional chief (Fon) of the Nso people. The cardinal was released the very next day, the Fon of Nso a few days later.

Unlike the preceding year, official sources were mostly silent on the topic of *negotiations* between the government and the Ambazonian fighters. In early July, Julius Sisiku Ayuk Tabe, one of the separatist leaders who had been sentenced to lifelong imprisonment, claimed that he and eight other separatist leaders, imprisoned like him in Yaoundé's Central Prison, had met with representatives of the Cameroonian government to discuss a ceasefire. The government denied this while professing to be open to peaceful solutions. Towards the end of the year, it was estimated that the war had already claimed 3,000 lives and forced 700,000 people to flee their homes.

In June 2020, public opinion was also shocked when a private media company announced that the journalist Samuel Wazizi had died in detention. Anchor of the regional channel Chillen Music Television (CMTV), Samuel Wazizi had been arrested by the police on 2 August 2019, in Buea, the capital of the Southwest. He had told his lawyer, the last person in his entourage to see him alive, that his arrest was linked to his critical coverage of the government's handling of the Anglophone crisis. Following the announcement of his death, the Ministry of Defence stated that Samuel Wazizi had been an active member of a separatist group and had died on 17 August 2019 at Yaoundé's military hospital as a result of severe sepsis, affirming that he had not been subjected to any act of torture. However, the ministry did not explain why the *journalist's death* had been concealed from his family, his lawyers, and the judicial authorities for nearly a year. According to Reporters sans Frontières (RSF), which was able to examine photographs of Samuel Wazizi taken on 13 August 2019, the day of his transfer from Buea to Yaoundé, the journalist had suffered numerous injuries.

Moreover, the security situation remained poor in the *Far North region* and even deteriorated compared with the preceding year, with an increase in raids by the armed group *Boko Haram*. At least 16 people, including five children and six women, were killed in early August in a suicide attack, attributed to Boko Haram, on a camp housing 1,500 displaced persons in the village of Nguetchewe. Seven days earlier, the Cameroonian army reported that it had killed five Boko Haram fighters. Violent incidents occurred almost daily over the course of the year, with dozens of attacks on villages, medical facilities, and positions of the Cameroonian armed forces, in addition to abductions, robberies, and the destruction of property. In the same region, at least 64 people also died in floods caused by unusually heavy rainfall.

Yaoundé was also plagued by unprecedented security problems: two *improvised explosive devices* were detonated in a poor neighbourhood in the night from 20 to 21 June, though without inflicting any casualties, while a second device exploded on 2 July in another area, injuring four people. On 14 August, another homemade bomb exploded in a bar, seriously injuring two people. A further nine people sustained injuries under similar circumstances on the evening of 1 November. The authorities reacted by stepping up police operations and vehicle searches, while at the same time intensifying the screening of people entering and leaving Yaoundé.

They did not provide any information on those who had planted the bombs or on their motives. Speculation that these incidents could be linked to the war in the Anglophone regions was voiced in the media.

The level of *corruption* remained high: Transparency International ranked the country 149th out of 180 in the 2020 Corruption Perceptions Index, making it one of the 30 most corrupt nations in the world. At the end of the year, the national anti-corruption commission (CONAC by its French acronym) published a report indicating that in 2019, the Ministry of Finance had been the most corrupt, followed by the ministries of State Property and Land Tenure, Defence, Justice, Transport, Public Procurement, Public Works, and Education. In April, Cameroon ratified the AU Convention on Preventing and Combating Corruption, which had been adopted in 2003 in Maputo.

Foreign Affairs

The war in the two Anglophone regions was a permanent source of tension between the government and its Western partners. The Ngarbuh and Kumba massacres provoked strong reactions abroad. The *United Nations* and international human rights organisations called upon Cameroon to take appropriate action on several occasions. This was particularly the case following the Ngarbuh massacre: the UNSG urged the government to open an investigation, while the Office of the UN High Commissioner for Human Rights declared that Cameroonian authorities need to ensure that their security forces comply with the norms of international law. The condemnations were just as numerous after the attack on schoolchildren in Kumba. Through its embassy in Cameroon, the US called for an end to the violence. The chairperson of the AU Commission, Moussa Faki Mahamat, expressed his horror at the attack, as did the French ambassador to Cameroon, who demanded that the perpetrators of this crime be brought to justice and sentenced accordingly. The EU, the UN, the UK, Canada, and Pope Francis also condemned the murders.

The Anglophone crisis was also one of the topics discussed at the UNSC meeting of 9 December. The report of the representative of the UN Regional Office for Central Africa (UNOCA) expressed his concern at the ongoing attacks on civilians by both non-governmental armed groups and security forces. The US advocated a political solution and called for a genuine dialogue between the conflicting parties, a position supported by Germany. The *Russian Federation and China*, for their part, opposed any interference in Cameroon's internal affairs.

On 31 December, in his traditional end-of-year speech, President Biya indirectly criticised his Western partners by urging them to take action against the sponsors and organisations which, according to him, finance and run the armed groups in the Anglophone regions – an allusion to certain members of the Cameroonian diaspora abroad whom the security services of Cameroon consider to be active in the armed conflict.

Tensions arose with *France* after the Ngarbuh massacre. Paris initially condemned these 'acts of violence' and demanded that 'those responsible be held accountable for their actions'. But a few days later, the French head of state, Emmanuel Macron, made rather undiplomatic comments while addressing an activist, leader of the 'Brigade anti-sardinards' (BAS, a group of activists living in France who sympathise with the MRC), who questioned him over the events in Ngarbuh while he was visiting the Paris International Agricultural Show. The French president spoke of intolerable acts of violence and promised to 'exert maximum pressure' on Paul Biya in order to ensure that an investigation was opened. The next day, the Cameroonian government responded to Macron's comments by issuing a communiqué explaining that it intended to remain master of its own destiny and asking 'friendly countries' not to grant credit to 'activists'. Relations between the two capitals appeared to improve somewhat after a telephone conversation between Emmanuel Macron and Paul Biya on 1 March. A few weeks later, another dispute broke out between Paris and opponents of the MRC. It began with a meeting, on 16 April in Yaoundé, between the French ambassador to Cameroon, Christophe Guilhou, and President Biya. Shortly afterwards, Christophe Guilhou gave an interview on national television in which he stated that the Cameroonian president was 'still alert'. At the same time, however, a rumour that President Biya had died a few weeks earlier, or was in any case incapable of leading the country, was circulating within the ranks of the MRC. The diplomat's statement was immediately criticised by MRC activists, who accused him of playing into the hands of the government. Certain activists even went as far as to claim that the images of the meeting between the two men that had been posted by the president's office were the result of a photomontage. They started a petition to demand the 'immediate departure' of the ambassador of France from Cameroon. On 27 April, during a press conference, the French ministry of foreign affairs was compelled to defend its ambassador in order to put an end to the polemic.

In early October, the government of CAR warned its Cameroonian counterpart that a rebel commander named General Fafour had created a new armed group that was said to have been baptised 'Mouvement de Libération du Cameroun' (MLC) and aimed to combat the Cameroonian government. On 23 December, shortly before the presidential election in CAR, over a hundred Central African soldiers fled to Cameroon by way of Garoua-Boulaï, a border town in the East region. They were disarmed and taken in charge by the Cameroonian army. Some 1,600 civilians also crossed the border, including about 200 Chinese citizens. A few days later, the minister of foreign affairs, LeJeune Mbella Mbella, gave the official position of his country on the conflict in CAR during an extraordinary CEEAC summit which was held by videoconference: he stated that Cameroon condemned any attempt, in whatever form, to destabilise republican institutions in CAR. Towards the end of the year, the Cameroonian army was engaged in military operations against rebels originating from CAR at the border between the two countries.

Socioeconomic Developments

Due to the Covid-19 pandemic, the Cameroonian economy experienced a *negative growth* rate of –2.5% according to the World Bank, as compared with +3.7% in 2019. The government was forced to revise its budget in the course of the year. The budget law for 2020 initially provided for a balanced budget of CFAfr 4,951.7 bn (about € 7.54 bn), a decrease of 5% compared with the revised budget of 2019 (such a decrease had not been seen in roughly ten years). Domestic revenues were set at CFAfr 3,545.2 bn, a drop of 2.3%. Loans and grants were expected to drop by 9.5%, as were oil revenues (–12.5% over the year, at CFAfr 443 bn), based on an anticipated oil barrel price of $ 55.3 (compared with $ 57.9 in 2019). Non-oil revenues were also expected to decline (–0.7%) due to the production stop affecting the National Refining Company (Sonara), the debt of which exceeded CFAfr 780 bn, meaning that revenues stemming from VAT and turnover tax would drop significantly. Debt servicing was scheduled to decrease from CFAfr 1,283 bn in 2019 to 1,011.9 bn in 2020. The servicing of foreign debt was set at CFAfr 472.2 bn (–12.7% over the year), that of domestic debt at CFAfr 539.7 bn (–27.3%). The budgets of several ministries increased: +12% for the Ministry of Public Works (+ CFAfr 50.7 bn for a total of CFAfr 459.6 bn), +8% for the Ministry of Water Resources and Energy (+ CFAfr 17.6 bn for a total of CFAfr 244.2 bn). The expenditures for education and health were also due to rise: +5% for education, +3.3% for health. Operating costs were to remain stable, but personnel expenses were to increase by 3.3% to CFAfr 1,066.2 bn.

In June, the budget was thus revised downwards to 4,049 bn (about € 6.17 bn) due to the pandemic. It provided for the creation of a Special National Solidarity Fund of CFAfr 180 bn for the fight against the coronavirus and its economic and social repercussions, which was intended to cover the expenses of the national action plan to stop the spread of the virus (case detection, care of those who contracted the virus, etc.). The country was nevertheless relatively spared by the pandemic, with very few people requiring hospitalisation and a rather low mortality rate at year's end (26,277 reported cases, 448 deaths). Covid-19 bed occupancy was around 1% at the end of the year.

The economic repercussions, on the other hand, were more severe due to the *falling commodity prices* (cocoa and oil) and the *decline in foreign trade*. Very early on, just after Cameroon announced its first case of Covid-19 infection, on 6 March, the authorities closed its land, sea, and air borders, with negative consequences for the economy. In August, the Groupement inter-patronal du Cameroun (GICAM), Cameroon's most important employers' organisation, concluded from a survey of more than 250 businesses (75% of which were small and medium-sized companies and 25% large enterprises) that 96% of them had been negatively impacted. Roughly 53,000 permanent employees were on short-time work, representing 13.6% of the total permanent workforce, and approximately 14,000 had been laid off. The GICAM estimated that in terms of absolute value, annual losses in the modern business sector could amount to CFAfr 3,139 bn (about € 4.77 bn) relative to 2019 and lead to a state revenue shortfall of CFAfr 521 bn (about € 791 m). The most affected sectors were food manufacturers, financial services, insurance companies, hotels, and restaurants. In April, the Cameroonian authorities relaxed the restrictions that had been imposed in response to the health crisis and announced a series of measures to help businesses whose existence was threatened by it. In May, the IMF approved a disbursement of $ 226 m under the Rapid Credit Facility (RCF) in order to help Cameroon deal with the crisis, which was aggravated by the sharp fall in oil prices. This was followed by a second disbursement of $ 156 m in October. Earlier in the year, it had also approved a Cameroonian request to extend an agreement concluded under the terms of the ECF, which was set to expire on 25 June, and granted an extension until 30 September. By the end of the year, Cameroon's *public debt* amounted to 40% of GDP.

Despite protests from the EU, Cameroon decided to *suspend the progressive tariff reductions* required by the EPA that had been concluded with the EU in 2006, invoking a case of force majeure, a provision laid down in the Vienna Convention on the Law of Treaties of 1969. This decision delayed the fifth stage of the timetable, in which Cameroon was to reduce the customs duties on products of the second category by 45–60% and to begin dismantling tariffs on products of the third category (fuels, cement, passenger and commercial vehicles, motorcycles). Products of the first category had been entirely exempt from duties since 4 August 2019. On 31 March, the customs authorities reported that the budget revenue shortfall resulting from the implementation of the EPA had reached CFAfr 16 bn.

The country also decided not to implement a reform advocated by the World Bank, which concerned the *remuneration of civil servants*. According to the World Bank, the wages of Cameroonian civil servants are among the lowest in sub-Saharan Africa, the highest monthly salary being CFAfr 330,000 and the lowest CFAfr 44,000. The government has adopted the practice of supplementing these low salaries with various allowances and bonuses, as exemplified by the system of daily allowances for public officials participating in committees, commissions, or special meetings. Having become an important source of income, this arrangement has led to a proliferation of committees and meetings, and to considerable delays in administrative and decision-making processes, according to the World Bank. It has also increased inequalities within the system, since not all categories of civil servants have benefited from the arrangement.

In late November, the government revealed its new *economic plan* for the next ten years (until 2030). Published under the name National Development Strategy (NDS), it replaced the Growth and Employment Strategy Paper (GESP) that had expired in December 2019. With this plan, Cameroon declared its intention to transform its economy by promoting 'an endogenous and inclusive development' that privileges local production. It aimed to pave more than 6,000 km of road, improve the rate of access to drinking water to 60%, guarantee access to primary education for all children of school age, create more than 300,000 jobs a year, reduce the unemployment rate to 25%, and boost oil production by exploring the Bakassi peninsula and the northern part of the country. Its goal was to achieve an annual growth rate of 8.1% (compared with 4% during the period 2010–19). Various economists expressed misgivings about the feasibility of this plan, particularly with regard to its monitoring and evaluation aspects, which they deemed too vague.

The *mining sector* witnessed a few innovations. The government created a national mining corporation (Sonamines), which was given the task of developing and promoting the sector and of representing the interests of the state in this domain. *Gold* mining remained an important economic factor in the East, involving thousands of artisanal gold panners as well as licensed mining societies. However, the sale of this gold remained largely unregulated: according to estimates, barely 5% of the country's gold production was sold through official channels. As a result, the BEAC did not recognise Cameroon as a producer or exporter of gold in a report published at year's end. In the *oil sector*, the search for new oilfields had to be interrupted in Bakassi (Southwest) and in Zina/Makary (Far North) due to the security crisis. With Hilli Episeyo, the floating natural gas liquefaction plant put into service off the coast of Kribi in 2018 and operated by the Franco-British Perenco Group, Cameroon's leading oil and gas producer, the country became one of Turkey's four African gas suppliers. A new gas platform named Sanaga 2 was installed off the coast of Kribi in order to help maintain the gas production levels necessary to supply the Hilli Episeyo plant.

Central African Republic

Andreas Mehler

General elections at year's end were contested by the opposition and violently interrupted by a new rebel coalition. The absence of any positive perspective was the responsibility not of ordinary people but of both government elites and rebel movements. The plight of CAR's citizens continued unabated. The internationally brokered peace plan of 2019 ultimately failed, representing a failure not only of the government but also of international mediators, who had courted ruthless rebel leaders and coup-makers. The consequences of the Covid-19 pandemic only added to an already bleak situation.

Domestic Politics

One main event of the last weeks of 2019 signalled more trouble to come. The country's erstwhile coup-maker and autocrat president *François Bozizé* (2003–2013) had returned to the country with obvious political ambitions. Only a few weeks later, the exiled rebel leader and short-term president (ten months in 2013–14) Michael Djotodia also returned to the country, on 10 January. President Faustin Archange

Touadéra met Bozizé and Djotodia on 21 January, earning international praise for this openness. The president's domestic popularity declined, however. Defections increased from Touadéra's support base across many political parties. At a press conference on 27 January, Bozizé alluded to the possibility of his standing again in upcoming elections and gradually extending his influence.

In parallel, the political opposition tried to close ranks. Touadéra's main rival in past years, Anicet-Georges Dologuélé attracted the support of Bozizé's Kwa Na Kwa party (KNK); he also gained official support from part of the former (1981–1993) ruling party Rassemblement Démocratique Centrafricain (RDC), though some RDC heavyweights remained loyal to Touadéra. On 11 February, 14 opposition parties formally launched the Coalition de l'opposition démocratique 2020 (*COD-2020*) as a new platform. Most prominently, KNK; the Convention républicaine pour le progrès social of former interim prime minister Nicolas Tiangaye; the deposed speaker of the national assembly Karim Meckassoua; and the Be Africa Ti E Kwe of former prime minister Mahamat Kamoun were among these parties. Bozizé assumed the presidency of the platform in late September.

Touadéra's camp reacted. On 15 May, 34 parties officially launched the *Be Oko* political platform, literally 'United Hearts'. Touadéra had used that label already last year. Be Oko was meant to make sure that one single candidate from the platform would be fielded in presidential elections, but also in each constituency at legislative elections. This aim proved futile when it became clear that at least four Be Oko supporters would want to stand in presidential elections, most prominently Touadéra himself and Martin Ziguélé of the established Mouvement de libération du peuple Centrafricain (MLPC).

The build-up of tensions within the political elite continued when the government backed a petition from a large majority in parliament to prorogate the mandate of the legislature and the president in the event of an instance of 'force majeure', which was obviously easy to demonstrate by invoking the Covid-19 crisis. However, the constitutional court declared the proposed amendment unconstitutional, arguing that any changes to the fixed electoral calendar should derive from broad national consultations and represent a consensus. Such a consensus was not in sight. The opposition complained about many non-transparent moves of the government in preparing the elections. On 7 August, Touadéra fixed the terms of the composition and organisation of the National Electoral Authority (ANE). A commission comprising representatives from political parties, the public administration, and civil society thereupon selected 11 new ANE commissioners on 14 October, who were subsequently appointed by presidential decree. On 26 October, the constitutional court permitted candidates of 27 political parties to run for the legislative elections, though most parties failed to meet the 35% quota for female candidates.

In the first half of the year, the government stuck to the peace plan. But in the *south-east* the government and the UN Multidimensional Integrated Stabilization

Mission in the Central African Republic (MINUSCA by its French acronym) had a hard time keeping up with the aggressive stance of the Union pour la paix en Centrafrique (UPC) rebel group. On 9 January, two soldiers were killed, reportedly by UPC elements, in Alindao, 20 civilians injured, and a displaced persons camp burned. Subsequently, MINUSCA dismantled illegal UPC barriers in the town. Further to the east, in Bangassou, local authorities, representatives of communities, and armed group leaders managed to sign a local peace agreement permitting the free movement of goods and people on the Rafai–Dembia–Zemio axis. Still further to the east, the situation remained problematic: on 20 May, MINUSCA and the armed forces exchanged fire with UPC elements in Obo. Six UPC combatants were arrested and transferred to Bangui, all others expelled from town. On 20 and again on 28 May, UPC leader Ali Darassa condemned alleged armed forces abuses of the civilian population in Obo and denied UPC involvement. Partly confirming such allegations, a soldier was arrested by local command for killing a civilian on 2 June. Nearly forgotten, the Lord's Resistance Army (LRA) still operated around Obo, ambushing traders but also attacking villages and towns, including Obo, and abducting people in July and September.

In the main eastern hotbed of intergroup violence, the Front populaire pour la renaissance de la Centrafrique (FPRC) and UPC struggled for influence, but the area also saw some ethnically coloured in-fighting: on 25 and 26 January, Kara and Runga factions of the FPRC clashed brutally in Bria, leading to about 50 casualties and the displacement of 11,000 people. On 10 March, UPC leader Darassa, travelled to Bria with heavily armed elements to broker a ceasefire between FPRC factions after a Fulani fighter of the FPRC had been killed in detention. This obviously was also meant to assert the UPC's dominance in the region. In July, the FPRC obstructed the recruitment of internal security forces in Bria, and one auxiliary checkpoint was burned down on 16 July. The UPC and its defiant leader were clearly a source of concern to the government. Prime Minister Firmin Ngrebada met Darassa on 30 July – with limited success. Instead, on 20 September, Darassa signed an agreement with another warlord, Mahamat Al-Khatim of the Mouvement Patriotique pour la Centrafrique (MPC), to establish a permanent framework of consultation.

In the far *north-east*, fighting between the Mouvement des libérateurs centrafricains pour la justice (MLCJ) and the FPRC resumed in Takamala and Bougaye in the second half of January. On 16 February, the FPRC attempted to retake control of the key town Birao from the MLCJ. MINUSCA intervened in a robust fashion, killing 11 FPRC combatants. On 14 March, government troops were deployed after the area had been declared a weapons-free zone. In Ndélé, the Goula faction of the FPRC attacked the Runga community and Arabs, killing at least 29, including 18 civilians, in a nearby village; in a nearby village, the same groups clashed on 25 March, also producing numerous casualties. On 15 March, Goula elements ambushed a

MINUSCA patrol. In Ndiffa, the smaller Parti du rassemblement de la nation centrafricaine (PRNC) armed group and the community of Misseriya Arabs clashed on 27 March; the chief of staff of the PRNC and six Misseriya were killed. The PRNC was held responsible for further violence in May and July. On 18 April, Misseriya herders ambushed five Goula merchants near Birao, killing three and seriously injuring two. Prime Minister Ngrebada started a mediation process between the Goula and Runga factions of the FPRC (24–27 April) in Bangui. Ngrebada also met with FPRC leader Abdoulaye Hissène, in Bangui on 25 April, permitting the deployment of national armed forces to Ndélé for the first time since 2013. However, on 29 and 30 April a further attack by Goula fighters killed at least 27 people, most of them civilians, in the area. On 9–10 November, the government held a peace conference in Bangui including representatives of Runga and Goula in the Vakaga, Haute-Kotto, and Bamingui-Bangoran prefectures. Thirteen ethnic communities and eight signatory armed groups agreed to a reconciliation pact to end violence.

The typical confrontation between Fulani herders and local communities, each supported by organised armed groups, continued in the *north-west*. Clashes in late February resulted in the deaths of at least four herders and two civilians near Batangafo. Control of precious resources was also a motivation for violent acts. On 29 March, clashes erupted between the MPC and FPRC around the Kouki gold mine, killing one person and leading to the internal displacement of about 100 individuals. The UPC saw a window of opportunity to extend its presence around Markounda. Partly as a response, a Markounda Coalition was announced on 9 July, comprising the MPC, Anti-balaka (Mokom branch), the FPRC, and the Révolution et Justice (Sayo branch). In the *west*, the 3R (Rétour, Reclamation et Réhabilitation) group extended its area of operation. Therefore, MINUSCA launched an operation against 3R on 10 April. In May, 3R temporarily occupied the gendarmerie station of Besson (Nana-Mambéré Prefecture) and extended its presence in western Ouham Prefecture to control gold mining sites. On 5 June, 3R leader Abbas Sidiki announced the suspension of his participation in the follow-up and monitoring mechanisms of the Political Agreement for Peace and Reconciliation until further notice; probably it was also 3R which attacked the camp of the special mixed security units in Bouar (injuring 15) and a MINUSCA checkpoint near Paoua, injuring two peacekeepers. Again in Besson, 3R killed three army soldiers during combat on 21 June. An anti-tank mine destroyed a MINUSCA vehicle on 13 July (killing one peacekeeper and injuring three) during an operation against 3R. This event was significant as it was the *first reported use of landmines* in CAR. Already on 17 June, Sidiki and Darassa had signed an MoU to formalise a 3R/UPC alliance, with the implicit aim of defending Fulani interests but officially to coordinate security and transhumance in their respective areas of operations. In mid-2020, it looked as if two solid coalitions of competing armed groups were forming, but later the game of knitting new alliances started anew. On 5 October, a government delegation and international guarantors of the Political Agreement met the 3R leader with limited success; in November 3R again extended its operations in three (North)Western prefectures.

Despite increased crime levels in its PK 5 neighbourhood and frequent violence against humanitarian organisations, *Bangui* was comparatively quiet until the hot election phase in December, but this was not the situation at some distance from the capital. On 15 March, Anti-balaka launched an attack on the town of Grimari (central CAR), killing a Burundian peacekeeper.

In cooperation with MINUSCA, the government also continued with *disarmament and demobilisation* processes and the build-up of the special mixed security units – again with limited success. Such special mixed security units remained non-operational in Bouar and Paoua. Many of their elements deserted or defected, often with their weapons. MINUSCA blamed the lack of internal cohesion, command, and control, but also interpersonal tensions, for this failure. Disarmament and demobilisation operations in the east (Bria, Kaga-Bandoro, Ndélé) included 773 combatants of different armed groups permitting the collection of 579 weapons of war, 16,134 rounds of ammunition, and 174 explosives – but this had limited effects on conflict dynamics. In sum, over half a year (April–September) the number of recorded violations of the Political Agreement went up from 504 in the previous reporting period to 644. Other elements of the peace plan progressed. On 7 April, Touadéra officially established the *Commission on Truth, Justice, Reparation and Reconciliation*, which *inter alia* was charged with identifying the root causes of human rights abuses; dignifying the experiences of victims; and proposing a reparations programme. Also, the Special Criminal Court was still active in investigating ten priority cases.

The presidential elections again became the most prominent bone of contention when, on 3 December, the constitutional court decided to invalidate five of the 22 *presidential candidates*, including Bozizé (but also armed group leader Armel Sayo). Quite stringently, the court argued that Bozizé failed to meet the 'good morality' requirement as he was under UN sanctions plus under an international arrest warrant issued in 2014 for alleged assassinations and other crimes. The KNK denounced the decision, but publicly called for restraint. From this point on, Bozizé officially supported the approved candidacy of Dologuélé (as the most promising candidate within the COD-2020). Other validated candidates included Touadéra, three sons of former presidents (Jean-Serge Bokassa, Sylvain Patassé, Désiré Kolingba), three former prime ministers (Kamoun, Ziguélé, Tiangaye), and a former parliament speaker (Meckassoua). The only female candidate was Catherine Samba-Panza, interim head of state, in 2014. The constitutional court also validated 1,504 candidates running for the national assembly, including 234 women (a nearly 16% increase).

Despite his declarations, Bozizé retreated to his stronghold Bossangoa, consulted with MPC leader Al-Khatim on 4 December, and also met other leaders of armed groups in a bid to rally their support. The *Convention des patriotes pour le changement* (CPC), created as a result, was hitherto the biggest armed coalition against a sitting government in CAR. It comprised UPC, FRPC, 3R, MPC, and two Anti-balaka groups – thereby uniting former arch-enemies with the sole aim of toppling Touadéra's government. Security incidents were augmented, not least in the north-west. National security forces searched the homes of several political figures (Bozizé, his eldest son, Anti-balaka leader Maxime Mokom), on unclear grounds. On 23 December, the house of Bozizé's son in Bangui was set on fire under the watch of the Presidential Guard.

The *elections* were overshadowed by violence. Already during voter registration, armed movements had disturbed the process, e.g. in Zemio (UPC) and Yalinga (FPRC). National armed forces abandoned positions in the prefectures of Bamingui-Bangoran, Lobaye, Mbomou, Nana-Grébizi, Nana-Mambéré, Ombella-M'Poko, Ouaka, and Ouham-Pendé. The electoral campaign (limited to a period of two weeks, 12 to 25 December) could not go smoothly under such circumstances. Several legislative candidates associated with the Be Oko platform (as well as independents) were physically attacked. Also, the COD-2020 suspended its campaign on 19 December, citing insecurity and irregularities. The heteroclite alliance called for a postponement of the elections and the holding of national consultations. Finally, coordinated military attacks on three main axes connecting Bangui and the hinterland hit the towns of Baboua, Bambari, Bossembélé, Bozoum, Grimari, and Sibut between 18 and 23 December; civilians were caught in cross-fire when they sought refuge. On 25 December, three peacekeepers were killed in fierce fighting in Dekoa, close to Bangui. A military conquest of the capital appeared possible, but – mobilising all their reserves – MINUSCA contingents efficiently fought back such attempts. Still, the constitutional court rejected calls to postpone the elections the next day. On 27 December (election day), CPC elements attacked voting centres in Ouham, Ouham-Pendé, Nana-Mambéré (north-west/west) and Ombella-M'Poko (centre) prefectures. In the east too (in Bria and Yalinga particularly), polling stations had to be closed after shootings and acts of destruction. While election results were not announced before the end of the year, the recorded participation rate was already telling: a total of 695,019 voters had cast their ballots, representing 37.4% of registered voters. Only 3,243 out of 5,448 polling stations (59.5%) were operational. With regard to legislative elections, the vote could not take place for 58 of the 140 seats. On the positive side, elections were peacefully conducted in Ndélé, pointing to the success of government-led mediation in the Runga–Goula confrontation. Predictably, the opposition called for the vote to be annulled, arguing that the process did not comply with constitutional and legal requirements.

On 31 December, the president revoked the appointments of Mokom as minister of disarmament, demobilisation, reinsertion, and repatriation and Abbas Sidiki (3R), Al-Khatim (MPC), and Darassa (UPC) as advisors to the prime minister.

The 2019 *peace plan ultimately broke down* – already on 15 December, the aforementioned groups had distanced themselves from the *Political Agreement for Peace and Reconciliation* in a joint declaration. It was no surprise, therefore, that several armed groups subsequently attempted to obstruct the elections, successfully in some places. Bozizé was clearly prepared for yet another coup (after unsuccessful attempts in 1982 and 2001, plus the successful one in 2003), though it was improbable that he controlled the four armed groups originating in the former Séléka alliance.

Foreign Affairs

Sponsors of the internationally brokered peace plan of 2019 did not openly acknowledge its failure, but some key lingering questions came to the fore again: why was former president Bozizé never arrested despite an international arrest warrant? On what basis rested the hope of taming the different armed groups whose leaders were courted in all sorts of negotiations, but who nevertheless constantly showed disrespect to the clauses of the pact? What political will to reconcile could be credited to a government that equally restricted political rights and sought international military support outside the peace plan?

The coronavirus prohibited the conducting of intense *travel diplomacy* in the second part of the year. Some highlights merit reporting, however. On 22 April, Touadéra officially visited the DRC and the *Congo*, both facilitators of the Political Agreement. In June, President Denis Sassou Nguesso of Congo – himself a two-times coup leader – met with Bozizé and Meckassoua in Brazzaville as part of efforts to advance political dialogue. In July, the UN under-secretary-general for peace operations, Jean-Pierre Lacroix, and the AU commissioner for peace and security, Smaïl Chergui, engaged with Prime Minister Ngrebada on the political and peace processes. On 24 September, Chergui, Lacroix, and the president of the CEEAC Commission, Gilberto Da Piedade Veríssimo (Angola), issued a joint call on national stakeholders to engage in political dialogue in order to conduct peaceful, credible, and inclusive elections within constitutional timelines. UNSG António Guterres himself convened a high-level meeting on the margins of the 75th session of the UNGA, including Touadéra, the chairperson of the AU, Moussa Faki Mahamat, and Da Piedade Veríssimo. The special representative of the UNSG for Central Africa and the CEEAC Commission president visited CAR in December and finally, amid the full crisis, Sassou Nguesso convened an extraordinary meeting of CEEAC heads of state on 26 December. All of these hectic diplomatic efforts did not produce the envisaged results.

CAR was constantly on the agenda of diverse *UN institutions*, from the UNSC to WFP and most clearly the UN peacekeeping mission itself. On 2 February, the

UNSC approved another slight relaxation of the arms embargo, under pressure from Russia. On 20 April, the UNSC sanctions committee added to their list warlord Martin Kountamadji, alias Abdoulaye Miskine, leader of the Front démocratique du peuple centrafricain (FDPC), who was an early spoiler of the peace agreement in 2019. On 5 August, Bi Sidi Souleymane, alias Abbas Sidiki, (3R) was also put under UN sanctions. Defections and desertions among the newly formed mixed security units compelled MINUSCA to assume all sorts of security tasks around the elections. During these, approximately 50 (out of 71) sub-prefectures were not covered by either the armed forces or internal security forces. Official security forces even abandoned their posts and sought protection in MINUSCA bases. MINUSCA increasingly opted for robust responses and was mostly effective in this. The mission also received two infantry companies and two military utility helicopters from the United Nations Mission in South Sudan (UNMISS). Over the year, MINUSCA suffered six fatalities (five peacekeepers, one civilian).

The government sought support from traditional and more recent partners. By the end of December, the government claimed that Russia and Rwanda were sending hundreds of troops into the country ahead of the presidential and parliamentary polls as a reaction to the attacks by the new rebel alliance. *Rwanda*'s President Kagame claimed that the additional support would operate 'within the legitimate and legal framework'. *Russia* had confirmed that it would send additional 'military instructors' only, but 300 of them. However, it was clear that Moscow was one of the strongest supporters of Touadéra: Russia had given military support to the government, including amphibious vehicles, earlier in the year. For Russia, a further set-back (after the futile involvement of mercenaries in Mozambique) in the CAR would have been a heavy blow to its reputation. The promise to deal with insurgents in a cost-effective manner had been the main selling strategy for a new engagement on the African continent. Russia, in 2020/21 holding the rotating chair of the Kimberley Process, meant to curb the trade of blood diamonds reportedly tried to get CAR removed fully from the diamond export ban list.

In some instances, mostly at year's end, defected soldiers crossed into neighbouring countries, and were disarmed, as was the case with about one hundred of them stranded in Cameroon (along with civilians and Chinese nationals). Direct neighbours obviously had to live with consequences of new waves of violence.

The *French government* – resenting the Russian influence in Bangui – was not openly supportive of the government, but sent war planes for a fly-over mission in December after President Emmanuel Macron had condemned attempts to disrupt the elections. However, just like the EU and member states Germany, Italy, and the Netherlands, plus Switzerland, France contributed to the € 300 m Békou Trust Fund, which was partially used to combat the Covid-19 pandemic.

Socioeconomic Developments

The pandemic did not spare landlocked CAR. President Touadéra announced a series of mitigation measures to combat the spread of the virus in March, including a 21-day quarantine for people entering the country and any suspected *Covid-19* cases and their contacts, a temporary ban on gatherings of more than 15 people, and the temporary closure of schools. On 27 April, authorities restricted commercial and passenger movements on key axes from Bangui to towns bordering Cameroon – the lifeline for all imported products – and on the Ubangi river. Overall, the drop in external demand resulted in a marked slowdown in economic activity in the first half of the year. According to the IMF, the most affected sectors were transport, tourism, hotels, and the mining sectors. In June, the EU allocated € 54 m as additional budgetary support to help the government to address the socioeconomic risks associated with the health crisis; an additional € 14 m was granted in December. Officially, close to 5,000 coronavirus cases (and about 60 deaths) were reported at year's end. The Covid-19 pandemic also had other negative repercussions: food prices went up, partly related to higher transportation costs, and inflation rose. Measures proposed by donor organisations to contain the pandemic, such as wearing masks, met with strongly limited means to procure such items, but also limited acceptance: keeping distance at social gatherings (like funerals or weddings) was considered difficult, according to a survey conducted by the NGO Ground Truth Solutions and funded by UNICEF and the Danish refugee council.

According to OCHA, the number of people in need had increased over the year from 2.6 m to 2.8 m, i.e. about 57% of the population relied on humanitarian assistance. But respondents among people in need to an enquiry again conducted by Ground Truth Solutions in four sub-prefectures and published in June saw the assistance as well below their needs: only 17% believed that assistance covered their essential needs, and only 15% that assistance was available when it was needed. In October, the WFP provided in-kind food assistance to over 500,000 affected people across the country, and some 280,000 people also received food assistance through cash-based transfers, but those in areas difficult to reach, e.g. in the north-east, were frequently left without assistance. In fact, about 1 m people in need were not even targeted by humanitarian organisations. The number of refugees and IDPs at year's end stood at equal numbers, namely 631,000 in each category.

Inundations in August and September hit five sub-prefectures in the east, and further torrential rains destroyed houses and harvest in four locations in different areas of the country in October.

The IMF projected a *decrease of GDP* per capita by 1.8% in the reporting year. Overall, it saw the perceptible negative impact of the pandemic contained in October. In a staff report issued on 9 October, it noted that the authorities were unable to meet the objectives set under the programme supported by the ECF due to the pandemic. This meant that most performance criteria could not be met and significant delays were experienced in the implementation of structural reforms. In fact, the budget and current account deficits increased (to 6% and 6.5% of GDP respectively).

The World Bank expected the demand for CAR's main export commodities (i.e., timber, but also diamond, coffee, and cotton) to fall significantly during the global crisis, particularly as China accounted for 44% of total exports. The pandemic effectively disrupted the legal trade of gold and diamonds. Prices fell abruptly, although those for *gold* recovered after a reopening of borders in May. In April, Amnesty International called on the government to suspend the operations of four Chinese firms at a gold mining site on the Ouham river close to Bozoum, which could impact on the local residents' livelihoods. This site was already the object of a parliamentary investigation in 2019, its report describing the situation as an 'ecological disaster'; that investigation had been dismissed by the government. In addition, armed groups competed for control of mining sites, e.g. near Markounda and Kouki in Ouham Prefecture. Media reports hinted at a sharp increase of child labour in diamond mines after the closing of schools as a response to the Covid-19 pandemic.

Chad

Ketil Fred Hansen

President Déby continued to rule by decree, fear, and personal loyalties. Using the fight against Covid-19 as a pretext, the regime restricted human rights for its opponents and critics. Demonstrations were not permitted, and protests were terminated by the police, sometimes even before they started. Elections for the general assembly, postponed numerous times since 2015 and now scheduled for December, were again postponed. Chad contributed to the international fight against terror by providing troops to both the UN-led Multidimensional Integrated Stabilisation Mission in Mali (MINUSMA) and the Nigerian-led Multinational Joint Task Force (MNJTF). Both the number of refugees and the number of IDPs continued to rise, to around 500,000 refugees and 400,000 IDPs respectively.

Domestic Politics

Media freedom was restricted by the regime throughout the year. For example, for writing on Facebook that President Idriss Déby was seriously ill and hospitalised in France, human rights defender Baradine Berdei Targuio was arrested by the National Security Agency (ANS) on 24 January and kept in custody awaiting charges and sentencing for the rest of the year. On hunger strike since 2 March, the director of the newspaper 'Salam Info', Martin Inoua Doulguet, was liberated on 23 April after spending 36 weeks in prison for publishing information about undisclosed public–private procurements of real estate. On 8 June, the High Authority for Media and Audiovisual (HAMA) accused the well-reputed N'Djamena-based newspaper 'Abba Garde' of spreading fake news and suspended its publication for 12 months. On 22 July, the government slowed down the speed of the internet, officially only 'temporarily', to reduce hate speech on social platforms. By mid-September, the speed was still not upgraded. On 7 September, the HAMA suspended another 12 newspapers for non-conformity with the law, stating, among other things, that the chief editor had to be a formally educated journalist.

The police used tear-gas and hit journalists at FM Liberté, a renowned private radio station in N'Djamena, on 27 November, as they interviewed human rights defenders and organisers of an alternative 'Forum Citoyen 2020', an event forbidden by the regime 'due to Covid-19'. Among those present on this occasion was human rights defender Alain Kemba Didah, who was imprisoned and charged with an 'act of rebellion and disturbance of public order' but found not guilty and released on 11 December.

Protesting against the police violence and arrests, private radio stations in Chad stayed off the air for the entire day on 1 December. Chad occupied rank 123 out of 180 on the World Press Freedom Index, one place down from the previous year.

Other human rights issues were also at stake. On 8 January, the renowned human rights defender Mahamat Nour Ibedou, imprisoned since 5 December 2019 and accused of complicity in murder, was found not guilty and released. Against the trend of imposing threats and harsh punishments, the national assembly voted unanimously, on 29 April, to abolish the death sentence, which had been legalised in 2015 as the most severe punishments for acts of terror. On 20 May, President Déby signed Law 003/PR, which formally eliminated the death penalty, making lifelong imprisonment the harshest penalty. On 13 November, Déby pronounced publicly that same-sex marriage was an unacceptable, negative Western value that had no place in African democracies like Chad.

During the second *Inclusive National Forum*, bringing together some 600 delegates invited by the regime and held in the three last days of October, police surrounded and surveyed the headquarters of opposition political parties. Succès Masra from the political party *Transformateur* was held in custody in his home to prevent him from trying to attend the forum. He was not formally invited to participate, as his party is not recognised as such by the regime. Human rights defenders at the Chadian League for Human Rights (LTDH) were intimidated and held hostage in their own offices by special police agents during the three-day forum, which discussed and evaluated the 2018 constitution. Suggested changes were later voted on by the national assembly and some of them incorporated into the constitution on

3 December. These included the creation of the post of vice-president, the establishment of a senate, and the lowering of the minimum age for presidential candidates from 45 to 40 years.

The presidency 'upgraded' its website. Compared with the former design, only a very few decrees and a sporadic sample of the president's speeches were made available on the new site, while it remained close to every step first lady Hinda Déby made and all of her public donations were widely published. This was in line with other developments: powerful and rewarding public positions were still filled with relatives of the president or first lady. Two examples included the nominations on 17 March of Fatimé Idriss Déby, one of the president's daughters, as vice-director of the oil refinery in N'Djamena and Abderahmane Mahamat Acyl, a brother of the first lady, as the vice-director of the Chadian Oil Company (SHT). President Déby's own position was also enhanced, as he was nominated 'Maréchal', the ultimate level in the military hierarchy, by the national assembly in late June and invested with the title on National Day, 11 August. Critics made comparisons to the lavishness of Zaïre's former president Mobutu and the CAR's former president Bokassa and called this symbolic militarisation of politics anachronistic.

The *personalisation of politics* also continued; Déby issued 2,285 decrees, some of them issued to change important positions within the bureaucracy or the government. Changing members of government at will on numerous occasions, the most important changes took place on 15 July when 14 new ministers were nominated together with six state secretaries. Among the most important was the nomination of Amine Abba Sidick as minister of foreign affairs. Sidick had until then been Chad's ambassador to France. Another was the creation of a ministry of security and immigration, given to Mahamat Tahir Orozi.

Boko Haram increased its violent attacks in Chad and the regime intensified its fight against the politico-military group and various splinter groups. On 20 January, a female suicide bomber blew herself up in the village of Kaiga Kindjiria, killing nine civilians. A week later, on 27 January, six soldiers were killed on Tetewa Island. In early March, a Boko Haram faction killed 14 in a village bordering Lake Chad. The deadliest attack, however, took place during the night between 23 and 24 March, when men aligned with Boko Haram killed 92 Chadian soldiers and officers in Bohoma, also near Lake Chad. During the seven-hour attack, Boko Haram also destroyed 24 military vehicles and stole massive amounts of military equipment, which they loaded onto five outboard motor boats.

Furious and upset, President Déby himself led a counter-attack named 'Bohoma Anger' (31 March to 8 April). Official information claimed that more than 1,000 Boko Haram militants were killed and some 40 motorised canoes ('pirogues') destroyed in the counter-attack. Costing the life of 'only' 52 Chadian troops, the operation was considered successful and contributed to restoring the army's honour. In the midst of Bohoma Anger, 58 Boko Haram elements were brought to N'Djamena for interrogation. On 16 April, 44 of them were found dead in their cells. According to the regime, the deaths were caused by self-poisoning. Human rights activists, however, believed that they died from cruel treatment, including lack of oxygen, food, and water. Three days later, Boko Haram killed four and captured five Chadian troops at Lake Chad near Ngouboua.

On National Day, 11 August, President Déby pardoned 538 prisoners, most of them condemned for rebellious activities and/or terror connected to Boko Haram, but not all. For example, former general Mahamat Abdoul Kadré Oumar, alias Baba Laddé, condemned in 2018 to eight years in prison for illegal possession of arms, assassination, and rape in southern Chad, was also pardoned. Despite the presidential pardon, Boko Haram continued to menace in the Lake region. On 19 October, six Chadian troops were killed. A month earlier, on 24 September, Chadian soldiers had killed 20 Boko Haram fighters in the same area. On 25 November, another four Chadian soldiers were killed when a mine blasted their boat as it patrolled on Lake Chad.

The national army also fought other groups within the country. On 20 February, fighting between regular troops and fighters belonging to the rebel group Conseil de Commandement Militaire pour le Salut de la République (CCMSR) took place near the village of Kouri Bougoudi in the northern part of the Tibesti region. While official sources claimed 40 rebels killed and 38 captured, the CCMSR's spokesperson claimed 50 national troops killed and only three of their own fighters. *Illegal artisanal gold mining* contributed to the escalation of violent conflicts in Tibesti, and on 9 October, the government announced the closure of all illegal gold mining sites and expulsion of the miners, including thousands of foreigners, mostly Libyans.

The regime used the judiciary at will, and it was often difficult to determine whether a judicial pursuit was an objective follow-up on legislation or destined to punish someone for being disloyal to the president or the regime. For example, the former prime minister Kalzeubé Pahimi Deubet, accused of corruption and arrested on 1 December 2019, was liberated after five weeks, on 9 January, after the supreme court discharged him. At the opposite end of the scale, former minister of oil Djerassem Le Benmadjiel, also accused of corruption and arrested on 3 September, was still imprisoned awaiting trial by the end of the year. Some speculated that the slow judicial process was related to the upcoming presidential elections, scheduled for 11 April 2021, and Déby's wish to clear away enemies beforehand. Arrested in January, ten army officers and intelligence agents at ANS were condemned on 25 July to respectively five and ten years of prison for smuggling quantities of the drug Tramadol worth close to € 20 m from Chad to Libya. In addition, the officers found guilty were fined between € 21,000 and € 42,000.

Farmer–herder conflicts were less numerous and less deadly than in previous years, but still represented a huge problem. One escalated in the village of Bémagra, leaving two dead and a dozen wounded on 7 and 8 June. On 23 November, villagers in Belegramme (Kabbia department) killed 11 herders accused of destroying a cultivated field. The herders took revenge two days later, killing 11 and burning down numerous villages. On 16 December, 13 people were killed in similar clashes in the Tandjile region.

Foreign Affairs

President Déby and his regime continued to diversify Chad's foreign relations. While France and the US were still among its prime collaborators, Turkey, China, Israel, and Russia continued to increase their importance in numerous areas.

The 4,700 troops of *France*'s Operation Barkhane were key in fighting armed groups across the Sahel. Meeting with G5 Sahel heads of state in Pau (southern France) on 13 January, President Macron confirmed France's military engagements in the region and increased the Barkhane force to 5,100 soldiers. Many of these were fighting in Mali, while the headquarters was in N'Djamena and detachments of the force were stationed in Abéché and Faya-Largeau. In addition to troops, Barkhane included three drones and seven fighter aircraft in addition to numerous helicopters and armoured cars. Both President Macron and Jean-Yves Le Drian, French minister of foreign affairs, met tête-à-tête with President Déby in France in early January. French minister of armed forces Florence Parly made a visit to N'Djamena (19–21 January), visiting the Barkhane force, and had talks with her Chadian counterpart, Mahamat Abali Salah. On numerous occasions in January–March, French ambassador Bertrand Cochery met with President Déby to discuss French military support to fight terror and other armed groups in Chad and the rest of the Sahel. A former vice-head of Barkhane, director of French military intelligence Jean-François Ferlet continued to work meticulously with the French intelligence service Direction Générale de la Sécurité Extérieure (DGSE) to geo-localise armed movements in Chad. The Chadian equivalent Direction Générale de Service and Sécurité des Institutions de l'Etat (DGSSIE) collaborated closely with DGSE. While France was of little importance in terms of Chadian exports, it remained the most important source of imports (19.8%).

USAID contributed $ 71 m in humanitarian assistance. The major part of this, $ 44 m, was transmitted through the WFP, while other UN agencies accounted for another $ 25 m. The *US* also donated some $ 11 m for development aid, mostly health related. In addition to civilian aid, military training and equipment were also supported. On 3 July, the US delivered 28 armoured vehicles, ten trucks, and other equipment worth $ 8.5 m to Chad's military. The US continued to train Chadian troops as part of their *Africa Command* military training and education programme. From 17 to 28 February, numerous Chadian special forces trained in Mauritania and Senegal as part of the annual 'Flintlock' exercise. In December, Chadian military personnel attended the US navy's technical training school on Pearl River in

Mississippi. Under Heidi Berg, Africa Command director of intelligence, the US also continued to help and collaborate with the DGSSIE. Africa Command army general Stephen Townsend met with President Déby in N'Djamena in mid-November to discuss further military cooperation and thanked him for 'continued leadership in regional security'. As a trading partner, Chad was of little and falling importance to the US. While Chad had exported goods to the US worth $ 133 m in 2019, in 2020 exports to the States shrank to a mere $ 3.3 m. Similarly, Chadian imports from the US, in 2019 still worth $ 84 m, were halved in 2020. Chad ranked around 160th among US trade partners.

The most prominent human rights case against businesses was the 20 September complaint against Glencore UK. The UK-based Rights and Accountability in Development (Raid), together with two other NGOs, accused Glencore UK of breaching OECD guidelines concerning human rights and the protection of the environment at their Badila oilfield in south-western Chad. Locals and workers had reported burns, sickness, and skin lesions after a waste-water basin holding a crude oil by-product collapsed two years ago.

In January, the Turkish Cooperation and Coordination Agency (TIKA) inaugurated the sponsorship of wells driven by solar-powered pumps and serving 26,000 refugees and locals around the town of Gore. In May, *Turkey* donated medical equipment to fight Covid-19, including 25 respirators and one ambulance. This more than doubled Chad's overall respiratory-help capacity. After talking for a long time on the phone with Déby on 24 November, President Recep Tayyip Erdoğan stated that Turkey wished to expand cooperation with Chad in all domains, including commerce.

China continued to be an important business partner to Chad, representing close to 16% of all imports (2019), thus making China the second most important origin of imports after France. Without signing any new imperative investment deals, China continued to invest in agriculture, energy, and the health sector. The China National Petroleum Corporation (CNPC) planned to increase its oil production and assured the regime that it could count 'more than ever before' on CNPC's contribution to social and economic development in Chad. In July, China donated 100 respirators and 60 oxygen concentrators destinated primarily to help Covid-19-affected patients.

One of Déby's sons, vice-president of his cabinet Abdelkerim Idriss Déby, met *Israeli* prime minister Netanyahu in Jerusalem on 8 September. Netanyahu expressed the wish that Chad would open an embassy in Jerusalem. Abdelkerim Idriss Déby and the director of ANS Ahmed Kogi met with the latter's counterpart in Mossad, Yossi Cohen, and the head of national security in Israel, Meir Ben-Shabbat. On 15 September, Israel sent Covid-19-related humanitarian aid to N'Djamena.

Déby renounced his planned visit to *Russia* to discuss increased cooperation between the two countries with his counterpart President Vladimir Putin. While his reasons for not travelling were not made public, dialogues around Russian nuclear technology continued. The Russian state corporation Rosatom planned to increase investments in nuclear infrastructure in Africa, including in Chad, significantly over the coming years.

Relations with Qatar, UAE, and Saudi Arabia developed steadily but without major changes, high-level meetings, or any particularly important new commercial deals. The level of bilateral economic aid from these counties remained a matter for speculation, as no official statements on these issues were given. Still, Chad received humanitarian aid from all three of them, but Qatar did not consider Chad a key partner.

Chad's military participated both in the UN Multidimensional Integrated Stabilization Mission in Mali (MINUSMA) and the MNJTF active in the Lake Chad area. Déby declared in April that Chad would bring home all Chadian troops, 1,200 in total, from the MNJTF forces, to fight Boko Haram in Chad only. The statement sparked off frustration and insecurity among the other countries – Nigeria, Niger, and Cameroon – contributing to MNJTF forces; Déby did not follow up on his speech. Former minister of foreign affairs Mahamat Saleh Annadif continued as special representative of the UN secretary-general in Mali and head of MINUSMA for the fifth consecutive year. Chad was the largest troop contributor to the mission, with more than 1,400 soldiers present. Appreciated for their courage and commitment, Chad was requested by France and the G5 Sahel in late April to send additional troops to MINUSMA. In mid-December, 1,450 soldiers ended their special training. Most of the training was delivered by American contractors in Chad, but for two weeks the French elite operational unit Eléments Français au Gabon also trained the future MINUSMA troops. Some 14% of Chad's GDP was military expenditure (2019). This was by far the highest percentage in sub-Saharan Africa.

Socioeconomic Developments

After 3.2% economic growth in 2019, Chad's economy declined (estimated −0.2 to −0.8 %) due to the outbreak of the pandemic caused by Covid-19 and the following steep reduction in the price of crude oil. Already on 14 April, the IMF approved the disbursement of $ 115 m under their Rapid Credit Facility to reduce the social impact of the economic crisis. The national budget expected a deficit of 0.8%, but was in fact estimated to be at a deficit of 13%. Inflation rose only slightly, from 1% in 2019 to an estimated 2.7%. Revenue from income tax decreased by some 80%.

While Chad lost an estimated 50% of its exports' value, oil still represented around 40% of government revenues. Thanks to oil, the US remained by far Chad's most important export destination (57%). Other important export destinations were India (8.9%) and China (6.7%). Cattle and dromedaries were also important components of exports, in addition to cotton. However, increased insecurity made exporters prioritise meat exports on lorries over the exporting of living animal on foot. The Singaporean company OLAN made CotonTchad SN a viable business after buying 60% of the parastatal company in 2018. Cotton production increased from 17,000 tons in 2017 to 115,000 tons in 2020, making it a living for some 4 m people.

Some 6.5 m people, 42% of the entire population, lived below the national poverty line.

The *number of refugees and IDPs* continued to increase. The 2,400 refugees arriving from Darfur in January were settled in Kouchaguine-Mora camp, some 40 km from Abéché. Another 16,000 arrived during the first six months. In total some 76,000 refugees from Nigeria, Cameroon, the CAR, and Sudan added to the already 400,000 refugees in Chad. The huge majority were from Sudan (367,400 refugees) and the CAR (96,100 refugees). In the Lac province, violence committed by Boko Haram and harsh climatic conditions increased the number of refugees and IDPs by 22%, making more than half of the population in the province displaced. By the end of the year, close to 400,000 Chadians were internally displaced.

On 23 December, Chad adopted a new law, conforming to the 1951 Refugee convention, aimed at protecting refugees and asylum seekers. The first ever asylum law guaranteed fundamental freedoms including education, justice, and healthcare to the huge IDPs and refugee population in the country.

Only 104 people died with Covid-19 while 2,113 were declared infected. Explanations varied for the relatively low numbers. Some pointed to the government's rapid reactions after the first case was discovered on 19 March. With economic and expertise support from various donors, the Ministry of Health rapidly developed a National Contingency Plan for Preparedness and Response to the Pandemic. A total lockdown was never used. At various periods, however, borders were closed, commercial activities restrained, internal displacements restricted, public transport shut down, nightly curfews imposed, schools and places of worship closed, and the use of masks made compulsory. Public health recommendations (handwashing, social distancing, etc.) were spread through billboards, radio, and television, but also by priests and imams, and professional storytellers. To help limit the social and economic consequences of all of these restrictions for the populace, electricity and water were made free for the poorest, Covid-19-related imports were exempted from taxes, a special nutrition fund was significantly increased, and a special € 150 m fund to help vulnerable population was created. In addition, most health-related NGOs transferred their priorities towards fighting Covid-19 and many international donors generously contributed with Covid-19-related equipment and material (respirators, masks, visors, hydroalcoholic gel, etc.). Other explanations focused more on the lack of equipment and personnel for testing for Covid-19 and thus proclaimed a huge discrepancy between the official number of cases reported and the probable actual spread of the virus.

Chad was the second most polio-affected country in Africa (behind Sudan), reporting 81 cases across 16 provinces. Close to half a million people were treated for malaria, a disease that took about 1,100 lives, ten times more than Covid-19.

Meanwhile, 8,500 people were treated for measles while vaccination continued at reduced speed due to Covid-19.

The indirect effects of fighting Covid-19 were plain to see. Three million schoolchildren lost 130 days of instruction due to nationwide school closures to halt the pandemic. Some 19,000 community teachers paid by parents' associations lost their jobs, and 50,000 pupils out of 87,500 who tried to pass the final high school exams (baccalaureate) in August failed. At the universities, the 40,000 students enrolled also lost precious months of education and many more than in a normal year failed to pass the exams.

Chad saw an extreme rise in the number of food-insecure people due to floods, droughts, and Covid-19-related impacts. From 2019 to 2020, there was an increase of 5.3 m food-insecure people, up from 0.6 m to 5.9 m. Some 2.1 m of them were severely food-insecure.

Heavy rainfalls in late July and August hit the Lac province and N'Djamena particularly hard. In Lac, some 30,000 people was displaced because of floods. In N'Djamena, the rising level of the rivers displaced around 20,000 people. The flooding destroyed an estimated 188,000 acres of cropland throughout the country. Insecurity and severe climatic conditions meant that basic foods like millet, maize, and sorghum were more expensive than the five-year average, throughout the country. However, locally produced rice, considered poor people's staple food, was around 10% cheaper than the five-year average.

Congo

Brett L. Carter

President Denis Sassou Nguesso, who has ruled the Republic of Congo for all but five years since 1979, spent much of 2020 preparing for the presidential election of March 2021. His efforts to transfer power to his son failed yet again, this time eliciting efforts by some in the presidential palace to depose the ageing president. To buttress his repressive apparatus, Sassou Nguesso supplied his Republican Guard with more than 100 tons of weaponry, purchased from the government of Azerbaijan with the aid of the Saudi ruling family and Turkish president Recep Tayyip Erdogan. To raise money for his electoral campaign, he levied a tax on oil tankers at the Djeno terminal, which would be paid to a company owned by his nephew and would generate nearly $ 10 m per year. The Covid-19 pandemic generated widespread popular frustration which the government struggled to contain. The national lockdown caused citizens' purchasing power to plummet, triggering widespread food insecurity. The government sought yet another $ 500 m bailout from the IMF. After having forgiven the government's debt in 2010 and provided a separate $ 449 m lending agreement in 2019, the IMF refused. With his family targeted by public corruption probes in France and the United States, Sassou Nguesso's foreign policy sought to diversify his alliance portfolio, which, he hoped, would render him less vulnerable to international sanctions.

Domestic Politics

The year in Congolese politics was marked by Sassou Nguesso's efforts to prepare for the March 2021 presidential election. He began early. In January, his Republican Guard received more than 100 tons of weapons from the government of Azerbaijan, including 775 mortar shells and over 400 cases of rockets. The Republican Guard, composed almost entirely of Sassou Nguesso's Mbochi co-ethnics, is directly responsible for his personal security. The shipment went through the Turkish port of Derince. He also continued his efforts to position his son, Denis Christel, as his successor. Long atop the oil apparatus, Denis Christel began his political career in 2012, when he claimed a seat in the national assembly representing Oyo with 99.88% of the vote. As before, Sassou Nguesso confronted opposition from within the senior ranks of the security apparatus, which, like the international community and most Congolese citizens, regarded Denis Christel as profoundly corrupt. Opposition within the presidential palace culminated in an aborted bid to force Sassou Nguesso from power in mid-March. This, and not simply the emergence of Covid-19, compelled Sassou Nguesso to impose a nightly curfew, ban gatherings of more than 50 people, and close Congo's borders.

These power struggles within the presidential palace were also the best explanation for an otherwise shocking prosecution for public corruption which marked the first half of the year. In February, the mayor of Brazzaville, Christian Roger Okemba, was accused by other elected municipal officials of having embezzled more than $ 2 m from the city's treasury. He was suspended and, shortly thereafter, arrested by security forces on charges of public corruption. In July, Okemba was sentenced to five years in prison; his wife was sentenced to three years in prison. They were also fined roughly $ 320,000. Given the Sassou Nguesso family's long record of corruption – and the extent to which public corruption has effectively been permitted for high-level appointees – the legal proceedings shocked most citizens. The prosecution appears to have been the outcome of a power struggle between rival sides of the Sassou Nguesso family. Elected in 2017, Okemba was supported by Edgar Nguesso, who is Sassou Nguesso's nephew, director of the presidential domain, and a one-time rival of Denis Christel as successor. Okemba's candidacy was opposed by the president's daughter Claudia Sassou Nguesso, who, as the full biological sister of Denis Christel, was also his close ally. It is most likely that Edgar was implicated in the power struggles within the presidential palace and that Okemba's conviction was intended as a signal to Edgar and others within the regime who might consider opposing Denis Christel's claims to succession.

Amid a persistent financial crisis – which, among other things, compelled former employees of the post office to protest the non-payment of their pensions in February – Sassou Nguesso needed to raise money for his 2021 election campaign. To do so, in August, he imposed a new tax on all Very Large Crude Oil Carriers (VLCC) and Suez Max oil tankers loading at Congo's Djeno oil terminal. The $ 84,000 tax, branded as a 'safety watch fee', would be paid to Congolaise des Prestations Maritimes (COPREMAR), a firm owned by Wilfried Nguesso, Sassou Nguesso's nephew. As of September, COPREMAR enjoyed a monopoly on towing operations at the Djeno terminal. The $ 84,000 tax, according to British NGO Global Witness, was between six and nine times more expensive than similar taxes levied at other regional ports. The move was estimated to yield Sassou Nguesso nearly $ 10 m per year.

Sassou Nguesso also rebuffed *calls to release political prisoners*. General Jean-Marie Michel Mokoko and André Okombi Salissa, Sassou Nguesso's two leading rivals in the 2016 election, remained in prison throughout the year, each having been sentenced to 20 years in prison for 'undermining state security'. General Mokoko nevertheless remained an active presence in Congolese politics. On 2 July, he was hospitalised in Brazzaville's military hospital. As his condition reportedly deteriorated, the Sassou Nguesso government refused to let him seek emergency medical care in France. In response, on 17 July, two human rights groups, the Observatoire Congolaise des Droits de l'Homme (OCDH) and Ras-le-Bol, planned a protest march to demand his evacuation. The government dispatched its security forces to block the march, though it cited 'risks of coronavirus infections' as justification. On 30 July, the Sassou Nguesso government was sufficiently scared that General Mokoko might die in custody that it arranged for him to be evacuated to Ankara, Turkey. The evacuation was shocking in part because of the destination. When members of the Congolese elite seek medical care abroad, they go overwhelmingly to France, in part because of the shared language. That the Sassou Nguesso government evacuated General Mokoko to Turkey suggests it wanted to conceal his condition from the French government, which, on several occasions, has pushed for his release. General Mokoko finally returned to his Brazzaville prison cell on 30 August.

Civil society groups called for the release of other political prisoners as well, most notably Celeste Nlemvo Makela, Parfait Mabiala, Franck Donald Saboukoulou, Guil Ossebi, and Meldry Dissavoulou. These five activists, all relatively young, were arrested between 23 November and 22 December 2019. They were accused of organising anti-regime protests and interrogated about their links to Andrea Ngombet, another young opposition activist based in Paris. Ngombet, who coordinates the 'SassouFit' collective, was among the first to announce his candidacy for the

March 2021 presidential election. In March, Trésor Nzila Kendet, executive director of the OCDH, described the activists as 'prisoners of conscience'. They were released in December, after a year in custody. OCDH called on the Sassou Nguesso government to cease its use of torture, which contravened its obligations under the United Nations Convention.

With widespread repression in Brazzaville, opposition activists took their struggle for political change to France. On 15 March, two young activists set fire to one of Sassou Nguesso's several mansions in France, located in Yvelines, a suburb of Paris. One of the mansion's walls was spray-painted with 'SASSOU ASSASSIN'. Five vehicles on the property were set aflame as well. French investigators had made no arrests by the end of the year.

The year witnessed the *death of two former presidents*. On 30 March, Jacques Joaquim Yhombi Opango died in Neuilly-sur-Seine, France, a casualty of Covid-19. Yhombi Opango had ascended to power in 1977 after the assassination of Captain Marien Ngouabi, Congo's first military dictator of northern descent. He was deposed in 1979 by Sassou Nguesso, incarcerated, freed in 1985, incarcerated again in 1987, and freed just before the National Conference of 1991. Yhombi Opango went into exile after the 1997 civil war, and was finally permitted to return in 2007. In August, Pascal Lissouba died at 88 years old, still exiled in Perpignan, France. Lissouba was elected in 1992 and deposed by Sassou Nguesso following the 1997 civil war. A southerner, Lissouba remains the only president in Congolese history to be elected in free and fair elections. Lissouba's death was largely ignored by the government-dominated media. 'Les Dépêches de Brazzaville', Sassou Nguesso's chief propaganda newspaper, marked Lissouba's passing by blaming him for the 1997 civil war, thus obscuring Sassou Nguesso's role in provoking it. The war, 'Les Dépêches' wrote, was a 'consequence of the disorganisation of the public administration and social services'.

The political year concluded in mid-December with three notable events. On 17 December, the government announced that it had cancelled a production permit for the *Nabeba iron mine* held by Sundance, an Australian mining firm that, in 2016, made international headlines for ceding a 30% stake of Nabeba's profits to a shell company owned by Denis Christel. Sassou Nguesso awarded the contract to Sangha Mining Development, a company owned by a single shareholder and domiciled in Hong Kong. Many observers speculated that the shareholder was either Denis Christel or someone closely linked to him, possibly with Chinese backing. Sassou Nguesso also awarded Sangha Mining Development two other permits: one for the Avima iron ore project, previously held by Core Mining, and an exploration licence for the Badondo iron ore project, previously held by Equatorial Resources. Strikingly, there were no records of Sangha Mining Development prior to these awards. On 21 December, Sundance announced that it would seek $ 8.76 bn in damages from the government. On 23 December, when Sassou Nguesso delivered his state of the nation address before parliament, he announced that the 2021 presidential election would be held on 21 March. Though he was widely expected to run, by year's end he had yet to announce his candidacy. Most of the emergency restrictions remained in place. Land and river borders were closed. Gatherings of more than 50 people were banned. Brazzaville and Pointe-Noire were subject to a night-time curfew. All non-essential businesses remained closed.

Foreign Affairs

Sassou Nguesso's foreign policy continued to be dominated by the country's persistent financial crisis. In January, Global Witness reported that the *government's debt* was some 30% greater than it had disclosed during debt relief negotiations with the IMF in 2019. With public debt likely exceeding $ 12.5 bn, the government's debt-to-GDP ratio was estimated at 102%. Between 2012 and 2018, according to Global Witness, the state-run Société Nationale des Pétroles du Congo (SNPC) reported only $ 123 m in profits despite $ 5.7 bn worth of sales, amounting to a yield of less than 3%. This revelation emerged at a particularly damaging moment. In July 2019, the IMF had approved $ 449 m in the framework of a three-year lending programme to help prop up the Congolese economy, but it had conditioned the loans on the government rescheduling its debt to Glencore, Trafigura, and the Chinese government. In January, just as the Global Witness revelations appeared, the government's talks with Glencore and Trafigura to restructure its $ 1.7 bn debt broke down, jeopardising more than $ 400 m in IMF loans and another $ 900 m from the World Bank, AfDB, and the French government. The impasse was resolved in April, when the government announced that Glencore and Trafigura had agreed to a 30% debt 'haircut', with payments to resume in October.

In May, just weeks after the government resolved its impasse with Glencore and Trafigura, Sassou Nguesso announced that his government had requested another $ 500 m from the IMF, this time to insulate the economy from the devastation of Covid-19. Congo is Africa's third leading oil producer, but the government projected that the average price of crude oil would halve, from $ 50 per barrel to $ 25. Accordingly, the parliament was forced to approve a revised budget that halved government expenditure. The IMF refused the request, citing Sassou Nguesso's persistent economic mismanagement and its 2010 debt forgiveness agreement under the HIPC initiative. The only additional support that the government received in 2020 was from the WFP, which provided $ 1 m to help the 83,000 citizens who were affected by flooding in the Likouala region in December. Reflecting its perilous financial position, Standard and Poor's downgraded Congolese government bonds to a CCC+/C rating in September.

Sassou Nguesso's foreign policy was also oriented by his lengthy record of corruption and human rights abuses. In February, two separate French newspapers reported that Denis Christel had been indicted in Paris in December 2019 as part of the ongoing '*biens mal acquis*' investigation. In addition, French authorities seized two apartments and one mansion owned by Denis Christel. A week later, Denis Christel's lawyers denied that he was currently under indictment. In June, the US government moved to seize a Miami penthouse condo worth some $ 3 m, purchased by Denis Christel's wife. Federal prosecutors alleged that the money for the purchase was embezzled from the SNPC, the state-run oil company, which Denis Christel has long controlled. Federal prosecutors worked throughout the year to bring a Racketeer Influenced and Corrupt Organizations Act (RICO) case against him. In July, the French government reopened its investigation into the attempted assassination of Ferdinand Mbaou, a senior military official in the Lissouba regime and opposition activist. As if to underscore the regime's frustration with the French government, in April a gendarme in Pointe-Noire shot at an Air France plane that was evacuating French citizens due to Covid-19.

To reduce his vulnerability to international sanctions, Sassou Nguesso has long sought to diversify his alliance portfolio, focusing in particular on the Chinese and Russian governments. The weapons shipments from *Azerbaijan* in January underscored that Sassou Nguesso has also cultivated bilateral relationships with the *Saudi and Turkish governments*. The weapons shipments listed the Saudi government as the 'sponsoring party', suggesting that it paid for either the weapons or the cargo delivery. Several similar weapons shipments, also sponsored by the Saudi government, were delivered between 2015 and 2018, as the Sassou Nguesso government sought Saudi support to join OPEC.

Socioeconomic Developments

Covid-19 devastated Congolese society. Official statistics were widely regarded as unreliable. Still, by the end of the year, Congo had experienced 7,107 confirmed cases and 108 deaths. Among these deaths were two of the society's most respected artists. In March, Aurélien Miatsonama died in Paris, 67 years old. Better known as Aurlus Mabélé, Miatsonama was regarded as among the founding fathers of soukous, a style of music derived from rumba. In June, Edouard Nganga died in Brazzaville, 87 years old. Nganga was a jazz icon in Central Africa, having founded three major ensembles: Negro Jazz in 1954, OK Jazz in 1956, and Bantous de la Capitale in 1959. Regarded as a father of rumba, Nganga remained active until 2019, when he performed at the Institut Français du Congo to celebrate the ensemble's 60th anniversary. His career was the subject of a 2019 documentary by Paul Soni Benga, one of Congo's most respected journalists.

The government announced a nationwide lockdown on 31 March, with markets in Brazzaville and Pointe-Noire open only three days per week. This had two major effects. First, citizens who relied on markets to sell textiles and agricultural products lost income. Second, because supply chains for both local and imported foods were disrupted, prices rose dramatically. The WFP estimated that between late April and early May alone, *food prices* rose by 10%. In turn, the number of people in Congo's urban areas who needed food assistance doubled, from 150,000 to 300,000. The lockdown had a range of other effects as well. With little disposable income left to purchase newspapers, for instance, many of Congo's independent media outlets – already struggling due to government suppression – stopped publishing. With citizens overwhelmingly at home, they were vulnerable to failures of the electric grid. In April, 20 people were killed when a lightning strike damaged a power line in Kintele, a suburb of Brazzaville that is governed by Stella Mensah Sassou Nguesso, one of the president's younger daughters.

The government's response to Covid-19 was otherwise rather tepid. With no additional financial support from the IMF, Sassou Nguesso advertised that his government had accepted a donation from the government of Madagascar of Covid-Organics, a herbal mix that Andry Rajoelina's government had claimed was a cure, despite the lack of any evidence. Sassou Nguesso's decision was opposed by scientists around the world, who expressed concern that the use of Covid-Organics could fuel a drug-resistant strain of malaria. Covid-Organics' chief ingredient is reportedly sweet wormwood, which is the basis for the anti-malarial drug artemisinin.

These shocks to both the national spirit and society's living standards compelled major frustration across the country. The government responded by repressing citizens who spoke out. In May, journalist Rocil Otouna, who worked for Télé Congo, a state-run television station, was fired for asking questions of the minister of justice, Aimé Wilfrid Bininga, that were deemed too critical of the government's response. Otouna's firing was even criticised by the Conseil Supérieur de la Liberté de Communication (CSLC), a constitutional body appointed by Sassou Nguesso that routinely justifies government sanctions against independent news outlets. The Ministry of Communication, overseen by Thierry Moungalla, later accused another Sassou Nguesso propaganda platform, Vox TV, of participating in a 'smear campaign' against the government. The irony was lost on few Congolese citizens: the government and its propaganda apparatus were criticising each other. The government's response to Covid-19 also occasioned a series of human rights abuses against citizens. Throughout the year, citizens disseminated videos that documented the regime's security forces beating citizens for failing to wear masks in public. In September, a 23-year-old woman in Nkayi died following injuries she sustained during one such beating.

Democratic Republic of the Congo

Janosch Kullenberg

Events in the DRC continued to be dominated by power struggles in the ruling coalition between President Félix Tshisekedi's Cap pour le changement (CACH) and former president Joseph Kabila's Front commun pour le Congo (FCC). Towards the end of the year, Tshisekedi had unexpected success in dismantling Kabila's power networks in the public institutions. In a way that had been inconceivable when he took office in 2019, Tshisekedi successfully challenged Kabila's dominance in the army, constitutional court, and parliament and among the governors. While this unprecedented string of victories clearly shifted the balance of power in Tshisekedi's favour, there were doubts as to whether he could permanently align elite interests behind himself and, therefore, would be able to move forward with a more constructive governance programme for the DRC. Although some Western governments supported Tshisekedi's advances, the international community failed to capitalise on the emerging window of opportunity. While the UN Organization Stabilization Mission in DRC (MONUSCO) continued to work on preparing its withdrawal, the security situation in eastern DRC further deteriorated, resulting in an increased number of civilian victims. As if that was not enough, the double health risks of Covid-19 and Ebola compounded the human suffering.

Domestic Politics

Tensions within the ruling coalition between President Tshisekedi's CACH platform and former president Kabila's FCC continued throughout 2020. At the beginning of the year, both sides reiterated their commitment to maintaining the coalition. However, already in January during a visit to London, President Tshisekedi expressed his intention to dissolve the parliament and dismiss ministers if his reform efforts continued to be blocked, to which the FCC's president of the national assembly, Jeannine Mabunda, countered that the prerogative of the president to dissolve the parliament was limited to situations of persistent crisis between the government and the parliament, and that doing so in the absence of such a crisis could prompt a trial for high treason.

Judicial authorities started *proceedings against two senior figures* of Kabila's security apparatus – both under international sanctions – in February. On 12 February, Kalev Mutond, the former head of the national intelligence agency (ANR; Agence Nationale de Renseignements), was briefly detained for illegal possession of a diplomatic passport, questioned by the ANR for suspected 'destabilisation', and finally, banned from travelling outside the country. On 27 February, the head of military intelligence, General Delphin Kahimbi, was suspended for allegedly spying on President Tshisekedi's government. The next day, Kahimbi was found dead at his house; diverging accounts about the cause of his death soon emerged, ranging from a heart attack to suicide to an assassination.

On 8 April, the president's chief of staff and head of the CACH-affiliated Union pour la nation Congolaise (UNC) party, *Vital Kamerhe, was detained* after numerous allegations of fraud and nepotism. Kamerhe, who had held key responsibilities in the $ 500 m emergency infrastructure programme during the first 100 days of Tshisekedi's presidency, was charged with the embezzlement of $ 51.2 m. Kamerhe had publicly displayed his flamboyant lifestyle – most notably through a video circulating on social media, in which his children played with bundles of $ 100 notes – yet the judicial proceedings against a politician on this level were highly surprising. While Kamerhe himself denied the charges, interpretations of the unusual judicial proceedings varied. His UNC party released a statement deploring his 'arbitrary arrest', and supporters continually referred to an unfair and politically motivated trial. Some civil society organisations welcomed the proceedings as a milestone in the fight against corruption and requested that similar measures be taken against other officials. Some observers saw the arrest as a major blow against President Tshisekedi, inflicting the loss of a major ally and the strategic mastermind of his platform. Others speculated that Tshisekedi himself might have taken the opportunity to show progress on his promise to fight corruption while also neutralising a future rival in the upcoming elections. In any case, a conviction would prevent Kamerhe from standing as a candidate in 2023, in which Tshisekedi had pledged to support him in exchange for loyalty during the current administration. On 20 June, Kamerhe was sentenced to 20 years in prison, a ruling against which he appealed immediately.

In May, a petition started by opposition MP Jean-Jacques Mamba of Jean-Pierre Bemba's Mouvement pour la libération du Congo (MLC) against interim president of the Union pour la démocratie et le progrès social (UDPS) and vice-president of the national assembly *Jean-Marc Kabund* escalated into the arrest of Mamba for alleged forgery and fist-fights in parliament. On 25 May, 289 parliamentarians voted to remove Kabund from his position as vice-president, attesting to the political nature of the procedure despite Kabund's technically problematic behaviour. Kabund objected judicially, but on 17 June the constitutional court ruled that the ouster was admissible.

In June, FCC deputies in the national assembly attempted to introduce *judicial reforms* that would have made judges answerable to the minister of justice, a political position held by the FCC. The proposal was widely criticised for attempting to undermine the judiciary and firmly rejected by the opposition, civil society, and international observers. The deputy prime minister in charge of justice, Kabila loyalist Célestin Tunda ya Kasende, bypassed the government and the president and endorsed the reform proposals. While the FCC majority in parliament wanted to push through the new laws, angry protesters erected barriers and burned tyres in front of the national assembly. On 27 June, justice minister Tunda was briefly detained by police after clashing with President Tshisekedi the previous day, which further exacerbated political tensions in the capital and prompted prime minister Sylvestre Ilunga Ilunkamba to threaten that the government would resign over the matter. After Tshisekedi stated informally that he would fire Tunda, the minister resigned on 11 July.

Further tensions emerged in July when Ronsard Malonda was proposed by discordant groups of religious dignitaries as the future *president of the Independent National Electoral Committee* (CENI). The appointment of Malonda, who has held different CENI positions in the last 15 years and was partially responsible for the rigging of the 2018 elections as then CENI secretary-general, could hardly be seen as a step towards democratic change. The parliament's confirmation of Malonda's status as CENI board member and presumptive future president on 9 July caused further large-scale demonstrations across the country, leading to at least three deaths, including the lynching of one police officer. President Tshisekedi stated that he would not sign the ordinance appointing Malonda and called for consultations and harmonisation between the members of the designating group and across the political spectrum. On 19 October, the Episcopal Conference of the Congo (CENCO), which had previously opposed Malonda's nomination, denounced the exertion of political influence to control the CENI as well as the lack of consensus on the necessary electoral reforms.

On 17 July, President Tshisekedi made several *appointments* to civilian, judicial, and military bodies during the absence of the FCC's Prime Minister Ilunga, instead having the deputy prime minister from his own party sign off the presidential ordinances. This method exacerbated tensions between the two sides of the coalition, prompting Ilunga to protest and call the appointments unconstitutional. The public TV announcement of the *army reshuffle* extended over two hours and included senior positions in charge of defence zones, units, bases, military schools, and training centres. Some of Kabila's top generals were moved from operational positions to administrative responsibilities. Most notable was the replacement of the sanctioned General John Numbi as the general inspector of the army by General Gabriel Amisi (alias 'Tango Four'), who is equally under international sanctions. Numbi did not receive a new post and seems to have been effectively removed from power. Another general under international sanctions, Charles Akili 'Mundos', became the deputy general inspector. General Fall Sikabwe Asinda – not sanctioned but previously accused of serious human rights violations and embezzlement – became the army's chief of staff. Rather than upsetting powerful stakeholders in the security sector and the former regime through more dramatic changes, Tshisekedi seemed to have opted to carefully yield *some* power and create loyalty in the military apparatus through a large number of conciliatory alterations. The approach seemed to be adequate, as the army subsequently vowed to remain apolitical during Tshisekedi's face-off with the old regime in December.

Most controversial was the nomination of three new *constitutional judges*, who have ultimate authority over the electoral process and other fundamental questions of political legitimacy. The inauguration of the three judges was thus delayed and hotly debated. On 13 October, the president of the national assembly, Jeannine Mabunda, and the president of the senate, Alexis Thambwe Mwamba – both FCC members and Kabila loyalists – questioned the constitutionality and legality of the nominations in a meeting with President Tshisekedi. In contrast, a delegation to the president from the Conseil supérieur de la magistrature confirmed the legality of the presidential ordinance the next day. On 21 October, the swearing-in ceremony of the three judges in the national assembly was attended only by the president and 60 parliamentarians from his CACH platform, with the noteworthy absence of the FCC-affiliated majority, the prime minister, the president of the senate, and the president of the national assembly.

Tshisekedi's take-over of the constitutional court subsequently turned out to have been a crucial move that allowed him to engage in a staggering *dismantling of the former regime*. On 23 October, during an address to the nation on television, Tshisekedi pointed to the continued tensions in the ruling coalition and announced consultation with all political and civil society stakeholders to form a 'Union Sacrée' (sacred union) and overcome the political impasse. These inclusive consultations took place between 2 and 25 November. On 6 December Tshisekedi then announced on state television that he was *ending the coalition* with Kabila's FCC and attempting to gain a parliamentary majority in order to be able to form a new government and implement crucial reforms. The president warned that if he could not form a new coalition, he might be forced to dissolve parliament and hold new elections. He also stated that he would shortly appoint an informant to identify a new parliamentary majority. A few days later, on 10 December, Congolese parliamentarians (MPs) voted to *dismiss the speaker of parliament* Jeannine Mabunda and the other members of her office, by 281 votes to 219 – meaning that many of the FCC's majority had voted against their own political camp. However, this was likely to be more the result of disgruntlement among the members of the FCC than a desire for real change. Over the last couple of years, Kabila's personalised and closed-off leadership style had left many people wanting a clearer political vision, more accessible decision-making, and, undeniably, also a better position for themselves. There were also persistent allegations that massive vote buying had swayed many parliamentarians. While resembling a political earthquake, Mabunda's ouster therefore did not mean that the tectonic plates of power were aligning behind President Tshisekedi. Much will depend on the ability of the future '*informateur*' to identify and unite the manifold interests. The fact that Tshisekedi appointed Modeste Bahati Lukwebo to this position on 31 December was encouraging. Bahati, an ambitious FCC dissident and the head of what was formerly its second-largest party, was widely perceived as a good choice because of his political influence and organisational capacities. Another reassuring albeit surprising development was that on 29 December, *24 of the 26 governors* (mostly FCC-affiliated) committed to support President Tshisekedi's vision and priorities in the framework of the Union Sacré.

Meanwhile, former president Joseph Kabila stayed remarkably *absent* from the quickly developing events and seemed to refrain from mounting a solid defence against the rolling Tshisekedi train. Some speculated that given the current momentum, Kabila was willing to let Tshisekedi try (and most likely fail) to bring together the various interests in a productive way. Moreover, Kabila could use his institutional influence behind the scenes to frustrate the junior president's efforts, thereby preparing his own political comeback in a less confrontational manner. Nevertheless, Kabila seemed to have underestimated the real gains that Tshisekedi was able to obtain during his absence.

In any case, Tshisekedi will have to deliver on his 2019 promise to improve his country's *security situation*. The number of violent deaths in the east markedly increased in 2020, exacerbating the political pressure on the president. The UN's Joint Human Rights Office (JHRO) documented 7,393 *human rights violations* in conflict-affected provinces, representing a 28% increase from the previous year. This includes the conflict-related deaths of at least 2,811 civilians – more than double the 2019 figure. Of the human rights violations, 51% (3,746) were committed in the province of *North Kivu*, which remained the hotbed of armed group violence.

The *Allied Democratic Forces* (ADF) continued to be the deadliest armed group in the DRC, committing regular atrocities against the civilian population supposedly in retaliation against military operations. The Kivu Security Tracker reported 113 ADF attacks, resulting in at least 599 civilian deaths (The JHRO reported 849 victims). While the group remained most active in the Beni area of North Kivu, the trend of ADF movement in the southern part of the province of Ituri (Irumu and Mombasa territories) and on the roads to Uganda (Mbau-Kamango and Beni-Kasindi) increased. The former was caused partly by the pressure of army operations and the latter was reportedly connected to the harvest of cocoa and other agricultural produce. Already during the first quarter of the year, 250,000 people were displaced in Ituri due to these ADF incursions. The group also continued to attack army patrols, involving looting and abductions, and resulting in over 100 soldiers from the Force armées de la République démocratique du Congo (FARDC) being killed and many more wounded. As previously, the ADF returned to areas that they had been chased away from when the army units there were redeployed elsewhere. On 22 June, suspected ADF elements attacked a MONUSCO convoy on the Beni-Kasindi road, killing one peacekeeping and injuring another. On 20 October, ADF elements attacked Beni prison, which allowed 1,335 prisoners to escape. Only 404 prisoners had been returned to the prison by 12 November.

As MONUSCO was unable to prevent the violence, political and civil society actors blamed the mission, criticised its purported uselessness, and, at times, even alleged involvement in the carnage. Multiple *demonstrations* were organised by civil society organisations in locations across the province, including in the town of Beni and in Mbau, Oicha, and Goma.

Also in North Kivu, the Forces démocratique de libération du Rwanda (FDLR) reportedly attacked civilians in Nyiragongo and Rutshuru territories, killing dozens and reportedly committing the most conflict-related sexual violence of any armed group. When the national army responded with military operations, the FDLR raised the costs of these measures by retaliating against the civilian population. On 24 April, alleged FDLR elements killed 13 rangers in Virunga National Park.

Meanwhile, fighting between *Nduma défense du Congo-Rénové* (NDC-R) and a coalition of Nyatura, FDLR, and the Alliance des patriotes pour un Congo libre et souverain (APCLS) continued in Masisi and Rutshuru and, as previously, resulted in gained territory for the NDC-R. By June, approximately 200 of these clashes had resulted in the loss of more than 160 civilian lives as well as other human rights violations, including conflict-related sexual violence. The military prosecutor of North Kivu issued an arrest warrant against NDC-R leader Guidon Shimiray Mwissa. On 8 July, the deputy of the group, Gilbert Bwira, then led an attempt to overthrow Guidon. Interestingly, the press statement by the Bwira faction used almost identical wording to explain the revolt to that Guidon himself had used against the previous head of the group, Ntabo Ntaberi Sheka, in 2014. Sheka was then sentenced to life imprisonment on 23 September for war crimes committed by the NDC between 2007 to 2017 in Walikale territory. Meanwhile, the two NDC-R factions clashed on multiple occasions around Pinga, Mweso, and Kashuga. On 18 August, approximately 485 NDC-R combatants surrendered to government authorities. Although the split weakened the NDC-R, it did not result in an improved security situation, as other armed groups took over its positions in Rutshuru, Masisi, and southern Lubero. In-fighting between the two NDC-R factions worsened in September and October around Pinga, displacing over 5,000 families.

In *Ituri*, Lendu armed groups, including the Coopérative pour le développement du Congo (CODECO), attacked security forces and civilians from other ethnic groups, particularly Hema, in Djugu and Mahagi territories. Between March and May, at least 333 civilians were killed in the area, including 70 women and 61 children. Approximately 300,000 people were displaced by the violence in the first half of the year alone. The FARDC launched military operations in March and successfully killed and arrested some of the CODECO leaders, disintegrating the group into various smaller factions that did not lay off the violence. Most dramatically, 37 civilians were killed on 8 July during a major attack in the village of Bunzenzele. The government dispatched a delegation of former armed group leaders, including the former head of the Force de résistance patriotique de l'Ituri (FRPI), Germain Katanga, to advocate for an end of the violence. As these negotiations were ongoing, the different militias continued to target civilians with extortion and killings. In August, violence against civilians ebbed after a pledge for peace in Mahagi territory that was signed by 42 Lendu chiefs and the adoption of a road-map by 60 leaders from the Alur community. On 4 September, over 100 Mai-Mai entered the provincial capital Bunia during the day to demand the release of CODECO prisoners. An armed escalation was avoided through negotiations and without freeing their comrades, the group was escorted out of the town by security forces. Towards the end of the year, different CODECO factions clashed over the control of several gold mines in northern and western Djugu territories.

In southern Irumu territory, progress was made on the demobilisation of the *FRPI*. On 28 February, the government and the FRPI's leadership signed a peace agreement. The process progressively improved the security situation. However, the reintegration of demobilised FRPI units stalled, resulting in sporadic exactions from communities living close to the pre-cantonment sites. The demobilisation and reintegration of 1,100 additional FRPI combatants was delayed due to Covid-19 as well as disagreements about prisoner release and the possibility of amnesty and integration into the army. In contradiction to the negotiations on the ground, the special representative of the UNSG (SRSG) Leila Zerrougui publicly spoke out against amnesty and integration in early September, prompting President Tshisekedi to follow suit, effectively preventing the implementation of an agreement that had been negotiated with MONUSCO support. When their stipends were subsequently not paid, frustrated FRPI elements looted and destroyed parts of the disarmament and demobilisation sites in Karatsi and Kazana on 30 September. After negotiations, payment of the pending stipends proceeded but continued to be an issue, impacting the willingness of FRPI elements to disarm.

Also in Irumu territory, the Front patriotique et intégrationniste du Congo (FPIC) attacked the army and civilians, causing further tensions between Bira and Hema communities and triggering retaliatory attacks by the Hema-based 'Zaire' armed group in Irumu and Djugu territories.

In *South Kivu*, inter- and intra-community violence continued in the middle and high plateaus of Fizi, Mwenga, and Uvira territories, specifically in Bijimbo, Mikenge, and Minembwe. The continued Rwandan and Burundian support of each other's rebel groups that collaborate with various militias in the high plateaus exacerbated the dynamics. An estimated 130,000 people remained internally displaced in the high plateaus, and militias targeted IDPs throughout the year. As previously, self-proclaimed indigenous Bembe, Fuliro, Vira, and Nyindu militias mobilised around the 'balkanisation' narrative, which postulates that foreign invaders want to divide and annex the DRC, while also fighting other 'autochthones' over local power disputes. On the other hand, Twigwaneho and Gumino militias usually 'defended' Banyamulenge (Tutsi) communities jointly, but also clashed with each other repeatedly. The former FARDC colonel of Banyamulenge origin, Michel Rukunda (alias Makanika), defected from the army in January and consolidated his control of the Twigwaneho militias. In Bijombo, Twigwaneho and Mai-Mai militias clashed frequently, triggering MONUSCO interventions. In July, Twigwaneho conducted a retaliatory attack against Kipupu village and killed at least 18, after Mai-Mai elements had raided Banyamulenge cattle. On Twitter, 2018 Nobel peace laureate Denis Mukwege denounced the incident as a massacre of 220 civilians and connected it to previous Rwandan attacks during the Congo Wars, demanding that the 'mapping report' of human rights violation between 1993 and 2003 be revised and those responsible brought to justice. Mukwege subsequently reported receiving death threats and saw his UN personal protection increased.

At the end of September, the situation in Minembwe deteriorated further when it was granted the status of a 'municipality' and a Banyamulenge mayor was installed during the visit of Azarias Ruberwa, the minister for decentralisation, who is himself of Banyamulenge origin. The fact that the long pending decision (since 2013) to create a decentralised territorial entity under Banyamulenge control was implemented by a Banyamulenge minister unleashed significant controversy and backlash against the perceived assault on the territorial integrity of the DRC, playing into the justifications for Mai-Mai 'resistance'. Ruberwa subsequently denied any responsibility, and President Tshisekedi overruled the decision on 8 October, announcing that a commission of independent scientific expects would retrace and redefine all the administrative boundaries in Fizi territory.

Multiple armed groups roamed the other parts of South Kivu (Kalehe, Mwenga, Shabunda, Uvira, and Walungu territories). Redeployments of FARDC units repeatedly created security vacuums and exacerbated dynamics of violence. For instance, the FDLR splinter group Conseil national pour le renouveau et la démocratie (CNRD) was able to recruit in the northern part of South Kivu, especially among local youth in Kalehe territory.

Several *Raia Mutomboki* leaders returned to the bush after failed demobilisation attempts, which caused a surge of violence, including conflict-related sexual violence, particularly in Shabunda territory.

On the *Ruzizi plain*, Mai-Mai Kijangala and local bandits conducted raids against cattle, imposed illegal taxes, and attacked villages.

In the border area between South Kivu and Tanganyika and Maniema provinces, Mai-Mai groups and Twa militias remained active, resulting in continued displacement. Following army redeployments, the humanitarian and security situation further deteriorated. Mai-Mai Malaika continued to operate in Kabambare and Kasongo territories in Maniema province, resulting in the displacement of more than 1,500 families.

In *Tanganyika* province, the conflict between Bantu and Twa communities about land rights and local power remained unresolved, leading to repeated clashes and about 70 victims and 40,000 displaced persons in the first quarter of 2020 alone. In April, the FARDC conducted military operations against Twa militias, successfully displacing them from the most populated areas but failing to stop their attacks on civilians. Twa combatants regularly conducted incursions from Tanganyika into Maniema province. In Kalemie territory (Tanganyika), different armed groups, including Mai-Mai Yakutumba, Apa Na Pale, and Fimbo Na Fimbo, conducted raids in mining sites and surrounding villages. Bendera remained the most affected area. On 5 October, the surrender of Mai-Mai Apa Na Pale leader Kasongo Amuri resulted in a reduction of violence in Nyunzu territory.

The security situation in Kasai, Kasai Central, Kwilu, Mai-Ndombe, and Sankuru provinces remained largely stable. Attempts to remobilise by former *Kamuina Nsapu* combatants towards the end of the year failed, after the arrest of their leaders and insufficient support among communities. The reduction of militia violence in the Kasai provinces is conducive to MONUSCO's foreseen withdrawal. However, the limited presence and legitimacy of state authorities make a re-emergence of violence possible. For instance, on 17 July and 4 August, clashes in Demba and Mweka territories led to the deaths of 11 civilians and the destruction of 263 houses.

In Haut-Katanga and Lualaba provinces, security forces killed 43 members of the *Mai-Mai Kata Katanga* when its leader Gédéon Kyungu Mutanga escaped his house arrest in Lubumbashi on 28 March. Gédéon, who has previously been sentenced for crimes against humanity, remains at large.

In Congo Central province, security forces killed 31 followers of the political-religious *Bundu Dia Kongo* movement and injured 40 more when they arrested its leader Ne Muanda Nsemi on 24 April. Nsemi, who was spectacularly freed from Kinshasa's central prison Makala in 2017, had prompted the intervention through his self-declaration as the president and tribal hate speech.

In this tense security situation, against the backdrop of 11 civilians having been killed the same morning in a village close to Beni and with the controversy around Minembwe still fresh, President *Tshisekedi arrived in Goma* for the second time on 5 October. He restated his aim to improve the security situation and reform the security sector, including through stating the intention to stay several weeks in the east. Tshisekedi met with the governors of North Kivu, South Kivu, and Maniema as well as civil society. Furthermore, he proclaimed his support for the community-based approach to disarmament, demobilisation, and reintegration (DDR), to which he intended to nominate a national coordinator, and alluded to $ 50 m of World Bank funding for the endeavour.

Foreign Affairs

President Tshisekedi continued his efforts in *regional diplomacy*, which is likely to have yielded international support for his domestic take-over. On 20 and 21 February, he participated in the third and fourth Quadripartite Summits with the presidents of Angola, Rwanda, and Uganda, resulting in the adaptation of measures to improve relations between Rwanda and Uganda, including prisoner release and commitments against the supporting of foreign armed groups.

In February, Tshisekedi was elected *vice-president of the African Union* and president of the continental body in 2021. While the exact implications and advantages of these offices remained unclear, it appeared that the president would use them and the connected international exposure to strengthen his position at home.

In mid-March, a *land dispute between the DRC and Zambia* flared up, with both sides deploying troops at the border around Moba territory, Tanganyika province. Several Congolese soldiers were killed during sporadic clashes. The two countries declared their willingness to resolve the dispute diplomatically and called on the SADC to mediate. The foreign minister of the neighbouring Republic of Congo, Jean-Claude Gakosso, visited Kinshasa, Lusaka, and Harare, encouraging the two disputing countries to resolve their issues peacefully. On 15 July, Tshisekedi then travelled on his third state visit to Congo-Brazzaville to meet with President *Denis Sassou Nguesso* of the Republic of Congo. They discussed the reopening of cross-river traffic, which had been closed for several months due to Covid-19 measures, as well as the presence of Zambian troops in DRC territory, for which Nguesso offered additional mediation. The SADC subsequently deployed a *technical team to the border* area from 23 to 29 July, Zambia committed to withdraw its troops, and a phased approach was started in September to improve the demarcation of the border.

Intermittent clashes also took place between the Congolese and *Angolan* armed forces in the Kasai borderlands. In June, an Angolan soldier was reportedly shot dead during an incursion into Congolese territory. Moreover, Angolan authorities forcefully returned approximately 4,468 Congolese, including 660 women and 308 children, to the DRC. On 16 September, the two countries signed a cooperation agreement on security and public order in the common border area and an agreement on the circulation of people and goods.

On October 7, Tshisekedi co-hosted a *videoconference* with the heads of state from Angola, Rwanda, and Uganda to discuss security matters. The summit had originally been planned to take place in Goma during Tshisekedi's visit there, but the format was adapted due to Covid-19 restrictions. Burundi declined to participate, requesting more bilateral engagement first. The four heads of state expressed their willingness to eradicate 'negative forces' in the Great Lakes region, including through strengthening national capacity, cutting the financial sources of armed groups, and increase security cooperation.

Western nations, in particular the United States but also France and former colonial power Belgium, continued to support Tshisekedi and his reform plans. During his visit in February, the US special envoy for the Great Lakes region Peter Pham reportedly requested the removal of several key allies of Kabila, including General Delphin Kahimbi and General John Numbi (see above), which, in addition to creating pressure, might just have assured Tshisekedi of the backing he needed to act. The *US ambassador* to the DRC Mike 'Nzita' 'Amani' *Hammer* was extremely active behind the scenes and gained popularity on social media through his public engagement with Congolese culture. Hammer was as explicit in his support of President Tshisekedi as he was outspoken in his criticism of the old regime. In return, Tshisekedi endorsed Donald Trump's peace plan for the Middle East. In August, the two countries resumed military cooperation, and a training programme for Congolese officers in the US was announced. Some rumoured that the US was also a financial backer of Tshisekedi's political take-over at the end of the year.

The rivalry within CACH eventually cumulated in a governance crisis and effectively paused other governance efforts, in particular during several weeks of national consultations in November. Accordingly, international partners spent most of the second half of the year on the *observers' bench*, although they had major projects to urgently move forward on. On the programmatic side, the delays in the development and implementation of a new DDR-Communautaire (DDR-C) programme were most unfortunate. In August, the three governors of Ituri, North Kivu, and South Kivu launched a *community-based DDR* effort through the Commission interprovinciale d'appui au processus de désarmement, démobilisation, réinsertion, réintégration et réconciliations communautaires (CIAP-DDRRRC). On 31 August, SRSG Zerrougui, President Tshisekedi, Prime Minister Ilunga, key ministers, and the three governors discussed this endeavour. Donors quickly came to appreciate the more bottom-up approach to the urgently needed but so far dramatically failed DDR programme. On the technical level, donors gave feedback on the draft of a presidential ordinance and, despite several technical concerns, remained eager to support it. However, FCC members in relevant positions, including the development ministry, defence ministry, and the previous DDR coordination, blocked progress. On 22 October, Western ambassadors expressed their support for DDR-C in a meeting with the president. The next day, President Tshisekedi announced the national consultations for the Union Sacrée.

Similarly, *MONUSCO's exit* and the required consultations for joint benchmarks and for the transfer of tasks and responsibilities to the government did not receive the necessary attention from the preoccupied Congolese side. In October, MONUSCO and the government agreed on a 'joint' strategy for the 'progressive and phased drawdown'. The public version appeared neither very strategic nor very joined up. It largely restated an independent strategic review from October 2019, and even international partners stated privately that they had hardly been consulted in the process. Further delays in MONUSCO's exit were expected also because the security situation in the eastern provinces had deteriorated.

On the operational level, joint military operations between UN peacekeepers, particularly the Force Intervention Brigade, and the FARDC also hardly manifested. The UN continued to be reluctant to conduct operations together with the Congolese army without joint planning, which the Congolese side appeared reluctant to do. MONUSCO thus supported the FARDC mainly through medical evacuations, intelligence-sharing (e.g. from drones), logistics, and more policing-like tasks.

MONUSCO contributed to the reduction and prevention of violence through supporting mediation efforts, deploying temporary *operating bases* and conducting more robust and frequent *patrols* in hotbeds of violence. In July, the mission's leadership approved specific *provincial strategies* to address the root causes of conflict and reduce armed group activity in Ituri, North Kivu, South Kivu, Tanganyika, Kasai, and Kasai Central.

In response to the *Covid-19* pandemic, MONUSCO and the UN Country Team were forced to reduce their activities, particularly in regard to community engagement. The movement of personnel was also reduced and troop rotations were suspended until mid-July, which impacted the generation of new units and the implementation of the recommendations of the dos Santos Cruz report on better protection for civilians against ADF attacks in the Beni area, including the deployment of the Geolocation Threat Analysis Unit (GETAU). In addition, significant staff shortages occurred at Force Intervention Brigade (FIB) and regular force headquarters due to military staff officers leaving MONUSCO before their replacements had arrived.

MONUSCO's *mandate* was renewed on 18 December (Security Council Resolution 2,556). While the mission's two priorities – the protection of civilians and stabilisation remained unchanged – the emphasis on the reconfiguration and transition of MONUSCO was palpable in the document.

Socioeconomic Developments

With a promising outlook and because of the ambitious government programme, the initial 2020 *budget* proposal had been increased from $ 10 bn to $ 11 bn on 31 December 2019. However, after a more realistic assessment by the finance ministry, the final approved budget was reduced to $ 8.2 bn in mid-February. The Covid-19 pandemic then further impacted the *economic situation* of the already fragile economy, mainly by weakening the exchange rate of the Congolese franc. The Congolese central bank rather optimistically projected a 2.4% contraction of the economy in 2020, but the World Bank later reported a 3.6% reduction of economic growth. Government investments fell by 10.2%. The government faced the dilemma of having to respond to the Covid-19 pandemic while its income declined due to fiscal relief measures and reduced growth. As a result, the fiscal deficit rose to 1.9% of GDP and the current account deficit increased to 4% of GDP. The government initially made do with advances from the central bank and then obtained emergency support from the IMF and the AfDB, which increased external debt and domestic debt by 15.9% and 8.9% of the GDP, respectively. In August, the prime minister instructed the financial authorities to adhere to the government's cash flow plan to stabilise the economy. Reportedly, the monetary stability pact between the government and the central bank was also successful in doing so. Growth of the extractive sector by 6.9%, mainly driven by strong Chinese demand, helped the Congolese economy as other sectors contracted by 1.6%. On 15 September, the 2020 budget was reduced to $ 5.7 bn. On 3 December, the 2021 budget was adapted to $ 7.1 bn, less than initially foreseen for 2020, but indicating some optimism. Real GDP was expected to grow by 3.3% in 2021 in an economic recovery which assumed that consumption and investments would recover and prices of raw materials, such as copper, would increase.

Major economic reforms to improve the business climate and the management of the mining sector were not manifested. The DRC was ranked 183rd out of 190 countries in the 2020 *Doing Business* report, with particular shortcomings in regard to trading across borders, paying taxes, and getting electricity.

The DRC's limited wealth is distributed in an extremely unequal way, and the country's pervasive and widespread *poverty* increased further due to the impact of Covid-19 on the economy. The World Bank reported that the country had the third-largest population of people living in poverty worldwide. Approximately 75% of the Congolese population (about 60 m people) lived on less than $ 1.90 a day.

Likewise, the already dire *humanitarian situation* was exacerbated by Covid-19. At the beginning of the year, an estimated 15.6 m people were in need of humanitarian assistance; this was subsequently raised to 21.8 m (approximately a quarter of the overall population). OCHA's 2020 humanitarian response plan foresaw the alleviation of suffering of 9.2 m Congolese. By August, only 22 % of the required $ 2.07 bn had been funded.

With more than 5.2 m people *displaced*, the DRC also continued to have the highest numbers of IDPs in Africa, constituting one of the largest displacement situations globally. UNHCR also reported 500,000 refugees from neighbouring countries in the DRC, notably due to the December elections in the CAR.

The double health crisis of *Covid-19* and Ebola viruses compounded human suffering in the DRC in the context of evolving political and security crises. The wealthy elite reportedly imported Covid-19 to the country through their travels, making Kinshasa the epicentre and prompting the general population to initially take the virus less seriously. Only a handful of cases were registered at the beginning of March, but numbers quickly rose into the thousands, while insufficient testing facilities and a generally high mortality rate (outside of Covid-19) hindered an accurate assessment of this pandemic. Health authorities were, however, able to build on the capacities acquired through several recent Ebola epidemics, notable adapting surveillance, tracing, and diagnostics, and managing intensive cases.

On 24 March, President Tshisekedi declared a public state of emergency in response to the Covid-19 epidemic. With the price of basic commodities soaring, an emergency food programme was established on 18 April on the initiative of the president. However, Covid-19 preventative measures further hindered humanitarian access due to travel and cargo restrictions, as borders were closed and a PCR test requirement hindered inter-provincial movement. The allocation of limited resources to the Covid-19 response, furthermore, meant that other health issues, notably vaccinations against polio, measles, and yellow fever, received less attention. MONUSCO provided logistical and security support for the Covid-19 response. Together with the Ministry of Education and UNICEF, the mission's Radio Okapi media outlet also developed a distance-learning programme, providing a daily two-hour programme for over 22 m primary school students across the country. On 9 October, the Council of Ministers established an institutional framework for the implementation of the multi-sectoral emergency mitigation programme. By 15 November, 11,838 Covid-19 cases had been confirmed in 22 of 26 provinces, leading to 322 deaths.

After almost two months without infections, a new case of *Ebola* was reported in the eastern territory of Beni on 10 April. Local populations reacted with mistrust and demonstrations, doubting the reliability of the new case. While six more cases were soon reported in the same area, the virus was subsequently contained successfully. On 25 June, health minister Eteni Longondo officially announced the end of this tenth Ebola outbreak, which had started in August 2018 in North Kivu and had also reached Ituri and South Kivu provinces. Overall, 3,400 people had been infected, of whom more than 2,200 died.

A new Ebola outbreak was declared in Mbandaka, Equateur province (over a thousand kilometres from Beni), on 1 June. The WHO cooperated with the Congolese health ministry to support an immediate response on the ground. Together with the UN Country Team, the government also developed a three-month $ 40 m multi-sectoral response plan, which remained only half funded by the end of August. By mid-November, over 40,000 people had been vaccinated in Equateur province. By the end of the year, the virus appeared to be under control, with 130 registered infections, including 55 deaths. Meanwhile, measles, cholera, and malaria remained prevalent, causing thousands of deaths.

Epidemics and particularly Covid-19 increased the pressure on already limited basic services and exacerbated the vulnerability of suffering populations. During the implementation of Covid-19 restrictions, including those entailed under the state of emergency, security forces committed 163 documented human rights violations, including use of excessive force and extrajudicial killings.

Although the government released 3,286 *prisoners* to reduce the risk of Covid-19 infections in the massively overpopulated prisons, the detention situation remained dire, particularly regarding lack of food and insufficient access to healthcare. The JHRO documented 76 deaths in custody (including one child) between July and October alone. In September, a mutiny took place in the prison of Lubumbashi during which at least 4 prisoners escaped, 3 were shot dead, 18 were wounded, and 21 women were gang-raped by rioting inmates.

Equatorial Guinea

Joseph N. Mangarella

The Covid-19 pandemic brought to the fore the country's most pressing issues. The government, led by the Essangui clan with President Teodoro Obiang Nguema Mbasogo at its helm, sought to stabilise internal politics by downplaying the real extent of the virus and by threatening dissident voices. As the oil industry suffered falling prices, President Obiang's son and oil minister Gabriel Mbaga Obiang Lima scrambled to find investors for the country's long-term goal of diversification. Lima's brother and rival for political power, vice-president and head of national security Teodoro Nguema Obiang Mangue ('Teodorín'), continued to silence and brutalise his detractors in a context of quarantine and lockdowns. Despite soured relations with the West, Teodorín's bid to replace his father, the world's longest-serving republican head of state, seemed all but certain to succeed.

Domestic Politics

The ravages of the *Covid-19* pandemic were compounded by *government neglect* and malfeasance, as on 4 June the regime expelled the local WHO representative, Triphonie Nkurunziza; it thereafter became impossible to assess the state of the virus or the country's management thereof. Two months later, *the entire cabinet resigned*, presumably forced to do so by President Obiang in a likely attempt to deflect blame for the government's handling of the crisis and the flagging economy. The move may also have reflected the ongoing internecine jostling for power between Teodorín and Lima. Teodorín was reportedly disappointed after President Obiang reappointed the entire cabinet on 19 August, including Prime Minister Francisco Asue, a Teodorín-inspired appointment who had failed to weaken oil minister Lima as Teodorín had intended.

Characteristically abusing his directorship of the country's security services, *Teodorín* drove the former president of the supreme court of justice, Juan Carlos Ondo Angue, into hiding. The judge had refused to change statements made in 2018 at the funeral of a persecuted fellow judge, in which he publicly supported the strengthening of judicial independence and praised his former colleague, who Angue claimed had been tortured to death for refusing to take part in a state-sponsored corruption scheme. In September, Teodorín ousted the agriculture and forests minister, Nicolas Hountondji Akapo, with reports suggesting that the minister had failed to give lucrative contracts to Teodorín's own logging companies. In November, Teodorín also moved on the oil industry, appropriating the discourse of maritime security to militarise the sprawling Punta Europa oil and gas complex; Marathon Oil, one of the complex's largest operators, appealed to Lima to have the forces removed. Widening the gulf with his half-brother, Teodorín continued to also appropriate the anti-corruption discourse by 'investigating' Lima's sale of offshore blocks to the Nigerian firm Levene Energy. Lastly, in November, 'Africa Intelligence' learned the circumstances of why Teodorín's uncle, ex-minister Candido Nsue Okomo, had moved to Dubai in 2019. The move had come as Teodorín revoked Candido's diplomatic passport and forced his uncle into political exile, later alleging that Candido was corrupt and had abused his position as CEO at GEPetrol from 2008 to 2016. But news in November revealed that Candido was opposed to Teodorín's rise within the family, and may have threatened to reveal damning information that might have concretised Teodorín's friendship and exploits with late financier Jeffrey Epstein. Past investigations of Teodorín in France and the US suggested frequent contact between the two in both Brazil and France.

The regime's attacks on *civil and political rights* continued to threaten the country's standing with the IMF. The desire to continue to benefit from IMF loans was most likely the motive behind the release of five political prisoners in June and Joaquin Elo Ayeto in February. Ayeto, an activist member of the NGO Somos+, had been arrested arbitrarily a year prior. Somos+ submitted an application to legally register as an NGO in June, which by year's end had not been granted. In November, an activist with the long-time opposition party Convergencia para la Democracia Social was found dead. The country's judicial independence continued to flounder, as in March a military court sentenced ten members of the Movimiento para la Liberacion de Guinea Ecuatorial Tercera Republic to a total of 734 years in prison for various crimes against the state. Two Spanish citizens were among the sentenced and were denied access to their embassy.

Citizens were also brutalised under the *pandemic lockdown* as the regime anticipated widespread backlash. In March, the government declared a state of emergency on Covid-19 grounds, severely and disproportionately restricting civil and political rights; many restrictions were not lifted until 15 June. Reports by US-based NGO EG Justice and various social media documented overzealous and physically brutal lockdown enforcements by the police, while the government stopped publishing case numbers in May shortly before expelling the WHO representative. Seven journalists for the TV channel Asonga were suspended after speaking out against excessive use of force in imposing the lockdown. On 14 April, Nuria Obono Ndong Andeme, a nurse, sent a WhatsApp message to a friend disparaging health services for the *lack of oxygen* for Covid-19 patients. After the message went viral, she was summoned a day later by the minister of health and was reportedly abused, intimidated, and humiliated. On 16 April, she was sent to pretrial detention without bail at the infamous Black Beach prison, before being released without charge on 21 April.

Faced with the Covid-19 pandemic, the government therefore appeared concerned more with its own longevity and less with that of its constituents. This view was further supported when the regime distributed CFAfr 85 m among the 17 legalised political parties with the stated intent of feeding those adversely affected by quarantines. For many, the gesture brought to mind the familiar practice of food distribution during election campaigns waged by the ruling and utterly dominant Partido Democrático de Guinea Ecuatorial.

Foreign Affairs

In 2020, the country took a seemingly more determined posture towards the East, both to obtain resources and for diplomatic cover. Despite its own socioeconomic crises, in February the regime donated $ 2 m to *China* to help its early Covid outbreak, while in October Chinese president Xi Jinping marked the 50-year anniversary of relations with Equatorial Guinea by congratulating President Obiang on his stewardship of the country. In June, the president expulsed the WHO representative for allegedly inflating Equatorial Guinea's virus tally. The country's charity coincided with more negative news related to Teodorín's misdeeds. In February, the ICJ ruled in favour of France in *Equatorial Guinea vs France*, declaring that Teodorín's 101-room mansion in Paris was not 'used for the purposes of a diplomatic mission' under the 1961 Vienna Convention on Diplomatic Immunity. Equatorial Guinea had therefore exhausted all appeals: Teodorín was formally convicted in France for ill-gotten gains and ordered to pay a fine of € 30 m as well as to serve a three-year suspended prison sentence. In the same month, the regime publicly lashed out at the US, France, and Spain for protecting *Judge Angue* from arrest. On 8 February, the ambassadors of the US, France, and Spain agreed to visit the dissident Judge Angue at his own home, thus preventing arrest by the gendarmerie on the official charges of crimes related to the attempted coup of 2017. Relations with *Spain* further deteriorated when Spain rescinded its outstanding arrest warrant for Candido, Teodorín's banished uncle.

Cultivating *regional allies* and stability continued to prove crucial. As tensions soured with The Gambia over Equatorial Guinea's continued refusal to extradite Gambian ex-president Jammeh, relations with others improved. In February, Obiang formally thanked Angola for helping to put down the alleged coup attempt of 2017. In September, an Equatoguinean delegation was sent to Zimbabwe, while cooperation with Morocco continued in October with further visits. Relations with Cameroon were improved in July when the regime ceased construction of its border wall – begun in 2018 on the pretext of national security following the alleged coup attempt of 2017 – and signed a cross-border pact with Cameroonian officials.

Regional *oil diplomacy* intensified, despite existential threats. In the spring, reports of piracy picked up, prompting President Obiang to meet with Nigerian president Buhari to discuss the Gulf's maritime security. As Covid progressed throughout the summer and oil markets dimmed, Lima expressed public concern for the future of the African Petroleum Producers' Organization and African oil in general. At an emergency videoconference requested by Lima on 15 June, Lima sought to ease divisions, address funding issues, and confront falling Western investment and the fallout of the COP21 climate summit in Paris. Despite this, the Joint Development Zone with São Tomé and Príncipe continued to evolve, while Lima joined other African producers in adhering to OPEC's production cuts in May. As the country's application to join the EITI was rejected in February for failing to meet transparency and governance requirements, non-Western industry allies became ever more critical.

Socioeconomic Developments

The Covid-19 pandemic caused among the most dramatic *crude oil price collapses* in recent memory, from an average closing price per barrel of $ 56.99 in 2019 to $ 39.68 in 2020, with a year's low of $ 11.26. Since the country continued to depend on the oil and gas sector for more than half of its GDP, export earnings fell by 13.5% of GDP, according to estimates by the EIU. GDP contracted by 12.7%, while government revenue fell from 19.2% of GDP in 2019 to 15.6% of GDP in 2020. Public and balance-of-payments deficits ensued, but the *IMF*'s Extended Fund Facility in the country, despite its June meeting having to be postponed, held the promise of bailing out the government. An IMF staff visit in February concluded that there had been some progress towards controlling expenditures and publishing oil and gas contracts, but also highlighted slow improvement towards a better business climate. However, other commercial initiatives brought added macroeconomic security for the future.

In a serious attempt to boost hydrocarbons exports, the country announced 2020 to be the *Year of Investment*. Oil minister Lima, riding the coat-tails of the January announcement that 53 memoranda of understanding had been signed for oil and gas blocks, reiterated his wish to see more *mid- and downstream investment*. The outcome of the series of proposal requests was an optimistic December announcement that $ 1 bn in investment was projected for 2021. The country also moved forward on its plans to become a major gas hub for the region, as in May British Gas Strategies was awarded the gas master plan. In November, state-owned Sonagas and Saipem (Italy) began construction of a gas line between the Alen oilfield and the Punta Europa complex. Five mining contracts were also signed in May, punctuating the regime's efforts to diversify from its historical dependence on upstream production.

As Covid-19 disrupted oil markets (prompting Lima to grant two-year extensions on all exploration contracts in May), and mature fields like Zafiro continued their decades-long production decline (Exxon began seeking to divest from Zafiro in July), successes were nevertheless seen in both the *downstream and upstream sectors*. In October, Teodorín attempted to threaten (French) Total's downstream near-monopoly by working with Marathon Oil and Noble Energy to construct a new modular refinery by 2023, while in May NexantECA was awarded the contract to build a methanol-derivatives plant. In the upstream sector, Lima continued searching for non-Western partners. Deals were reached with Levene Energy (Nigeria) in March and with RosGeo (Russia) in November to conduct seismic studies, which the company finished only weeks later. Attempts at limited nationalisation and reinforced local content proceeded, as in April Lima launched new regulations focusing on local content and the management of maturing fields. In December, Teodorín launched an attempt to acquire the Zafiro oilfield for state-owned GEPetrol.

Despite the boons to Equatorial Guinea's extractive industries, the country continued to have the world's *largest gap between per capita wealth and the country's HDI as published by the UNDP*. With the onset of the pandemic, chronic overcrowding in public schools became a health concern, while hospitals were lacking in equipment, protective gear, and adequately paid staff. Lockdowns had an outsized effect on *public health* and often were not possible to respect, given the lack of running water in most households and the prevalence of communal water taps.

The country suffered 5,277 cases of Covid-19 in 2020, and 86 deaths, according to the WHO and the government. As several reports suggested that these statistics had been deflated, it remained to be seen whether the continent's per capita richest country would protect its poor and vulnerable.

Gabon

Douglas Yates

The country witnessed the fourth cabinet reshuffle since the failed coup of 2019, but a dynastic change of key members of the presidential staff caused a greater stir in the capital. The appointment of a new prime minister came during dual health and economic crises caused by the Covid-19 pandemic and a subsequent fall in the prices of oil, manganese, and timber, the country's three main exports.

Domestic Politics

On 16 July, *Rose Christiane Ossouka Raponda was named as prime minister*, becoming the country's first woman to hold that position. She had previously served as the first female mayor of the capital city, Libreville, and was serving as the country's first female defence minister at the time of her appointment. Raponda was born in the capital city to a prominent Mpongwe family, and her appointment sealed the fate of the Bongo dynasty's former use of the prime ministerial nomination in its electoral strategy of ethnic balancing, denoted in the local patois as '*géopolitique*'. The Fang are the largest ethnic group in the country (ca. 40%) and during the decades in power of current president Ali Bongo's father, the late Omar Bongo, the prime minister's position had always been given to a member of the Estuary Fang. This had been the case for Raponda's immediate predecessor, Julien Nkoghe Bekalé. But since 2016, when numerous Fang ex-prime ministers and other leaders of the powerful Fang community opposed Ali Bongo in presidential elections, three out of Bongo's last four prime minister have been, like Raponda, non-Fang.

Legally speaking, it is not formally forbidden for the head of state to name members of his family to powerful state office, but there was nevertheless ongoing debate around the *nomination of the president's eldest son Noureddin as 'general coordinator of presidential affairs'* on 5 December 2019, a nepotistic post created for the occasion. His father had assigned him the objective of monitoring presidential chief of staff Brice Laccruche Alihanga, whose downfall and arrest in the anti-corruption 'Operation Scorpion' in 2019 had led to the latter's replacement by Noureddin, who was suspected of being behind this operation. The general coordinator's position has been described as a 'super chief of staff' and as the 'number two in the regime'. More controversially, Noureddin's appointment was seen as a further step in his future designation as his father's dynastic successor. One indicator of this dynastic lineage strategy came on 20 November, when President Bongo fired his half-brother Alex Bernard Bongo Ondimba from the Agence nationale des infrastructures numériques et fréquences (the telecommunications agency), which he had directed since its creation in 2011. This followed last year's dismissals of the president's older sister Pascaline Mférri Bongo from the post of high representative of the head of state and his half-brother Frédéric Bongo from the directorship-general of special services. No one in the ruling clan now remains powerful enough to oppose Noureddin as the heir presumptive.

Unsurprisingly, the presidential palace presented this nepotism as an integral part of the fight against corruption. On 21 October, the Paris-based 'Jeune Afrique' reported that the taskforce run by Noureddin had refused to acknowledge € 367 m of internal private debt. Much of this debt, the president's son claimed, had been corruptly embezzled by Laccruche Alihanga and his henchmen during the one-year absence of his father following Ali's stroke in October 2018. The fight against corruption continued against the backdrop of political battles with, for example, the placement in preventative detention, in September, of the mayor of Libreville, Léandre Nzue. But behind the scenes, the appointment of Noureddin is believed to have been the handiwork of first lady Sylvie Bongo, a result of her desire to keep a close grip on the reins of power during her husband's long recovery from his stroke and the flurry of money-grabbing which the impunity of his absence had inspired.

Cyriaque Andjoua became the new head of security for President Bongo, of whom he is the first cousin, succeeding South Korean Park Sang-chul, who was retired in February 2020. Andjoua's father, Fidèle Andjoua, brother of the late Omar Bongo Ondimba, is considered the eldest patriarch of the Bongo clan, and as such, both the father and son retain a significant influence on the elites of Haut-Ogooué, the

Bongo clan stronghold. At the presidential palace Cyriaque Andjoua was previously in charge of the head of state's mission.

The government response to the Covid-19 crisis was better than expected. On 7 and 8 March, the government announced the implementation of a series of measures aimed at preventing the spread of the coronavirus in its territory. No systematic containment was imposed. However, a compulsory health check (heat flashing, in particular) was carried out on newly arriving passengers. In the event of fever or any other symptom that suggested infection, passengers were then placed into confinement. There was a curfew imposed by the government from 6 PM to 5 AM. This was suffered as a hardship by many in the merchant community, who complained regularly about it in the media. After about four months of curfew, on 1 July, the government announced a partial de-confinement after reports of 5,394 people having tested positive for Covid-19, including 2,420 recoveries and only 42 deaths. *By year's end, fewer than 70 people were reported to have died from the coronavirus.*

In March, when the epidemic broke out, Gabonese health authorities initiated a daily public briefing on the evolution of the presence of the coronavirus in the country. This was held every day at the end of the afternoon by Dr Guy-Patrick Obiang Ndong in his dual capacity as secretary-general of the Ministry of Health and spokesperson for the steering committee of the monitoring plan and response against the epidemic, before he was appointed minister of health on 17 July. His press briefings, which thereafter took place three times a week due to the reduced circulation of the virus, were maintained throughout the remainder of the year. This exercise in public health made it possible to dispel false information and respond to the often complacent and unconscious comments which abounded on social networks.

President Bongo made mass testing a priority in the Covid-19 response. A high-capacity laboratory was set up in Libreville capable of carrying out up to 10,000 tests a day. Testing centres were initially set up at the airport, the capital city's hospitals, military bases, and health centres. Diagnosis clinics were soon expanded beyond the capital. Mobile sample collection teams were formed to complement testing centres.

According to the WHO, by 20 October, with over 60 sample collection sites and a network of laboratories, including the high-capacity one, the government had tested nearly a tenth of its 2 m people.

On 3 March, President Bongo announced an arsenal of measures intended for businesses and households in order to counter the economic crisis forecast to result from the health shock of the coronavirus, 'exceptional massive aid measures' that his government implemented to cope with Covid-19. This included CFAfr 250 bn (€ 381 m) to assist companies in financial difficulty through an emergency account created for this purpose. Those firms which had ceased activity or otherwise were suffering because of the health crisis benefited from a moratorium on the repayment of their bank debts, without penalties. Tax breaks were granted to those who preserved jobs for their employees. Private services companies and small businesses saw their final tax obligations and licensing fees reduced by half. The Covid relief package also helped ordinary Gabonese households. Employees placed on technical unemployment received an allowance representing between 50% and 70% of their gross salaries, while income of between CFAfr 80,000 and 150,000 was simply maintained by the public treasury. Around CFAfr 4 bn and CFAfr 2 bn were allocated each month to cover electricity and water bills respectively, while CFAfr 2.5 bn compensated small landlords who were asked to suspend the collection of rent from people without any income. The latter benefited from free public transport and a 'food bank' into which CFAfr 5 bn was injected.

Foreign Affairs

On 17 August, *Gabon celebrated 60 years of independence from France*, marked by a military parade in the capital attended by the president. The French ambassador, Philippe Autié, present at the celebration, evoked a deep cultural proximity: 'This kinship is lasting because it affects history and identity', he insisted, 'but also because it is expected and it is wanted by our two countries'. As the former colonial power, the source of Gabon's Francophone culture, and a long-time supporter of the Bongo regime, France remained the most important ally on the international scene. But the strength of the Franco-Gabonese alliance was declining in terms of bilateral trade between the two countries. The coronavirus crisis, of course, affected exports from France to Gabon, which fell to € 399 m (down 12.5%). French imports from Gabon also fell, to € 105 m (down 25%). As a sign of the lack of diversity in French imports from Gabon, manganese and wood represented 85% of French imports. Also, following the reconfiguration of the local oil landscape and the economic context, oil and gas imports from Gabon fell sharply (down 99%) and represented only 7% of total imports. French purchases of manganese ore (22% of the total) also fell by 57%. Wood was France's largest import from Gabon (62% of total imports), at € 65.4 m, up 10% compared with the previous year. In sum, declining world demand for Gabon's commodities, an indirect effect of Covid-19, had a spillover effect on relations with France. French non-residents of Gabon were strongly recommended by the French embassy to postpone their visit plans as long as they were not essential. Meanwhile the Gabonese diaspora in France, a force of political influence, continued to criticise Ali Bongo's regime and the weak organisation of the opposition within Gabon.

The Covid-19 crisis also had a negative effect on bilateral relations with China, because the origin of Covid-19 was believed to have been in Wuhan, China. So, on 7 February, the government announced an indefinite ban on entry of all travellers from China. This ban was eventually lifted on 11 May. There were some other small incidents, such as when pirates boarded four vessels owned by Sigapeche (formally known as Société Sino-Gabonaise de Pêche) on 21 December 2019 and killed one freighter master and took four Chinese nationals hostage. The four captives were aboard a Chinese trawler awaiting a licence to fish in Gabonese waters. A hotline at the Chinese embassy in Libreville was staffed throughout 2020 to advise Chinese fishing companies worried about safety, according to Hu Changchun, the Chinese ambassador to Gabon who was serving as China's liaison with its fisheries companies operating in the region. When it came to strategic issues of importance to China, Gabon appeared ready and willing to accommodate Beijing. In June, *Gabon was one of 53 countries backing the Hong Kong national security law* at the UNHRC in Geneva, a clear sign that the Bongo regime was willing to support Beijing despite Western criticism of that law.

In a virtual videoconference on 24 December, Indian foreign minister V. Muraleedharan and Gabon's foreign minister Pacôme Moubelet Boubeya discussed and reviewed the entire spectrum of their countries' bilateral relationship, including further strengthening cooperation during the Covid-19 pandemic and possibilities of cooperation in the post-Covid era. They also discussed the huge potential of joint projects in sectors such as manganese, fertiliser, railways, agriculture, and timber. Bilateral trade with *India* had been progressing steadily and had reached $ 511 m in 2019. During the meeting, both leaders also reviewed the utilisation of the Indian Technical and Economic Cooperation Programme to advance aid to Gabon, and Boubeya extended an invitation to Muraleedharan to visit Gabon and also raised the issue of opening of an Indian embassy in the country. The two leaders also discussed India–Gabon cooperation at international level and reaffirmed their commitment to continue to support one another's candidature at the UN and in other international fora.

On 30 April, Serge Thierry Mickoto was named Gabonese ambassador to Belgium, having been the managing director of the Gabonese Strategic Investments Fund, Gabon's sovereign wealth fund, since 2012. Mickoto had been sacked from the fund by President Bongo after he had poorly supervised the purchase of France's BNP Paribas's 37% stake in the country's second-largest bank, Banque Internationale pour le Commerce et l'Industrie du Gabon (BICIG). BNP Paribas received only € 39 m from the sale – less than expected. Looking for a lateral promotion out of important matters of international finance, Mickoto was now responsible for managing cooperation both between Libreville and Brussels and also with the EU, an eminently strategic function in foreign affairs.

Socioeconomic Developments

Gabon has a highly oil-dependent economy, with crude oil revenues providing around a third of the state budget and allowing the country to post one of the highest per capita income figures on the African continent: € 7,425 (or $ 8,030) per inhabitant. Offshore oil production from the Dussafu block came online in early March, when crude prices stood around $ 60 a barrel. Then the outbreak of the economic crisis caused by Covid-19 led to a 25% fall in global energy demand, and African producers saw their exports decline. Prices collapsed by half, reaching as low as $ 25 per barrel by May. So instead of increasing, as had been hoped, Gabon's output instead fell over the course of the year from 200,000 to 150,000 barrels a day. In April, French oil company Perenco announced a lucrative contract to supply gas from Port-Gentil to the Owendo power station serving Libreville. It followed this with the purchase of several offshore oilfields, suggesting a strengthening relationship, in the light of the government's plan for joint investments in real estate, between senior political figures and commercial enterprises.

Living under a state of health emergency from 9 April onwards, despite investments like the gas pipeline to Owendo and new offshore blocks coming on line, oil capital Port-Gentil could well retain the scars of this unprecedented crisis for a long time. Businesses, commerce, transport, tourism, and many other sectors struggled to survive the lockdown, and Covid-19 worsened the social situation of a city usually kept on artificial respiration thanks to public spending. The ECA estimated that this crisis cost Gabon more than 17% of its GDP. Initially, the IMF projected a growth rate of 3.8% of GDP in 2020, down from 3.4% last year. Falling oil prices prompted Fitch to downgrade its sovereign rating from B to CCC on 1 April, as the agency argued that the ensuing drop in liquidity increased the risk on the country's debt repayment. The rating agency expected a budget deficit of 4.6% of GDP in 2020, compared with a budget surplus of 2% in 2019.

Despite being rich in natural resources (or perhaps because of that), Gabon is *now the tenth most indebted country in sub-Saharan Africa*, with $ 174 m in bilateral debt, $ 71 m in multilateral debt, $ 157 m in outstanding bonds, and $ 250 m in private debt to commercial banks. On 8 June, the IMF published a damning report on the poor management of public investments between 2010 and 2019 – i.e. the Ali Bongo era – which concluded that the regime and its collaborators had dilapidated the public coffers, with over $ 5 bn of debt spent on the president's ambitious 'Gabon Emergent' development plan and much being wasted on the multiplication of strategic and operational bodies (agencies, general directions) with unclear management roles, as well as on grand corruption, as revealed by Operation Scorpion.

On 15 April, the G20, under the influence of French president Emmanuel Macron, offered deferment of payment of interest but not debt cancellation to increasingly indebted sub-Saharan African countries. Gabon received over $ 100 m in ECF from this French-inspired international gesture. But the IMF estimated that Gabon's public debt would exceed the high risk benchmark and reach 74.7% of GDP in 2020 and 2021 'due to the past domestic arrears that were validated in the outstanding debt in 2019, widening budget deficits and slowing growth'.

In a report published in February, the World Rainforest Movement accused Singapore-based Olam of making meaningless 'zero deforestation' pledges about a major palm oil plantation and neglecting the rights of local communities. Olam was failing to fulfil commitments made to villagers in the central-southern province of Ngounié before tens of thousands of hectares of new palm plantations were to be established. Oil Palm Gabon, a joint venture between Olam and the government of Gabon, has total concessions of 144,000 hectares, of which 56,000 have been planted with oil palms and 72,000 are permanently protected. Olam is said to have hired a logging company to cut down trees with any commercial value, and it is said that the profits generated were then shared between the logging company, the Gabonese state, and local notables or 'big men'.

São Tomé and Príncipe

Gerhard Seibert

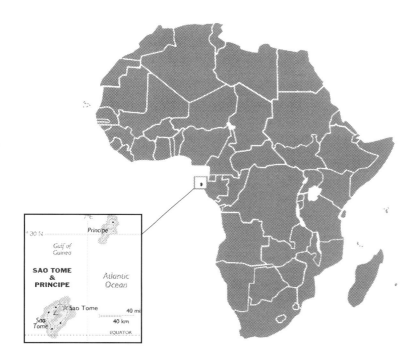

Like everywhere else, the socioeconomic crisis provoked by the Covid-19 pandemic largely dominated domestic politics and foreign affairs. The cohabitation between President Evaristo Carvalho and the government headed by Prime Minister Jorge Bom Jesus was largely conflict free. Nevertheless, when the government meddled in presidential competences Carvalho forced a government reshuffle. Another headline story was that former prime minister Patrice Trovoada regained full control of the opposition Acção Democrática Independente (ADI). However, the government-controlled constitutional court refused to recognise his election as party leader, in an obvious attempt to impede his political comeback.

Domestic Politics

The authorities quickly reacted to the pandemic declared by the WHO. On 19 March, the government imposed a *state of emergency*, including social confinement, closure of the borders, and a flight ban, in an attempt to avoid the spread of Covid-19 in the country. On 21 April, the health authorities confirmed the first three cases of

Covid-19 infection, while nine days later the first death caused by the disease was reported. On 16 June, the government replaced the state of emergency that had been extended five times consecutively with a state of public calamity that in turn was in force until 15 December. With the exception of occasional individual violations of a few restrictive measures in the beginning, there were no popular protests at all against the restrictions of movement. By the end of the year, 1,014 Covid-19 cases and 17 deaths were reported.

Pressured by the dominant rival party faction led by former party leader Patrice Trovoada, on 10 July Agostinho Fernandes, who had been elected ADI president by a dissident faction on 25 May 2019, declared his resignation, paving the way for new leadership elections. Although Fernandes' election had officially been recognised by the constitutional court, his position had already been weakened when on 28 September 2019, the majority faction re-elected Trovoada uncontested *in absentia* as party leader. Nevertheless, the constitutional court refused to recognise Trovoada's election, arguing that it had already approved Fernandes' election. Consequently, at another extraordinary ADI congress held in São Tomé on 3 October, about 600 delegates present elected Trovoada – again unopposed and *in absentia* – as party leader by simple acclamation. However, twice, on 18 November and on 16 December, *the constitutional court again denied the approval of Trovoada's election*, this time on the grounds that he had been elected by a simple show of hands instead of by secret ballot, as demanded by the ADI statutes.

On 3 September, the government triggered a *conflict with President Evaristo Carvalho*, who before his election in 2016 had been ADI vice-president, when it announced a withdrawal of confidence in attorney-general Kelve Nobre de Carvalho due to supposed institutional malfunctioning and failure to proceed with several corruption cases involving members of the former ADI government. The government assumed Kelve de Carvalho's partiality since he had been appointed by the Trovoada government in 2018. On 5 September, President Carvalho classified the government's declaration as a clear act of institutional disloyalty to his office. He argued that the declaration was unconstitutional, since according to the constitution the government could only propose the attorney-general's name, while the latter's appointment and dismissal were presidential competences. On 9 September, President Carvalho held a meeting of the 13-member Council of State, an advisory body, to discuss the affair. Subsequently, the president threatened Prime Minister Bom Jesus with dismissal if he would not reshuffle his government.

Consequently, on 19 September, the latter announced a *government reshuffle*. The ministers of foreign affairs, cooperation, and communities, Elsa Pinto, and of tourism and culture, Maria da Graça Lavres, were dismissed and replaced by Edite dos Ramos Ten Jua, a former justice minister, and Aerton do Rosário Crisóstomo, hitherto secretary of the national assembly, respectively. Minister Osvaldo Abreu maintained his portfolios of infrastructure and natural resources, while a newly appointed secretary of state directly subordinate to the prime minister, Eugénio Vaz do Nascimento, a former director of the Joint Development Authority (JDA) in Abuja, took over public works and environment and received a third new portfolio, territorial planning. Minister Wando de Andrade Castro's competences were also restructured. He became minister of the presidency of the council of ministers, media, and new technologies, while a newly appointed minister, the jurist Cílcio Pires Santos, took over parliamentary affairs, state reform, and decentralisation. During the inauguration of the new government members on 21 September, Bom Jesus declared that it was necessary to draw lessons from the political crisis and promised his executive's constructive institutional relationship with the presidency.

On 15 December, the government parties in the national assembly approved a revision of the 1990 electoral law. During the parliamentary discussion of the bill, the opposition ADI and civil society groups fiercely criticised amendments that they considered unconstitutional. On 2 December, a civil society initiative publicly called upon President Carvalho to veto the bill. Among the contentious issues was the exclusion from presidential elections of independent candidates and those without permanent residence within the country during the three years preceding the elections. The latter restriction was widely interpreted as a measure to impede the candidature of Patrice Trovoada, who has been in voluntary exile in Portugal since November 2018. On 30 December, *President Carvalho vetoed the controversial law*, arguing that it included provisions that were incompatible with rights and liberties and respective guarantees fundamental to the rule of law.

Foreign Affairs

The pandemic significantly affected diplomatic travelling, while China, the country's major bilateral donor, capitalised on the crisis by demonstrating the image of a reliable partner in times of need. On 22 January, as a clear sign of *São Tomé's political support for Moroccan territorial claims to the Western Sahara*, foreign minister Elsa Pinto presided over the inauguration of her country's general consulate in Laayoune, the largest city in the disputed territory, occupied by Morocco since 1975. In 1978, São Tomé had recognised the Sahrawi Arab Democratic Republic, but in 1996 the recognition was withdrawn in exchange for Moroccan development assistance.

On 4 February, Bom Jesus received the Luanda-based *Russian ambassador Vladimir Tararov*, who manifested his country's availability to resume bilateral cooperation in education, maritime security, and international diplomacy. Tararov also mentioned the possibility of granting scholarships for the Moscow-based Peoples' Friendship University of Russia (formerly Patrice Lumumba Peoples' Friendship University). With regard to maritime security, he spoke about the possibility of creating a surveillance company to combat illegal fishing and to install radars to monitor the archipelago's vast territorial waters. On 9 August, São Tomé and Russia commemorated the 45th anniversary of the establishment of bilateral diplomatic relations. On the occasion, Tararov recalled that the Soviet Union had been one of the first countries to recognise São Tomé and Príncipe's independence in 1975.

On 21 February, the resident *Chinese ambassador Wang Wei* and the minister of public works, infrastructure, environment, and natural resources, Osvaldo Abreu, signed an agreement on the modernisation of São Tomé's international airport, including a 600-m extension of the runway. The works at the airport, estimated to last four years, were expected to start in the course of the year; however, a concrete date was not mentioned. On 31 May at the local airport, Wang Wei, Pinto and health minister Edgar Neves welcomed a 12-member Chinese medical team that had been deployed in direct response to São Tomé's request for foreign assistance in the fight against the pandemic. Between June and his departure in September, Ambassador Wang Wei publicly handed over several donations of medical equipment and supplies for the fight against Covid-19. On 5 November, Chinese President Xi Jinping appointed Xu Yingzhen, hitherto secretary-general of the Forum for Economic and Trade Cooperation between China and Portuguese-Speaking Countries (Macao Forum), as new ambassador in São Tomé. On 9 December, Ambassador Xu Yingzhen presented her credentials to President Carvalho, and the following day she was received by Bom Jesus. During both meetings, she guaranteed China's willingness to further strengthen bilateral cooperation in all sectors.

On 25 February, a government delegation headed by Bom Jesus paid an *official visit to Malabo in Equatorial Guinea*. Bom Jesus was received by President Teodoro Obiang Nguema, with whom he discussed questions of bilateral cooperation, including joint oil exploration, the participation of the airline Ceiba Intercontinental in the capital of STP Airways, the creation of a joint shipping company, professional training, and direct budget support. During his visit, Bom Jesus also met his counterpart Prime Minister Francisco Pascual Eyegue Obama Asue, and in his role as leader of the Movimento de Libertação de São Tomé e Príncipe/Partido Social Democrata (MLSTP/PSD) he visited the headquarters of the ruling Partido Democrático de Guinea Ecuatorial (PDGE), where he was welcomed by the latter's secretary-general Jerónimo Osa Osa Ecoro. The delegation included the ministers Osvaldo Vaz (finance), Osvaldo Abreu (natural resources), and Julieta Rodrigues (education), and the secretary of state for trade and industry, Eugénio Graça.

During an official four-day visit to Luanda on 21 December, foreign minister Edite Ten Jua and her Angolan counterpart Téte António signed an agreement on *mutual visa waivers* between their countries. Already in 2013, São Tomé had unilaterally introduced a visa waiver for Angolan citizens for visits of up to 15 days. The new agreement extended this period to 90 days for the citizens of both countries. During her visit, Ten Jua was also received by Angolan president João Lourenço.

Socioeconomic Developments

On 28 February, the government of Prime Minister Bom Jesus announced the postponement *sine die* of the introduction of a 15% value-added tax (VAT) scheduled for 1 March. The government justified the decision by arguing that the computer software necessary for its implementation was not yet operational. The introduction of VAT approved by the national assembly in mid-October 2019 was one of the preconditions imposed by the IMF for the signing of a new 40-month ECF of $ 18.2 m earlier in the same month. During a parliamentary session on 13 March, finance minister Osvaldo Vaz showed his embarrassment and declared that his ministry would work together with the IMF to solve the technical problems. As a consequence, the IMF expects the government to finally introduce VAT in July 2021.

On 14 April, the government approved a batch of economic and financial measures budgeted at $ 84.8 m to mitigate the socioeconomic impact of the pandemic. On 28 July, the 28 parliamentarians of the ruling parties in the national assembly approved the revised 2020 national budget of $ 152.7 m. Due to the pandemic, the revised budget was 7.2% less in value than the previous 2020 budget approved in December 2019. Current expenditure of $ 90.7 m accounted for 59.5% of the budget, and $ 50.7 m (37.2%) was allocated to public investment projects (PIP). The PIPs, including 14.2% for health projects, were 96.1% externally financed, of which 80.4% was grants and 15.7% loans. China (contributing 52.6% of grants) was by far the major donor, while the IMF (55.9% of loans) was the PIPs' principal creditor. Expenditure on personnel represented 51.7% of total current expenditure, while education and health accounted for 16.1% and 12.9% respectively of total expenditure. Total revenue was composed of current revenue of $ 63.3 m, grants of $ 68.2 m, and financing of $ 21.2 m, of which $ 17.1 m came from external sources. On 24 November, the IMF expected the country's economy to contract by about 6% due to the drastic decline in tourism and pandemic containment measures.

The pandemic also prompted the postponement of scheduled oil exploration activities in the Exclusive Economic Zone (EEZ), while the financial constraints provoked by the crisis in the international oil industry resulted in a *major shift of oil block ownership* within the zone. On 1 September, the US oil company Kosmos Energy farmed out several interests in oil blocks in four countries to Dordtsche Petroleum Maatschappij BV, a subsidiary of Royal Dutch Shell, for approximately $ 100 m plus future contingent payments of up to $ 100 m payable upon commercial discovery. In São Tomé, the deal included Kosmos' interests in EEZ block 6 (25%), and EEZ blocks 10, 11, and 13 (35% each). In addition, earlier in the year before the outbreak of the pandemic, Kosmos decided to exit block 12 before the beginning of exploration phase 2. Consequently, Kosmos' 45% stake in this acreage was proportionally awarded to the other two stakeholders, Equator Exploration and Galp Energia, which increased their stakes accordingly from 22.5% to 46.3% and from

20% to 41.2% respectively, while the National Petroleum Agency (ANP) kept its 12.5% interest. In the end, Kosmos, since 2015 the major investor in the EEZ, only kept a 58.85% stake in EEZ block 5. On 25 October, Aerton do Rosário, the minister of tourism and culture, chaired the laying of the foundation stone of the construction of a 2.5 ha, 20-bungalow tourism project at Praia Tartaruga, Cantagalo district, a € 2.4 m investment by the resident French businessman Bruce Rosique. At the ceremony, Siomara Viegas Le Roux, the French honorary consul in São Tomé, claimed that the investment in the south-eastern district would create about 150 new local jobs. At a second stage, Rosique planned to construct another 28 bungalows budgeted at € 3.5 m.

On 3 December, the second anniversary of his government, Prime Minister Bom Jesus inaugurated *the country's first mineral water factory*, called 'Bom Sucesso', located on the former Monte Café estate in Mé-Zóchi district. The project was initiated by Libya in 2009 but interrupted for several years due to the political crisis in that country. The factory, completed by a consortium of the Libyan Africa Investment and Trade Company and the Italian company Zarco with an investment of about $ 2 m, had an average production capacity of 4,000 1.5-litre bottles per hour. In the initial phase, the plant employed 30 local people. The output was destined both for the domestic market and for export to neighbouring countries. Bom Jesus expressed his hopes that the plant would soon make redundant the importing of mineral water.

PART 5

Eastern Africa

Benedikt Kamski

Encouraging signs of peace and reconciliation were overshadowed by open conflict and a deteriorating security environment across large parts of the sub-region. But not all was dim, for instance, the prospects for Sudan to harness the dividends of the revolution were promising and a new transition government in South Sudan restored hope. The first half of the year was characterised by governments' uphill battle to halt the spread of the coronavirus and absorb the immediate socioeconomic repercussions of the pandemic. Key sectors such as tourism, hospitality, and air transport were hit the hardest. Government revenue dropped and debt increased, along with inflationary pressure, shattering generally hopeful developments of recent years. Overall growth contracted by 4.6% and averaged 0.7%. While the Covid-19 pandemic disrupted public life, affected economic performance, and threatened livelihoods, in addition to that, Eastern Africa experienced intense weather extremes. Floods and landslides affected at least 4 m people in the second half of the year in at least eight countries of the region, as well as bordering eastern DRC. Moreover, no end was in sight to the desert locust infestation that had been ravaging especially Somalia, Ethiopia, and Kenya since the end of 2019. This 'triple shock' further weakened food security. Growing numbers of IDPs and refugees put more pressure on hosting nations such as Sudan, where more than 50,000 people from conflict-ridden northern Ethiopia sought refuge from November onwards. The multi-actor war in Tigray, which besides federal and regional troops reportedly also involved Eritrean forces on Ethiopian soil, threatened stability across the Horn of Africa and could end in a dangerous stalemate. Negotiations between the three riparian states of the Blue Nile over the use of the river's waters stalled again, while visible progress on upstream dam construction was reported. Elections that were held despite the public health crisis did not bring notable political changes except in Ethiopia, with the unilateral decision of Tigray to go to the polls that triggered the ongoing war. On the contrary, the year saw increased levels of repressive legislation against the media and an increasingly limited space for opposition groups in many countries. Looking ahead, post-pandemic recovery plans will provide an opportunity to initiate deep economic reforms in Eastern Africa. However, economic recovery will be slow, and substantial additional financing, especially from the private sector, will be needed to adapt existing growth models to novel configurations of global value chains.

Political Developments

The region entered the year with mixed prospects. *Several countries in the region were scheduled to hold elections in 2020* amid growing socioeconomic challenges. The outbreak of the Covid-19 pandemic in Eastern Africa constituted a major disruptive shock from mid-March onwards, resulting in large-scale job losses in the region and amplified debt vulnerabilities. The electoral year became a testing ground for democratisation and the safeguarding of human security and created uncertainties through polling delays and the suspension of elections. While public health concerns were given as the major reason for postponed polls, the pandemic was in many cases not the only factor but added to a bundle of security challenges faced by governments in the region.

Ethiopia postponed legislative elections twice and eventually announced that the long-awaited polls would take place in 2021. Due to the pandemic and deteriorating security situation in many parts of the country, prime minister Abiy Ahmed, appointed by parliament only in 2018, would therefore only be standing for election after his constitutional mandate had already expired in October 2020. Similarly, in Somalia, ongoing armed conflicts resulted in the delay of the November parliamentary and presidential elections, originally scheduled to take place before February 2021, by one year. In Kenya, county assembly and national assembly by-elections did not take place as planned between April and July. Prospects for national elections in Eritrea remained, as in previous years, largely unchanged in the absence of any democratic reforms. Isaias Afewerki is still the only president of Eritrea since independence from Ethiopia in 1993.

Political campaigning for next year's elections took off in the second half of the year in Uganda, and Djibouti also set the course for the upcoming presidential polls. Djiboutian president Ismaïl Omar Guelleh was not yet designated as an official candidate by the end of the year. However, no candidate had declared an intention to contest him in April 2021 either. There were speculations that Guelleh, who has been in power since 1999, would nominate a successor in his party, the Rassemblement populaire pour le Progrès (RPP), yet there was nothing to indicate a transition within the ruling party. By contrast, the campaign for the 2022 elections in Kenya had an early start, while several events surrounding the violence-ridden 2017 campaigning and election period were still unresolved. Campaigning activities in Kenya for individual candidates continued to grow towards the end of the year, and the so-called Building Bridges Initiative shaped the political discourse; however, no agreement was reached as to when the announced constitutional referendum would take place. Casting a dark shadow ahead, the campaign for the January 2021 general elections in Uganda, electing parliament and president, was marked by violence, with dozens of casualties and reports of unprecedented levels of repression of the opposition. It remains to be seen if and how the government will account for the victims during the build-up to the elections. Uganda will see a stand-off between long-term ruler, president Yoweri Museveni, and political newcomer and popular musician Robert Kyagulanyi Ssentamu (known as Bobi Wine), who was arrested multiple times throughout the year, including for violating Covid-19 prevention protocols on public gatherings.

Such clampdowns on the opposition under the pretext of the pandemic came in two contrasting extremes. On the one hand, as seen in Uganda and increasingly in Kenya, opposition politicians were accused of breaching public health protocols. The other end of the spectrum could be witnessed, for instance, in Tanzania: elections went ahead as planned at the end of October in a bizarre environment that was nothing less than 'official Covid-19 denialism' during the campaigning period and on election day. The president and chairperson of Tanzania's Revolutionary Party (Chama cha Mapinduzi, CCM), John Magufuli, was re-elected, with the CCM recording overwhelming results in parliamentary elections. Magufuli had declared the country free from the coronavirus only one month after the first case was reported in May. Significantly, the media was prohibited from reporting on the extent of the health crisis; the pandemic and its effects on the country were not mentioned by the candidates, given the likelihood of repercussions backed by the official restrictions put in place. Tanzania did not enforce any health precautions during campaigning and voting.

Despite an evolving Covid-19 situation across the region since the beginning of the first quarter of the year, the election calendars of Burundi, Comoros, and Seychelles remained largely unaffected. In Burundi, the ruling party maintained its grip on power. Four-term president Pierre Nkurunziza gave way to Évariste Ndayishimiye who was sworn in ahead of his tenure following the sudden death of Nkurunziza in June. Promising news for a peaceful power transition came from Seychelles. Incumbent Danny Faure, whose United Seychelles party faced increasing pressure due to allegations of corruption, lost the presidency to the opposition leader Wavel Ramkalawan and handed over power without notable disruptions. President of Comoros Azali Assoumani and his party the Convention pour le renouveau des Comores (CRC) won the majority in the national assembly in an early legislative election; however, the poll was boycotted by large parts of the opposition. While the absence of a parliamentary opposition shed a controversial shadow on the rule of Assoumani, the banning of opposition rallies in the run-up to the elections in other countries was indeed a clear sign for a further restriction of democratic space.

South Sudan will hold general elections, both parliamentary and presidential, next year. The prospects for sustainable peace and stability, however, have remained relatively bleak since the country gained independence in 2011. The Transitional

Government of National Unity was replaced by a Revitalised Transitional Government of National Unity (RTGoNU) with four vice-presidents appointed by president Salva Kiir Mayardit in February.

In Sudan, the three-year power-sharing agreement between civilian representatives and the military entered its second year. A gradual shift towards a civilian administration took place and prime minister Abdallah Hamdok replaced acting military state governors in 18 states by mid-year. The announcement in December of the establishment of a so-called Transitional Partners Council (TPC) once more illustrated the complex dynamics of the transitional period Sudan entered in early 2019. The chairperson of Sudan's Sovereign Council, Lieutenant General Abdel Fattah al-Burhan was accused of shifting influence to the TPC.

Governments applied widely divergent approaches in the handling of the Covid-19 pandemic, as the decisions to delay elections clearly illustrate. Overall, the pandemic enabled authoritarian practices, which led to the restriction of political protest and of the campaigning of opposition parties. Health-related emergency measures were enforced with excessive use of violence in Rwanda, Kenya, and Uganda, and other countries saw new laws governing assembly rights and a shrinking space for media freedom. In Burundi, the official narrative was that god would protect the country and hence no measures to restrict community gatherings were imposed during the election campaigning period – a pattern that could be observed not only in the sub-region but globally. The sudden illness of sitting Burundian president Nkurunziza, described by official sources as a cardiac arrest but later suspected to be Covid-19, was no isolated incident in the region. Towards the end of the year, the number of coronavirus-related deaths of members of political elites made more and more headlines. For instance, Kenya officially recorded several deaths of politicians, including members of parliament and country assemblies.

High-profile *corruption* cases relating to Covid emergency funds made the headlines. Officials of the Kenya Medical Supplies Agency were accused of embezzling funds through opaque procurement processes for protective equipment, a case that dominated the news in Kenya for several weeks. On *TI's Corruption Perceptions Index*, again most countries of the region ranked relatively low in 2020, with Seychelles best placed and unchanged from the previous year (27th out of 180) followed by Rwanda (49th) and, at the bottom without meaningful changes, Sudan (174th), South Sudan, and Somalia (jointly ranked 179th).

The scores on the main indexes regarding the status of political and media freedoms, civil rights, and democracy were also rather mixed and overall showed little improvement. Several countries performed particularly poorly especially with regard to the *safety of reporters, human rights, and access to political rights and civil liberties*. For instance, on the World Press Freedom Index for 2021 (based on 2020 data), Eritrea occupied the last rank (180th out of 180 countries), followed by Djibouti (176th), and Somalia (161st), whereas Seychelles (52nd) and Comoros (84th) stood out positively in the sub-region.

Restrictions on social media, human rights violations, and harassment of journalists, civil society, and opposition members during the campaign in Tanzania were openly criticised by international actors, including the EU, US, and Commonwealth secretariat. An amendment to the Electronic and Postal Communications Regulations limited the collaboration between local and foreign journalists; the latter were required to be accompanied by government officials assigned to them during their reporting in the country. Similarly, in Burundi, journalists were severely limited in covering information relating to the elections and were obliged to follow an official code of conduct. In Rwanda, the work of social media reporters became more precarious and potentially more dangerous, as YouTubers are officially not recognised as journalists by the Rwandan Media Commission. Press freedom and the security of journalists, both local and foreign, suffered severe set-backs. Well intentioned as a means to counter disinformation, Ethiopia's so-called 'hate speech law' sparked serious concerns following the detention of several journalists throughout the year. Little progress can be reported from Djibouti compared with previous years with regard to press freedom. Journalists working with La Voix de Djibouti, a radio station broadcasting from outside the country, continued to face intimidation and arrest by Djiboutian security forces.

A positive sign was the extension of the mandate of the Commission of Inquiry (CoI) in Burundi, which presented its findings to the UNHRC on human rights violations in the country since 2015. Coming to terms with history remained an essential part of state–society relations in Burundi, with the Commission Vérité et Réconciliation taking a central role. In Rwanda, suspected genocide perpetrators hiding in Europe were brought to justice nearly a quarter of a century after the Rwandan civil war.

The outbreak of the pandemic did not pause *conflict*; at the end of the year the Horn of Africa in particular was again caught up in a spiral of violence involving multiple actors. Insecurity, armed confrontations, and regional flare-ups of intercommunal violence reached a new peak in Ethiopia, with the federal government gradually losing its ability to exercise control in several parts of the country. Tensions between the northern regional state of Tigray and the federal government had been growing for months, culminating in a decisive rupture when the formerly ruling Tigray People's Liberation Front (TPLF) conducted regional elections in September despite a nationwide postponement of polls. Armed conflict between the Ethiopian National Defence Forces (ENDF) and troops loyal to the regionally ruling TPLF erupted in the night between 3 and 4 November following an attack by Tigray Defence Forces (TDF) on the ENDF's northern command stationed in Mekelle. In November, the TDF confirmed rocket attacks on Eritrea's capital Asmara, targeting the airport and military facilities. The conflict in Tigray and events evidently also involving Eritrean forces in Ethiopia and civilians further deepened the existing rift within the diaspora communities of both Eritrea and Ethiopia. Moreover, Amhara militias, rumours of the deployment of Somalian forces, and air support reportedly provided to the ENDF through UAE drones based in Asab, Eritrea, illustrate the complexity of this new conflict, which is likely to drag on for an indefinite time.

Armed activities and combat were by no means limited to the Horn of Africa; Rwanda, Burundi, South Sudan, and Sudan also experienced repeated flare-ups of violence during the year. The rebel movement RED–Tabara claimed two attacks against security forces and armed incursion in Rwanda. Members of the movement were arrested in Rwanda in September, and another incident involving Burundian militiamen in Southern Province was reported. The situation eased somewhat in South Sudan, with the new transitional government bringing new hope for reconciliation. UNMISS, the UN Mission in South Sudan, remained intact for another year. On the other hand, violence and armed conflict continued in different states of Sudan. The AU-UN Hybrid Operation in Darfur (UNAMID) was not extended. With the closure of the peace mission, the complex process of mediating intercommunal conflicts became another key challenge for the Sudanese government.

Operation Atalanta, formally the EU Naval Force Somalia, continued its engagement at the Bab al-Mandeb Strait that links the Gulf of Aden and Indian Ocean with the Red Sea. Protecting one of the main trading routes between Asia, the Arabian Peninsula, and the Mediterranean Sea, Operation Atalanta had recorded noteworthy achievements since its inception in 2008 and was extended until the end of 2022 with an adjusted mandate. There were few reports of attempted *piracy* attacks during 2020, and the number of actual attacks fell drastically compared with 2010. While the threat of piracy along the Somalian coastline visibly decreased, the capabilities of Somali Islamist militant group al-Shabaab to carry out attacks remained surprisingly strong. Troops from Burundi, Djibouti, Ethiopia, Uganda, and Kenya, under the AU Mission in Somalia (AMISOM), were deployed across south and central Somalia; no massive coordinated offensives against al-Shabaab cells were conducted during the year. AMISOM's mandate formally expires at the end of 2021, yet conflict dynamics in Ethiopia in particular are likely to define the further trajectories of Somalia's security situation. The withdrawal of Ethiopian troops not under AMISOM towards the end of the year allowed al-Shabaab to regain strength and prevail in areas under the control of the Somali National Army (SNA) and AMISOM. Several attacks were reported across Eastern Africa, mainly in Somalia and Kenya, with the latter seeing intensified attacks in the first quarter of the year. For instance, in January, al-Shabaab targeted a military base in coastal Kenya that is jointly used by US and Kenyan forces. The porous border between Kenya and Somalia, not yet secured by the controversial border wall, remained an entry point for militants to recruit within the country. The rise of Covid-19 cases in Somalia also played into the hands of al-Shabaab and led to a quick adaptation of propaganda strategies. Covid-19 was labelled a disease brought by the invading forces and their allies.

Transnational Relations and Regional Conflict Configurations

The vision of peace and unity for the *Horn of Africa* outlined since the ascent to power of Ethiopian prime minister Abiy Ahmed in 2018 has been dampened. Unrest, instability, and a stagnating reform course in Ethiopia reverberated across borders and triggered a downward spiral of conflicts. Allegations that Eritrean forces had joined the ENDF in what the federal government called a 'law enforcement operation' against the TPLF in Tigray were not officially confirmed by the end of the year. However, they fuelled speculations about the peaceful rapprochement between Asmara and Addis over the past years. After nearly four weeks of heavy fighting that commenced on the eve of the US elections, the federal government announced that it had regained control over major parts of the region, including the regional capital of Mekelle. However, the war continued until the end of the year and reports of mass atrocities resulted in international calls for an immediate end to hostilities and peace talks, including by the AU; the latter had appointed three high-level envoys to resolve the conflict, yet without success.

With mounting tensions between Sudan and Ethiopia in the border area of al-Gedaref over the al-Fashaga triangle, there can be no doubt that peace and security in the region was increasingly at stake in 2020. Albeit troop movements on both sides of the border and clashes between Ethiopian (federal and regional) forces and the Sudanese military were reported, there were still valid hopes for a diplomatic solution to this conflict between Addis Ababa and Khartoum following bilateral talks between Abdallah Hamdok and Abiy Ahmed in Djibouti in December.

The border dispute added to the ongoing conflict between the neighbours over the filling of the *Grand Ethiopian Renaissance Dam (GERD)* at the headwaters of the Blue Nile and its operation during future droughts. Ethiopia went ahead with the first-phase filling of the reservoir mid-year amid stalled talks that continued to circle around the same narratives. Ethiopia insisted on its right to a 'fair' share of the waters of the Nile, while Egypt stressed the importance of the river for its water security and any obstruction to its flow as an imminent threat to the nation. Significantly, the GERD was also deemed a national security issue in Khartoum after years of leaning towards Ethiopia in the dispute between the three riparian states. Following talks mediated by the US and the World Bank at the beginning of the year, the AU, under the leadership of South Africa, took a more prominent role in the negotiations, yet no agreement for a multi-year drought mitigation scheme could be reached. Ethiopia also announced that it would go ahead with the second phase of filling the dam, scheduled for July–August 2021, and with plans to generate electricity for domestic supply and regional export as soon as technically possible. Fears over armed confrontations between upstream and downstream states grew, notably after US president Donald Trump's reckless remarks on Ethiopia's refusal to accept the proposed agreement.

New alliances were forged and existing ties strengthened. Relations between Juba and Khartoum showed promising prospects, and the Juba Peace Agreement was officially signed in October. Significantly, Egypt and South Sudan also forged closer ties and Egyptian president Abdel Fattah el-Sisi called for a lifting of international sanctions following discussion with Kiir in November. Eritrea and Sudan moved visibly closer together, as evidenced by high-level visits to Khartoum, and relations with Egypt remained firm, showing the complexity of alliances in the region – visible evidence for a re-emerging role for Eritrea in the region.

Besides the conflicts involving Ethiopia and its neighbours that received considerable attention globally, several other countries of the region continued to be entangled in bilateral and regional disputes, yet often less in the spotlight of the international media. Relations between Rwanda and Uganda were finally on a better footing following a regional summit facilitated by Angola and the DRC. However, allegations of continued support for militant groups were not resolved, and borders remained closed. Repeated clashes were reported between Burundian and Rwandan security forces, but relations also improved somewhat and Rwanda announced its readiness to resolve bilateral disputes, resulting in the first bilateral summit for five years. Efforts to ease tensions between Burundi and the DRC were less successful, and Burundi's President Ndayishimiye did not attend a regional summit organised by DRC president Félix Tshisekedi on the issue. Reports of Ugandan forces entering South Sudan (Eastern Equatoria) soured relations between the two governments notably. Salafi-jihadi militants from the Islamic State group (IS) entering Tanzania also became a cause for concern. Following attacks in October in southern Tanzania, the two countries agreed to collaborate in joint anti-terror operations.

The public hearings at the ICJ in The Hague on the Kenya–Somalia border dispute were postponed from June to next year on the request of Kenya, with the pandemic cited as the major reason. Relations between Somalia and Kenya reached a new low due to the lack of progress in the case. Similarly, bilateral relations between Kenya and Tanzania were strained and the governments banned their national carriers from landing on a reciprocal basis. Throughout the year, the cross-border movement of people and goods was affected by the further deepening row between the two countries.

Again, on a negative note, the border conflict in the region of Ras Doumeira between Djibouti and Eritrea, looming since 2008, was far from being resolved despite the positive outlook and regional peace initiatives led by Abiy Ahmed in the previous year.

Despite a year overloaded with negative trends, some promising developments can be reported. Somalia and the self-declared state of Somaliland (officially part of the Federal Republic of Somaliland), at odds for decades, moved closer together following the mediation of Djibouti, which formed the basis for future talks on resource management, security cooperation, and disputed territories.

Overall, *donor dynamics were largely influenced by the global fight against the pandemic and first planning exercises for post-pandemic recovery*. China provided fast and desperately needed medical and technical assistance to the continent. The Jack Ma Foundation, linked to the privately owned Alibaba Group, particularly stood out. China–Africa relations during the year were also marked by rather unusual incidents, such as open criticism of Beijing by African governments. For instance, Kenya questioned the quality of Chinese-supplied personal protective equipment (PPE), and the reported mistreatment of Africans in China during the first weeks of the pandemic prompted official criticism directed at Beijing. Several countries of the region made attempts to renegotiate lending terms in 2020, yet China balked at major talks of debt relief or restructuring of lending terms.

The political and economic influence of China in the region is well documented. What is new is the growing presence of Turkey in recent years. Ankara successfully managed to create an overwhelmingly positive image of its engagements. Turkey stands out especially in the export of construction materials, industrial machines, foodstuffs, and textile and is a central source of FDI inflow to the EAC. The announcement by Turkish government officials at the end of 2019 that 2020 would be the 'Africa Year' for the country, albeit ultimately knocked off course by the pandemic, points to growing engagement in economic, humanitarian, and military areas.

The UAE continued to be a central protagonist across the Horn of Africa, intervening openly and covertly to varying degrees, for instance in Sudan, Somalia, and Ethiopia/Eritrea. Russia's influence is also growing, as new security and energy agreements between Moscow and countries of the region illustrated. The Covid-19 pandemic brought Russia prominently onto the scene, and announcements that it would provide Sputnik V vaccines enhanced its standing in the region, as did the supplying of foodstuffs and testing kids to member states of the SADC. There were growing reports that Russian military contractors are also present in the region, especially across the Horn, albeit less visibly than in West Africa. This caused growing concerns in the US that Washington could be pushed into the background, losing geopolitical influence in the region at the end of a Trump administration that had largely neglected the continent. However, USAID provides long-term funding to most of the region to strengthen livelihoods and enhance food security, and was also visible during the year through financial assistance to control the locust invasion in Somalia, Kenya, and Ethiopia. Yet announcements by the government in

Washington of the halting of funding to countries in the region could contribute to the US's declining standing and the growing influence of other actors.

Socioeconomic Developments

All countries of the region had reported *positive Covid-19 cases* by the end of March, except South Sudan (5 April) and Comoros (30 April). Countries were quick in enforcing health protocols, yet to varying degrees. Containment measures included travel bans, mandatory quarantine for travellers from high-risk regions, the closure of public offices and schools, and the compulsory wearing of face masks. Pandemic fatigue could be seen in several countries by the end of the year. Albeit restrictions were still in place, the public health crisis in the region was overshadowed by other issues, including conflict, elections, and campaigning, and the fatigue was no less due to the overall low (officially) reported numbers of severe cases and fatalities. Rumours and official statements by governments about the effectiveness of 'traditional' medications circulated especially in rural areas, with an initial flare-up of anti-foreigner sentiment reported in several countries. Judging from official figures, no massive outbreak was witnessed despite reports of increasingly overwhelmed health facilities and quarantine centres.

Prior to the pandemic, tourism and travel contributed substantially to employment in several countries of the region. Reduced global aviation, the cancellation of conferences, and the absence of tourists led to the temporary closure of hotels, directly affecting, for instance, Kenya and Ethiopia – both hotspots of international conference tourism in the region. The frequent daily flight links between Eastern Africa and China were stopped until further notice by Kenyan Airways and RwandAir at the end of January. Notably, Bole International Airport, the major passenger hub of Ethiopian Airlines, maintained air transport links to China without interruption, albeit at a reduced capacity, throughout the year.

UNICEF estimated that schools in Eastern Africa were fully closed for an average of 101 days in 2020, making it, together with Southern Africa, the third most affected region globally after South East Asia (where the average was 146 days) and Latin America and the Caribbean (average of 158 days). *The long-term educational effects still cannot be determined.* However, two extremes are evident. On the one hand, a huge digital divide within and between countries of the region manifested itself in limited (or no) access to technologies. This included, for instance, internet coverage and high prices for data packages, as well as the availability of computers and radios that would allow students to participate in remote learning. On the other hand, blended learning techniques were developed and new technologies were used successfully in teaching and learning. This could open up novel opportunities in the future for educators and the education sector on the continent. However, most sub-regions of the continent, and the Eastern African in particular, are still far from the digitalisation standards needed.

Partial *lockdowns and restrictions on movement* entailed the most visible impacts on livelihoods, especially in urban areas. Women faced the highest degree of economic vulnerability, as more than 90% of women are employed in the informal sector, according to UNOCHA estimates. In the absence of reliable data, it is difficult to ascertain trends and impacts; however, this points to higher risks of sexual exploitation and abuse. Threats to food insecurity increased due to a combination of natural disasters (drought, floods, locust invasion), conflict, and displacement. The WFP warned in May that the outbreak of additional effects of the pandemic could double the number of people facing acute food insecurity to 20 m by the end of the year in Burundi, Djibouti, Ethiopia, Eritrea, Kenya, Rwanda, Somalia, South Sudan, and Uganda.

The *macroeconomic performance* of the sub-region remained divergent, according to AfDB data, and average GDP growth contracted by 4.6% (against 5.3% growth in 2019). The pandemic considerably confounded the positive growth projections for the region of more than 5%, with growth averaging 0.7% in 2020. In terms of economic downturn, most affected were the economies of Seychelles (–12% real GDP growth) and Sudan (–8.4% real GDP growth), with growth still positive in Ethiopia (6.1%), Tanzania (2.1%), and Kenya and Djibouti (both 1.4%). While in 2019 the sub-region recorded overall falling inflation rates, in 2020 inflationary pressures amplified existing macroeconomic challenges. Similarly, all countries of the region registered state current account deficits with growing debt; however, this could gradually narrow in 2021 because of the resumption of key economic activities. The pandemic tied up financial resources, affected budgetary and debt positions, and naturally resulted in the delay of national development initiatives.

FDI to the continent declined by $ 7 bn to $ 40 bn between 2019 and 2020, according to UNCTAD's World Investment Report 2021. While this was a reduction of 16% compared with the previous year, the sub-region received combined investments of around $ 6.5 bn. Again, Ethiopia performed well, receiving one-third of FDI to the region, despite looming insecurity in large parts of the country and political instability during the long-awaited election year. Future FDI inflows into the sub-region will be largely determined by rising demand for commodities and commitments made by investors before the pandemic. On the upside, Tanzania and Comoros were upgraded to 'lower-middle-income' and 'middle-income' status respectively by the World Bank.

Conflicts and environmentally induced displacement resulted in growing numbers of IDPs and refugees crossing state boundaries. The number of displaced people in the region reached new heights, and refugees put additional pressure on the hosting countries. By year's end, South Sudan recorded more than 1.6 m IDPs, compared with Burundi's estimated 114,000 IDPs (UNOCHA data). The armed conflict in northern Ethiopia led to an unprecedented cross-border movement from Tigray to Sudan, which hosted an estimated 1.1 m refugees at the end of the year. In addition to more than 4.6 m refugees and asylum seekers, UNOCHA estimated the number of IDPs at 8.8 m in the Greater Horn of Africa region alone. At the same time, reports on the abduction of Eritrean refugees in Ethiopia emerged in the early weeks of the conflict. Several incidents were reported of refugees attempting to cross the Red Sea (via Somali Region in Ethiopia to Djibouti), as well as the forcible return of undocumented migrations to the region.

The region also retained its sad record as home to some of the largest refugee settlements in the world, including the Dadaab refugee complex (Hagadera, Dagahaley, Ifo) and Kakuma refugee camp in Kenya, as well Yida in South Sudan and Katumba in Tanzania.

The pandemic was just one of multiple crises affecting the refugee crisis, livelihoods, and economic development in the region. *Weather extremes* and other ecological catastrophes tested the disaster management capacities and resilience of governments and people. Sudan and South Sudan faced devastating floods during the rainy season, causing large-scale displacement, destroying crops, and reducing yields. Other countries experienced extreme weather patterns, with floods and landslides reported in Ethiopia and Rwanda and drought in parts of Kenya. The biggest threat to rural livelihoods was clearly the desert locust invasion. Despite coordinated regional measures led by the FAO and IGAD, swarms continued to spread across the region, affecting pasture and agricultural land especially in Somalia, Ethiopia, and parts of Uganda, Sudan, South Sudan, Eritrea, and Kenya. The impact of harvest loss in areas affected by maturing swarms and hopper bands will be visible in 2021.

Sub-regional Cooperation and Organisation

The continental approach in the fight against the Covid-19 pandemic was coordinated by the AU; however, *regional organisations* successfully complemented this role, especially by limiting trans-border transmission of the virus (i.e. closure of borders, health checks) and contributing to the sharing of information and resources between national health bodies. For instance, COMESA launched a digital platform for information-sharing among member states. In May, the heads of state of the EAC proposed the establishment of an emergency relief fund for affected business. July also marked the 20th anniversary since the EAC entered into force; over the course of 20 years it has become a customs union and led to the establishment of a common market. These are remarkable and promising achievements for regional economic integration; however, trade conflicts between member states continue to be daily fare. The EAC Heads of State Summit, mandatorily held at least once per year, was again postponed. Paul Kagame, president of Rwanda, thus remained chairperson until 2021, when all six partner states (Burundi, Kenya, Rwanda, South Sudan, Tanzania, and Uganda) are expected to meet. DRC's application for membership is hence still pending, and Uhuru Kenyatta remains 'chairperson-in-waiting'. Throughout the year, exchanges between the EAC member states took place virtually, yet never with the attendance of all heads of state. Following an established tradition, the member states all presented their budgets for the 2020/21 budgetary year on 11 June, except Rwanda, where cabinet approval was pending, and Burundi, which was in national mourning following the death of the sitting president.

The Eastern Africa Standby Force (EASF) held a ministerial council meeting in December to approve its next five-year strategic plan. Sudan became a contributor, so that the EASF now comprises Burundi, Comoros, Djibouti, Ethiopia, Kenya, Rwanda, Seychelles, Somalia, Sudan, and Uganda.

An unexpected development in January 2020 was the proposal from Eritrea, Ethiopia, and Somalia to form a tripartite alliance – again, a sign of the diplomatic re-emergence of Asmara after decades of isolation. The so-called *Horn of Africa Cooperation* is meant to jointly address security challenges in the Horn of Africa. However, given the challenges faced by existing regional blocs in implementing coordinated responses, it remains to be seen if the initiative will further amplify the problems of 'overlapping regionalism' or actually complement the efforts of organisations such as IGAD and the EASF.

IGAD went through a challenging year with the outbreak of the war in Tigray, the extremely strained relations between Kenya and Somalia, and the impacts of the pandemic. Kenya broke off diplomatic relations with Somalia in December and reports on the rapidly deteriorating humanitarian situation in northern Ethiopia determined the agenda of the 38th Extraordinary Assembly of Heads of State and Government at the end of the year. Other topics addressed during the summit were the progress and set-backs of the peace process and security situation in South Sudan and Sudan. While IGAD was accused of putting pressure on Somalia to resolve the diplomatic dispute with its neighbour, Ethiopia refused to tolerate any interference in internal matters. Videoconferences and virtual meetings were held on different subjects throughout the year to discuss the trajectories of the pandemic that had by mid-year affect the member states to a lesser extent than expected.

The East African Legislative Assembly (EALA) also held most of its sessions in virtual format. Similarly, the heads of state and government of the SADC meet virtually for the 40th Ordinary Summit in August, and Mozambique took over the chair from Tanzania. From April onwards, SADC chaired the tripartite group of the SADC, EAC, and COMESA that oversees the implementation of the Tripartite Free Trade Area Agreement (TFTA). Significantly, there will be overlapping memberships between the TFTA and the AfCFTA. The latter was scheduled to enter its operational phase on 1 January 2021 after several months of delay. Once ratified, the TFTA could result in unique trade liberalisation agreements among its members. At the same time, it could evolve into one of the regional trade agreements of the AfCFTA, as detailed in Article 19 of the agreement.

Existing regional economic communities are crucial components of the AfCFTA, as continental integration must be seen as a parallel process of bottom-up and top-down initiatives. The delay of the operational phase of the AfCFTA due to the pandemic did not hamper the sense of euphoria in the region, as large parts of East Africa are in a good position to implement and benefit from the trade agreement. At the end of the year, five countries in the region (Djibouti, Ethiopia, Kenya, Rwanda, and Uganda) had deposited the documents of ratification of the AfCFTA and were legally ready to start the gradual reduction of tariffs on intra-regional trade flows as defined in the agreement. This was beyond doubt an important milestone for regional economic integration, yet several challenges remain, most visibly in the internal dynamics of the EAC.

Burundi

Antea Paviotti and Réginas Ndayiragije

Burundi was marked by three major developments in 2020. Firstly, the *2020 elections* were awaited with apprehension by many, both inside and outside the country, especially after the 2015 electoral period had been marked by significant episodes of violence, and considering the uncertainty around the CNDD–FDD (Conseil National pour la Défense de la Démocratie – Forces pour la Défense de la Démocratie) presidential candidate until just a few months before the elections. However, for the first time in history, the country experienced a peaceful transfer of power from one elected president to another, when Évariste Ndayishimiye replaced incumbent Pierre Nkurunziza, both belonging to the CNDD–FDD. Secondly, on 8 June, the unexpected *death of President Nkurunziza* left a significant void in the political system, which had become increasingly centralised around his figure. This void was promptly filled by Ndayishimiye, who situated himself in a position of both continuity and change within the administration system that developed under Nkurunziza. Thirdly, all this happened in the context of the global *Covid-19 pandemic*, towards which the Nkurunziza government adopted an attitude of denial and kept soliciting god's protection, while Ndayishimiye, after the death of Nkurunziza, faced the virus with more substantial measures.

Overall, the security situation of the country remained under control in 2020, despite two incidents of armed violence claimed by the rebel movement RED-Tabara (Résistance pour un État de Droit – Tabara). International relations with Rwanda as well as with other international partners showed significant improvement, as illustrated by the UNSC decision to drop Burundi-specific deliberations from its agenda. The socioeconomic situation of the country did not present major developments.

Domestic Politics

Burundi's political context was essentially dominated by the *general elections* (presidential, legislative, and municipal) in 2020. Speculations about the CNDD–FDD presidential candidate had been circulating since President Pierre Nkurunziza's announcement (on 7 June 2018) that he would not run for an additional presidential term, which aroused incredulity among most political commentators and analysts. Some believed that the president would ultimately change his mind, while others speculated about potential alternative candidates: the then first lady Denise Bucumi Nkurunziza; the secretary-general of the CNDD–FDD, General Évariste Ndayishimiye; the president of the national assembly and former president of the CNDD–FDD (2010–15), Pascal Nyabenda; and the president of the senate, Révérien Ndikuriyo, to name but a few.

Nkurunziza's commitment not to run for a fourth term was given more credence after the national assembly approved a law (on 21 January) on the benefits reserved to former presidents of Burundi who had been democratically elected. In practice, the only beneficiary of this law among the living former presidents of Burundi was Nkurunziza, as the other three living former presidents had come to power through a coup d'état (Pierre Buyoya) as a replacement for a deceased head of state (Sylvestre Ntibantunganya), and in the context of a transitional government (Domitien Ndayizeye). The benefits, considered excessive and severely criticised by many political opponents, included a lump sum of 1 bn Burundian francs (BIF; around $ 530,000), a monthly allowance, a luxury villa, and the immunities of a sitting president. Thanks to this law, Nkurunziza could have secured his financial and political stability for the rest of his life. A couple of days after this law was approved, the name of the CNDD–FDD presidential candidate was revealed: General Évariste Ndayishimiye, named as 'samuragwa' ('heir').

Despite these announcements, the real impact of Nkurunziza's retirement from the public scene was not clear. On 20 March, a law consecrating Nkurunziza as Burundi's 'Supreme Guide of Patriotism' made the soon-to-be-retired president an 'ideal reference in terms of patriotism, social cohesion, and national wisdom'. In this capacity, Nkurunziza had the ultimate say on 'questions related to the safeguarding of national independence, to the consolidation of patriotism, and to national unity', thus obtaining a political status more or less equivalent to that of the incumbent president.

The outbreak of the *Covid-19 pandemic* did not put into question the appropriateness of holding elections either for the ruling party or for the political opposition in Burundi. A key argument advanced by many government representatives was that god would protect Burundi from the hecatombs that Covid-19 was provoking elsewhere. In addition, by postponing elections and thus recognising the seriousness of the pandemic, the government would have had to take more severe measures to fight Covid-19, and measures like lockdowns and curfews would have been unpopular and were therefore not an option during the electoral period. Thus, the electoral calendar was maintained as planned: presidential, parliamentary, and municipal elections on 20 May; senate elections on 20 July; local elections (at the hill and neighbourhood levels) on 24 August. The political opposition in Burundi also never questioned the government stance and conducted its electoral campaign as well. Several opponents in exile denounced on social media the irresponsibility of the government, which did not take any major measures to fight the virus and carried out the electoral campaign as if Covid-19 did not exist: political gatherings were allowed without any measure of social distancing or obligation to wear masks. Online, opponents criticised the government's inadequate resources to face the pandemic and questioned the real state of the pandemic in the country, where those who contracted Covid-19 would have not been able to admit it because it would have contrasted with the government's narrative.

The electoral campaign started on 27 April in accordance with the planned electoral calendar. In total, seven candidates ran for president: five candidates from political parties (Évariste Ndayishimiye for the CNDD–FDD; Agathon Rwasa for the CNL/Congrès National pour la Liberté; Gaston Sindimwo for UPRONA/Union pour le Progrès national; Léonce Ngendakumana for the Sahwanya FRODEBU/Front pour la Démocratie au Burundi; Domitien Ndayizeye for the coalition Kira Burundi) and two independent candidates (Francis Rohero and Dieudonné Nahimana). Former CNDD–FDD president (2007–12) Jérémie Ngendakumana, in exile in Belgium since 2015, also announced his intention to participate in the electoral process and, to this end, founded the party PDG–Girubuntu (Parti pour la Démocratie et la Bonne Gouvernance – Girubuntu) in January. On 15 February, Ngendakumana was denied entry to Burundi by the Burundian embassy in Kampala (Uganda), where he had solicited a laissez-passer, and his presidential ambitions were thus thwarted.

The months before the elections were characterised by a climate of political tension between the ruling party and the CNL. The CNDD–FDD accused members and supporters of the CNL of committing violence during the electoral campaign, while the CNL accused the CNDD–FDD of vandalising its local party headquarters (*permanences*), harassing its members, and undermining the organisation of its political gatherings. Non-governmental media outlets denounced bias in the distribution of electoral cards, the unexpected rejection of some candidacies at the legislative and municipal elections, and the arrest of more than 200 CNL electoral observers the day before elections and on election day.

According to the official results approved by the constitutional court, Évariste Ndayishimiye (CNDD–FDD) was elected with 68.70% of the votes in the presidential elections of 20 May. Agathon Rwasa (CNL) received 24.18% of the votes, while each of the other candidates garnered less than 2% (1.63% for Sindimwo, 0.54% for Ndayizeye, 0.47% for Ngendakumana, 0.41% for Nahimana, and 0.16% for Rohero).

In the national assembly, the CNDD–FDD obtained 86 out of the 123 seats while the CNL obtained 32 seats, the UPRONA secured two seats, and three seats were allocated to the Twa ethnic group through co-optation. In the senate, the CNDD–FDD obtained the large majority of the seats (34 out of 36, or 94.4%), while CNL and UPRONA obtained one seat each. Many CNL supporters were disappointed with the relatively low number of votes obtained by their party and suspected electoral fraud. The results of the 2020 elections also confirmed the important loss of their grip on power of historical parties like UPRONA and FRODEBU.

The regularity of the elections was questioned by many. External observers were awaited from the EAC but on 8 May, 12 days before the scheduled elections, the government 'reminded' the EAC secretary-general that their electoral observers would be placed under 14-day quarantine upon arrival in Burundi, as part of the measures taken in the fight against Covid-19. This prevented them from being operational at polling stations and counting centres on 20 May. Ultimately, no external observers were accredited. Domestic observers were deployed by the Conference of the Catholic Bishops of Burundi, which denounced several electoral irregularities in a communique of 26 May, putting into question the results of the elections. The official results were also contested by Agathon Rwasa through an appeal to the constitutional court on 28 May. Despite these claims, on 4 June, the constitutional court validated the results of the presidential elections as proclaimed by the Commission Électorale Nationale Indépendante (CENI), thus confirming the victory of the CNDD–FDD.

A few days later, on 8 June, *Pierre Nkurunziza died* under unclear circumstances. According to the government's announcement, he died from a heart attack; many opponents claimed that he actually died of Covid-19, which the ruling party could not have admitted without contradicting its own narrative. Some even suspected he was assassinated because he was trying to gain too much influence. The death of Nkurunziza left an important void within the CNDD–FDD and in Burundi's political arena, where the late president had become an increasingly central figure. Some feared that this sudden void would lead to a crisis in the middle of the electoral period and at a moment when the transition between presidents was not yet completed. The death of the former president also raised the question of who should replace him, since Nkurunziza's term was expected to end only in August. According to the constitution, Pascal Nyabenda, as president of the national assembly, should have replaced the deceased president, and the election of a new president should have been organised within three months. However, a new president had just been elected and recognised by the constitutional court. On 12 June, the constitutional court established that Évariste Ndayishimiye could take up the position ahead of the planned date. Thus, Ndayishimiye was sworn in as new president of Burundi on 18 June.

The new president assumed a position of both continuity and change in relation to his predecessor. The adoption of the motto 'Leta Mvyeyi, Leta Nkozi' ('The parent-state, the worker-state'), sometimes completed by 'Leta Nsenzi' ('the prayer-state'), was an excellent illustration of this: it replaced 'Dusenga dukora, dukora dusenga' ('We pray by working, we work by praying'), previously adopted by Nkurunziza, and it modifies the message about the state, although its main elements, notably working and praying, remain present. Once in office, in order to secure the most important basis for his political support, Ndayishimiye nominated high-ranking military and police officers into positions of political responsibility, as members of the government or provincial governors. Thus, Alain-Guillaume Bunyoni was named prime minister, a position reintroduced after more than 20 years by the 2018 constitution, and Gervais Ndirakobuca was appointed minister of the interior, community development, and public security. Both Bunyoni and Ndirakobuca are under US sanctions, and Ndirakobuca is under EU sanctions too, for human rights violations committed in the context of the violence that characterised the 2015 electoral period. The further centralisation of power in the hands of the CNDD–FDD compared with the 2015–20 period also became clear at the institutional level: the new government included only members of the CNDD–FDD, and a significant amount of power was placed in the hands of the president. The office of the secretary of state, the office of the inspector-general, the central bank, and even tasks like the partnership with Burundi Backbone System, the consortium working for the installation of optic fibre in Burundi, fell under the responsibility of Ndayishimiye. The expansion of the functions of the president may represent a way to limit the influence of Prime Minister Bunyoni, like Ndayishimiye a heavyweight of the CNDD–FDD system, and to ensure that the president is not relegated to a ceremonial function.

At the same time, Ndayishimiye took some initiatives that showed the will to represent an inclusive government. In mid-July, the president met the Conference of the Catholic Bishops of Burundi, signalling an attempt at reconciliation after tensions emerged during the 2020 electoral period. On 27 July, Ndayishimiye received former presidents Domitien Ndayizeye and Sylvestre Ntibantunganya, an unprecedented event since the CNDD–FDD has been in power. In addition, Imelde Sabushimike was appointed minister for solidarity, social affairs, and human rights – the first Twa, and the first Twa woman, to hold a ministerial post.

Two main incidents of armed violence took place in 2020 in Burundi. Between 19 and 23 February, clashes took place between an armed group and security forces in the province of Bujumbura Rural. According to official sources, 22 armed men and two police officers were killed during the combat and six members of the armed group were captured. Between the end of August and mid-September, armed incursions were reported in the southern provinces of Rumonge and Bururi and in parts of Bujumbura Rural. The official number of casualties was unknown. Both attacks were claimed by the rebel movement RED–Tabara.

Hearings of two important judicial proceedings were held in 2020. On 4 February, a hearing was held at the supreme court, *in absentia* and without legal representatives, as part of an ongoing process against 12 lawyers, activists, and journalists in exile accused of being involved in the organisation of the 2015 coup d'état. On 19 October, in the context of the trial of those accused of involvement in the assassination of President Melchior Ndadaye in 1993, the supreme court sentenced former president Pierre Buyoya and 18 other Tutsi politicians and former army officers to life imprisonment and a collective fine of BIF 102 bn (around $ 54 m). They were accused of 'attack against the head of state, attack against the authority of the state, and attempt to bring about massacre and devastation'. Three other people were sentenced to 20 years' imprisonment, while one person was acquitted. On 24 November, Buyoya resigned from his role as AU high representative for Mali and the Sahel, which allowed him to dedicate himself to his defence. On 17 December, Buyoya died of Covid-19.

In parallel with these processes, the Commission Vérité et Réconciliation (CVR) continued its exhumations throughout Burundi. A first report on the activities of the commission was presented to the public on 14 February. Many activists and government opponents repeatedly accused the CVR of conducting selective exhumations by focusing on the 1972 massacres of the Hutu, possibly in support of the predominantly Hutu ruling party.

The human rights situation remained worrisome throughout 2020. The Commission of Inquiry (CoI) on Burundi, created in 2016 to investigate human rights violations and abuses in the country since April 2015, documented 'numerous serious human rights violations' and episodes of political violence (summary executions, arbitrary arrests and detention, torture, sexual violence, hate speech) in its report presented in September to the UNHRC. On 6 October, the mandate of the CoI was extended for another year. On 2 October, the arrest of Fabien Banciryanino, a former independent parliamentarian who in March had voted against the law that nominated Nkurunziza as 'Supreme Guide of Patriotism', and his imprisonment on charges of threats to state security, slander, and rebellion aroused the concern of many human rights defenders.

A positive sign of respect for human rights, however, was represented by the supreme court's rejection and request for revision of Germain Rukuki's sentencing to 32 years in prison on 30 June. Rukuki was working for a local association for the abolition of torture when he was arrested in 2017; a petition for his release was launched by AI. Another positive sign was the liberation of four journalists working for Iwacu Press Group who had been arrested and imprisoned in October 2019, while they were trying to report on two armed attacks on military and police posts in the north-western province of Bubanza. On 30 January, the journalists were sentenced to 2.5 years of prison and a fine of BIF 1 m (around $ 530) but were released on 23 December on presidential pardon.

The government's relationship with local media remained difficult in 2020. Local media had to respect a specific code of conduct in the coverage of the 2020 elections, publishing only information that was provided by the national electoral commission. Burundi ranked 160th out of 180 countries in the 2020 World Press Freedom Index elaborated by Reporters Without Borders, dropping one position from 2019. The country was still classified as 'not free' by Freedom House in 2020, with a 'global freedom' score of 13/100 (as of 31 December 2019), one point less than in 2019.

Foreign Affairs

Burundi's relations with foreign countries showed significant changes in 2020, despite some elements of continuity with the past. Relations with the neighbouring DRC were marked by some tensions. On 26 April, the Burundian army attacked the RED–Tabara rebel movement in South Kivu (eastern DRC). Congolese president Félix Tshisekedi was not open to an active collaboration with the Burundian army in the eradication of Burundian rebel groups, and Burundi withdrew its troops. When Tshisekedi tried to organise a summit of the heads of state of the region (DRC, Rwanda, Uganda, Angola, and Burundi) on 13 September in Goma (eastern DRC), Ndayishimiye refused to attend, declaring a preference for bilateral discussions with the Congolese president.

Relations with Rwanda, severely strained since 2015, showed signs of improvement in 2020. On 8 May, shooting took place between the Burundian and the Rwandan armies on Lake Rweru (in the northern province of Kirundo, on the border between the countries), after Rwandan defence forces ordered Burundian fishermen who were allegedly fishing in Rwandan waters to return to their country. On 26 June, clashes took place at the border with the Rwandan district of Nyaruguru, during which the Rwandan defence forces claimed to have pushed back to Burundi around 100 unidentified armed men. Notwithstanding these incidents, Rwandan president Paul Kagame declared on 10 July that Rwanda was ready to work with Burundi to address their strained relations. On 26 July, 331 refugees from the Mahama camp in Rwanda who had fled Burundi in 2015 sent a letter to President Ndayishimiye asking him to facilitate their return to Burundi. On 7 August, in reaction to this letter, Ndayishimiye declared that Burundi would not hold relations with a 'hypocritical state that takes refugees hostage and that hosts criminals who harmed Burundi'. Nevertheless, on 26 August, Rwandan and Burundian military intelligence chiefs met at the border at Nemba to discuss security issues affecting the two countries. On 29 September 2020, the Rwandan defence forces apprehended 19 Burundian rebels, self-identified as RED–Tabara combatants, in the Rwandan district of Nyaruguru. The ICGLR Expanded Joint Verification Mechanism (EJVM) intervened to investigate the incident, although Burundi was seeking the rebels' extradition. On 20 October, the Burundian and Rwandan ministers of foreign affairs met on the Nemba–Gasenyi border, with the aim of normalising bilateral relations between the two countries.

Burundi's relations with Tanzania and China remained strong. On 26 June, Burundi received the support of Tanzania, which said it would back Burundi's attempts to enter the SADC, after Burundi was said not to meet the admission requirements in 2019. On 20 September, Ndayishimiye made his first state visit to Tanzania, with the aim of 'strengthening brotherhood and cooperation'. Burundi's relations with China were also strengthened during the Covid-19 pandemic, with China providing important quantities of medical supplies. Despite the government's attitude of denial towards the pandemic, Burundi received a first supply of medical equipment from the Jack Ma Foundation on 24 March; within the framework of the bilateral cooperation between the two countries, on 3 April and on 4 June China sent additional medical equipment to Burundi worth more than $ 400,000.

Burundi's relations with other *international partners* also showed significant improvement in 2020. It notably achieved an important diplomatic victory on 4 December, when the UNSC decided to drop Burundi-specific deliberations from its agenda, following many years of lobbying on the part of the Burundian government and its UNSC allies China and Russia. Burundi was thus included in the reporting on the broader Central Africa and the Great Lakes region. In its official communique, the UNSC based its decision on its observation 'of the improved security situation in Burundi and of the six principal priorities presented by President Ndayishimiye' after 'the broadly peaceful elections which marked a new phase for Burundi'. The measure came after the OIF resumed its multilateral cooperation with Burundi on 4 November, after four years of suspension as a result of the 'democratic crisis' and 'gross and continuous human rights violations' that followed the 2015 electoral period. The OIF was convinced by the fact that the 2020 elections 'led to the election of a new president of the republic and to the setting up of new authorities and of a new parliament' and that 'the new authorities' took action 'in favour of Burundians' well-being, independence, [and] daily security, as well as of the guarantee of their rights and freedoms'. In addition, on 27 July and on 7 December, Ndayishimiye met different European ambassadors, renewing ties with European diplomacy in Burundi after a five-year break. All these signs of openness, in both regional and international diplomacy, clearly broke with the hard line that Burundi's government had privileged under Nkurunziza, especially after the 2015 crisis.

Socioeconomic Developments

Burundi's socioeconomic situation did not show significant improvement in 2020. Most of the indicators of reference remained stable: Burundi ranked 185th out of 189 countries on the 2020 Human Development Index (data refer to 2019), as in 2019; in the 2020 World Bank Doing Business Index, Burundi ranked 166th out of 190 countries (benchmarked to 1 May 2019), as it did in 2019; in the Corruption Perceptions Index elaborated in 2020 by TI, Burundi had the same score as in 2019 (ranking 165th out of 180 countries, with a score of 19/100, where 0 means 'very corrupt' and 100 'very clean'). Internet penetration also remained low, with a rate of 10.4% as of 30 September, according to Burundi's Agence de Régulation et de Contrôle des Télécommunications. According to the IMF, real GDP growth was negative in 2020 (–3.2 annual percentage change), while general government gross debt reached 69.5% of GDP, confirming an upward trend (+9.4 percentage points compared with 2019). The IMF's last report on debt sustainability (April 2015) identified a high risk of debt distress; the last Article IV consultation took place on 25 August 2014. On 15 May, the state budget for the period 2020/21 was established at BIF 1,576.03 bn (around $ 1.67 bn), showing a 3.8% increase as compared with 2019.

In continuity with the preceding years, the government strived to contain the *depreciation of local currency*. In February, $ 1 could be exchanged on the official market for around two-thirds of its value on the black market. Since September 2019, the government had been implementing stricter measures against unauthorised exchange dealers, by fining or arresting them. On 15 February, the central bank announced the closure of all foreign exchanges, leaving the monopoly of foreign-currency exchange to the banks. The measure provoked discontent among both foreign exchange employees and clients. On 18 March, the central bank announced that international money transfers via Western Union and MoneyGram were to be done in BIF. These measures were aimed at tackling the lack of foreign currency in Burundi, which was the outcome of the reduction of foreign investment in the country since 2015. Many perceived these measures to be a way for the government to have exclusive control over the increasingly reduced inbound cash flows.

The government took some initiatives aimed at boosting the local economy. On 15 April, the Bank for the Youth (BIJE, Banque d'Investissement pour les Jeunes) was inaugurated in Gitega, offering youth access to credit at a preferential interest rate (7%) in order to facilitate access to capital for the implementation of projects of economic development. On 15 September, a partnership was established between the BIJE and the Agence de Promotion des Investissements (API). After an important market in the Kamenge neighbourhood of Bujumbura burned down on 3 October, President Ndayishimiye organised a fundraiser for the rehabilitation of the market, for which a commission was established.

The country's economy continued to rely mainly on agriculture, from which more than 90% of the population derived its livelihood, according to IFAD. According to the FAO, subsistence farming contributed around 40% of the country's GDP and 80% of its production is used for consumption. Burundi exports coffee, tea, and sugar, as well as rare-earth elements, nickel, and gold. The exportation of these products was affected by the Covid-19 pandemic to the extent that Burundi's main commercial partners took quarantine and lockdown measures that slowed down or temporarily put international trade exchanges on stand-by. On 3 December, the LATAFIMA project (Lake Tanganyika Fisheries Management, EU-funded) was launched by the Authority of Lake Tanganyika (to which Burundi, DRC, Tanzania, and Zambia adhere) through the Ministry of Environment, Agriculture, and Livestock, with the aim of improving fisheries management and production in Lake Tanganyika. At the same time, the LATAWAMA project (Lake Tanganyika Water Management, EU-funded) aimed to improve the utilisation and management of Lake Tanganyika's cross-border waters and fight against water pollution. As a result of both climate change and seasonal rains, the water level of Lake Tanganyika rose significantly in April and September, obliging some families to leave their homes on the lakeside and affecting the economic activities of bars and restaurants situated on Bujumbura's lakeshore.

The outbreak of the *Covid-19 pandemic* was officially recognised in Burundi on 31 March. Between 5 and 20 March, the government imposed a period of quarantine on passengers on arrival in Burundi; 'highly recommended' handwashing kits at the entrances of public spaces (health structures, schools, stadiums, private and public offices, churches, bars, markets); and closed international borders. Mass gatherings remained allowed; masks were not required anywhere. In mid-May, Burundi expelled four WHO representatives because they seemed to interfere in the government's management of the pandemic. According to data provided by the Ministry of Health, two people died of Covid-19 in 2020. Only after Ndayishimiye came to power was the campaign 'Ndakira, sinandura kandi sinanduza' ('I recover, I do not get contaminated and I do not contaminate [others]') launched, made possible by $ 5 m from the World Bank. Mass testing was carried out and information was regularly shared about new Covid-19 cases and deaths. On 20 July, the IMF approved $ 7.63 m in debt relief to Burundi to help the country free up resources for its public health sector. On 6 May, the WHO reported a measles outbreak in the north-western province of Cibitoke, allegedly brought in by refugees from measles-affected provinces of the DRC. The outbreak affected at least 857 people, especially children, in Cibitoke and other provinces. Although malaria is endemic in Burundi, the number of cases declined in 2020 (1.2 m cases reported as of 22 March, compared with 1.7 m in the same period in 2019), according to data provided by UNOCHA.

In the months before the 2020 elections, around 3,000 people fled Burundi. This added to more than 300,000 people who had previously sought refugee status, mostly in connection with the 2015 crisis, and were still living outside Burundi. As of 31 December, around 150,000 refugees were residing in Tanzania, 65,000 in Rwanda, 50,000 in Uganda, and 47,000 in the DRC. After the 2020 elections, a significant number of people voluntarily returned to Burundi from Tanzania, Rwanda, and DRC under the framework of the tripartite agreements between the governments of these countries and UNHCR. As of 31 October, 106,588 refugees had returned to Burundi. Inside Burundi, according to IOM data, 113,841 IDPs were counted in December. Most of them (81%) had left their place of origin following natural disasters, and 88% of them were living in host communities throughout the country.

Comoros

Simon Massey

While, the year was dominated by the Covid-19 pandemic, the health implications of the virus for the populations of the three islands of the Union of the Comoros were limited throughout the year. The main effects of the pandemic were the economic, social, and external consequences of the preventative and control measures imposed by the government of President Azali Assoumani. Curfews and transport restrictions in and out of the country meant that most projects funded by the World Bank, the IMF, and the private sector intended to generate growth under the Emerging Comoros Plan (Plan Comores Emergent, PCE) were unable to start. Likewise, the same anti-Covid measures undermined the infrastructural projects that were part of the Cyclone Kenneth recovery plan. The usual amount of activity between Comoros and its international partners also diminished as a result of travel restrictions and the Comoros' limited capacity to transfer its diplomacy online. An exception was increased communication with the World Bank and IMF, which were forced to incorporate the challenges of Covid-19 with the existing planning for regeneration after Cyclone Kenneth. The major political event at the start of the year was the legislative elections, brought forward three months by the government. When they were boycotted by the opposition, the inevitable result was a landslide for the government party and its allies. The strategy of forcing the government into a position where it controlled all the levers of state in order to demonstrate its illegitimacy to the wider world was explicitly adopted by a new anti-Assoumani platform – styling itself a resistance rather than an opposition – the *Front Commun des Forces Vives Comoriennes*.

Domestic Politics

After he secured the first of two further potential terms as president through victory in the disputed 2019 election, the final branch of government outside Assoumani's grasp was the *national assembly*. His party, the *Convention pour le renouveau des Comores* (CRC), held only two seats in the assembly, with the highest number of seats being held by the parties of former president Ikililou Dhoinine, the *Union pour le Développement des Comores* (UPDC), and former President Ahmed Abdallah Sambi, the *Parti Juwa*. Despite the opposition having a clear parliamentary majority and the assembly's mandate officially not due to end until March 2020, political horse-trading allowed 'enabling' legislation to pass granting the government the power to rule by decree and to take any measures necessary to organise new legislative elections.

The national assembly was peremptorily closed by the government on 31 December 2019. On the day before its closure, the opposition sought to bring a vote on an amnesty bill aimed at preventing further arbitrary arrest and imprisonment of Assoumani's opponents. Despite having passed all of its committee stages, the bill was withdrawn from the parliamentary agenda by minister of interior Mohamed Daoudou, a parliamentary manoeuvre condemned by the opposition as interference in the prerogative powers of the national assembly.

The assembly comprised of 33 members, elected using two methods. Firstly, 24 members were directly elected in single-member constituencies using the two-round system with a first round of voting on 19 January and a second scheduled for 23 February. The remaining nine members were elected by the island assemblies of Ngazidja, Nzwani, and Mwali. Since all three assemblies were solidly pro-Assoumani, there was an assumption these members would be government supporters.

With many of their number in prison or exiled, the opposition combined in calling for a boycott of the legislative election. Rejecting as mere rhetoric calls from Assoumani for the opposition to participate, opposition leaders offered to take part in the election only if its demands, including transparent elections and the extension of the franchise to the Comorian diaspora community, were met and guaranteed by a credible international organisation. This was not acceptable to Assoumani.

The boycott had a chilling effect on Comoros' usually animated political campaigning. The campaign was described by Radio France International (RFI) as lacking the 'slightest enthusiasm', citing one voter's damning verdict that 'there were no elections, just nominations'. The African Union Election Observer Mission noted 'the lack of interest of the population' and the 'unusual absence of effervescence'. Despite the boycott and the apathy, voter turnout was measured by the *Independent National Electoral Commission* (CENI) as unexpectedly high, at 62.42% in the first round and 62.80% in the second round.

Ultimately, 81 candidates contested the 24 seats in the single-seat constituencies. However, of these, 35 came from the umbrella *Alliance de la Mouvance Présidentielle* (AMP), a grouping of parties supporting Assoumani that included 21 candidates from his own CRC; seven from the *Rassemblement pour une Alternative de Développement Harmonieux et Intégré* (RADHI), led by Houmed Msaidie, Assoumani's campaign manager in 2019; and seven from the Orange Party, led by Daoudou. Only one candidate from a recognised opposition party stood – El-Anrif Mohamed of Mouigni Baraka's *Rassemblement Démocratique des Comores* (RDC). The remaining 45 candidates ran as independents.

The final results were announced by CENI after the run-off polls on 23 February. The CRC won a total of 20 seats, the Orange Party two seats, and two independent members were elected. As anticipated given the boycott, Comoros was left with no more than a rubber-stamped parliament and negligible legislative scrutiny of Assoumani's policies going forward.

The absence of a parliamentary opposition will remove the legislative obstacles that have held up policy-making under previous administrations, but also the last layer of checks and balances within Comoros' governance. However, if the purpose of the boycott was to draw attention to the illegitimacy of governance under Assoumani, it has had only limited success.

Based on the country's position in a set of international league tables, *corruption* continued to grow in Comoros over the past year. The country dropped yet further down on *Transparency International's Corruption Perceptions Index 2020*, published in January 2021 based on data collected between May 2019 and May 2020, from 153rd out of 180 countries in the 2019 CPI to 160th in the 2020 ranking.

Reporters Without Borders rated Comoros at 75th out of 180 countries in its *World Press Freedom Index 2020*, a sharp drop from a ranking of 49 in the 2018 index based on an analysis of deteriorating media freedom between January 2017 and December 2019. Reporters Without Borders' reported 'an unusual and dramatic surge in press freedom violations, including intimidation of journalists, attacks, arrests and censorship, forcing some Comorian journalists to flee abroad for safety reasons'. While Comoros had previously been considered a model of *media freedom* in the region, the coronavirus pandemic cast further light on Assoumani's determination to deprive Comorian journalists of the freedom to conduct independent investigation, with journalists investigating the government's handling of the pandemic being threatened with prosecution.

Finally, in terms of *political rights* and *civil liberties*, Freedom House rated Comoros as 'partly free' in its 2020 Freedom in the World survey, with a *Global Freedom Score* of 44, down from 50 the previous year. The most visible case of human rights abuse remained the continued pretrial detention, for 28 months between May 2018 and the end of the 2020, of former president Sambi, accused of the embezzlement of more than € 800 m of public funds and held in his own house, declared an annex of Moroni prison. Since Comorian law sets pretrial detention at a maximum of four months, renewable once, by the end of the year Sambi had already been held for three times the permissible period of detention.

In July, a new *anti-Assoumani platform*, the *Front Commun des Forces Vives Comoriennes*, was established that explicitly linked Sambi's continued incarceration with what the Forces Vives claim to be the constitutional coup of the 2018 referendum. Their argument was that 2021 should be treated as a presidential election year, since if the constitution had not been changed then the next legitimate presidential poll according to the rotating presidency system should take place on 26 May 2021 and should be restricted to candidates from Nzwani. They claimed that the most likely victor would be Sambi. Referring to Assoumani as merely a 'tenant' in the presidential palace, the Forces Vives declared that 'the fight today is no longer that of the opposition. It no longer exists. It's now *resistance*. Opposition exists only in a democracy.'

The three main sources of support for the Forces Vives are the tacit anti-Assoumani sentiment within the electorate, the Comorian diaspora, and the international community. Extrapolating from the votes for Assoumani at the 2015 presidential election – the last poll widely accepted as free and fair – suggests that Assoumani does not enjoy large-scale popular support, especially outside his home island of Ngazidja.

Given the restrictions on political activity within the archipelago, the Forces Vives will seek to tap into the large Comorian diaspora in France. Anti-Assoumani protests have become a weekly occurrence in Paris and Marseilles. Members of the Comorian diaspora often have a complex relationship with their homeland, but many of them retain an interest in Comorian politics, so the size and regularity of diaspora protests are likely to concern Assoumani. It is telling that Assoumani once more pushed back against the franchise being extended to the diaspora prior to the 2020 legislative elections.

Foreign Affairs

However, these efforts by the Forces Vives to represent the government as illegitimate failed to register with the international community. The bilateral partner most likely to be receptive to the Force Vives' stance was France. Yet formal Franco-Comorian relations ended on a high in December 2019 with the successful organisation in Paris of the *Comoros Development Partners Conference* (CPAD) in December 2019, an investment conference co-sponsored by France which pledged $ 4.3 bn towards Comorian emergence by 2030, including extensive promised investment from a number of major French companies. While the anticipated commencement of CPAD projects was, for the most part, frustrated by the Covid-19 prevention measures forced on the Assoumani government, relations between the two countries remained cordial. In October, when French foreign minister Jean-Yves Le Drian was confronted in the national assembly by the French *député* Jean-Paul Le Coq about the absence of a constitutional opposition in Comoros, Le Drian reportedly looked embarrassed, but chose to make no further comment.

The most contentious issue between Comoros and its most important partner remained the seemingly intractable dispute over the sovereignty of Mayotte, claimed as the archipelago's fourth island by Comoros and as a full department by France. The large-scale informal maritime migration from Comoros to Mayotte has been a cause of tension for many years, but this tension was exacerbated by the Covid-19 pandemic, with Comorian migrants suspected by the Mahorais of importing the virus and the migrant community on Mayotte blamed for additional pressures on the island's social and health services.

The government sought to further strengthen links with the UAE. In November, the first defence pact between the two countries was signed. Apart from the UAE offering training and equipment, the focus of the agreement was counter-terrorism and intelligence-sharing. In the commercial sector, however, the government cancelled its contract with the UAE's Armada Group, which, after three years, had failed to start construction on the Galawa resort, pivotal to the regeneration of the Comorian tourist industry.

The Russian ambassador, resident in Madagascar, attended a handover ceremony for a gift of rice, beef, and generators. Addressing the Comorian ministers present, he announced that 'the relationship will improve even more between the two countries'.

Relations with *China* remained robust. The most senior Chinese figure to visit was the president of Huawei in Southern Africa, who visited Assoumani to further strengthen existing links with Comoros and to guarantee China's key role in emergence by 2030. The meeting concentrated on cooperation between the Chinese tech giant and Comoros Telecom, and in particular the delivery of fibre-optic technology to Comorian households. Discussions also touched on Huawei's strategic role in a major project, the Moroni smart city project, that originally stemmed from the CPAD.

Also following on from discussions initiated at the CPAD, Comoros and Morocco established full diplomatic relations, with the exchange of ambassadors and the opening of embassies. The new relationship will involve mutual investment in agri-foods and health, as well as the provision of 3,000 scholarships to the Union of the Comoros by 2030 to cover the studies and vocational training of young Comorians in Morocco.

Socioeconomic Developments

The first case of Covid-19 in Comoros was confirmed on 30 April 2020. The number of infections remained stable and relatively low throughout the summer months, reaching a cumulative total of 611 cases and seven deaths by the end of November. The government nonetheless instigated rigorous protective measures, including a curfew and a ban on incoming flights.

Comoros was ill-prepared to handle Covid-19. According to the 2019 *Global Health Security Index*, Comoros was ranked 160th out of 195 countries overall, 166th out of 195 countries in terms of 'robustness and capacity to treat diseases', and 141st for 'rapid response capacity to contain the spread of an epidemic'.

The country was already dealing with the fallout from a previous disaster in April 2019, when the country was hit by *Cyclone Kenneth*. Estimates of an economic rebound in 2020 were frustrated by the stringent measures taken by the government to prevent Covid-19. Indeed, far from rebounding, the economy contracted.

Comoros' *current population* is estimated at 850,000, with annual growth of 2.23%. At an estimated –2.1% according to the EIU, *real GDP growth* in 2020 was significantly lower than the figure for GDP growth in 2019, at 2.7%, mainly as a result of the impact of the Covid-19 pandemic on trade, tourism, and domestic demand. For 2020, the EIU estimated a *current account deficit* of 5.5% of GDP, set against 2.8% in 2019. In 2020, the ILO-modelled estimate of *total unemployment* as a percentage of the total labour force was 8.4%. Unofficial estimates from media and diplomatic sources estimated a much higher level of unemployment, ranging between 20% and 40%.

Economic activity in priority sectors such as infrastructural projects and tourism, already hindered by the destruction caused by Cyclone Kenneth, were inhibited by the anti-Covid-19 measures. In April, the executive board of the IMF approved a disbursement under the Rapid Credit Facility (RCF) of about $ 4.05 m and a purchase under the RCF of $ 8.08 m to address Comoros' balance-of-payments needs resulting from the pandemic. The IMF had already disbursed $ 1.2 m under the Catastrophe Containment and Relief Trust (CCRT). The Board's deputy managing director stressed the need for 'timely support by donors and development partners', and that the Comorian 'authorities should use all tools at their disposal to safeguard the stability of the banking system, including by providing liquidity to banks facing liquidity pressures'.

The last Article IV Executive Board Consultation was on 18 March 2020. The IMF stressed that 'weak governance and the resulting vulnerability to corruption can undermine macroeconomic performance'. In particular, the IMF focused on weakness in five areas of governance prevalent in Comoros: the rule of law, the regulatory framework, fiscal management, anti-corruption efforts, and management of the civil service. The IMF's conclusion was that if Comoros could address these five governance issues, it would 'likely derive large long-run growth benefits'.

At the end of July, a $ 247 m funding package, partially paid out of the International Development Association 19th Funding Cycle (IDA-19) was agreed with the World Bank to enable Comoros to respond to the socioeconomic consequences of both Cyclone Kenneth and Covid-19. The funding was aimed at 'promoting economic recovery', but also 'inclusive growth by improving governance and the business environment, promoting private sector growth and improving connectivity', reflecting World Bank good governance priorities under the Assoumani government.

The onset of Covid-19 undermined the Cyclone Kenneth recovery plan, as well as projects intended to generate growth under the PCE, the pivotal strategy mapping the country's progress to an emerging economy by 2030. The World Bank's stated goal was to offer necessary support 'to contain the effects of this double shock to enable the country to return to a new trajectory in its ambitions of emergence'.

Early in 2020, a general strike was called following a joint decision on the part of the National Trade Union of Traders (Synaco) and Comoros' main employers' organisation (Opaco). The primary complaint was malpractice by the customs authorities intended to inflate the amount of customs duties to be paid on a range of products. An ensuing consequence of media coverage of the strike was the suspension from their roles of the director of information and editor-in-chief of the main state television channel, accused of granting a disproportionately greater amount of airtime to the strikers than to the government.

In the *oil and gas* sector, the UK/Irish oil exploration company Tullow Oil made no explicit announcement about the results of the 3D seismic survey conducted in Comorian waters in 2019. However, Tullow was forced to make far-reaching staff cuts and sell or close a number of its worldwide projects to counter heavy debts. At the time of writing, Tullow remains operational in Comoros with a new head transferred from its Mauritanian operations, which have closed.

In 2019, Comoros was raised by the *World Bank* from the income category of 'least-developed country' to 'middle-income country', defined as having a per capita gross national income of between $ 1,026 and $ 12,475. The country retained this status in 2020. It also maintained its ranking of 156th out of 189 countries in the UNDP's *HDI*, based on data collected in 2019. Comoros also retained its position of 160th out of 190 countries in the World Bank's 2020 *Ease of Doing Business rankings*. The data for the 2020 index was captured between January 2018 and May 2019.

Djibouti

Nicole Hirt

Djibouti's authoritarian political system was stable and President Ismaïl Omar Guelleh remained the strongman, with no strong competitor for the 2021 presidential elections in sight. Journalists and members of the political opposition were regularly intimidated. Djibouti lost in its competition with Kenya to gain a non-permanent seat in the UNSC, and the border conflict with Eritrea was not resolved. President Guelleh cautiously backed Ethiopia's military operation in Tigray but pledged for peace as the best option. The Covid-19 pandemic slowed down the economy, but the coronavirus-related death rate was relatively low. The government strengthened its investment in renewable energies, including wind, photovoltaic, and geothermal energy. The government continued its legal disputes with UAE-based port management company DP World with little success. Poverty and unemployment were endemic and in addition to the pandemic, the countryside was hit by locust infestation.

Domestic Politics

Ismaïl Omar Guelleh (widely dubbed IOG), who had served as Djibouti's president since 1999, remained firmly in office and controlled the public sphere and all institutions of the country, including the judiciary and the security apparatus as well as the economy. His extended family played a dominant role in the economy, and the Union pour la Majorite Presidentielle (UMP) retained its position as the dominant political party one year ahead of presidential elections that were scheduled for April 2021. Guelleh was the head of the *Rassemblement Populaire pour le Progres* (RPP) and remained the party's strongman, with no serious contender in sight. There was growing evidence that he planned to run for election for another term. The political opposition was weak and largely inactive. On 16 March, the *Rassemblement pour l'Action, la Démocratie et le Développement Ecologique* (RADDE) planned a demonstration in front of the national assembly in favour of transparency and civic freedom before the upcoming elections, but it was banned by the Ministry of the Interior for security reasons. On 9 March, Dileyta Tourab, a member of the *Alliance Républicaine pour la Démocratie* (ARD), was detained by security forces, allegedly to silence political dissent.

The *political climate* remained repressive, and civil liberties were limited. Human rights defender and journalist Kadar Abdi Ibrahim suffered from repression, according to the UN Human Rights Council, and his passport was confiscated by the security forces to prevent him from travelling abroad. Press freedom remained absent, and 'La Nation' was the only newspaper, closely monitored by the government. The same was true for state-owned radio and television stations, and as in previous years, the opposition internet radio station La Voix de Djibouti was forced to broadcast from France. Reporters Without Borders ranked Djibouti 176th out of 179 in its press freedom report, and the Freedom House index of 2020 labelled Djibouti as 'not free'. On 26 August, the Committee to Protect Journalists (CPJ) reported that journalist Charmarke Saïd Darar, who worked for La Voix de Djibouti, had been held for two weeks from 14 July to 4 August and was mistreated during his detention. There was constant harassment and intimidation of journalists working for the opposition radio.

Due to the presence of international military bases, Djibouti was hit relatively early by the *Covid-19 pandemic*, with the first case being discovered on 18 March in a member of the Spanish special forces and further cases appearing among Spanish and US military personnel; by the end of the year, 6,102 people had been diagnosed positive. Yet due to preventative measures, mortality was relatively low, with 63 Covid-related deaths. Immediately after the outbreak, the government stopped commercial passenger flights and train travel. Schools and places of worship were also closed, and a country-wide lockdown was in place from 23 March to 17 May. Djibouti, along with Tanzania and Somalia, was among the first countries in Africa to open schools again, on 6 September, with strict social distancing measures in place. On 4 October, at least eight Ethiopian *labour migrants* drowned off the Djiboutian shore and 12 were missing after people smugglers had forced them off a boat, while 14 migrants survived. Djibouti served as a travel hub for labour migration towards Saudi Arabia, but due to the pandemic and the deteriorating situation in Yemen many migrants tried to return. By November, more than 700 had been stranded in Djibouti due to border closures by Ethiopia, according to the IOM.

Foreign Affairs

Djibouti's role continued as a host of *international naval and military bases* that aimed to protect the strategically important sea passage at the Bab al-Mandeb Strait, and the country served as Ethiopia's only sea outlet. The prolonged conflict between President Guelleh and *UAE-based DP World*, a company which had previously managed the Doraleh Container Terminal until it was seized by the government in 2018, resulting in losses of $ 1 bn, according to the UAE's government. The case was litigated at the London International Court of Arbitration, and on 15 January the court ordered that Djibouti should restore the rights and benefits under a 2006 agreement between both parties. It was the sixth ruling in favour of DP World, almost all of which have been ignored by Djibouti.

Ethiopia remained Djibouti's main economic partner, and relations were stable. In an interview published by 'The Africa Report' on 24 November, Guelleh stated that the aim of Ethiopia's prime minister Abiy Ahmed to implement a policy of togetherness in a country plagued by centuries of ethnic divisions was probably over-optimistic. However, he expressed understanding for Abiy's law enforcement operation in Tigray, but also voiced concern that his country could be affected by the conflict and his wish that peace would be restored soon.

On 20 December, the regional organisation IGAD held an extraordinary meeting in Djibouti to discuss the ongoing conflict in Ethiopia's Tigray Region and the rift between *Kenya* and *Somalia*. Tensions between the two countries had erupted after Mogadishu accused Nairobi of supporting militias that were supportive of the Jubaland administration and had attacked a Somali army base in the border town of Beled Hawo. Djibouti was mandated by IGAD to send a fact-finding mission to the border area.

Djibouti also mediated in a conflict between *Somalia* and the unofficial government of *Somaliland*. The relations between the two territorial entities had deteriorated since Somali president Mohamed Abdullahi Mohamed Farmajo came to power in 2017. Djibouti hosted a reconciliation meeting between Farmajo and Muse Bihi, the unofficial president of Somaliland. The event was attended by senior US diplomat Donald Yamamoto and representatives of the EU, AU, the regional organisation IGAD, and Ethiopia on 14 June, and ended in partial success with a decision to instal committees for further talks. The persistent border conflict between Djibouti and *Eritrea* that erupted after military clashes in 2008 remained unresolved, and no efforts took place to resume negotiations between the parties.

Jean-Baptiste Lemoyne, *France*'s minister of state for tourism, French nationals abroad, and the Francophonie, paid a three-day visit to Djibouti from 12 to 14 December to strengthen the close ties between the two nations in the fields of economic, political, cultural, and security cooperation. He held talks with President Guelleh and visited the armed forces stationed at the French military base. The US maintained its military base at Camp Lemonnier, which hosted some 4,000 military personnel and strengthened its engagement in Djibouti by donating tactical vehicles worth $ 31 m to Djibouti's Rapid Intervention Batalion, which was trained and equipped by the Combined Joint Task Force – Horn of Africa (CJTF-HOA).

All other military bases that were established in previous years in Djibouti due to its strategic location at the *Bab al-Mandeb Strait* were maintained, and the small country remained one of the most militarised places on earth. China stationed about 2,000 troops at its naval base, which had a maximum capacity of 10,000 people. The EU's *Operation Atalanta*, with the purpose of containing piracy in the region, continued, and *Japan* and *Italy* upheld their military presence with 180 and 80 stationed personnel, respectively. Djibouti remained one of the five troop-contributing countries to the *AU peacekeeping mission in Somalia* (AMISOM), with most of its troops stationed at Belet Weyne.

Turkey further strengthened its cooperation with the government of Djibouti in an attempt to increase its influence in the strategic Horn of Africa region. On 19 February, the two governments signed an agreement on maritime cooperation with the aim of strengthening bilateral trade and improving relations in transportation, including in the aviation, railway, and maritime sectors. Turkey also had plans to establish a free economic zone in Djibouti. As a first step, the Djibouti Shipping Company established a shipping line in October that was supposed to operate exclusively between Turkey, Djibouti, and Somalia and would substantially reduce shipping times between the countries.

On 30 December, the president of Djibouti's national assembly, Mohamed Ali Houmed, led an AU delegation to *Pakistan*. During his visit, Pakistani prime minister Imran Khan affirmed his interest in enhancing cooperation with Africa and declared his readiness to open an embassy in Djibouti soon.

Socioeconomic Developments

Due to its strategic position and the strong presence of foreign actors, Djibouti's *development strategy* was based on FDI with a focus on infrastructure projects and port development. A new port in Tadjoura close to the border with Ethiopia's Afar Region became operational in July and was supposed to ease the high utilisation of the main port in Djibouti City. The country's emphasis on *sustainable development* gained momentum. The Djibouti Wind Company was set up to establish the

Goubeh Wind Project, supported by a $ 63 m investment by the Africa Finance Corporation with an investment guarantee of $ 91.6 m provided by the Multilateral Investment Guarantee Agency, a subsidiary of the World Bank. The Spanish company Siemens Gamesa Renewable Energy was in charge of constructing a wind park in Arta Region with a capacity of almost 60 MW. In May, the government also approved a photovoltaic solar power plant worth € 360 m in Grand Bara with a capacity of 30 MWp (megawatt peak) to be installed by the French company Engie in a private–public partnership. Another project approved in May and financed by the AfDB with $ 3.22 m was a geothermal exploitation plant around Lake Assal intended to reach a final capacity of 50 MWe (megawatt electrical) in two phases. All three projects were part of the development plan *Vision Djibouti 2035*, the target of which is not only to establish the country as a leading logistics and commercial hub in East Africa, but also to achieve the goal of producing 100% of Djibouti's energy needs through renewable energy by 2030. On 14 September, the government officially launched another flagship component of Vision Djibouti 2035, the *Djibouti Sovereign Fund*, with the purpose of modernising the country's economy, boosting the growth of a competitive private sector, and enhancing the development of the public productive sector. It was headed by Senegalese economist Mamadou Mbaye and aimed at reducing the country's dependency on foreign donors in the long term. In June, Djibouti Telecom launched D-Money, a digital mobile money service that could be used to transfer money or to manage payments. On 29 May, the *World Bank* approved an IDA loan of $ 25 m to improve Djibouti's statistical data base as a way to create economic growth and reduce poverty.

China continued to act as a *major foreign investor*. The Djibouti International Free Trade Zone was operated as a joint venture of the Djibouti Ports and Free Zone Authority and Chinese enterprises including China Merchants Holdings and Dalian Port Corp Ltd. It covered one-tenth of Djibouti's land area and more than 20 companies had settled in the zone, including commerce, logistics, and processing businesses. The Chinese-built Doraleh Multi-Purpose Port that had been inaugurated in 2017 continued to play an important role in handling import-export activities. However, the performance of the Ethiopia–Djibouti railway, another infrastructure project financed by China, lagged behind expectations. Its operation was slowed down by the *Covid-19 pandemic*, which reduced the quantity of trafficked goods, and it suffered from acts of vandalism on the Ethiopian side.

The pandemic arrived in Djibouti in March, and the economy suffered from a slowdown. The World Bank estimated a decline in Djibouti's economic growth to 1.3%, down from an initial expectation of 7.5%. According to the *IMF*, this was caused by a large negative external demand shock due to global recession that weakened the country's macroeconomic prospects. In the domestic sphere, virus prevention and containment measures affected both demand and supply, causing a situation of reduced spending needs while government revenue declined.

Accordingly, on 8 May the IMF approved a disbursement of $ 43.4 m to help Djibouti meet the urgent balance-of-payment needs created by the pandemic. The *African Development Fund* also granted $ 41 m to bolster the national budget in order to alleviate the consequences of the pandemic under its Covid-19 Response Facility.

Unsurprisingly, *endemic poverty* remained high, with a prevalence of 40% according to the WFP, although Djibouti had reached the category of a low-middle-income country. Yet the country's distribution of income was extremely unequal, with the extended Guelleh family clan dominating all major sources of income. The WFP supported some 108,000 people, including refugees and migrants, with direct food distribution. Almost 30% of the population suffered from chronic food insecurity, especially in the rural areas, which were also affected by locust infestation, further heightening the levels of food insecurity among agro-pastoralists. The World Bank's *Doing Business report* of 2020 ranked Djibouti 112nd out of 190 countries; the 2021 report did not indicate a ranking for the country.

In late January, Djibouti hosted the International Summit of Balanced and Inclusive Education, attended by 30 governments and NGOs. It ended with the signing of a Universal Declaration of Balanced and Inclusive Education (UDBIE) with the aim of promoting better education in the Global South. In March, the *sub-marine cable system* Djibouti Africa Regional Express was inaugurated. The 5,000 km cable connected Djibouti, Somalia, and Kenya and was supposed to boost connectivity.

Eritrea

Nicole Hirt

The State of Eritrea remained a dictatorship with no implemented constitution ruled with an iron fist by President Isaias Afewerki. The open-ended national service which had depleted the country of its productive youth remained in place and the human rights situation was dire, despite the release of some prisoners detained for their religious beliefs who had served long prison sentences. The government used the Covid-19 pandemic to introduce an indefinite harsh lockdown in April, with all businesses closed without compensation and all kinds of public meetings prohibited. The Ministry of Health claimed that only three Eritreans had died due to the virus, but nevertheless the lockdown, which led to a hidden famine, was not eased. Schools remained closed and no alternative means of education were provided for the youth. In November, Eritrean soldiers became part of Ethiopian prime minister Abiy Ahmed's so-called law enforcement operation in Tigray against the Tigray People's Liberation Front in an undeclared war against the people of Ethiopia's northern region bordering Eritrea. The EU's support for road construction projects carried out by national service conscripts came under increased scrutiny.

Domestic Politics

Once again, Eritrea's autocratic political system did not undergo any kind of reform. *President Isaias Afewerki's rule* over the country remained uncontested, and he continued to rule without an implemented constitution supported by a small circle of advisors. The national assembly, in theory the country's legislative organ, remained inactive, and the ruling *People's Front for Democracy and Justice* (PFDJ) was largely inactive. Only the party's financial head, Hagos Gebrehiwot 'Kisha', and the head of political affairs, Yemane Gebreab, who was also in charge of diaspora affairs and accompanied minster of foreign affairs Osman Saleh on most of his official journeys, maintained their political influence. No elections were envisaged to be held and there were no plans to reform the national service without time limit, which had been in place since 2002. The last official meeting of the cabinet of ministers was held in April 2018, which meant that the president seemed to have abandoned the last impression of public participation in his decision-making processes. No cabinet reshuffles were announced, and it was obvious that Eritrea was fully under the one-man rule of the president.

Following the outbreak of the *Covid-19 pandemic*, Eritrea's first case was registered on 21 March, when a Norway-based diaspora Eritrean visiting the country developed symptoms. The Eritrean government declared a strict lockdown on 2 April that remained in place throughout the year. International travel, including diaspora visits, ceased and the borders were closed. All schools and businesses except for groceries were shut down; public transport, including buses and taxis, was discontinued and the use of private cars was prohibited. This meant that people had to resort to horse and donkey carts to transport daily commodities. Restrictions on travel from one location to another were extremely tight, and agro-pastoralists and pastoralists were unable to perform their seasonal movements.

At the same time, the government claimed that the country was hardly affected by the spread of the pandemic. Nevertheless, fundraising campaigns to help fight the pandemic were conducted throughout the year among diaspora Eritreans, with no transparency as to how the funds were being used. Despite grave economic consequences due to a lack of compensation for individuals affected by the lockdown and a drop in agricultural production, no opening strategy was envisaged by the end of the year.

Aid organisations warned that the lockdown, which deprived people of the ability to engage in all kinds of informal business opportunities and leave their homes to look for food, led to *famine conditions* with far more dangerous implications than the pandemic itself. In early September, the BBC reported that there was most probably a hidden famine in Eritrea – denied by the government, which did not grant independent journalists and aid organisations access to the country. The diplomatic community in Asmara had been banned from travelling to Eritrea's countryside for more than a decade.

The *human rights situation* remained dire, and civil liberties, which had been extremely restrained even before the Covid-related lockdown, became even more restricted due to the prohibition on meeting other people in public in the absence of any possibility to communicate online. The indefinite lockdown further tightened the totalitarian grip of the regime on the population. All internet cafés were closed, removing one of the few possibilities to gather information and communicate with the outside world, even if only 2% of all Eritreans had internet access. The telephone system was unreliable, and most Eritreans feared that all communication was traced by the state security. Eritrea was ranked 178th out of 180 countries in Reporters Without Borders' *press freedom* ranking. There were no improvements in religious freedom, and Jehovah's Witnesses and Pentecostal churches were denied the right to practise their faith actively. However, in September the government released 20 members of Pentecostal congregations from prison, and on 4 December it freed 28 Jehovah's Witnesses, two of them women, who had been behind bars for between 5 and 26 years without trial. No explanation was given as to why these individuals were pardoned while large numbers of Eritreans remained in prison due to religious persecution. The legal religious denominations, namely Orthodox, Catholic, and Lutheran Christianity and Sunni Islam, remained under the close surveillance of the government. All of Eritrea's surviving long-term political prisoners remained in prison, including the reform group of the G15 and the journalists of the independent press who were put behind bars in 2001.

In September, Dr Mohamed Abdelsalam Babiker, a Sudanese professor of international law, was appointed as the new *special rapporteur on Eritrea* by the UNHRC. His predecessor, Daniela Kravetz, published her final report on 11 May, stating that there had been no tangible improvements in the human rights situation. In September, a lawsuit filed in 2014 against Nevsun Resources, a Canadian mining company that ran a gold and copper mine at Bisha in a joint venture with the state-owned Eritrean Mining Corporation (ENAMCO), was settled out of court, with the plaintiffs receiving compensation from Nevsun. Amnesty International welcomed the decision as a landmark settlement because it held international companies responsible for their activities abroad. The former miners, who had been conscripts of the Eritrean national service, had claimed to have been subjected to forced work, torture, and human rights abuses during the construction of the mine.

Eritrea's *judicial system* remained in a state of obsolescence in the absence of an implemented institution, rule of law, and ordinary legal processes. There was still no institution of higher education in charge of educating judges and other jurists. *Corruption* remained high, and TI's Corruption Perceptions Index ranked Eritrea 160th out of 180 countries. Due to the strict lockdown, which included the closure of administrative buildings, Eritreans had no access to public services starting from April. In the absence of online services, communication inside the country and with relatives abroad was only possible for those who had a telephone connection.

The *Eritrean diaspora* remained deeply split between government supporters and opponents, and the opposition was weakened by splits along ethnic, religious, and regional fault-lines. Eritrea's involvement in the armed conflict in Ethiopia's bordering Tigray Region (see below) caused further splits, but many diaspora Eritreans residing in North America and Europe participated in demonstrations demanding an end to the conflict, while many government supporters celebrated the demise of the Tigray People's Liberation Front (TPLF).

Foreign Affairs

The *Joint Declaration of Peace and Friendship* signed by Eritrea's president Isaias Afewerki and Ethiopia's prime minister Abiy Ahmed with the aim of establishing close political and economic ties and fostering cooperation in the fields of social and cultural activities remained unimplemented. No lasting transport, trade, or communication links were established, and the border was not demarcated on the ground. However, in the field of security cooperation it seemed that both leaders, whose personal relationship was strong, were pursuing unforeseen strategies.

On 27 January, Abiy and *Somalia*'s President Mohamed Abdullahi Farmajo met with Isaias in Asmara and forged a tripartite alliance with the official aim of fighting terrorism, human and arms trafficking, and drug smuggling. On 3 May, Isaias travelled to Addis Ababa to discuss the Covid-19 pandemic and locust infestation. On 18 July, it was Abiy's turn to visit Eritrea again, and he became the first foreign leader to be allowed to visit Eritrea's infamous *Sawa military training camp* in the western lowlands, where national service recruits received their military training. On 12 October, Isaias met with Abiy in Ethiopia once again and visited various projects, including the controversial Grand Ethiopian Renaissance Dam (GERD) and the military facility at Bishoftu which hosts Ethiopia's national air force. When Abiy Ahmed launched what he called a law enforcement operation in Tigray against the TPLF leadership on 4 November, rumours of Eritrean participation soon emerged. On 14 November, the TPLF launched several rocket strikes against Asmara, targeting the airport and other strategic locations. TPLF leader Debretsion Gebremichael accused Eritrea of rendering military support to the Ethiopian National Defence Force, but Eritrea denied involvement and remained silent about the shelling of Asmara. On 8 December, Reuters reported that the US government had accused Eritrea of being involved in the war in Tigray, citing evidence from satellite images, intercepted communications, and eyewitness reports from Tigray and from refugee camps in Sudan. However, presumably due to the imminent change of the US government, no further action was taken by the Trump administration.

Eritrea's relations with *Sudan*, which had improved after the ousting of President Omar al-Bashir in 2019, remained close, and President Isaias was anxious to retain his influence on Sudanese policies, specifically in the eastern part of the country bordering Eritrea. Beginning on 25 June, he paid a three-day visit to the government in Khartoum, holding talks with the head and the deputy chairperson of Sudan's Sovereign Council, Abdel Fattah Al-Burhan and Mohamed Hamdan Dagalu (known as Hemedti), and Sudan's prime minister Abdallah Hamdok about regional issues and enhanced cooperation. On 21 July, a high-level delegation of the Eritrean Defence Forces, including chief of staff General Filipos Woldeyohannes, General Romodan Osman Awliya, navy commander General Humed Karikare, and head of the National Security Agency General Abraha Kassa, travelled abroad to hold talks with General Hemedti about defence and security issues. It was highly unusual that Eritrea's military elite jointly travelled abroad. Further meetings took place on 7 September, when General Abdel Fattah al-Burhan arrived in Asmara for a one-day visit, and on 11 November, when Eritrea's minister of foreign affairs Osman Saleh and his constant companion, presidential advisor Yemane Gebreab, travelled to Khartoum to discuss the evolving conflict in Ethiopia.

Eritrean relations with *Saudi Arabia and the UAE*, which maintained a military base at Eritrea's port city Assab, remained close. On 19 November, Getachew Reda, the spokesperson of the TPLF, claimed that drones stationed at Assab by the UAE had been employed during the military campaign in Ethiopia's Tigray Region with the aim of toppling the TPLF administration. On 20 February, President Isaias met Crown Prince Mohammed bin Salman bin Abdulaziz in Riyadh to discuss bilateral cooperation, and on 15 December a delegation from Saudi Arabia headed by foreign minister Prince Faisal bin Farhan Al Saud travelled to Asmara for talks.

Relations with *Egypt* also remained strong, and Isaias, accompanied by Yemane Gebreab and Osman Saleh, paid a visit to Cairo and met President Abdel Fattah el-Sisi and other officials on 8 June and again on 5 July to discuss regional relations and the situation in Sudan. On 18 November, Yemane and Osman travelled to Cairo once more to discuss, *inter alia*, the GERD and the situation in Ethiopia.

The *European Union's* relations with Eritrea remained stable, but no high-level visits took place. Eritrea's Ministry of Information once again accused Germany of a biased stance against Eritrea because the development committee of the Bundestag had claimed on 22 April that no bilateral development cooperation could be considered due to the poor human rights situation in the country and a lack of cooperation by the Eritrean government, a statement which was considered an insult by the latter. The *United States* maintained little diplomatic interaction with Eritrea during the year, but the US administration was the first international actor to officially raise the issue of Eritrea's military involvement in Ethiopia on 8 December.

The situation of *Eritrean refugees* stuck in Libya deteriorated further due to the Covid-19 pandemic, which drastically diminished the possibility of migrating further to Europe, and a decline in sea rescue operations. Evacuation flights of refugees from Libya to Rwanda via the Emergency Transit Mechanism also came to an intermittent halt due to the pandemic, but in November 79 asylum seekers, including Eritreans, were evacuated from detention centres in Libya by the UNHCR and received protection in Rwanda. According to UNHCR Sudan, the country hosted close to 123,000 Eritrean refugees, but there was a high number of unreported cases because many Eritreans tried to settle in the cities rather than staying at refugee camps. The armed conflict in Tigray had devastating effects on the approximately 100,000 Eritrean refugees hosted in four camps in northern Tigray. On 8 December, the UN's High Commissioner for Refugees Filippo Grandi said that he was alarmed about alleged abductions of Eritrean refugees to their homeland by Eritrean military forces, killings, and abductions. The Eritrean leadership did not comment on these allegations, but the Ethiopian government denied them, although satellite images showed that massive destruction of housing and infrastructure had occurred in the Hitsats and Shimelba refugee camps.

Socioeconomic Developments

The *command economy* dominated by the military and the ruling PFDJ was not reformed during the year. Borders with Ethiopia remained closed, and no border trade was possible. The national service was not reformed and remained open-ended, which meant that large numbers of Eritreans had to serve for decades without the freedom to choose their occupation or their residence. The government used the outbreak of *Covid-19* to further restrict the possibility of moving from one place to another and carrying out business activities. In spite of claiming that only small numbers of the population were affected by the spread of the coronavirus, the government extended the initial lockdown imposed in April for an undisclosed period of time. At the end of the year, the Ministry of Health announced that so far 1,320 Eritreans had been diagnosed with Covid-19 and three had died from the disease. Reportedly, there were 41 quarantine centres in the country, which were apparently also in charge of carrying out the tests, but their exact locations were not disclosed. It was unclear which testing strategy the ministry had followed and why measures were not lifted in the face of an allegedly extremely low Covid-related death rate, while the harsh lockdown caused a looming famine.

In July, Human Rights Concern Eritrea warned that up to two-thirds of the population might be living under *famine conditions*. Daily labourers and people surviving through street-vending activities were prevented from working, and agricultural and pastoral activities were restricted due to the restrictions on movement. In urban areas, people were not allowed to leave their immediate neighbourhoods, and all public transport including buses and taxis was stopped. Consequently, people had to use horse and donkey carts to transport food products and water. The scarcity of *consumer goods* such as cooking oil, sugar, and other basic commodities continued, and the capital Asmara suffered a severe shortage of potable water due to decades-long poor maintenance of the water supply system, which made it impossible to follow WHO recommendations to washing hands frequently as a precaution against the coronavirus.

The AfDB's rather optimistic outlook on the economic development of Eritrea, including an *economic growth* rate of 3.9% based on economic cooperation with Ethiopia after the peace agreement and the lifting of sanctions against the country – which had actually consisted of an arms embargo with no economic component – did not materialise due to the pandemic, the stalled peace with Ethiopia, and Eritrea's involvement in the Tigray war since November (see above).

In the face of Eritrea's extremely weak economy, the president continued to receive *support from the UAE and Saudi Arabia* as renumeration for the use of the military base at Assab in their anti-Houthi war in Yemen. President Isaias even used UAE's Royal Jet aircraft for his international travel. As usual, no state budget was published, and it was unclear how funds generated through the diaspora tax levied on millions of Eritreans in exile and local income from mining activities were spent. The *banking system* remained in a rudimentary state, with no ATMs available and no possibility to pay by debit or credit card. The pandemic made it more difficult for diaspora Eritreans to remit money through Hawala systems, and many had to resort to official money transfer companies such as Western Union, increasing the cost of remittances. The use of cash remained under heavy restrictions and the maximum withdrawal allowed was 5,000 Nakfa (ERN; $ 333) per month for families and businesspeople alike. Most Eritreans depended on diaspora remittances for their survival, especially in the urban areas where all economic activities had come to a complete halt.

In addition to the pandemic, parts of Eritrea were affected by *natural disasters*. In August, the coastal areas were hit by flooding, and agricultural areas around Bada were damaged. Minister of local government Woldenkiel Abraha toured the Northern Red Sea Region from 21 to 26 September and promised to alleviate social service shortages. Eritrea was also affected by *locust invasions* in different regions of the country, including Central Region (Ma'akel), but the government claimed to have brought the infestation under control by spraying large areas with pesticides.

The focus of the EU's support for the Eritrean government shifted from the *National Indicative Programme* (NIP) under the EU's 11th EDF to the European Emergency Trust Fund for Africa (ETUF), which had been established in 2015 with the aim of curbing irregular migration by improving 'migration management' and socioeconomic conditions in refugee-producing countries. The EU allotted € 30 m for job creation in the agricultural sector, € 5 m to economic governance, and € 15 m to promote Eritrea's culture and heritage. The bulk of the support, comprising € 125 m, was allocated to infrastructure development – more precisely, to the construction of new roads that were supposed to connect Eritrea and Ethiopia in the aftermath of the 2018 peace agreement. The EU Commission was fully aware that the national service had not been reformed and that those who were employed as construction workers were forcibly recruited members of the national service.

However, this decision came under scrutiny, and on 15 June the *EU's Parliament Committee on Development* (DEVE) discussed development cooperation with Eritrea with the European Commission and Europe External Action Service (EEAS). As a result, the Commission decided to stop funding road construction in Eritrea and declined a request by the Eritrean government for € 50 m for this purpose in addition to € 80 m which had already been allocated. Instead, the EU allocated € 19.7 m to apparently less controversial areas, including diaspora engagement in national development, enhancement of the efficiency of the judiciary administration – mainly in the field of crime prevention – and promotion of a dubious UNDP-managed programme with the purpose of promoting economic growth, jobs, and public finance management. UNDP Eritrea was known to be playing into the hands of the government. On the other hand, the *World Bank* did not resume its lending programme to Eritrea, officially due to repayment arrears.

The *Covid-19 pandemic* had an adverse impact on the living conditions of the people. UNICEF reported that throughout the year, almost 70,000 children under five were treated for acute malnutrition, up from 58,000 the year before. Among those affected, 17,800 children suffered from severe acute malnutrition and 51,500 from moderate acute malnutrition. Probably the true situation on the ground was even worse, because Eritreans were often prevented by security forces from leaving their homes in search of food or medical treatment under the pretext of the pandemic. The Global Hunger Index was unable to provide any data for Eritrea.

Schools were closed in April and did not reopen throughout the year, with no substitute educational programmes offered to students, who were forced to simply remain at home. Eritrea's educational system had already suffered for many years from the outflow of educated teachers, and often, unqualified national service recruits have been obliged to teach large numbers of students without renumeration. Against this background, it could be assumed that the prolonged closure of schools would lead to a further drastic increase of illiteracy. As usual, the government did not publish any reliable statistical data.

The only exception was the *Ministry of Health* (MoH): it regularly published Covid-19-related data on the Ministry of Information's website shabait.com, which is predominantly addressed to diaspora Eritreans. According to the ministry, Eritrea was hardly affected by the pandemic, with only 1,320 cases and three deaths by the end of the year; yet there was no public discussion of the consequences of the unlimited severe lockdown. It was unclear if the numbers presented by the MoH were reliable and reflected the reality on the ground. The Sawa military camp, which hosts thousands of national service recruits who are forced to live in extremely crowded conditions, did not put in place any measures to protect their health. When Jack Ma, the head of the *Alibaba Group*, donated large quantities of *Covid-related supplies* such as face masks and test kits to African countries, Eritrea did not accept this support, refusing landing permission to the plane carrying the supplies. No explanation was given by the government. It seemed that the political leadership relied on diaspora donations to curb the pandemic, but no information was made available as to how much money was collected, nor was there any transparency about how the funds were used.

The *Bisha Zinc Polymetallic Mine*, which had been operated by ENAMCO in collaboration with Canadian Nevsun since 2011, was now run as a joint venture with Chinese Zijin Mining, and no information was published about the impact of the pandemic on mining activities or financial revenues generated by the mine. The *Colluli Potash Mine* in the Southern Red Sea Region did not commence production. Australian-owned Danakali was supposed to run the mine in a joint venture with ENAMCO and issued a statement in July, stating that it had received the necessary licences from the government but that progress in construction had been slowed down by the pandemic. Eritrea's HDI rank was 182nd out of 189 countries, and the last available information about Eritrea's total debt was from 2019, indicating that it stood at 248.9% of GDP. The radical lockdown had an adverse impact on the ailing economy, but the government showed no signs of preoccupation with the wellbeing or even the mere survival of the population.

Ethiopia

Jon Abbink

Ethiopia continued to be marked by a volatile political situation, interethnic unrest and an uncertain 'reform agenda' trajectory under prime minister Abiy Ahmed and the reigning Prosperity Party. Some of the political actors invited back into Ethiopia in 2018 reverted to armed struggle, and certain political murders and ethnic-based killings disturbed the country. The global Covid-19 pandemic reached Ethiopia in March, leading to socioeconomic damage and the declaration of a 'state of emergency' for five months. Economic growth continued, although at a more reduced rate, and many new urban and infrastructural projects were started. The agrarian sector did well due to a favourable rainy season. Expansion was also seen in the mining and industrial sectors, despite a decline in foreign investment. The external debt burden became a prominent issue. The controversy with Sudan and notably with Egypt over the Grand Ethiopian Renaissance Dam (GERD) continued, with no negotiated settlement in sight. In November, a serious armed confrontation unfolded in Tigray after an unprovoked attack by the Tigray armed forces on the federal army camps and military infrastructure in the region, producing a massive and highly disruptive conflict, with incomplete media reporting and social media disinformation having a nefarious impact. This conflict also led to a decline in the international reputation of Ethiopia and its prime minister and to economic stress.

Insecurity in areas in western Ethiopia was evident in the many killings and the property destruction by insurgent groups with no clear agenda. National parliamentary elections scheduled for May 2020 were first delayed to 29 August, then postponed to 2021 because of the coronavirus pandemic.

Domestic Politics

Extraordinary political volatility and unpredictability continued to mark Ethiopian political life during the year. This was related partly to violent incidents, power changes at the federal level, opposition parties manoeuvring in view of the parliamentary elections planned (originally) for May 2020, youth activists' protests, and interethnic clashes in various parts of the country. There was controversy over the legitimacy of the mandate of the federal government and the pushing back of the date of the May 2020 elections (due to the Covid-19 pandemic), with opposition parties pleading for broad, multi-party talks and a transitional government. Prime minister Abiy Ahmed stayed in power and in August reshuffled his cabinet, also appointing a new, young attorney-general, Dr Gedeon Timotewos. The prime minister's close friend and defence minister Lemma Megersa, who had expressed reservations over the formation of the Prosperity Party (PP) the year before and over the *Meddemer* ('synergy') philosophy as expounded in Abiy's book on the subject, was removed from the ministry and replaced by Dr Kenea Yadeta. Lemma was also removed from the central committee of the party. On 8 November, another round of reshuffling was seen, with the leadership of the entire security sector replaced: Temesgen Tiruneh became director of the National Intelligence and Security Service (NISS), General Berhanu Jula army chief of staff, and Demelash Gebre-Michael federal police chief. Vice-premier Demeke Mekonnen replaced Gedu Andargachew as foreign minister; the latter became the prime minister's national security advisor.

There was a continuation of the broad reform process of Abiy Ahmed and his PP, formed in November 2019 as a successor to the Ethiopian People's Revolutionary Democratic Front or EPRDF (minus the Tigray People's Liberation Front/TPLF, which left this coalition on 7 January), but there were ups and downs. Due to the persistent security problems, Abiy's popularity waned and his reform agenda was contested, but it remained strong.

Very serious *violent incidents occurred in Benishangul-Gumuz* during the year, mainly aimed at ordinary, non-combatant people of Amhara, Agaw, or Gurage background, who were the victim of harsh confrontations if not 'ethnic cleansing' operations. Culprits were said to be 'Gumuz militias'. Problems in the state of Benishangul-Gumuz came to a head because of decades-long purposeful institutional and political neglect of this region by the previous EPRDF government. In various parts of *western Oromia (e.g., Wollega zone)* there were also *numerous violent incidents*, victimising non-Oromo residents and descendants of Amhara-speaking people, all of them civilians, of whom hundreds were killed in terrorist-like violence. In some parts of Oromia, internet shutdowns were imposed from January for a three-month period.

In addition, *internal divisions among political actors and movements led to outbursts of violence*, e.g. the *targeted killing* on 29 June of *Hachalu Hundessa*, a very popular Ethiopian-Orthodox Oromo singer, apparently undertaken by sectarian youth activists of Oromo background. His killing, after he had given a nationally televised interview where he criticised an emerging alliance between TPLF agents and certain Oromo opposition circles, was shocking. It led to an orchestrated campaign via Facebook and other social media by certain opposition figures, as well as to *'revenge killings': at least 150 mainly non-Oromo people were killed* by young activists or alleged *qerroos* (members of the Oromo youth protest movement), often on the basis of prepared target lists. Wilful destruction of property (with businesses and even schools set ablaze) accompanied the killings. In this period of unrest, the internet and mobile data were shut off on 30 June (to prevent coordination of the protests and killings) and restored only partially on 17 July in Addis Ababa and some other parts of the country. On 23 July, mobile data were restored across the country. Shocking incidents also occurred around the burial of Hachalu. His family wanted him buried in their home town of Ambo, but members of the Oromo opposition party the Oromo Federalist Congress (Jawar Mohammed and others) went with a group of followers to attack the funeral group and force them to head back to Addis Ababa, in order to get Hachalu buried there and make a big political manifestation of it. In this skirmish, they killed one Oromo police officer. This degrading spectacle was followed by the arrest of the perceived main instigators Jawar Mohammed and Bekele Gerba for assault and violence. They were also already known for social media incitement, and by year's end they were awaiting trial. On 10 July, two of the alleged killers of Hachalu were arrested. On 1 July, the journalist-turned-politician Eskinder Nega, heading the Balderas Party for Genuine Democracy, had been detained on charges of inciting violence in Addis Ababa after the Hachalu killing. On 10 September he was also charged, on tenuous evidence, with preparing the assassination of a former acting mayor of Addis Ababa and of 'inciting ethnic and religious conflict to try and illegally take power in the capital'. Ethiopian Democratic Party politician Lidetu Ayalew was arrested and charged in September 'for unlawfully preparing for regime change' but was released on bail on 11 December by the Oromia Supreme Court.

In terms of local administration, the country saw, as usual, *a high turnover and reshuffling of personnel*, including in high positions (in the cabinet; see above), often on the basis of non-transparent criteria and making policy follow-up difficult. On 28 October, Adanech Abebe (formerly the attorney-general) was appointed as the new acting mayor (officially 'deputy mayor') of Addis Ababa, replacing Takele Uma, who became minister of mines and energy.

Due to the coronavirus pandemic, which reached Ethiopia in March 2020 and rapidly expanded, the original *date for the parliamentary elections in May 2020 was first postponed to August*, based on constitutional interpretation, as requested by parliament to the Constitutional Inquiry Commission. The problem was that the constitution did not foresee circumstances under which the election might not be held before the end of the five-year term of parliament. But the commission ruled the date extension acceptable under the constitution (referring to Article 93), due to the pandemic conditions. This delay was not accepted by many opposition parties and activists, including the TPLF: they refused to recognise the authority of the federal government and the Commission after the election date of 20 May, saying that they had 'outlived [their] mandate'. Many opposition parties and activists pleaded for a 'transitional government' based on inter-party negotiation. The issue also caused the TPLF government in Meqele – opposed to the federal government since the change of premiership in April 2018 – to organise its own regional elections on 9 September (where it won 189 of the 190 seats), in their turn not recognised by the National Electoral Board and the federal House of Peoples' Representatives, as they flouted the federal constitution.

During the year, political parties continued to manoeuvre for election campaigning but experienced problems – not only pressure from local PP branches and sometimes unauthorised police actions, but also internal disarray and lack of clear party politics and programmes. The Oromo Liberation Front (OLF) suffered from in-fighting among its factions and in December was on the verge of splitting into two or three parts, and the Oromo Federalist Congress, never clear about a comprehensive national political programme apart from an 'Oromo first' agenda, was weakened and in perpetual complaint mode. Like the OLF, it repeatedly stated that it wanted 'an all-inclusive national political dialogue'. On 3 January, the three main Oromo parties – the Oromo Federalist Congress (OFC), the OLF (the Dawud Ibsa faction), and the Oromo National Party (ONF, Kemal Gelchu) – formed a 'Coalition for Democratic Federalism' (CDF).

Interethnic tensions, partly a continuation of existing land and border problems as well as of EPRDF-created divide-and-rule politics in the previous decades, continued, with new fault-lines marking the South (e.g., Konso), the south-west, Benishangul-Gumuz (Metekkel), Afar, and Somali-Oromo. For example, on 7–8 August, 16 people were killed in Guba *woreda* (district) in Benishangul-Gumuz. Again, on 24 September, 20 people were killed in Dangur *woreda*, in Metekkel, followed by another 12 in Mandura *woreda*. Law enforcement was weak, and on 24 September, 45 members of the local administration were dismissed due to neglect of duty. On 24 December, 207 people were murdered in the community of

Bakuji in Metekkel. In early August, attacks occurred in the Arsi zone of Oromia, and the killings of ca. 35 people appeared to have a religious dimension: of these, 35,22 were ethnic Oromo-Christians and 13 were ethnic Amhara-Christians, revealing an often underexposed aspect of Muslim–Christian rivalry, with Muslim radicals targeting Christians.

In the border areas of the Afar and Somali regions, there were also repeated clashes, e.g. on 28 October, with at least 27 people killed. And on 27 December, in the same area, 39 people, both Somali special force members and civilians, were killed and dozens injured. The local authorities of Afar and Somali blamed each other for having started it. Other 'ethnic' violence was seen in Konso, where from 10 to 15 November, 66 civilians were killed in an appalling manner and more than 94,000 displaced, against the backdrop of a complex pattern of local conflict between population groups. In some other areas of the Southern region (formally, Southern Nations, Nationalities and People's Region), state-affiliated army units in so-called 'law enforcement' operations regularly meted out excessive violence on agro-pastoral peoples, dozens of whom were killed, often with impunity.

Violence also occurred in places not previously known for such bloodshed, such as the Bench Gurafarda district (Bench-Sheko Zone) in south-west Ethiopia, with ca. 31 people killed in October. The killings were followed by an exodus of more than 4,600 people to other places, leaving their property (homes, coffee farms, cattle) behind. Local security forces could not or did not act appropriately to protect people and arrest the culprits.

All such clashes seemed again to be the fruit of decades of ethnic divide-and-rule politics, now being fought out because of a relaxation of the previous repressive law-and-order regime of EPRDF.

In general, the more open post-2018 political space and the as yet unsettled political dispensation gave ethnic radicals a chance to pursue their sectarian agendas and foment unrest, and this sometimes evokes harsh responses from federal security units. While this year the effects of the concrete political and judicial reforms instituted by the Abiy government were clearly seen and created conditions for intensified political debate, party organisation, and critical media presence, a large part of the Ethiopian people, impacted by the past 'ethnic politics' of the EPRDF-TPLF regime, seemed not up to the challenges of Abiy's reform agenda. Also, sections of the PP, the (reformed) successor to the EPRDF, retained elements of an undemocratic and hegemonic approach towards their constituents and towards other political parties. On the other hand, some opposition parties/movements invited back to Ethiopia in 2018 abused the new freedoms and refused to participate in a democratic process. Instead, they went back to armed action, intimidation, and subversion. The TPLF retreated gradually to Meqele, leading the autonomous regional government and trying to protect its (economic) interests and evade court cases on past abuse, and disengaging from the federal government.

There were also reports of growing repressive measures towards opponents and activists by the police, although reports by global human rights organisations were often not accurate and lacked context to assess the criminality of the acts of some of the arrested persons (e.g. Jawar Mohammed, Bekele Gerba). There were also reported cases of police abuse and 'ethnic profiling'. In February, a new 'Hate Speech and Disinformation Prevention and Suppression Proclamation' was passed by parliament. On the *Freedom House list*, Ethiopia was categorised as *'not free'*, as in the previous year. The *World Press Freedom Index* of Reporters Without Borders listed the country at rank 99 (of 190 countries), a rise of 11 places. The *Mo Ibrahim Foundation Index on African Governance* noted on 16 November that Ethiopia was one of the eight countries that had improved on all 16 sub-categories of good governance, although it expressed concern about the worsening Tigray situation on 19 November.

The new 'ethnic-nationalist' forces continued to assert themselves – besides the OFC, the OLF, and the Oromo Liberation Army (OLA), also the National Movement of Amhara (NaMA) founded in 2019, the Wolaitta National Movement (2020), and some others. The OLA, an alleged splinter group of the legal party OLF, turned to full-scale violence and perpetrated many mass killings in western Ethiopia, based not on clear 'grievances' or a constructive political agenda but on negative ethnicism and population expulsion. It seemed like a return to the agenda of the 1970s, but this time directed more towards non-Oromo civilians. The law enforcement efforts of the Oromia police and militia were often half-hearted and slow, and populations of non-Oromo (and of non-Gumuz in Metekkel) were not well protected, suffering property destruction and hundreds of killings in an often appallingly cruel manner.

The government accused TPLF-linked agents of compromising national security by illegally facilitating various insurgent groups and violent actors across the country (e.g. in Wollega, Metekkel, Qemant, and North Shewa). It also pointed to foreign-supported agents and several radical religious actors operating under the radar.

Religious politics took a back seat in public life and was not very visible; communal relations were accommodative but not necessarily cordial. Behind the scenes the leaders of religious communities tried to reposition themselves and explore what the new politics of democratisation and openness could bring them. Among the younger Muslim generation, radical ideas about enhancing Islam's role in Ethiopia were gaining ground. The rights of expression of religious communities were, overall, respected by the government. Religion-based clashes were rare, but major communal rivalries and competition persisted in many places.

The last two months of the year were blighted by a dramatic *bloody armed conflict between Tigray's TPLF government and army and the federal army*, the outcome of an unresolved political stand-off caused by the TPLF leaders' intransigence and incapacity to change with the times. They begrudged the new PP its dominant position on the federal level, and were especially afraid of losing the vested interests and privileges they had built up in their 27 years of rule, politically, economically, and financially. The loss of the federal power of the TPLF meant the ongoing decline of its role in security and surveillance matters, in the economy, and on the international scene – although it remained well entrenched there.

The start of the conflict was an unprecedented night attack by TPLF troops on federal army bases and soldiers on 4 November: hundreds were killed in their sleep and stores of key military hardware of the national army in the bases of Meqele and Dansha (and 198 other smaller bases and army stations) were captured.

The federal army response, however, was swift and for the TPLF unexpected: its initial advantage (its 'lightning strike', as boasted about on Tigray TV by TPLF leader Sekuture Getachew) was undone in a matter of days. The federal army regained ground, rescued many of the encircled federal troops, and recovered most of the hardware. But much equipment was also destroyed so as to prevent the TPLF from using it. Simultaneously, TPLF forces had also attacked the region of Amhara, e.g. with a raid on the town of Kirakir. This provoked Amhara militias into the war. The TPLF aimed to march on Addis Ababa and counted on a cascade of other armed rebellions within Ethiopia that it had supported, e.g. in Metekkel, Afar, Wollega, northern Shewa, Qemant, and elsewhere. This did not happen.

On 9 November, a *mass killing of people of Amhara background and other non-Tigrayan inhabitants took place in the town of Mai Kadra* in Wolqait, western Tigray. Over *700 non-combatant people were killed in targeted attacks*, often in a grisly manner, as documented in an Amnesty International report. The psychological shock was great, the military advantage zero. It led to the further involvement of militias from neighbouring Amhara that aimed to return 'western Tigray' (Wolqait, Ts'ellemt, and T'egede) to the Amhara region. Revenge killings also took place in this area, and a process of tit-for-tat violence was the result.

The effects of the Tigray conflict were dramatic and by year's end had taken a huge human toll on the military and civilians. The conflict caused antagonism beyond hatred for the TPLF, between ordinary Tigrayans and others, reinforced by the 'ethnic' killings of Mai Kadra. It also led, on 17 November, to the seizure or freezing of the bank accounts of 34 TPLF-affiliated companies, among them Sur Construction, Gunna Trading, Mesfin Industrial, Selam Bus, and Mega Printing.

On 28 November, Tigray's capital Meqele was taken over by the federal army. A campaign of stabilisation and recovery began, hindered by the covert presence of TPLF sympathisers within the region and even partly within the Tigray Interim Administration appointed by the federal government in November. These officials, headed by interim president Dr Mulu Nega, were all of Tigrayan background. The defeated TPLF armed militias partly left to find refuge in Sudan or retreated to inaccessible rural areas. Offers to surrender and requests for amnesty were rejected. At year's end, around 60,000 Tigrayan refugees, partly from Wolqait and among them perpetrators of the Mai Kadra massacre, had assembled in refugee camps in Sudan.

Several ex-TPLF commanders also tried to rebuild military supply lines from Sudan to TPLF units in Tigray.

The conflict, dubbed a 'law enforcement operation' (which it technically was), also led to a flood of social media/cyber-warfare, with a well-organised TPLF-affiliated group of activists filling social media with misinformation and unreliable reports about abuse and killings, with little solid evidence provided.

Foreign Affairs

A key concern of Ethiopia's foreign policy was to defuse *the row over the Blue Nile dam, the GERD*, with Egypt and Sudan. Notably, Egypt blocked any progress on the dam and its filling schedule, categorically asserting that the GERD constituted an existential threat to Egypt. Sudan toed this line. The new Sudanese prime minister and co-reformist Abdalla Hamdok rejected Abiy's request to conclude a partial bilateral agreement prior to the first filling process in July, saying that the three countries would need a tripartite accord first. Under pressure from Egypt, no amount of argument based on analysis on the impact of the dam and its flood-reducing capacity could convince him. But hydrological arguments were not strong in the Egyptian narrative. President Abdel Fattah el-Sisi of Egypt kept on systematically undermining Ethiopia's position and proceeded to internationalise the issue. He thereby effectively abandoned the Cooperative Framework Agreement (CFA) signed in 2010 by the Nile Basin countries. Various meetings on the GERD issue were held, e.g. direct talks in Addis Ababa in early January and mediation on 28–31 January in Washington under the auspices of the USA and the World Bank and involving the foreign ministers of Ethiopia, Sudan, and Egypt, and, at the request of the Ethiopian side, the water ministers. To no avail.

US president Donald Trump's mediation efforts on the GERD in Washington in January were a failure, as he had no full grasp of the dossier and ultimately sided with Egypt. As a result of the failure, he announced on 2 September that the US would cut a promised $ 100 m in aid to Ethiopia because of its intention to start filling the basin before reaching agreement with Egypt and Sudan. On 25 August, Abiy had visited Khartoum to discuss the GERD issue with prime minister Abdalla Hamdok. US secretary of state Mike Pompeo was also there, but reportedly avoided meeting Abiy. In a telephone conversation on 23 October with Hamdok, Trump talked about the likelihood of Egypt bombing the dam due to Ethiopia's refusal to accept a new filling scheme and rejecting Trump's own proposal.

In July, another mediation round was held under the auspices of the AU, chaired by South African president Cyril Ramaphosa. But no progress was made, mainly due to Egypt's systematic blocking of any change in the status of the (colonial-treaties-based) status quo and to both Sudan and Egypt not accepting the data and predictions of the hydrological analysis on the dam's impact. Since the January direct talks in Addis Ababa, Egypt had unrealistically asked Ethiopia to extend the time to fill the dam reservoir from 12 years to 21 years – a demand they already knew would never be accepted.

Another issue spoiling Ethio-Sudanese relations was the flare-up of a *border conflict in the al-Fashaqa triangle*, a piece of land in a fertile border zone between Sudan and Ethiopia with as yet unsettled official status, but understood as belonging to Sudan. For many decades, the presence of Ethiopian farmers had been condoned, in a mutual agreement between the two countries based on their diplomatic 'Exchange of Notes' in 1972. In the context of the Tigray conflict, the status quo was suddenly fractured by Sudan, which proceeded to chase out the Ethiopian farmers, thus putting pressure on Ethiopia. Sudan's Transitional Council (part military, part civilian) bringing up the issue in a time of conflict was widely perceived as having been instigated by Egypt, in its aim to put maximum pressure on Ethiopia so as to frustrate the (filling of the) GERD. The al-Fashaqa area was thus destabilised by frequent skirmishes between Sudanese and Ethiopian army units, and people were killed on both sides. Ethiopia repeated its aim to de-escalate the issue and come to a diplomatic solution. The issue was not resolved by year's end.

Ethiopia's relations with South Sudan, Kenya, Somaliland, and Djibouti remained stable. On 24 November an important new 60 km asphalt road (costing ca. $ 23 m) was completed between the southern Ethiopian town of Dima and the town of Rad in South Sudan – the first of its kind in the region. IGAD's activities showed no notable impact in the Horn of Africa except for efforts to coordinate the response to the locust plague, alert members to the spread of Rift Valley fever, and assist in Covid-19 response, e.g. with EU-donated equipment (ambulances, field laboratories, millions of surgical masks, protective gloves, test kits, hair covers, 70,000 safety boxes, 14,000 shoe covers, etc.). IGAD Ethiopia's standing in the world was *negatively impacted by the Tigray conflict* in November–December, with often hasty and ill-informed condemnations in the global press and by donor country spokespeople, attacking Abiy's course and accusing the Ethiopian federal army of abuses before these were properly checked or demonstrated. One example was the fictitious discourse on social media around a so-called Aksum massacre, alleged to have occurred on 28–29 November 2020. While there had indeed been a confrontation between local Tigray militia and Eritrean troops on the outskirts of the city, the occurrence of a civilian massacre could not be verified by the end of the year. *Cyber-warfare* initiated by TPLF-affiliated digital activists mainly in the Ethiopian diaspora targeted global reporters, international organisations, and policy-makers, with narratives of abuse that were not verified but made an impact.

Foreign visits to and from Ethiopia were restricted due to the Covid-19 pandemic. Trips abroad made by Abiy were mostly within Africa, e.g. to Guinea on 9 January, to Equatorial Guinea on 9–10 January, to South Africa on 11–12 January, to Eritrea on 18 July, to Sudan on 25 August, and to Kenya on 9 December. On 16–17 February, he visited the UAE for discussion of bilateral economic relations and to attend the *Expo 2020 Dubai*.

A limited number of *foreign diplomatic visitors* came to Addis Ababa, e.g. Canadian prime minister Justin Trudeau to discuss 'democracy, women's empowerment and gender equality, fighting climate change, and economic growth'. Trudeau's visit coincided with the 33rd AU Summit in Addis Ababa. On 8–9 October, EU High Representative for Foreign Affairs Josep Borrell and EU crisis manager Janez Lenarčič met with the Ethiopian leadership, and donated 7.5 tons of coronavirus testing kits. It was a problematic visit, with some meetings cancelled and afterwards the news that one member of the EU delegation to Addis Ababa had been infected with the coronavirus. The EU delegation also met with AU commissioner for peace and security Smaïl Chergui and AU Commission chair Moussa Faki Mahamat. On 13 December, Sudanese prime minister Abdalla Hamdok came to Addis Ababa to try (unsuccessfully) to broker a ceasefire in Tigray. AU envoys, among them South Africa's president Cyril Ramaphosa, came to Addis Ababa on 21 November also to try to 'mediate', but they were not accepted by the Ethiopian government, which rejected any idea of 'parity' between the federal army and the Tigray insurgent forces. Eritrean president Isaias Afewerki visited Addis Ababa on 3–5 May, officially to discuss bilateral ties, the fight against Covid-19/locust infestation, and regional matters. He visited Bishoftu military base and also attended the opening of a 2,000 ha irrigation project in Batu Dugda, Oromia. Eritrean troops allegedly entered the country at the beginning of the confrontation, yet this was not officially confirmed by the Ethiopian federal government by year's end.

Ethiopia kept an army contingent of ca. 5,500 military in *Somalia* under AMISOM (AU Mission in Somalia) but withdrew some personnel towards the end of the year.

Socioeconomic Developments

The coronavirus pandemic expanded gradually in Ethiopia from mid-March and was tackled rapidly by the Ministry of Health and the health services, according their (limited) ability in monitoring, testing, and treatment. A country-wide state of emergency was declared on 8 April. *By year's end, there were 124,264 coronavirus cases registered, with 10,245 infected people counted, 112,096 recovered, and 1,923 deaths officially recorded*. Although people adjusted to the pandemic with cautious behaviour and the medical services did their utmost to register and treat cases, including post-mortem autopsies done on deceased people and imposing the quarantining and social distancing rules, the real figures were likely higher. Nevertheless, in the countryside, cases were far fewer in number. One reason for this was the partial ban on public inter-regional transportation to contain the spread of the virus. The economic effects of the pandemic were felt mainly in the services sector (e.g. transport), travel, and tourism/hospitality services. Over a million people lost income or jobs. The government issued a first $ 150 m stimulus package, removed import taxes on all Covid-19-related items, and promised faster VAT refunds for businesses. It also readied a $ 630 m fund to support banks with expected liquidity shortages. As in several EU countries, the government decreed that employees could not be dismissed during the pandemic.

Despite multiple crises, such as armed conflict, coronavirus backlash, and receding FDI, and varying sources for the financial data, there was overall *economic (GDP) growth* of an estimated 3.5% (World Bank data). Total GDP reached ca. *$ 96 bn*, meaning per capita GDP of ca. $ 602. GDP growth outstripped population growth by only 0.8 % (for the budget year in Ethiopia ending on 1 July).

GDP by sector consisted of *agriculture ca. 33%, industry 24 %, and services 43%*. Coffee exports again generated the largest revenue, closely followed by minerals (notably gold), agrarian/horticultural products (sesame, oilseeds, vegetables including *khat*, and flowers), and live animals, leather, and meat. Agricultural production benefited from good rains but was impacted by locust plagues, flooding, and conflict. In Tigray the agricultural cycle was seriously disturbed by the armed conflict from early November, with much of the ripening crop lost. Industrial production rose slightly, but the performance and productivity of the industrial parks lagged behind projections, partly because of Covid-19.

The government budget for 2020/21 was 476 bn birr (ca. $ 16.4 bn), with 160.3 bn birr allocated for capital expenditure, 133.3 bn for recurrent spending, 176 bn to subsidise regional states, and 6 bn birr for Sustainable Development Goal (SDG) projects. It was a budget that was 89 bn birr higher than last year.

At ca. $ 15 bn, imports were about 3.5 times the value of exports. Imports consisted mainly of fuel, machinery, metal products and electrical materials, motor vehicles, chemicals and fertilisers, consumers electronics, and clothing. Due to coronavirus and rumours about security conditions, *foreign tourism* notably *declined*.

In November, a ten-year economic plan entitled *Ethiopia: An African Beacon of Prosperity* was approved by the Council of Ministers (awaiting parliamentary approval), according the private sector a more important role as the motor for economic growth and foreseeing a larger GDP-generating share for manufacturing and industry.

World Bank figures suggested an official unemployment rate of 2.8%, but this was entirely fictitious (as was that for youth unemployment, at 3.26%). No reliable data were available (with many sources providing different figures), and informal estimates by local economists put the figure rather at 22–24% (the same for youth unemployment).

Digitalisation of the economy proceeded. In the agrarian sector, the government expanded its mobile-phone-based advisory platform for farmers, the *8028 IVR/SMS service*, a kind of hotline and helpdesk system to access information about crop types (including cereals, pulses, oilseeds, and household irrigation crops), with livestock advisory and Covid-19 health advisory contents.

The country's *external debt* rose slightly to about *$ 28 bn*, enhanced by Covid-19 expenses and related economic damage, lagging foreign investments, and the Tigray conflict in November and its humanitarian fallout. About half of this was owed to China, which built the larger part of Ethiopia's industrial parks. The overall debt remained quite high in terms of the debt-to-GDP ratio (60%), although it went down to 26.8% this year compared with 37.7% in 2018. According to the IMF, the danger of external 'debt distress' remained very high. The annual debt repayment obligations amounted to almost $ 2 bn, around 30 bn birr domestically. There was also still $ 538 m in external debt arrears dating from before the 1970s owed to East European countries and to Libya. In November, *Fitch Ratings* downgraded Ethiopia to CCC status, after a government announcement that it wanted to apply to the G20's Common Framework for Debt Treatments, beyond the Debt Service Suspension Initiative (DSSI). This was approved and saved Ethiopia a payment of $ 470 m.

On the *TI Corruption Perceptions Index* published in 2020, Ethiopia had a 'score' of *38 out of 100* and took *rank 94 of a total of 180 countries*, meaning a clear improvement and a rise of five places since 2012. The World Bank's Doing Business report noted that Ethiopia scored *58* (with 100 the best performance) and was *at place 159 (of 190)*. This also meant improvement, but still with much work to do. On the UNDP's HDI, Ethiopia's value for 2019 (published 2020) was 0.485, positioning it as 173rd out of 189 countries, in a continuation of the slow trend upwards.

As the IMF said in a report, Ethiopia under the EPRDF had a debt-financed growth model, but at the cost of *increasing debt vulnerabilities*. Massive investment schemes inherited from the previous government, such as the Kuraz Sugar Development Project and factory schemes, the Addis Ababa light-rail and the new Ethio-Djibouti railway (China-financed and built), were all loss-making, contributing to the debt problem. The failure of these large state-supported schemes under the EPRDF was one reason why Abiy's government continued to base its 'Home-Grown Economic Reform Agenda' more on the private sector, and on privatisation to generate money. To this effect, further talks continued with foreign parties to, for instance, partly privatise Ethio-Telecom (under preparation). Other privatisation plans regarding state-owned companies also stalled, like Ethiopian Airlines (suspended), the Ethiopian Sugar Corporation (delayed), and the Ethiopian Shipping and Logistics Service Enterprise (cancelled).

The EU decided on 28 December to *block a promised sum of $ 107 m budget support*, because it was of the opinion that the federal government was preventing humanitarian aid from reaching all civilians in Tigray.

The *FDI* value in the first six months of the fiscal year reached *$ 1.1 bn*, a decline of 12%, although this was below the African average of a 21% decline (due to the coronavirus effect). China was a still big lender, but the amount invested/loaned declined strongly during the year due to disappointing returns. The government also expressed growing scepticism about the opaque conditions of Chinese financing and the speed and rate of repayment.

Remittances sent by the 3–4 m Ethiopians living abroad reached an estimated *$ 4.5 bn* officially and at least the same sum came informally, again making the diaspora the largest source of income for the country, for both family and social support and business investments.

Inflation on an annual basis was an estimated 20.9% in 2020 (World Bank data), leading to a steady depreciation of the birr, to a rate of 38–40 to the euro in December. There was a constant lack of foreign currency, hindering economic expansion.

Progress was made this year by the new Ethiopian Financial Intelligence Center, a government unit *combating illicit financial flows* from Ethiopia to abroad. According to Transparency International, in the years 2005–14, for instance, the illicit outflow was between $ 1.25 bn and $ 3 bn annually (most of it via trade mis-invoicing and illicit transfers by government-connected or -protected people, e.g. via embassies). The new government under Abiy made a priority of controlling and curbing this clandestine outflow, based on large amounts of cash (an estimated 110 bn birr, or $ 2.7 bn) circulating outside the banking system. Part of the effort was a $ 97 m operation in September to *change the birr currency notes*, whereby the public had three months to exchange the old banknotes.

The GERD dam was the focus of a continued national effort, with multiple appeals to the public and the Ethiopian diaspora for financial contributions. It was about 70% completed by year's end.

In February, the IMF disbursed the first part of a huge loan to Ethiopia – one of the highest possible under its own rules, to the tune of $ 2.9 bn. Later in the year, it accorded $ 411 m in emergency assistance and also approved a request for a suspension of Ethiopia's debt service payments of $ 12 m under its Catastrophe Containment and Relief Trust.

The humanitarian and economic situation in Tigray predicably deteriorated after the start of the armed conflict on 4 November. Reliable data were scarce and not transparent but the damage done by all sides concerned – the remnant TPLF, the federal army, and Eritrean troops – was substantial. The TPLF government in Meqele had also opened all Tigrayan prisons, releasing over 21,000 prisoners of all kinds, often without family support or income. This contributed to the disturbances, the looting, and the scale of violence that was also reported from some federal and Eritrean troops. At year's end, the situation in Tigray had not yet stabilised but the federal government had restored telephone and ICT connections partly destroyed by the TPLF remnants since 4 November 2020.

Population growth in selected (urban) areas showed decline but remained substantial, at *2.5 to 3.3 %: a growth of 10,600 people per day*. No recalibration of population policy was seen, although the constrained natural resource base of agriculture and its slow pace of intensification produced a worrying trend that was unsustainable in the long term. There was a growing unmet need for contraception among women, although certain religious leaders continued to argue against it. Population density reached 105.4 people per km². Ethiopia's population was 116.4 m by year's end, i.e. 2.8 m people more in one year (an increase of 2.53%). The population under 15 years of age reached 46.3%. There was limited *official* outmigration of 14,759 people only (UN figures).

Human trafficking and illegal/undocumented labour migration remained serious problems, with tens of thousands again 'trying their luck' at reaching the Middle East and elsewhere, and many caught in involuntary networks of exploitation and low pay. During the year, there were several campaigns of repatriation of Ethiopians in distress in the Arab peninsula.

Environmental problems were undiminished due to erosion of top soils, land degradation, overcultivation, loss of biodiversity, and encroachment of cultivation in natural areas. New policies were announced by the government to implement 'Green economy plans', including campaigns of tree planting and pollution reduction and sustainable energy production plans. In the government policy plans there was a definite turn towards a green, sustainable economy, but implementation was difficult. Sufficient funds were lacking to radically tackle the growing environmental decline, land degradation, and overpopulation in certain areas marked by long-standing patterns of 'predatory' resource use and deforestation.

Humanitarian challenges continued to plague the country, with high numbers of IDPs in regional border zones, and with numerous foreign refugees, Tigray conflict victims, and conflict-induced displacements or 'ethnic-based' expulsion and killings in the rest of the country, among them the ca. 94,000 displaced in Konso. The UN reported that at year's end there were ca. 797,000 refugees from abroad (mostly from South Sudan and Somalia, but even including Syrians) and 1.8 m IDPs (but there were also 1.2 m returnees by December). UNHCR reported that in late December there were 60,348 refugees from Tigray in Sudanese camps. Ethiopia's appeal on 9 June for $ 1.65 bn to meet the humanitarian requirement needs of 16.5 m people – compounded by the Covid-19 pandemic problems, displacement, disease outbreaks, etc. – was not met in full.

Kenya

Njoki Wamai

The Covid-19 pandemic and its effects dominated Kenyan politics, its foreign relations, and its socioeconomic developments. Kenya registered its first case of the novel coronavirus on 13 March 2020. The pandemic led to significant loss of life not only from health complications but also as a result of police brutality and health issues arising from the attendant loss of livelihoods in an economy that is largely informal and dependent on tourism. Dominant political issues in 2020 were nation-building, devolution, corruption, terrorism, and economic downturn due to the pandemic. The Covid-19 pandemic had far-reaching political consequences. The pursuit of a united Kenya continued through the proposed Building Bridges Initiative (BBI), resulting in new elite alliances and divisions. These divisions were exacerbated by the devolution disagreements that emerged from the planned revenue-sharing formula among different counties. On foreign affairs, Covid-19 strained and promoted relations between Kenya and other states in equal measure. Relations with neighbouring Tanzania were strained over different pandemic containment measures, while relations with the US and China were strained by the increasingly nationalist and protectionist policies of the great powers. Macroeconomic indicators weakened as the economy took a downturn, along with other development indicators.

Domestic Politics

The year 2020 was defined by President Uhuru Kenyatta's economic and political legacy projects, branded the *Big Four Agenda*. The Big Four Agenda included affordable housing, food security, universal healthcare, and industrialisation. The reconciliation of Kenyans and an end to divisive ethnic politics became another legacy agenda after Kenyatta and Raila Odinga, the former prime minister and Kenyatta's political opponent, ended their rivalry in March 2018 – publicly symbolised by the famous 'handshake'. The *Building Bridges Initiative (BBI)* was conceived after that public handshake between Kenyatta and opposition leader Odinga in an attempt to end the 2017 post-election tensions and enduring divisions resulting from winner-takes-all elections in Kenya. As a background, the BBI acknowledged ethnic antagonism and competitive elections as destructive to Kenya's politics. It recognised corruption as an existential threat to Kenya; the lack of a national ethos; support for devolution by Odinga and Kenyatta; the role of divisive elections in ethnic polarisation; the need to guarantee safety and security from natural and human-made disasters; the importance of implementing the BBI to ensure respect for human and civil rights; and that income inequalities prevented Kenyans from having shared prosperity, which was important in ending conflict.

New divisions in the ruling Jubilee Party emerged following the Kenyatta–Odinga rapprochement. The partnership of President Kenyatta and Deputy President William Ruto, conjured before the March 2013 elections and ICC trials in 2013, finally ended in 2020, leading to a strained relationship between the two despite their political friendship during turbulent times with the ICC. The death in February 2020 of Kenyatta's and Ruto's mentor Daniel arap Moi, Kenya's longest-serving president (1978–2002), whose leadership was defined by oppression, corruption, and ethnic exclusion, did little to heal the unfolding political divisions between former members of the *Kenya African National Union (KANU)* party.

The relationship between Kenyatta and his deputy president, who plans to succeed Kenyatta in 2022, deteriorated further as several scandals involving Ruto's close associates further alienated him. Without clear opposition in 2020 after the handshake, William Ruto and his allies stepped into the opposition role despite being in government, while Odinga became a trusted partner in the government despite having no formal position within it. In May 2020, President Kenyatta demoted Deputy President Ruto's allies from powerful positions in parliament, including party whips and members of house committees. Odinga also demoted members of his *Orange Democratic Party (ODM)* who were not supportive of the BBI. As President Kenyatta and Odinga continued to pursue the BBI and other initiatives, the isolated Ruto started crafting a new political agenda away from Kenyatta's legacy projects. These included infrastructure development projects such as the Nairobi Expressway and the Nairobi Commuter Railway to tackle traffic congestion in the capital, the affordable housing fund, and universal healthcare.

As a result of the Covid-19 pandemic, the Jubilee leadership shelved the rollout of a country-wide Universal Health Coverage Programme, ICT and electricity infrastructure projects, and the establishment of the National Housing Development Fund for affordable housing. The pandemic forced Kenyatta to abandon some of his legacy projects to prioritise the emergency hiring of frontline health workers and the purchase of Covid-19 emergency response equipment like ventilators and personal protective equipment (PPE) for health workers.

Kenya was ranked 124th out of 180 in the 2019 TI Corruption Perceptions Index released in 2020. In August 2020, an investigative journalist revealed a corruption scandal at the Ministry of Health after Covid emergency funds were released by the World Bank in May 2020. The media report, popularly known as the *'Covid millionaires scandal'*, exposed how the Kenya Medical Supplies Agency (KEMSA), a government institution, lost money through suspicious procurement of low-quality PPE at inflated prices. Members of the political elite and officials at KEMSA were also accused of conflict of interest as they engaged proxies to secure procurement contracts. According to the Ministry of Finance, Kenya secured $ 2 bn in aid and grants from the World Bank, WHO, and Chinese billionaire Jack Ma's foundation for Covid-19 mitigation. The media report, which alleged the theft of funds meant for Covid management, led Kenyan activists and medical professionals to organise protests and a country-wide strike in August 2020. By September 2020, more than 1,000 medical professionals had been infected by the virus and ten had died. The health workers criticised the corruption in government while they lacked much-needed personal protective equipment (PPE), allowances for health workers, and other equipment. The Kenya Medical Practitioners, Pharmacists and Dentists Union (KMPDU) called a strike from 10 September to protest delayed salaries and lack of PPE. Kenyatta ordered an investigation into the corruption incident while the police tear-gassed and arrested 12 protesters demonstrating in Nairobi.

Kenya was ranked 'partly free' with a score of 48 out of 100 in the Freedom House Index on freedom of speech and assembly for 2020. Kenya continued to score poorly on political rights, at 19/40, and on support for civil liberties, with a score of 29/60. Kenyan police violently enforced curfews and movement restrictions after the onset of the pandemic. In March 2020, 20 people were killed by police enforcing the lockdown. A 13-year-old boy, Yassin Moyo, was killed by stray police bullets in Nairobi's informal settlements as the police enforced the lockdown measures using excessive force. This led to protests, and to police arresting activists in July for protesting against police brutality during the lockdown period.

The *pandemic aggravated existing political divisions* as Kenyatta and Odinga continued to pursue their BBI project oblivious to the unemployment and loss of livelihoods and the increased cost of healthcare and resultant poverty caused by the pandemic in a country without universal healthcare. As Kenyatta's erstwhile Jubilee Party partner William Ruto now turned rival, he took advantage of the public mood of indignation over the KEMSA corruption scandal and BBI campaigns during the pandemic. He seized the opportunity presented by the corruption scandal to criticise the Kenyatta-led Jubilee faction. Ruto initially appeared ambivalent towards the BBI but later opposed it and continued to champion his populist 'hustler narrative'. The hustler narrative is a campaign advanced by Ruto highlighting class divisions between Kenya's elite families, like those of Kenyatta and Odinga, and those like Ruto, who sells himself as a hustler who will transfer power from the ungrateful dynasties to the hustlers – the ordinary people. The 'hustler–dynasty' division led to the formation and consolidation of other political coalitions across ethnic elites, such as the Ruto-led Tanga Tanga faction and the Kenyatta-led Kieleweke faction, within the ruling Jubilee Party back in 2019. When the two factions, both drawn from across ethnic groups, first formed, they were considered a spectacle that would quickly fade away. But in 2020, they consolidated themselves into formidable political camps that could guarantee their political survival beyond the forthcoming 2022 election.

A stand-off on the *revenue-sharing formula* also emerged in the senate between July and September 2020 that created an impasse. The debate pitted senate members from well-resourced, population-rich counties against those from sparsely populated, semi-arid, under-developed counties. The Kenyatta-supporting Kieleweke Jubilee faction members and the Ruto-led Tanga Tanga members failed to pass the revenue allocation formula 11 times as their divisions played out. They finally passed the government formula on 17 September 2020, after the coercion and demotion of the Tanga Tanga faction by Kenyatta, further dividing the Jubilee Party.

Still on devolution, the senate impeached two governors – a first in Kenyan politics after the 2010 constitution was implemented. The senate heard three impeachment cases against three governors, Ferdinand Waititu for Kiambu County, Anne Waiguru for Kirinyaga County, and Mike Sonko for Nairobi County, in January, June, and December respectively. The senate then successfully impeached former Kiambu governor Waititu for violation of the constitution and abuse of office and flamboyant Nairobi governor Sonko, while failing to impeach Kirinyaga governor Waiguru. The motion against Waiguru, filed by members of her own county assembly and citing corruption and violation of procurement laws, failed the impeachment test. Divisions between Kenyatta and Ruto also played out as senators aligned to the Odinga-Kenyatta alliance outvoted the Ruto-aligned supporters opposed to Waiguru.

Sonko was impeached in December 2020 after 88 members of the county assembly out of 122 voted him out. After his ouster, Sonko was arrested and charged with several offences, including abuse of office, gross misconduct, and economic crimes of corruption. Kenyatta and Odinga then appointed Major General Mohammed

Badi, a military man, to lead a team of professionals to run the city. This decision by the central government to run Nairobi County attracted criticism and court litigation from civil society and the Law Society of Kenya, on the grounds that it usurped the democratic power of the citizens to elect their governor. The Ruto-led Tanga Tanga faction also criticised the move by the Kenyatta-Odinga alliance. A female deputy governor, Anne Kananu, was hurriedly appointed and promoted to become the acting governor. Many Nairobi residents equally supported the military running the city if the move would address rampant corruption and enhance service delivery for residents. The two governors who have run Nairobi since 2013 faced corruption charges in 2020. Sonko's predecessor, Evans Kidero, faced corruption charges from his time in office in 2013–17. Nairobi is often fiercely contested due to the high voter population and resource levels and proximity to the central government. The emerging divisions and realignments between Kenyatta, Odinga, and Ruto continue to play out in Nairobi County politics as interested parties plan for December 2022 elections.

Another effect of the Covid-19 pandemic was the deaths of several politicians, including members of county assemblies, members of parliament, senators, and the governor of Nyamira County. Although general elections are scheduled for 2022, electoral polls to replace these politicians overshadowed other political activities as coalitions realigned to ensure a win in the by-elections in anticipation of the December 2022 elections.

On security, the *common border with Somalia* remained porous despite the ongoing construction of a wall by the Kenyan government. Sixty-nine terrorist attacks in Kenya were reported in 2020, according to the Centre for Human Rights and Policy Studies (CHRIPS) Observatory on terror attacks. This was a 49% increase compared with the 34 attacks recorded in 2019. According to CHRIPS, the attacks intensified at the beginning of the year, decreasing from April to August but later increasing in September and December. By March 2020, *al-Shabaab* had launched 16 attacks in the North Eastern and Coast regions in the counties of Mandera, Wajir, Garissa, and Lamu. Garissa County recorded the highest number of attacks, which resulted in the deaths of ten people including teachers, pupils, and security officers. According to the CHRIPS report, 58 militants were reported dead along with 25 security officials across the four counties, including ten police officers, eight police reservists, three Kenya Defence Forces soldiers, and six unspecified security officials. This was a decrease from 2019, when Kenya lost 42 security personnel to terror-related attacks. Twenty-four civilians were victims of kidnapping along with one government official, according to the CHRIPS report. Due to the Covid-19 pandemic, the attacks did not disrupt education as most children were at home. Previously in some parts of northern Kenya, militants have targeted teachers from other counties as well as security forces and communication masts. The terror group attacked the Westgate Mall in 2013, the University of Garissa in 2015, and Dusit Hotel in Nairobi in 2019. Despite these attacks, the president did not publicly address the country's security situation.

The ICC also issued warrants of arrest on a Jubilee-supporting lawyer, Paul Gicheru. As divisions between Kenyatta and Ruto continued to emerge, the ICC cases against Gicheru and Walter Barasa, a journalist, were reopened. The two were accused of witness-tampering during the ICC investigations against Kenyatta and Ruto, among others. Ruto's defence lawyer at the ICC, Karim Khan, was elected as the ICC prosecutor with the support of the government. Khan's win was met with disappointment and disapproval by Kenyan civil society and victims of the 2007–08 post-election violence, owing to his support for and defence of Ruto for crimes against humanity at the ICC between 2013–16.

Foreign Affairs

Before the pandemic struck, *2020 was celebrated as Kenya's diplomatic moment* following various multilateral leadership positions Nairobi secured at the UNSC, the AU Peace and Security Council (AUPSC), and the ACP.

In June 2020, Kenya was elected as a non-permanent member of the UNSC for the third time. Kenya beat Djibouti by 67 votes to join India, Ireland, Mexico, and Norway for two years (2021–22) as non-permanent members of the council. Kenya is expected to champion the African agenda along with Niger and Tunisia by pushing for reforms at the UNSC to increase African representation and support for peace and security initiatives in the continent. Kenya joined the UNSC at a time when the global pandemic had caused great power rivalry between the East and the West that would inevitably affect African states through the distribution of vaccines and aid. According to the Horn Institute, Kenya will face a diplomatic dilemma given its cordial relationships with the USA, China, and Russia, all of whom hold permanent positions at the UNSC. The pandemic not only had economic consequences but also peace and security consequences, as states retreated to nationalist and protectionist policies, reducing vaccine distribution and economic support to African states. Diplomats in Nairobi proposed developing a common agenda for the three African member states at the UNSC. The agenda would address conflict crisis in the Horn of Africa, governance, climate change, support for sustainable peacekeeping operations, and strengthening transitions in countries like South Sudan.

At the regional level, Kenya was embroiled in *diplomatic disputes with its neighbours Somalia and Tanzania*. Relations between Somalia and Kenya declined further as the maritime border dispute at the ICJ remained unresolved following Kenya's insistence on delaying the case due to Covid-19. The border dispute is a disagreement over the direction in which the border extends into the Indian Ocean, with Somalia favouring a south-easterly path over Kenya's preference for a border parallel to the latitudinal line. The disputed area covers 100,000 square kilometres and is believed to be rich in oil, gas, and fish, with both countries accusing the other of selling off the blocks before the court ruling.

Differing Covid-19 containment measures further strained the foreign relations between Kenya and its southern neighbour Tanzania. Kenya followed the WHO guidelines for daily reporting of Covid-19 incidents and mass testing, while Tanzanian president John Magufuli publicly criticised the WHO demands, using a postcolonial critique while supporting indigenous practices for dealing with respiratory viruses, such as steam baths. Kenya closed the border between Kenya and Tanzania to avoid increasing cross-border infection from Tanzania but later reinstated cordial relations.

The *AU Mission in Somalia (AMISOM)* continued operations in 2020. Kenya contributed 3,697 soldiers to AMISOM in 2020, according to the UNSC. The Kenyan troops continued to support the training of Somalian forces for counter-terrorism operations as they organised a smooth transition out of Somalia. The Kenyan government, in partnership with bordering counties, resumed construction of the controversial 700 km wall at the Kenya–Somalia border, which had stalled after border communities protested.

The cost of overseas trips by President Kenyatta was expected to reduce drastically after the 25 March 2020 flight ban at the start of the Covid-19 pandemic. However, presidential travel costs increased ten times between March and June to $ 587,637, up from $ 55,438 in the same quarter last year, as the state hired chartered flights, according to data from the Office of the Controller of Budget. Kenyatta's trip to Paris for bilateral talks in October 2020 was the first public trip after the travel ban.

In Paris, President Kenyatta and President Macron signed three *bilateral agreements* that focused on infrastructure development in Kenya. Earlier in 2020, President Kenyatta held talks with US President Donald Trump to renew a bilateral free trade agreement that would allow preferential trade for Kenya's products. The current trade agreement between many African states and the US, the African Growth and Opportunity Act (AGOA), expires in 2025. The AGOA allows countries to export goods to the USA without quotas and tariffs. According to Africa Report, Kenya was one of the few countries whose contract was renewed after renegotiation with the Trump leadership. In December 2020, president-elect Joe Biden reached out to Kenya as chair of the AUPSC promising support in ending conflicts in Ethiopia and Sudan. Biden promised a lasting partnership with Kenya focused on cooperation on security, climate change, and refugees to ensure regional peace and stability in the Horn of Africa, but his economic relations agenda on the continent remains unclear.

Meanwhile, on citizenship, Kenya retained its position as a *leading refugee host country in Africa* due to instability in Somalia, South Sudan, Burundi, and DRC.

Advocacy for stateless persons led to the registration of 4,500 Shona people and 1,300 members of Rwandan communities who had moved to Kenya in the 1930s and 1950s. About 490,000 refugees and asylum seekers were registered in 2020. The Covid-19 pandemic slowed the government's controversial planned repatriation programme for refugees.

Socioeconomic Developments

Before the pandemic, *Kenya was one of the fastest-growing economies in the region*, with GDP having grown at 5.7% for the past five years. According to the AfDB Economic Outlook Report, Kenya's economy decelerated from 5.4% in 2019 to 1.4% in 2020 due to the Covid-19 pandemic. The fiscal deficit widened to 8.3% of GDP as a result of revenue shortfalls and pandemic-related spending. Unplanned government spending increased to deal with the health crisis and to mitigate business and household income damage. Foreign exchange reserves decreased from $ 8.96 bn in 2019 to $ 7.8 bn in 2020. The Kenyan shilling (Ksh) also weakened by 8.9%, to Ksh 110 to the dollar compared with Ksh 101 in November 2019. The AfDB reported that Kenya's financial sector was affected by spillover effects from major sectors, but the capital market was the hardest hit. The Nairobi Securities Exchange share index fell by 20% between 30 September 2019 and September 2020, and market capitalisation fell by 2% over the same period. Despite the pandemic, Kenya's economy, with a GDP of $ 109 bn, remained the largest in Eastern Africa, having overtaken that of Ethiopia in 2017. Overall, the economy contracted by 5.7% in the second quarter of 2020, its first quarterly contraction since the global financial crisis 12 years ago.

Kenya's *public debt* continued to be a major concern in Kenya in 2020. The country's debt burden continued to increase, while the macroeconomic environment and financial sector weakened due to the pandemic. The high debt burden and widening budget deficit left the government little space to deal with Covid-19 and the locust invasion without external support. The country's public debt rose by $ 11.8 bn due to increased borrowing in response to the pandemic and the implementation of planned infrastructure projects, including roads and railways. Kenya borrowed $ 54.3 bn in January 2020 before Covid-19, and a year later a $ 66.1 bn debt was recorded. Most of this debt ($ 34.4 bn) was external, provided for by multilateral and bilateral lenders like the World Bank, while the rest was domestic.

The IMF raised Kenya's risk of *debt distress* from moderate to high in 2020 due to the impact of the coronavirus pandemic on Kenya's financial stability. A virtual country visit was held in November 2020 which concluded that though the Kenyan economy was often resilient, the pandemic had had an unprecedented impact, causing reduced government revenue from taxes and rising public debt – 65.9%

of GDP in 2019/20. The IMF provided Kenya with the conditional ECF arrangement for three and a half years. Kenya was expected to mobilise more taxes, strengthen its monetary policy framework, and restructure inefficient state-owned enterprises such as the Kenya Railways, Kenya Airways, Kenya Power, and sugar companies, whose underlying financial weaknesses were exacerbated by the pandemic. These recommendations were questioned by parliament for their expected impact on unemployment, with the Ministry of Finance cautioned against similar outcomes to those of the structural adjustment programmes (SAPs) of the 1990s.

The World Bank Ease of Doing Business Report for 2020 ranked Kenya 56th out of 190 countries reviewed. The report evaluates the extent to which a country enhances or constrains business activity. Of the 190 countries reviewed in 2019, Kenya improved by five positions, with a score of 73.2, from position 61 in the previous year. In Africa, Kenya's rank declined by one position to 4th, after Mauritius, Rwanda, and Morocco. The World Bank reported that Kenya's improvement was a result of improved processes in application for registration permits, construction permits, credit access, access to electricity, tax payments, cross-border trade, resolving insolvency, labour market regulations, enforcing contracts, and protection of minority shareholders. Analysts and small and medium-sized enterprises (SMEs) in Kenya disputed the report, arguing that it only represented large businesses with large capital while SMEs continued to face myriad challenges due to delays and inefficiencies in the registration of licences, electricity, and cross-border trade challenges.

On its *Vision 2030*, with barely ten years remaining to accomplish the vision, the government embarked on the third Medium Term Plan (MTP) despite the impact of Covid-19. Launched in 2008, the strategy document aims to transform Kenya into an industrialised middle-income economy with high-quality lives for Kenyans. The pandemic has forced the Vision 2030 secretariat to rethink the continued investment in infrastructure projects, including rail, roads, ports, and the LAPSSET (Lamu Port-South Sudan-Ethiopia-Transport) Corridor project, without a commensurate emphasis on human development projects such as in healthcare systems and education. Despite this realisation, Vision 2030 continued to support the LAPSSET Corridor programme that was adopted as an AU infrastructure project. After the adoption, the transport corridor from Lamu Port to Isiolo, Addis, and Juba was redesigned to link the port of Douala on the Atlantic Ocean in West Africa with Lamu in the Indian Ocean on the East African coast.

The adoption was praised by Raila Odinga, the AU's envoy for infrastructure, because it would attract FDI and catalyse the realisation of the planned AfCFTA.

On the HDI rankings, Kenya was ranked 143rd out of 189 countries and territories in the 2020 report, based on 2019 indicators. Kenya's HDI for 2019 was 0.601, putting the country in the medium human development category. This was an increase of 0.1 from 2018 but still low compared with the highest country index, with Norway at 0.957. Kenya's HDI fell to 0.443 when discounted for inequality, a loss of 26.3%, as the country continued to be highly unequal. On gender inequality, Kenya had a Gender Inequality Index (GII) of 0.518, ranking 126th out of 162 in the 2019 index.

Kenya's unemployment rate doubled from 5.2% in 2019 to 10.4% two months after the first Covid-19 case was recorded in March 2020, according to the 'Labour Force Report' by the Kenya National Bureau of Statistics. The rate of unemployment in June 2020 was 10.4% due to Covid-19, compared with 4.7 % in June 2019. The report noted that unemployed increased to 4,637,164 between April and June 2020, compared with 2,329,176 in 2019, as a result of lay-offs linked to the pandemic. Job entrants aged 20–29 years were most heavily affected by the rising unemployment as employers laid them off first. The AfDB estimated that nearly 2 m people fell into poverty and nearly 900,000 lost their jobs in Kenya. The pandemic had disproportionate effects on the urban poor: 47% of urban residents in sub-Saharan Africa live in informal settlements that are ill equipped to cope with a disease outbreak due to high population density and inadequate housing and sanitation facilities, according to Reuters Foundation. The urban informal traders in Kenya's cities bore the high economic costs of lockdowns and physical distancing policies. Female low-income earners were faced with an extra care burden in their households as a result of the pandemic. While mitigation policies may have slowed the transmission of the virus, the poor, especially women, were forced to bear the heavy social and economic burdens due to the lack of a safety net. A survey by the Kenya Private Sector Alliance (KEPSA) on the impact of the coronavirus pandemic on Kenya's economy indicated that 61% of businesses had been affected by the restriction measures taken to contain the virus. The survey featured 95 locally owned businesses from 17 different sectors of the economy. According to the report, businesses were disrupted in various ways: lay-offs, work-from-home policies, reduced demand for their products, increased costs of production, and reduced capital flows.

Kenya Airways, the national carrier, cancelled 65% of flights and reduced the salaries of all staff while forcing non-core staff to take compulsory leave. The Covid-19 pandemic had a profound effect on the tourism sector – the leading foreign exchange earner for Kenya. The Ministry of Tourism was reported to have lost $ 999 m in revenue between January and October. The travel bans and lockdowns affected tourism and Kenya's economy significantly, with the loss of jobs and closure of hotels.

At the beginning of the year, swarms of desert locusts invaded the northern and north-eastern parts of Kenya. The swarms of locusts began to cross the border in December 2019 from Somalia and Ethiopia, and in 2020 they spread to 28 Kenyan counties. According to the FAO, the desert locust invasion was the worst in 70 years. It posed a severe food security threat across the entire sub-region and reduced economic growth. The Ministry of Agriculture reported that swarms had flattened approximately 175,000 hectares of crop, while 164,000 households were at risk of food insecurity. In response to the locust attack, the government, in collaboration with county governments and development partners, undertook control measures. Working with the World Bank, FAO, WFP, and UN, the ministry deployed spraying and surveillance aircraft targeting breeding grounds in Wajir, Isiolo, Turkana, Marsabit, and Garissa counties. Regional organisations such as IGAD and the Desert Locust Control Organisation of East Africa (DLCO-EA) were also involved. The losses from the locust invasion will have a significant impact in 2021 as farmers seek coping mechanisms to meet their income and livelihood losses.

Despite the effects of the pandemic and the locusts, the agriculture sector grew from 5% in 2019 to 6.3% in 2020, according to the Kenya Bureau of Statistics, with increased exports of tea, coffee, and fruit. Tea was the leading foreign exchange earner, contributing 23% of foreign earnings according to the Ministry of Agriculture. Kenyatta's government proposed regulatory and administrative reforms in the tea and coffee sector to enable farmers to increase their incomes through value addition. The Ministry of Agriculture proposed to eliminate the dysfunctional and inefficient tea auction system that is often manipulated by insider trading and cartels, leading to low prices and poor earnings for tea farmers. A $ 3 bn coffee fund was launched to cushion coffee farmers from delayed payments as well as the value addition of horticultural produce. Heavier taxes were imposed on milk products originating from outside the EAC region, as farmers accused Kenyatta and his family of interference in market competition in the milk sector.

On climate change, ecological disasters which started in 2019 continued in 2020, with relentless droughts and torrential floods in Northern Kenya and the Rift Valley respectively. The dry season in the north intensified in 2020, killing more animals and crops than in previous years, causing food insecurity. It also increased vulnerability to conflict, as neighbouring communities routinely raided each other for remaining cattle. Deforestation, loss of wetlands, and urban growth intensified in 2020, resulting in rising water levels and flooding. Floods in the eight lakes on the floor of the Rift Valley resulted in the loss of livelihoods and food insecurity. Schools, farms, homes, health centres, churches, and shops were flooded around Lake Baringo, which rose by several metres and claimed 34 square miles of land. Members of more than 1,250 households were forced out of their homes, adding to the numbers of global climate change refugees and displaced persons.

The education sector was greatly affected by Covid-19. The Kenyan government closed schools abruptly on 15 March as a nationwide response to the pandemic. According to the Right to Education Initiative (RTE), the closure disrupted 17 m learners, with public school learners and teachers bearing the socioeconomic burden due to lack of training and resources that could be quickly adapted to an online learning system. The closure of schools exposed the income, regional, and gender inequality in Kenya's education system. It affected the health of learners who relied on school feeding programmes as their main source of nutrition in informal urban settlements and marginalised rural areas. Learning for those from underprivileged households was interrupted for the year due to a lack of online learning equipment, homelessness, increased house chores, and an increase in sexual exploitation and teenage pregnancies among girls. Teenage pregnancies in Kenya became a national concern in June, when Machakos County health officials reported that 4,000 teenage pregnancies had occurred during the pandemic. In addition to the Covid-19 pandemic, teen pregnancies were a result of insufficient reproductive health services, as resources were diverted to dealing with the pandemic.

The *health sector* was already struggling to offer quality, affordable healthcare before the pandemic. Immediately after the first Covid-19 cases, the Covid-19 Emergency Response Fund was set up and a National Coronavirus Taskforce was formed to evaluate the evolving risk and advise the government on appropriate measures for preparedness, prevention, and response in order to mitigate the public health impact. Health institutions country-wide reported insufficient medical facilities, including personal protection kits for frontline health workers and community health workers, laboratory testing kits for mass testing, and logistical support for quarantine facilities, with increasing numbers of new cases every day. The pandemic exposed the neglect of the public healthcare system, as the planned universal healthcare remained a dream and corruption scandals in the health ministry were unearthed. By 31 December, 96,458 Covid-19 cases had been confirmed in Kenya and 1,670 had succumbed to the disease. There was reduced uptake of other essential health services such as medication for chronic conditions, which threatened to reverse investments made in control of communicable diseases like tuberculosis and non-communicable diseases like diabetes. In conclusion, Kenya's leadership in 2020 was constantly faced with the dilemma between the need to fully reopen the economy and the rapid spread of the coronavirus, without adequate health facilities to mitigate the disease.

Rwanda

Erik Plänitz

President Paul Kagame underpinned his ambitions in both domestic and foreign policy, as Rwanda once again confidently laid claim to leadership roles on the continent. It used the UN peacekeeping mission in CAR to underscore this claim with an increased military presence in the country. At the same time, the regime change in Burundi brought a new dynamic in the bilateral relations and led to direct talks between the two countries. The dispute with Uganda eased slightly this year but persisted. Domestically, the political opposition continued to be subject to the strong pressure of persecution. This was illustrated by the trial of Paul Rusesabagina, whose story inspired the movie 'Hotel Rwanda'. He was accused of supporting armed militias. The coronavirus pandemic brought economic development to a halt, reversing years of progress. The economy, which is primarily based on tourism and exports, suffered from the decline, and the country slid into recession.

Domestic Politics

President Paul Kagame continued to show little patience with *underperforming cabinet members*. He announced on 18 February that he would no longer tolerate 'lying, carelessness and indiscipline' in his administration. Following this, a *major cabinet reshuffle* on 26 February led to a changing gender balance within the Rwandan government. Following the reshuffle, 55% of cabinet members were female. As a former WHO official, Dr Daniel Ngamije was appointed minister of health, while Valentine Uwamariya replaced Eugene Mutimura as minister for education. The previous minister of health, Diane Gashumba, was caught lying about the availability of coronavirus test kits. Patrick Nyamvumba was sacked as minister of internal security on 27 April after having assumed office only in November 2019. Nyamvumba was blamed for incompetence. His dismissal could be related to indiscipline within the armed forces during the coronavirus lockdown imposed on 22 March. Soldiers allegedly assaulted, robbed, and raped slum dwellers in Kigali. On 9 April, Kagame dismissed Olivier Nduhungirehe, the minister of state in the Ministry of Foreign Affairs and International Cooperation in charge of the East African Community. The reason given for the decision was Nduhungirehe's actions contrary to government policies. His successor was Professor Nshuti Manasseh. The governors of Southern Province, Emmanuel Gasana, and Northern Province, Gatabazi Jean Marie Vianney, were suspended on 25 May due to pending investigations over accountability issues. Gasana had faced criticism over his leadership since he assumed office. Several development projects had been delayed and the poverty levels in the region remained high.

On 26 August, Kagame appointed Lynder Nkuranga as the director of external intelligence. She is the first woman to hold the office, replacing Anaclet Kalibata. Nkuranga had previously worked in the ranks of the Rwanda National Police.

On 22 October, six new senators were sworn in. Four of them were appointed by Kagame and two by the Consultative Forum for Political Parties in Rwanda: Alexis Mugisha, a member of the opposition Democratic Green Party of Rwanda (DGPR), and Clotilde Mukakarangwa, who belonged to the Centrist Democratic Party and thus to the ruling coalition.

The capture of *suspected genocide perpetrators* in Europe remained a focus of Rwandan politics. On 16 May, Felician Kabuga was arrested in France. He was wanted over the genocide, and it was announced that he would be transferred to the war crimes tribunal in Arusha once Covid-19-related travel restrictions were eased. Kabuga is accused of using his business empire to facilitate the genocide in 1994. In July, Aloys Ntiwiragabo was captured in Orleans, France. Ntiwiragabo commanded the Kigali gendarmerie until 1993 and is believed to be one of the masterminds behind the genocide. In Belgium, police forces arrested the wanted génocidaires Pierre Basabose, Seraphin Twahirwa, and Christophe Ndangali in October.

On 31 August, Rwandan police publicly announced the detention of *Paul Rusesabagina* over terrorism allegations. Rusesabagina resided in Belgium and was abducted in Dubai before being transferred to Kigali. The background to his journey to Kigali remained mysterious. However, the operation proved the power of the Rwandan intelligence services and their ability to act globally. The movie 'Hotel Rwanda' was inspired by the story of the polarising hotel manager who created a safe haven for Tutsi during the genocide. Rwandan investigators claim that the suspect had financed and supported terror groups in East Africa. Rusesabagina is a founding member of the National Liberation Front (FLN), the aim of which is to overthrow the Kagame government. In their indictment, the investigating authorities mentioned, among other things, incidents of murder, kidnapping, and terrorism allegedly committed in the districts of Nyaruguru in June 2018 and Nyamagabe in December 2018. Although the FLN formed the armed wing of the Mouvement Rwandais pour le Changement Démocratique (MRCD), Rusesabagina denied that the group aimed to organise terror attacks. His trial began on 14 September in Kigali.

The *Rwandan opposition* remained the target of investigations this year. Rwandan opposition heavyweight Victoire Ingabire and leader of the Development and Liberty for All (Développement et Liberté pour tous, or Dalfa Umurinzi) party remained under suspicion by the investigating authorities. On 13 June, police officers searched her residence for evidence of links to terrorist organisations. The investigation against Forces Democratiques Unifiées – Inkingi (FDU-Inkingi) continued this year. Seven members of the party were sentenced to seven to ten years' imprisonment on 23 January. Three members, Théophile Ntirutwa, Léonille Gasengayire, and Venant Abayisenga, were released from custody and gave video interviews about their experiences made in various detention centres. Later in the year, Abayisenga disappeared in early June and Ntirutwa was rearrested for spreading false information. On 17 February, a popular Rwandan singer allegedly committed suicide in police custody. Kizito Mihigo was arrested and sentenced for conspiracy. He was granted a pardon and released from prison. During an attempt to leave the country he was again captured, and he died in police custody on 17 February.

The *media remained under the tight control* of the Rwandan government. In March and April, six bloggers were arrested. Four of them had reported on the misconduct of security forces and two organised private food distribution events in marginalised neighbourhoods of Kigali. Online journalism suffered another setback in April. The Rwanda Media Commission announced that YouTubers are not recognised as journalists. This means that they do not enjoy any special legal protection. Despite these incidents, Rwanda was able to maintain its 155th place in the World Press Freedom Index.

In September, minister of justice Johnston Busingye apologised for recent incidents of *police violence* against civilians. He assured that proper investigations would take place into any cases of misconduct among the Rwanda National Police. Kigali city authorities continued to evict slum dwellers from parts of the town to make space for development under the country's long-term development strategy, 'Vision 2050'. Demolitions in late December 2019 sparked protest. Victims claimed that they had not received compensation, which was denied by city officials. Human rights groups stated that this was in line with the policy of detaining marginalised groups in camps, so-called transit centres, outside the city. On 13 February, the UN Committee on the Rights of the Child urged Rwanda to stop the detention of street children in these transit centres. In response, Rwandan authorities invited international observers to the camps. These events were also reflected in the Freedom House Index, which classified Rwanda as 'not free'. The aggregate score deteriorated by one point, from 22 in 2019 to 21 out of 100.

Rwanda continued its good performance in the *Corruption Perceptions Index* of Transparency International and was listed as the fourth least corrupt country on the continent in 2020. But it dropped by three positions compared with 2019 and was ranked 54th in 2020, and the Rwandan chapter of TI was concerned about a sharp increase in perceived corruption in the process of granting building permits and among the traffic police.

Activities of *armed groups* within Rwanda were reported from Southern Province. On 26 June, around 100 militiamen crossed over from Burundi and clashed with the Rwanda Defence Force (RDF) in the district of Nyaruguru. According to military sources, the heavily armed group targeted an IDP village in Yanza. The gunmen were reported to be carrying official Burundian military equipment and withdrew back to Burundi after having lost four fighters in the shoot-out. In Nyungwe Forest, the RDF arrested 19 members of Résistance pour un État de droit-Taraba (RED-TARABA) as they entered Rwanda from Burundi on 29 September. Rwanda invited a team of the ICGLR Expanded Joint Verification Mechanism to investigate the incident. An expert group consisting of military officials from Burundi, DRC, Congo-Brazzaville, Rwanda, and Kenya took over and interrogated the militiamen. Burundi later demanded the expulsion of the group on 5 October.

Cyprien Leo Mpiranya, the leader of the RUD-Uranana militia that was behind the Kinigi attacks in 2019, was killed in an operation by Congolese security forces in the border area with Uganda on 29 August. In the 2019 attacks, 14 civilians had been killed, 18 wounded, and 19 members of the group died in clashes with the RDF. Uganda is accused of supporting the militia, which is believed to be the armed wing of the FDU-Inkingi.

Foreign Affairs

Efforts to normalise relations with its neighbours Burundi and Uganda defined Rwanda's foreign policy this year. Tension grew in 2019 between the presidents, who accused each other of destabilising the domestic political situation in their respective countries. *Relations with Uganda* eased slightly in 2020. While Uganda showed some signs of appeasement early this year, Rwanda remained hesitant. In January, the president of Uganda, Yoweri Museveni, announced via social media that he would do his best to ease relations between the neighbours. In consequence, Uganda released nine prisoners on 8 January. Although Kagame acknowledged the move as good progress, he insisted on substantial changes before considering the reopening of the borders.

The process received a major boost in a regional summit facilitated by the president of Angola, João Lourenço, and the president of the DRC, Felix Tshisekedi, on 21 February. Uganda agreed to verify allegations on the operation of anti-Rwandan militias from its soil within 30 days and, if such militias were found to be present, to stop their activities. Additionally, Uganda revoked the passport issued to the commissioner of the Rwanda National Congress (RNC), Charlotte Mukankusi. The RNC is believed to be responsible for the grenade attacks in Kigali between 2010 and 2013.

On 4 June, Uganda announced that it would release a group of 130 Rwandan prisoners. The agreement was reached during a conference between Rwandan and Ugandan foreign ministers. The progress in normalising the relationship was described by Rwandan foreign minister Vincent Biruta on 12 August as one step forward, two steps back. The statement followed reports on the continued harassment of Rwandan nationals and support for anti-Kagame activities in Uganda. In October, Biruta stated that relations had improved slightly with the release of some migrants from Ugandan custody, but pointed out that militant groups still received support from the Ugandan authorities.

The unexpected death of the president of Burundi, Pierre Nkurunziza, on 8 June led to a sudden *improvement in bilateral relations between the two countries*. In the first half of the year, Burundi repeatedly accused Rwanda of supporting armed militias in their efforts to topple the president. In return, Kagame blamed Burundi for supporting the Democratic Forces for the Liberation of Rwanda (FDLR) group in the DRC. Although not directly blaming Burundi, Rwanda noted that it was very likely that Burundian soldiers were behind the border attacks on 26 June.

As a first sign of rapprochement, Kagame congratulated Évariste Ndayishimiye on his victory in the presidential elections and expressed his hope for a resumption of direct talks. Mediated by the ICGLR, military intelligence chiefs of Burundi and Rwanda met on 26 August and discussed security issues at their border. Both sides agreed to restore security in the area. The new spirit in the bilateral relations was accompanied by the repatriation of Burundian refugees that was negotiated between Burundi, Rwanda, and UNHCR on 13 August. Foreign minister Vincent Biruta and his Burundian counterpart Albert Shingiro brokered a ground-breaking deal in Kigali on 20 October. At the first bilateral summit since 2015, both sides agreed to normalise relations and maintain contacts. Shingiro also invited Biruta to Burundi.

The *improved relations with DRC*, which were also expressed in Tshisekedi's mediation role in the Uganda–Rwanda conflict, proved sustainable in 2020. On 13 January, the RDF and Congolese Armed Forces (FARDC) conducted a joint military operation against the FDLR. On 1 March, the FARDC arrested Marc Nizeyimana, who served as deputy commander of the FLN militia. After the killing of 12 rangers in the Virunga National Park in the east of DRC, the FDLR blamed the Rwandan military for being responsible for the massacre on 24 April. Kagame harshly rejected these claims. A UN report published in December by the Group of Experts on the DRC referred to the presence of Rwandan soldiers in North Kivu from the end of 2019 until October 2020. According to the report, witnesses from MONUSCO, FARDC, and civil society confirmed RDF activities in the region. Accordingly, on 2 October, 60 heavily armed RDF soldiers were seen in Rutshuru territory.

On May 27, Rwandan and DRC officials agreed to reopen the border despite the Covid-19 pandemic. The border had been closed since the beginning of the lockdown on 22 March to stop the spread of the coronavirus.

The *security situation in the Great Lakes region* was addressed in a virtual summit on 7 October, bringing together the heads of Rwanda, DRC, Angola, and Uganda. In a joint statement, all parties agreed to cut funding for 'negative forces', and to fight criminal organisations that exploit natural resources on the regional and global level.

The ambitious integration plans of the EAC suffered again this year from the closure of the borders between Rwanda, Uganda, and Burundi. The postponement of the Summit of the East African Community Heads of State to 2021 implied that Kagame would retain the role of chairperson in 2020. A special online conference on the coronavirus crisis was held in May without Tanzania or Burundi. The dismissal of Olivier Nduhungirehe, who played a leading role in the previous year's negotiations between Rwanda and Uganda, could be interpreted as a sign intended to give new impetus to Rwanda's relations with its neighbours and the EAC.

Similarly to the EAC, the *African Union*'s agenda was dominated by the joint fight against Covid-19. Rwandan economist and former AfDB president Donald Kaberuka was appointed by the chairperson of the AU, Cyril Ramaphosa, as one of four special envoys on the Covid-19 pandemic. Rwanda contributed $1 m to the AU Covid-19 Solidarity Fund and the Africa Centre for Disease Control. In the upcoming 2021 election for deputy vice chairperson of the AU Commission, Rwanda proposed Dr Monique Nsanzabaganwa, who is running against Ugandan Pamela Kasabiiti Mbabazi, among others.

Rwanda made use of bilateral channels and the *UN peacekeeping forces*, in addition to regional organisations, to further *strengthen its role on the continent*. The president of Zambia Edgar Lungu rejected accusations of supporting Rwandan rebel groups. In his hearing at the high court in Kigali on 14 July, the FLN leader Callixte Nsabimana claimed that Lungu had promised $1 m to bolster their activities against the Kagame government. The Rwandan side did not reiterate the accusation. One of the few state visits this year took Kagame to Malawi in August. President of Malawi

Lazarus Chakwera showed interest in Rwanda's development model and his counterpart's leadership style. After the extradition of the genocide suspect Vincent Murekezi in 2019, Kagame is likely to have pushed for further extraditions.

In preparation for the December elections in CAR, Rwanda massively increased its military footprint in the country. The deployment of hundreds of additional RDF units under a bilateral agreement underpins Kagame's intention to strengthen Rwanda's influence on the continent. Besides France and Russia, Rwanda became the strongest player in the CAR. In December, 1,382 soldiers and 446 police officers from Rwanda were deployed to the UN Multidimensional Integrated Stabilization Mission in the Central African Republic (MINUSCA). On 13 July, a Rwandan peacekeeper was killed and two others injured in an attack by the 3R armed group in CAR. Other major deployments in 2020 include the UN Mission in the Republic of South Sudan (UNMISS). Here, too, Rwanda was the largest troop contributor, with 3,371 soldiers and 581 police officers. At the end of the UN–AU Mission in Darfur, Sudan (UNAMID), which terminated on 31 December 2020, Rwanda was providing 1,125 soldiers and 38 police officers. In 2020, five Rwandan police officers and six soldiers were deployed for the UN Interim Security Force for Abyei (UNISFA).

The country's pan-African ambitions since its AU chairship were reflected in the strong commitment to free trade, free movement, and, not least, the deployment of Rwandan troops under the UN flag and through bilateral arrangements.

On 28 May, the *United States and Rwanda* signed a Status of Forces Agreement. From then on, US military personnel and contractors could operate in Rwanda without the oversight of the Rwandan authorities. They operate with impunity and all imports are duty free. Plans for a US base have been denied in this context. However, in the light of the Russian presence in Central Africa, the signing could certainly be seen as underlining the US interest in the region. USAID and Rwanda signed a deal worth $ 643.8 m on 2 July. Under the grant scheme, USAID supports the implementation of the National Strategy for Transformation, with a focus on education and health. The deal was signed two months after the Status of Forces Agreement.

New financing agreements were concluded with the *Bretton Woods institutions* in 2020. Under the Rwanda Country Framework 2021–2023, the World Bank Group agreed to provide $ 1.2 bn to support economic recovery and development. The first IMF reviews took place this year under the Policy Consultation Instrument (PCI) scheme concluded with the organisation in 2019 in support of the National Strategy for Transformation (NST). The reviewers acknowledged the government's strong macroeconomic performance and its sound Covid-19 strategy to revive the economy. At the same time, they urged a focus on private-sector-led growth to overcome the crisis. The last Article VI consultations took place in 2019.

The *European Union* pledged its support for job creation in the digital economy and tourism sector. The € 10 m project aimed at fighting youth unemployment in Rwanda.

Paul Kagame participated in the UK–Africa Investment Summit on 20 January. At the summit, the World Bank announced the issuance of its first bond in Rwandan francs (RWF) that is to be listed on the London Stock Exchange.

On 3 July, Rwanda condemned the French plans to investigate the plane crash of President Juvénal Habyarimana on the eve of the genocide in 1994. Rwandan minister for justice, Busingye Johnston, called it a farce. Despite the case being rejected at the appeals court in Paris, lawyers of the victims' families announced that they would bring it to the supreme court. However, the initial rejection of the case in the Paris court was welcomed in Rwanda and foreign minister Biruta spoke of an important step towards further improving relations.

Socioeconomic Developments

Due to its heavy dependence on exports, tourism, and conferences, Rwanda suffered badly from the global coronavirus restrictions from February onwards. The country went into its first *national lockdown* on 22 March, during which all non-essential movement was restricted. Violators were punished with fines and arrest. Also, borders were completely closed except to goods and cargo. On 27 April, 1,673 prisoners were released to defuse the situation in detention centres. On 4 May, the lockdown was eased for selected businesses. However, schools remained closed and transport between Kigali and the provinces remained banned. The restrictions particularly affected the national carrier RwandAir. From January, connections were gradually suspended until the airline was completely grounded in April, operating only cargo flights from Kigali. Government support for RwandAir has increased from RWF 122 bn to RWF 145 bn to respond to the Covid-19 situation. From 1 August, commercial flight operations resumed.

The corona crisis seriously *disrupted the Rwandan economy*. Years of major achievements in poverty reduction were put at risk in 2020. The projected GDP growth for 2020 went down to –0.2%. In the second quarter of the year alone, GDP contracted by 12.4%. While agriculture fell by only 2%, industry dropped by 19% and services by 16%. The IMF concluded that there had been a sharp economic decline in the second quarter of the year, with signs of recovery in October. Under the coronavirus pandemic, *economic growth* is expected to slow down in 2020. Minister of finance Uzziel Ndagijimana declared on 21 May that the anticipated growth rate for 2020 would not exceed 6.3%. At the end of the year, Rwanda slipped into recession, with projected growth of –0.2%. Before the pandemic reached Rwanda, projected economic growth had stood between 8 and 9.4%.

The government set up a special economic recovery fund of over $ 200 m to support the most affected sectors of the economy. Among others, the hotel and catering sector was hit hardest, suffering a decline of 62%. The transport sector lost a total of 41%, with the air transport sector, including RwandAir, falling by 96%. The construction sector got off relatively lightly, losing around 20%.

Years of positive development in the *labour market* were halted by the corona crisis. While the official unemployment rate fell from 17.8% to 13.8% between August 2017 and February 2020, it rose rapidly when the crisis began. In May, it reached 22.1%, the highest level since 2016. According to the National Institute of Statistics of Rwanda, it had dropped again to 16% by August.

International donors responded to the situation in Rwanda with *aid pledges*. On 8 May, the EU committed € 52 m to address the challenges arising from the coronavirus crisis. The fund targeted government efforts to cushion the effects of the pandemic and was expected to reach about 630,000 people. The IMF contributed a loan of about $ 110 m. The World Bank responded to the health crisis with $ 100 m in budget support. The government provided food to about 20,000 residents of Kigali. Despite the tense bilateral relations, France supported the Covid-19 response with € 49.5 m. € 40 m was paid as a budget loan for prevention measures against the coronavirus. The AfDB approved a loan of about $ 98 m for mitigation efforts.

The coronavirus pandemic had serious ramifications for regional trade. Cross-border trade with Tanzania was disrupted by the Rwandan–Tanzanian dispute over Covid-19 testing. Both states rejected the other's testing, which brought trade to a complete halt until a driver-swap system was installed.

To counter the challenges, national spending increased by 7.5% to RWF 3.245 bn in the 2020/21 fiscal year compared with 2019/20. To return to pre-crisis growth, Rwanda would need to invest $ 962 m. In the parliamentary debate, Ndagijimana presented the strengthening of the health system, increasing agriculture productivity, social protection, and support for Covid-19-affected enterprises as key priorities for the budget. Accordingly, 15.2% of the budget was to be contributed by development partners.

For economic transformation, 55.5% of the budget was earmarked. This included job creation, Covid-19 recovery, support for the Made in Rwanda strategy, and promotion of digital infrastructure. The Made in Rwanda strategy is deemed to be particularly important against the background of the implementation of the AfCFTA in 2021. Rwanda hopes to secure a share of the common market of 1.2 bn people.

The IMF projected an overall fiscal deficit of 8.5% of GDP in the 2020/21 fiscal year and public debt of 67% of GDP by late 2020. In the Human Development Index published in 2020, using data from the previous year, Rwanda fell three positions to rank 160.

Rwanda suffered from the drop in international *commodity prices*. The revenue from tin, tantalum, and tungsten decreased by almost 30% in January and February compared with the same months in 2019. Other minerals dropped by 4–15%. The same was witnessed for the prices of tea, which fell to an all-time low. In the first half of 2020, Rwanda received $ 31.6 m in mineral revenues, almost $ 25 m less than in 2019 for the same period. In general, trade recovered relatively quickly from the coronavirus pandemic. As announced by the Ministry of Trade and Industry, trade in 2020 increased by as much as 13.6% compared with 2019. Between the second and third quarters alone, non-mineral exports grew by 46%, according to Trademark East Africa.

In the wake of the coronavirus pandemic, *local and foreign direct investment* declined. The Rwanda Development Board (RDB) reported a drop of 41% compared with 2019. Notable FDI took place in the real estate and manufacturing sectors in particular. Instead of the targeted 214,000 new jobs, only 24,703 new jobs were created through investment. One of the highest levels of FDI, $ 193 m, came from the One Acre Fund. This non-profit organisation supports local farmers and now operates a seed production plant in Rwanda. This will reduce the import of seeds. In a move to enhance productivity in the export of coffee, the government initiated the replacement of 3 m old coffee trees. The agricultural sector remained the most important economic factor. Due to the coronavirus crisis, the number of people employed in subsistence agriculture even increased. In August, around 1.9 m people were employed in the sector.

Extreme weather events from January to March caused flooding and landslides in Kigali and various districts. According to the Ministry of Emergency Management, over 50 people were killed; 858 homes and 196 ha of crops were destroyed by March. Towards the end of the rainy season, parts of the Northern, Western, and Southern provinces were again flooded. After heavy rains between 6 and 7 May, 65 people died in the affected regions. Crops and houses were repeatedly destroyed.

In this context of severe devastation caused by *natural disasters* in the first half of the year, Rwanda submitted a *climate action plan* worth $ 11 bn to the UN Framework Convention on Climate Change, as part of Rwanda's obligations under the Paris Agreement. About $ 6 bn is required for mitigation measures, while the remaining $ 5 bn is reserved for adaptation to climate change. The country plans to reduce its gas emissions by 38% by 2030 and identified 24 measures to improve adaptation to climate change.

In 2020, the National Institute of Statistics reported 12.66 m inhabitants. At the end of the year, UNHCR counted 146,831 *refugees and asylum seekers* in Rwanda; 69,666 came from Burundi and 76,845 from DRC. Additional refugees from Libyan camps arrived throughout the year and were transferred to Rwanda under the Emergency Transit Mechanism.

Under an agreement between Rwanda, the AU, and UNHCR, about 600 asylum seekers who had been evacuated from Libya left for Norway. Sweden later accepted 28 refugees. France and Canada also showed the intention to accept migrants evacuated to Rwanda.

To further modernise the financial sector, the parliament passed a law on the establishment of a Financial Intelligence Centre on 3 January. Primarily, the newly established centre aims to combat money laundering or financing of terror groups. The establishment of the agency may also be linked to recent accusations against foreign bodies of funding armed opposition and terror groups in and outside of Rwanda.

In March, the UN and Rwanda signed an MoU to establish a big data regional hub for Africa at the National Institute of Statistics in Kigali. The centre is part of the UN strategy to develop data hubs for official statistics. Other centres are to be established in China, Brazil, and the UAE.

The transformation and development of the energy sector continued in 2020. The AfDB approved an € 8 m grant for the Ruzizi IV hydropower plant that will be located at the DRC–Rwanda border and will have the capacity to produce up to 287 MW. This came as the Ministry of Infrastructure announced its plans to connect all households to the national grid by 2024. About $ 1.5 bn is to be mobilised to achieve that target. In September, the World Bank announced that it would support access to affordable energy with $ 150 m.

Seychelles

Anthoni van Nieuwkerk

Seychelles had the highest GDP per capita in Africa in 2020, at $ 12,323, even though it dropped significantly from the $ 17,448 recorded for 2019. Continued shared prosperity remained of concern. Climate change continued to pose long-term sustainability risks to this archipelago of 115 islands in the Western Indian Ocean. Seychelles' newly elected leader, former opposition leader Wavel Ramkalawan, was sworn in as the country's fifth president in October. The government's immediate priority was the containment of Covid-19 and recovery from its economic and social impact on the country.

Domestic Politics

Wavel Ramkalawan, whose coalition party the Linyon Demokratik Seselwa (LDS) won a landslide victory in the October presidential and legislative elections, won the presidency with 54.9% of the valid votes. The victory elevated an opposition leader to the presidency for the first time in 43 years. The LDS won 20 out of the 26 directly elected seats in the national assembly and five proportionately elected seats. Although the LDS had won control of parliament in 2016, it was now in control of the executive branch as well.

Outgoing president Danny Faure lost, with 43.5%. This was the first defeat for United Seychelles since 1977, when it came to power through a coup d'état. United Seychelles, formerly known as the Seychelles People's Progressive Front, changed its name in 2009 to People's Party, or Parti Lepep, and again in 2018.

The government's handling of the coronavirus and its economic impact had a direct impact on the election. In July, the president announced that presidential and legislative elections (due 2020 and 2021 respectively) would be run together in 2020, as a cost-saving measure. The Ministry of Health banned election rallies, and candidates campaigned mainly through social media. Apart from the struggling economy, corruption was a key theme of the campaign. Faure struggled to distance himself and United Seychelles from allegations of corruption and mismanagement dating back to when the Seychelles was a one-party state. These emerged during the hearings of the Truth, Reconciliation and National Unity Commission (TRNUC) established in 2018.

Ramkalawan's victory and that of his party in the national assembly represented a shift in political power for the island nation. A spokesperson for the civil society organisation Citizens Engagement Platform said that the political landscape in Seychelles had changed after the LDS won a majority in the parliamentary election in 2015, which forced the executive branch to become more open with regard to public affairs. She noted that the creation of the Anti-Corruption Commission and TRNUC had provided information that had not been in the public domain before.

Seychelles' governance was recognised as exceptional by the Mo Ibrahim Foundation; it declared the country one of eight in Africa which have managed to improve their governance in the past decade. In the 2020 ranking in the Ibrahim Index of African Governance, the island nation was third out of 54 African countries for overall good governance. Building on this track record, the new government led by Ramkalawan identified its top priorities as reviving the economy, damaged by the Covid-19 pandemic crisis; addressing rampant corruption and cronyism prevalent in the civil service; reducing the growing crisis of drug addiction; and securing the Seychelles' sovereignty as it faced geopolitical competition in the Indian Ocean.

Seychelles' unchanged score in the two most recent Corruption Perceptions Index surveys (2019 and 2020) made the island nation the country with the highest score in sub-Saharan Africa. The 2020 CPI gave Seychelles 66 points, ranking it 27th out of 180 countries globally. According to Freedom House's 2021 rating of people's access to political rights and civil liberties, Seychelles' status improved in 2020 from 'partly free' to 'free' (with a rating of 77 out of 100) because a strengthened electoral framework had contributed to a more open and competitive presidential election, resulting in the country's first transfer of power to an opposition party. Media pluralism and funding was limited by Seychelles' size and population. According to Reporters Without Borders, self-censorship reflexes, inherited from decades of single-party rule and close control of the media, was gradually dissipating and gave way to a broader range of opinion and more editorial freedom. There were only a few private broadcast media outlets and the government maintained its influence on the country's state-owned TV channel and its two radio stations. Although Seychelles has strict defamation laws, they have not been used for years. There were few reports of abuses against journalists.

Foreign Affairs

In January, Seychelles hosted negotiations between the EU and eastern Southern African states Madagascar, Mauritius, Seychelles, Zimbabwe, and Comoros on the implementation of an interim economic partnership. Two areas of difficulty, relating to the fisheries sector and trade barriers, were addressed. Seychelles received € 10 m from the EU under a new contract signed in November in 2019 to support the implementation of the EPA.

At a high-level side event during the AU summit in February, co-hosts Seychelles, Morocco, and Gabon explored means of capacity-building in the development of early-warning systems and enabling senior policy-makers to deal with adaptation strategies in Africa. The meeting also addressed ongoing climate actions on adaptation, mitigation, and building the resilience of the African continent. During the event, Seychelles announced a coastal management plan costing $ 15 m, aimed at protecting its coastline from ongoing erosion.

The new government confirmed its intention to focus on the country's enduring strategic foreign policy objectives – namely, establishment and maintenance of strategic partnerships to promote the blue economy, cooperate on environmental mitigation strategies, and enhance maritime security.

In a speech in October following his swearing-in ceremony, President Ramkalawan said that Seychelles was looking to strengthen relations with its neighbours, in particular Madagascar and Réunion. In order to ensure a smooth continuation of diplomatic relations, in November President Ramkalawan met with the diplomatic corps with a presence in the island nation. At the meeting, President Ramkalawan identified climate change, the environment, and the fight against organised crime (including drugs, arms, terrorism, and human trafficking) as top priorities for bilateral cooperation between Seychelles and other countries. He also requested practical support in dealing with maritime threats. He further noted that obtaining necessary financial resources to assist Seychelles' recovery from the Covid-19 pandemic, renegotiating foreign debt obligations, and engaging with international development partners to fund new initiatives to boost the economy were key foreign policy priorities. Securing external assistance to aid economic recovery would require a careful diplomatic balancing act. Seychelles had always attracted the interest of great powers – first France and Britain as colonial powers, then the US and the Soviet Union during the Cold War, and more recently India and China. The latter maintained a strong interest in the Seychelles and facilitated the delivery of several batches of the Sinopharm vaccine and personal protective equipment to Seychelles between July and December, at the height of the Covid-19 crisis. Russia similarly maintained a cordial relationship with Seychelles and focused on strengthening tourism exchanges and offered to cooperate in space technology to mitigate the impact of climate change.

More recently, Seychelles has maintained close relations with the UAE and Japan, which opened a new embassy in November 2019. Meanwhile, the US, which regards the Indian Ocean and African east coast as a strategic domain given the piracy threat to sea traffic, violent extremism, and drug trafficking, continued its security cooperation with Seychelles.

Seychelles became the new home for the Fisheries Transparency Initiative (FiTI) after the signing of a headquarters agreement in November. FiTI is a global multi-stakeholder partnership seeking to increase transparency and participation to promote more sustainable management of marine fisheries.

Socioeconomic Developments

According to the World Bank, Seychelles had the highest per capita GDP in Africa, at $ 12, 323. However this represents a significant drop from $ 17,448 in 2019 and $ 16,390 in 2018, reflecting the economic downturn following the Covid-19 crisis. It was classified as an upper-middle-income country and had the highest literacy rate and the best healthcare system in the East Africa region. According to the Heritage Foundation's 2020 Index of Economic Freedom, in 2019 Seychelles' score was 64.3, making its economy the 72nd-freest in the index. Its overall score had increased by 2.9 points due to higher scores for government integrity and property rights. Seychelles was ranked 4th among 47 countries in the sub-Saharan Africa region, and its overall score was well above the regional average and slightly above the world average. The country was ranked 67th (second-highest in Africa) in the UNDP's 2020 HDI report, based on data collected in 2019.

The Seychelles' economy grew by an average rate of 4.2% per annum between 2009 and 2019. With the help of an IMF programme, the government maintained its target of 2.5% primary balance and, according to the IMF, was on target to reduce the debt-to-GDP ratio to 50% by 2021. However external debt increased to 10.06 bn Seychellois rupees (SCR) in December from SCR 9.90 bn in November.

According to the National Bureau of Statistics, the unemployment rate dropped to 3.5% in 2018, largely due to the reintroduction of the unemployment relief scheme in 2017. The IMF estimated unemployment to be 3% in 2019 and 2020, despite the negative economic impact of the Covid-19 pandemic.

The austerity policy applied by the government – namely, reduction of the number of public employees and privatisations – allowed the country to reduce its public debt from 183% of GDP in 2011 to a relatively high estimated 53.8% for 2019. The government aimed to reduce the ratio to less than 50% by 2020 through fiscal discipline coupled with an improved debt management strategy. The IMF anticipated government debt to be 49.7% in 2020 and 45.4% in 2021. The government had a surplus of 0.9% of GDP in 2019, which was expected to reach 1.6% in 2020. The inflation rate decreased to 1.8% in 2019 and was expected to increase to 4.5% in 2020 and decrease slightly to 3.1% in 2021, according to the World Economic Outlook of the IMF in April.

However these estimates were impacted negatively by the Covid-19 crisis. An increase in Seychelles' external debt resulted in its credit rating being downgraded by Fitch, in December, from B+ to B. The key drivers for the rating were a slow recovery in tourism, an extension of fiscal measures, and greater exchange rate depreciation.

The SCR continued to depreciate significantly against foreign currencies. The governor of the central bank noted that this last happened in 2008, when Seychelles embarked on an economic reform programme with the IMF. In November, the cost of $ 1 was on average SCR 21.44 while € 1 stood at SCR 25.38. In 2019, the cost of $ 1 was SCR 13 and the cost of € 1 was SCR 15, representing about a 66% loss in value. The governor of the reserve bank noted that this was a consequence of the global crisis caused by the Covid-19 pandemic. She said that the foreign exchange the country was earning with fisheries and the tourism sector was not enough for the amount of forex the country needed in order to function at the individual, business, and governmental levels.

In December, the national assembly approved amendments to the Business Tax Act. The main reason for the amendments was to meet EU obligations concerning taxation. The tax system was viewed by the EU's Code of Conduct on Business Taxation grouping as 'harmful' or not in line with tax standards. As a result, Seychelles was placed on a list of countries not cooperating with the EU tax system.

Seychelles avoided the outbreak of Covid-19 inside the country, following the first cases recorded in early March. The government adopted containment measures, including social distancing, travel bans on visitors from high-risk regions, screening at ports of entry, and school closures. Given that about 30% of GDP directly or indirectly related to the tourism sector, the disruption to global tourism had an adverse impact on the economy. Mandatory working from home was lifted in April. In May, all schools were reopened and in June, the country reopened its borders to passenger flights, limited to chartered flights only from low-risk countries. Some commercial flights from low-risk and medium-risk countries were allowed to enter the country starting in August.

The economic and social shock to the Seychellois economy from Covid-19 was severe due to strong dependence on international tourism. Tourism accounted for approximately 30% of GDP in 2019, making the country highly vulnerable to the current Covid-19 pandemic. The global outbreak drastically reduced economic activity in 2020, as tourist arrivals were projected to decline by more than 50%. At the end of November, the total number of visitor arrivals to the Indian Ocean archipelago reached 102,246 – a 71% drop compared with the same period in 2019. This affected other sectors, such as transportation; art, recreation, and entertainment; wholesale and retail trade; and the financial and insurance sector. On the positive side, a survey by the Seychelles Tourism Board found that 100% of respondents said they felt safe in Seychelles during the pandemic.

Due to the outbreak of Covid-19, GDP growth fell to –13.8 % in 2020.

The World Bank delivered a $ 15 m Development Policy Loan in July to support Seychelles in its Covid-19 response. The bank disbursed $ 7 m in April from a Catastrophe Draw Down Option (CAT-DDO) emergency credit line that had been in place since 2015.

In April, the government announced the Financial Assistance for Job Retention (FA4JR) programme – to subsidise wages for companies facing distress caused by Covid-19. From July, the Seychelles Employee Transition Scheme (SETS) was set up to facilitate reskilling. Initially planned to last three months, wage subsidies were fully extended to February 2021. In September, additional measures were introduced to support households and firms.

The Central Bank of Seychelles (CBS) reduced the policy rate by 100 basis points to 4% in March and to 3% in July. It announced a credit facility of approximately SCR 500 m to assist commercial banks with emergency relief measures. The CBS also announced that commercial banks, the Development Bank of Seychelles (DBS), and the Seychelles Credit Union had agreed to consider a moratorium of up to six months on the repayment of principal and interest on loans to assist businesses in impacted sectors.

Among Seychelles' development challenges was the need to focus on greater productivity of, participation in, and performance of its economy as a means to increased shared prosperity. Some of the main institutional challenges in this regard were barriers to opening and operating businesses; inefficiencies in public sector management, such as limited statistical capacity; scope for a more strategic and sustainable approach to social protection; and the need to broaden access to quality education and skills development. Climate change adaptation, including through strengthened disaster preparedness systems and enhanced coastal management, was also key.

An independent ocean authority was expected to be set up in Seychelles by 2025 to ensure proper monitoring and protection of the Seychelles Exclusive Economic Zone (EEZ). The proposed authority was being considered given that the island nation has reached its target of 30% ocean protection around some of its outer islands as part of the Seychelles Marine Spatial Plan (SMSP).

Seychelles tripled the UN Convention of Biological Diversity target of effective and equitable conservation of 10% of marine areas by 2020, and UN Sustainable Development Goal 14 of 10% coastal and marine protection. The 30%, or 410,000 square kilometres of the island nation's EEZ of 1.4 m square kilometres, was meant to be safeguarded to encourage sustainable development and to support adaptation to the effects of climate change. The protected areas were split into two 'zones'. The first was High Biodiversity Protection Areas, where almost no extractive human activities will be allowed. These Zone 1 areas included the waters around the Aldabra group – a UNESCO world heritage site. The second was Medium Biodiversity Protection and Sustainable Use Areas, designed to conserve natural ecosystems while allowing some economic activities, including fishing, tourism charters, renewable energy, and others.

Under the South West Indian Ocean Fisheries Governance and Shared Growth Program (SWIOFish3), the World Bank supported the management and conservation of marine areas and strengthening seafood value chains in Seychelles. The project was co-financed by a Seychelles Blue Bond ($ 15 m), which was supported by a $ 5 m guarantee from the International Bank of Reconstruction and Development and a further $ 5 m concessional loan from the Global Environment Facility.

The Southwest Indian Ocean (SWIO) region was one of the most active areas globally in terms of tropical cyclone formation. The science journal 'Nature' reported that hurricanes were becoming more powerful than those of 30 years ago, due to global warming.

Located just south of the equator, Mahé was not within the direct path of the tropical cyclones. However, Assumption, Bird and Denis islands and the Aldabra atoll were affected by the feeder bands of tropical cyclones in the region, and this resulted in gale-force winds, flash floods, and severe thunderstorm activity.

In December, the African Risk Capacity Group proposed a new insurance mechanism to African countries in the SWIO region to cope with the devastating effects of tropical cyclones. The mechanism was seen as a significant milestone in building resilience to climate-related disasters in Africa.

Money laundering, drug use, and trafficking remained problems. In August, the minister for finance, trade, investment, and economic planning announced the country's first National Anti-Money Laundering and Countering the Financing of Terrorism Strategy. He noted that the Covid-19 pandemic had the potential to increase anti-money laundering risks.

The Seychelles Anti-Narcotics Bureau (ANB) seized 30 kg of cannabis in December. The biggest seizure of cannabis was 180 kg during an operation by a Seychelles Coast Guard vessel along with ANB officers in July. The importation of illegal drugs remained a challenge for the authorities in Seychelles, with a vast EEZ of 1.4 m square kilometres. Seychelles maintained a zero-tolerance policy towards trafficking and importation of illegal drugs.

Somalia

Jon Abbink

Somalia's political instability continued, but the federal government kept its ground and solidified some of its services and administrative structures, although still in a limited area of south-central Somalia. Its population remained vulnerable to poverty and insecurity and was mainly dependent on its own socioeconomic resourcefulness and on support from abroad (donor aid and remittances). Somaliland retained its separate, independent status and, despite several meetings, saw little rapprochement with the Somali Federal Government. Economically and politically, Somaliland was again more stable and functional than its southern neighbour. There was no let-up in the violence of the Islamist terror movement *Harakat al-Shabaab al Mujahideen* in south-central Somalia, which remained an important presence in Somali society. But while it carried out a range of attacks on government personnel and the general public, costing the lives of hundreds, it did not make territorial or political gains. The humanitarian situation remained grave, with a high number of IDPs, economic insecurity, and widespread poverty, all aggravated by the spread of Covid-19. Environmental issues and climate change dangers were hardly addressed. International interest in the country receded somewhat, with fewer international visitors due to lack of major political progress, insecurity, and the Covid-19 restrictions. However, international support for the AU's peacekeeping force, the African Union Mission in Somalia (AMISOM), was maintained, and associated private security companies also remained active. The USA, the EU, Turkey, and some Gulf countries also gave developmental and budgetary assistance alongside security assistance, and as usual, various Western countries also supported the federal government with humanitarian relief provision.

Domestic Politics

The Somali areas remained divided into the same autonomous political units, largely following their own political destiny: Somalia under the Somali Federal Government (SFG), Somaliland de facto independent since 1991 but still not gaining international recognition, and several states nominally recognising the SFG federal dispensation but autonomous in political decision-making, local administration, (preparations for) elections, and regional economic policy. Puntland and Jubaland were the strongest units, with the states of Galmudug, HirShabelle, and South West of lesser importance. The SFG claimed normative authority over Somalia as a whole and continued to be headed by President Mohamed Abdullahi 'Farmajo', in power since 2017. He retained his position despite an ongoing balancing act with parliament and his prime minister. The SFG struggled to solidify its authority and institutional rule and to gain more control over the federal political process, security issues, tax revenues, and the economy. Some headway was made with the formation of a constitutional court, the Judicial Services Commission, and the independent Human Rights Commission, and a review of the federal constitution was completed. But the planned National Human Rights Commission was not formed, and neither was a planned review of the old Criminal Code carried out. In addition, the practical effects of these measures were hardly felt on the ground. In general, the judicial system of the SFG underperformed and lacked independence. It was understaffed and fractured and had low esteem in the eyes of the public, partly due to perceived corruption. Court rulings were regularly ignored by the state administration and the police.

Some progress was made in reconciliation efforts on the federal and local levels. For instance, AMISOM troops helped to set the stage for a successful clan reconciliation conference in Galmudug. In various other local areas, violent clan conflicts were also mediated via conferences, as on 5–12 June in the villages of Taaroge and Saho-Kurun (west Mudug), where members of the Leelkase and Sa'ad clans signed an agreement to end the cycle of violence and promote local peace. In Jubaland, President Ahmed Mohamed 'Madobe' and opposition figures from the Ogadeni clans reached a settlement meant to lead to mutual recognition and cohabitation. More evidence of a desire to solve differences was shown in the meeting of Puntland president Said Abdullahi Deni and President Ahmed Abdi Karie of Galmudug in Gaalkayo on 27 June, committing to cooperation on keeping the peace, security, and economic development, especially regarding the shared border region of Mudug. On the federal level, a virtual meeting was held on 22 June between President Mohamed and the leaders of the five federal member states and the governor of the region of Banadir. It was the first kind of comprehensive political dialogue on this level since 2018, when a structure of federal cooperation was put on the agenda. It served to prepare for a follow-up summit on 18–22 July, where the format and timing of the parliamentary elections (for 2021) were discussed.

The SFG was again strongly supported by the international donor community, with development funding and security assistance to AMISOM in its perpetual campaign to contain the radical Islamist insurgent movement Harakat al-Shabaab, still allied to al-Qaida. The latter again made many victims with its terrorist attacks and hit-and-run actions against SFG targets and public facilities. It did not politically engage the SFG or any other potential civil society partners but retained its presence in the rural areas, through imposing its role in local communities and some religious leaders. It thereby claimed the role of mediator/arbiter in criminal cases or local disputes between sub-clan/(descent) groups in the countryside via an appeal to Muslim Sharia law as normative. It maintained its economic base via an extortionate economy of imposed local levies and (road) taxes and contraband activities, with exports of local commodities such as ivory, charcoal, and wildlife products, and it also received undisclosed sums from Somali diaspora communities and politico-religious connections in the Middle East. The movement also sought a rapprochement with Iran, as evident in various messages emanating in January from its leader Ahmed Diriye ('Abu Ubaidah').

Al-Shabaab also continued to provide services to local people in the absence of the SFG, notably in the domain of justice (land, property and business disputes, resource access), where according to local people and observers it had a reputation for delivering swift, effective, non-corrupt, and fair rulings, though exclusively based on Sharia. In matters of family law, gender-violence rulings, and criminal law, al-Shabaab's role was less popular.

The SFG retained control of south-central Somalia in and around Mogadishu and extended its authority and territory somewhat. Its governmental services, however, reached only a few sections of the population, necessitating the large majority to continue to fend for themselves. Within the SFG, rivalry based on personal antagonisms, interest groups, sub-clan competition, and regional divisions made for frequent in-fighting and lack of a unified political and security agenda. The underlying segmentary nature of Somali political society was still evident and also influenced by outside factions and foreign players (such as Qatar, UAE, Turkey, and Kenya). This was seen in the Somali National Army (SNA) as well, which still showed a tendency towards devolved authority due to different regional/clan allegiances and lack of strong overall coordination and command.

On 20 July, it was announced by the SFG that the planned direct, one-person-one-vote elections, foreseen for November, were again *delayed, until 2021*, officially due to lack of resources and preparation and the problems caused by the Covid-19 outbreak.

The popular prime minister Hassan Ali Khayre was dismissed by the Somali parliament on 25 July, in a 170-to-8 vote. Allegedly, this was due to his failure to organise the elections and to 'not establishing a better national security force', but in reality it was because of the long-standing tensions with President Mohamed on election delays and personal ambitions. The EU and the US condemned the parliamentary procedure of Khayre's dismissal as 'irregular'. Puntland president Said Abdullahi Deni labelled this vote of no confidence in Khayre 'illegal'. On 23 September, Khayre was officially *succeeded by political newcomer Mohamed Hussein Roble* (of the Hawiye-Hilowle-Sa'ad-Habr Gidir sub-clan). Mohamed, a 57-year-old engineer and Swedish citizen who had previously worked at the ILO office in Nairobi, announced his new cabinet on 19 October, with 15 of the 26 ministers under Khayre retained. In September Khayre announced that he would challenge President Mohamed in the presidential elections of 2021.

Somaliland politics was more stable, but the electoral process stalled. Following the trajectory of delay seen in the presidential elections, the parliamentary elections which had been due in October 2018 were delayed to May 2021.

Somalia scored low again on the *Freedom House index* of 2020, with the label 'not free', and showed little if any improvement over previous years. In particular, the repeated delays of elections were seen negatively, in addition to the restrictions on civil society, the media, and political activity. The corruption and impunity of security forces in cases of abuse were also seen as stifling freedom and political life. In al-Shabaab-controlled areas, the situation was the worst.

Somaliland scored much better on the index, as 'partly free', but the report noted an 'erosion of political rights and civic space', as evident in the pressure on journalists and public figures. Also, minority clans were still subject to marginalisation, and gender-based violence (against women) remained widespread.

Journalism was a precarious occupation. On 16 February, journalist Abdiwali Ali Hassan was shot and killed by unknown attackers in Afgooye. There were also arrests of journalists on 17 March and 29 July on dubious charges of murder and of producing 'fake news'. About 25 pending cases of murdered journalists were still unsolved by year's end. In Somaliland, journalism was also under fire, with government restrictions on news gathering and reporting and with three journalists arrested. Somalia was ranked 163rd out of 180 countries in the *World Press Freedom Index* of *Reporters Without Borders*. In a meeting with Reporters Without Borders on 27 October, President Mohamed promised to improve the SFG's record.

Religious diversity was very limited in a country with 99.5% (Sunni) Muslims, but there was much intolerance towards Christian and other religious minorities. Islam is the state religion in Somalia. There was no religious freedom, as exemplified in a decision by Somaliland's Youth and Sports Ministry on 18 December to cancel a women's football tournament as 'un-Islamic'. Proselytisation by other religious faiths than Islam was forbidden, as were Christmas celebrations.

Al-Shabaab actions were again marked by excessive violence and targeted killings and hit-and-run attacks on smaller bases and government institutions and foreign forces assisting the SFG. There were hundreds of attacks. For instance, on 4 January, al-Shabaab units attacked a base on the island of Manda in the Indian Ocean used by US and Kenyan troops. Four attackers were killed, but there were report of planes and equipment damaged. On 23 June, a suicide bomber killed two Somalis near a Turkish military training facility. On 13 July, a VBIED (vehicle-borne improvised explosive device) attack by al-Shabaab in the district of Hodan targeted the convoy of the head of the SNA, Brigadier General Odowa Yusuf Rageh. He escaped, but three SNA soldiers and three civilian bystanders were killed and ten others injured. On 3 August, another al-Shabaab suicide bomber blew himself up inside the Luul Bar and Yameni Restaurant in Mogadishu, with two guards killed and three civilian bystanders seriously injured. In other areas of Somalia, more al-Shabaab violence was seen: on 29 March, the governor of Nugal was killed in Garoowe, and on 17 May in Gaalkayo in the Mudug region, the convoy of the governor of Mudug was killed in an al-Shabaab VBIED attack with four of his bodyguards. Further attacks occurred on 23 and 24 May when, during the *Eid* celebrations in Baidoa and Dinsoor, at least seven civilians were killed and over 40 injured. On 21 June, another VBIED exploded near a police station in the Hobyo district, killing two soldiers. There were also abductions and killings of local and regional politicians throughout the year. On 16 August, al-Shabaab car-bombed and stormed the Elite Hotel in Mogadishu, killing 17 civilians and injuring many more. On 18 December, an al-Shabaab suicide bomber blew himself up near a political gathering at a stadium in Galkayo, killing 17 people, among them high-ranking officials, civilians, and three soldiers. Al-Shabaab, incapable of engaging in open battle with the SNA and AMISOM, limited itself to such (daily) terror attacks and to targeting convoys. It also carried out about a dozen mortar attacks on Mogadishu international airport.

Al-Shabaab showed flexibility and adaptiveness as a socio-political and fighting force but had no political strategy of engagement or compromise. The movement could afford this position due to its relatively successful economic base and its regular recruitment of young, unemployed Somali men, seeking some kind of stable income – which the movement was in a position to offer. It continued to coercively recruit children into its forces, routinely threatening retaliation on parents and communities that refused to cooperate.

But *al-Shabaab's military activities were degraded* by SNA action and by frequent US-supported airstrikes, which notably increased in number this year. The SFG recovered some territory, for example capturing the strategic town of

Janaale (in the Lower Shabelle region), with allegedly 140 al-Shabaab troops killed. On 20 March and 18 July, AMISOM and Somali security forces near the villages of Koban and Bula Haaji (Lower Juba region) inflicted heavy casualties on al-Shabaab forces. Another al-Shabaab attack on 18 July on an Ethiopian AMISOM base in the town of Halgan in Hiraan region was repulsed, with an unknown number of attackers killed. Due to drone strikes, some al-Shabaab masterminds were killed, such as Bashir Qorgab, who had planned the 4 January Manda airbase attack, and one al-Shabaab *Amniyat* (security) chief, Yusuf Jiis. On 25 August, the notorious commander Abdulkadir Osman Yarow (Abdulkadir 'Commandos') was killed. Whether the (very slow) extension of SFG authority and control in former al-Shabaab areas would last was dependent on its delivering acceptable services and justice. In August, there were reports that al-Shabaab's leader Abu Ubaidah, ill with kidney failure, had been replaced by his deputy, militarist hardliner 'Sheikh' Abukar Ali Adan (Hawiye-Gaal Jael sub-clan), although this choice was contested by another (Hawiye-Habr Gidir-Ayr-based) faction within the movement.

There were also attacks by militants affiliated to the 'Islamic State in Iraq and the Levant' (ISIL), a 'competitor' of al-Shabaab – for instance, two in Mogadishu and one in Boosaaso – but the number was much lower than in the previous year.

On 5 March, AMISOM carried out a further troop reduction of 1,000, leaving 19,626 uniformed personnel in service. Logistic support from donors via the UN Support Office in Somalia (UNSOS) continued. Also, 10,900 troops of the Somali Security Forces were supported by UNSOS. The expansion of Covid-19 slowed down the training of SNA forces needed to fight al-Shabaab.

Foreign Affairs

Somalia and Somaliland foreign affairs were primarily geared to keeping relations with the donor community in order to enhance stability and economic and humanitarian support, and in the case of Somaliland to enhance its international recognition. Both received a lot of attention from the global community, but the two governments themselves did not play an active role in regional or global affairs. Foreign relations were low-key due to Covid-19 restrictions, although online virtual meetings were held with donor country partners and UN agencies.

On 27 January, president Mohamed met with Eritrean president Isaias Afewerki and Ethiopian prime minister Abiy Ahmed in Asmara over a joint plan of action concerning security cooperation, economic and social development, and enhancing regional cooperation.

Relations of the SFG with Kenya remained difficult, if not hostile, due to disagreements on AMISOM and the case of the dispute *over the maritime delimitation in the Indian Ocean (Somalia vs Kenya)*, brought to the ICJ. It was announced on 22 May that a ruling on this was delayed and was to be expected only after March 2021. The SFG also resented Kenya's continued support for Jubaland president Ahmed Madobe. On 1 December, Somalia recalled its ambassador in Nairobi and ordered the Kenya envoy in Mogadishu to leave in protest against Kenya's 'interfering in the electoral process'. But on 7–9 November, a Kenyan economic delegation visited Somalia to discuss investment opportunities and boost bilateral ties between the two countries.

Somaliland tried to maintain good relations with Ethiopia and Kenya, but on 16 February it signalled that it was rejecting a planned joint visit by President Mohamed and Ethiopian prime minister Abiy to Somaliland's president in Hargeisa.

The country made no progress in its efforts to gain international recognition, but *it began diplomatic relations with Taiwan* and a representative office was opened in Hargeisa in September. This drew condemnation from China and led to a rapprochement of this country and the SFG in Mogadishu.

An economic issue with foreign relations impact was *Ethiopia's closer involvement in the DP World (Dubai) investments in developing the port of Berbera*, in which it held a 19% stake, with the aim of eventually handling 30% of its export cargo. This meant competition with Djibouti, and on 1 December its president Ismaïl Omar Guelleh reacted negatively to the Berbera port developments. Also notable was the economically driven *rapprochement between Ethiopia's Somali Region* (under its dynamic president Mustafa Omer) *and Somaliland*, via rapidly expanding trade channels between the two, enhanced by a new road between Jijiga and Berbera via the border town of Togochale.

On 11 May, James Swan, the special representative of the UNSG for Somalia and head of the UN Assistance Mission in Somalia, visited Mogadishu's UN Level 2 hospital to discuss its capacity and needs for Covid-19 response.

A consultative meeting was held in Djibouti on 14 June at the behest of President Guelleh, with SFG president Mohamed, Somaliland president Muse Bihi Abdi and Ethiopian prime minister Abiy Ahmed attending. The aim was to prepare a resumption of the political dialogue between the two countries and thus enhance stability and cooperation. The two sides agreed to form a joint committee, which proceeded to meet over the next few days (15–17 June), with 'facilitators' from the US and the EU also present. But a second meeting on 12 July did not materialise; only on 14 September was an agreement reached on the modalities for the 2021 elections.

On 13 November, Ethiopia announced that it was withdrawing some 3,000 of its AMISOM soldiers, to be redeployed to the insurgent Tigray Region.

The US acting secretary of defence Christopher Miller visited Somalia on 27 November, coming from US Camp Lemonnier in Djibouti, but did not meet with the Somali government. On 4 December, US president *Donald Trump announced the withdrawal of American military personnel* from Somalia, estimated at about 700 in number, in early 2021. Many Somali politicians voiced their opposition to this.

On 6 December, an *Egyptian diplomatic delegation* headed by assistant foreign minister for African affairs Sherif Issa visited Mogadishu to boost bilateral relations and counter Ethiopian influence.

Socioeconomic Developments

The economy was severely hit by the Covid-19 pandemic in Somalia, eliminating economic growth. With some reservations about the reliability of the data, GDP reached $ 4.6 bn, a decline of ca. 1.5% (AfDB data) compared with the previous year. This translated into a 4.4% decline in real *per capita* income.

Somaliland had a GDP of about $ 2.5 bn, with GDP per capita estimated at about $ 560. GDP growth was also slightly negative due to Covid-19, locust infestation, and export restrictions.

Trade and incomes were affected also by reduced FDI, a decline in remittances, and unpredictable bans on livestock imports from Somalia by the Gulf countries. The pastoral and agrarian sector was hit by locust invasion and major flooding. On 23 June, the World Bank approved a supplemental sum of $ 55 m to the SFG to deal with the shocks and with the impact of the coronavirus.

Somalia's state budget was $ 476.2 m, with half of it provided by donors, mainly for developmental efforts and security support. In October, it was announced that the projection for the 2021 budget would be a staggering 40.9% higher, again with half of it supplied by donor grants and loans.

Donor funding again propped up the SFG budget (about 40% in loans and grants), and the government received $ 170.9 m in project and direct budget support from the international donor community. Additionally, the donors promised support for development projects worth $ 240.8 m, in the context of the SFG's current National Development Plan (NDP 9, running from 2020 to 2024). Despite this continuity in the steady flow of external finances, there were few indications that Somalia was building up a solid and sustainable economic base by itself.

Although significant oil and gas reserves had been discovered in previous years, there were no major activities to exploit this wealth, except for the Ministry of Petroleum and Mineral Resources announcing the launch of an offshore licensing round (from 4 August 2020 to 12 March 2021). While (in)formal services expanded, investment in productive enterprises (commodities, minerals) remained scarce. Imports were again much higher than exports, and the current account deficit was estimated at 12.8%. Inflation went down slightly, to 4%.

Remittances covered another large chunk of Somalia's income, supporting more than 40% of the population, and made up 34% of GDP. The remittances continued to flow in, but they were down by 7–9% compared with last year, from about $ 1.4 bn to some $ 1.3 bn. Due to Covid-19, there was a shift from cash-based transfers via the informal *hawala* system to digital transfers e.g., via the SWIFT system.

Somaliland's state budget was about $ 328 m, about 92% of which was financed domestically (taxes and import duties) and only 8% from foreign sources. The country received a remittance sum of around $ 1.3 bn, meaning a 6.8% drop compared with the previous year.

Somalia was officially a country in 'debt distress'. In March 2020, the SFG secured *debt relief under the HIPC initiative*. The aim was to gradually reduce its external debt, from $ 5.2 bn to $ 557 m by the end of 2023 (when the HIPC scheme ends). The IMF announced in March that Somalia would get a financing package worth $ 395 m under the joint ECF and the extended fund facility (EFF).

On the World Bank's *Ease of Doing Business Index*, Somalia was ranked lowest, 190th of 190 countries, but the value of such an index was limited, perhaps relevant for foreigners wanting to start a business in the country. In practice, starting an enterprise and running a business was easy, and Somalis went about this in innovative ways.

Corruption was one of the major obstacles. It remained rampant, as shown on the TI *Corruption Perceptions Index,* where Somalia was at the last but one position (179th). It showed no sign of diminishing and remained an essential ingredient of economic life, due also to the nature of this fractured society with weak public trust. Although there were no reliable data, it seemed that Somaliland (not listed in the CPI) suffered lower levels of corruption. However, in September, several high-ranking officials were arrested on corruption charges.

The still under-developed and under-funded *medical infrastructure* could not handle the coronavirus pandemic, of which the first case was registered on 16 March. Testing capacity and hospital care facilities were extremely inadequate. But great efforts were made and news on the disease and the precautions needed spread rapidly. Community surveillance teams undertook active case searching, contact tracing, and awareness raising. In November, according to UN information, community rapid response teams giving information on prevention had reached over 2 m people in 9,840 settlements, including 43,225 people in IDP settlements.

After the first coronavirus case was registered in Somalia on 16 March, Turkey sent four planes of medical equipment, including intensive care unit beds, ventilators, protective gear, surgical face masks, face shields, and useful materials, during April.

During the year, various packages with materials to deal with coronavirus arrived from other donors. The WHO supported four biosafety level 2 PCR testing laboratories in Mogadishu, Hargeisa, and Garowe. In December, some 4,580 cases of Covid-19 were confirmed nationwide, with total fatalities a comparatively low number in view of a population of 15.4 m, although this was partly due to lack of testing.

While vaccination campaigns on measles and polio proceeded in some areas (such as Banadir), by year's end no significant number of vaccinations had happened against Covid-19.

Somalia's population reached approximately 15.4 m, based on a growth rate of 2.92% this year (World Bank data) and a fertility rate of 6.12: very high and a partly a reflection of the serious lack of (female) education, ignorance, and lack of contraceptives, and religious conservatism and pressure. In total, 46.8% of the population was urban (7,431,038 people in 2020). The median age in Somalia was 16.7 years.

Gender-based violence remained a widespread problem, with coercive (and child) marriage and sexual abuse of women very frequent. Female IDPs were especially vulnerable. Not only government soldiers and militia members but also ordinary Somali men were perpetrators. Only extreme cases of (gang) rape and murder came to the courts. Despite a legal ban, female genital mutilation operations, seen as culturally/religiously necessary by many, were also routinely done. In al-Shabaab-controlled areas, forced marriages remained common, whereby local women were wedded to fighters. A new Sexual Intercourse Related Crimes Bill was introduced in parliament in August, but it fell far short on addressing gender-based abuse in light of internationally agreed upon norms: it would allow for child marriage, reduce penalties for forced marriages, exclude a broad range of sexual offences, and include weak procedural protections for survivors. Remarkably, *in Somaliland* an equally controversial Rape, Fornication and Other Related Offences Bill was tabled and even approved by the lower house on 25 August, inspired by Muslim religious figures but displeasing many women and lawyers. In it, same-sex sexual relations were made punishable by death, child and forced marriages were allowed, and the definition of rape was made very vague.

Human trafficking (for purposes of sexual exploitation or forced labour) and child labour remained common as well, and law enforcement action on this was sparse and inadequate.

Humanitarian needs in the country remained extremely high: at year's end, *about 3.9 m people faced acute food insecurity*. The UN said that 5 m people required assistance. Of the $ 1.05 bn funding requested by the UN, only $ 567 m was secured. Humanitarian workers again faced serious challenges in their work, due to general insecurity, targeted attacks, and various restrictions such as blockades by al-Shabaab of some government-controlled towns. Alongside cases of kidnapping, at least 11 humanitarian workers were killed on duty (UN figures).

The country's *IDP population* of 2.6 m (UN figures) increased by about 620,000 people due to locust infestation, flooding, and Covid-19 problems. IDPs and those lacking sufficient food and services were severely tested again but showed continued resilience and survival skills.

South Sudan

Daniel Large

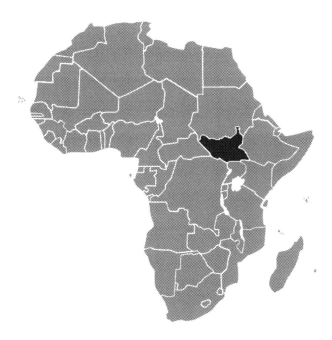

Any hope generated by the official formation of a new transitional government in February dissipated in the face of political disagreement between and within the main government and opposition political groupings and limited implementation of the peace agreement amid prevailing insecurity, impunity, severe flooding, and economic dire straits. Falling global crude oil prices had political repercussions in terms of power struggles and, combined with the Covid-19 pandemic, badly affected an already struggling economy. With no budget agreed, and international agencies providing humanitarian services, the government struggled to pay civil servants and to manage debt and the economy. The Covid-19 pandemic provided an easy official explanation for the atrophy of the peace agreement, and hindered many aspects, but non-implementation was in reality a consequence of intractable political disagreements.

Domestic Politics

In January, the government and the South Sudan Opposition Movements Alliance (SSOMA), including the National Salvation Front (NAS) led by Thomas Cirillo

Swaka, which did not sign the September 2018 Revitalised Agreement on the Resolution of the Conflict in the Republic of South Sudan (R-ARCSS), signed the Rome Declaration committing to a cessation of hostilities and political talks. This came amid concern about whether or not a new transitional government could be formed in Juba under the terms of the R-ARCSS.

On 21 February, however, Salva Kiir Mayardit dissolved the Transitional Government of National Unity and appointed Riek Machar, chairperson of the Sudan People's Liberation Movement/Army in Opposition (SPLM/A-IO), as first vice-president (for the third time since South Sudan's independence), together with three vice-presidents: Taban Deng Gai, James Wani Igga, and Rebecca Nyandeng de Mabior. The next day the *Revitalised Transitional Government of National Unity (RTGoNU)* was sworn in. On 23 February, following disagreement within the South Sudan Opposition Alliance (SSOA), Kiir appointed Hussein Abdelbagi as the fourth vice-president from a list submitted by the SSOA.

After negotiations about the latest iteration of a power-sharing government, President *Salva Kiir* announced a new cabinet on 12 March. The former government, or Sudan People's Liberation Movement – in Government (SPLM-IG), retained 20 ministries; the SPLM/A-IO held nine, including defence minister Angelina Teny (Machar's wife and the first woman to hold this position) and minister of petroleum Puot Kang Chol; the SSOA held three, including minister of public service and human resources development Joseph Bangasi Bakasoro; the SPLM 'Former Detainees' (SPLM-FD) held two; and the Other Political Parties (OPP) coalition held one. With nine women (25%), the RTGoNU missed the 35% quota for women envisioned in the Revitalised Agreement. On 27 March, President Kiir established a new security mechanism, the National Transitional Committee, to coordinate and implement transitional security arrangements

The government moved to respond to the *Covid-19 pandemic* when Kiir created a high-level task force headed by Machar on 20 March. Five days later, interior minister Paul Mayom imposed a nationwide curfew to prevent the spread of Covid-19. On 15 May, Kiir appointed a new 13-member task force led by vice-president Abdelbagi. On 20 May, Machar, Teny, and the minister of information and communication, Michael Makuei Lueth, confirmed that they had tested positive for Covid-19, along with other cabinet ministers. By the end of December, 3,558 people were confirmed to have tested positive with Covid-19.

Prior to the formation of the RTGoNU in February, Salva Kiir had broken a political deadlock with a concession on the vexed issue of state boundaries, by *reducing the 32 states that had been created in 2017 amid much controversy to 10*, the number of states before the civil war. In June, agreement was reached on the political allocation of the states. The incumbent SPLM-IG was allocated six (Central Equatoria, Eastern Equatoria, Lakes, Northern Bahr el-Ghazal, Warrap, and Unity), the SPLM/A-IO three (Upper Nile, Western Bahr el-Ghazal, and Western Equatoria), and the SSOA one (Jonglei). Later in June, Kiir appointed governors of eight of the ten states and chief administrators of the administrative areas of Abyei, Ruweng, and Pibor. The new governor of Jonglei, Denay Jok Chagor, was appointed in July, but Kiir refused to appoint Johnson Olony, a controversial former leader of a Shilluk militia who defected to join the SPLM-IO in 2015, as governor of Upper Nile, contributing to a delay in the creation of state governments.

The lack of functioning state-level political authority exacerbated tensions and intercommunal violence. The security situation deteriorated, even though South Sudan's permanent ceasefire more or less continued to hold. In April, the truce established by the January Rome Agreement broke down after NAS forces attacked SPLM/A-IO forces in the county of Yei River. In May, clashes occurred between government forces, at times together with those of the SPLM/A-IO, and the NAS in central and western Equatoria.

Shifting, fluid *power struggles* continued, not just between the main parties but within them as well. Reduced oil revenues compounded this. There was discord within the SPLM/A-IO. This occurred at different levels, but one indication came when its secretary-general, Tingo Peter Regbigo Limbo, resigned in November, citing Riak Machar's 'lack of display of good leadership'. Tensions and a power struggle within the SPLM-IG and Dinka political elite around Kiir became evident. In May, amid tensions over Angelina Teny's appointment as defence minister, Salva Kiir removed the chief of defence forces Gabriel Jok Riak without explanation (but reportedly due to a failure to respond quickly enough to a coup attempt) and replaced him with Johnson Juma Okot, the former deputy chief of defence forces. Kiir appointed Nhial Deng Nhial as minister of presidential affairs in the RTGoNU in June; this was widely seen as an attempt to counterbalance *Akol Koor Kuc*, the powerful director-general of South Sudan's National Security Service (NSS) Internal Security Bureau. In August, Kiir removed Akol Koor Kuc from the board of directors of the Nile Petroleum Corporation (or Nilepet, South Sudan's national, state-owned oil company) and appointed loyalists in an attempt to ensure control of the main source of state revenue. He named Nhial Deng Nhial as the new chairperson of the board and Josephine Napwon Cosmas, minister of environment and forestry, as deputy chairperson. In September, Kiir appointed Bol Ring Mourwel Kon as the new managing director of Nilepet. A presidential executive order relieved minister of finance Salvatore Garang Mabiordit of his post, replacing him with Athian Diing Athian, and sacked the head of the Revenue Authority.

Negotiations between the government and umbrella non-signatories SSOMA ended in Rome on 12 October without agreement. Following the January 2020 ceasefire, fighting had restarted in April and featured significant government offensives and guerrilla responses. The Rome talks had resumed on 9 October. The meeting took place after recent frictions within the SSOMA. The South Sudan United Front, led by Paul Malong, was suspended and the Real SPLM, headed by Pagan

Amum, refused to sign the charter of the opposition movement alliance in solidarity with Malong. The SSOMA had three main components: the National Salvation Front led by Thomas Cirillo, the South Sudan United Front/Army, and the Real Sudan People's Liberation Movement. However, partly due to efforts by Nhial Deng Nhial to get Malong to rejoin the government, these splintered into one faction led by Cirillo and another led by Malong and Amum, producing parallel negotiations at the Rome talks. In November, the SSOMA joined the ceasefire monitoring agreement after talks in Rome, amid doubt about whether it would hold in the field. In December, talks continued amid differences over the nature of the conflict and the new constitution.

South Sudan's *National Dialogue*, which had begun early in 2017, came to an end. In December 2020, the South Sudan National Dialogue Steering Committee published its concluding report regarding the National Dialogue process. This was forthright. It argued that South Sudan and its people are caught in a 'tragic vicious cycle' of political deadlock between President Kiir and Riek Machar, and it was 'glaringly obvious that this dysfunctional government cannot deliver peace, security, and stability which the country desperately needs'.

While the February formation of the RTGoNU appeared to indicate some progress, as ever what mattered most was whether or not such formal events were followed by meaningful implementation. As 2020 advanced, the lack of any proper functioning of the central and lower levels of government became more evident amid worsening economic conditions. Even Salva Kiir, in his 8 July Independence Day speech, acknowledged that 'peace implementation remains painfully slow and far below your expectations'. By November, *the implementation of the R-ARCISS was widely deemed to have 'stalled'*. This was true particularly for security sector reform, a critical area. The South Sudan People's Defence Force (SSPDF) and SPLM/A-IO violated the cessation of hostilities agreement. Violence increased in Lakes, Unity, Warrap, Western Bahr el-Ghazal, Western, Eastern and Central Equatoria, Jonglei, and the Greater Pibor Administrative Area, with the latter two illustrating how political competition within Kiir's coalition played out in conflict via rival factions supplying arms to militias. The RTGoNU did not function well, with the opposition in effect excluded from government decision-making. The Transitional National Legislative Assembly was not established, which delayed the constitution process.

Another issue, the lack of progress establishing the hybrid court for South Sudan with the AU Commission, was indicative of *prevailing impunity*. In one example, an executive order in June promoted 12 SSPDF commanders to military high command, six of whom were identified by the UN Mission in South Sudan (UNMISS) Human Rights Division as having been involved in serious human rights violations and two of whom were included on the UN sanctions list. Freedom House's Freedom in the World 2020 rankings listed South Sudan's status as 'not free' in 2019 (with a total score of 2/100: -2/40 for political rights, 4/60 for civil liberties). The NSS harassed, censored, and arbitrarily detained critics and activists. In June, for instance, NSS officers detained Moses Monday, director of the Organization for Non-Violence, for erecting billboards demanding financial transparency in government spending. There were reports of enforced disappearances and extrajudicial killings, such as of Kerbino Wol Agok, a businessman from Tonj who had been detained by the NSS but pardoned in February 2020, after which he published a manifesto in June launching 'the 7 Oct Movement' (after a protest at the Blue House, or NSS headquarters, in 2018) and setting out a 'model for revolutionary change'. Not long afterwards, Wol was executed by a force of NSS, army, and Gelweng youth in Rumbek, Lakes State.

Media were also targeted; in January, for example, local Voice of Eastern Equatoria radio journalist Ijoo Bosco was arrested for six days not long after airing news about US sanctions against the first vice-president, Taban Deng Gai. In June, the government blocked access to local news website the 'Sudans Post' after the publication of an article deemed defamatory by the NSS. According to the Reporters Without Borders World Press Freedom Index 2020, South Sudan ranked 138th of 180 countries in 2019 (having been 139th in the previous year's rankings).

Foreign Affairs

Relations with the US continued to be strained. In January, the US Treasury sanctioned vice-president Taban Deng Gai for serious human rights violations. Later in the year, amid speculation about the impact of US presidential election on US policy on South Sudan, the new *chargé d'affaires* at the US embassy in Juba reiterated its support for peace and humanitarian aid. Salva Kiir Mayardit congratulated American president-elect Joe Biden on his election victory.

The new RTGoNU was finally realised following mediation efforts led by IGAD and the deputy president of South Africa and special envoy, David Mabuza, as parties continued to miss deadlines agreed in the R-ARCSS and mediation process. The Community of Sant'Egidio mediated talks in Rome, with a delegation of the Catholic body also visiting Juba in December.

The revitalised peace deal did not translate into renewed donor support, as some in the government of South Sudan had hoped; wary donors, especially in the West, were prepared only to contribute humanitarian funding and aid. In July, a joint local statement by the EU delegation, France, Germany, the Netherlands, Sweden, Canada, and the UK expressed 'deep concern regarding recurrent reports of high levels of sexual and gender-based violence affecting young children and women in South Sudan' and 'the prevailing culture of impunity'.

In contrast, when then minister of foreign affairs and international cooperation Awut Deng Acuil visited Moscow in January for talks with Sergey Lavrov the tone was upbeat, with talk of future cooperation between South Sudan and Russia. Awut

Deng Acuil was replaced in March by Beatrice Khamisa Wani, who continued to engage China, one of South Sudan's most important existing partners. Anti-Covid 19 medical supplies were donated by Jack Ma and the Alibaba Foundation as well as the Chinese government, which maintained its medical cooperation programme. In September, South Sudan and China signed a new deal to renovate the Jur River Bridge in Wau. The Shandong Hi-Speed Group Company resumed work on the Juba–Terekeka–Yirol–Rumbek road in December.

In March, the UNSC renewed the mandate of UNMISS for another year; overall force levels (17,000 troops and 2,101 police) and the mission's core mandate were mostly unchanged. In May, the UNSC renewed the arms embargo on South Sudan for another year by a 12–0 vote (Russia, China, and South Africa abstained) and individual sanctions on eight South Sudanese nationals for their role in the conflict. In June, the UNHRC renewed the mandate of the Commission on Human Rights in South Sudan.

A *backlash against the UN* followed the reporting of South Sudan's first Covid-19 case on 5 April, an UNMISS member of staff who had arrived from the Netherlands via Ethiopia in February. The UN was accused of spreading the virus; it was unclear how far this was directed by government officials, since Kiir called for people to not engage in hate speech against foreigners, but such accusations and xenophobia were prominent in social media reactions. In June, UNMISS was sheltering 181,231 IDPs in its protection of civilian sites in Bentiu, Juba, Malakal, Bor, and Wau. In September, UNMISS announced that it had started 'to progressively withdraw' troops from 'protection of civilians' camps in Bor and Wau; these were to become camps for IDPs under government, not UN, control. UNMISS also established a temporary base in Lobonok, Central Equatoria, in response to fighting there. The protection of civilians sites in Juba were also redesignated as camps for IDPs in November. Elsewhere, amid the pandemic, government-imposed restrictions continued to impede peacekeeping and humanitarian activities. Nine humanitarian aid workers were killed in 2020.

South Sudan's relations with the AU and the EAC were affected by its economic dire straits. In June, the AU sanctioned South Sudan for not paying its yearly financial contributions and the East African Legislative Assembly censured the country for defaulting on its annual payment; by August, South Sudan owed the EAC over $ 24 m.

One important axis of South Sudan's external relations concerned *enhanced relations with Egypt*. In August, Egypt's chief of general intelligence services, Abbas Kamel, visited Juba with a delegation featuring minister of health Hala Zayed. Egyptian president *Abdel Fattah el-Sisi then paid a historic visit to Juba* in November for talks with Kiir. Their subsequent statement saw el-Sisi call for international sanctions on South Sudan to be lifted. It made no mention of conflict in Ethiopia, at a time when federal forces had captured Mekelle, but stated that the use of Nile waters had been discussed at a time when many wondered how Cairo might exploit Ethiopia's crisis to strengthen its own position, particularly over Egypt's Nile waters dispute with Ethiopia.

By contrast, South Sudan's relations with Uganda were more challenging. The Uganda People's Defence Force (UPDF) continued to enter South Sudan. In October, South Sudan accused Uganda of making a 'major incursion' after the UPDF and SSPDF clashed in Magwe County, Eastern Equatoria.

Relations with Sudan stood out. The government of South Sudan continued to be active as a mediator in Sudan's peace process. In August, Salva Kiir chaired a signing ceremony in Juba for the initial peace agreement between the transitional government of Sudan, represented by chairperson of the Transitional Sovereign Council *Abdel Fattah al-Burhan* and the Sudanese prime minister *Abdullah Hamdok*, and the Sudan Revolutionary Front, an umbrella group featuring groups from Darfur (the Justice and Equality Movement, Minni Minawi's Sudan Liberation Army, and the Sudan People's Liberation Movement-North). On 3 October, the *Juba Peace Agreement* was officially signed in Juba. Steps were taken to improve relations between Juba and Khartoum. There were signs of official rapprochement over the contested area of Abyei, a free trade zone in Mokhaleef, El Jebelein, to promote cross-border trade, and a memorandum on defence cooperation signed by Sudan's minister of defence Yasin Ibrahim and his South Sudanese counterpart Angelina Teny.

Socioeconomic Developments

Falling global crude oil prices and the Covid-19 pandemic negatively affected the economy.

The IMF revised the projected GDP growth rate for 2020 down from 8.2%, and in October stated real GDP growth in 2020 was −2.3%. By December, there was still *no budget for the July 2020/21 financial year*; expenditure was made via a combination of a presidential extension of the 2019/2020 budget and opaque off-budget processes.

The second deputy governor of South Sudan's central bank, Daniel Kech Pouch, announced in August that the bank had *run out of foreign exchange reserves* and could not stop the South Sudanese pound's depreciation. He said that inflation stood at 35% and that there were three exchange rates: from the central bank at 165 South Sudanese pounds (SSP) per US dollar, from commercial banks at around SSP 190, and from the parallel market at SSP 400.

South Sudan struggled to secure new finance and manage its external and domestic debt. In August, the government requested a $ 250 m loan from the African Export-Import Bank, under its Pandemic Trade Impact Mitigation Facility, and secured an additional $ 63 m in September. In early September, the then finance minister Salvatore Garang told a parliamentary committee that civil servants had not been paid since April because of the drop in oil revenues. In November, the IMF approved $ 52.3 m in emergency assistance to South Sudan under the Rapid Credit Facility, the first lending since South Sudan joined the IMF in 2012. On debt, South Sudan was ordered by the high court in London in June to pay the commodity giant Trafigura $ 9.7 m in unpaid debts. According to the IMF, in July South Sudan reached a debt restructuring agreement with the Qatar National Bank and as a result was no longer in debt distress, although it remained at 'high risk' of external and overall public debt distress. In October, however, in an effort to recover loans of some $ 700 m incurred between 2012 and 2015, the Qatar National Bank initiated arbitration proceedings with the World Bank's International Centre for Settlement of Investment Disputes.

The World Bank's Doing Business report 2020 ranked South Sudan 185th (out of 190, as of May 2019), and the country was at the bottom of TI's Corruption Perceptions Index in 2020 (with a score of 12 out of 100, based on data from 2019 and 2018). In September, the UN Commission on Human Rights in South Sudan revealed 'the misappropriation of a staggering $ 36 m since 2016 'by high-ranking bureaucrats and politicians', noting this was what they could trace and that it 'may not reflect the whole picture'.

South Sudan ranked 185th out of 189 countries in the 2020 Human Development Index Ranking (with an HDI value in 2019 of 0.433). However, this provided only a broad indication of the severity of the situation. Access to services such as healthcare, water, and sanitation was already limited, and in 2020 this worsened due to damage, destruction, or closure of service infrastructure. Women and girls continued to face extreme levels of violence. Restrictions imposed due to Covid-19 were partially lifted from May; flights resumed and markets, shops, and bars were allowed to reopen, but churches, mosques, and nightclubs remained closed. Schools were closed for six months due to Covid-19, forcing some 2.2 m children out of school.

In December, according to OCHA, 1.63 m South Sudanese were displaced internally and approximately 5.8 m were food-insecure. According to UNHCR, at the end of December, there were some 300,000 refugees in South Sudan and 2,202,479 South Sudanese refugees: 40.3% (889,054) in Uganda, 33.4% (736,685) in Sudan, 16.5% (363, 198) in Ethiopia, 5.6% (123,968) in Kenya, and 4.1% (89,574) in the DRC.

Despite new plans concerning agricultural production, food insecurity affected most parts of the country. In July, South Sudan signed an agreement with the WFP to help accelerate agricultural production under its Comprehensive Agricultural Masterplan, which seeks to improve food security. In December, South Sudan and Egypt agreed to cooperate on agriculture, starting with an action group to identify how this could be done. However, overall food security worsened and some communities were facing catastrophic needs. As of December, 1,392,259 children were considered acutely malnourished, according to the Integrated Food Security Phase

Classification. Coinciding with the outbreak of the Covid-19 pandemic in April, prices for staple foods and basic commodities escalated drastically. In March, the price of a 50 kg bag of maize grain in markets had already reportedly increased by 36%. After the spread of Covid-19, the price of a kilogram of maize in Juba shot up from SSP 159 in April 2019 to SSP 298 in April 2020. Such price increases provoked demonstrations, including in the town of Bor, by civilians blaming traders for taking advantage of the pandemic.

In March, the Ministry of Petroleum postponed plans to tender the rights to 14 new oilfields because of Covid-19. Nilepet was slated to take over operations from the Dar Petroleum Oil Operating Company consortium oilfields (3 and 7 in Upper Nile), with CNCP, Petronas, Sinopec, and Tri-Ocean due to leave in 2027. South Sudan produced around 165,000 barrels per day for export in September. It could sell only about 42,500 barrels per day to finance its budget, however, after subtracting the oil obligated to the government's commercial partners and Sudan. The government was accused of ignoring reports connecting oil pollution and birth defects in oil-producing states. The NGO Hope for Humanity Africa filed a legal suit in April in the East African Court of Justice, which demanded $ 720 m in compensation for affected communities from the companies and the government for pollution in the states of Unity and Upper Nile; in June, a temporary injunction was filed calling for the government of South Sudan and the two major producing consortia, Greater Pioneer Operating Co. and Dar Petroleum, to halt oil flows.

In February, desert locust swarms spread from Uganda to South Sudan. Alongside local responses and international efforts led by the FAO, IGAD was mandated to coordinate desert locust control in the region by the 34th Extraordinary Summit of IGAD Heads of State and Governments in February 2020. Following unusually heavy rainfall from July to October, the Nile, Pibor, Sobat, Lol, and other rivers overflowed mainly in the eastern and central parts of South Sudan. The flooding caused large-scale displacement of people and cattle and damaged or destroyed crops and property. OCHA estimated that 1,042,000 people were affected, with Jonglei State and the Greater Pibor Administrative Area (495,000 people) the worst affected. Finally, in December, the Famine Review Committee said that Pibor County was likely in a famine amid wider concern over the impact of conflict, flooding, and economic deterioration.

Sudan

Jean-Nicolas Bach and Clément Deshayes

This was a difficult year for the political transition in Sudan, but it was also marked by decisive steps forward. The institutions of transition remained divided between civilians (government) and the military (half of the Sovereign Council). This fragmentation did not facilitate the implementation of important reforms: the Legislative Council, one of the key institutions provided for by the Constitutional Declaration, was not formed. In October, the political scene was further shaken by the historical agreement signed in Juba between the transitional institutions and armed groups of the Sudanese Revolutionary Front. But this agreement did not include the most influential armed groups, the Sudanese People's Liberation Movement-North led by Abdul Aziz al Helou (SPLM-N al Helou) and the Sudanese Liberation Movement led by Abdel Wahid Nur (SLM-AW), and the costs of the implementation were not secured.

In terms of external relations, 2020 represented a turning point for the diplomatic normalisation, as Sudan was delisted from the US State Sponsors of Terrorism List (SSTL) after 27 years. This success occurred in December after a year-long normalisation process between Khartoum (the Sovereign Council military branch played a decisive role), Tel Aviv, and the US that was facilitated by the UAE. Sudan also redefined its geostrategic position in the Horn of Africa, with a clear rapprochement with Cairo and a growing critical attitude towards the Grand Ethiopian Renaissance Dam. Relations with Addis Ababa were further damaged by armed clashes on the Ethiopia – Sudan border, notably in the region of al-Fashaga.

The delisting of Sudan from the SSTL raised hopes of improvements as the socio-economic situation continued to deteriorate dramatically. The economic challenges remained huge: the new civilian government could not reverse the collapse of the currency, inflation, or fuel/diesel shortages. The end of public subsidies on fuel provoked a significant increase in fuel/diesel prices. The country was hit by Covid-19 (officially, 23,316 people were infected, 1,468 died, and there were 13,524 recoveries by the end of December).

Domestic Politics

After 2019, marked by the Sudanese Revolution and the implementation of transitional institutions, *2020 was a year of stabilisation at the governmental level, with major progress in terms of accountability, transparency*, and the cleansing of the establishment of elements supporting the previous regime. However, the general trend of reform was blurred by the fragmentation between military and civilian actors and by the revival of competition among political forces supporting the civilian government. In addition, the restructuring of the state and of the economy did not go unchallenged.

After months of intense negotiations between the components of the transitional bodies, the prime minister *Abdallah Hamdok nominated the 18 state governors on 22 July* to replace acting military governors. These nominations were welcomed by most parts of political forces but also triggered protests especially in the east of the country. Against a backdrop of tribal and ethnic tension (between the Beni Amer and the Beja), the nomination of the Kassala state governor led to massive demonstrations (generating at least three dead) and several days of the blockading of the highway connecting Port Sudan to Khartoum in August and at the beginning of October.

The reshaping of the state included several purges in the administration during the year, in the Central Bank of Sudan, in the Zakat chamber, and in the Ministry of Education and the Ministry of Justice. Leading members of the previous regime and members of the National Congress Party (Ali Osman Taha, Bakri Saleh, and eight others military and officials) were prosecuted over the 1989 coup. In order to dismantle the security apparatus of the former regime, on 8 June the Sudanese Armed Forces (SAF) dissolved the paramilitary Popular Defence Forces that were used extensively during Omar al-Bashir's rule.

Following this change and reacting to financial cuts, members of the elite units of the former National Intelligence Security Services rebelled on 14 January in

Khartoum and El Obeid. The situation was quickly resolved by the intervention of the army and the Rapid Support Forces (RSF). *In March, Prime Minister Hamdok faced a failed assassination attempt in Khartoum.* This event provoked demonstrations in support of the civilian government across the country.

Peace negotiations, the coronavirus crisis, and political instability led to a cabinet reshuffle in July. Abdallah Hamdok dismissed minister of health Akram Ali Eltom and accepted the resignation of six others. Interim ministers were appointed, including Heba Mohamed as minister of finance, in preparation for the result of the peace process. The head of police was also replaced following police violence during peaceful demonstrations.

The government issued a major reform of the penal code inherited from the previous regime. The main points of the bill were the abolition of the crime of apostasy, the suppression of articles of the 'public order laws' including public flogging and the ban on non-Muslims drinking or selling alcohol, and the suppression of the death penalty for children. A second law was enacted, the Fundamental Rights and Freedom Act, which included the abolition or amendment of laws concerning women's dignity and the criminalisation of female genital mutilation. The government strengthened existing bills concerning freedom of belief and religion.

Abdel Fattah al-Burhan, head of the Sovereign Council, announced in December the setting up of the new Transitional Partners Council (TPC). This new body did not replace the Sovereign Council or the civilian government but had the task of gathering all the forces supporting the revolution. The TPC was composed of five military members of the Sovereign Council, one member of the RSF, six members of the Forces of Freedom and Change (FFC), and seven members of former rebel groups, and one seat remained open pending the negotiations in the eastern part of the country. The launch of the TPC received a qualified or hostile reaction in the country. Several political parties, resistance committees, and the Sudanese Professional Union (SPA), including members invited to be part of the TPC, denounced it as an initiative designed by the military that betrayed the Constitutional Declaration signed in 2019.

The FFC, the main political alliance supporting the civilian transition, faced turbulence during the year. This very eclectic force lost one of its main parties with the freezing of all activities of the National Umma Party (NUP) within the coalition. Several parties, including the Sudanese Congress Party (SCP), pushed for the replacement of civilian members of the Sovereign Council and of the government. *The reconfiguration of the political sphere was ongoing*, but some trends and political alliances can be schematically drawn. First, the SPA and the resistance committees presented themselves as the guardians of the legacy of the revolution. They lobbied, sometimes through demonstrations, for the Constitutional Declaration to be respected and for the acceleration of state reform and the prosecution of former regime members. Second, the FFC gradually reorganised itself around the alliance between the SCP, the Unionists, and the Ba'ath Party. This alliance pushed for a more political government and the replacement of experts by political figures to improve communication and the legitimacy of the transition, but also to give more weight in the head-to-head with the military. Third, despite the corruption cases against their main leaders, the Islamist forces tried to reorganise themselves as political entities. Fourth, two main parties of the political sphere, the NUP and the Communist Party, decided to distance themselves from the FFC, ending the appearance of unity among the political parties supporting the revolution.

Sadiq El-Mahdi, leader of the NUP, died on 26 November of Covid-19 in Abu Dhabi. Sheik of the Ansar and prime minister twice (1966–67 and 1986–89), he had been incarcerated several times as a leading opponent of Omar al-Bashir's regime and one of the founders of the Sudan Call, a platform gathering political parties, civil society organisations, and rebel groups.

Concerning the peace process, the year started with a *highly symbolic visit by Abdallah Hamdok to Kauda*, a stronghold of the SPLM-N in the Nuba Mountains.

After delay and difficult negotiations in Juba in South Sudan, a *Comprehensive Peace Agreement was initiated on 31 August and officially signed on 3 October in Khartoum*. The agreement was signed by the Sudanese government and the Sudan Revolutionary Front (SRF), an alliance of armed groups from different areas of Sudan. The accord includes eight protocols and five 'tracks' (Darfur, the Two Areas, Eastern Sudan, Northern Sudan, and Central Sudan). *The transitional period was extended to three years starting from the date of the signing.* The agreement reshuffled the distribution of power by according to the SRF three new seats in the Sovereign Council, 25% of seats in the future Legislative Council, and five ministerial positions. *Both parties agreed about the federal organisation of the country.* They also worked on *security protocols* to build a joint force of former rebels and army to provide security in Darfur: the rebel combatants were to be progressively incorporated into the army following several phases planned to end after 40 months. Darfur was to be reorganised as one region and the Darfurian signatories were to be a part of the government of this region. Fifty per cent of the governmental positions were to be filled by members of the Darfurian peace track and 30% appointed by the federal government. Concerning South Kordofan and Blue Nile, the SPLM faction under the leadership of Malik Agar (SPLM-N Agar) was to be given the positions of governor of Blue Nile and deputy governor of West and South Kordofan, as well as 30% of the ministerial positions in these three states.

The peace agreement did not include the SPLM-N al Helou, which controlled large parts of South Kordofan, or the SLM-AW. Negotiations continued throughout the year with the SPLM-N al Helou and an agreement is still conceivable according to Abdallah Hamdok, but the SLM-AW continued to refuse the preconditions of the peace talks.

Despite the peace process and the signing of the comprehensive agreement, *levels of violence remained high in South Kordofan and increased in Red Sea State and in Darfur* for different reasons. In the eastern region, tribal clashes between the

Nuba and the Beni Amer provoked the death of dozens of people despite the tribal reconciliations launched by the state and the curfew in Port Sudan. In Darfur, the year started with a bloody attack on Geneina, the capital of West Darfur, by Arab tribesmen who targeted Masalit people in retaliation after the murder of one of their kin. Over 80 people were killed and 200 injured, according to the Sudanese Doctors' Union. Several raids on villages and refugee camps increased the feeling of insecurity. *Demonstrations and sit-ins spread in the area, demanding security, rights, and better living conditions.* Two of these sit-ins, in Misterei and near Kutum, were violently attacked by militias, and nine protesters were killed. The protesters accused members of Hemedti's RSF of being involved in this endemic violence and the attempt to prevent the relocation of refugees on their lands. The protests gradually decreased after the promises of the government to improve the security situation, the nomination of civilian governors, and the signing of the peace document in October.

The articulated issues of security, reform, and economic difficulties fuelled substantial contestation across the country. The climax of the demonstrations occurred during the celebrations of the revolution, especially on 6 April and 30 June, when thousands of protesters took the streets in the major towns. The main demands were for the implementation of the August 2019 Constitutional Declaration, a complete civil power, and investigation of the violent dismantlement of a sit-in on 3 June 2019. Demonstrators asked for better wealth redistribution and for the end of cuts in the electricity, gas, and oil supply. The police reacted violently during the protests and at least one demonstrator was killed in Khartoum on 30 June. Facing the outrage on the streets, Hamdok formed a commission to investigate police violence during the demonstrations and sacked the head of police in July. Demonstrations over commodity prices and shortages continued until December.

In 2020, the country confirmed the significant improvement in the main world indexes (based on 2019 data) induced by the political changes. Reporters Without Borders ranked Sudan 159th out of 180 for press freedom. As repressive laws regulating the press are still in place, the organisation expressed concern and encouraged the government to accelerate the pace of reform. Freedom House gave Sudan a score of 17 out of 100 in its Global Freedom Index 2021 (based on 2020 data, compared with 12 in 2020 and 7 in 2019) and 30 out of 100 in its Internet Freedom Index. It pointed to the global development of freedom of speech in Sudan while expressing concern over the role and the action of the military and militias. Despite this progress, several cases showed the limits of the opening up of freedom of speech in Sudan. One of the most emblematic of these was the imprisonment of five members of the Feed Arts group for public disturbance after a happening in a neighbourhood of Khartoum. The 2021 TI Corruption Perceptions Index (based on 2020 performance) showed the stagnation of Sudan at 174th position out of 180 (stable since 2017), illustrating the deep concerns of the Sudanese people over this issue.

Several Sudanese organisations were rewarded last year. The Sudanese Professional Association and the Organization of the December Revolution Martyrs' Families received Freedom Awards from Freedom House. The Sudanese Journalists Network received the Press Freedom Award from Reporter Without Borders-Sweden. Last but not least, the National Endowment for Democracy awarded three organisations for their work to 'strengthen civil society in Sudan': Sudan's Regional Center for Development and Training, the Darfur Bar Association, and the Nuba Women for Education and Development Association.

Foreign Affairs

The internal *political reconfigurations remained dramatically influenced by international and regional politics*, notably in the Gulf states. In January, the Sudanese minister of animal resources visited Riyad, while an official delegation led by Qatar's head of staff visited Khartoum, followed a few days later by a delegation led by the UAE's state secretary for foreign affairs, Anwar Gargash, on 14 January. This was the second official visit by UAE diplomats since the fall of Omar al-Bashir in April 2019. Confirming the growing relations between Khartoum and Abu Dhabi, this visit was preceded by a three-day official visit by the Sudanese vice-president of the Sovereignty Council, Mohamed Hamdan Dagalo (known as Hemedti), to the UAE at the beginning of January. The head of the Sovereignty Council, General Abdel Fattah al-Burhan, also visited the UAE later in the year, on 22 September. On 8 December, the minister of foreign affairs of the Kingdom of Saudi Arabia (KSA) visited Khartoum, the first Saudi visit at this diplomatic level since the formation of the Sudanese transitional government in September 2019. *This active diplomacy by the Gulf countries, especially the UAE, was related to their firm interest in the Red Sea's strategic importance, and their desire for Sudan's stability and 'successful' transition.* Such success means, for Abu Dhabi, continued support for the military branch of the Sudanese transition institutions, considered more experienced than the civilian branch of the government. The military branch and its leaders – though divided between Hemedti's RSF and Burhan's SAF – represented trustworthy, well-known, and long-term partners because of their involvement in the coalition led by the UAE and the KSA in Yemen in recent years. The UAE played a dramatic role as a facilitator for the Juba peace negotiations between the SRF and Khartoum's transitional institutions, during which the military branch – especially Hemedti – unsurprisingly played a leading role.

The military branch of the Sudanese transitional institutions was also obvious through the diplomatic manoeuvres of the UAE in order to facilitate the historical rapprochement between Sudan and the Israeli state. This rapprochement started with news received with huge surprise by many parties and Sudanese civil society:

General Burhan met the Israeli prime minister Benjamin Netanyahu on 3 February in Entebbe, Uganda. The civilian government of Adballah Hamdok initially denied any involvement or having been informed of such a meeting. Sudanese Islamists and traditional groups strongly condemned the diplomatic move and what it revealed about the growing influence of the military branch within the transitional institutions. The meeting also revealed divergences within the FFC coalition: the Communist Party and the FFC central committee opposed the normalisation of relations between Israel and Sudan, considered a trade for the delisting of Sudan as a state sponsor of terrorism. However, the SPA announced that such normalisation was unavoidable if Sudan was to rejoin the international community.

In fact, discussions between political groups in Sudan and at the diplomatic level revolved around a complex articulation of a couple of key issues: on the one hand, the payment of financial reparations by the Sudanese state to the victims of the 'USS Cole' and terrorist attacks on US embassies in Dar es Salaam and Nairobi in 1998, the normalisation of Sudan's relation with Israel; and on the other hand, the positive effects expected for Sudan, i.e. the delisting from the US SSTL after 27 years, and the recognition of Sudan's sovereign immunity in order to avoid reparations related to the 11 September 2001 terrorist attacks. The delisting of Sudan from the SSTL was a *sine qua non* for the opening of the country to foreign investment, international finance, IMF's HIPC initiative, and the expected restructuration or even cancellation of the $ 60 bn debt. During the following months, it became clear that the Sudanese Sovereign Council and Israel were organising a series of meetings abroad facilitated by the UAE, Egypt, and the USA. On 24 November, an Israeli delegation eventually landed in Khartoum for an official visit.

From the beginning of 2020, diplomats carefully underscored the complexity and long delays to be expected for a country like Sudan in being delisted from the SSTL. And though the normalisation of diplomatic relations between Khartoum and Tel Aviv appeared to be a reality in the short run, the announcements of Mike Pompeo, during a visit to Sudan in August, about the necessity for Khartoum to pay for the damages of the 1998 bombing, seemed to add new delays. The Sudanese government responded positively to the US demand to pay $ 335 m, once the US Congress had voted in favour of the sovereign immunity of Sudan. A few months earlier, in April, the case of the 'USS Cole' attacks had been closed, as agreement had been reached between the families of the victims and the Sudanese regime. *The US embassy in Khartoum officially announced the removal of Sudan from its SSTL on 14 December and accepted the nomination of the first Sudanese ambassador to the USA for 22 years, Dr Noureddine Satti.* On 27 December, President Trump signed a law re-establishing the sovereign immunity of Sudan and announced $ 931 m of US bilateral aid for Sudan.

The EU and European states adjudicated for the normalisation of Sudan at the diplomatic level. High-level European figures visited Sudan, like the head of European humanitarian affairs Janez Lenarčič in June and December. During his first visit, an € 11 m agreement was signed with the WHO to support Sudan against Covid-19, and he announced the official start of the humanitarian air bridge between Europe and Sudan (a project notably supported by Sweden and France). An additional € 80 m was announced later on. The EU pledged € 250 m in development assistance, and an additional € 100 m was announced in March on the occasion of the visit of the EU high representative Josep Borrell in order to support the political transition.

Ali Mohammad Ali Abd-Al-Rahman (commonly known as Ali Kushayb), subject to an ICC arrest warrant since 2007, was detained in neighbouring CAR and transferred to The Hague. Fatou Bensouda, the ICC prosecutor, visited Khartoum in October to discuss the case of former leaders detained in Sudan and also subject to an ICC arrest warrant for war crimes and crimes against humanity in Darfur, including the former president Omar al-Bashir. She declared in June in Khartoum: 'The ICC has outstanding arrest warrants against Omar Al Bashir, Ahmad Harun, Abdel Raheem Muhammad Hussein, and Abdallah Banda Abakaer Nourain. These suspects are still wanted for the atrocity crimes listed in their ICC warrants of arrest. They must all face justice without further delay. We look forward to continuing our dialogue with the Sudanese authorities to ensure we make progress on these cases with full respect for our respective roles and mandates and the principle of *complementarity*.' Earlier, al-Bashir had been tried and sentenced by Sudanese justice for embezzling public funds.

The UN Mission in Darfur (UNAMID) was not extended, following the demands of the Sudanese transitional institutions to stop the hybrid operation in the region and any mission involving foreign military troops under Chapter 7 of the UN Charter. A resolution adopted by the UNSC thus extended UNAMID for the last term on 3 June, until 31 December. The same day, another resolution was adopted, responding positively to Sudanese demands to initiate a new mission under Chapter 6, whose aim was to be the facilitation of the Sudanese transition. *The UN Integrated Transition Assistance Mission in Sudan (UNITAMS) was thus adopted as a civilian mission to start on 1 January 2021.*

At the regional level, *tensions continued about the filling of the Grand Ethiopian Renaissance Dam (GERD), a decade after Ethiopia started building (2011). Negotiations failed as Ethiopia continued to reject proposals for a multi-year drought mitigation scheme*, and no agreement was reached about the legal status of the text. Ethiopia announced in April that it would start the 'first stage filling' in July, with 18.4 bn cubic metres of the Nile over the next two years (the total capacity of the reservoir will be about 74 bn cubic metres). While Cairo condemned this initiative, arguing that it threatened its national security, Addis Ababa denounced Cairo's systematic 'obstructionist' positions. From 2011 to 2020, Khartoum's position on the GERD has been ambivalent due to the balanced consequences of the dam for the country: Sudan would lose its historical share of the Nile (along with Egypt) but would also benefit from the expected regulation of water, enabling better control of floods and new possibilities for irrigation projects within Sudan. It was also expecting to benefit from electricity imported from the Ethiopian dam in the short term. This geopolitical situation of Sudan, between Cairo and Addis Ababa, and the internal political and economic risks due to the ongoing transition, explained the continued attempts of Khartoum to avoid supporting either neighbour, aiming to impose itself as a mediator between Egypt and Ethiopia, but, sponsored by the US, it eventually supported the initiative at the beginning of the year.

In fact, *Washington got more involved in the GERD issue* in 2020, as the filling of the reservoir was supposed to begin in July, as announced by the Ethiopian authorities. The USA had been pushing diplomatically for an agreement to be signed before the filling of the dam, and it held two months of talks in Washington as a facilitator. *But the negotiations broke down again*: the Washington text was considered supportive of Cairo's position and was rejected by Abiy Ahmed's government in Addis Ababa. Cairo put significant diplomatic efforts into relations with external partners and the Ethiopian government in order to convince the latter to reconsider the draft agreement. Khartoum, on its side, rejected the propositions of both neighbours: a resolution of the Arab League sponsored by Cairo, and a resolution sponsored by Addis Ababa. The three countries agreed to meet on 21 June at ministerial level, as tensions rose between Egypt and Ethiopia, the former declaring a state of alert and the latter deploying anti-aircraft missiles in order to protect the dam. But again, talks remained in a deadlock.

The issue was brought to the UNSC by Egypt, followed by Ethiopia and Sudan. Sudanese prime minister Hamdok invited both countries to come back to the negotiation table, which happened in June, including new observers within the talks (each of the three countries inviting its own observer, Sudan the EU, Egypt the US Treasury Department, and Ethiopia South Africa). Along with Egypt, Sudan continued to underscore the necessity of signing an international agreement before starting the filling of the lake. But according to the International Crisis Group (ICG), no agreement was reached as Ethiopia's government did not bow under international pressure and continued to present the filling of the dam as part of the construction – a construction 'agreed' by downstream countries.

The Sudanese rhetoric on the GERD shifted progressively but radically during the year. The ministers of the transitional government and the prime minister made unprecedented and repeated official declarations that the GERD could affect negatively the hydroelectric production of the Sudanese Roseires dam and, most importantly, endanger 20 m people living downstream from the GERD. For the first time since 2011, the GERD officially became a national security issue for Sudan. This pragmatic approach against Addis Ababa was an important shift in the relations between Sudan and its neighbours. Since the late Ethiopian prime minister Meles Zenawi announced the building of the dam in 2011, the former regime of Omar al-Bashir had sided with the Ethiopians at the expense of Cairo.

The evolution of Khartoum on the GERD issue illustrates a rapprochement with Cairo, along the Cairo-KSA-UAE axis, and with the US. This was partly facilitated by the military branch of the transitional institutions, perceived by Cairo as solid partners and opponents to Islamist groups – Khartoum, for instance, facilitated the deportation of Egyptian opponents of the Muslim Brotherhood. The Egyptian president Abdel Fattah el-Sisi visited Khartoum on 15 August, while General Burhan and Hemedti visited Cairo several times. Declarations were issued about the GERD as a common national security issue, and common military manoeuvres were announced.

Furthermore, *bilateral tensions with Addis Ababa increased along the eastern Ethiopian–Sudanese border*, in the region of al-Fashaga particularly, where deadly clashes multiplied at the beginning of the year. These rich agricultural lands have been long time disputed territories, officially belonging to Sudan but claimed by Ethiopian Amhara nationalist groups. A military delegation led by General Burhan visited the region in April after several clashes occurred. The visit was followed by a visit to Khartoum by the Ethiopian chief of staff on 11 April. But clashes between Sudanese forces and local militias supported by Ethiopian forces continued to multiply in the region. Sudanese militaries were directly attacked in May (a Sudanese military detachment) and in June (the Sudanese Gallabat military camp). Troops were deployed along each side of the border, and General Burhan was invited for an official visit to Addis Ababa on 1 November. Three days later, in Tigray Region, Tigray People's Liberation Front troops attacked Ethiopian National Defense Forces and prime minister Abiy Ahmed launched a large-scale military campaign in the region, which evolved into a civil-war-like situation by the end of the year and provoked the exile of tens of thousands of Ethiopian refugees fleeing to Sudan – estimated at about 50,000 at the end of the year (UNHCR). The situation along the Ethiopian border with Sudan became extremely tense, even if large-scale combats did not occur between armed forces and diplomacy remained the priority – prime ministers Hamdok and Abiy met in Djibouti on 20 December to discuss IGAD's possible involvement in the crisis, but no concrete engagement for peace was undertaken.

The year 2020 thus marked the normalisation of Sudan and the redefinition of its foreign strategy. The long list of high-level diplomatic visits to Sudan illustrates this radical evolution: by heads of state (Egypt, Germany, Ethiopia); foreign affairs ministers (KSA, Qatar); the EU high representative, Commission vice-president, and head of humanitarian affairs; the International Committee of the Red Cross (ICRC) president; the US state secretary; and the ICC prosecutor. But diplomatic activities abroad also reflected the internal divisions between civilian and military actors, and the significant role played by the head of the Sovereign Council and its deputy – respectively General Burhan and Hemedti – in Sudan and abroad. In fact, while PM Hamdok visited Cairo, Addis Ababa, and Djibouti, General Burhan visited Cairo, Addis Ababa, Asmara, and the UAE, and initiated the historical rapprochement with Israel. Hemedti also visited Cairo, Addis Ababa, and the UAE to discuss key issues (counter-terrorism, GERD, economic cooperation etc.) with regional leaders and led the peace talks in Juba. His growing influence at the international level echoes the influence he has within Sudan – Hemedti was also vice-president of the Supreme Committee for Health Emergency and president of the Emergency Economic Committee.

Socioeconomic Developments

Despite Hemedti's promise to offer $ 300 m from his own account to the central bank, the IMF considered the economic prospects of Sudan 'alarming'. GDP fell (–7%), and inflation accelerated: by February, inflation had risen to 71%, by April it had almost reached 100%, and it progressively increased to reach 230% in October, according to the National Statistics Office. In April, the Sudanese Ministry of Finance raised the minimum wage from 425 Sudanese pounds (SDG) to 3,000 and announced an average 600% rise in public salaries.

The value of the SDG dramatically decreased. The central bank raised the official exchange rate with the US dollar from SDG 45 to 51 in February, but the gap with the black market rate skyrocketed, approaching SDG 300 for $1 by the end of the year. Following the announcement of the delisting of Sudan from the SSTL, the black market rate decreased to SDG 247 for $1. Zain, one of the main phone/internet providers, announced a 50% increase in its prices in December.

Discussions between the IMF and Sudan revolved around a programme that would eventually lead to international support, and the revaluation of Sudan's debt (about $ 60 bn) with the IMF, the World Bank, and the AfDB. Such initiatives remained conditioned by the delisting from the US SSTL (which occurred in December) and the end of some public subventions.

Debates remained very tense about Sudan's economic restructuration and the end of subventions (notably for fuel and electricity) advocated by the minister of finance and strongly opposed by the FFC coalition. A national economic conference organised by the government in September recommended the end of subventions and their replacement by direct support for the most vulnerable branches of society. This echoed EU, IMF (Staff-Monitored Program), and World Bank ($ 400 m to support the families affected by the economic reforms) initiatives in support of such restructuration of the economy.

Though no agreement was reached between these political forces, the prices of fuel and diesel suddenly increased in October: from SDG 28 to SDG 120 per litre of imported fuel and SDG 106 for imported diesel, SDG 6 for local fuel, and SDG 106 for local diesel. In November, the government again adjusted the prices, which stabilised at SDG 106 for imported fuel and SDG 99 for imported diesel.

To soften the combined effect of inflation and subsidy cuts, the government gradually established the Samarat Family Support Programme. The programme was based on a direct allowance of SDG 500 for every family member. After a year of pilot projects (targeting 900,000 families) the support programme was implemented with grants from the World Bank and EU of $ 200 m and $ 170 m respectively.

Another significant debate related to economic restructuration was initiated between Hamdok and Burhan, regarding the reform of the Defence Industries System. A huge industrial conglomerate had been built under the former regime, said to control no less than 80% of the national GDP. Hamdok made public declarations on the necessity of partly nationalising the industry still under the control of the military – those related to civilian industries especially – while General Burhan strongly defended the preservation of the current industries.

In May, the Emergency Economic Committee headed by Hemedti with his vice-chair, Hamdok, announced the liberalisation of the gold market and its adjustment on international market exchanges; a salary rise supported by money collected from trafficking (10%); and a reform of customs, including the end of previous exonerations by the former regime. The government took control of the Jebel Amer gold mines, which had been exploited by different militias over the preceding years.

UNICEF Sudan announced that more than 2 m children were suffering malnutrition in the country; 6.2 m people suffered extreme poverty, with the proportion of families unable to feed themselves on a daily basis estimated at 58% of the population, and the number of people in need of humanitarian assistance was estimated at 9.3 m by USAID. In 2020, Sudan was ranked 170th in the UNDP HDI (life expectancy at birth was 65.3 years; expected years of schooling 7.9; mean years of schooling 3.8; and gross national income per capita SDG 3,829).

This catastrophic socioeconomic situation was further aggravated by Covid-19. On 13 March, after the first case was detected in Sudan, the state immediately closed its border with Egypt and cancelled air flights with European and infected countries. Schools, kindergartens, and universities were also closed, while public meetings were forbidden. Later in March, the state of Khartoum decided to close markets, commercial zones, and restaurants, and a curfew was imposed from 8 pm to 6 am, then extended to 6 pm to 6 am. A lockdown was decided on 18 May and lasted until 16 August. By the end of December, official statistics announced 23,316 people infected, 1,468 dead, and 13,524 recovered. According to the government, state revenue decreased by 40% during the lockdown.

Sudan again faced devastating floods during the rainy season. Sixteen of the eighteen states were declared 'natural disaster areas'. Around 100 people died, according to the government. Sudan's High Committee for Rainy Season Emergencies confirmed that 770,000 were affected by the floods.

In terms of people's mobility, the UNHCR estimated the total number of *refugees and asylum seekers at about 1,106,000 at the end of 2020*, still mostly composed of 'South Sudanese' (773,000), followed by Eritreans (124,000), Syrians (93,000), Ethiopians (82,000), and CAR citizens (27,000). The civil war in north-east Ethiopia (Tigray, Amhara) since November explained the significant increase in Ethiopian refugees (14,000 in 2019). The country is ranked sixth among host countries worldwide. The total number of IDPs reached 2,552,000, according to UNHCR. This organisation also underlined that 8% of the Sudanese population in 2020 were refugees or displaced people. In December, General Burhan, announced the cancellation of Sudanese citizenship granted to 3,549 foreigners by the former regime. He also announced the end of visa exemptions for Syrians formerly considered 'brothers and sisters' by the al-Bashir regime.

The Central Bank of Sudan announced in January that the institution had begun substantial structural changes to bring itself in line with the international banking system. The crisis of hard currency was stabilised and reserves now cover two to three months of imports.

The 2020 Doing Business Index of the World Bank (assessing performance in 2019) was still ranking Sudan 171th, with a general score of 44.8. The country lost ground in the 'getting electricity' and 'resolving insolvency' categories. Sudan also received poor rankings in the categories 'starting a business', 'getting credit' and 'paying taxes'. This illustrates the economic difficulties faced by the country.

The state budget was planned to increase up to SDG 568 bn, with a deficit of SDG 73 bn. The defence allocation dropped from 9% to 7% despite the rise in the total amount allocated. The education and health ministries received substantial increases in their budget, up to 7% and 2% of the total budget respectively. The total amount allocated to defence, security, health, social housing, and education represented 34% of the planned budget, while subsidies took 36 % and 30 % was directly dedicated to the regional states.

The Sudan Anti-Corruption Committee (SACC) gained a major institutional role over the year. Pushed by public opinion and by the government, the SACC accelerated its work with the objective of fighting the system of corruption inherited from the previous regime. The committee set up branches in 15 of the 18 states. The SACC dissolved the administrative boards of 11 banks and dismissed nine heads of banks. Nine administrative boards and managers of semi-public corporations were dismissed for their links with the former regime. The SACC confiscated 390 private properties in Khartoum and froze dozens of bank accounts registered under the names of leading members of the previous regime. Several private hospitals and schools owned by ex-followers of Omar al-Bashir were also seized. These increasing efforts remained limited in their ambition, as the SACC had no power to prosecute members of the armed forces, militias affiliated to Hemedti, or armed groups.

Tanzania

Kurt Hirschler and Rolf Hofmeier

The government's unorthodox policy reactions to the global Covid-19 pandemic and the run-up to and conduct of national elections in October were the dominant themes in 2020. President John Magufuli flatly denied the utility of science-based medical protective measures against the virus and advocated prayers and traditional healing methods. No lockdowns of public life or economic activities were decreed, while the number of Covid-19-related cases remained unknown. Anyone voicing dissent from this approach was severely reprimanded. Magufuli's authoritarian leadership style continued unabated, but he was undoubtedly popular among substantial (particularly rural) population groups. Elections in October were held in accordance with constitutional requirements, but in a political atmosphere which did not allow a level playing field for opposition parties. Magufuli and his long-ruling CCM (Chama Cha Mapinduzi/Revolutionary Party) won with conspicuously high numbers of votes in comparison with previous elections. All opposition forces rejected the results as fraudulent, but with limited protests the government remained in undisputed control. In the absence of rigid anti-coronavirus restrictions, economic activities were largely undisrupted. The GDP growth rate nevertheless slumped markedly, although remaining positive (a rare exception in Africa). Ambitious goals of pushing large infrastructural projects were further pursued.

Domestic Politics

Initially, the government reacted with the usual *protective measures* to the global spread of *Covid-19*. Incoming travellers had their body temperature scanned at entry points, and the government appealed to the public to regularly wash their hands, to refrain from shaking hands, and to avoid unnecessary contact. *President John Pombe Magufuli* urged the media to educate the public about the virus. After a first Covid-19 case was reported on 16 March (a Tanzanian returning from Belgium), measures were intensified and schools and universities closed, sports events cancelled, and all forms of public gatherings suspended. A contact-tracing and testing system was put in place, and isolation centres were established. These mechanisms had been developed to react to a possible Ebola outbreak. A 14-day quarantine period for incoming travellers was also imposed, and in mid-April, all international passenger flights were suspended. The infection rate nevertheless increased, initially through returning travellers, but soon through local transmissions.

Magufuli, a PhD-holder in chemistry and a devout Catholic, simultaneously embarked on a *faith-based approach* towards the pandemic and recommended the use of *traditional herbal medicines* and steam inhalations. On 22 March, during a church service, he stated that the virus was 'satanic' and not able to 'survive in the body of Jesus'. He called upon the faithful to assemble in churches and mosques to pray. On 16 April, he called for three days of national prayers, urging people to trust in god and not in face masks. The popular reaction to these calls was mixed. Whereas many people in Tanzania's deeply religious society welcomed Magufuli's approach, others were sceptical and tried to privately implement different personal safety measures. Magufuli's Covid-19 strategy was severely criticised by the opposition parties. After the deaths of three MPs, Freeman Mbowe, chairperson of the major opposition party CHADEMA (Chama cha Demokrasia na Maendeleo/ Party for Democracy and Progress) called for the suspension of parliament for at least three weeks. He and other opposition members recommended lockdowns. Magufuli, however, rejected opposition calls to impose stricter measures and insisted that only hard work, fasting, and praying could stop the virus; no development activities or major projects were to be affected by the pandemic.

Tanzania's unique response to the pandemic obtained a further turn on 4 May, when Magufuli fired the director of the national health laboratory and the deputy health minister. He accused the laboratory of having returned *false positive test results from fake samples* (from a goat, a quail, and a papaya) which had been deliberately submitted to the lab. Magufuli accused unnamed foreign imperialist powers of sabotaging Tanzania's efforts to control the disease by either providing ineffective testing kits or bribing laboratory staff. Tanzania stopped collaborating with international health organisations and *stopped reporting case numbers*. From May onwards, the number of officially confirmed Covid-19 cases remained at 509, of recovered patients at 183, and of deaths at 21. Concurrently, Tanzania received a consignment of Madagascar's herbal Covid-Organics 'remedy', which was, however, used for research and not publicly distributed. Nevertheless, dozens of untested herbal Covid-19 'treatments' were produced and sold in the country. On 8 June, the president declared Tanzania *free of the coronavirus*, attributing this to the citizens' successful prayers and divine intervention. All preventative measures were stopped by the end of June.

The *international community* followed Magufuli's unique approach with concern. The WHO and the Africa Centres for Disease Control and Prevention (CDC) called upon the government to take the pandemic seriously, protect its population, and resume international cooperation. The governments of neighbouring countries, which had implemented strict measures to contain the disease, distanced themselves from Tanzania and closed the borders, while Western countries issued travel warnings but also offered and delivered support.

In pursuance of *restricting the circulation of information and controlling opinion* about the pandemic and the government's response, *repression of the media* and civil society was increased. Several media outlets were banned or fined and journalists suspended for reporting about the Covid-19 pandemic. Numerous individuals were arrested for disseminating information about the pandemic through social media. The Electronic and Postal Communications (Online Content) Regulations of July 2020 introduced – among other restrictive provisions – a *long list of prohibited content*, including information about the 'outbreak of a deadly or contagious disease' distributed without the approval of the authorities. Due to the government's restrictive information policy, the *real situation on the ground* became extremely difficult to assess. Not even hospital staff were allowed to speak about the situation. The blocking of any information gave room for widespread uncertainty. Rumours circulated about secret night burials of Covid-19 victims, overwhelmed hospitals, and patients with specific symptoms being turned away from hospitals. However, the truth of such rumours was difficult to verify. It nevertheless appeared that – like in other African countries – the pandemic had by and large *not caused a massive outbreak* with huge numbers of patients and deaths.

Presidential and parliamentary elections for the entire country (Union), separate presidential and parliamentary elections in the semi-autonomous archipelago of Zanzibar, and district and town council elections were scheduled for 28 October in accordance with the regular election cycle. Given the specific political circumstances, the pandemic remained a non-issue in the elections. Neither was it an issue during the campaigns, nor were any precautions to avoid spreading the virus taken during voter registration, campaigning, and voting.

As expected, the president and party chairperson *Magufuli was nominated unopposed* as *Union presidential candidate* and endorsed with a 100% approval rating at the CCM congress (11–12 July) in Dodoma. He re-selected vice-president Samia

Suluhu Hassan (the first woman in this position) as his running mate from Zanzibar. The congress did, however, have to select a new *candidate for the Zanzibar presidency*, since the incumbent Ali Mohamed Shein was constitutionally barred from contesting for a third term. The nomination process followed a well-established procedure, which ended with the choice of the long-serving defence minister *Hussein Ali Mwinyi* from among a list of 31 contestants, including several Zanzibari political heavyweights. Despite being the son of the popular former Zanzibar and Tanzania president Ali Hassan Mwinyi, his nomination was not unanimously well received in Zanzibar. Since he had spent most of his private and political life on the Mainland, he was perceived by sections of Zanzibar's CCM as Dodoma's choice rather than a genuine Zanzibari candidate. In late August, the local CCM organs nominated their *candidates for the parliamentary elections* in Zanzibar and on the Union level, as well as the candidates for the local and town councils. More than 10,000 CCM members had applied for nomination as parliamentary candidates for the 264 seats in the national assembly, almost 800 for the 50 seats in the Zanzibar house of representatives, and over 33,000 for the local councils. The party dropped some big names from the list, including several outgoing MPs and cabinet ministers.

On 3 August, *CHADEMA*, the main opposition party on the Mainland, nominated its former chief whip Tundu Lissu as its presidential candidate from among seven contestants. A popular figure, Lissu had barely survived an assassination attempt in 2017. He had then been taken to a hospital in Nairobi and later flown to Belgium for further rehabilitation. Lissu returned to Tanzania on 27 July 2020, three months before the polls, and was enthusiastically received at the airport by supporters. The CCM, however, characterised him as an agent of Western interests.

In early August, the *ACT-Wazalendo* (Alliance for Change and Transparency) national conference named Seif Sharif Hamad as its candidate for the Zanzibar presidency and former foreign minister (2007–15) Bernard Membe as its Union presidential candidate. It was Hamad's sixth attempt to win the Zanzibar presidency; the previous five nominations had been on the CUF (Civic United Front) ticket. Membe had sought nomination as CCM's presidential candidate in 2015, but was beaten by Magufuli. He had remained in the CCM as a rather backbench critic of Magufuli but was expelled in February, either for violating the party's ethics (according to the CCM) or to prevent him from challenging Magufuli's nomination as presidential candidate (according to Membe). In July, he finally returned his CCM membership card and joined the ACT-Wazalendo.

The *CUF* had been Zanzibar's main opposition party since the reintroduction of the multi-party system in 1992, representing about half of Zanzibari voters, with a stronghold in Pemba. This was mainly due to the popularity of its charismatic secretary-general Hamad, who had, however, defected to the ACT-Wazalendo in March 2019 after a leadership conflict with chairperson Ibrahim Lipumba. Lipumba had already run in four previous elections and was again nominated as CUF's Union presidential candidate on 27 July, together with the relatively unknown Haji Mussa Kombo as presidential candidate for Zanzibar. Neither the party nor its candidates were expected to gain significant support in the polls.

Despite the positive experience in 2015, when all major opposition parties had formed an anti-CCM alliance (UKAWA: Umoja wa Katiba ya Wananchi or Coalition for the People's Constitution) with joint candidates on all levels, *no formalised cooperation* was organised in the 2020 polls. However, CHADEMA and ACT-Wazalendo declared their readiness to cooperate. After numerous constituency opposition candidates were barred by the authorities, both parties sorted out ways to cooperate without conflicting with the restrictive laws. CHADEMA finally announced its support for ACT-Wazalendo's Hamad in the Zanzibar poll, whereas ACT-Wazalendo dropped its support for its own candidate Membe and supported Lissu in the Union presidential race.

The *electoral process* was conducted against the backdrop of an *extremely hostile political environment*. Since President Magufuli had assumed power after the highly competitive 2015 elections, the country had witnessed continuously increasing restrictions of civil rights and political freedoms, and a deterioration of the human rights situation. Magufuli's administration *severely limited the space for political party activities*, such as party meetings, information events, campaigns, and demonstrations. Political party activities had been banned since mid-June 2016 until the 2020 election campaign period started in August. In practice, however, the ban was applied only to the activities of opposition parties, whereas CCM was not affected. Politicians from the opposition, civil society actors, and journalists were constantly threatened, harassed, obstructed, (temporarily) arrested, abducted, and even killed. Amendments to several laws restricted the right to assembly, freedom of expression, and the right to information, and aimed at bringing political parties, civil society organisations, artists, societies, and companies under control of the government – which demanded the monopoly over most sectors in state, economy, and society. These restrictive laws posed a constant threat to opposition politicians, media workers, civil society actors, and even the broader population, and were frequently used to legitimise clamping down on any independent or dissenting opinion. With regard to the government's severe crackdown on critics in the political opposition, the press, and civil society, *Freedom House* characterised Tanzania as 'partly free', with a further reduced score of 34/100, compared with 40/100 in 2019 and 63/100 in 2015.

This hostile environment, against the experience of violence and fraud during several by-elections since 2016 and the November 2019 local elections (which were boycotted by the main opposition parties after the authorities banned over 90% of their candidates on dubious grounds), increased fears that the *general election would be neither free nor fair*. The opposition had for many years demanded the formation of independent *electoral commissions*, which the government rejected.

Opposition parties accused the commissions of having arbitrarily *disqualified* numerous of their council and parliamentary *candidates* on petty grounds, such as using abbreviations in registration forms. In some instances, opposition candidates were reportedly even attacked and robbed of their application documents while on the way to the local election office. Although appeals against the disqualifications were successful in some cases, 28 CCM parliamentary candidates and 873 councillors stood unopposed. In Zanzibar, opposition voters reported that they were denied the issuance of voter ID cards.

The *authorities systematically obstructed* efforts of the *opposition parties* to organise their activities and to mobilise their supporters, before and during the official campaigning period. Party activities were still banned until the campaigning period officially started on 26 August. The ongoing *harassment and intimidation of the opposition* continued throughout 2020 and increased towards the election date. On 10 March, a Dar es Salaam court sentenced CHADEMA chairperson Mbowe and eight other party leaders to five months in prison or to fines totalling 350 m Tanzanian shillings (Tsh; $ 152,000) on charges including sedition and unlawful assembly. The party immediately started a successful online-based fundraising campaign; however, the convicts were taken to jail, where they remained until the fine was paid. When Mbowe was released on 13 March, the police violently dispersed attendant CHADEMA supporters with tear-gas and wooden batons. Reportedly, some 25 CHADEMA members were arrested and later released on bail. The OHCHR strongly condemned the sentence against the eight leaders as 'further troubling evidence of the crackdown on dissent and the stifling of public freedoms in the country', and called upon the government to abide by its international obligations to respect human rights. On 12 June, ACT-Wazalendo party leader Zitto Kabwe was summoned by the police to explain his meeting with the British high commissioner. In late June, police arrested him and seven party members in Kilwa, where they had held an internal party meeting, for 'unlawful assembly'. The following day, they were released on bail. A few weeks earlier, a court had found Kabwe guilty of sedition and banned him from making 'seditious' statements for one year. Seven members of CHADEMA's youth wing were arrested on 7 July for allegedly ridiculing the national anthem and flag. They were only released in late November after 133 days in detention, whereby the police violated a court order of 26 August which had granted them bail. Numerous politicians from all major opposition parties were harassed, beaten, intimidated, or temporarily arrested; women political candidates were physically assaulted, verbally attacked, arrested, and harassed by security agents.

On 8 June, Mbowe was attacked and injured by unknown assailants on his way to his home in Dodoma. This attack was a reminder of the 2017 assassination attempt against then CHADEMA chief whip Lissu, also in Dodoma, which had never been thoroughly investigated.

Lissu's *electoral campaign was continuously obstructed* by the authorities, security forces, ruling party supporters, and unknown people. Lissu's campaign convoy was attacked by stone-throwing people on at least three occasions; the CHADEMA offices in Arusha and Mbeya were torched by unknown people. On 28 September, Lissu's motorcade was tear-gassed by police on the way to a rally in Tarime District. Heavily armed security forces blocked Lissu's convoy in Dar es Salaam for nine hours on 6 October on the way to a campaign rally in Morogoro. On 23 October, police dispersed his rally in a village near Kilwa with tear-gas. Several other candidates also had their campaigns temporarily suspended by the electoral commission.

In *Zanzibar*, tension was particularly high, and heavily armed security forces and military patrolled the streets and arrested and beat several people. ACT-Wazalendo's opposition presidential candidate for Zanzibar, Hamad, was briefly arrested at a polling station in Zanzibar on 27 October, during early voting for security forces and electoral commission officials.

Polling day itself was, by and large, peaceful. However, the atmosphere outside polling stations was generally tense, with some incidents of violence, intimidation, and threats, as well as widespread *allegations of irregularities*. Opposition parties complained that their polling agents were denied entry to about 75% of all polling stations. The internet, social media, and other communication platforms were widely disrupted. However, videos and photographs circulated on partially accessible social media, showing evidence of pre-filled ballots and pre-signed statements. Cases of repeat voting and ballot-box stuffing were also reported.

After *preliminary results from Zanzibar* were released on the morning of 29 October, Hamad, in a press conference, called on Zanzibaris to protest against what he called a sabotage of the elections. Immediately afterwards, *Hamad and 40 others were arrested*. Hamad was later released on bail. ACT-Wazalendo central committee member Ismael Jussa Ladhu was beaten by police and admitted to a hospital with broken limbs. *Protests against the conduct of the elections* also occurred on the Mainland. Post-election clashes between security organs and protesters in various parts of the country left several people injured, and hundreds of members and supporters of the two main opposition parties were arrested. Human rights organisations reported that over *20 people were killed by the security forces and hundreds injured* during the elections. However, none of the many incidences before, during, and after the elections was thoroughly and impartially investigated.

On 30 October, the NEC (National Electoral Commission) declared *Magufuli the winner* with 84% of the votes, against 13% for Lissu. This was the best result of any CCM presidential candidate since the reintroduction of the multi-party system in 1992. Five years earlier, Magufuli had only achieved an embarrassing 58% vote – the worst CCM presidential election result ever. The voter turnout was at 50.7%, the lowest in Tanzania's electoral history. According to the NEC, the CCM also secured a landslide victory in the *parliamentary elections*, winning 256 of 264 constituencies. CHADEMA won a single constituency (compared with 32 in 2015), CUF obtained three seats (one on the Mainland and two in Pemba), and ACT-Wazalendo got four seats in Pemba. On the Mainland, CCM won all but two seats. Based on the results of their respective presidential candidates, CCM was allocated an additional 95 'special seats' for women, and CHADEMA received a further 19 'special seats'. The *CCM also won overwhelmingly in Zanzibar*. Mwinyi was declared Zanzibar president with 76%, against Hamad's 20%.

A victory for Magufuli and the CCM had widely been expected. The scale of this victory, particularly in the parliamentary elections, was nevertheless *not plausible*. The officially announced results saw the CCM victorious in constituencies which had long been opposition strongholds, and where the opposition had nominated strong and popular candidates. The almost complete wipe-out of the opposition from parliament (and from the political space) raised fears about a *return to a de-facto one-party state*. It was also feared that the elimination of the opposition had laid the ground for possible attempts to alter the constitution to remove the term limit to allow Magufuli to extend his rule – something which he denied.

Both major opposition parties and many observers, including the international community, received the *official results with scepticism*. In a joint press conference on 31 October, ACT-Wazalendo and CHADEMA rejected the election results over what they termed irregularities, and called for peaceful country-wide demonstrations and a re-run of the elections. However, any protests were foiled by the presence of heavily armed police, the temporary arrests of several leaders, including Mbowe, Lissu, and Kabwe (later released on bail), and further disruptions of social media. Both opposition parties appealed to the international community not to accept the results and to press for a re-run of the elections. The *international community*, including the US embassy and State Department, the EU, the UK government, the Commonwealth secretary-general, and the OHCHR, expressed deep concern about the electoral conduct, the restrictions of social media, and the human rights violations, and demanded investigations into the allegations. China and several African states congratulated Magufuli on his victory.

Citing credible death threats, *Lissu sought refuge* in the German ambassador's residence, after he had been arrested by police (later released after an interrogation) outside the German embassy some hours before. After three days in the residence, he *left for Belgium* on 10 November for security reasons. Defeated Arusha MP Godbless Lema (CHADEMA) fled with his family to Kenya in early November, where he was temporarily arrested before he was granted asylum in Canada.

Magufuli was inaugurated on 5 November and on 13 November he reappointed prime minister Kassim Majaliwa, foreign relations minister Palamagamba Kabudi, and finance minister Philip Mpango. He completed his *cabinet* on 5 December, appointing 21 cabinet ministers and 23 deputies. The cabinet list included several new names, but no significant changes were made in key ministries.

Both major opposition parties declared that their elected MPs would not take up their parliamentary and council seats. CHADEMA was thereby thrown into *crisis*, when 19 female party members were surprisingly *sworn in as special seats MPs* on 24 November. The group was led by prominent former MP and CHADEMA women's wing chairperson Halima Mdee; it included several former MPs and female party heavyweights. The 19 declared that they had received the party's blessings for taking the oath – which the party leadership denied. After several crisis meetings, CHADEMA's central committee finally expelled the 19 women on 27 November for contravening the party's positions. However, the group appealed against the decision on 27 December.

Unlike Magufuli, the new Zanzibar president *Mwinyi introduced several changes in his cabinet*, including the creation of a new Ministry of Blue Economy and Fisheries. More importantly, he appointed completely new cabinet members, disregarding several political heavyweights from his predecessor's era. This raised some discontent within the Zanzibar CCM but symbolised the new spirit that Mwinyi had promised in his campaigns. He *invited ACT-Wazalendo* to join the constitutionally required Zanzibar *Government of National Unity* (GNU) and left the position of first vice-president (constitutionally reserved for the second-strongest party) and two cabinet posts vacant for ACT-Wazalendo nominees. After long internal discussions, the ACT-Wazalendo central committee finally agreed on 6 December to join the GNU and to allow its MPs and councillors to accept their mandates. The decision to participate in the GNU was driven by the pragmatic acknowledgement that security forces would suppress any attempt at popular protests, and that strong international pressure was very unlikely to happen. The previous boycott (2015–20), after the controversially annulled 2015 election and the boycotted 2016 re-run, had deprived the opposition of any possibility to influence the electoral conduct in their favour. Mwinyi immediately appointed *Hamad as first vice-president*.

New regulations had been decreed to *limit international media coverage* of Tanzania's elections. On 10 August, an amendment to the Electronic and Postal Communications Regulations was published which obliged the media to re-register and seek a separate licence if they wished to broadcast *content from foreign media* (such as the BBC) through local partner channels. The amendment further required foreign journalists to be *accompanied by a government official* when working in relation to broadcasting content. The amendment came after a private radio station had aired a BBC interview with Lissu. The regulatory body placed four BBC partner stations under three-month observation. After Tanzania had consistently dropped in Reporters Without Borders' *World Press Freedom Index* for years (54 ranks in seven years), the 2020 issue saw Tanzania's position unchanged, ranked 124th of 180 countries as in 2019.

Restrictions against CSOs were also further tightened, targeting mainly organisations perceived as critical of the government. New guidelines for the coordination of NGOs were aimed at further increasing government control over the CSO sector. On 23 June, the NEC stopped several CSOs from conducting election-related activities, such as voter education and training of lawyers to handle election petitions. The Registrar of NGOs threatened several organisations with deregistration if they failed to disclose details about their activities, funding sources, and financial records. Prominent NGOs were deregistered or threatened with deregistration and their bank accounts frozen by the regulatory authority.

Several high-profile *international election observers*, such as groups from the EU and the Commonwealth, were not invited by the government, unlike in previous elections. However, some international bodies (such as the AU and EAC) and private African institutions sent observers. On 5 June, the NEC published (without the legally required consultation with relevant stakeholders) regulations which *prohibited observers* from commenting on any aspect of the elections until the official announcement of results.

On 24 July, Tanzania's third president (1995–2005) *Benjamin William Mkapa died* aged 81. He had steered the country during a difficult transitory period from the socialist past to a liberal democracy and was well respected for taking on honorary public roles long after leaving office.

Foreign Affairs

Relations with the *EU*, Tanzania's biggest development partner, improved somewhat. In February, the EU released € 52 m in development aid as its first major funding since having withheld € 88 m in December 2018. The long-established relations had soured as a result of the deteriorating human rights situation. In mid-December, the EU announced a € 30 m grant to support the energy sector. *France* promised three concessional loans totalling € 230 m for electrification and water and sanitation programmes. *Sweden*, in contrast, adopted a changed five-year strategy in reaction to 'negative democratic developments in the country', which entailed reduced support and a focus on non-state actors in the fields of human rights, democracy, gender equality, environment, and climate. On 22 October and 2 November, the EU and several member states expressed their concern about the run-up to and conduct of the elections. The EU parliament's foreign affairs committee, on 19 November, discussed the deteriorating situation in the aftermath of the election as well as the EU's Covid-19-related aid assistance. It demanded an explanation for why the EU had provided € 27 m to fight the pandemic (and how the money was spent) despite Tanzania denying the existence of Covid-19 in the country and stopping cooperation with international health institutions.

The government's unique response to the pandemic also *negatively affected relations with neighbouring countries*. Since most EAC partner states had imposed strict preventative measures, Tanzania's refusal to cooperate provoked criticism.

On 12 May, Magufuli skipped a videoconference of the EAC presidents which was intended to develop a regional approach to contain the spread of the virus. The following day the *Kenyan government* declared the Namanga border a Covid-19 high-risk area after several Tanzanian truck drivers had been tested positive by Kenyan authorities. Truck drivers and traders had to line up at the border and wait for up to two weeks to get tested. About 150 Tanzanian truck drivers tested positive and were denied entry into Kenya. The Tanzanian authorities, however, declared that they had tested these drivers upon their return – with negative results. On 16 May, Kenya closed its borders with Tanzania except for vehicles carrying essential goods. An agreement to resolve the dispute over tests for truck drivers was handled by both presidents and agreed by the transport ministers on 22 May. The conflict escalated again on 1 August, when Kenya resumed commercial flights. Kenyan authorities listed all countries whose citizens were allowed to enter Kenya without a mandatory 14-day quarantine, excluding Tanzania from the list. As a result, Tanzania banned Kenya Airways (and subsequently three further Kenyan airlines) from entering the country.

To curb the spread of the virus by long-distance truck drivers coming from Tanzania, *Rwanda*, depending heavily on imports via the Dar es Salaam port, proposed in May that Rwandan drivers should take over the Tanzanian trucks at the border. However, Tanzanian truck owners refused to hand over their vehicles to Rwandan drivers, and more than 1,000 trucks destined for Rwanda got stuck at the border. On 16 May, the two governments abandoned the proposed swapping of drivers and agreed to offload and tranship the freight from Tanzanian to Rwandan trucks, except for perishable goods and petroleum products. In addition, drivers had to undergo mandatory testing in Tanzania. A smooth trade flow was again impeded when both countries refused to accept each other's testing certificates and insisted on carrying out their own tests – with the results taking between four and seven days. In mid-September, the two governments eventually agreed to settle the issue.

Burundi and Tanzania discussed the construction of a joint nickel-processing plant during the new Burundian president Évariste Ndayishimiye's first visit on 19 September. This working visit was aimed at strengthening investment and trade relations. Ndayishimiye called upon the nearly 200,000 *Burundian refugees* in Tanzania to return home. International human rights organisations accused the Tanzanian authorities of being responsible for severe human rights violations against Burundian refugees.

On 17 August, Tanzania routinely handed over the rotating SADC chair to Mozambique. Tanzania had held the chair for one year, but with very little impact on the bloc's activities. Having unsuccessfully requested that SADC chairperson Magufuli hold an emergency SADC summit meeting on Covid-19, South Africa's president Cyril Ramaphosa convened a virtual meeting with South Africa's neighbour states.

About 300 Islamist fighters from *Mozambique* attacked a border village in southern Tanzania on 14 October, killing at least 20 people and forcing scores of people to abandon their homes. Some of the attackers were arrested by Tanzanian police. In late November, police chief Simon Sirro stated that the police had detained several Tanzanians who had attempted to join the insurgency in Northern Mozambique; allegedly, some local people had been involved in the October attack on the Tanzanian village. On 22 November, Sirro and his Mozambican counterpart signed an MoU regarding joint efforts in the battle against the Jihadist insurgents, providing for joint operations across the border.

Malawi's new president Lazarus Chakwera met Magufuli on his first state visit (8–9 October) to intensify bilateral relations and discuss joint infrastructure and development projects. The unresolved boundary dispute on Lake Nyasa was, however, not discussed.

A new US ambassador in April ended a three-year period without an accredited US ambassador. Nevertheless, relations with the *USA*, Tanzania's largest bilateral donor, remained difficult due to the deterioration of human rights and democratic principles, as well as Tanzania's handling of the Covid-19 pandemic. On 31 January, the USA barred the controversial Dar es Salaam regional commissioner Paul Makonda from entry for involvement in the oppression of the political opposition, crackdowns on freedom of expression and association, and gross violations of human rights. In 2018, Makonda, a close Magufuli ally, had launched an anti-gay surveillance force. However, the frosty relations had no impact on the US aid programmes in Tanzania.

China continued to be Tanzania's biggest trading partner and largest source of FDI. The two countries celebrated the 55th anniversary of the signing of the China–Tanzania friendship treaty. In a meeting with the Chinese ambassador, foreign minister Palamagamba Kabudi underscored the 'need for other countries to respect each other and refrain from encroaching on internal freedom under the pretext of human rights, democracy or anything else'.

Socioeconomic Developments

In July, the World Bank upgraded Tanzania to *lower-middle-income status*, since its gross national income per capita had increased to $ 1,080 in 2019 and thus exceeded the threshold of $ 1,036 for this category. The government celebrated the upgrade as a confirmation of its policies, emphasising that this had been achieved five years earlier than projected in the Tanzania Development Vision 2025 (TDV 2025). The World Bank attributed the success to continuous GDP growth and macroeconomic stability, but also underscored the fragility of the newly achieved status. It also reminded the Tanzanian government that the TDV 2025 development goals were much broader, and that despite passing the threshold, only a small portion had been achieved, while substantial investments in human development and physical capital were necessary to consolidate the newly attained status. This status did not, however, reflect the widespread endemic poverty or the economic uncertainties caused by the pandemic. Additionally, doubts existed about the reliability of the official economic data provided by the government, including the GDP growth rate. In the 2020 Human Development Report, Tanzania ranked 163rd out of 189, in the 'low human development' category, with a HDI score of 0.529, with only very little improvement over the past years.

Despite Magufuli's anti-Western rhetoric and his denial of the pandemic, Tanzania received considerable *support from Western donor countries to cope with the effects of Covid-19*. Several donors, such as Ireland, the Netherlands, and others, disbursed additional financial assistance, and in September the EU granted € 27 m in support. On 22 April, Magufuli thanked the World Bank for making loans available to help the country cope with Covid-19, but suggested that the Bank should instead cancel the debts of developing countries. In June and October, the IMF approved debt relief of $ 26 m under the Catastrophe Containment and Relief Trust. In addition, Tanzania received support through participation in the Debt Service Suspension Initiative. In October, the AfDB approved a $ 50.7 m loan to finance the nation's response to the Covid-19 pandemic. Tanzania pledged to use contingency reserves to *fund additional health spending* and to *expand its social security schemes* to mitigate the impact of the pandemic.

The negative effects of Covid-19 on *macroeconomic performance* were comparatively modest. Unlike in many other countries, an economic recession was avoided. However, the *gdp growth rate* declined from 5.8% (2019) to an estimated 2.0%, and GDP per capita contracted for the first time since 1994. This was due to the global economic slowdown, decreased demand for Tanzanian exports, reduced investments, and a slump in tourism receipts, but also to reduced domestic economic activities. Companies and consumers adopted precautionary behaviour, although the government refrained from imposing strict measures. The number of Tanzanians living below the *poverty line* increased as the pandemic caused weaknesses in sectors with high employment figures, notably agriculture and manufacturing. The World Bank estimated that the pandemic could push an additional 600,000 people below the national poverty line ($ 1.35 per person per day in PPP terms), increasing the previously modestly declining poverty rate from 26.1% (2019) to an estimated 27.2%. According to a World Bank survey, about 140,000 formal jobs were lost in June, and another 2.2 m non-farm informal workers suffered income losses. The government introduced only limited measures to support the private sector's efforts to cope with the economic impact of the pandemic, and most affected firms could not benefit. Growth was driven mainly by huge public investments in major infrastructure projects. Private sector activities declined, suffering from the impact of the pandemic and the government's unfriendly and unpredictable policies towards the sector. Tanzania ranked 141st out of 190 in the World Bank's 2020 Doing Business Report (ranking benchmarked to May 2019), a slight improvement against the 2019 ranking (144th/190). TI's 2020 Corruption Perceptions Index ranked Tanzania 94th of 179 countries (score 38), hardly improved compared with the 2019 ranking (96th) and score (37).

Inflation averaged at 3.2% for the year (3.7% in 2019) and remained well below the official 5% target. The *current account deficit* slightly narrowed to 1.6% of GDP in December, from 1.9% in December 2019. The mainly Covid-19-related decline of imports outpaced the decline in exports. Increased earnings from gold exports partly offset reduced traditional exports. The deficit was primarily funded by external (mostly concessional) borrowing, with the total external debt stock increasing from $ 22.4 bn (December 2019) to $ 24.0 bn in December 2020. However, the joint IMF – World Bank Debt Sustainability Analysis (updated in April) indicated that Tanzania's *risk of debt distress was low*, implying that the debt level was quite sustainable.

Finance minister Mpango submitted the *2020/21 budget* to parliament on 12 June, stressing the government's focus on infrastructure development, enhanced accessibility of social services (health, education, water, and sanitation), and the development of industries by utilising local agricultural and mineral resources.

Total *expenditure* was budgeted at TSh 34,879.8 bn (about $ 15.2 bn), an increase of 5.3% over the previous year, taking into account increased expenditure for Covid-19 interventions, repayment of government debt (up to 30% of the budget from 18.7%), and requirements for the elections, which were completely funded from domestic resources. As in the previous fiscal year, 37% of the budget was earmarked for development expenditure. In 2019/20, only about 75% (6.4% of GDP) of the budgeted development expenditure was realised; the implementation shortcomings of development projects were primarily due to an under-execution of the locally funded components. Development spending slowed in the first half of 2020/21, partly due to Covid-19-related shortfalls in domestic revenue and external financing.

The *revenue forecast* encompassed tax and non-tax revenue projections (66.7%), domestic and external non-concessional borrowing (22.8%), and external grants and concessional loans (8.2%), consistent with the previous fiscal year. According to the Bank of Tanzania, the government's budget was hardly affected by the pandemic. *Revenue collection* remained within the set target and was projected to increase to 15.3% of GDP (14.3% in 2019/20). The World Bank estimated that the *fiscal deficit* had in 2019/20 narrowed to 1.4% of GDP, due to increased revenue collection and lower expenditure, particularly in development spending. However, the pandemic entailed a reduction in domestic revenue in 2020, and the fiscal deficit was expected to widen to 2.6% of GDP in 2020/21.

Tourism, for years Tanzania's leading foreign exchange earner and Zanzibar's main economic sector, was severely hit by the pandemic, and the 2020 peak season was largely lost. Earnings from tourism decreased by almost 60% compared with 2019. After an initial suspension of incoming flights, the government reopened its airspace in mid-May, attempting to attract tourists, albeit with very limited success. The government nevertheless tried to find new markets and also promoted domestic tourism. Growing numbers of tourists from Russia, China, and the Middle East helped to reduce the losses.

Tanzania benefited from increased *gold exports*, which replaced tourism as the major foreign exchange earner. Gold export earnings increased by 33.5% in 2020, due to higher global gold prices and resumed mineral exports. On 24 January, the government signed an agreement with the major gold producer Barrick Gold to settle their long-standing dispute. Exports of the stockpiled containers of concentrate resumed in April, and in late May Barrick paid the first tranche ($ 100 m) of the agreed $ 330 m to settle a long-delayed tax dispute.

On 31 March, the World Bank approved a *controversial $ 500 m education sector loan*. It was one of several loans which had been withheld since November 2018 in reaction to Tanzania's policy of banning pregnant students from public schools and to a restrictive Statistics Act. According to the World Bank, the terms of the loan now gave pregnant schoolgirls a chance to complete their schooling through 'alternative public education programs'. Civil society actors, however, criticised the Bank's decision and demanded an end to the discrimination against pregnant schoolgirls and teen mothers. CCM leaders publicly called for the elimination of ACT-Wazalendo leader Kabwe, after he called upon the World Bank to withhold the loan over human rights concerns.

An agreement to commence construction of the Uganda–Tanzania *East African Crude Oil Pipeline* at an estimated cost of $ 3.5 bn was signed by the presidents of the two countries on 13 September. On 27 October, Tanzania and the French oil company Total followed up by signing a Host Government Agreement. The envisaged 1,445-kilometre oil pipeline was criticised by conservation groups, who feared that the project threatened valuable livelihoods and fragile ecosystems.

Tanzania was spared from the locust plague which devastated large parts of East Africa.

Uganda

Moses Khisa

Two major developments dominated public discourse in Uganda in 2020, one domestic – elections – and the other global – the pandemic. Domestically, campaigns for general elections and globally, the Covid-19 pandemic defined and disrupted socioeconomic and political engagements. During the election campaign season, Uganda's political status quo came under heavy strain and a strong spotlight. The combination of a general election campaign season and a novel pandemic created a tense and turbulent environment for a country facing grave political uncertainty and enormous socioeconomic difficulties, ranging from runaway youth unemployment to population pressures on the environment and limited national resources. In preparation for general elections, where incumbent president Yoweri Museveni faced renewed challenge to his stay at the helm, and in seeking to tackle the Covid-19 pandemic through enforcing standards and protocols, Uganda's police and security agencies engaged in gross human rights abuses and excesses that included deadly shootings. Economically, the pandemic compounded the already difficult living conditions for the majority of Ugandans as the government instituted a national lockdown at the end of March 2020. While the country's overall macroeconomic outlook remained promising, several economic variables, including worsening public debt and sluggish progress in the emerging oil and gas sector, among others, were a great cause for worry. In regional geopolitics and security, the country continued to play a leading role in Somalia under the African Union Mission (AMISOM) and in other unspecified military adventures in Equatorial Guinea, CAR, and South Sudan. Ongoing frosty relations with Rwanda remained a top security sore following the latter's unilateral closure of the two countries' main border post.

Domestic Politics

In December 2017, *Uganda's parliament* removed the age limit provision from the national constitution in highly controversial circumstances, including violent and chaotic scenes on the floor of the legislature. After an unsuccessful challenge in court by opposition leaders and civic activists, incumbent president Yoweri Museveni got the green light to stand for another term in the 2020–21 election cycle. On 18 April 2019, Uganda's highest court, the supreme court, upheld the constitutional court's ruling in favour of the December 2017 parliamentary vote that removed the age limit for presidential candidates. Museveni's move to run for president again cemented his position as Africa's third-longest-surviving president, just behind Equatorial Guinea's Teodoro Obiang and Cameroon's Paul Biya in first and second positions, respectively.

The *ruling National Resistance Movement (NRM) party* conducted its primary elections for parliamentary and local government candidates in September and took a controversial decision to ditch secret-ballot voting for lining up behind contestants or their agents. As previous cycles had been, the 2020 NRM primaries were chaotic, highly contested, and violent. On his part, Museveni was on course to be 're-elected' in yet another controversial election scheduled for 14 January 2021. This meant that he was firmly on course to have ruled this East African nation of more than 40 m people for a staggering 40 years uninterrupted by the end of his expected next term in 2026. Museveni has already ruled Uganda for more than half of the country's 58 years of independence from Great Britain, a period longer than the combined time of the seven previous governments between 1962 and 1986.

The political contestations over Museveni's long rule and the struggles for succession in a country that has never had a peaceful transfer of power intensified during the 2020–21 election cycle, compounded by the uncertainties and anxieties of the Covid-19 pandemic. In addition to the pandemic environment, which entailed an initial lockdown in the second quarter of 2020 and severe restrictions on public activities throughout the second half of the year, there were other features of the political landscape and social terrain that made this round of electioneering stand out in quite significant ways from previous electoral cycles. First, Museveni faced a deepening crisis of legitimacy after 35 years at the helm, presiding over a decayed and corrupt system of government unable to convincingly tackle the country's endemic socioeconomic problems.

Second, a youth bulge and acceleration in the share of young people, the majority of whom are unemployed yet who are exposed to modern tastes and aspirations through social media, constituted a stupendous demographic nightmare for an incumbent who had previously harked back to Uganda's chequered political history as a justification for his rule. Increasingly, this argument about how bad Uganda's past was no longer appeals to young Ugandans, born after Museveni came to power in 1986.

Third, and related to the second factor, the *force of youth* served as fuel for a youthful challenger to Museveni – the pop star musician cum member of parliament since 2017 *Robert Kyagulanyi Ssentamu, also known as Bobi Wine*, who took Uganda's political scene by storm, emerging as the popular (and populist) candidate around whom the disparate forces seeking to unseat Museveni coalesced. Throughout 2020, local and international news headlines and opinion commentaries on Ugandan politics focused – inordinately – on Bobi Wine, producing a fourth major feature of the election season: an unprecedented level of reporting and commentary on Uganda in the Western media (and academia). The 2020 Uganda election season attracted a great deal of Western media and diplomatic attention, comparable with that devoted to only a few other African elections.

The general election campaign season as a whole was largely characterised by numerous and repeated arrests of the two main opposition presidential candidates, Bobi Wine, contesting under the newly launched National Unity Platform (NUP), and Patrick Amuriat Oboi of the then main opposition party, the Forum for Democratic Change (FDC). In a surprise announcement in August 2020, Dr Kizza Besigye, the former leader of the FDC, bowed out of contesting against Museveni again in what would have been his fifth consecutive challenge, in a race where the odds are always stacked against the opposition. In October, the FDC endorsed its president, Patrick Amuriat Oboi, to run on the party's ticket. Besigye's move of snubbing the election effectively handed the mantle of challenging Museveni to 38-year-old Bobi Wine as the candidate to rally behind for those urgently seeking to topple Museveni. While Oboi stayed in the race along with his predecessor in the FDC, Mugisha Muntu, now leading a new party, the Alliance for National Transformation (ANT), and seven other candidates (11 in total), the race was squarely between Bobi Wine and Museveni.

In the final weeks of the campaign season in late 2020, violent confrontations between opposition supporters, particularly followers of Bobi Wine, and security personnel became commonplace and fatal. For example, two days of protests and riots in November, following the arrest and detention of Bobi Wine on the campaign trail in the Eastern Uganda district of Mayuge, claimed the lives of more than 50 Ugandans according to official reports, but the opposition claimed a higher figure.

Among the dead were innocent bystanders caught by indiscriminate and unprofessional use of live ammunition by the police and military personnel. Hundreds of opposition supporters were arrested and detained indefinitely.

As the *political situation became hot, hostile, and volatile going into the 2021 polls, on 16 December 2020*, President Museveni brought back his son, Lieutenant General Muhoozi Kainerugaba, to command the Special Forces Command (SFC), widely considered the most powerful department of Uganda's military apparatus. The SFC had been commanded by General Muhoozi previously, but he was dropped from the position in 2017. Along with the first son's redeployment were other critical appointments. These included putting Major General Kayanja Muhanga, former commander of Ugandan forces in Somalia and South Sudan, in charge of security in Kampala, and Major General Paul Lokech, another veteran of the Somalia conflict who was recalled from special assignment in South Sudan, was appointed as deputy head of the Uganda Police Force, replacing Major General Sabiiti Muzeyi. President Museveni also reappointed Martins Okoth as the inspector-general of police. These appointments further strengthened the militarisation of law and order in Uganda and the pre-eminence of the military in otherwise civilian processes.

At the end of 2020, election campaigns drew to a close amid heightened uncertainty and anxiety and increased human rights violations at the behest of the armed forces. Abuses of and assaults on civilians by the military and the police, including fatal shootings, were officially justified as a result of the enforcement of Covid-19 standards and protocols, albeit they were selectively applied against opposition supporters and not those of the incumbent president and his NRM. As the initial extreme restrictions wore out and the pandemic took a toll on the public imagination, Uganda soon entered the election campaign season, starting with party primaries ahead of general elections slated for January 2021.

At the beginning of the campaign season in late summer 2020, the country's Covid-19 status was generally less worrying. Positive cases remained low and there were no officially confirmed deaths. Rather than fighting the virus as the security threat that Museveni had initially conceived it, which would have meant limiting or even postponing campaigns, primary elections went on uninterrupted but produced violent confrontations and controversies, as has happened in past election cycles, especially in the ruling NRM, as noted above. At this point, the Covid threat took a back seat for a while. As the season moved towards campaigning for the general elections, the incumbent seized on the pandemic as a weapon and an excuse for repressing his opponents using the military and police forces. It became more about protecting Museveni than fighting the virus. Brutality against journalists attracted attention as scenes of physical assault were captured and shared on social media platforms. Museveni appeared on the back foot as the excesses of his security forces generated condemnation both at home and abroad. Bobi Wine and other opposition leaders, along with their allies and supporters, were successful in mobilising Western media attention on Uganda as well as diplomatic pressure, with the US Congress and Senate taking keen interest in political developments in Uganda.

However, even with the youth momentum whipped up by the candidature of Bobi Wine, and the waning legitimacy and fading appeal of Museveni, without any meaningful political reforms or a major exogenous shock that would drastically alter the political landscape, it was unquestionable that Museveni remained fully in charge and was unlikely to be unseated in the January 2021 polls. In all, Uganda's civil and political landscape deteriorated further in 2020. For the year 2019, *Freedom House* had downgraded Uganda from 'partly free' in 2018 to 'not free' in 2019. Given the events of 2020, the ranking for the country's freedom standing could only get worse. Bureaucratic and political corruption remained a major problem for the country. *Transparency International's Corruption Perceptions Index* had previously ranked Uganda 137th out of 180 countries, and the ranking fell further to 142nd in 2020. Early on in the pandemic, on 9 April 2020, top officials of the Office of the Prime Minister were arrested on allegations of inflating prices for Covid-19 relief food and accused of causing losses to the government of over half a million dollars.

Foreign Affairs

Given the continuing volatile and violent security situation in the *wider Great Lakes region of East and Central Africa as well as the Horn of Africa*, Uganda remained a critical actor in the region's geopolitics. In 2020, President Museveni maintained his status as an indispensable Western ally, a proven reliable pointsman in navigating the region's security complexities, and a master at tackling regional terrorism threats. However, the events of the 2020 election campaign put Museveni on the spot, as various media and human rights activists ramped up campaigns aimed at diplomatically alienating him from his Western allies and benefactors. Yet except for the usual statements 'expressing concern' and 'urging the government to respect the rights and freedoms of citizens', neither the US nor the EU rocked Museveni's diplomatic boat in any substantial manner. In March 2020, Uganda hosted the first ever *Europe–Uganda business forum* and signed three grant financing agreements with the EU worth $ 97.5 m, aimed at improving the standards of Ugandan products so as to increase and sustain exports to the EU market. The growing and predominant role of China in Uganda's economy continued in 2020, which complicates relations with the West. As with other African countries, China is Uganda's top trading partner.

Uganda's regional economic and security engagements in 2020 remained exclusively under the grip of Museveni. If he has personalised internal domestic political and economic processes, this is even more the case in foreign policy matters and external relations – bilateral and multilateral, formal or informal – where he operates with almost no oversight or check from parliament.

A key highlight of Uganda's foreign affairs was the relations with its southern neighbour, *Rwanda*. Relations between the two countries had warmed up since the deadly clashes during the second Congo war, 1999–2003, only to deteriorate rapidly in 2018, culminating in Rwanda's unilateral closure of the two countries' most important commercial border post at Katuna in March 2019. Mediation efforts by Angolan president João Lourenço and the DRC's Félix Tshisekedi led to a quadripartite summit in Luanda on 2 February 2020 and a follow-up summit at the closed Katuna border post on 21 February. At the conclusion of the Luanda summit, presidents Paul Kagame and Yoweri Museveni agreed to free prisoners, especially those detained in Uganda on various allegations, and that the two governments would refrain from aiding dissident activities in either country. Each side has accused the other of aiding rebel activities and destabilising forces against each other. Rwanda accuses the Ugandan authorities of allowing Rwanda dissidents to operate on Ugandan soil while Uganda accuses Rwanda of infiltrating its security and intelligence agencies and engaging in espionage activities.

In addition to the mediation efforts of the presidents of Angola and the DRC, other initiatives to repair the strained relations between Rwanda and Uganda included a flurry of shuttle diplomatic activities, notably by Uganda's permanent representative to the UN, Ambassador Adonia Ayebare, who formerly served as Uganda's chief diplomat in Kigali. Despite these interventions and efforts, relations between these two otherwise natural allies remained sour and hostile throughout 2020.

The actual root of the hostile relations between Rwanda and Uganda remains somewhat puzzling, and there are often contradictory postures in the overarching foreign policy orientations of the governments of the two countries. A constant set of allegations touch on espionage, intelligence, and counter-intelligence infiltrations on the part of both governments, whose leaderships share a historic bond and some familial ties. It is worth noting that the military and political elites in charge in Kigali and Kampala have not only intimate intra- and interethnic relations but also a shared history and ideological provenance in the guerrilla fighting that saw victory in Uganda in January 1986 prepare the ground and inspiration for a Rwandan campaign, launched from Uganda four years later in October 1990, and eventual victory in July 1994 in the shadow of genocide. This shared history and close social connection should make for harmonious, not hostile, relations.

As diplomatic relations with Rwanda dipped and cross-border trade flows declined, the Ugandan government sought to shore up alternative commercial ties with other neighbouring states, particularly with the DRC. In office since January 2019, DRC president Félix Tshisekedi visited Uganda in late 2019, after which the two countries started discussions on improving the road infrastructure in eastern DRC to improve commerce between the two countries. Consequently, in September 2020, Uganda's cabinet approved proposals for works on a string of roads connecting Uganda's border with the eastern DRC towns of Beni, Butembo, and Goma. Some of these planned works went into Uganda's 2021 budgetary proposals. Uganda's push for closer economic connections with the DRC is linked to the latter's move to join the EAC customs union and future political federation, a project for which Museveni has been the most aggressive advocate and promoter. In continuing to push for the expansion of regional economic partnerships, in September 2020, Uganda and Tanzania signed a $ 3.5 bn agreement for a crude oil pipeline to facilitate movement of Uganda's (yet to be pumped) oil from the Albertine Graben in the country's Western Region to the coast of East Africa.

South Sudan remained of strategic significance to Uganda as a market, but the security situation in the former continued to pose tremendous concerns for the Ugandan business community and the Museveni government. Over the years, Ugandans travelling between northern Uganda and the South Sudanese capital of Juba have suffered armed attacks, particularly road ambushes, from unknown violent actors. In a related twist to the security situation, in June and October 2020, Ugandan and South Sudanese soldiers clashed at two separate border locations in the South Sudanese states of Central and Eastern Equatoria. There were deaths in both incidents, four South Sudanese in the first and two on either side in the second. The actual cause of the clashes was not very clear, but there were allegations by each side of the other's soldiers straying past the international border. The security landscape in South Sudan remains characterised by the proliferation of armed groups and violent activities that greatly hamper commerce with neighbouring Uganda.

Socioeconomic Developments

The first officially registered positive case of Covid-19 in Uganda was on 21 March – an individual who travelled from Dubai. The number of positive cases rose rapidly in the weeks following this, but the total case count remained very small compared with global trends. At Entebbe International Airport, the initial response was to screen arriving passengers using a simple temperature check. Also, some basic travel information was collected. However, the health team at the airport soon became overwhelmed and the Ministry of Health deployed additional personnel. The president brought on board the military, including the military's medical personnel.

Testing and isolation were part of the early attempts to confront the virus. Passengers arriving at Entebbe airport were subject to mandatory quarantine, but because of lapses and alleged bribery, there was suspicion that some people were able to get through without quarantining. It appears that the very first possible cases of Covid-19 likely slipped through undetected. Following the first officially registered positive test, the government attempted to contact-trace and detect individuals who had travelled from the same country and all those who had been in contact with such persons, but this was difficult in a country with porous borders, poor record-keeping, and limited logistical resources compounded by institutional inefficiencies, including corruption.

From March through to June, testing capacity was limited to a few thousand samples per day. For weeks, most of the daily testing reports returned no positive cases. This was to change starting in June 2020 as cases emerged from government institutional quarantine centres and among truck drivers crossing the border, especially from Kenya and Tanzania. However, even as the virus spread, the number of *officially registered cases* in Uganda remained quite low, reaching only 100 cases on 6 May, a month and a half after the first positive case was reported.

From the outset, President Museveni and his government treated the *pandemic as a security matter* in which the military and security agencies had to play critical and central roles. Museveni defined the pandemic as a war, thus making a discursive construction of Covid-19 as a security operation that necessitated a supplementary budget, complete with classified expenditure. On 29 March 2020, the government tabled before parliament a 284 bn Ugandan shilling (UGX) supplementary budget, approximately $76 m, of which the Ministry of Health was allocated UGX 82 bn and security UGX 81 bn (29% and 28%, respectively). In the end, parliament approved UGX 104 bn ($28 m) for health and UGX 77 bn ($20 m) for security.

Museveni's approach to the Covid-19 pandemic as a security problem was in line with his overall understanding of his government's remit as primarily one of ensuring security. The military played a range of roles, but most important of all was enforcing Standard Operating Procedures (SOPs) and implementing restrictions on public gatherings imposed by the government.

By July, the government lifted the more *restrictive lockdown regime* and instead shifted to curfew enforcement, which initially ran from dusk to dawn, then extended to 9 pm until 6 am. The curfew was still in place at the end of the reviewing period. As with the lockdown, the task of implementing curfew hours fell on the police and the military, with Local Defence Unit (LDU) soldiers the primary source of personnel charged with enforcement. They erected roadblocks on major roads leading to and from the capital, Kampala, and along highways across the country. This was a huge law enforcement undertaking, which the police could not manage on its own. In addition to conducting arrests at roadblocks, the police and military carried out operations to arrest people engaged in social activities that ostensibly violated SOPs and the different decreed restrictions, such as home parties and other forms of social gatherings. These operations constituted blatant violations of personal freedoms and the right to privacy in the name of enforcing presidential directives to restrict movement and activities that were ostensibly contributing to spread of the virus. A blanket ban on public transportation created difficulties for people who needed urgent healthcare, such as expectant mothers and individuals with underlying health conditions like HIV, as any movement had to have the explicit permission of a presidential representative, the Resident District Commission. In part because of a securitised approach to the pandemic in line with presidential directives, the enforcement mechanisms endangered people's lives in some situations to a greater extent than the danger posed by the virus.

The extent of the impact of the Covid-19 pandemic on Uganda's overall macroeconomic standing is a little unclear but, like other economies, Uganda's suffered substantial contraction as a national lockdown went into effect at the end of March 2020. According to the World Bank, *real GDP was estimated to have contracted by 1.1% and real GDP per capita by 4.5% in 2020*, portending ill for the country's poverty levels. The tourism and manufacturing sectors were among the most hurt. With the pandemic causing all sorts of disruption, GDP growth, initially projected at more than 6%, performed at a modest 3%, less than half of the projection. Government revenue underperformed in all areas except stamp duty, and the fiscal deficit grew by more than 30%. Heavy reliance on agriculture, accounting for 25% of GDP and 70% of employment, means Uganda's economy is vulnerable and volatile.

According to the Bank of Uganda's mid-fiscal-year report for July 2020 – January 2021, Uganda's 'current account deficit deteriorated by $ 1,276.0 m to $ 3,430.1 m largely due to the widening of the services account deficit by $ 1561.6 m as activities in the tourism sector were affected by social distancing restrictions imposed to contain the spread of the Covid-19 pandemic'. This deterioration was expected to continue as the pandemic continued to dictate the course and pace of economic activity. By contrast, the Bank reported, 'the trade account and primary income account improved by $ 310.2 m to $2,435.0 m and $ 107.5 m to $ 602.8 m, respectively'. The Bank of Uganda further noted that the country's financial account surplus increased by $ 1302.4 m to $2,938.2 m due to an increase in the budget support loan disbursements of $2,444.2 m, largely targeted at mitigating the impact of the pandemic. In May 2020, the IMF extended a $ 491.5 m emergence disbursement under the *Rapid Credit Facility* to help with balance-of-payments and fiscal needs. On the other hand, FDI inflows declined by 26.3% over the same period to $ 893.1 m. Uganda was ranked 166th out of 190 countries in the World Bank's Doing Business report of 2020 (data from 2019); irregularities in the reporting of data resulted in a temporarily halt to the publication of the 2021 Doing Business report, and hence, no updated ranking for 2020 is available. Overall, the balance of payments recorded a surplus of $ 429.2 m, resulting in a build-up in reserve assets (compared with a deficit of $ 107.2 m in the prior year). The central bank reported that total stock reserves as at end of January 2021 stood at $ 3.6 bn, equivalent to 5.3 months of import cover.

The *Uganda shilling* was on average stable against the US dollar but made some marginal appreciation in the second half of the year, pointing to the contraction in demand for imports due to the lockdown and other pandemic restrictions. Headline inflation grew mid-year, perhaps driven by a drop in domestic output and an exponential rise in public transport fares due to restrictions imposed on passenger vehicles, but it dropped and stabilised in the second half of the year, estimated at about 3.7% at the end of 2020.

The World Bank noted that *Uganda's Human Capital Index (HCI)* is low: a child born in Uganda today is likely to be 38% as productive when she grows up, as she could be if she enjoyed complete education and full health. Beyond disrupting the economy, the World Bank further noted, 'the Covid-19 pandemic risks rolling back the recent gains in health and human capital development if effective prevention and control measures do not continue to be implemented rapidly and at scale'. Uganda's HDI for 2019 (published in 2020) was 0.544, putting the country at 159th out of 189 countries and in the low human development category, according to the UNDP.

Arguably, the biggest point of debate remains Uganda's soaring public debt, which has closed in on 50% of GDP, considered the threshold for red flags. Total public debt stood at more than $ 17 bn. The Bank of Uganda projects that the country's debt portfolio will to grow to just under 55% of GDP in the next two fiscal years. A major driver of Uganda's public debt is President Museveni's singular focus on transforming Uganda's otherwise poor and under-developed road infrastructure. In the past years, the government has committed huge budgetary resources to road projects, but these have been plagued by endemic corruption and long delays, both problems contributing to inflating project costs and a spike in loan acquisitions. The entry of China into the foreign financing market and aggressive take-over of the road construction industry has accelerated the indebtedness of poor countries like Uganda. The Chinese approach has been to tie its loans to guarantees of contract awards for its construction companies. China is Uganda's second-largest creditor, with about one-fifth of the country's debt. In the face of criticisms and questions about debt sustainability and the burden that debt servicing places on the national budget, Ministry of Finance political leaders and technocrats have insisted that Uganda's debt status remains within manageable levels and is not a cause of for concern. While presenting budget estimates for 2020/21 financial year, finance minister Matia Kasaija revealed that the government was negotiating with major creditors to suspend debt servicing in the face of the pandemic. The country expressed interest in joining the Debt Service Suspension Initiative spearheaded by the World Bank and the IMF and approved by the G20 to provide temporary relief from debt servicing for poor countries.

In the oil sector, which has been a key issue for debate on Uganda's economy since 2006 when commercially viable oil reserves were confirmed, a UK-based think tank, Climate Policy Initiative (CPI), warned in a December 2020 report that Uganda's planned $4 bn oil refinery was too costly and would undermine the value of the East African crude oil pipeline. The Ugandan government and especially President Museveni remained committed to the refinery project even as they signed the pipeline agreement. In the same report, the CPI also noted that the value of Uganda's oil had dropped by 70% between 2015 and 2020, from $ 61 bn to $ 18 bn. Earlier in April, Total announced its acquisition of Tullow's remaining stake in Uganda's oil for $ 575 m.

Uganda maintained its status as a leading host of *refugees*, with numbers estimated at 1.4 m in 2020 and drawn from across a region that remains turbulent and unstable, from DRC and South Sudan to Burundi and Somalia. Uganda was the largest refugee host nation in Africa and the third-largest in the world in 2020. The country's pro-refugee stance has earned the Museveni government plaudits and praise among international humanitarian circles and Western aid agencies. But given Uganda's own precarious and uncertain political situation, the country may well become a net producer of refugees in the near future, especially if the transition from Museveni's rule is not properly handled.

Hosting huge numbers of refugees places enormous pressure on the environment, local resources, and host communities in Uganda, a country whose own population is growing rapidly at a 3% annual rate, one of the highest in the world. It is estimated that at least 8 m Ugandans lack access to safe and clean water. With the pandemic disruptions, irregular rainfall, and a new round of desert locust invasion in early April 2020, food insecurity was a problem for many Ugandans. Inadequate rainfall in the north, parts of the west, and West Nile affected cultivation and harvest, while heavy rainfall caused displacements in the east and parts of the west. Locust invasions affected mainly the north-east (Karamoja) sub-region. Environmental degradation, particularly deforestation, remained another major problem. Between 1% and 3% of trees were cut down and an estimated 3.59 kha (thousand hectares) of primary forest and 73.6 kha of tree cover lost in 2020.

PART 6

Southern Africa

David Sebudubudu

Overall, this was an extraordinary year that was defined by the Covid-19 pandemic and characterised by uncertainty. Consequently, the sub-region's political attention and economic resources were largely focused on efforts to contain the pandemic, with power further concentrated on the executive owing to the associated restrictions imposed. Undoubtedly, apart from absorbing a substantial amount of resources, the pandemic disrupted and stalled regional economies – demonstrating their vulnerability to external shocks. In the sub-region, South Africa registered the highest number of deaths associated with Covid-19. The sub-region sustained its relative stability, but governance and security challenges and associated human rights abuses were evident in some countries, especially Angola and Mozambique, where insurgencies presented a major security threat in some provinces. Equally, regional cooperation was hampered by the Covid-19 pandemic because countries were mainly focused on containing it.

Elections, Democracy, and Human Rights

In *Malawi*, presidential elections were held on 23 June following a 3 February high court decision that invalidated the results of the disputed 2019 presidential elections, which had been won by Peter Mutharika of the Democratic Progressive Party (DPP). The domestic political environment was largely characterised by conflicts and protests, especially in the lead-up to the presidential elections and thereafter. The elections were won by Lazarus Chakwera of the Malawi Congress Party (MCP), part of the Tonse Alliance, with 59% of the votes while Peter Mutharika obtained 40%. Corruption led to criticism of Chakwera's government.

In *Angola*, a damning investigation regarding the dubious business dealings of Isabel dos Santos, the daughter of former president Jose Eduardo dos Santos, and her family attracted headlines at the beginning of the year. Furthermore, other high-profile cases of corruption and wrong-doing were in motion. Despite this, President João Lourenço's anti-corruption posture was considered wanting as it excluded some of those implicated in wrong-doing, including some of his relatives and members of his government and party, sparking protests in Luanda. Violence and human rights abuses continued to diminish domestic politics and the quality of governance, especially in the province of Cabinda, where an insurgency was in motion. Unsurprisingly, the long-anticipated local elections, mandated by the 2010 constitution, were deferred, with the Covid-19 pandemic cited as the reason.

Although local government elections were deferred in Angola, those in *Mauritius* proceeded. Corruption was a major issue in Mauritius, especially associated with Covid-19-related procurement, as structures of accountability were diminished owing to emergency measures introduced to contain the virus. Assertions of corruption regarding a power-generation plant led to the dismissal of the deputy prime minister, Ivan Collendavelloo.

In *Namibia*, an attempt by independent candidate Panduleni Itula and others to challenge the 2019 presidential elections results in court was not successful. The country held its regional and local government elections in November. Consistent with the national assembly and presidential election results of 2019, the regional and local government election results showed that support for the ruling South West Africa People's Organisation (SWAPO) was declining. In the 14 regional councils, SWAPO's vote decreased to 57%, from 83% in 2015, while it obtained 40% of the votes in the local government elections compared with 73% in 2015.

The inauguration of Moeketsi Majoro as prime minister of *Lesotho* revived prospects for stability and presented an opportunity for the country to deal with its long-standing political crisis. Majoro was voted into parliament through an alliance of the All Basotho Convention (ABC) and the Democratic Congress (DC). His inauguration followed several unsuccessful attempts by the embattled Tom Thabane to hold on to power despite mounting pressure for him to quit as prime minister owing to an impending charge against him for murdering his former wife.

In *Eswatini*, governance challenges persisted, and pressure for reforms was stamped out. As in the previous year, the country registered demonstrations, protests, and strikes, and all of these were quashed using the law, and use of force. Corruption intensified, and a curtailment of freedom of association and assembly and freedom of expression persisted; this was a major blight on the country, diminishing the quality of governance.

The democratic credentials of *Zambia* continued to diminish as intolerance of the opposition and media was sustained throughout the year. Apart from efforts to contain Covid-19, the political environment was preoccupied with the voter registration for the 2021 general elections, and for the first time the right to vote was extended to those in custody. Meanwhile, an attempt to extend the powers of the executive through a constitution amendment bill was without success, as it failed to secure the required support and approval in parliament.

Similarly, in neighbouring *Zimbabwe*, the main preoccupation was with Covid-19 and measures to contain the pandemic. An effort was equally made to further concentrate power on President Emmerson Mnangagwa through the discordant Constitution of Zimbabwe Amendment Bill No. 2 of 2019, which attracted disapproval even from President Mnangagwa's Political Actors Dialogue (POLAD) allies. The country's governance continued to deteriorate and the domestic political scene remained tense. The suppression of opponents and those critical of the government, including the media, and a violation of human rights continued to be business as usual. Those who engaged in protests were repressed. The opposition, especially the Movement for Democratic Change Alliance (MDC-A), had a tumultuous year, with suggestions of interference by the ruling Zimbabwe African National Union – Patriotic Front (ZANU-PF) in the affairs of the opposition. Divisions were also evident within ZANU-PF. Meanwhile, corruption remained a major issue and there were calls for government to take action against it.

Although the focus in *Mozambique*, as elsewhere, was also on containing the Covid-19 as a matter of priority, the country faced a major security challenge because of an ongoing and intense insurgency in Cabo Delgado Province, in the face of an ill-equipped and poorly trained army, that sent shivers across the region. The insurgency displaced around 583,000 people, resulted in the utilisation of the second-largest gas reserves in Africa being discontinued, and diminished prospects of development. In the meantime, the government also faced challenges in attracting aid money owing to corruption.

In *Madagascar*, President Andry Rajoelina succeeded in consolidating power around him by decreasing the size of the senate, a move which was endorsed by the High Constitutional Court (HCC) following a challenge by opposition senators. This gave him the leeway to make decisions without involving the opposition. Strangely, while other countries worked closely with the WHO in tackling the Covid-19 pandemic, Rajoelina's government had an adversarial relationship with it, claiming that the country had a remedy for Covid-19 in Covid-Organics (CVO). CVO and other Covid-related products such as personal protective equipment (PPE) presented prospects for his government to pursue a state-led industrialisation plan. Despite schoolchildren and adults being made to take CVO, the country recorded a rise in cases of Covid-19, thus eroding assertions made by Rajoelina regarding CVO.

In *South Africa*, domestic politics equally grappled to contain the Covid-19 pandemic using the Disaster Management Act. The country recorded the highest number of Covid-19 cases in the sub-region. The Zondo Commission of Inquiry investigating state capture was sustained, with costs associated with it becoming a public issue. Divisions and dissension within the ruling African National Congress (ANC) were apparent, with one faction associated with president Cyril Ramaphosa and the other with former president Jacob Zuma. The other faction, which was advancing the Radical Economic Transformation (RET) agenda, seemed to be irked by President Ramaphosa's anti-corruption posture, which was considered to be directed at those associated with the RET. The divisions within the ruling party gave rise to a proposition that Ramaphosa could be president for only one term, suggesting that there could be a plan to recall him. Meanwhile, Jacob Zuma's corruption case was in motion and his supporters stood by him. The main opposition, the Democratic Alliance, had an active year, holding its policy conference and national elective congress. Among other concerns, the party was confronted by the issue of internal transformation, which seemed to work against its electoral fortunes as it was not considered inclusive of black people, especially in positions of leadership. The other key development for the year was that the country's electoral law was subject to scrutiny. At the constitutional court, the New Nation Movement (NNM) organisation successfully challenged a section of the electoral law that did not allow independent candidates to compete in national and provincial elections if they were not members of a political party.

Despite President Ramaphosa's anti-corruption stance, reports of corruption across different levels of government intensified throughout the year, including those associated with the procurement of PPE, needed to combat the Covid-19 pandemic. Overall, the pandemic compounded the country's frail and uncertain socio-economic system.

In *Botswana*, President Mokgweetsi Masisi's government resorted to a state of public emergency, as provided for in the country's constitution, to contain Covid-19, because the Public Health Act was considered inadequate. Yet the state of public emergency, which was initially for six months (April–September) and was extended for a further six months, could not halt the spread of Covid-19. Consequently, the country's measures to contain the virus, as well as the Presidential Task Team, attracted criticism from certain quarters. Strangely, President Masisi engaged in external travel despite travel restrictions that his government had put in place to curb Covid-19, attracting condemnation as his trips were considered unnecessary.

Reports of corruption became more intense, and President Masisi maintained an anti-corruption rhetoric without much evident success, as most of those associated with high-profile cases were discharged. Furthermore, President Masisi engaged in dubious business relations and interests that attracted public disapproval, with some doubting his commitment to combating corruption. Meanwhile, the spat between Masisi and former president Ian Khama continued, although it seemed to have eased somewhat.

According to the 2020 Fund for Peace *Fragile States Index*, which considers 'risk and vulnerability' in countries, Mauritius was the only country in the sub-region considered 'very stable', emerging 153rd out of 178 countries, Botswana was 'more stable' at 121st position, Namibia attracted a 'warning' at 105th; South Africa, Lesotho, and Madagascar were on an 'elevated warning' at 85th, 60th, and 57th respectively; Eswatini, Malawi, Zambia, and Angola were under a 'high warning' classification at 45th, 43rd, 41st, and 34th respectively; and Mozambique and Zimbabwe were in the 'alert' category at positions 27th and 10th respectively. The rankings suggest that most countries in the sub-region remain vulnerable to instability, with Mozambique among the 'most worsened' countries, owing in part to the insurgency in the northern part of the country. Despite its perceived flaws, the index is considered 'a critical tool in highlighting not only the normal pressures that all states experience, but also in identifying when those pressures are pushing a state towards the brink of failure'. Pressures for development are quite evident in developing countries such as those in the sub-region under review and in the rest of the African continent.

The 2020 EIU *Democracy Index* report declared that democracy further suffered because of measures to curb Covid-19 globally, noting that the democracy midpoint score registered a record low since the introduction of the index in 2006. In sub-region, there was no change from the previous year regarding the categorisation of regimes. Mauritius remained a 'full democracy'; Botswana, South Africa, Namibia, and Lesotho were 'flawed democracies'; Malawi, Madagascar, and Zambia were 'hybrid'; while Angola, Mozambique, Zimbabwe, and Eswatini were considered 'authoritarian'. Overall, the future of democracy in the sub-region remains uncertain and unstable.

Considering the *Ibrahim Index of African Governance (IIAG)* of 2020, the sub-region continued to rank favourably compared with other regions in the continent, despite evident challenges and the flaws of the index. The sub-region obtained an overall governance score of 53.3, being the highest. Out of the 54 countries assessed, the sub-regional countries were ranked and scored out of 100 as follows: Mauritius, 1st/77.2; Botswana, 5th/66.9; South Africa, 6th/65.8; Namibia, 7th/65.1; Lesotho, 20th/52.3; Zambia, 21st/52.0; Malawi, 23rd/51.5; Mozambique, 26th/49.0; Zimbabwe, 33rd/46.1; Madagascar, 35th/44.4; Eswatini, 36th/43.8; Angola, 43rd/40.0. Only four countries (Mauritius, Botswana, South Africa, and Namibia) obtained a score above that of the sub-region, an indication that governance remains uneven across the sub-region.

Socioeconomic Developments

As elsewhere, countries in the sub-region had to tackle the Covid-19 pandemic that caused unparalleled havoc across economies. According to the African Development Bank (AfDB), the *growth* of Southern African economies was projected to decline by –6.6% in 2020 because of measures taken to control the spread of Covid-19 and other challenges that stifled economic activities, with some sectors such as tourism brought to a standstill. The contraction of regional economies associated with Covid-19 had ripple effects within and across countries because of the interconnectedness and interdependence of economies. It also compounded long-standing challenges, particularly unemployment and poverty, which soared across the sub-region.

In addition, the sub-region was afflicted by challenges associated with adverse climatic conditions such as drought, which gave rise to hunger and food insecurity in a number of countries in the sub-region, such as Angola, Eswatini, Madagascar, Malawi, and Zimbabwe. Other countries such as Malawi and Zimbabwe were afflicted by floods, which also had an adverse effect on food production. Mozambique and Zambia recorded an increase in food production but the insurgency in northern Mozambique gave rise to hunger. Owing to an economic collapse and the uncertainty associated with the Covid-19 pandemic, the need to contain the pandemic and introduce measures to revive economies intensified the debt burden across the region.

Meanwhile, most regional leaders adopted anti-corruption postures without any evident successes realised. Reports of corruption intensified during the year across the region, including in relation to procurement of PPE for Covid-19. Botswana, Mauritius, and Namibia were the only sub-regional countries that were among those considered 'least corrupt' by the 2020 Transparency International Corruption Perceptions Index, which measured and ranked 180 countries globally, on a range of 0 to 100, where 100 was the highest score, meaning that a country is free of corruption. Botswana, Mauritius, and Namibia scored 60, 53, and 51 out of 100 and ranked as 35th, 52nd, and 57th, respectively. The other countries in the region were in the range of those regarded as 'more corrupt', ranked and scored as follows: South Africa, 69th/44; Lesotho, 83rd/41; Eswatini, 117th/33; Zambia, 117th/33; Malawi, 129th/30; Angola, 142nd/27; Madagascar, 149th/25; Mozambique, 149th/25. Zimbabwe emerged as last in the region at 157th, with a score of 24. Zambia, Malawi, Madagascar, and Mozambique were among 'significant decliners', while Angola was listed as one of the 'significant improvers' in the SSA region. The scores and rankings attest that corruption remained a major constraint to the development of the sub-region.

The World Bank's 2020 *Ease of Doing Business* evaluation of 190 countries in terms of how their regulatory framework facilitates or impedes business shows that most sub-regional economies remained largely unfavourable to business and continued to slip but compared favourably with their peers in SSA. Mauritius was ahead its peers, ranked 1st in SSA and 13th globally. It was followed by South Africa at 4th/84th, Zambia at 5th/85th, Botswana at 6th/87th, Namibia at 9th/104th, Malawi at 10th/109th, Eswatini at 14th/121st, Lesotho at 15th/122nd, Mozambique at 20th/138th, Zimbabwe at 21st/140th, Madagascar at 31st/161st, and Angola at 40th/177th.

Sub-Regional Organisations

The Covid-19 pandemic equally affected the activities of sub-regional organisations, and in turn the sub-region's development trajectory. Participation in sub-regional activities was in the main done virtually. An Extraordinary Troika Summit of Heads of State and Government of the SADC Organ on Politics, Defence and Security was held in Harare, Zimbabwe, on 19 May. This was followed by a virtual SADC Troika

Summit on 5 August. The virtual 40th SADC Ordinary Summit of Heads of State and Government, under the heading 'SADC: 40 Years Building Peace and Security, Promoting Development and Resilience in the Face of Challenges' and its associated meetings, including the Organ Troika Summit, were held on 10–17 August, hosted by Mozambique. This was a fitting theme considering the insurgency in northern Mozambique that posed a security challenge with the potential to destabilise the region, and the urgent but unsuccessful attempt to contain it. Mozambican president Filipe Nyusi succeeded Tanzanian president John Magufuli in the rotational position of chairperson, while president of Botswana Mokgweetsi Masisi took over from Zimbabwean president Emmerson Mnangagwa as chairperson of the SADC Organ on Politics, Defence and Security.

The SACU region was equally not spared by the Covid-19 pandemic, which affected its activities as well. According to the 2020 SACU annual report, economic growth within the SACU regional economies was projected to shrink by −7.4% in 2020, owing to the Covid-19 pandemic. As part of its efforts to improve its effectiveness and processes, on 20 January SACU and the UK entered into an MoU intended to revamp the SACU customs initiative. In line with this MoU, the 1st SACU Regional Workshop of Accredited Preferred Traders was held on 5 November.

Meanwhile, South Africa replaced Namibia in the rotational positions of the SACU Summit chairperson, Council of Ministers chairperson, and Commission chairperson on 15 July 2020, for a one-year period. The succession of these positions was conducted virtually. The virtual 4th SACU Council of Ministerial Retreat was held on 21 September, while the virtual 41st SACU Council for Ministers took place on the 29 October. Undoubtedly, the Covid-19 pandemic has not only disrupted and in some instances stalled the regional agenda of sub-regional organisations but it has once again demonstrated the vulnerability of regional economies, which put further pressure on regional countries and governments to transform their economies in order to be able to withstand external shocks.

Angola

Jon Schubert

While the public health impact of the Covid-19 pandemic was ultimately not as catastrophic as anticipated, the ensuing restrictions to public and economic life negatively affected the lives of citizens, resulting in rising police repression, increased hardship and dissatisfaction, and the postponement of the planned local elections. Powers were concentrated in the hands of the executive, as many emergency measures were initially passed as presidential decrees, only to be approved later by the parliament, dominated by the MPLA (Movimento Popular de Libertação de Angola). This in turn led to a hardening of the social climate and a more aggressive stance by security forces towards citizens, who sought to protest against continued corruption in public life.

Domestic Politics

The year started with the publication of the *#LuandaLeaks*, an investigation by the International Consortium of Investigative Journalists. Based on a trove of 715,000 confidential financial and business records leaked from offshore jurisdictions, the investigation detailed how the daughter of the former president José Eduardo dos

Santos, *Isabel dos Santos*, had built up a business empire of more than 400 companies and subsidiaries, benefiting from access to no-strings-attached government loans and preferential access to public works and consulting contracts, often without any public tender. The leaks finally provided tangible proof of what most Angolans already knew, and in January the attorney-general decided to prosecute dos Santos for money laundering, document fraud, abuse of power, and influence-peddling.

Isabel and her family had been living in exile in London and Lisbon since President João Lourenço's accession to power. In January, she assumed Russian citizenship, to which she was entitled through her mother, with the intention of protecting some of her investments, notably in Azerbaijan. From undisclosed locations, she kept sniping on social media against Lourenço's policies (and, ironically, in support of anti-government protests) while mobilising an army of lawyers to contest the seizure of her economic assets in Angola, as well as ongoing investigations in Portugal and the Netherlands. In July, she lost an appeal at the International Arbitration Court in Paris, and shortly afterwards she resigned from the board of Angola's major mobile phone company, Unitel, which she had until then controlled. In August, her brother and the former head of Angola's Sovereign Wealth Fund, *José Filomeno 'Zénú' dos Santos*, was sentenced by the Angolan supreme court to five years' imprisonment for fraud and influence-peddling, truly marking the downfall of the dos Santos family.

In October, Isabel dos Santos's husband, *Sindika Dokolo*, died at the age of 48 in a diving accident in Dubai. Dokolo and Isabel dos Santos had been Angola's wealthiest and glitziest power couple in the heyday of dos Santos's rule. Before the leaks, many Angolans still somehow admired the couple, despite doubts about the provenance of their fortunes, as they epitomised the aspirations of the 'New Angola' on the international stage – an image carefully crafted and managed by international consultancy and audit firms that had been more than happy to take the Angolan coin. Although Isabel had been vilified in public discourse, Dokolo's death came as a shock to many, with even her fiercest critics expressing their sympathy for the family.

In addition to the investigations prompted by the Luanda Leaks, some other notable cases of *corruption* came to light, with mixed results. In January, the governor of Cunene Province, Virgílio Tyova, was dismissed for embezzling funds destined to help fight drought in the province. However, rather than face trial, Tyova was shortly afterwards nominated to the government's Commission of Constitutional Affairs. In September, a former governor of Lunda-Sul, Ernesto Kiteculo, was also arrested on suspicion of corruption. Other reports were made of corruption by provincial governors, but were not followed up.

However, in February, reserve general and 'youth entrepreneur' *Bento Kangamba* was arrested on the border with Namibia carrying a pistol and an undisclosed amount of Angolan and South African currency, and was accused of trying to flee the country after embezzling around $ 6 m of MPLA campaign money. Kangamba denied the accusations and was set free but prohibited from leaving the country pending an investigation. In September, Swiss authorities froze accounts worth $ 900 m owned by Carlos São Vicente, the husband of Irene Neto, daughter of Angola's first president. The attorney-general placed São Vicente in preventative prison pending trial and confiscated his Angolan assets. Neto complained bitterly about the 'witch hunt' in the Angolan media, saying that this was a vendetta against her family. Angolan observers noted, however, that São Vicente had long benefited from a monopoly in providing insurance to the oil sector, and that an inquiry was only opened after the Swiss seizure of assets had come to the attention of the international media. The attorney-general also opened an investigation into the assets of *Manuel Vicente*, the former vice-president under dos Santos. President Lourenço stated that the Angolan state had suffered damages over and above the $ 24 bn that had been discovered in the investigations thus far.

Nonetheless, an international study suggested that these measures had no lasting effect and that judicial reforms were necessary. Opposition parties and civil society also criticised Lourenço for being selective in his fight against corruption, which had no positive impact on citizens' lives. This was especially the case after his daughter *Cristina Dias Lourenço* was appointed executive administrator of the new Angola stock exchange BODIVA in August. Civil society activists said that Lourenço had 'lost his way', although, unsurprisingly, BODIVA and the ministry of finances, which oversaw her nomination, affirmed that Cristina Dias Lourenço had been chosen for her track record and competencies. More spectacularly, Portuguese television channel TVI reported in September that the president's chief of cabinet, *Edeltrudes da Costa*, had illicitly enriched himself under both dos Santos and Lourenço. According to the report, Costa's 'service delivery' company, EMFC, had benefited from government contracting, allowing him to amass a fortune of around € 20 m. Despite public outcry, calls for his dismissal and an investigation were not acceded to. A media report in July also said that 95% of MPLA cadres owned property abroad. Below the radar of such high-profile cases, citizens also complained about continued corruption in their everyday lives, for example when trying to purchase social or state-subsidised housing.

The public's patience had already increasingly been tested by the restrictions imposed to curb the pandemic, and persistent economic challenges (see below, 'Socioeconomic Developments'). The Edeltrudes da Costa case proved to be the proverbial final straw, and in October and November the residents of Luanda repeatedly took to the streets demanding his dismissal, as well as a general improvement of living conditions. Justified by the interdictions of mass gatherings to prevent the spread of Covid-19, the police forcefully intervened on all occasions. At the first gathering, over 100 people were detained, including four journalists who were covering the event. The governor of Luanda province, *Joana Lina*, deplored the damage caused by the demonstrators and vowed that 'violent episodes' of the past would never be repeated, alluding, unsubtly and completely disproportionately, to the – largely MPLA-orchestrated – post-electoral violence of 1992. One hundred and three detainees were then summarily judged, with their legal defence saying that some had been tortured during detention; 26 accused were acquitted, 71 sentenced to a fine. A second, peaceful demonstration, marking the 45th anniversary of the country's independence on 11 November, was met with increased police violence. In addition to the use of tear-gas, some demonstrators were injured and hospitalised, and one youth protester, Inocêncio de Matos, was fatally shot in the head.

To defuse tensions, President Lourenço met with civil society representatives at the presidential palace in late November. The state-controlled 'Jornal de Angola' wrote that a frank and open dialogue was 'the best form of demonstration'. It also cautioned the youth not to allow themselves to be manipulated by 'political interests'. More independent sources, however, reported that only a minority of the invited speakers seized the opportunity to clearly state the problems the country was facing. Accordingly, civil society representatives were sceptical, characterising the meeting as a mere diversion. For the International Day of Human Rights (10 December), youths again protested in Luanda and some provincial capitals against the high cost of living, unemployment, and a lack of progress in combating corruption. Contrary to the last rally, the police did not intervene against demonstrators. Nonetheless, the minister of justice said that protesters would be charged with vandalism because they had 'desecrated' the statue of the country's first president, Agostinho Neto, when they dressed the statue in a t-shirt bearing the effigy of the protester who had been killed in the November demonstration.

Although in March the country adopted a National Human Rights Strategy and passed the Universal Periodic Review at the UNHCR in Geneva, overall, *human rights* and *media freedom* registered retrogressions. While the authorities justified this as the result of measures against the spread of Covid-19, the hardening of the government's position against any form of dissent was seen as an attempt to deal with mounting popular dissatisfaction, three years into Lourenço's mandate. In February, before the lockdown, several youth organisations accused the police of excessive violence in repressing a planned demonstration against the nomination of a new head of the National Electoral Commission. In March, Amnesty International warned that emergency measures should not serve as a pretext for human rights violations, and in April civic activists complained about the gratuitous use of violence by the police. Amnesty also warned of the continued high incidence of *extra-judiciary assassinations*, especially in Lunda-Norte Province. In Cazengo, Kwanza-Norte, the provincial government in April relocated families rendered homeless by heavy rainfall and started destroying houses built in 'precarious' zones. The resettled families complained about insufficient compensation and that some people had been waiting for four years to receive their new houses. *Housing demolition* also took place in Luanda and Benguela provinces, which the Catholic Church condemned as acts of social injustice that benefited only a small elite. In May, various human rights agencies also addressed an open letter to the government to denounce the violence and death threats made against MBAKITA (Missão de Beneficência Agropecuária do Kubango Inclusão Tecnologias e Ambiente), a local human rights NGO in Cuando Cubango Province. Throughout the year, there were reports of youths being killed by the police for violating curfew regulations. In September, the police in Luanda detained a paediatrician, Sílvio Dala, for driving without a face mask. Dr Dala then died in police custody. While the police claimed that he had died of cardiac arrest, his body was found bruised and covered in blood, leading to calls for an enquiry and a peaceful street protest against *police brutality* on 12 September.

In the oil-rich northern enclave province of *Cabinda*, the heavily militarised counter-insurgency and concomitant repression and human rights abuses continued. In June, confrontations between government troops and a unit of the Liberation Front for the Cabinda Enclave – Cabindan Armed Forces (FLEC-FAC) resulted in the deaths of six civilians, four government soldiers, and two FLEC fighters. According to FLEC, the movement had declared a unilateral truce on account of the Covid-19 pandemic, in response to an earlier appeal by UN secretary-general António Guterres. FLEC-FAC was in the process of commemorating the fourth anniversary of the passing of its founding leader, Nzita Tiago, when government troops attacked. Another attack in September claimed the lives of two FAC fighters, three government soldiers, and one civilian. Accordingly, the independent deputy Raúl Tati, a member of the parliamentary faction of UNITA (União Nacional para a Independência Total de Angola), stated in an interview that Cabinda was still at war, and accused the ruling party of downplaying the seriousness of the situation. Similarly, the endemic violence and *human rights abuses* by public and private security forces against the population in the diamond-rich eastern provinces of *Lunda-Norte and Lunda-Sul* continued. In April, for example, an artisanal miner was fatally shot by a private security guard from the company Mosquitos.

Although Angola slightly improved its standing in different rankings, *press freedom* remained a challenge. In March, independent online news portal Correio Angolense crashed because of a cyber-attack after reporting on the Edeltrudes da Costa case. In October, six journalists and one driver were arrested while covering a popular protest (see above), and journalist Carlos de Rosado was twice uninvited for media debates when he sought to speak on the da Costa case. Generally, the state-controlled media returned to being more subservient to the ruling party line after two years of relative openness following Lourenço's election: when the public television station TPA reported in October on the demonstrations, all its invited commenters, including those from an alleged youth organisation called the Angolan Association of Moral Values, strongly repudiated any idea of demonstrations. The

Union of Angolan Journalists also expressed concerns about media pluralism after the newspaper 'O País', TV Zimbo, and Rádio Mais were expropriated by the government in the course of corruption investigations against their previous owners.

As part of efforts to curb government spending, in April the *number of ministries* was reduced from 28 to 21 by merging, for example, agriculture with fisheries, and oil and mineral resources with gas. Manuel Augusto left the foreign ministry and was replaced as minister by his former secretary of state, *Tete António*. More notably, *Adjany Costa*, a young marine biologist, was nominated to head the new super-ministry for culture, tourism, and environment. Costa, born in 1989, became Angola's youngest ever minister. She was at the time completing a doctoral degree in wildlife conservation at Oxford, and in 2019 was the recipient of a United Nations Young Earth Champions award for her work in the Okavango Delta. This represented a marked change in governance style, and raised hopes for more decisive environmental action by the government. Yet Costa was dismissed from the position only six months later and in turn made a 'consultant' to the presidency. Independent media speculated that Costa had faced obstruction from the two former ministers of culture and environment, respectively, who had found themselves subordinate secretaries of state in the new super-ministry. Costa was replaced at the ministry by Jomo Fortunato, a literary critic, university professor, and long-time consultant of the former Ministry of Culture, who appeared more likely to be able to reconcile the opposing forces at the ministry. In November, former minister of finance *Armando Manuel* took up the post of executive director of the World Bank Group for Angola, Nigeria, and South Africa. In other political news, in July the constitutional court turned down an appeal against the non-legalisation of the planned opposition party Partido do Renascimento Angolano – Juntos por Angola (PRA-JA) by former CASA-CE leader Abel Chivukuvuku.

The main political fallout from the pandemic was the *postponement of local elections*. The 2010 constitution foresees regular local elections, but these have never taken place. In previous years the government had always cited technical reasons for not holding them, but in late 2019 it appeared to finally prepare some legislation on their organisation. In February, Mário Pinto de Andrade, the secretary for electoral affairs of the MPLA Politburo, was still affirming that local elections would be called and held in the time frame determined by the 'competent organs' of the state. In March, parliament appointed a new head of the National Electoral Commission (CNE), with 111 MPLA votes in favour, after all opposition parties had walked out of the session in protest. The appointee, Manuel Silva Pereira 'Manico', was at the time of his nomination being investigated for corruption, in which the central figure accused was the former minister of public works and former governor of Luanda, Higino Carneiro. Moreover, Silva Pereira did not fulfil the formal criteria to serve as head of the CNE, and opposition parties and civil society associations called for protests and the annulment of his appointment – without success. Nonetheless, in

April opposition parties stated that the pandemic should not stand in the way of institutionalising laws on local elections.

The Covid-19 pandemic, however, justified *postponing elections* once again: in August Pinto de Andrade said that the 'objective conditions' to hold local elections were not met, and in September the elections were officially postponed until 'conditions allow it'. Although most apart from the MPLA protested and called the decision into question, President Lourenço declared that elections had not been postponed, as they had not been called in the first place. Moreover, as an MPLA deputy wondered on social media, how could the government's commitment to local elections possibly be doubted, given that the cornerstone of the first building for local elections had been laid? However, when the 2021 budget was approved on 14 December, against the votes of opposition parties UNITA and CASA-CE, it did not include local elections. Accordingly, Angolan commentators said that there was a lack of political will to hold the elections, and doubted they would be held before 2023. Undeterred, UNITA continued to call for the establishment of a new, independent national electoral register, also in view of the scheduled general elections of 2022.

Foreign Affairs

Engagement with the SADC continued to present a somewhat mixed picture. Again, Angola failed to join the SADC free trade zone, although it said, for the umpteenth time, that its adhesion was 'imminent'. Still, in January it took the lead in plans for the regional body to share satellite infrastructure, as to date only Angola and South Africa had their own communications satellites. In October, President Lourenço attended a virtual meeting with his counterparts from DRC, Uganda, Rwanda, and Burundi to discuss peace and security in the Great Lakes region.

Bilateral ties with *Namibia* were good as always; in January, the two countries discussed the establishment of a joint chamber of commerce and an Angola/Namibia private investment forum, and in March President Lourenço flew to Windhoek for Hage Geingob's second-term presidential inauguration – just one day after Angola had suspended all passenger flights because of the pandemic. Links with *South Africa* equally remained important. Despite travel bans in South Africa, in October Angola became one of the privileged countries exempt from the ban. However, in December Angola suspended direct flights again because of the appearance of the new Covid-19 variant.

In September, three agreements on security, defence, and migration were signed with the *DRC*, in the presence of provincial governors from either side of the border in the east. This was to avoid possible 'hiccups' in the fight against 'illegal migration'. In June, an Angolan military unit followed some women into the fields on the

Congolese side of the border, and in the ensuing skirmish with DRC soldiers, one Angolan soldier was killed. The agreements also indicated that the repatriation of illegal immigrants would henceforth be carried out 'in full respect of human rights'. In neighbouring *Republic of Congo*, a new international airport in Pointe-Noire was inaugurated in September and named António Agostinho Neto Airport, after Angola's first president and national hero.

Further afield, ties with *China* remained central, especially economic ties, as China remained Angola's most important commercial partner. By May 2020, the volume of bilateral trade since January had already exceeded that of the period January–June 2019, at $ 120 m. Throughout the year, Angola sought to renegotiate its debt to China, which was Angola's single largest foreign creditor. As part of this, the number of crude oil shipments for debt repayment were reduced from June. In December, a team of Chinese doctors visited to offer some training in support of the fight against the pandemic.

The traditionally strong ties with *Portugal* were also marked by the Luanda Leaks (see above), which were revealed by a Portuguese hacker in January. This, together with a visit to Lisbon by Angolan attorney-general Hélder Pitta-Grós, put pressure on the Portuguese public ministry to also launch an investigation into Isabel dos Santos's Portuguese business interests, freezing her assets at the end of January. Shortly afterwards, a Portuguese banker named in the investigations hanged himself. In July, Portugal announced that it would nationalise and then sell off the energy company EFACEC, which had played a central role in dos Santos' deals with the Angolan state. Further leaks later in the year revealed major failures in Portugal's anti-money-laundering mechanisms. The leaks also dominated the relationship with *Switzerland*, even prior to the São Vicente case (see above), as it was revealed that Isabel dos Santos had used the Angolan state diamond company Sodiam to take out a $ 98 m loan from a commercial bank, BIC, to buy a controlling stake in the Geneva-based jeweller Di Grisogono. Shortly afterwards, Di Grisogono filed for bankruptcy.

Relations with *Brazil* were more tense than usual, after the Angolan attorney-general opened an investigation into the Brazilian Universal Church of the Kingdom of God (IURD) in Angola. IURD was suspected of fiscal fraud, criminal association, and capital flight. This enquiry came on the heels of a rift in the church, after 300 Angolan IURD bishops and pastors had complained of racial discrimination by their Brazilian counterparts and had broken away. In August, the attorney-general seized seven IURD temples in Luanda, leading Brazilian president Jair Bolsonaro to write a letter of concern to President Lourenço. Despite such high-level intervention, in September the government closed all IURD churches in Angola. In October, some Angolan bishops revealed to the press how Brazilian pastors had physically smuggled US dollars collected during the church services via South Africa to Brazil. In December, the National Institute for Religious Affairs confirmed the election of the Angolan bishop Valente Bezerra Luís as the new leader of the church in Angola, a decision formalising the 'Angolanisation' of IURD and contested by the church leadership in Brazil.

US secretary of state Mike Pompeo visited Angola in February to strengthen business ties and support Angola's fight against corruption. In December, President Lourenço, via videoconference, underscored the manifold investment opportunities in Angola to the (US) president's consultative council on business in Africa. The two countries also agreed to pursue bilateral cooperation and strengthen their efforts against corruption and for human rights.

The *German* chancellor, Angela Merkel, visited Luanda in February. This was her second visit since 2011 and served to further reinforce political and economic cooperation, with agreements entered into in the areas of traffic and mining and collaborations also planned for the education and justice sectors. German companies also signed contracts worth € 900 m on this occasion. President Lourenço expressed renewed interest in acquiring armed naval patrol boats from Germany. Though the deal was not closed by year's end, German and Angolan NGOs severely criticised the German government for wanting to sell weapons to Angola despite ongoing human rights abuses, notably in Cabinda. A state visit by *French* president Emmanuel Macron, planned for May, had to be postponed on account of the pandemic. Macron had been slated to travel to Malanje Province to take part in the inauguration of a new Higher Institute for Agribusiness Technology which the two countries had established together; the institute was finally inaugurated in October, in the presence of President Lourenço and the French ambassador.

Furthermore, *Russia* announced that it was building a second communications satellite for Angola, Angosat-2, after Angosat-1, launched in 2017, became inoperable three days after the launch. The MPLA also took part in a meeting with Russia's ruling party, Russia United, in September, to share experiences in dealing with the economic contraction precipitated by the Covid-19 pandemic. Cooperation with *Vietnam* was slated to increase after a bilateral meeting in June, especially in the areas of textile production, timber processing, mining, tourism, fishing, agroindustry, and telecoms.

Socioeconomic Developments

In March, the global oil price dropped from $ 45 per barrel to $ 32, thereby reducing Angola's GDP by 6% overnight. This economic contraction was further compounded by the slowdown resulting from Covid-19 restrictions: all sectors contracted, and unemployment, especially among the youth, rose sharply. As such, the country could not pull itself out of the recession it has been in since 2015, despite successful negotiations of new loans with the IMF and debt rescheduling by its largest creditors. The initial 2020 budget had been based on an oil price of $ 55 per barrel, and so the government found itself incapable of maintaining spending levels. In July, parliament ratified a revised budget, with a 15.7% cut overall and a 23% reduction in government spending. However, debt servicing, budgeted at 56.8% of spending in the original budget, remained the largest government expenditure, greater than the sum of all other expenditures, with the debt-to-GDP ratio estimated at 120% at year's end.

In July, new *kwanza bills* were introduced; the new series included the portrait of the country's first president, Neto, but the face of José Eduardo dos Santos, which together with Neto had graced previous series, no longer figured. Despite this symbolic change, the general economic slowdown increased inflationary pressures, with the rate of exchange of the kwanza to the US dollar rising from about 450 to 1 to a peak of 666 to 1 in late November. In September, the national air carrier TAAG decided not to accept payments in kwanza for international flights. In November, foreign exchange reserves stood at their lowest, at around $ 8.5 bn.

The oil industry remained dominant in the country's economic life, despite an October presidential speech hailing (again) Angola's ambitions to become an agricultural power in the region. Despite renewed pledges to diversify the economy, oil majors advanced with new discoveries, offshore in the Namibe Basin, off the southern coast, and in the protected Okavango Delta, which Angola shares with Namibia and Botswana, raising concerns about the conservation of that ecosystem. The diamond mining sector also suffered losses, with several mines suspending production. One of the few sectors that saw growth was that of online platforms for *food delivery* – apps like Tupuca, Garçom, Vono, and Mamboo saw growth of up to 100% after the introduction of emergency measures to curb the spread of Covid-19.

In February, Angola imposed a quarantine period for travellers coming from China. A *State of Exception* because of Covid-19 was introduced on 27 March; this was followed in May by a National State of Calamity, which remained in place till year's end. These measures provided justification for further curtailing the right of assembly, emboldening the police to freely use violence against people who violated lockdown restrictions (see above). Although the WHO suggested in April that Angola was likely to see at least 10,000 cases of Covid-19, which would push the *health system* past breaking point, the measures taken to prevent the spread of the virus appeared to have a positive effect.

In March, the World Bank released $ 15 m to help the country buy personal protective equipment (PPE) and lab equipment, and in April 250 Cuban medical doctors arrived to help bolster Angolan capacity, which reminded Angolans of the Cuban help during the times of the civil war. In June, however, it was revealed that the total cost of this Cuban contracting amounted to € 71 m. By June, the country had recorded 176 cases, rising to 1,852 by mid-August and 17,553 cases with 371 recorded deaths by year's end – a still manageable number by regional comparison.

However, this was dwarfed by *malaria* deaths, which averaged over 2,500 per quarter, making up 3% of malaria deaths worldwide. Generally, the fight against the pandemic seriously reduced the resources for tackling the three major causes of death in Angola – malaria, HIV/AIDS, and tuberculosis. Polio and cholera equally remained health concerns. In January, it was reported that President Lourenço had signed a decree for the construction of a hospital reserved for political leaders at a cost of $ 128 m, a decision criticised by the opposition. Meanwhile, in September, it was reported that residents of a remote eastern province, Moxico, had to cross into neighbouring Zambia to access primary healthcare services. In December, the *Order* of Psychologists stated that they were at the end of their tether, as the organisation had been waiting for legalisation for ten years, with no progress, despite the evident need for mental health provision. The education sector was also not spared, after schools were closed in March and gradually reopened in late October.

In January, aid agencies suggested that *drought* in southern Angola continued to affect local communities, leading to famine and forcing girls as young as 12 into prostitution to survive. In September, Father Pio Wacussanga of the NGO Construindo Comunidades said that the € 30 m government programme introduced in late 2019 to mitigate against drought was ineffective, as local communities had not been involved, and that it was not transparent in its expenditure. Bernardo de Castro, of Rede Terra, said that most of the funds had been embezzled. At the same time, heavy *rainfall* in the central and northern part of the country led to deaths, destroyed houses, and loss of crops – such that in February, prices for vegetables such as tomatoes, onions, and garlic rose by 400% at Luanda markets. In April, a drainage channel in the Zango district of the capital claimed the lives of more than 30 residents, with locals complaining about government inactivity in securing the 'gully of death'. *Hunger* remained a problem, aggravated by the pandemic restrictions, with a reported average of 46 children dying per day of malnutrition. In December, Voice of America reported that rural residents in Namibe Province had to eat 'weeds' to survive after their livestock had perished in the droughts. In the Lunda provinces, pandemic restrictions led to shortages of almost everything, including salt and cooking oil.

Only one-third of the population had access to running water, and half of the population had no access to electricity. Meanwhile, the government announced in February that it would invest in the construction of swimming pools across the country to promote swimming sports. Generally, *spending priorities* were questionable. For example, the draft budget for 2021, debated in parliament from late October, initially included 3 bn kwanza (ca. $ 4.8 m) for the construction of a presidential library. Following an outcry, the budget was amended. On closer examination, it emerged that only the designation of the budget item had changed, to 'planning and building of infrastructures for the preservation of heritage', but the budgeted amount had remained the same. In September, on Twitter, MPLA deputy

João Pinto criticised the 'hateful rhetoric of Angopessimists', holding up instead the 'first-world social housing, hospitals, schools, and dams that supply regular electricity' of the country as proof of 'good governance'. Citizens ridiculed this as 'hypocrisy' and responded with tweets of pictures of precarious, informal housing, potholed and rain-filled roads, and heaps of uncollected garbage.

In February, the Ministry of Transport signed a contract with Siemens for the construction of a planned *surface metro* in Luanda, and in November the minister announced that works would commence in January 2021. In December, however, the newspaper 'Valor Económico' reported that works were unlikely to start in January, and that the metro would cost *$ 24 m per kilometre* to build and operate. Construction of the new *Luanda International Airport*, which had been ongoing since 2005, was still halted, but transport minister Ricardo d'Abreu promised an 'imminent' resumption of construction.

In August, the nation mourned two titans of Angolan music. On 10 August, *Waldemar Bastos*, the composer of, among many others, 'Velha Chica', lost his year-long battle against cancer at the age of 66, and on 12 August, at the age of 67, semba legend *Carlos Burity* died after a protracted illness. Another notable loss was in December, when the entrepreneur *António Segunda Amões* passed away in a South African clinic, after complications from a vascular incident. Segunda Amões had decided in 2019 to reinvest some of his family's fortune to revive Camela Amões, a village in the central Huambo Province from where his family originated. Within a short time, he managed to transform Camela Amões into a model village, with a functioning school and health centre, solar energy, social housing, and sustainable agri- and pisciculture. Accordingly, his untimely death at the age of 51 was received with consternation, as it threw plans for the continuation and expansion of model villages into jeopardy. In Camela Amões, a group of youths burned alive a distant cousin of the late entrepreneur, accusing the former of witchcraft and having had a hand in the latter's death.

Finally, in January, the cartoonist *Sérgio Piçarra* received the French-German prize for human rights and rule of law. And in February, the Luandan dance troupe Fenómenos do Semba recorded their *#JerusalemaDanceChallenge* video. The video showed the dancers eating a Cabo Verdean stew, cachupa, in the courtyard of an informal house, and then breaking out into a dance routine to the track 'Jerusalema' by South African producer Master KG with the vocalist Nomcebo Zikode, while they continued to hold their plates to eat. The video rapidly went viral, sparking inventive takes on the initial dance challenge across the globe.

Botswana

David Sebudubudu and Dithapelo L. Keorapetse

This was an unprecedented year that was dominated by efforts to contain the Covid-19 pandemic through the use of a public state of emergency and associated regulations that centralised power around the presidency but without much success. Owing to Covid-19, the domestic economy almost came to a halt as the key revenue earners for the country, mainly minerals and tourism, were negatively affected to the extent that the economy shrank by 8.9%. Corruption, maladministration, and money laundering seemed to increase during the state of public emergency, as there was no accountability and transparency in government processes. Despite the challenge of Covid-19, the country sustained its foreign policy.

Domestic Politics

On 29 January, the court of appeal decided not to consider 14 *Umbrella for Democratic Change* (UDC) parliamentary candidates' appeals petitions, arguing that it had no legal authority over appeals of petitions, in terms of the constitution and the Electoral Act. The appeals emanated from the 2019 election petitions that were dismissed by the high court in December 2019. On 30 January, the remaining parliamentary petition was withdrawn by the candidate, Noah Salakae. The controversial October 2019 elections were considered fraudulent by the opposition. Subsequent to this, in February the chief justice, Terence Rannowane, was criticised by the opposition and some members of the legal fraternity for taking part in politics after he stated that 'whilst the unsuccessful petitioners in the 2019 elections might remain aggrieved ... the Judiciary ensured that peace and tranquillity prevailed and that the democratic process of ushering in new leaders was facilitated'. The judiciary has, in some quarters, been criticised for not being independent and had 'become an extension of the executive'. Rannowane was perceived to be 'assuming the role of the Independent Electoral Commission (IEC) by declaring the elections as free and fair'. Subsequently, the legal costs associated with the petitions made headlines throughout the year, as the UDC had challenges in settling the costs.

As expected, Botswana, just like other countries, was not spared by the *Covid-19 pandemic*. On 24 March, the government introduced 14 days' compulsory quarantine for travellers as a way of containing the pandemic. On 30 March, three cases of Covid-19 were affirmed by health authorities. Consequently, on 31 March, President Mokgweetsi Masisi announced a *state of public emergency* from 2 April for an unspecified period, under the terms of Section 17 of the constitution, in an effort to contain the pandemic. He further declared that he would call a meeting of parliament to seek an extended state of emergency. President Masisi also declared a 28-day lockdown and attendant intense social distancing. Section 17(2) of the constitution empowers the president to declare a state of emergency for 21 days, and this can be extended to six months with the approval of the majority of members of the national assembly as per Section 17(3). President Masisi also established a *Presidential Covid-19 Task Force* to coordinate activities relating to the containment of the pandemic. On 7–8 April, the president summoned *parliament* to discuss the state of emergency and consider prolonging it for six months. On 9 April, parliament approved a six-month state of emergency as requested by President Masisi, which further entrenched the centralisation of power around the presidency. The opposition did not support the extension, preferring a 28-day state of emergency in line with the lockdown period or at most a three-month state of emergency. Surprisingly, on 9 April, it was also announced that all those who had attended parliamentary proceedings had been exposed to Covid-19, as a nurse who was testing members of parliament for the coronavirus on 8 April had tested positive for the virus herself; this resulted in all members of the national assembly and the whole executive and accompanying officials being quarantined for 14 days immediately after the parliamentary meeting. In some quarters, it was considered suspicious that the nurse had tested positive for Covid-19, and it was perceived as a ploy to persuade members to approve the six-month state of emergency. Interestingly, on 13 April it was reported that an acquaintance of the nurse had tested negative for Covid-19. In May, media reports suggested that the nurse concerned had questioned the Covid-19 results. On 21 April, President Masisi summarily dismissed the permanent secretary of the Ministry of Health and Wellness, Solomon Sekwakwa, and his deputy, Dr Morrison Sinvula, without disclosing the reasons. Media reports immediately suggested that they were dismissed for undermining the director of health services, who had earlier required quarantine for travellers and in turn reversed this requirement. At the time of their dismissal, the country had registered 22 cases of Covid-19 and one death. In October, parliament agreed to extend the state of public emergency by a further six-month period in order to control Covid-19. As expected, the opposition was opposed to the extension of a state of public emergency.

In May, the member of parliament for the Nata-Gweta constituency, Polson Majaga, was put on 60 days' suspension after he was arraigned for defilement, and his suspension was increased in September by another 60 days as the case was still in progress. On 15 July, the member of parliament for Francistown West, Ignatius Moswaane, and former cabinet minister Vincent Seretse were suspended from the Botswana Democratic Party (BDP) for 60 days. In August Moswaane left the BDP, and in September he decided to join the opposition UDC. In August, the BDP put the member of parliament for Jwaneng Mabutsane, Mephato Reatile, on suspension after he voted with the opposition in parliament, and Reatile in turn left the BDP in December, immediately joining the Botswana Patriotic Front (BPF), which increased the party's members of parliament to four. In September, the UDC decided to suspend Tonota member of parliament Pono Moatlhodi from his position as opposition chief whip, to allow him to deal with a case of assault that involved a minor. As expected, in December, Moatlhodi quit the UDC and joined the BDP. Meanwhile, in August, the minister of international affairs and cooperation, Unity Dow, decided to quit her ministerial portfolio, and some reports associated her decision with the controversial 100 bn pula (P) fraud and money laundering case (see below). Dow rejected these suggestions. She was replaced by Lemogang Kwape. Edwin Dikoloti was moved to the Ministry of Health and Wellness while Karabo Gare became minister of agricultural development and food security. Molebatsi Molebatsi was made assistant minister of investment, trade, and industry following reports that he wanted to resign from the ruling party.

On 17 July, a *Constitutional Amendment Bill* meant to end floor-crossing by elected political officials was hurriedly published, despite President Masisi having pledged a constitutional review during his 2019 election campaign. In terms of this bill, and the associated 2020 Local Government (Amendment) Bill, a decision to switch party allegiance by an elected political official at national and council levels would lead to a vacancy and in turn a by-election. This move attracted widespread criticism especially from the opposition because it was considered to have been introduced for reasons of political expediency. On 17 October, three opposition parties, the Alliance for Progressives (AP), the BPF, and the coalition UDC, held a meeting and decided on ways to cooperate during *by-elections*, which were to be considered by the parties before entering into an MoU and before holding joint council and parliamentary caucuses. They agreed that the parties would be allowed to consult their members regarding cooperation during the 2024 election. The three parties also decided on holding a 'People's Court' on 24 October at which they pledged to release evidence regarding rigging of the 2019 general elections. They also urged their supporters to 'wear black on October 23 and 24, to symbolise the death of democracy, as a result of the rigging that took place'. Subsequently, the People's Court was deferred twice. Meanwhile, the BPF sustained its aggressive recruitment of new members during the year.

Corruption, money laundering, and questionable business dealings or interests attracted newspaper headlines. In June, President Masisi's *business dealings, relations, and interests* became a political issue and were disapproved of in certain quarters, particularly with the chief executive officer of the supermarket chain Choppies, Ramachandran Ottapathu, widely known as Ram. Those apprehensive about Masisi's business relations and interests felt that they had the potential to give rise to conflict of interest, undue influence, and corruption. Ram had previously had a business relationship with former president Festus Mogae, which was also disapproved of and which ended after an acrimonious tussle between the two. In June, media reports suggested that former president Mogae was apprehensive about President Masisi's business relations, but Mogae immediately rebuffed these reports. In June, owing to his questionable dealings, there were calls made, among others by the BPF, for President Masisi to step down. Masisi's business dealings were not only a public issue but a subject of discussion in parliament when an extension of the state of public emergency was being considered. In October, the leader of the opposition, Dumelang Saleshando, even cautioned President Masisi that his engagement in questionable business relations could lead to ruin as did that of former president of South Africa, Jacob Zuma. Saleshando quipped, 'I am just warning President Masisi that you are also treading towards state capture just like a former President of our neighboring country'. When quizzed about President Masisi's business dealings, including doing business with government, his press secretary declared that the 'law does not preclude him', a clear indication that he offered a narrow interpretation and understanding of the issue.

While controversial Directorate of Intelligence and Security Services (DISS) agent Wilhelmina 'Butterfly' Maswabi had been charged in October 2019 in connection with the P 100 bn fraud and money laundering case, in February the 'Weekend Post' newspaper suggested that in 2019 two South African men, who presented themselves as private investigators, had defrauded the DISS of an 'undisclosed' amount of money and thereafter disappeared after they claimed they had evidence that associated former president Ian Khama, former director-general of DISS Isaac Kgosi, South African businesswoman Bridgette Motsepe, and associate of Motsepe Malcom X with corruption, and that they had embezzled P 100 bn. It was further reported that on the basis of this 'fabricated information' and without scrutiny, charges were prepared against Maswabi, with damning accusations made against Khama and associates. These accusations were immediately rejected by Ian Khama and Motsepe.

Remarkably, in June, the director of public prosecutions (DPP), Stephen Tiroyakgosi, announced that government had engaged *AfriForum's Private Prosecution Unit*, a South African right-wing Afrikaner organisation, to assist in facilitating 'mutual legal assistance' in the Maswabi investigation. The money was presumed to have been stolen from Bank of Botswana, in association with Ian Khama, Kgosi, and Bridgette Motsepe, and kept in South African banks and offshore bank accounts. Motsepe publicly denounced the investigation by AfriForum, declaring that the accounts she was being associated with at the South African banks Absa and Nedbank were non-existent. Earlier in 2019, Motsepe was reported to have financially supported an attempt to plot a coup against President Masisi, and to have funded Masisi's challenger for the position of party leader, Pelonomi Venson-Moitoi. Despite being widely reported, these allegations were not substantiated. The decision to involve AfriForum – widely condemned in Botswana by, among others, the Law Society of Botswana, which considered it 'alarming', and in certain quarters in South Africa – was reported to have been taken after South Africa had failed to cooperate despite receiving a request for 'mutual legal assistance' in September 2019 through its Department of International Relations and Cooperation. In August, Stephen Tiroyakgosi maintained that the agreement between Botswana and AfriForum was still in force. The decision to engage AfriForum appeared to have caused a diplomatic tiff between the two countries, with South Africa publicly declaring its disapproval. Meanwhile, BPF leader Biggie Butale described the P 100 bn money laundering case the 'corona' of the economy. In August, media reports suggested that former president Khama intended to seek P 25 m for defamation from the government of Botswana, after being implicated in the P 100 bn fraud and money laundering case. Equally, in October, media reports suggested that Maswabi and Motsepe were seeking P 30 m and P 20 m respectively from the government of Botswana for defamation in relation to the case.

Surprisingly, on 24 November, the DPP decided to retract a charge of financing terrorism charge against Maswabi, in relation to the scandal because it did not have enough evidence, but it sustained two other charges against her: false declaration of passports and failing to account for property in her possession. In November, the 'Mmegi' newspaper called for the resignation, sacking, or even prosecution of the heads of the DISS, the DPP, and the Directorate on Corruption and Economic Crime (DCEC) for fabricating evidence against Maswabi. The newspaper further noted that failure to sack the three heads would suggest that President Masisi 'was also involved in the fabrication of evidence' against Maswabi.

In July, the director-general of the DCEC, Joseph Mathambo, decried limited funding for the agency, which worked against its efforts to contain corruption – thus sustaining his previous concerns that the DCEC lacked capacity to tackle corruption. He further declared that there had been a rise in cases of corruption during the state of emergency meant to contain Covid-19, with 47 cases reported to the DCEC associated with Covid-19. His declaration was consistent with reports of increased corruption raised by the opposition, especially by Dumelang Saleshando, in parliament, including damning allegations that relatives of President Masisi were involved in corruption. Moreover, the *stability of tenure* of the head of the DCEC attracted newspaper headlines during the year. In August, Joseph Mathambo was redeployed back to the army without reasons being given, as had also been the case with previous heads following his appointment to that position in April 2019. He was replaced with a former head of the DCEC, Tymon Katholo, who had retired. Consequently, the independence of the DCEC once again became a public issue. As a result, reports of obstruction of the affairs of the DCEC in November and December by the permanent secretary to the president (PSP), Elias Magosi, were not surprising given the nature and history of the institution, especially in relation to the Maswabi case. Following his redeployment, Mathambo validated this obstruction of the affairs of the DCEC by the PSP, Elias Magosi, and the head of the DISS, Peter Magosi; Elias Magosi and Peter Magosi are related. According to Mathambo, the DCEC did not sanction the involvement of the controversial DCEC investigator Jako Hubona in the P 100 bn case – which was quite baffling and strange – to the extent that the institution made an attempt to discipline him.

The *P 500 m Botswana Public Officers Pension Fund (BPOPF)* and *Capital Management Botswana (CMB)* scandal and associated cases continued to attract newspaper headlines. Of particular interest was the case in which the former PSP Carter Morupisi and his wife, Pinny, were charged with corruption and money laundering in connection with the BPOPF and CMF. In November, the high court decided that the state had proved that there was a strong case against Morupisi and his wife for which they needed to answer, allegedly for receiving a land cruiser motor vehicle bought using BPOPF funds. Carter Morupisi and Pinny, who was a BDP councillor, decided to join the BPF.

The *P 250 m National Petroleum Fund* money laundering case also continued to make newspaper headlines. In February, former director-general of the DISS Isaac Kgosi was finally arraigned in relation to the case. In July, the high court did not approve a request by the key accused person, Bakang Seretse, to have President Masisi and Ian Khama testify in this case. On 27 October, a high court judge, Zein Kebonang, and a former minister and former member of parliament for Lobatse constituency, Sadique Kebonang, were acquitted in connection with the case because of lack of evidence associating them with the charge. The court accused DPP Stephen

Tiroyakgosi for failing to read the charge sheet before charging them. In November, the high court acquitted Kgosi and a former executive director of the Botswana Energy Regulatory Authority, Kenneth Kerekang, in connection with the case. The court declared the charges against them 'irrational and unreasonable' and stated that 'prosecutors are not persecutors'. These acquittals led to plausible reports that the charges were 'politically motivated'. In November, the high court decided that Bakang Seretse be paid back P 82 m held by the DPP since January 2018. The state decided to appeal the decision. Consequently, Masisi's anti-corruption crusade was found wanting as he lost some of the high-profile corruption and money laundering cases and was also criticised for being involved in dubious business relations.

In June, reports suggested that World of Oath (Pty) Ltd was owed P 15 m by the DISS for a service relating to the 2019 general elections. In July, media reports suggested an easy relationship between one of President Masisi's closest political allies and former army commander Tebogo Masire and the controversial director-general of the DISS, Peter Magosi, who seemed to have thrived by advancing lies, including a suggestion that the life of President Masisi was in danger. Yet no one was charged in relation to this allegation. Masire was reported to have called for the removal of Magosi from the DISS, as he was said to have been concerned by, among other things the way the DISS had dealt with the P 100 bn Maswabi case. In July, it was further reported that a senior state prosecutor, Priscilla Israel, and a dubious investigating officer, Jako Hubona, in the P 100 bn case were accorded state security as their lives were considered to be in danger.

In August, Ian Khama declared his intention to bring legal action against the investigator Jako Hubona for harming his reputation after an inquiry by Cherie Blair's Omnia Strategy LLP, an international firm, established that allegations against Khama, Bridgette Motsepe, Isaac Kgosi, and Wilhelmina Maswabi had been made up. The inquiry further stated that 'the claims of financial impropriety originating with accounts at the Bank of Botswana are pure fiction. It is impossible to avoid the conclusion that if Jako Hubona's allegations had been properly investigated, it would have been obvious to any reasonable and fair minded prosecutor or court that the case should be abandoned for lack of credible evidence and doubts over the integrity of the State's witness.' In October, media reports suggested that DISS director-general Peter Magosi was likely to be sacked, but these reports were dismissed by the DISS. Meanwhile, in November the opposition declared its disapproval of the state media for not extending its attention to former president Ian Khama, particularly his philanthropic activities, arguing that by not focusing on these activities President Masisi's regime's intended to frustrate Khama – owing to public differences between the two leaders. In December, Ian Khama maintained that there was a plot to assassinate him using 'undetectable poisons sourced from Russia and China'. On 1 October, the EU finally placed Botswana among countries that were at high risk in relation to money laundering and financing terrorism, affirming the country's porous framework of anti-money laundering and counter-financing of terrorism. This was after the country had failed to satisfy suggestions of the Financial Action Task Force (FATF) that were based on the 2016 evaluation of its framework. Despite these events, President Masisi in December maintained his devotion to making corruption an issue of priority at the UN Anti-Corruption Day.

Tensions resurfaced between President Masisi's government and public sector unions, particularly *the Botswana Federation of Public, Private and Parastatal Sector Unions (BOFEPUSU)*. On 21 October, the president of BOFEPUSU, Johannes Tshukudu, criticised the government for failing to restore the Public Service Bargaining Council (PSBC), despite President Masisi's undertaking on assumption of office in April 2018. Tshukudu declared that this was the case because there was 'a leadership vacuum' in the country. Similarly, reports of President Masisi's intolerance were sustained, especially by the private media. For instance, two 'Weekend Post' journalists, David Baaitse and Kenneth Mosekiemang, were charged with 'common nuisance' for 'taking pictures of an unmarked building allegedly belonging to the Directorate on Intelligence Services (DIS)'.

Foreign Affairs

President Masisi attended the inauguration of Mozambican president Filipe Nyusi on 15 January; took part in the 50th World Economic Forum annual meeting from 21 to 24 January in Davos-Klosters, Switzerland; travelled to Addis Ababa, Ethiopia, on 7–11 February, taking part in the High Level Forum on Agenda 2063 on 8 February, the 33rd AU Ordinary Session of the Assembly of Heads of State and Government on 9–10 February, and the Third Africa Business Forum on 11 February; and hosted the 2nd session of the Botswana – Zimbabwe Bi-National Commission on 25–28 February in Kasane. On 21 March, media reports suggested that President Masisi had secretly travelled to Namibia to attend the inauguration of the Namibian president, Hage Geingob, despite his appeal to citizens urging them to restrict travel to countries affected by Covid-19. Masisi's travel to Namibia also came immediately after his government had decided to suspend international travel by government employees and state-owned entities. The trip was widely condemned, as it was considered unnecessary and also went against travel restrictions imposed by Masisi's government. President Masisi and his entourage were put on 14 days' self-isolation on their return from Namibia on 21 March. The presidency defended the trip on the basis that the president needed to meet other heads of states who were attending the inauguration to consider measures put in place in those countries to contain Covid-19, an explanation that was difficult to comprehend as the president did not need to travel to discuss those measures. Masisi came out of isolation on 1 April after testing negative for Covid-19, before the expiry of the 14 days. On 19 May, President

Masisi attended the Extraordinary Summit of the Troika of the SADC Organ on Politics, Defence and Security in Harare, Zimbabwe. The minister for presidential affairs, governance and public administration, Kabo Morwaeng, attended the inauguration of Malawian president Lazarus Chakwera on 6 July. President Masisi visited Mozambique on 14 December, and vice-president Slumber Tsogwane attended the inauguration of Tanzanian president John Magufuli on 4 November.

President Masisi took part in the inaugural WEF 2030 Vision leaders' virtual meeting on 9 June; the virtual United Nations Global Compact 20th Anniversary Leaders Summit on 15–16 June; the virtual SADC Troika Summit plus Force Intervention Brigade Troop Contributing Countries on 5 August; the virtual 40th SADC Ordinary Summit of Heads of State and Government on 17 August; the virtual 75th session of the UNGA in September; and the virtual African Human Rights Day celebrations on 21 October. On 7 November, Masisi congratulated Joseph Biden on his election as president of the USA. He also took part in the virtual summit of the Global Investment Promotion Conference (GIPC) of the United Nations Conference on Trade and Development (UNCTAD) in collaboration with the World Association of Investment Promotion Agencies (WAIPA) on 7–8 December, and the virtual Climate Ambition Summit on 12 December. Four ministers took part in the virtual SADC Ministerial Committee of the Organ (MCO) on Politics, Defence and Security Cooperation on 26 June; the minister of international affairs and cooperation, Lemogang Kwape, took part in a virtual SADC and UN meeting on the reconfiguration of the Force Intervention Brigade on 28 August. He also led the virtual SADC Electoral Observation Mission to Seychelles and Tanzania on 22–24 and 28 October, respectively; the Botswana delegation to the virtual 37th session of the AU executive council on 13–14 October; the virtual Forty-Fourth Annual Meeting of Ministers for Foreign Affairs of the Group of 77 on 12 November; the virtual 73rd session of the World Health Assembly on 9–13 November; and the 147th executive board of the WHO on 16 November; the virtual 111th session of the Organisation of African, Caribbean and Pacific States (OACPS) Council of Ministers. The minister of environment, natural resources conservation and tourism, Phildah Kereng, took part in the virtual meeting of the Commonwealth Foreign Affairs Ministers (CFAMM) on 14 October, and the minister of investment, trade, and industry, Peggy Serame, took part in the virtual High-Level Stakeholder Conference on Strengthening African Economies on the same date.

Socioeconomic Developments

The advent of Covid-19 disrupted the performance of the economy. On 30 January, Botswana approved the Tripartite Free Trade Area (TFTA) Agreement. However, owing to Covid-19, the date for the implementation of the AfCFTA was altered from

1 July to 1 January 2021. In terms of the 2020 budget speech delivered on 3 February, the economy was initially expected to register modest *growth* at 4.4%, but this was not realised as a result of the Covid-19 pandemic that resulted in the economy decreasing by 8.9%, according to the government. *Inflation* was contained below the 3–6% Bank of Botswana target, put at 2.5%, 1.8%, and 2.2% in April, September, and December, respectively. On 1 April, electricity tariffs were raised by 22%. In May, Moody's rating agency reduced the country's rating to negative, from stable. Owing to interruptions associated with the Covid-19 pandemic, in June and July the country registered a shortage of fuel, and in turn the government decided to ration fuel from 10 July. Interestingly, the country's long-standing foreign reserves plummeted from P 65.2 bn in December 2019 to P 58.7 bn in November, presenting a source of discomfort for the government in a country that has faced challenges in weaning itself from mineral dependency. In terms of the 2020 budget proposal, minerals made P 20.0 bn of the P 62.4 bn in revenue. Botswana continued to slide internationally. It was ranked 87th out of 190 countries by the 2020 World Bank Ease of Doing Business report.

In order to encourage production, the country maintained long-standing programmes such as the Economic Diversification Drive (EDD) and citizen empowerment initiatives that take advantage of the government's purchasing power. As part of its attempt to reduce the disruptive effects associated with Covid-19 and to revive the economy, the government decided on a P 4 bn economic relief package in April and a P 14.5 bn Economic Recovery and Transformation Plan (ERTP) in November. In September, the draft mid-term review of the eleventh National Development Plan (NDP11) was approved by parliament. On 15 September, parliament approved a motion to authorise an increase of the bond issuance programme from P 15 bn to P 30 bn to allow government to increase revenue streams.

The government also maintained its social relief programmes meant to reduce hardships for vulnerable groups, including those resulting from Covid-19. In April, the Covid-19 Response Plan included food baskets for those eligible. Also in April, the minister of local government and rural development, Eric Molale, declared that around 800,000 people were supported by the state – almost half of the population in a country with around 2.2 m inhabitants,. However, in September, it was reported that the number of recipients benefiting from various social programmes was 229,622.

Covid-19 had the potential to worsen socioeconomic challenges. Although the national poverty rate was put at 16.3%, a study by an Institute of Development Studies (IDS) researcher suggested that the country's poverty rate stood at 46.2%. Equally, other challenges persisted. According to government, 89% of 384,110 people who had HIV accessed treatment, while transmission from mother to child was put at 1.9% in November. Although employment creation was deemed a priority by government, it remained elusive. There was no evident shift in the prevalence rate. With respect to the unemployment rate, it remained at 17.6%. However, it was put at 23.2% by the Statistics Botswana Multi-Topic Survey of Quarter 1. This puts even more pressure on government to consider expediting job creation. However, the Covid-19 pandemic seems to have made the unemployment situation in the country even more precarious and to have further shown the susceptibility of the domestic economy to external shocks.

Eswatini

Marisha Ramdeen

The Kingdom of Eswatini is a landlocked country with an approximate population of 1.16 m people. In 2020, the country faced severe challenges that included but were not limited to poverty, chronic food insecurity, financial mismanagement, and severe drought. Eswatini has the highest HIV prevalence in the world and was ranked 139th out of 189 in the 2019 Human Development Index. While ranked a lower middle-income country, 63% of the population live below the national poverty line. The consequences of the coronavirus pandemic exacerbated challenges for the health sector as well as worsening the livelihoods of the majority of the citizens in the country.

Domestic Politics

Various sectors of society engaged in *protests*, owing to the challenges that afflicted the country in governance, livelihoods, and health services. The government made efforts to stem *pro-democracy protests* by allocating additional funds to internal security. Earlier in the year, trade unions had called for pay increases to meet the rising costs of living. However, the industrial court banned the strike as it was considered to be against 'the national interest'. The unions involved included the National Public Service and Allied Workers Union (NAPSAWU) and the Swaziland National Association of Teachers (SNAT). In March, members of the Swaziland Democratic Nurses Union were involved in a demonstration over a lack of personal protective equipment (PPE) needed to contain the coronavirus, and in turn refused to treat patients.

At the time of the nurse's strike, however, King Mswati III declared *a state of emergency* to contain the spread of the coronavirus after it was rapidly detected in countries across the Southern African region. This resulted in a partial lockdown being imposed. The lockdown included restrictions on movement, on gatherings of 50 or more people, and on trade, as well as the closure of schools, colleges, universities, and borders with other countries. In September, the police forbade a protest march that was organised by the Swaziland National Liquor Association (SNLA) against the ban on the manufacture and sale of alcohol during the lockdown.

In November, *students* from the University of Eswatini were involved in a demonstration to petition government after more than 1,500 of them were refused scholarships. Only about 1,000 students for the new intake were awarded the scholarships, which cover tuition, books, and living expenses. In response to the protest, the university suspended in-class teaching and students were dismissed from the campus until further notice.

The police were heavy-handed and used excessive force against citizens to enforce lockdown restrictions. Soon after the lockdown was instituted, an estimated 41 people were arrested for violating the lockdown rules and regulations. In April, it was reported that armed military police officers forced members of the public to do press-ups when they were found at a bus rank, and in a separate incident an 85-year-old woman collapsed and died when security forces raided her home. In September, police fired tear-gas and rubber bullets to disperse a crowd that was protesting at being made to pay fines for jay-walking while a broken pedestrian bridge was left unrepaired. According to Swaziland Human Rights Watch, in December, at the height of the second coronavirus wave, police resorted to using 'whips, batons and teargas to break up groups of revellers who had gathered together breaking new stricter coronavirus regulations'.

Corrupt activities surfaced in relation to the coronavirus relief efforts, when it was found that people in employment had registered for a food aid scheme that was meant for those who had lost their jobs and were facing starvation due to the lockdown. According to Transparency International's Corruption Perceptions Index, which ranks countries from least to most corrupt, Eswatini's rank increased from 113th in 2019 to 117th in 2020 (based respectively on 2019 and 2018 data), further indicating an increase in corruption in the public sector.

Restrictions on freedom of association and assembly remained in place in 2020. According to Human Rights Watch, Eswatini Sexual and Gender Minorities (ESGM) registered a case at the high court against the Eswatini Registrar of Companies for its refusal to register ESGM as a company. ESGM is a human rights community-based advocacy organisation working to advance the protection of the rights of lesbian, gay, bisexual, transgender, and intersex (LGBTI) people in the kingdom. The registrar argued that ESGM could not be registered as a company due to the fact that 'ESGM's objectives were unlawful because same-sex sexual acts are illegal in the country'. In October, LGBTI activists returned to the high court in an attempt to have their advocacy group officially registered and made legal. At the time of writing, no further information was forthcoming.

Women remain oppressed, and continued to be under-represented in leadership and decision-making positions in both the public and private sectors in spite of the 2018 Election of Women Act. In February, a 19-year-old woman was sentenced to three months in jail with the option of a fine for wearing a miniskirt in public. In May, during the peak of the coronavirus and subsequent lockdown, it was found that domestic abuse cases had doubled. According to the Swaziland Action Group Against Abuse (SWAGAA), at least 40 cases had been reported to them between 30 March 2020 and 24 April. On a more hopeful note, in September a high court judge recommended that the country should consider legalising abortion, following a case in which a mother who was unable to provide for her four-year-old son ended his life. While the constitution provides for abortion in certain instances, there is no law that enables it. *Freedom of the media and freedom of expression* remained under threat, and the police used heavy-handed tactics against people who expressed dissent and who criticised King Mswati III. Opponents of the government turned to social and print media to express concerns over governance and human rights issues. The president of the Economic Freedom Fighters-Swaziland (EFF), was charged with sedition for criticising King Mswati on the Swati Newsweek website. In March, the editor of the 'Swaziland News' fled Eswatini for the second time after being arrested and tortured by police who accused him of sedition. In 2020, Reporters Without Borders ranked Eswatini 141st out of 180 countries on media freedom, partly because of constraints that journalists face under the absolute monarchy and the fact that courts are not permitted to prosecute representatives of the monarchy. In August, Eswatini authorities gazetted a new omnibus cybercrime bill, with implications in terms of severe penalties against people who engage in cyberbullying or spreading fake news. The most controversial section of the bill set out to make it unlawful for any person to publish any statement or 'fake news' through any medium, including social media, with the intention to deceive any other person or group of persons. On conviction, a person would be liable to a fine not exceeding 10 m emalangeni (E; $ 600,000), imprisonment not exceeding ten years, or both. However, in November a committee of members of the Eswatini parliament withdrew the parts of the bill that could impose the exorbitant fine or jail time on people publishing 'fake news' and agreed to allow further consultation before the bill would be passed into law. The Harmful Digital Communications Bill 2020 was prepared by the Ministry of Information, Communication and Technology. The bill is intended to deter, prevent, and mitigate against harmful digital communications and provide victims with a quick and efficient means of redress.

Meanwhile, Prime Minister Ambrose Dlamini died after testing positive for the coronavirus. Themba N. Masuku, who had served as the deputy prime minister since 2018, was appointed as the acting prime minister following Dlamini's death.

Foreign Affairs

The *EU ambassador* to Eswatini joined LGBTI rights supporters at the high court for a landmark hearing on LGBTI rights. In January the EU announced that it would provide €1m in aid for people who had been affected by the drought and who were facing a severe food crisis.

Eswatini sustained close ties with Taiwan, much to the disapproval of China. In February, the Chinese government threatened Eswatini with *diplomatic, travel, and economic sanctions* for maintaining diplomatic relations with Taiwan.

In March, the prime minister announced the *closure of all informal border crossings* with South Africa to stop the spread of the coronavirus. In August, Eswatini *received 20 Cuban doctors* who spent three months in the country assisting with both Covid- and non-Covid-related diseases. The arrival of the Cuban doctors was part of a partnership between the two countries that goes back 14 years. The IMF approved a loan of $110m to help Eswatini cope with shortages in its financial budget, in light of the economic devastation caused by the coronavirus.

The *US ambassador to Eswatini* Lisa Peterson called for the kingdom's constitution to be reviewed to curtail King Mswati III's lavish spending. Furthermore, Jeanne Marie Maloney, the incoming US ambassador, pledged to engage the kingdom on political reform.

Socioeconomic Developments

The economy remained heavily reliant on agricultural and industrial production. Eswatini's main agricultural products include sugar cane, corn, cotton, citrus, pineapples, cattle, and goats. Its industrial products include soft drink concentrates, coal, forestry, sugar processing, textiles, and apparel.

GDP stood at $3.85bn, while GDP growth was projected at 2.5% for 2020, spurred by industrial growth and agricultural expansion, but was expected to slow to 1.2% in 2021. Public debt continued to rise, domestic arrears grew, and international currency reserves fell 'below adequate levels'. According to the AfDB's economic outlook, in Eswatini 'poverty, inequality, high unemployment (youth unemployment at 47.4%), and HIV/AIDS prevalence at 27.2% among adults aged 15–49 remained key challenges'. More than 18,000 workers in the Swazi textile industry were in danger of losing their jobs or faced salary cuts, according to the secretary-general of the Amalgamated Trade Union of Swaziland (ATUSWA).

In June, the government announced an E 25 m ($ 1.5 m) *relief fund* to help people who had lost their jobs. In an attempt to save their businesses, bus operators defied coronavirus social distancing regulations and ran vehicles at full capacity to sustain their livelihoods.

On 29–30 October, as a means to *promote women in business*, Swaziland Gender Links hosted a two-day summit and launched the Women in Local Economic Development (WLED) network, in collaboration with the Commonwealth Local Government Forum (CLGF) and the Eswatini Local Government Association (ELGA). The summit focused on the importance of mainstreaming gender in different areas, including sexual reproductive health and rights (SRHR), climate change, gender-based violence, economic justice, and the media. Sex workers in Eswatini wanted to be formally registered so they could work legally and pay taxes. At present, sex workers face fines of up to E 100,000 ($ 6,500) or up to 20 years' jail time.

Apart from the threat to livelihoods and economic deterioration, *the health sector* also faced numerous challenges as a result of the coronavirus. Hospitals across the country were in a state of crisis both because of existing challenges and in light of the strain placed on them due to the coronavirus. Nurses and other healthcare workers lacked protective clothing and equipment and as a result refused to treat patients at the onset of the pandemic, as they felt that their lives were at risk. At least four public hospitals stopped treating patients on 19 March 2020. Patients at a major hospital were left without food for at least a day due to the government's inability to pay its service providers. This was a recurring issue from previous years. Ambulances were grounded due to a lack of fuel at the height of the pandemic. By October, hospitals faced a shortage of coronavirus test kits and ventilators as positive cases and deaths continued to rise. On a positive note, a new research project commenced that was aimed at improving care for people with diabetes through strengthening eye and foot screening.

According to the FAO, the levels of *malnutrition* increased to the extent that nearly a quarter of the total population needed food assistance. The FAO reported that 300,000 people were affected. Food insecurity was largely a result of the ongoing drought, which had an impact on food production and, coupled with rising food prices, has left people facing a dire food shortage.

A *ritualist tendency* surfaced targeting bald-headed people in a way that raised fears of ritualistic practices. In February, the 'Times of Eswatini' reported that a man who had died of natural causes later had his scalp cut off. His family believed that it was used in a ritual or as part of a 'magic potion'. This was similar to the situation where people with albinism were targeted in the past. In 2018, ahead of the national election, there was widespread reporting of abductions across the kingdom. It was believed that body parts were being used to bring good luck to candidates running for the House of Assembly.

While the majority of the Swazi people live below the poverty line, King Mwsati III remained one of the world's richest people, with an estimated net worth of $ 500 m. He is widely known for his luxurious lifestyle and has 15 wives. He is also known for celebrating his birthday lavishly; however these celebrations were cancelled this year due to the outbreak of the virus. On 17 March, Prime Minister Dlamini issued a statement that the money budgeted for the celebration was to be used in the fight against Covid-19.

Lesotho

Roger Southall

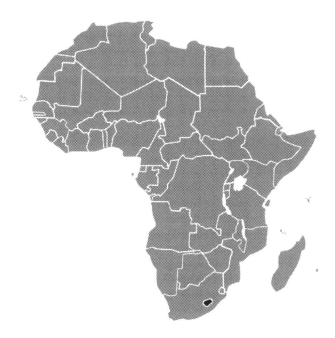

The installation of Moeketsi Majoro as prime minister on 20 May 2020 was widely welcomed as providing a way out of the long-running political crisis which had resulted from the efforts of Tom Thabane, Majoro's 80-year-old predecessor, to cling on to power in defiance of he and his wife being charged with murder, his losing support from within his All Basotho Convention (ABC) party, and charges that he had manipulated the judiciary. The peaceful transfer of power, enabled by a vote in parliament, was consolidated by Majoro's forging a coalition between the ABC and the Democratic Congress (DC), whose leader, Mathibeli Mokhothu, became deputy prime minister.

Nationally, the two parties' holding 78 out of the 120 seats in the national assembly offered the prospect of the new government being enabled to serve out the term of the present parliament, which ends in 2022, and hence being well placed to manage the crisis inflicted on Lesotho by the Covid-19 pandemic. However, given that Majoro's own standing within the ABC was far from secure and that Thabane retained the support of a minority faction within the party, an era of political stability was far from guaranteed.

Domestic Politics

Thabane spent the early months of 2020 attempting to prevent his ouster. The police had let it become known that he was going to be charged with the murder of his former wife, Lipolelo Thabane, who had refused to stand down as the country's first lady in favour of his current wife, Maesaiah. Faced with increasing pressure from within his own party, Thabane had announced on 20 February that he would step down on 31 July if 'all the requisite preparations' for his retirement were completed (by which, it was widely speculated, he was bargaining for immunity from prosecution). However, when his political opponents, including his rivals within the ABC, made it plain that they wanted him to resign immediately, he sought to neutralise them by suspending parliament for three months. He justified this by referring to the emergency caused by the Covid-19 pandemic, yet the suspension took place just after the House of Assembly had passed a bill barring him from calling fresh elections if he were to lose a looming vote of no confidence. However, when parliament's suspension was challenged in the constitutional court on Friday 17 April, his action was overturned on the grounds that it was irrational. Parliament was duly reassembled, bringing forward the likelihood of the no-confidence debate.

With his position increasingly untenable, Thabane now chose to gamble. On the day after the court decision, he ordered troops onto the streets of the capital, Maseru, proclaiming in a broadcast that certain law enforcement agencies were undermining democracy, and that correspondingly there was a need to restore order. The police replied that the army had been deployed to intimidate them. Whether or not this was true, the Lesotho Defence Force – which so often in Lesotho's troubled history had been more than happy to intervene politically – chose to withdraw to the barracks on Sunday 19 April. Thabane's last gambit had failed.

The army's withdrawal had doubtless been encouraged by South Africa's dispatch of a delegation to Maseru over the weekend for high-level talks aimed at calming the situation. In a joint statement, the South African delegation, representatives of the coalition government, and other stakeholders declared that they had agreed to guarantee a 'dignified, graceful, and secure exit' for Thabane. Although Thabane's immediate reaction was to hit back by declaring that he would not be driven from office by people who had no authority over him, it was clear that he had now run out of road. Within a short space of time, the senate passed a new constitutional amendment that empowered the national assembly to form a new government without holding fresh elections. Although thereafter Thabane continued to play for time, he reluctantly announced his resignation on 18 May. Two days later, he was out of office, seemingly without gaining the immunity from prosecution for which he had hoped. Thus ended a long career which had seen him serve in senior positions in the civil service or in the cabinet, with only brief interruptions, since 1966.

In the wake of Thabane's resignation, the speaker of the national assembly, Sephiri Motanyane, accepted an agreement between the ABC and the DC to work in coalition. Majoro, previously minister of finance and before that an executive director at the IMF, assumed office as prime minister on 21 May and announced a 24-member cabinet immediately. Composed of 12 ministers from the ABC and 8 from the DC, it also included the leaders of the small Patriotic Front for Democracy, the Movement for Economic Justice, and the Reformed Congress of Lesotho, the last two both being breakaways from the Lesotho Congress for Democracy. An additional eight deputy ministers brought up the rear, one of whom was drawn from the Basotho National Party.

The extension of the coalition beyond the ABC and DC was intended to stabilise governance after the disarray of the last years of the Thabane government. For his part, Majoro was widely regarded as more a technocrat than a politician capable of managing tensions between rival political parties and factions. Nonetheless, he got off to a good start, declaring his commitment to a 'new version of leadership' and restoring people's trust in government, and promising to make tackling Covid-19, poverty, and unemployment his major priorities. Yet the prospects for a peaceful tenure of office were uncertain.

The truth was that Majoro was very much a compromise candidate from within his own ABC, whose leadership was still being bitterly contested between Thabane and Professor Nqosa Mahao (now appointed minister of justice) prior to the party holding a new leadership contest. He was not even a member of the ABC's National Executive Committee. Furthermore, to cap it all, Thabane's former deputy prime minister, Monyane Moleleki, leader of the Alliance of Democrats, who had angled for a position in the new cabinet but been denied (and hence now became leader of the opposition), was manifestly disgruntled and was rumoured to be refurbishing his working relationship with the former prime minister. Accordingly, there was much talk that Majoro was merely a caretaker prime minister until both the final resolution of the ABC leadership battle and the coming of the next election in 2020. Indeed, the fragility of his position was put on public display when, merely ten days after he had appointed Prince Maliehe from the ABC as minister of defence, he was compelled by his own party to dismiss him in favour of Lekhetho Mosito, on the grounds that the former had been installed without consultation with either of the major parties in the coalition.

Even so, Majoro's elevation to the premiership augured well in one regard. His appointment, aged just 43, signified the transfer of power to a new generation of leaders, all of Lesotho's previous premiers having been born before the Second World War and being steeped in the culture of patronage and factionalism that had consistently pervaded the country's politics. Nonetheless, the challenges he faced were daunting.

Among these were the crisis in the judiciary, whose leadership had become entangled in the leadership battle which was taking place within the ABC. Thabane had appointed judge Maseforo Mahase as acting chief justice in September 2018. Various of her judgments had proven highly controversial, and Nqosa Mahao had attacked her as politically biased, a charge which he deemed to have been substantiated when she ruled against the legality of his February 2019 election to the leadership of the ABC. This had been appealed and overturned by Justice Kananelo Mosito, president of the court of appeal, only for the latter, in turn, to be suspended by Thabane. But now Mahao was minister of justice, and a trial of strength now ensued between him and the acting chief justice.

In late August, Mahase and the attorney-general, Haae Phoofolo, sat as the Judicial Service Commission (JSC) and recommended five people for appointment as judges by King Letsie III. There was no doubt that there was a severe shortage of judges, which severely hampered the administration of justice. However, when he heard of the recommendations, Mahao was enraged, asserting that Mahase and Phoofolo had breached all procedures, had not constituted a quorum of the JSC, and had made their recommendations without the knowledge of the other members of that body (the chairperson of the Public Service Commission and a nominated judge). Furthermore, he asserted that Mahase's and Phoofolo's actions were contrary to the government's stated commitment not to appoint any new judges until after the implementation of judicial reforms. (The latter was envisaged as part of the wider multi-sector reforms recommended by the SADC to achieve lasting peace and stability within the country.) Mahao insisted that before the JSC recommended new appointments, it had to be restructured to have a wider representation of stakeholders, provision for which had been catered for by tabling an Administration of the Judiciary Bill before the cabinet the intent of which would be to ensure that the appointment process was depoliticised.

Ultimately Mahao's position prevailed when the king, acting on the advice of the prime minister, declined to approve the appointment of the five recommended candidates. Furthermore, Mahase suffered a further set-back when, in September, Mahao confirmed the appointment of high court justice Sakoane Sakoane as chief justice, explaining that although the government had committed to making substantive appointments only after the enactment of judicial reforms, it had concluded that it could not replace one acting person (i.e. Mahase) with another in an acting capacity. Overall, Mahao's reasoning seemed sound, providing some reasonable grounds for trusting that the recent politicisation of the judiciary would be reversed.

Foreign Affairs

Apart from the dispatch of the South African delegation to Lesotho to mediate in the latest political crisis in April, political relationships between Maseru and Pretoria were largely dictated by the Covid-19 emergency (see below). There were, however, two other developments of significance.

The first was the cancellation by the Lesotho Highlands Development Authority (LHDA) of prequalification for the construction of the Polihali Dam and transfer tunnel because it did not meet the requirements for lenders. Although phase two of the dam, part of the Lesotho Highlands Water Project, should have been finished by 2020, there had been major delays in getting it started, severely imperilling the supply of water to Gauteng, which was now at risk of experiencing water restrictions until at least 2026. The LHDA stated in its announcement that a company which had been appointed to take part in the design phase of the project had been selected after the prequalification exercise had already commenced. The irregularity had come to light as a result of Nomvula Mokonyane, the South African minister of water affairs, firing Zodwa Dlamini, the country's chief delegate to the Lesotho Water Commission, allegedly because she would not assist in the selection of one of Mokonyane's favoured companies, LTE Consulting, despite the latter having had its lack of the necessary capabilities to undertake the project revealed by its participation in the much smaller Giyani water supply project in South Africa. Knowledgeable observers welcomed the development as indicating that the Polihali Dam project, the major funding for which would be provided by the AfDB and the New Development Bank, would not become tarnished by rent-seeking. With these two bodies looking over the shoulders of the LHDA, it boded well that repayment of their loans would be underpinned by the sale of water by Lesotho to South Africa, as intended, rather than its being drained away by corruption.

The second interruption of smooth relations with South Africa was the decision by the Lesotho Communications Authority (LCA) to revoke the operating licence of Vodacom, the major South African mobile phone operator, which owned 80% of its subsidiary in Lesotho, citing the failure of the latter to pay a portion of a 134 million rand (R) fine in connection with an alleged conflict of interest relating to the company's external auditors. A third of the payment (R 40.2 m) had been due on 7 October, and when it was not forthcoming the LCA immediately withdrew Vodacom's permit to operate. (The remaining R 98.8 m had been suspended for five years on condition that the company did not commit any further contraventions of the regulatory commitments.) The crux of the issue was that Vodacom Lesotho had used an external auditor whose partner was a sister-in-law of the company's board chairperson, the LCA maintaining that this compromised its independence. Faced with a crisis, Vodacom had rushed to the high court, which proceeded to temporarily block the LCA from revoking its licence, subject to Vodacom being able to show why the revocation should not be made a final order of the court. The judgment remained pending at year's end, and it remains to be seen whether Lesotho bends to South African pressure.

Socioeconomic Developments: The Impact of the Covid-19 Pandemic

Lesotho was the last country in Africa to record a case of the Covid-19 virus, but this was probably more a function of the lack of local testing capacity than of its absence. In reality, the country was severely at risk of experiencing a Covid-19 disaster because of the high number of border crossings from South Africa.

Responding to the loud ringing of alarm bells regionally, the government announced the closing of its borders with South Africa on 6 March, before declaring a national emergency 12 days later, despite there having been no confirmed cases as yet. Prime Minister Thabane also announced a national lockdown from 29 March, that arriving travellers were to be quarantined upon arrival for 14 days, and that schools were to be closed until 17 April. Meanwhile, Lesotho began sending samples to South Africa's National Institute for Communicable Diseases for testing. Some aspects of the lockdown were lifted on 5 May, but only a few days later the first case of Covid-19 was confirmed.

Thereafter the number of cases began to rise steadily. By the end of July, the number of confirmed cases had climbed to 604 and the death toll to 13; by the end of December, there had been a total of 3,206 confirmed cases, with the death toll having risen to 51. However, given the lack of local testing capacity and that many Basotho had returned home and dispersed across the country over the Christmas holiday period, as well as the likelihood that there were numerous illegal crossings over the border after it was closed, these statistics were almost certainly an undercount.

Lesotho's economy is significantly open to global trade, and Covid-19 was expected to have a marked impact upon supply chains, thus hampering exports, as most textile and apparel firms in the country sourced their raw materials from China. Exports to major economies such as the euro area and the United States were also likely to be negatively affected.

According to the World Bank, Lesotho's real GDP growth rate is estimated to have averaged a mere 1.6% during 2015–19. It was predicted that this would fall to 0.6% between 2019 and 2021, largely as a result of the impact of the pandemic.

Madagascar

Richard R. Marcus

In 2020 Madagascar faced comparatively few Covid-19 cases but significant impacts from the pandemic on both the economy and politics. GDP fell for the first time in over a decade, the current account balance dropped to alarming levels, the value of the currency (the ariary) slipped, manufacturing slowed, agricultural production slowed, and services declined. As a result, social conditions worsened in a country already suffering as one of the poorest in the world, and the government was ill equipped to provide a robust response to famine in the south of the country. The year was positive for President Rajoelina, who made great strides in consolidating power. Having already secured decisive victories for the presidency, in taking control of the national assembly, and in local elections throughout the country, the only remaining opposition space was in the senate. The president received support from the High Constitutional Court (HCC) to reform the senate before winning a decisive victory in the indirect elections on 11 December. The year ended with deep concerns about economic recovery, worsening social conditions, high levels of engagement by international donors, rising concerns about the health risks of Covid-19, a demoralised and highly fractured opposition, and President Rajoelina indisputably at the helm, relying on a small coterie of loyalists.

Domestic Politics

President Andry Rajoelina entered 2020 in an enviable political position. Having served as the illegitimate president of the Transition (2009–13), he had much to prove to the populace and the international community when he was elected in 2019. His political party, Miaraka amin'i Prezida Andry Rajoelina (MAPAR), and its coalition, Isika Rehetra Miaraka amin'i Andry Rajoelina (IRD), had just won political control of the national assembly. Madagascar is divided into 22 regions, 1,695 communes, 18,333 fokontany, and 24,852 electoral districts, and Rajoelina's IRD was already dominant at every level. The remaining space for the opposition in January was in the senate, where its president, Rivo Rakotovao, continued to present a challenge and the party of former president Hery Rajaonarimampianina was in the majority. In January, President Rajoelina reduced the number of senators from 63 to 18 (including six appointed by President Rajoelina). Early 2020 contestations between the president and the senate effectively received split decisions from the HCC, with both Rajoelina and Rakotovao able to claim victories. However, in October, a court challenge by 19 opposition senators against the right of the president to reduce the size of the senate was decisively defeated in the HCC. The reforms were put in place and the indirect elections were held on 11 December. The president's platform won 10 of the 12 seats and the Malagasy Miara-Miainga (MMM) won two seats. The platforms of the primary opposition leader, former president Marc Ravalomanana and of Rajoelina's predecessor Hery Rajaonarimampianina both boycotted the elections. The success of President Rajoelina and his party in the senatorial elections meant that all possible institutional avenues in which the opposition could compete were closed until the presidential elections of 2023.

Madagascar has long been a paradox, with significant resource wealth but one of the highest levels of poverty in the world. President Rajoelina ran on a campaign for state-led development via the Madagascar Emergence Initiative (IEM). He promised 'lasting and effective' solutions through the IEM's large-scale projects but recognised immediate concerns such as rice and petrol prices. While the successful centralisation of power meant that President Rajoelina could make decisions without negotiating with the opposition, it also put pressure on him to deliver on his promises, with no scapegoats to take the blame for failures. In early 2020, the pressure on the president was apparent. He often acted defensively, there was continual discussion about a cabinet reshuffle, and there was wide speculation that he would finally have to expand his coterie from the small group of loyalists he had come to trust. The Covid-19 pandemic provided a new opportunity.

From the onset of the pandemic, President Rajoelina was combative and even openly hostile to the WHO, global efforts, and international norms around the virus. Seeing the WHO warning as a barrier, he stated that 'nothing will stop us moving forward, neither a country nor an organization'. The Malagasy government was going to forge its own path.

A state of emergency was declared on 21 March, based on a legal definition consistent with a state of war. This meant that there were no automatic ends to increased executive authority in decision-making. Covid-19 was framed as a national security threat, and enforcement of Covid-19 measures fell to a Council of Ministers led by a military general. Thirty-eight Covid-19 Operational Command Centers (OCCs) were set up across prefectures and districts. While there is an established process through decentralised authorities to set up emergency responses, the OCCs were set up outside of institutions with clearly designated legal authority. In Madagascar, military leaders are permitted to hold civilian posts, effectively creating a martial elite. Successive presidents have taken advantage of this to lash bureaucratic authority to dominant political networks, and this was an opportunity for President Rajoelina to do the same. The military presence in urban areas, surveillance of citizens, muting of opposition, and challenging of journalists increased. Restrictions on freedom of movement and mass demonstrations followed global norms on confinement, but with these freedoms the only way for opposition to foment outside of the senate, the political implications were significant. The Varieties of Democracy Pandemic Backsliding Project acknowledged this challenge, ranking Madagascar in the top third of countries in the world in terms of experiencing democratic backsliding due to specific pandemic-related actions.

President Rajoelina made progress on campaign promises. He sought changes to the Finance Law in the face of losses of more than $ 700 m, even while he championed the idea of a national car company, GasyCar; negotiated land for the state-led development of a new community, Tanamasoandro, near the capital; and gained strength to control the outcome of the rebuilding of Lapa Masoandro, a culturally important palace. Part of the nearly $ 650 m in Covid-19-related foreign aid flowing into the country could be used for *sosialim-bahoaka* (public social aid) and *vatsy tsinjo* (subsidies on basic goods), which benefited a population in desperate need but also was doled out with great fanfare to the political benefit of the president.

While President Rajoelina's ideology is difficult to pin down, he is a nationalist and has benefited from the rise of nationalism throughout the world. For him, his Covid-19 response was immediately tied to his version of nationalism. On 20 April, Rajoelina made an announcement that Madagascar had found a cure for Covid-19 in an artemisia-based drink dubbed Covid-Organics (CVO). On 21 May, the WHO director-general Tedros Adhanom publicly agreed to enter CVO into a testing regimen, but warned of using untested drugs. Pharmalagasy was already part of the state-led industrialisation plan, but the CVO and personal protective equipment were an opportunity for rapid expansion. President Rajoelina required all schoolchildren to take CVO and sent the military door-to-door in the capital to convince adults to drink it. As of the end of 2020, no data confirmed its efficacy and Madagascar's sharp increase in Covid-19 cases appeared to undermine the president's claims. It nonetheless continued to provide an important political foothold for the president to claim that there are Malagasy answers to Malagasy challenges, and that he was best placed to offer them.

Christian Ntsay was appointed prime minister under former president Hery Rajaonarimampianina, but he retained his post under Rajoelina. This was seen as a move to please the international community, particularly donors. It quickly became clear that the political power of the cabinet was marginal, as the president turned to his close advisors, notably then foreign minister and former president of the corporation GEM (Groupement des Entreprises de Madagascar) Naina Andriantsitohaina (now mayor of the capital, Antananarivo) and businessman Maminiaina Ravatomanga (also known as Mamy). Much concern was raised both locally and in the international community about the role of Mamy in official functions despite his lack of portfolio, his legal challenges in Mauritius, and the favourable contract his company, Sodiat, received in 2020. There was speculation through 2020 that the president would reshuffle the cabinet to expand his political network, but in the end there were only routine changes, Prime Minister Ntsay remained in post, and decision-making remained in the hands of a few.

Corruption continued to be a salient issue in 2020. While Madagascar's score in the TI Corruption Perceptions Index improved from 24 to 25, it remained on TI's list of countries with the greatest negative change since 2012 and in the lowest performance quintile. At root, corruption in Madagascar is caused by inefficient governance and economic instability. TI Madagascar logs areas of pervasive corruption such as contracting, appointment and holding of office, and budgeting. In August, it raised concerns that the long-term increase in corruption may irreparably damage citizen trust.

Foreign Affairs

The health impacts of Covid-19 in Madagascar were relatively modest in 2020, with a total of 17,700 cases and 261 deaths by year's end, but the political and economic impacts were significant. GDP shrank by 3.8%, the first negative growth in over a decade. The last recession, in 2009, was at least in part politically driven and the response of the international donor community was to freeze aid or limit communication with the government. In 2020, the international community robustly engaged with the government and increased both development and humanitarian assistance.

Madagascar's economic engagement with the international community was already on an upwards trajectory before the pandemic. ODA was $ 756 m in 2019 (most recent aggregate figures), an increase to 5.5% of gross national income. In

2020, the World Bank remained the largest donor with new dispersal of $ 174.4 m, followed by the US at $ 109.4 m, the EU at $ 82.3 m, France at $ 76.4 m, the IMF at $ 44.6 m, and UNICEF at $ 25.9 m. Portfolio commitments showed an even stronger response, with 2020 World Bank commitments rising from $ 310 m to $ 548 m.

The international donor community expressed collective concern particularly about vulnerable populations in urban areas and new exposure to economic hardship and poverty traps in these circumstances. Madagascar entered 2020 with 74.3% of the population living in extreme poverty ($ 1.90 per day), and according to World Bank figures, the pandemic pushed that figure to an estimated 77.4% due to losses in manufacturing, agriculture, and services. The informal economy recorded widescale collapse. Global trade decreased. Travel was disrupted. Tourism was halted. In all, a World Bank survey showed in December 2020 that on average 97% of surveyed companies reported a decline.

In December, UNICEF clarified its response and funding status, with its focus on accessing essential healthcare, safe water, support for children, and outreach. It also joined the World Bank and the US in supporting household direct cash transfers.

On 29 January, the IMF completed its sixth review under the ECF arrangement for Madagascar. This enabled the dispersal of $ 43.2 m, bringing the total of the ECF to $ 344.5 m. Despite some concerns, the overall assessment was positive, asserting that Madagascar's performance on its economic programme was broadly satisfactory and mitigated internal and external risks. It was largely complimentary about the IEM, the president's initiative to raise economic growth. With this positive assessment, Madagascar was well placed in its relationship with the IMF when the pandemic hit. On 27 August, a statement by the IMF acknowledged the economic deterioration due to the pandemic, but, in contrast to the perspective in 2009 that economic crisis was endogenous, it clearly saw Madagascar as a victim of circumstances in need of balance-of-payments support. The IMF approved an additional release of funds under the 'exogenous shock' window of the Rapid Credit Facility. The balance-of-payments support was critical, but it also sent a signal to bilateral donors, the ambassadorial community, and private investment that the IMF saw a need to increase engagement.

On 20 April, US ambassador Michael Pelletier pledged $ 2.5 m in assistance to Madagascar to address the Covid-19 outbreak. While important, this did little to increase the role of the US, which had carved out an important space in humanitarian support but not development decision-making. Africa was not a priority for the Trump administration, and the leadership vacuum left by the US under the administration had a significant impact on the international community in Madagascar. Though the US administration referred frequently to its effort to compete with China for global influence, this was not apparent in Madagascar.

China's involvement in Madagascar was already on the upswing going into 2020, with commitments from the Chinese special envoy, He Wei, to extend support to a level that rivalled that of the EU. The new ambassador, Guo Xiaomei, arrived on

20 October. In December, she marked significant ground by committing to increase Madagascar's benefit in the Belt and Road Initiative and as part of global development efforts. China is the largest funder of the Initiative for the Emergence of Madagascar, critical both to Madagascar's primary development objectives and the perceived success of the president.

French–Malagasy relations continued to deteriorate in 2020. Andry Rajoelina's relationship with President Nicolas Sarkozy during his time as president of the Transition a decade ago was strong, bringing out ire and accusations of French meddling from the opposition. However, the shift in *FrancAfrique* policy under President Emmanuel Macron has left points of conflict. This was exacerbated at the end of 2019 when the French president announced the classification of a nature reserve of the island of Grande Glorieuse, one of the Scattered Islands. The contested territory is thought to be rich in hydrocarbons, which Madagascar claims and wants to exploit. In January, foreign affairs minister Djacoba Liva Tehindrazanarivelo invited French ambassador Christophe Bouchard to discuss a way out of the impasse. Yet on 23 October, Macron reaffirmed France's sovereignty over the Scattered Islands, despite a 1979 UN resolution stating that the islands were arbitrarily separated and calling on France to reintegrate them with Madagascar. The issue continued to heat up at the Joint Commission on the Scattered Islands on 18 November. As the rift grew with Paris, President Rajoelina made it clear that he was increasingly looking towards Russia, China, and other countries for new contracting opportunities, particularly in the oil and mining sector. Growing these relations remained a difficult balancing act, as the president continued to rely on his relationships with the Bretton Woods institutions.

Socioeconomic Developments

The majority of Madagascar's population remained in subsistence agriculture, with 64% living in rural areas, but agriculture accounted for only 25.7% of GDP. Services accounted for 51.4% of GDP but employed a comparatively small percentage of workers. As a result, unemployment, which neared 50% in 2020 according to EIU figures, underestimated hardship and disparities. Madagascar's Gini coefficient of 42.6 (comparable to that of DRC and Peru) was an indicator of how poorly the economic gains over the past decade have been distributed. It was a signal about how poverty could deepen even during times of economic growth. With Madagascar's pandemic-fuelled recession in 2020, the poverty rate ($1.90 per day or less) increased by an alarming 3.1%. Less than a quarter of the population could meet its basic human needs. Inflation remained in check (3.8%) and the exchange rate continued its slow slide, avoiding currency collapse, but concern rose not just for the rural poor but for the new urban poor, who suffered losses in manufacturing, exports, and services. Madagascar's ranking continued to fall in the UNDP HDI (measuring life expectancy, years of schooling, and gross national income) in 2020, to 164th out of 186 countries, down from 162nd in 2019, 161st in 2018, and 158th in 2017, marking development concerns. The 2020 UN Global Multidimensional Poverty Index data dated from before the pandemic impact, but showed a high 55.6% intensity of deprivation and noted that 45.5% of the population were in severe multidimensional poverty. Measured as a combination of health, education, standard of living, relationship to the national poverty line, and the percentage of the population living on $1.90 per day or less, it was clear that the poverty rate is sticky. The additional 1.38 m people who entered poverty in 2020 will not have the structural support or opportunities to rapidly exit from poverty when the economy enters post-pandemic recovery.

There are three large industrial mining interests in the country: Ambatovy (led by Sherritt International), QMM (led by Rio Tinto), and Toliara Sands (led by Base Resources). The independent EITI, which appointed Herinarahinjaka Eryck Randrianandrasana its new coordinator on 15 September, reported in its most recent figures earnings of $ 44.7 m from extractive industry taxation, and showed that it contributed 4.6% to the country's GDP. The goal has been to grow industrial mining's share of GDP to 14% by 2025 in order to fund state-led development initiatives. For that to have an effective impact, the government called for reforms to the mining code and the Law on Large Scale Mining Investments in Madagascar (LGIM). The year began with combative negotiations over an increase in royalty rates to 4% and in the requisite government share to 10%. The Rajoelina government insisted that this was a core part of its IEM development strategy, and that the mineral wealth of Madagascar was the patrimony of the Malagasy people. Mining companies insisted that it would drive capital flight, and the World Bank, long seminal in the writing of Malagasy mining law, attempted to broker agreement. At the same time, the government faced a significant backlash against Base Toliara for potential impacts on the environment and local livelihoods, leading the government to temporarily suspend the Toliara Sands project. By year's end there was no resolution, and there were concerns of a heightened sectoral rift and social conflict in communes impacted by extraction.

Beyond the pandemic, the most critical socioeconomic development in 2020 was the famine in the south of the country. The regions of Anosy, Androy, and Atsimo-Andrefana faced drought conditions and food shortages not seen in a generation. According to Integrated Food Security Phase Classification (IPC) data, in Androy 83% of the population experienced food insecurity in 2020, with 43% at level 3 ('crisis') or higher, while in Anosy 71% of the population experienced food insecurity with 34% at level 3 or higher. In total, more than 2.4 m people faced a food crisis. There have been 16 famines in the region since 1896, but eight of them have been in the past decade. With each one successively worse, concerns were raised in

2020 that they had undermined regional gains for years while exacerbating vulnerability in one of the most fragile parts of the country. Prices of rice (the food staple) in the south more than doubled when it was available, and areas not serviced by the JIRAMA electricity and water parastatal or UNICEF water projects saw private water prices rise as much as twentyfold. The long-term impacts, including the sale of cattle and other reserves, a higher percentage of the population slipping into extreme poverty, high regional migration, an increase in insecurity in some areas, and a rise in cattle theft, will impact the region long after 2020 and post-pandemic economic recovery.

Malawi

George Dzimbiri and Lewis Dzimbiri

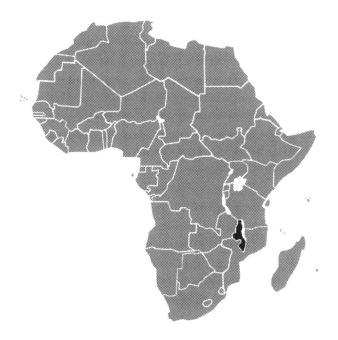

The nullification of the 2019 presidential elections by the high court was the most dramatic event that drew the attention of Malawians over the year. Peter Mutharika was declared the winner in the May 2019 polls amid widespread allegations of irregularities and vote-tampering, particularly the use of corrective fluid called Tipp-Ex. The opposition Malawi Congress Party (MCP) and United Transformation Movement (UTM) filed a petition challenging the election results at the high court, and on 3 February a panel of five judges unanimously nullified the May 2019 presidential elections and ordered that fresh elections be held in 150 days. Intra- and inter-party conflicts ensued as preparations for the elections were underway. The fresh elections took place on 23 June, and Lazarus Chakwera of the MCP won under the banner of the nine-party grouping called the Tonse Alliance. The composition of Chakwera's cabinet and parastatal board of directors attracted criticism from Malawians for lack of merit and gender balance. The country also witnessed an escalation of the coronavirus pandemic during the first half of the year, leading to job losses, loss of business, and closure of companies. Mutharika declared the coronavirus pandemic a national disaster, and announced a 21-day lockdown to stem the spread of the coronavirus, a decision opposition parties saw as a strategy to postpone fresh elections. Consequently, there was widespread protest against the lockdown by vendors, human rights groups, and opposition parties.

Domestic Politics

The nullification of the *2019 presidential elections* dominated the political scene. On 3 February, the high court nullified the presidential polls and declared that new elections should be held within 150 days, because of widespread irregularities and vote-tampering. Following the nullification, in March the Malawi Electoral Commission (MEC) announced 2 July as the new election date, one day before the 150-day limit to hold elections set by the constitutional court or high court. However, on 21 May the Legal Affairs Committee of parliament decided on 23 June rather than 2 July as the date for fresh presidential elections. The elections were won by Lazarus Chakwera of the MCP with 59% votes, while Peter Mutharika of the Democratic Progressive Party (DPP) secured 40%.

Intra-party and inter-party conflicts dominated the domestic scene before and after the fresh elections. Intra-party conflicts were noticeable in both the *Democratic Progressive Party (DPP)* and opposition parties. On 16 January, some 220 DPP members in the Chikwawa and Nsanje districts left to join the MCP, citing poor leadership in the DPP. On 23 January, President Peter Mutharika reprimanded camps that emerged in DPP ahead of the 2025 presidential election. There was in-fighting within the party as some were against Mutharika standing again as a presidential candidate for the party in 2025, while others were in full support of his candidature. Mutharika described their squabbles as a sign of hunger for power, and he advised that they should be brought to an end. The DPP also expelled the vice-president for Southern Region, Kondwani Nankhumwa, over in-fighting on 26 November at Mutharika's retirement home in Mangochi. Also expelled from the party was Gelzeder Jeffrey, who was replaced by Samuel Tembenu as secretary-general. Yusufu Nthenda, Mulanje North legislator, was also expelled for defying the party in parliament when he opposed the imposition of Francis Kasaira as leader of the opposition in parliament. However, in October both Nankhumwa and Jeffrey were reinstated by the court to their former positions.

The opposition MCP was also beset by internal squabbles. On 17 October, members of the MCP constituency committee for Karonga central resigned and joined the UTM, citing poor leadership especially at the district level, and that the MCP executive committee was not only disrespectful but was also monopolising everything.

Inter-party conflicts became a typical feature of the year. On 26 November, the leader of the opposition in parliament, Kondwani Nankhumwa, called on President Chakwera to address the challenges faced by farmers through the use of cheap fertiliser and seeds under the Affordable Input Programme (AIP). Nankhumwa described the AIP as a disaster and called upon the Tonse Alliance government to introduce workable solutions to the crisis within a reasonable time frame. On 9 December, the DPP regional governor for the east of the country cautioned that the government would be letting down Muslims if it were to follow through on its decision to open an embassy in the Jerusalem – a decision that attracted local and international criticism. This was because Palestine considers Jerusalem its future capital city, and the governor felt that Malawi should not fuel the enmity between Israel and Palestine.

The government was also in collusion with civil society organisations (CSOs) over governance. On 2 January, Mutharika accused the *Human Rights Defender Coalition* (HRDC) of bringing chaos in the country and operating like a terrorist organisation. But HRDC vice-chairperson Gift Trapence accused Mutharika of fuelling disunity among Malawians. Since the announcement of the 21 May tripartite elections, HRDC had been orchestrating protests aimed at forcing the resignation of MEC chairperson Jane Ansah for mismanaging the election results. On 3 December, an influential youth rights activist, Charles Kajoloweka, called on President Chakwera to bring to an end to the recruitment of Tony Blair and his team as advisors to the Malawi government. He observed that Chakwera's administration had failed to mention the challenges that his government was facing, describing the government's decision to hire the Tony Blair Institute (TBI) as an insult to the presidency. On 20 December, HRDC took the government to task for allegedly betraying the trust of Malawians on both social and economic fronts as its administration was losing direction. The HRDC argued that there were signs that Chakwera and his Tonse Alliance partners were unwilling to combat corruption as they had promised. It also observed that the administration appeared clueless as to how to grow the economy to create the promised one million jobs to reduce poverty.

Various acts of legislation kept parliament busy. In February, parliament passed the *Parliamentary and Presidential Elections Act (PPEA) Amendment Bill*, setting 19 May as the date for the new presidential elections and extending the terms of MPs and local councillors by one year to allow for harmonised presidential, parliamentary, and local elections in 2025. In August, President Chakwera assented to 12 bills that parliament passed into law. Among the bills was the much-awaited Taxation Amendment Bill, which would see workers benefiting from the 100,000 kwacha (MK) free tax band. The Constitutional Amendment Bill endorsed the fact that the next tripartite elections would be conducted on 19 May of 2025. And another electoral law would see the MEC applying the 50%-plus-1 rule to presidential elections, where winners would have to receive over 50% of total votes cast.

During the six months to the end of the year, Chakwera's administration came under severe criticism over the calibre of cabinet and parastatal board members. There was a delay in appointing the 31-member cabinet, raising questions about the unpreparedness of the president although he had had sufficient time to decide on cabinet members before and after the elections. The composition of the cabinet was not well received, as it had a high concentration of members from Central Region, President Chakwera's home region, and traces of family connections were evident among cabinet members. The appointment of a husband and wife as ministers, as well as other family-related persons to cabinet roles, meant that Chakwera was committing the mistakes he vigorously campaigned against – nepotism, regionalism, and tribalism. Worse still, although Chakwera signed a commitment to gender balance in line with the Gender Equality Act before the elections, only three female cabinet ministers and four deputy ministers were appointed. Although the public was not persuaded, the president defended his decision by defining merit in his own way and promised to reshuffle what he called an interim cabinet within five months – a promise he did not fulfil. Moreover, the appointment of the parastatal board of directors attracted uproar from women's groups for ignoring gender balance. Out of over 70 parastatal boards, only 11 had women chairpersons, and a good number of parastatals had no female appointee.

Foreign Affairs

The EU Election Observation Mission (EU-EOM) arrived in Malawi on 8 January to issue a fresh report on the disputed 21 May presidential polls. The delegation came as the country awaited the judgment of the constitutional court sitting at the high court in Lilongwe within 45 days from 21 December 2019. the EU-EOM preferred to arrive earlier but found that the airport had been closed, as workers were on strike calling for wage increases.

Malawi continued to enjoy good relations with other countries and international agencies, and received financial and material support. In April, China made a donation of 2,000 Covid-19 testing kits and hospital equipment to the Malawi government, stating that it was ready to help Malawi fight the Covid-19 pandemic and promote education among girls. The kits were meant to equip the Malawi government with kits for testing at the borders and airports, to facilitate progression in terms of overall testing programme. On 5 November, the Malawi government signed a $ 343 m about (MK 259 bn) grant from the United Kingdom for the implementation of projects in the three ministries of Local Government, Forestry and Natural Resources, and Finance.

On 3 November, over 10,000 Malawians were repatriated from South Africa. The repatriation exercise started in early May, following the outbreak of Covid-19. Since the pandemic had emerged, South Africa had been in a series of lockdowns, thereby affecting many foreigners, including Malawians. The government of Malawi and the South African government made an agreement on the repatriation process. Returnees were transported in 30 buses, and key border agencies ensured that coronavirus cases were not imported into the country. However, many returnees were not cooperative with the government's Covid-19 preventative measures, fleeing from isolation camps where they were supposed to stay for 14 days before proceeding to their respective destinations. Despite the Covid-19 pandemic challenge, on

5 November transport minister Sidik Mia and information minister Gospel Kazako represented President Chakwera at the inauguration ceremony of the president-elect of Tanzania, John Magufuli.

As the chairperson of the Least Developed Countries group, President Chakwera addressed the Biodiversity Summit of the 75th Session of the UNGA via a pre-recorded speech on 25 September. Among other things, he appealed to developed nations to consider debt cancellation for the least-developed countries, stating that it would assist them in recovering from the effects of the Covid-19 pandemic.

On 6 October, President Chakwera visited Mozambique. He held bilateral talks with President Filipe Nyusi in the town of Songo, visited the Cahora Bassa hydro-power dam and a transformer station through which Malawi was likely to connect electricity under the Malawi–Mozambique interconnection project.

Palestinian president Mahmoud Abbas urged Chakwera not to go ahead with the decision to open an embassy in Jerusalem, Israel. On 5 November, Abbas sent a special envoy, Hanna Jarrar, who delivered a letter to Chakwera at Kamuzu Palace in Lilongwe. Jarrar stated that the decision to open an embassy in Jerusalem defied international law and United Nations resolutions. She said that Security Council Resolution 475 of 1980 and Resolution 2334 of 2016 speak against any action that seeks to alter the character and status of Jerusalem.

Chakwera visited South Africa on 11–12 November to strengthen bilateral relations between the two countries. On 25 November, Chakwera visited Botswana, to attend an extraordinary SADC Troika Summit meeting. The meeting was scheduled to tackle emerging challenges faced by the region, and as an incoming SADC chair it was vital for Chakwera to attend the summit.

Socioeconomic Developments

On 23 January, the country suffered heavy rains resulting in floods that affected many families. A total of 1,519 people were affected by heavy rains in Lilongwe. The Department of Disaster Management Affairs (DMA) confirmed that a total of 63 houses had been damaged. The most affected areas were Kaliyeka, Mgona, Area 25, and Ngonamo. Floods also displaced over 2,187 households in the district of Chikwawa. Some of the victims were evacuated by boat. The affected families sought shelter in schools and churches.

Malawi registered a decline in the 2019 Transparency International Corruption Perceptions Index (CPI) released on 23 January. The country emerged as 123rd out of 180 countries, down from position 120 in 2018. Malawi's performance on the CPI has been dismal since 2012.

Inflation declined from March onwards. The year-on-year inflation rate for June stood at 8.5% (compared with 9% in June 2019), the lowest level since January 2018, when it reached 8.1%. In May, food and non-food inflation rates stood at 13.4% and

4.5% compared with 13.7 and 4.5%, respectively, the previous year. In August, inflation decreased to 7.6% from the 8% recorded in July. This was due to a decrease in food inflation.

In April, the IMF approved an additional $ 101.96 m in disbursements under the Rapid Credit Facility (RCF), bringing total IMF Covid-19 emergency support to Malawi to $ 193 m. This was the second disbursement since the onset of the pandemic and to help finance Malawi's urgent balance of payment and fiscal needs. Since the first RCF, Malawi's economic outlook had worsened with the spread of the pandemic in the country and the deteriorating global and regional economic situation. The additional $ 101.96 m was expected to help close part of the increased external financing deficit and provide the fiscal resources needed to address critical spending needs. Owing to the Covid-19 pandemic, the IMF, in its World Economic Outlook (WEO) report, also revised Malawi's economic growth downwards for the years 2020 and 2021, from a projected 6% to 7% in the medium term to 1% and 2.5% in 2020 and 2021, respectively.

President Mutharika declared the coronavirus pandemic a national disaster and announced a 21-day lockdown to stem the spread of the coronavirus by enforcing preventative measures such as social distance measures, closure of schools, and a ban on gatherings of more than 100 people. This affected all sectors negatively, including through loss of jobs. Consequently, there were widespread violent protests across the country as informal business owners, particularly vendors, complained that a 21-day nationwide lockdown would make them starve. They wanted the government to provide them with upkeep money to survive during the 21 days. Further, the opposition parties described the lockdown as a tactic by the DPP to delay the presidential polls scheduled for 2 July. The high court, on 17 April, temporarily barred the government from implementing the 21-day lockdown following a petition by a human rights group. The HRDC argued that its action was based on the government's failure to announce any measures to cushion the poor during the lockdown. The escalation of Covid-19 resurfaced towards the end of the year and the government closed its borders after confirmed cases of Covid-19 increased by 75% in November. The surge was attributed to relaxed preventative measures and increased cross-border traffic for the holidays. However, the government mandated everyone to wear face masks and use hand sanitiser. In October, the government reopened borders and eased restrictions on social gatherings following a drastic decline in the number of confirmed Covid-19 cases.

A damning Covid-19-related report was released by the Malawi Ombudsman's office, titled 'Misplaced Priorities: A Report on an Investigation into Allegations concerning Lack of Transparency and Accountability in the Implementation of Malawi's National Covid-19 Preparedness and Response Plan'. The main conclusion of the report was that priorities were misplaced – rather than spending MK 6.2 bn on Covid-related equipment and essential supplies, 79% of the money had been spent on personnel allowances.

The uncertainty surrounding the performance of the kwacha in the short to medium term continued. After a period of stability, the currency depreciated against the US dollar in July, moving from an average of K 737.7 to $ 1 to K 738.9, with further depreciation in September. This depreciation followed an intensification of demand and supply mismatch in the month following the closure of the tobacco marketing season, and the continued decrease in inflow of donor funds. The kwacha also depreciated against the UK pound in July, averaging K 947.1 to £ 1, down from the previous month's recorded average of K 934.7. The kwacha opened the month of August at K 922.8 against the pound and progressively depreciated, reaching a two-year low of K 994 by the end of August. The depreciation was occasioned by the fact that the pound sterling appreciated on the global market after the dollar slipped to a two-year low. The local currency also depreciated against the South African rand in July. It moved from an average of K 44.3 recorded in June to an average of K 45.4 in July.

The official forex reserves in September decreased to $ 546.99 m (2.6 months' worth of import cover) from $ 641.88 m (3.1 months of import cover) at the end of August. The private sector reserves increased to $ 318.47 m (1.5 months of import cover) at end of September from $ 316.74 m (1.5 months of import cover) in August. On 30 September, total forex reserves stood at $ 865.46 m (4.1 months of import cover), a decrease from $ 959.60 m (4.6 months of import cover) at the end of August.

The tobacco season made K 130 bn, about 27% lower than the K 182 bn earned in the preceding season. The country sold a total of 112.89 m kilogrammes of tobacco last season, down from the 165.67 m kilogrammes traded the season before. This was due to reduced tobacco output and high rejection rates, leading to forex reserve declines. Additionally, subdued demand for locally made products and increased appetite for imports also contributed to the decrease of forex reserves, which left the kwacha in a buffering state. Nineteen weeks after the opening of the tobacco, the average price trailed at $ 1.53/kg in 2020, compared with $ 1.47/kg recorded over the same period in 2019. A total volume of 114.02 m kilograms of all tobacco types valued at $ 174.97 m had been sold by the end of 19 weeks in 2020, compared with 143.98 m kilograms sold at $ 211.49 m during the same period in 2019. The cumulative average price of all tobacco types went up by 4.08% in the current season compared with the prices that prevailed over the same period in 2019.

Tea production also dropped during the year. In July, tea amounting to 1.1 m kilograms was produced. This was less than in June 2019, when the amount was 1.4 m kilograms. Tea sales through the Limbe auction market amounted to 0.3 m kilograms, at an average price of $ 1.45 per kg from total sales of 0.2 m kilograms in June. Total average tea sales earnings realised at the Limbe auction market were $ 227,357.94 in June 2020 compared with $ 403, 471.90 in June 2019.

Labour disputes escalated in all sectors of the economy. On 14 April, health workers in Malawi's commercial capital, Blantyre, staged a sit-in to protest against working conditions during the coronavirus pandemic, including a 'critical' shortage of personal protective equipment (PPE) needed to treat patients. The action came despite the National Organisation of Nurses and Midwives (NONM) asking its members on 13 April to return to work following a brief strike over the weekend. The organisation said that the government had provided assurances to resolve their grievances, which include demands for PPE and a risk allowance of 70% of their basic salary.

On 18 July, airport workers went on strike demanding that government improve their working conditions. Malawi's government came under intense pressure. Staff members were demanding, among other things, promotions, risk allowances, and revision of allowances. Investigations revealed that cargo planes, including those meant to bring in Covid-19 materials such as testing kits, were cancelled because of the strike.

On 18 October, truck drivers in Lilongwe started a strike over what they called unfair treatment by both government and their employers. They close the M1 road at Kanengo, where no heavy-duty vehicle was allowed to pass. Among other grievances, they wanted to be regarded not as labourers but as permanent employees, adding that some of them were receiving as low as K 25,000 per month in wages. Professional Drivers Union chairperson Major Mkandawire told the press that the strike was nationwide and that they would continue with the it until authorities intervened. The strike had the potential to affect the inflow of fuel and other essential goods in the country, hence putting Malawians in a state of panic.

Mauritius

Roukaya Kasenally

This was an exceptional year on all fronts, as the whole world felt the effects of Covid-19. Mauritius an island to a large extent dependent on external exchanges, be it for tourism, importation of food and other commodities, or the export of its garments, felt the wrath of a global economy in lockdown. The ruling coalition that was elected at the end of 2019 faced a challenging year that culminated in street protests in August and September.

Domestic Politics

This was a different year. Considerable attention and resources were essentially devoted to dealing with the Covid-19 pandemic at the national level. Mauritius, as one of the 54 countries of Africa, received precious medical supplies from the Jack Ma Foundation at the outset of the Covid-19 pandemic in March. One of the major gains for the government led by Pravind Jugnauth was the early containment of *Covid-19* on the island, which was in turn celebrated as one of the few 'Covid-safe' destinations in the world. The Covid-19 Bill was hurriedly passed in parliament and became law on 16 May. Under the *Covid-19 Act* (2020), some 56 amendments were brought to existing laws giving the government a sort of carte blanche to act in the name of national security and interest. The opposition parties, civil society, and other civic organisations decried the total absence of discussion and engagement around the Covid-19 Act (2020).

This carte blanche approach put a major strain on the practice of *accountability and transparency*. Parliament, one of the key institutions supposed to act as an oversight body especially against executive excesses, was severely constrained. On several occasions, parliament was suspended. The leader of the opposition (a constitutional position) and members of the opposition were ejected from the house, and perhaps more damaging to the autonomy of parliament was the inherent pro-government bias exhibited by the speaker. Furthermore, a number of civil rights and liberties were reigned in, with examples ranging from the multiple suspension of the licence fee for a private radio station, to the arrest of civilians for sharing content online deemed defamatory, to the imposition of tax on digital services. Meanwhile, the political calendar was marked by the holding of local elections across 130 villages on the island. These elections did not see the participation of the mainstream parties, but most candidates and parties who were subsequently elected aligned themselves with the ruling party.

An *oil spill* caused by the 'MV Wakashio' drew local and international attention. On 25 July, the Japanese oil tanker, flying under a Panamanian flag and carrying some 1,000 tonnes of oil, ran aground on the south coast of Mauritius. This event caught both local and international attention and was essentially spurred by the failure of the government to deal with the matter in a timely manner. Thousands of Mauritians took it upon themselves to manufacture artisanal booms to contain the oil spill before the government started to act. What is important to note is that the oil spill unleashed an unprecedented series of anti-government protest marches across the island, demanding the resignation of the prime minister. The hashtag BLD (bourre li dehors/kick him out) went viral and was used as a means of stirring up mobilisation among the 800,000 or so Facebook users on the island. The mobilisation among the citizenry was led by activist Bruno Laurette – the initiator of the protest marches and a vocal critic of the opacity surrounding the oil spill. In December 2020, Laurette officially launched the Linion Sitwayen Morisien (Union of Mauritian Citizens), putting pressure on established, mainstream political parties to change their methods of engagement with Mauritian citizens. With the next general election due in December 2024, only time will tell whether Laurette's platform will be a serious contender to these established, mainstream political parties or a mere flash in the pan.

Graft, corruption, and drugs gained in prominence. In fact, this was exacerbated by the sanitary emergency caused by Covid-19. A number of emergency procurements were authorised (a measure provided for under Section 21 of the Public Procurement Act 2006). Questions that were subsequently asked in parliament by the leader of opposition and local media exposed the extent of malpractice and favouritism in the awarding of contracts to unqualified parties, worth millions of US dollars. The deputy prime minister Ivan Collendavelloo was sacked over alleged corruption in a local power-generation project. Although the ruling party thus had to part with one of its most senior members, this did not have an impact on Pravind Jugnauth's majority in parliament. The use and spread of drugs within and outside the small island state has been a recurrent problem. The Organised Crime Index Africa (2019) ranked Mauritius first on the continent in relation to the use of synthetic drugs. Matters escalated considerably during the year, to the point that the head of the Catholic Church in Mauritius Cardinal Piat on several occasions publicly declared his concern over how 'drugs are so freely available'.

The government initiated a number of measures to support the flagging economy, adversely affected by almost a year of closed borders. To that effect, two schemes were introduced – *the Government Wage Assistance Scheme* (GWAS) and the Mauritius Investment Corporation (MIC). The GWAS was an economic measure to provide a government wage subsidy applicable to employees in the private sector who became technically unemployed during the Covid-19 lockdown period. The employer was eligible to receive funding equivalent to one month's basic wage bill for each employee drawing a monthly basic wage of up to 50,000 rupees (MUR) subject to a cap of MUR 25,000 per employee. The main aim of the MIC, which was set up under the aegis of the Bank of Mauritius, was to support financially distressed medium- to large-sized companies. The MIC was endowed with initial capital of MUR 80 bn. Meanwhile, the expansion of the light railway commonly referred to as the Metro Express was initiated, although works were considerably delayed by Covid-19.

Foreign Affairs

India, one of Mauritius' key partners, continued to support the island on multiple fronts. The new building of the Supreme Court of Mauritius, financed by India, was inaugurated in July. The courthouse's construction was one of the five projects under the Special Economic Package (SEP) to the tune of $ 353 m extended by India in 2016. Due to Covid-19, the signing of the Comprehensive Economic Cooperation and Partnership Agreement (CECPA) was delayed. Indian presence on the island of Agalega continued to generate many questions among civil society and the media in Mauritius. Agalega is a dependency of Mauritius and situated about 1,000 kilometres away. In 2018, India began infrastructure-related works to extend an existing runway and build port facilities on one of the two islets. It had been confirmed by Prime Minister Jugnauth that Afcons, an Indian company, had won the MUR 3 bn contract for works that would be 'fully funded by the government of India on a grant basis'. From the outset, the nature of the construction has been shrouded in secrecy and has only fuelled speculation on the intentions of India. In late 2020, the Outer Islands Development Corporation (OIDC) (responsible for the management and development of the outer islands, namely Agalega and Saint Brandon) decided to make a MUR 403,000 bank guarantee mandatory for any Mauritian citizen wishing to visit Agalega. This decision was subsequently revoked after public uproar.

Despite the UNGA in May 2019 voting in favour (by 116 to 6) of urging the United Kingdom to 'withdraw its colonial administration from the Chagos Islands within six months', the UK maintained its presence and, on the contrary, reaffirmed its sovereignty over the group of islands. In 2020, the UN issued a new world map (Map 4170 Revision 18.1 of February 2020) where the Chagos Islands were marked as Mauritian territory. Prime Minister Jugnauth publicly criticised both the UK and the US, labelling them 'hypocrites and champions of double talk for the way they behaved over the Chagos Islands'.

Japan's foreign affairs minister visited Mauritius in early December as part of a tour encompassing four African countries. This visit was deemed significant in the wake of the oil spill caused by the Japanese freighter 'MV Wakashio'. Discussions centred around Japan offering a $ 289 m loan to Mauritius in light of the oil spill. The president of Seychelles, Wavel Ramkalawan, also visited Mauritius; the two countries are part of the Indian Ocean Commission that also includes Madagascar, the Comoros islands, and the island of Réunion. A series of MoUs were signed on matters pertaining to maritime security, combating crime, and sharing of intelligence, among others.

Socioeconomic Developments

The economy of Mauritius contracted significantly despite its classification as a high-income country by the World Bank in July (classification based on 2019 data). The government initiated measures to keep the economy afloat which came at a high cost, and there is no doubt that their impact will be felt in the future. Already struggling to maintain its traditional economic pillars (sugar, tourism, and textiles) in pre-Covid-19 times, the Mauritian economy will have to imperatively reinvent and adapt itself and its workforce. The unemployment rate stood at 21% in 2020 compared with 6.7% the previous year. Meanwhile, public debt ballooned to 83.5% of GDP by the end of 2020. It should be noted that under the Covid 19 Act (2020), an amendment was made to the Public Debt Management Act (2008) whereby the public sector debt ceiling clause was removed.

The tourism sector, one of the island's core pillars, was adversely affected. Visitor numbers declined from 1.3 m in 2019 to around 300,000 in 2020 (essentially representing arrivals between January and March, prior to the borders being closed). Some 39,000 people were employed in the tourism sector and a fair number of them were able to retain their jobs through the GWAS. Around MUR 2 bn was disbursed to the sector under the GWAS in 2020. Mauritius kept its borders closed from March, and instituted a very strict mandatory 14-day quarantine for all travellers entering the country. There is no doubt that this measure helped to keep Mauritius a 'Covid-safe' destination, but in the process it caused irreversible long-term damage to the tourism industry. The grim fate faced by the tourism sector was further exacerbated by the national airline Air Mauritius going into voluntary administration. Air Mauritius' creation and evolution is closely tied to that of the tourism sector and its fate casts additional uncertainty about the sector that contributed 24% to Mauritius' GDP in the pre-Covid-19 era.

In 2020, 270,000 tonnes of sugar were produced – down from the 325,000 tonnes produced the previous year. This figure confirmed that sugar production had stalled and is a far cry from the industry's heyday, when production reached 700,000 tonnes and accounted for up to 25% of GDP. The island has four sugar mills, down from 11, and these have over the years diversified into more lucrative segments such as selling electricity to the national grid and the production of special sugars. The FTA with China caters for the export of special sugars to China.

The year marked half a century of the presence of the textile industry in Mauritius; the industry has significantly shaped the small island state and allowed large numbers of women to be employed. However, this celebratory year was undermined by the fact that most of the global economy underwent contraction. This added to the woes of an already fragile sector facing critical challenges due to its relatively expensive labour and the closing down or relocation of a number of textile factories to less expensive locations. There was a decline of 9% in the textile sector from January to August 2020 compared with the same period in 2019. To palliate the hardship faced by textile operators, the government extended a number of measures such as the reimbursement of 60% of freight costs instead of 40%, a Special Relief Fund of MUR 5 bn, exemption from port charges from July to December 2020, and the extension of 15% of Investment Tax Credit to all manufacturing enterprises for a period of three years.

Mauritius was listed by the Financial Action Task Force (FATF) as a 'jurisdiction under increased monitoring', adding it to the 'Grey List' of such countries in February 2020. This listing relates to the Anti-Money Laundering/Counter-Terrorist Financing (AML/CFT) framework and follows the findings on 'strategic deficiencies' with respect to the effectiveness of the framework identified by the Mutual Evaluation Report of the Eastern and Southern Africa Anti-Money Laundering Group in July 2018. Following the FATF listing, the European Commission placed

Mauritius on the list of high-risk third countries, externally referred to as the 'Black List', in May 2020. The repercussions were adverse for the global business sector in Mauritius – an important economic pillar that had directly contributed 5.8% to GDP in 2019. The reputation of Mauritius as an international financial centre was thus undermined: already, the latest Global Financial Centres Index downgraded Mauritius' ranking by 26 places to rank 89. The government of Mauritius responded rapidly to address the deficiencies outlined and has engaged with the FATF to develop a road-map towards removal from the Grey List. Legislation to reinforce the AML/CFT framework was introduced in July 2020, establishing risk-based supervision for entities that were previously not subject to AML/CFT regulations, such as real estate, gambling, and jewellery operators. However, the real challenge will be for law enforcement agencies to effectively and independently undertake financial investigations that culminate in the prosecution of offences.

There was no real change to Mauritius' key metrics because the borders remained closed, and many of its key economic sectors remained idle. The country retained its lead position in the Ibrahim Index of African Governance (IIAG) 2020 and its status in the EIU Democracy Index 2020 as the only 'full democracy' in Africa, as well as its 13th position in the World Bank's Ease of Doing Business rankings.

With unemployment up at 21%, increased inequality between low- and high-skilled workers, and the number of Mauritians who had lost their jobs growing, Mauritius risked sliding into a severe economic and social depression. Poverty, once under control at 10.5% in 2019, rose to 13% in 2020.

Mozambique

Joseph Hanlon

The civil war in Cabo Delgado Province escalated, with 583,000 people displaced and seven districts virtually depopulated; debate on the roots of the war intensified. Work on the natural gas developments was curtailed by war and falling gas prices. Stringent measures that adversely affected that economy were imposed to successfully limit the spread of Covid-19. New data showed that Mozambique was growing poorer and more unequal. Corruption largely stopped any aid money going directly to government.

Domestic Politics

Defence forces failed to prevent a major escalation of the *civil war in Cabo Delgado Province* in the north-east of Mozambique. The uprising started slowly in 2017 but by the end of 2020, total deaths had reached 2,530, of which more than two-thirds (1,728) were in 2020. The war is concentrated in an area 200 km (north–south) along the coast and stretching 50 km inland to the west. Nearly all of the population in that zone has been pushed out by insurgents and government defence forces; 583,000 people were displaced during the year. UN OCHA estimated that because of the war, 1.3 m people were in urgent need of humanitarian assistance, with 950,000 'facing severe hunger', including 242,000 children with acute malnutrition. OCHA said that the insurgency had damaged or destroyed 36% of health facilities across Cabo Delgado Province and there were no functional clinics in Mocimboa da Praia, Macomia, Muidumbe, or Quissanga.

Off the coast of Cabo Delgado is the *second-largest gas reserve in Africa* (after Algeria), which is now being developed; Total of France is the lead company for half of the gas reserves, and was moving ahead with building a gas liquification plant on the coast on the Afungi Peninsula. The discovery of the gas presented hopes for igniting development, ending poverty, and wealth for the elite. The notorious $ 2 bn secret debt was justified with the claim that the gas would repay the debt. But 2020 was the year the bubble burst. (See 'Socioeconomic Developments' below).

By mid-year, insurgents had taken control of Mocimboa da Praia town, port, and district, just south of Afungi. The only paved road north from the provincial capital and main port, Pemba, the N380, was closed. This left a circuitous dirt road which was also closed late in the year. Afungi and its nearby town Palma could only be reached by boat and air. On 31 December, insurgents reached the gates of the Afungi construction camp, and Total pulled out its workers, halting the project.

The defence forces proved corrupt as well as poorly trained and motivated, and were sharply divided. Most of the fighting was done by the paramilitary riot police under the Interior Ministry, who were better trained and paid and somewhat more successful. The army, under the Defence Ministry, often fled under attack, not willing to risk their lives for a low salary in a war they did not understand. Insurgents were able to equip themselves with weapons, ammunition, and vehicles taken in raids, and began wearing army uniforms similarly acquired.

The division in the army was evident at the top. Formally, the Interior Ministry was in charge of the war, but the Defence and Interior ministries did not cooperate centrally, and riot police and the army were not cooperating on the ground. The split was both doctrinal and a power struggle. The Defence Ministry wanted a long-term project with major investment to build a large professional army and much larger ministry, which would take several years. The Interior Ministry looked for a quicker solution to the war by using private military companies (PMCs). The Interior Ministry (not the central government) hired the South African PMC Dyke Advisory Group (DAG) to provide air support. Late in the year, the Defence Ministry was allowed to sign a contract with another South African company, Paramount, to provide equipment and training.

Local civilians bore the brunt of the war, attacked by all sides. This escalated, causing the large number of displaced people in 2020. Amnesty International reported 'violations of international humanitarian law, including *war crimes*, by all sides of the conflict'. The insurgents are known locally as al-Shabaab, which simply means 'the youth' and has no connection to groups in other countries with the same name. Amnesty found that al-Shabaab fighters routinely killed civilians, often beheading or quartering them, and looted and burned down their homes. In November, more than 50 civilians were killed in one incident at a football pitch in the district of Muidumbe.

On the government side, residents said that they were subjected to constant harassment and extortion by police. Soldiers mistreated civilians and often beat them. Videos taken by the soldiers themselves showed beatings and executions. Perhaps the strongest accusation by Amnesty was that in April, after the army retook Quissanga from insurgents, the house of the permanent secretary (number two in the district) 'would come to be known to villagers as a place where government security forces took women to be raped, and men detained, beaten, and in some cases, summarily executed as well'. Witnesses described a mass grave behind the home, a 'big hole' under the trees, where people would be taken to be shot and dumped directly in the pit. The executed included an imam and community leaders.

Amnesty said that DAG helicopters and light aircraft had directed machine gun fire at civilian infrastructure, including hospitals, schools, and homes. Witnesses described them 'hand-dropping explosive ordnance out the side of the helicopters' on civilians – apparently Syria-style barrel bombs. DAG and the military denied the allegations.

With a major outbreak of *Covid-19* in neighbouring South Africa, Mozambique moved quickly to impose restrictions on travel and public gatherings, and made attempts to persuade people to wear masks and maintain social distancing. These measures appeared to have been successful in containing the pandemic. New cases and deaths remained low until September, but even then reached only two deaths per day. Numbers began to fall again in November, and restrictions were eased over the Christmas-New Year holiday period – despite warnings that it was too early and might cause a large second wave in January. The disease proved to be largely urban, with 84% of deaths in the Maputo metropolitan area. Most deaths were of people over 60 years old.

Mozambique had 17,477 Covid-19 cases and 147 deaths. But the country had 9.3 m malaria cases and 15,000 deaths in 2019, according to the WHO World Malaria Report 2020. And it registered 130,000 new HIV/AIDS cases in 2019, and the Centers for Disease Control (CDC) estimates 45,000 deaths per year. Malaria thus causes 100 times as many deaths as Covid-19, and HIV/AIDS 300 times as many.

The re-elected President Filipe Nyusi *named his government* on 18 January, with a few new appointees. Three key people retained their posts – Carlos Rosario as prime minister, Adriano Maleiane as economy and finance minister, and Celso Correia (one of Nyusi's most trusted advisors) heading a super-ministry of Agriculture and Development (dropping environment and taking on agriculture in a restructuring of two ministries). In March, Nyusi set up the Northern Integrated Development Agency (Agencia de Desenvolvimento Integrado do Norte, ADIN) for the provinces of Cabo Delgado, Niassa, and Nampula, under Celso Correia, but it did nothing for the rest of the year.

Max Elias Tonela remained minerals minister while João Osvaldo Machatine retained the Ministry of Public Works, Carmelita Rita Namashulua moved from State Administration to Education, and Carlos Mesquita moved from Transport to Industry. Two former senior officials in parliament, speaker Verónica Macamo and party bench head Margarida Talapa became foreign and labour ministers, respectively.

Mozambique's constitution restricts a president to two terms, and this has been consistently followed. Thus, the internal Frelimo battle to choose Nyusi's successor began soon after the government was formed, with groups around former presidents Joaquim Chissano and Armando Guebuza, a Nyusi group, and a loose group opposing the growing corruption all trying to control the selection.

On 5 March, the National Statistics Institute (NSI) published figures that showed Nyusi's votes in the 2019 election were hugely inflated. In the previous year, the National Elections Commission (CNE) said that it had registered 1,166,011 voters in Gaza Province, which overwhelmingly voted for Frelimo. But in its report, the INE (Instituto Nacional de Estatística) said that there were only 717,635 voting age adults in Gaza, 448,375 fewer than were registered. These ghost voters played a significant part in Nyusi's landslide victory.

Foreign Affairs

As the insurgents gained ground, Mozambique *looked desperately for foreign help* to control them. It appealed broadly for international military help and for humanitarian assistance for the hundreds of thousands displaced. Foreign governments with specific programmes such as training or equipment supply, mercenaries on contracts, and UN agencies caring for displaced people were welcome – if they stayed strictly under Mozambican control. Frelimo feared that the UN, EU, or SADC would look closely at Cabo Delgado, draw their own conclusions, and make unacceptable demands for strategy and policy changes. By November, there were public complaints that humanitarian aid workers could not get visas and that NGOs could not import medicines and other relief goods. Under EU pressure, on 1 December the government agreed to issue special humanitarian visas, but none were issued. In response to appeals for military help, the EU wanted to send an investigating mission, but this was not approved by government.

The most telling confrontation was with the SADC. President Nyusi was chair of the SADC (August 2020–August 2021) and various meetings were called and often postponed. The SADC said it would support Mozambique against the insurgents, but wanted a plan for how they were to be defeated. Nyusi did not attend an extraordinary SADC summit on 27 November which he had called, sending the defence and interior ministers, and presenting what was dismissed as a 'shopping list' of military hardware that Mozambique wanted.

The problem for the Mozambique leadership was that it saw the response to the insurgency as purely military, and it presented the war as being driven entirely by external Islamist terrorism, hoping to gain support because Islamic State was the new global enemy. But the *roots and solutions of the war* were widely seen as internal. Amnesty caught the mood when it noted in its war crimes report that 'Al-Shabaab is primarily a home-grown armed group fighting over local issues, an insurgency sparked by the long-term under-investment in the Muslim-majority province by the central government. The group uses jihadist ideology as an organising tool. While Islamist ideologies have been growing in Cabo Delgado for decades, the movement did not gain traction until the arrival of resource extraction industries that provide little subsequent benefit for the local communities.'

On 5 March, Myrta Kaulard, the coordinator of the UN in Mozambique, posed a stark choice: should donors support the continuing but still unsuccessful attempt to defeat the insurgents by force, or should they support a rapid UN-led programme to create jobs and development to take away the grievances fuelling the war? In an explicit challenge to President Nyusi's portrayal of the war in Cabo Delgado as a military issue, she said the need was to 'completely change the situation in Cabo Delgado' through a joint donor effort for 'development and job creation'.

'The cause of so much suffering [in Cabo Delgado] has deep roots in the time when the people were forgotten', declared the Catholic bishops' Episcopal Conference of Mozambique (Conferência Episcopal de Moçambique, CEM) on 15 June. The bishops were directly challenging government claims that the causes of the war were foreign, and they called for the use of mineral and gas resources to develop Cabo Delgado. Luiz Fernando Lisboa, Catholic bishop of Pemba, said on 15 June: 'So far, the resources have been a curse ... It seems that the whole province is being divided up and given to big multinational companies. How much land is left in Cabo Delgado for cultivation, for people to plant and make a living? The province is looking like a Swiss cheese, full of holes because of these mines ... Mozambique is very rich in resources. Here we have a few millionaires, but we are one of the poorest countries in the world ... If there is no job creation policy, especially for the youth, we will continue to lag behind and our youth will be co-opted for delinquency, for drugs, for the insurgency.' The bishop had become increasingly outspoken and came under increasing attack from social media trolls supporting President Nyusi.

Government was anxious to keep out anyone who questioned its line. Journalists and researchers were barred from Cabo Delgado and sometimes arrested. The independent media was under increasing pressure. 'Canal de Moçambique' (11 March) published a contract between the gas companies and the military in which the former paid for military and police protection, but the money went not to the ministries but to a special account held by the then defence minister, vice-minister, and permanent secretary. 'Canal de Moçambique' was firebombed on 23 August. 'Zitamar' editor Tom Bowker was expelled in December, effectively for reporting on Cabo Delgado.

Senior leaders made it clear in private that they did not want interventions from large international organisations, such as the EU, SADC, or UN, because they were powerful enough to publish their own reports. The EU, for example, published a highly critical report of the 2019 re-election of Filipe Nyusi. Individual countries and PMCs can be more tightly controlled, and told that they should provide support and remain silent. Foreign diplomats have been warned not to give press briefings.

'The *standard of governance* in Mozambique is low', warned Tomas Tobé, chair of the European Parliament Development Committee, at a meeting on 3 December of the European Parliament's development and foreign affairs committees. It is wrong to 'privilege security', the new managing director for Africa at the European External Action Service (EEAS, the foreign ministry), Rita Laranjeira, told the meeting. It is necessary to 'confront the crisis and its root causes'. She stressed the need to create jobs. Tobé added that 'development and security are tightly linked together'. The European Commission's acting director for international cooperation and development, Francesca Di Mauro, told the committees that there 'cannot be just a security response'. There must be 'economic prospects for young people who now have no prospects and no jobs'. She stressed the need to involve young people in political life. This message was not acceptable to the government.

The *Portuguese and South African military* wanted to intervene, in part because both were defeated in Mozambique and would like to show that now Mozambique needs their help. But both foreign ministries are reluctant. Defence minister João Gomes Cravinho said on 24 June and 1 December that Portugal could send troops to help Mozambique fight terrorism. Portugal held the presidency of the EU from 1 January to 30 June 2021, and unsuccessfully used the build-up period at the end of 2020 to use the EU as an umbrella for Portuguese intervention. The US under President Trump promised anti-ISIS support, but this was unlikely with a new president in that country.

It had been widely predicted that France would provide maritime patrols, as Total is French and there are French islands in the Mozambique Channel, which the French navy is already patrolling. This has not yet happened. However, 200 South African navy personnel are now patrolling the Mozambique Channel as part of Operation Copper.

Government corruption, notably the $ 2 bn secret debt and failure to use government funds to reduce poverty, have led to *a reduction in foreign aid*, from $ 762 m in 2018 to $ 622 m in 2019 to only $ 330 m in 2000. UN coordinator Myrta Kaulard pointed on 5 March to the reluctance of donors to give money to the government. Of the $ 700 m needed for reconstruction after cyclones Idai and Kenneth, only

$ 100 m was made available. In April, health donors informed the government that they would not provide cash for Covid-19; instead, donors undertook the procurement and routed money through existing donor-controlled programmes. Government was no longer trusted even to buy basic medical equipment.

Donors would not give money to a corrupt government, and their election observers were highly critical of the 2019 re-election of Filipe Nyusi as president. But donor priorities had changed; they were interested no longer in good governance or credible elections but only in contracts and investment. Despite the war and bad governance, Nyusi, Frelimo, and the government received political support because of the huge gas project.

For two decades, Mozambique was a major transit centre for *heroin*, with the trade tightly controlled by the Frelimo leadership. Heroin from Afghanistan was carried in dhows from the Makran coast of Pakistan to the coast of Cabo Delgado, and thereafter transported by road to South Africa, where most of it was sent to Europe. An estimated 40 tonnes per year of heroin passed through Mozambique annually, adding up to $ 100 m per year to the local economy. Two changes occurred in 2020. First, the insurgency's closure of key roads forced a shift in the drop zone in Mozambique, south along the coast to Nampula Province. Second, crystal methamphetamine is being smuggled alongside heroin. The ephedra plant, a common shrub that grows abundantly across northern and central Afghanistan, contains a naturally occurring form of ephedrine, a key precursor required to produce methamphetamine. This allowed the local production of high-quality crystal meth.

Mozambique began campaigning to be elected in 2022 to one of the non-permanent seats on the UNSC.

A newly released document confirmed reports of Turkish diplomats spying in Maputo on members of the opposition Gülen movement just after the visit to Maputo on 24 January 2017 of Turkish president Recep Tayyip Erdogan.

The Global Solidarity Forest Fund (GSFF) was founded by Norwegian and Swedish churches in 2006, and the following year promised an incredible 13% real rate of return on ethical forest investment in Mozambique. The troubled project was taken over by the Norwegian company Green Resources, with 360,000 ha in Mozambique. But it finally admitted that it could not manage, and in July proposed to give most of the land back to communities it had been taken from.

Socioeconomic Developments

The *gas chimera disappeared* in 2020. The second-largest gas field in Africa was founded off the coast of Cabo Delgado in 2010. Gas was to be compressed into liquefied natural gas (LNG) and exported across the world in tankers. LNG plants are hugely expensive, and there were serious projections of $ 100 bn in foreign investment in the largest project in Africa. At first, the climate crisis led to support for the project, because gas is a transition fuel with half the carbon of coal. But by 2020 gas was being treated as just another fossil fuel, and consumption projection fell. Prices fell as Saudi Arabia and Russia increased production to take control of the remaining market. ExxonMobil of the US is the lead company for the other half of the gas reserve, and in April it decided to indefinitely postpone its final investment decision on the $ 27–30 bn. The Exxon half of the project may never go ahead, bursting Mozambican dreams of a gas bonanza. The lead company for the other half had been the US company Anadarko, which sold its Cabo Delgado assets to the French company Total on 3 August 2019 for $ 3.9 bn. Total moved ahead with its $ 20 bn first phase, which include two gas liquification 'trains' (plants with a series of compression and purification units acting sequentially, and thus called 'trains' – one train costs $ 3–5 bn) on the Afungi Peninsula, wells 50 km offshore, and pipes to connect them. On 17 July, Total announced that it had agreed a $ 14.9 debt financing package, and work on Afungi started in earnest – only to be halted at the end of the year by the insurgency.

The start was already three years late, and projections showed that the Mozambique government would only begin to earn large amounts of money a decade later than had been hoped, in the 2030s. Although $ 20 bn is a huge investment, it is only one-fifth of the dreams. Another rude awakening was on the number of local jobs that would be created. In a 14 May report, Total estimated that the five-year construction project would employ 12,000–13,000 people, of whom fewer than 2,500 would be Mozambicans and the rest would be foreigners. On 14 May, the United States Export-Import Bank (Exim) approved a $ 4.7 bn loan, for both onshore and offshore parts of the project. All Exim-supported goods and services would have to be provided by the US, and the loan was said to support 16,700 US jobs. As well as creating US jobs, the Exim statement notes that 'China and Russia were slated to finance this deal [but] the project now will be completed without their involvement and instead with "Made in the USA" products and services'. On 26 June, it was reported that UK Export Finance (UKEF) would guarantee a $ 1 bn loan for a pipeline to link the gas wells to the LNG plant, supporting 2,000 British jobs. This suggests that more than 29,000 foreign jobs and fewer than 2,500 Mozambican jobs would be created in the $ 20 bn Total LNG gas project.

In November, it became clear that none of the projects to use Mozambique's share of the physical gas, which were approved in 2016, would go ahead. Norwegian fertiliser giant Yara abandoned plans to develop a fertiliser plant using Cabo Delgado gas. Shell, which was planning to develop a gas-to-liquids project at the LNG site in Palma, and Great Lakes Africa Energy, which was planning a gas-fired power plant in Nacala, had not moved on their projects.

Despite challenges, Total was the only bright spot in an otherwise *grim economic year*. GDP fell by 1.3%, with the biggest fall in the extractive industry (–17%, with notably big drops in coal, graphite, and rubies) and tourism, hotels, and restaurants (−23%, mainly due to Covid-19 restrictions). The fall was less than the −5.5% SADC average. Inflation was 3.5%, mainly due to rising food prices. The World Bank estimated that 850,000 people fell into poverty. The metical fell by 18% against the US dollar, and in turn increased the value of external debt.

Aid was only 59% of what was expected. Government planned on $ 557 m of aid but received only $ 330 m. It planned on foreign loans of $ 730 m but obtained only $ 515 m. Part of the shortfall was made up with increased government revenue at 110% of what was planned ($ 315 m above plan), but it was not enough to close the foreign gap. Domestic borrowing was $ 770 m, largely in treasury bonds – double the level of 2019, pushing domestic debt to $ 2.8 bn.

The civil war had an impact on the state budget, with defence and security rising from 14% to 17% of the budget. Health and social spending also rose, from 9% to 13%. But education and general public services were cut. Spending was only 90% of plan, with the investment budget cut by 27%.

Mozambique was officially in *debt distress*. On 24 April, the IMF announced that it would disperse $ 309 m under the IMF's Rapid Credit Facility for Covid-19. The government was forced to make unprecedented concessions on transparent use of the money, including an independent audit, which will be published. Tao Zhang, IMF deputy managing director and chair, noted that this was to 'prevent corruption and misuse of emergency financing, by strengthening transparency and accountability'. He also indicated that did not suggest a new IMF programme for Mozambique. That would require 'strengthened debt management and transparency' and "structural reforms"'. Later in the year, negotiations with the IMF were suspended. Currency depreciation and borrowing by the state hydrocarbons company ENH (Empresa Nacional de Hidrocarbonetos) to fund its share of the gas projects pushed external debt from 89% to 103% of GDP (2019 to 2020) and total public debt to 120% of GDP.

The country has increasingly become dependent on what it calls '*megaprojects*' and mineral and energy exports, with little growth in agriculture and the domestic sector. GDP growth had been falling steadily, from 6.9% in 2015 to 2.3% in 2019, and the number of people in poverty had been steadily increasing. Coal and aluminium accounted for half of exports, and prices had been falling; megaproject exports fell from $3.9 bn in 2018 to $2.2 bn in 2020.

The fall in global demand caused by Covid-19 accelerated the shift to renewable energy. Coal production had already been falling and in 2020 was half the 1998 level. Investment in gas slowed. The contribution of the megaprojects to the state budget fell by 72% – from 26% of the budget in 2019 to only 9% in 2020.

Domestic food production rose by 12%. Commercial fishing fell by 60% when compared with 2019. Reserves of $ 4 bn were sufficient to cover six months of imports.

The Covid-19 squeeze particularly hit the service industry – tourism, hospitality, and transport. It caused 1,075 companies to close, according to the business association CTA. At least 120,000 jobs were lost and 63,000 contracts suspended. This had a knock-on effect on the large informal sector. The World Bank reported low-income urban households being hardest hit, with more than 50% of urban households running out of food. Mozambique increased its cash transfer programme; the 560,000 exiting beneficiaries received an additional $ 50 and an additional 290,000 households not in the programme received $ 150.

The UN University World Institute for Development Economics Research (UNU-WIDER) published a set of studies in April, May, and June showing Mozambique *becoming poorer and more unequal*. In terms of welfare poverty ('multidimensional poverty' in the jargon) based on sanitation, water, electricity, assets, housing, and cooking fuel, the number of poor people increased from 20.1 m in 2011 to 22.2 m in 2018. In the 2018 survey, only 37% of urban people were poor (in welfare terms) and 42% of people in the south were poor, compared with 93% of rural people and 86% of those in the north. 'A significant, and striking, result of our analysis is that rural poverty incidence for children aged 0–17 is more than three times that of urban areas, and the four poorest provinces are about 50 times poorer than the richest', wrote the WIDER authors. 'Mozambique continues to have multidimensional poverty levels that exceed those of its neighbours – Malawi, Tanzania, Zambia, and Zimbabwe – by a large margin.' Two other studies showed that inequality in Mozambique increased between 2009 and 2015, due to consumption disproportionally increasing among the better-off. The top 5% had 38 times the income of the bottom 5% in 2009, but this increased to 56 times in 2015.

Part of the secret debt, $ 1.2 bn to Mozambique Asset Management (MAM) and Proindicus was declared 'null and void' by the Constitutional Council (CC) on 8 May. That means that the highest court in Mozambique has ruled that the loans and the guarantees should be treated as if they had never existed. The case was brought by 2,000 citizens and the NGO N'weti, part of the Budget Monitoring Forum which has taken the lead on the debt issue. Eighteen people who had been charged in relation to the secret debt case, including former president Armando Guebuza's son Ndambi, remained in preventative detention in Maputo throughout the year. Former finance minister Manuel Chang spent the year in a Johannesburg jail, and both Mozambique and the US wanted to extradite him.

The Extractive Industries Transparency Initiative (EITI) report for 2019 (published in 2020) said that the government had cheated communities of $ 443,000. Under the law, communities with mines are to be paid 2.75% of revenue from two years before. The 2.75% of 2017 revenue should have been $ 1,555,000, but the government 2019 budget execution report says only $ 1,112,000 was paid to communities.

The dominance of foreign and parastatal companies, plus a couple of key Frelimo oligarchs, was shown in KPMG's '100 biggest companies in Mozambique 2020'. Only two in the top 20 had major Mozambique shareholdings – Intelec Holdings (ranking 9), controlled by former president Armando Guebuza, and Montepuez Ruby Mining (20), part owned by Raimundo Pachinuapa, a member of Frelimo's ruling Political Commission.

Mozambican parastatal companies were prominent in the top ten: EDM/Electricidade de Moçambique (3) (third-largest by 2019 turnover), Hidroeléctrica de Cahora Bassa (4), Petromoc/Petróleos de Moçambique (5), and CFM/Portos e Caminhos de Ferro de Moçambique (8). The state also had significant holdings in the Mozambique operations of some of the foreign-owned companies.

Foreign mineral-energy companies dominated: Mozal (1) (the largest company by 2019 turnover), Vale (2), Sasol (6), Petrogal (15), Total (16), and Puma Energy (17). Three foreign banks are key: BIM/Banco Internacional de Moçambique (7), BCI/Banco Comercial e de Investimentos (12), and Standard Bank (14). Foreign food and construction companies complete the rest of the top 20: Cervejas de Moçambique (10), Mota/Engil Engenharia Construção África (11), Mozambique Leaf Tobacco (13), CMC Africa Austral (18), and Coca-Cola Sabco Moçambique (19).

Namibia

Henning Melber

This was a challenging year for the governing South West Africa People's Organisation (SWAPO) and citizenry in general. The political landscape changed in terms of the new legislative period that started on 21 March and the composition of the new government and parliament. Even more so, the governance map was considerably redrawn following the regional and local authority elections held at the end of November. This dramatically reinforced shifts which were manifested with the national assembly and presidential election results of November 2019. The rise of opposition parties was indicative of the growing frustrations among ordinary citizens concerning the degree of corruption revealed by #fishrot, as well as the hardship that the continued recession, exacerbated by the consequences of Covid-19, inflicted on them.

Domestic Politics

Afrobarometer survey results of August 2019, published on 24 March, confirmed an *erosion of political trust*. Trust in the country's president dropped from 81% in 2014 to 60% in 2019. Trust in the national assembly was put at 46%, the lowest since the first survey in 1999 (when it stood at 48%; it peaked in 2012 and 2014 at 74% and declined to 47% in 2017). A decline in trust was also registered in the army (from 74% in 2012 to 61% in 2019), the police (from 76% in 2012 to 60% in 2019), and the courts of law (from 75% in 2012 to 54% in 2019). While in 2014 trust in the Electoral Commission (ECN) was 74%, this declined to 54% in 2019.

The ECN caused a *legal dispute over the presidential election results*. The controversy was over the use of electoral voting machines (EVMs) in the national assembly and presidential elections of November 2019 without a paper trail, as required by the Electoral Act. Panduleni Itula – a prominent SWAPO member who had competed with Hage Geingob as an 'independent' candidate in the presidential elections – had taken almost 30% of Geingob's previous support from him. Together with other claimants, Itula had challenged the results in court, but without success. On 17 January, the supreme court heard the arguments. On 5 February, the court decided that the electoral procedures were in violation of the law. But the court found the claimants' argument of gross irregularities unconvincing, and that there was a lack of sufficient evidence that the absence of a paper trail affected the election results to an extent which would invalidate them. It therefore did not revoke the elections but ruled that elections be required from 21 March to be in full compliance with the Electoral Act or that EVMs be abandoned until they are equipped with the ability to provide a paper trail. On 11 February, Itula filed an objection to the ruling. On 4 March, the registrar of the supreme court confirmed that the proceedings had been finalised and that the court decision of 5 February was binding. This cleared the way for Hage Geingob as re-elected president of Namibia for a second term, and he was inaugurated on 21 March (Independence Day). Notably, no similar claim was registered in court against the national assembly election results, which were also conducted without a paper trail.

As a first step towards forming the *new government*, on 18 March, Geingob reappointed the three most senior members of his government: the deputy president (Nangolo Mbumba), the prime minister (Saara Kuugongelwa-Amadhila), and the deputy prime minister, who also serves as the minister of international relations and cooperation (Netumbo Nandi-Ndaitwah). These were loyal supporters throughout his first term in office. This gave rise to assumptions that he was 'playing safe' and that these appointments signalled continuity more than change. However, the assumptions were partially wrong. Rather, the appointments seemed intended to create a point of departure rooted in familiarity before other roles were infused with fresh blood. This was illustrated by Geingob's appointment of the eight members of parliament (MPs) without voting rights on 22 March, as part of his presidential privileges. Out of the eight, Veikko Nekundi (former deputy minister of public enterprises) and Kalumbi Shangula (former minister of health) were the only two previous law-makers who were brought back. The other six new appointees were Yvonne Dausab (law reform and development commission director), Emma

Kantema-Gaomas (executive director of the Ministry of Sport, Youth, and National Service), Emma Theofilus (former deputy chairperson of the Children's Parliament), Natalia Goagoses (former chief regional officer for Erongo Region), Iipumbu Shiimi (governor of Bank of Namibia/BoN), and Peter Hafeni Vilho (rear admiral). All of them were much younger than the veterans, who were close to retirement. Four of the eight were appointed ministers: Dausab (justice), Shangula (health and social services), Shiimi (finance) and Vilho (defence and veteran affairs). Three became deputy ministers: Kantema-Gaomas (sport, youth, and national service), Theofilus (information and communication technology), and Nekundi (works and transport). The 23-year-old Theofilus, a law graduate from the University of Namibia, became the youngest MP in the whole of the SADC region. This clearly signalled the intention to counteract the image of a gerontocratic party.

Geingob also followed through on his earlier promise to downsize the *cabinet*, though not as rigorously as was expected. After some mergers, reorganisations, and redefinition and renaming of ministerial portfolios, on 22 March the number of ministries was reduced from 24 to 21, and the 28 deputy ministers to 17. The appointment of the BoN's governor, Ipumbu Shiimi, came as a surprise to many. Shiimi replaced Calle Schlettwein, who was transferred to a new consolidated Ministry of Agriculture, Water, and Land Reform. While Shiimi is a trained economist, Schlettwein had graduated in zoology/botany and then entomology at the University of Stellenbosch. His appointment was welcomed by stakeholders in the commercial agricultural sector. It is not without irony that the only cabinet member from the German-speaking minority was tasked with the thorny and sensitive issue of land reform. In another surprise move, Geingob replaced Shiimi as governor of the BoN with 64-year-old Johannes !Gawaxab for the remaining 18 months of Shiimi's term of office at the bank. !Gawaxab is considered a friend of Geingob and, since the early 1980s, has been an influential player in a variety of positions in the private financial sector. This was considered a potential conflict of interest.

Following the poor electoral showing in late November 2019, President Geingob assured the electorate through his New Year message that 'I have heard you'. He declared 2020 'the year of introspection'. Yet during the year, more details emerged regarding the scale of corruption in the infamous #fishrot saga, hitherto by far the country's largest bribery scandal, involving billions of Namibian dollars. Two ministers and several leading officials of state-owned enterprises were implicated. Geingob's proclaimed introspection was limited to an internal self-examination by the party, with no visible results. Party leaders and high-ranking state officials continued to brush aside dissatisfaction with their lacklustre performance and resorted to a *blame game* distracting from their own failures. Speaking on the occasion of a meeting of the Southern Africa Regional Police Chiefs Cooperation Organisation in Windhoek in mid-February, the inspector-general of Namibia's police, Sebastian Ndeitunga warned of 'the phenomena of radicalisation of the youth in our region who are singing the song of regime change'. The defensive rhetoric also drew the race card. Addressing soldiers on 28 August, defence minister Peter Hafeni Vilho accused the country's white minority community of being supporters of 'regime change', 'misguided intellectuals', and 'unpatriotic' citizens bent on seeing the government fail. He held the white minority responsible for all governance failures and current inequalities. In mid-October, Geingob bemoaned the growing number of whites (estimated at less than 5% of the population) registering as voters. He claimed that they intended to support anything but SWAPO, and threatened: 'I will not forget that. People are declaring war against SWAPO.' Martin Shalli, the former commander of the Namibian army, urged the crowd attending a rally in early November to slit the throat of SWAPO defectors. Public outrage forced him to apologise on national television.

Despite a worrying increase in hate speech, mobilisation by *other political forces* gained ground. Further to the Itula drama, on 20 March SWAPO expelled him from the party. He subsequently formed a new party, the Independent Patriots for Change (IPC), which held its maiden convention on 31 July. It was officially registered by the ECN on 22 September and joined the competition for support in the *regional and local authority elections* of 25 November. For the first time in Namibia's 30 years of democracy there was a meaningful and vibrant election campaign, with several parties as well as a growing number of independent candidates competing in the 14 regions and 53 municipalities and towns. While shifts were predicted, SWAPO's landslide loss came as a surprise.

Many of the country's *14 regions* have remained spatial hubs for culturally and linguistically distinct groups. Their voting behaviour, to some extent, has reproduced existing identities. Up until fairly recently, SWAPO was the only organisation among the 14 parties (and numerous independent candidates) competing for votes that had significant support among almost all population groups and in the urban 'melting pots'. This came to an end. SWAPO's vote share dropped from 83% in 2015 to 57% in the 14 regional councils, which are the second tier of government. The elected council members appoint three representatives each to the National Council, the upper house of parliament, composed of regional delegates. SWAPO previously held 40 of 42 National Council seats; this changed fundamentally, with the party's number of seats dropping to 28. The southern regions of Hardap and //Karas went to the Landless People's Movement (LPM). Central-western Erongo went to the IPC, which also made some inroads in SWAPO's northern strongholds. Kunene in the north-west went to a coalition of the United Democratic Front (UDF) and the People's Democratic Movement (PDM), which is the official opposition in the national assembly. SWAPO also lost its absolute majority in the central and eastern Khomas, Omaheke, and Otjizondjupa regions.

There are 57 *local authorities* in Namibia, among which SWAPO garnered just 40% of the votes, down from 73% in 2015, in competition with close to 30 other parties and associations. It maintained full control only in 20 of the 52 municipalities and town councils it held previously. Most urban centres, including Walvis Bay and Swakopmund, went to other parties or coalitions. The loss of the capital Windhoek was a major embarrassment. Having held 12 of the 15 seats in the municipality since 2015, SWAPO won only five. The fact that Job Amupanda, a social movement activist and senior lecturer at the University of Namibia in his early 30s, became the new mayor of Windhoek's municipality for the year to come pointed to the dramatic changes.

SWAPO's spokesperson Hilma Nicanor accused 'outside forces' of trying to unseat the 'victorious' governing party. Frustrated members of the SWAPO establishment suggested that the party, which controls the central government, should make the fiscus withhold funds to financially starve towns and regions governed by other parties. This underlined the emerging *centrifugal tendencies*, fuelling regional if not tribal animosities. Notably, Geingob dismissed such suggestions. He categorically declared that all those elected into office are supposed to serve all people and that no funds would be withheld.

Foreign Affairs

Despite strict lockdown rules to control the Covid-19 pandemic, on 21 March several hundred invited guests attended the inauguration of Namibia's president for a second term in office, including a few heads of state from neighbouring countries, some of whom were in violation of their own country's travel restrictions. The atmosphere testified to the *close relations in the sub-region*. However, due to the pandemic, international relations during the year were mainly limited to exchanges in the virtual space, and no visits for bi- or multilateral events were recorded.

At the commemoration of the *75th anniversary of the UN* on 21 September, president Geingob stressed the role of the organisation in the progress towards the self-determination of the country. He also recalled the contribution of the United Nations Institute for Namibia, of which he was the director for 12 years prior to independence. He reiterated that it remained unacceptable that Africa had no permanent seat on the Security Council. At the opening session of the UNGA in his recorded message on 23 September, President Geingob emphasised Namibia's continued solidarity with the people of *Palestine and of Western Sahara* in their struggles for self-determination. He stated: 'The 17 interconnected Sustainable Development Goals and their promise to leave no one behind by 2030, ring hollow for the people of Palestine and Western Sahara, who still remain under occupation. They are left behind.' He also reaffirmed a strong commitment to multilateralism.

Bilateral *German–Namibian negotiations* continued over how to come to terms with the genocide committed by the German empire in its colony, South West Africa, between 1904 and 1908. An eighth round of talks was held on 12/13 February by the special envoys in Swakopmund. In a statement on 11 August, President Geingob summarised the progress made. The German government, as he declared, has out of 'political and moral responsibility … agreed to render an unconditional apology to the Namibian government, her people and in particular the affected communities'. At stake remained the form of redress, since Germany had declined to accept the term 'reparations'. Instead, the terminology 'Reconciliation and Reconstruction Programme' was submitted for debate. The amount of financial compensation also remained a matter for further negotiations. All affected communities were invited for a feedback session at the state house. But a statement of 13 August by the Nama Traditional Leaders Association and the Ovaherero Traditional Authority dismissed the invitation as a 'waste of time' as long as the recognition of unconditional reparations was avoided. This was echoed in a statement of 24 August by the Nama Genocide Technical Committee. While the two governments seemed to have come closer to a mutually agreed compromise, the representatives of the descendant communities remained confrontational, not least because they continued to feel excluded from the direct negotiations. In contrast, in a statement on 18 August the OvaHerero/OvaMbanderu and Nama Council for the Dialogue on the 1904–08 Genocide, a body collaborating with the government, regretted the continued intra-Namibian disagreements.

In the wake of rearranging trade relations with the UK for the *post-Brexit* era, Namibia's national assembly ratified on 20 October a SACU–Mozambique and United Kingdom EPA. It entered into force on 1 January 2021 when the UK officially left the EU. This secured continued market access for the signatories. Namibia mainly exported beef, dates, grapes, and charcoal to the UK, which amounted to the value of 6.1 bn Namibian dollars (N$) in 2019.

Economic factors also affected *relations with Iceland*. Samherji, the biggest Icelandic fishing company, which had been benefiting from a grand-scale corruption scheme for years, was exposed in late 2019 by investigative journalists, and has since made headlines in the #fishrot saga. This caused a legal dispute when Namibia's prosecutor-general seized one of the company's fishing vessels to compensate for the loss created by the illegally obtained fishing quota. In the course of the investigations, a warrant of arrest was issued for two Icelandic citizens involved in the bribery scandal. Samherji rejected cooperation and pointed out that there was no extradition treaty between the two countries. The matter was pending at year's end.

Tensions with Botswana emerged on 5 November when four Namibian fishermen were shot dead by members of the Botswana Defence Force in the Botswana border territory along the Chobe River. They were accused of poaching, which upon instructions from the Botswana government was met with a 'shoot to kill' response. President Geingob had a phone exchange with Botswana's President Mokgweetsi

Masisi to seek clarification, and also discussed the matter with Botswana's former president Ian Khama. Masisi extended condolences to the families of the deceased and regretted the incident. The two countries agreed to conduct a joint investigation. This was of no comfort to infuriated locals, who on 13 November held a demonstration. In a press statement, the state house criticised this as 'pointless and wholly misplaced'. This provoked strong dismissals by civil society organisations, who stressed the civil right to express peaceful protest as a fundamental constitutional right. In a statement read at a funeral service on 16 November, President Geingob condemned the 'shoot to kill' policy as 'inconsistent with the international and regional core principles of peaceful co-existence and stability' and demanded that the transgressors be brought to justice. Reportedly, with this latest event the number of Namibians killed in similar incidents had risen to 37. On 1 December, President Geingob received the report of the joint investigation by the two governments. Its findings were not made public, which triggered new demonstrations by a regional protest group in Zambezi Region on 23 December.

Socioeconomic Developments

Drought and recession have during recent years created a much more vulnerable socioeconomic environment, and large-scale corruption scandals have added to the growing frustration among the electorate. In November 2019, six accused for their involvement in the *#fishrot* saga (including the former ministers of fisheries and justice) were arrested, and they remained in custody throughout the year awaiting trial, while investigations continued. The amount involved was estimated at least N$ 10 bn, as proceeds of the crime, with devastating results for the local fisheries sector and those employed in it.

As a result of the economic deterioration, the hitherto rather stable social contract became more fragile and contested. The devastating effect of the *Covid-19 pandemic* added further pressure. President Geingob declared a six-month-long state of emergency on 17 March, with strict lockdown regulations for the first 38 days. The restrictions included a ban on liquor and cigarette sales. As Geingob informed a cabinet meeting on 1 December, an economic stimulus package had been rolled out during the year of N$ 8.1 bn, easing the negative effects. But he also declared: 'it is not an exaggeration to say that Covid-19 has thrown us off balance', with considerable job losses and business closures.

Figures issued by the BoN illustrated an *economic decline*. It was estimated that the economy would shrink during the year by 7.8%. It was further assumed that the economy would reach the 2015 level again only by 2024. Tourism was among the hardest-hit sectors. Having been a reliable contributor to GDP in the past, it recorded massive losses, with a decline of foreign visitors of 75% for the first eight months and no decisive increase in sight. Manufacturing and the wholesale and retail trade sectors also registered a decline in employment. According to figures released by the BoN in October, by mid-2020 losses had been sustained of 6.8% and 4.8%, respectively, compared with a year before. The Construction Industries Confederation reported in October that the sector's contribution to GDP had decreased from 7.2% in 2015 to 2.9%, and that employment had decreased since 2016 by one-third to 5,783 workers.

Tabling his first *annual budget* on 27 May, finance minister Shiimi could not be envied. The total volume of N$ 72.8 bn was estimated at 42.5% of GDP (N$ 171.1 bn). Public debt, which was estimated at 54.8% for the last financial year, was expected to rise in an unprecedented way to 68.7% of GDP or N$ 117.5 bn. The annual budget tabled amounted to N$ 64.3 bn, with an additional N$ 8.4 bn earmarked for debt services. The continued contraction of the economy was expected to add further pressure to growing unemployment. Namibia was applauded by observers for its crisis management, and in particular the immediate measures to ease the social misery triggered by the lockdown through a N$ 750 grant to those in need – euphemistically labelled 'low-income groups' (though as it emerged, not all who should have been entitled were among the beneficiaries). This might have, for a limited period, eased the pressure slightly, but it was not going to solve the immense problems of growing poverty and the frustration which grows alongside it. The budget allocations, however, very much followed the philosophy of 'business as usual' even in these very unusual times. The highest allocations remained those for education, with N$ 14.18 bn (plus N$ 3.3 bn for higher education), health and social services (N$ 7.95 bn), defence (N$ 6.23 bn), and police (N$ 5.43 bn).

To cover the Covid-19 subventions, the finance ministry received an increase from N$ 4.4 to 6.22 bn. The budget deficit was estimated at N$ 21.4 bn, 12.5% of GDP, raising overall *debt* to 69.6% of GDP; official policy has always maintained that overall debt should not exceed 30%. With this being declared an emergency budget, debt services amounted to N$ 8.4 bn, exceeding public investments of N$ 6.4 bn. In October, *state debts* amounted to N$ 119.8 bn, and were expected to escalate further to N$ 134.4 bn in 2021 and N$ 156.7 bn by March 2024. The Mid-Year Budget Review tabled by the finance minister in October estimated that by March 2024 the annual credit payments for debts accumulated would exceed N$ 10 bn.

The *credit ratings* further deteriorated during the year. In May, Moody's downgraded Namibia from Baa3 Stable to Ba2 Negative. On 4 December the rating agency downgraded the country's junk status even further to Ba3, which is three notches below investment grade with a negative outlook. As the agency observed, 'very large gross borrowing requirements ... point to material liquidity risks'. Moody's expected an increase in the debt burden to 72% of GDP and an increase of the interest bill to 15.5% of revenue income (it was at 5% five years ago) in the 2020/21 fiscal year. As a frustrated local economist commented: 'while the sun shone on the global economy for the last half decade, Namibia has languished, scoring a number of major policy-own-goals that have left all and sundry worse off'. In early December, Fitch Ratings affirmed Namibia's long-term foreign-currency issuer default rating at BB with a negative outlook.

The *Human Development Report 2020*, released by UNDP on 15 December, placed the country, with a GNI (gross national income) per capita of US$ 9.357 (2017 PPP), at rank 129 in the HDI. This was a decline of two ranks over the 2014–19 period. Adjusted for inequality, the drop of 14 ranks was the seventh-highest of all countries. On assumption of office for his second term in March, a frustrated Geingob felt offended by 'ungrateful Namibians'. As he claimed, he would be praised outside the country for the progress in fighting poverty, inequality, and corruption despite taking over a 'broke' country. This provoked scathing attacks. After all, Geingob, in concert with his finance minister and others, had always claimed that Namibia's fiscal and economic situation was sound and that there was nothing to be worried about. In his State of the Nation Address on 4 June, he clearly scaled down ambitions when he declared: 'I remain confident that with sufficient resources and concerted efforts, Namibia can one day achieve the goal of a more equal society'. It remains to be seen if and when this will happen.

South Africa

Sanusha Naidu

South Africa started the year in a technical recession. This was the second time that the country had recorded a recession under the presidency of Cyril Ramaphosa. Politically, the state of the nation was far from where the government had hoped it would be when the 2019 State of the Nation Address was delivered. Factional politics deepened in the ruling party, the African National Congress (ANC), revelations of corruption and state capture at the Zondo Commission of Inquiry exposed the complex nature of patronage networks between the state and political and non-political actors, and the country's bleak socioeconomic landscape became more dire with, *inter alia*, rises in basic food costs due to fuel hikes and currency volatility, wasteful government expenditure, and increases in electricity tariffs. The Covid-19 pandemic found the country's political and socioeconomic stability in a fragile state. A small reprieve was on offer in the foreign policy ambit of the country's engagements in the UN, the AU, and the WTO.

Domestic Affairs

Like most countries around the world, South Africa saw business as usual in the first two months of 2020. As much as the Covid-19 epidemic was becoming a global concern, for the government authorities it seemed it did not warrant serious reflection since no infection had been recorded in the country. And so the usual political events marked the calendar for the months of January and February.

Beginning with the usual ANC birthday celebrations known as the January 8th Statement, the ruling party delivered a confident and cohesive message to show unity in the organisation, strengthening the capacity of a capable state, advancing an inclusive society around job creation, improving lives and livelihoods, bringing about skills upliftment, and redressing the inequities of the past, while not ignoring the need to end gender-based violence (GBV), fight corruption, and ensure effective governance mechanisms. Unfortunately for most commentators, the statement did not offer any road-map on how this would be achieved. It became just another litany of promises that did not synchronise with realities on the ground. Rather, it seemed as if the statement was dusted off each year and set on repeat. As one commentator put it, 'unfortunately, the January 8th Statement showed a political movement out of its depth, failing to realise that the country is drowning, and how it is pushing it under'.

Meanwhile, the ANC could not hide the fractures caused by power battles between factions aligned with former president Jacob Zuma and groups supporting President Cyril Ramaphosa. Despite attempts to illustrate that all was well in the party, it was becoming abundantly clear that the Radical Economic Transformation (RET) bloc that comprised senior heavyweights like the secretary-general Ace Magushule, Kebby Maphatsoe of the uMkhonto weSizwe Military Veterans' Association (MKMVA), members of the National Executive Council (NEC) such as Tony Yengeni and Malusi Gigaba, as well as provincial structures in the Free State and KwaZulu Natal and constituencies like the ANC's Women's League, were defiant towards Ramaphosa's fight against corruption. This was partly due to perceptions that the anti-corruption stance was aimed at purging those connected with the RET faction, including Zuma, from the party.

The intensity of the political rambunctiousness saw the party caught in a dilemma over whether Ramaphosa would remain a one-term president. The internal faultlines in the ANC spilt over into the institutional architecture of the country, blurring the lines of separation between the party and the state. A case in point was former president Jacob Zuma's non-appearance in a court case relating to charges of corruption. In February, the high court in Pietermaritzburg, KwaZulu Natal, issued an arrest warrant against the former president after Zuma's lawyers had explained that he was unable to attend due to medical reasons. The presiding judge refused to accept the sick note as grounds for Zuma's absence, noting that the document from the military hospital in Tshwane was inadmissible due to inconsistencies since it had no date that could be verified. In deciding on the issue, the judge noted that this was standard practice. But not everyone saw it that way.

Family and supporters of the former president went on a vitriolic attack, challenging the ruling, and accused the judge of being biased, levelling allegations of corruption against him. As much as the claims were seen as baseless and with the KwaZulu Natal acting judge president weighing the situation, noting the independence of the judiciary, the die had been cast regarding the judiciary also being captured and a political witch hunt being waged against those in the RET camp. This became a rallying point and remained an issue of contention throughout the year, with the integrity of the courts called into question and aspersions cast that judges were being influenced by public opinion and by certain political and economic stakeholders with vested interests.

In February, President Ramaphosa delivered his fourth State of the Nation Address (SONA). The 2020 SONA would be remembered more for the chaos that preceded its delivery than for some of the tangible actions that the president mentioned as the road-map for the year.

In its objection to former president F.W. de Klerk being one of the dignitaries invited to the event, the opposition party the Economic Freedom Fighters (EFF) disrupted proceedings for more than an hour, demanding that de Klerk vacate the national assembly. As if that were not enough, the leader of the EFF, Julius Malema, then turned on the minister of public enterprises, Pravin Gordhan, with a verbal onslaught about the parlous state of affairs at public entities like South African Airways and the load-shedding crisis at the state electricity utility, Eskom. The EFF warned that stability would only prevail in the national assembly if Ramaphosa fired Gordhan immediately. After what seemed like a protracted stand-off coupled with acts of violence with water bottles being thrown, members of the EFF left the chamber. Most political parties were in agreement that the flagrant violation of the rules of the house and disrespect shown by the EFF warranted urgent action against the party's members, including punitive measures. Some commentators cautioned that the EFF had planned the disruption weeks in advance. The speaker of the house, Thandi Modise, summed up the feelings of the nation when she declared: 'I'm sure South Africa is not very proud of us tonight'. The address was resumed without the EFF in the chamber.

The speech was not considered spectacular. It articulated the usual realities that confronted the country's body politic. The president emphasised that a social compact was needed to drive inclusive growth. The idea that the speech was to instil confidence and hope among the nation did little neither to inspire or to reverse levels of distrust towards the government. As much as the electorate remained apathetic towards government, the South African Reconciliation Barometer Survey conducted by the Institute for Justice and Reconciliation released a report in November showing that the citizenry was anything but apolitical. Over 50% of respondents acknowledged that they were actively engaged in local politics and community-based issues, while 71% noted that relying on each other was more significant than relying on political elites.

The survey results suggested that ordinary South Africans were actively involved in politics and well aware of the critical issues underpinning the governance of the country based on their everyday struggles. Although the Barometer Survey confirmed that the level of distrust in the governing elite was still high, it also reaffirmed the stark reality that the citizenry should not be seen as complacent, unsophisticated, or out of touch in their assessment of the country's governance deficit and lack of socioeconomic service delivery.

Commentators immediately suggested that Ramaphosa's 2020 SONA was thin on substance, with one newspaper describing the content as 'empty promises, impossible dreams'. It seemed that it would be left to the finance minister to provide the detail on the implementing of plans that the president outlined in the SONA.

In March, the first case of the coronavirus was confirmed in the country. It was just a matter of time before South Africa also became part of the global pandemic. For two weeks, government monitored the situation, using the period to define and formulate an intervention strategy. As infection rates rose, on March 23 President Ramaphosa addressed the nation in what was to become known as a regular 'family meeting' where he announced a 21-day hard lockdown. This was the beginning of an ongoing cycle of shifts between different levels of lockdown measures, ranging from level 5 (the most stringent set of regulations) to level 1 (a more flexible set of interventions).

The first wave of Covid-19 infection took place between May and July. During this period, the government instituted the National Command Council on Covid-19 as an inter-ministerial body that would take decisions relating to the management of the pandemic through the various lockdown levels. This was in alignment with the government's adopting the Disaster Management Act, which characterised the response to the epidemic as a national emergency. In preparing for the level 5 lockdown and addressing the security cluster, including the deployment of the national army in managing the stringent regulations, Ramaphosa referred to the pandemic as a 'war against an invisible enemy'.

President Ramaphosa and his government were applauded for their decisive action, which saw only essential services and workers being allowed to continue with their daily operations, while long curfew hours were put in place and strict bans were placed on sale of alcohol and cigarettes. For the services industry, the lockdown was a heavy blow, and it impacted negatively on small business and informal township entrepreneurs.

The government argued that the level 5 lockdown was necessary to flatten the curve and allow for emergency services like the medical health sector to be prepared as infection and transmission rates increased.

Initially, all political parties welcomed the restrictions following broad consultation by President Ramaphosa relating to the decision. But as the uncertainty of the pandemic loomed and the debate of lives versus livelihoods became more significant regarding the socioeconomic situation of ordinary citizens, the question at hand was whether South Africa could afford to keep the economy insulated while containing the virus. The official opposition, the Democratic Alliance, was quick to point out that the ANC-led government had lost touch with realities in the country and was fuelling an already fragile state of socioeconomic affairs.

The Ramaphosa government, however, recognised the debilitating effect that the pandemic had on an ailing socioeconomic landscape and the precarious situation that faced many households. With this in mind, the government introduced a 500 bn rand (ZAR) relief package to assist vulnerable sections of the population with the socioeconomic costs of a faltering economy.

Unfortunately the scourge of corruption and financial irregularities and tender fraud in relation to government contracts for personal protective equipment (PPE) reared its ugly head. For instance, payments through the temporary employment relief programme were frozen when it was discovered that the scheme was being defrauded by unscrupulous business owners who were not giving the money to their employees. Then there were the PPE corruption scandals, ranging from price collusion between retailers on masks and sanitisers to large-scale contracts that deviated from tender processes and were awarded to individuals with close links to the ruling party.

Some senior members in national and provincial government, others in the ANC, and the partner of the president's spokesperson Khusela Diko were implicated in the looting of government tenders. This led to the Special Investigating Unit (SIU) assessing ZAR 2.2 bn in contracts linked to irregular tenders associated with PPE, while another ZAR 30 m in alleged irregular contracts awarded at the provincial level were also being investigated. Despite households struggling to feed themselves, some ANC cadres were accused of using the distribution of food parcels as the basis for buying votes.

It became unconscionable that at a time of an unprecedented crisis, selfish material interests were put ahead of the poor, vulnerable, and marginalised. In addition, the scorecard on government achieving its implementation goals on the rescue package was viewed with mixed reactions. Bureaucratic inertia and institutional bottlenecks made the distribution of grants and relief much harder. In turn, the Institute for Economic Justice declared that 'government needs to radically reduce onerous requirements, cumbersome processes, and stringent eligibility criteria'.

At the time of the second wave at the beginning of December, the easing of lockdown measures did little to mitigate the risks in social behaviour, while the economy faced further debilitation. If anything, as less-stringent lockdown regulations took effect, the idea of a new economic normal gave way to business as usual. The toll of the first wave saw people wanting to enjoy their civil liberties, while for the many employed in low-paid industries, the necessity of keeping a job and earning a living became more difficult to sustain.

The second wave also saw a new variant of the virus emerging called NY501Y, which exacerbated the situation in the country. The new variant was also detected in other countries, leading to travel bans being instituted against South Africans. This even led to Emirates airline grounding all inbound and outbound fights. In all of this, the South African authorities were struggling to contain the pandemic. As the situation become more acute, the festive holiday season saw another adjusted level 3 lockdown with mask-wearing made mandatory. By the end of 2020, the country had recorded 1,057,161 cases with the fatality rate standing at just under 30,000. The peak was to come in January 2021.

As much as the pandemic dominated much of the political, economic, and social landscape of the country throughout the year, with limited political activities registered, the domestic affairs of the country shifted into a hybrid level of engagement. Working online and using platforms like Zoom allowed for policy work to continue.

It was an eventful year as well for the Democratic Alliance (DA). The party hosted its much anticipated policy conference and national elective congress. The DA also grappled with its internal transformation agenda and spent most of the year trying to rebuild itself following its weakened performance in the 2019 national and provincial elections. The elective conference presented serious questions regarding the party's retention of black leaders and the perception that it was catering for the needs of minority interests only. As much as the party tried to steer away from race as overarching identity in South Africa's political landscape, it could not ignore the polarising narrative of racial politics in its own deliberations. This saw senior black members like Herman Mashaba and John Moodey, as well as other African members, leave the party, citing irreconcilable racial differences.

The question of race also became evident in the leadership contestation of the party. In the build-up to the leadership challenge, questions emerged on whether the party was ready for a young black woman, Mbali Ntuli, to lead it. Speculation was rife that the old white guard were orchestrating issues behind the scenes to ensure that the party's new young guard compromising mainly aspiring white individuals would succeed. Accusations were levelled against party executives of shutting down spaces to prevent Ntuli from actively lobbying with various constituencies in the leadership race. Consequently, John Steenhuizen, the party's chief whip in parliament, was elected the new leader of the DA, with Helen Zille re-elected as chair of the Federal Council. Some commentators pointed out that having a mix of an old and a young white guard in the executive structures of the party implied that the party was leaning more to the right of the ideological political spectrum when it came to race and transformation.

For other political parties, the impact of the Covid-19 virus meant refocusing their presence online. In the wake of the pandemic, the EFF was able to harness its populist footprint through its social media outreach. The party's presence on social media morphed into a significant online presence, including key policy desks on labour, GBV, and structural racism. While the party deepened its social media populism, it was unable to win a single ward during by-elections.

Other smaller political parties were hardest hit by the pandemic because they did not have sufficient resources (monetary or otherwise) to maintain a sustained online presence. Meanwhile, the political landscape also recorded a new political formation led by Herman Mashaba, called ActionSA. This was an anticipated move following his decision to quit the DA. But as soon as the political organisation was announced, it ran into difficulties with the Independent Electoral Commission (IEC). The IEC refused to register the party due to the organisation's flag and logo having close similarities to those of another political party and the South African flag. Initially vowing to challenge the IEC decision, Mashaba ultimately accepted the outcome. ActionSA was eventually registered in December.

The country's electoral laws attracted headlines with a landmark decision by the constitutional court. The question of whether independent candidates can contest national and provincial elections was brought by the New Nation Movement (NNM), a non-partisan organisation formed in 2017. The issue was first heard in the Western Cape High Court, a month before the 2019 elections could be held. In their court application, the NNM together with two other applicants had contended that their rights were infringed because they could not stand for public office given that the Electoral Act did not allow for independent candidates to participate in national and provincial elections. They argued that a mixed electoral system would be preferred, as it was more flexible in enabling both individuals from political parties and independent candidates to stand for elections.

In delivering his judgment, the Western Cape High Court judge noted that the issue was *sub judice*, as parliament was deliberating on a report addressing the reform of the electoral system. Therefore, it would be difficult and not justifiable for the court to reach a decision on the matter.

An appeal to the constitutional court took a different trajectory to the position of the Western Cape High Court judge. The constitutional court declared that the Electoral Act was unconstitutional 'to the extent that it requires adult South African citizens to be elected to the national assembly or provincial legislatures only through their membership of a political party'. The court gave parliament two years to go through the necessary processes to address and revise the act for the 2024 national and provincial elections. Meanwhile, the constitutional court remained active in critical cases that impacted on the democratic integrity of the country's institutions. The court had to deal with legal challenges from industry actors like the tobacco sector, academics, and postgraduate students, as well as the official opposition and other stakeholders, disputing the constitutionality of the lockdown measures.

In other matters, the court had to deal with an application by the Zondo Commission of Inquiry regarding former president Jacob Zuma absconding from a hearing before which he had been summoned to appear. Tensions between the commission chair and the beleaguered former president had been fermenting prior to this flagrant violation of the summons and rules of the commission, as Zuma had questioned the integrity and credibility of Deputy Chief Justice Zondo.

Zuma's legal team alleged a conflict of interest in Zondo overseeing the proceedings due to the latter having a familial connection to the sister of one of Zuma's wives. This led to a war of words between the two individuals in which Zondo refuted the claims, noting that while a relationship did exist with an extended member of Zuma's family, this did not have any bearing on his impartiality in hearing Zuma's evidence since the relationship had ceased to exist many years prior. This, however, did not deter Zuma and his legal team from pursuing the matter even further by alleging that Zuma would not be given a fair hearing at the commission. Zuma and his legal team noted that their issue was with Zondo and not the commission itself.

The showdown intensified when Zuma, appearing before the commission in November, left the proceedings without the permission of the chair. In response, Zondo instructed that criminal charges be instituted against Zuma since this constituted an offence in terms of the Commissions Act of 1947. Zondo also noted that the offence would be communicated to the National Prosecuting Authority, and he went to the extent of issuing a new set of summons against Zuma and asking the constitutional court to issue an order that would force the former president to appear before the commission.

The public protector's legal woes continued in 2020, which also constituted an active year for the judiciary. There were eight legal challenges that saw the courts either overturn or set aside advocate Busisiwe Mkhwebane's reports and recommendations. These ranged from investigations not properly undertaken and failing in her duties to execute the mandate of her office, to allegations that her conduct in certain cases, like that on the South African Revenue Service (SARS) rogue unit, was 'egregious' and sometimes akin to bias. The most important of these was her investigation into President Cyril Ramaphosa's campaign funding relating to his bid to become president of the ANC in 2017, known as the CR17 funding campaign. The public protector had issued a report citing that the president was obliged to disclose records of the donations made to his campaign. In the report, she argued that as much as it was an internal party issue, it did have serious implications for the state given the relationship between the party and the state. The Pretoria High Court 'disagreed with her findings and set aside all other findings and remedial actions contained in the report'. The decision was taken on appeal by the public protector, and in December the constitutional court reserved judgment in the matter.

In August, dynamics in the ANC reached a tipping point when President Ramaphosa noted in an explosive revelation in his weekly letter that the 'ANC stands as accused No. 1' when it came to corruption. Analysts declared this revelation an unprecedented move by the president to expose and disclose the intensity of disunity in the organisation. Perhaps the most telling insight that emerged from the letter was how President Ramaphosa was using the corruption issue as a driver to get implicated persons like secretary-general (SG) Ace Magushule, factions aligned to him, and the RET to step aside. By appealing to a sense of morality and ethics, the president went further to highlight that 'corruption was robbing the most vulnerable of citizens' and warned 'those using the party as a steppingstone to power to leave the ANC'. Some understood this as Ramaphosa reinforcing his position as president of the party and also letting opponents know that he would not be a one-term president. This was compounded when the president wielded his influence by making sure that decisions from the NEC's meetings were communicated by him in media briefings. This again pointed to the president being unsure of whether the SG would provide an accurate reflection of the discussions and decisions. It became a telling point in the situation that had gripped the party and the levels of distrust across the factional battle lines in the organisation.

As the year drew to a close, the government's handling of Covid-19 vaccine procurement began to raise questions about whether the state had dropped ball in not being part of clinical trials so that it could take advantage when a vaccine became available. The DA continuously raised questions as to why South Africa seemed slow out of blocks when it came to the procurement process and securing purchase of the vaccine. Criticisms were levelled that the procurement strategy was riddled with bureaucratic weaknesses and that the government had no coherent plan. Government defended itself by saying that it was in negotiations with pharmaceutical companies and relevant stakeholders, and that such deliberations take time. But none of this seemed to appease opposition parties and civil society actors.

Things spiralled out of control when the chief justice of the constitutional court Mogoeng Mogoeng made inflammatory remarks questioning whether the vaccine would be an appropriate intervention to mitigate the spread of the virus. Speaking at a religious event, the chief justice noted that 'if there is any vaccine that is being manufactured or advances a satanic agenda of the mark of the beast, 666; if there is any vaccine, anything manufactured for the purpose of corrupting the DNA of people, then that vaccine must be burned, it must die [sic]'. He defended his position along the lines of freedom of religion, speech, and thought but also noted that he was not an 'anti-vaxxer'. The issue remained contentious, as some commentators felt that by implication because of the position he occupied, the chief justice needed to be impartial and not let his personal views influence the debates regarding vaccine hesitancy.

By the end of the year, questions were also raised about the inflated costs of the Zondo Commission of Inquiry into State Capture. With the price tag of nearly ZAR 800 m and escalating, some witnesses appeared to give trivial responses on issues raised regarding their implication in state graft, at times not complying with the mandate of the commission. But nevertheless, it was an eventful year for the commission as some high-profile officials appeared before it. Pravin Gordhan was one of the senior members of cabinet reprimanded by the chair for not making himself available to the commission. When he ultimately appeared, it was to be cross-examined by the former SARS commissioner Tom Monyane regarding his claims that Monyane was pursuing a state capture agenda that the commission should investigate. The cross-examination became a showdown between Monyane's lawyer, Adv Dali Mpofu, and Gordhan, given their hostile relationship.

Others included the former board chair of South African Airways Dudu Myeni, former minister of water affairs and member of the ANC NEC Nomvula Mokoyane, members of parliament Vincent Smith (who subsequently resigned) and Cedrick Frolick, and former senior executives from Eskom. The biggest scalp was Angelo Agrizzi, former senior executive of Bosasa. According to Agrizzi, the company, now known as African Global Operations, paid kickbacks to Smith and Mokoyane in return for their 'influence in the company's state business'. Eventually, Smith was charged and arraigned on corruption charges. What was perhaps most disturbing was when the identity of a whistle-blower was revealed during the appearance of Myeni. It was unprecedented, and the commission chair had to intervene and remind Myeni that her admission, whether by accident or deliberate, had serious consequences. This exposed some of the criticisms that the commission faced regarding the protection of whistle-blowers and why those who had vital information were afraid to come forward and assist the commission. The deliberations at the commission revealed a deeply complex web of money laundering using corporate entities, state-tendered projects, and bank accounts, among other instruments, to siphon money out of the country. The domestic affairs further exposed the faultlines of the country's fragile democracy.

Foreign Affairs

When it came to the country's international affairs, the state seemed to fair a little better, despite having to navigate, at times, an intractable global landscape. The Ramaphosa presidency was entering the second year of its third term as a non-permanent member of the UNSC. This was accompanied by South Africa assuming the chair of the AU and of the Indian Ocean Rim Association and joining the Troika of the SADC's Organ for Politics, Defence and Security in August 2020.

The country's presence in these global, continental, and regional institutions boosted its international presence in terms of aligning and strengthening the partnership between the UNSC and the AU Peace and Security Council relating to 'financing peace operations, and advancing debates on thematic issues including security sector reform and the women, peace and security agenda'. Key to South Africa's positioning on the UNSC was the reform of the Council itself based on the need to significantly transform the multilateral agenda on global governance.

South Africa stuck to its overall mandate based on the constitutional values defining its global affairs and, more importantly, in line with its membership of and 'entrenched … promotion of multilateralism through the various multilateral organisations in which it plays an active part, including the African Union, G20, BRICS, India-Brazil-South Africa Dialogue Forum (IBSA) and the UN' (according to the Heinrich Böll Foundation).

The Department of International Relations and Cooperation (DIRCO) had noted that engagements on the UNSC had become increasingly politicised in the year under review. Despite these difficulties, South Africa managed to galvanise its position through closer cooperation on Africa's objective of 'Silencing the Guns'. The minister of DIRCO, Naledi Pandor, had reflected on the country's performance on the council as 'partly successful and somewhat challenging'. In reviewing South Africa's overall engagements during its two-year tenure (2019–20), Pandor noted that the impact of Covid-19 compounded the reorientation of some of South Africa's priorities towards pursuing a safer world.

The linkages between South Africa's non-permanent UNSC term and its chairing of the AU during 2020 were to deepen collaboration for 'the peaceful settlements of conflict through preventative diplomacy, inclusive dialogue and post conflict reconstruction'. The minister noted that challenges faced by Africa in relation to peace and security interventions had to do with financing instruments. To this end, it was evident that the continent needed to strengthen the mobilisation of its finance mechanisms.

Nevertheless, critics immediately pointed out that as much as South Africa tried to play a bridging role between the continent and the UNSC, as well as in the maintenance of international peace and security, the country grappled with its identity as an African actor. One issue that remained a constant blight for the government was that there was little representation of South African personnel in the AU Peace and Security Council. This pointed to the fact that it may not be enough for South Africa just to call for closer engagement between the UNSC and the AU: clarity is needed regarding how cooperation between the two institutions would be structured.

With regard to its chairing of the AU, the Ramaphosa presidency had to address the impact of the Covid-19 pandemic on the continent's fragile public health architecture. A key consideration was to facilitate a coherent response to the pandemic. In addition, South Africa had to consider the corresponding impacts that the pandemic had on the fiscal durability of African countries. With this in mind, according to DIRCO minister Pandor, 'the Bureau of the AU Heads of State and Government appointed Special Envoys to support the continent in the mobilisation of debt relief measures and securing recovery resources, financial resources, maintaining economic activities and reviving African economies'. In particular, Ramaphosa used South Africa's membership of the G20 to ask for more debt relief and economic aid measures to be afforded to the continent. The overarching measure was the Debt Service Suspension Initiative (DSSI) to assist medium to high debt-distressed countries in sub-Saharan African. There were various instruments linked to the DSSI, such as the sovereign debt restructuring framework. But critics suggested that the financial fallout from the pandemic would create a burden on Africa's prospects of economic sustainability, especially considering that, as noted in British newspaper the 'Financial Times', 'the DSSI lays the burden of repayment on official bilateral creditors ... [and] success will depend on whether there is appropriate burden sharing by private lenders'.

In keeping with its AU theme, 'Silencing the Guns: Creating Conducive Conditions for Africa's Development', South Africa engaged with the *Trilateral Negotiations on the Grand Ethiopian Renaissance Dam (GERD)*. Tensions between Egypt, Ethiopia, and Sudan soared over the construction of the dam and the impact this would have on access to the Nile river. South Africa mediated the negotiations in trying to find an amicable solution and possible negotiated settlement to the conflict. As much as South Africa saw this as part of aligning its positioning between the UNSC and the AU, an Egyptian newspaper was scathing about South Africa's role in brokering a resolution of the tensions, citing that the Ramaphosa presidency lacked a coherent plan, seemed to be meagre in its efficacy, and at times was seen as favouring the Ethiopian side by allowing Ethiopia to renege on its promises.

Perhaps the biggest success for South Africa was its handling of the pandemic and engaging with the WHO to ensure that Africa was not left behind in the procurement of a vaccine. This saw the establishment of the Covid-19 African Vaccine Acquisition Task Team (AVATT) in support of the Africa Vaccine Strategy. The strategy would also assist Africa in its call for vaccines to be identified as a global public good, especially in addressing possible resistance from the richer countries.

The COVAX (Covid-19 Vaccines Global Access) Facility, a WHO and Gavi Vaccine Alliance initiative to help low- and middle-income countries secure access to vaccines on a fair and equitable basis, secured 600 m doses of the vaccine for distribution in the continent. But the more pressing concern was the increasing shift towards vaccine nationalism and hoarding by some developed countries. President Ramaphosa noted that this was a worrying sign that Africa would be left at the back of the queue once again. Civil society groups like the Social Justice Initiative for Public Health played a crucial role in their advocacy for more equitable distribution of the vaccine. This extended to civil society supporting South Africa's joint proposal with India for a temporary waiver of the intellectual property rights on access to the Covid-19 vaccine. The proposal seemed to enjoy support from many countries, especially developing countries. The proposal was seen as way to also advocate for access to health to be seen as a global public good.

Closer to home, South Africa had to contend with the security crisis emerging out of the northern part of Mozambique. The insurgency in the Cabo Delgado region represented a regional security threat. The crisis not only led to a human security dilemma for South Africa and SADC, but also saw the emergence of climate refugees as a significant outcome from the conflict. Addressing parliament, the DIRCO minister noted that the South African government pledged to assist Mozambique in its intervention against the insurgency. This, she argued, would be based on what assistance the Mozambican government needed. But South Africa also had to deal with a backlash from the insurgents, who warned South Africa not to get involved. At the regional level, South Africa's role in the Troika of the Organ for Politics, Defence and Security seemed to be a more protracted approach to engaging with the Mozambican head of state. The Mozambican president did not attend the SADC summit on the crisis in November and did not provide a roadmap on how the situation would be addressed. In fact, it was reported that the only communication from the Frelimo government was a list of military equipment that it needed. The inability of the Troika specifically and SADC in general to actually engage with Mozambique was seen as the regional body once again not having sufficient influence over member states, leaving it with a muted strategic response to the situation. At times, the Mozambican president made it clear that the conflict was a sovereign issue that did not require intervention from the regional body. As the situation worsened, advocacy groups lobbied the South African government to adopt a stronger stance and prevail on its counterparts in the Troika and SADC to intervene pragmatically rather than only symbolically.

In November, the country faced an embarrassing situation when the Bushiris, a Malawian pastor and his wife, skipped the country, violating their bail conditions, and fled to Malawi. The well-known couple were charged with fraud and money laundering. The Bushiris were known for claiming to have cured HIV/AIDS with miracle oil, and for restoring sight to a blind person. It was coincidental that the Bushiris fled the country during a state visit of the Malawian president to the country. Speculation was rife that the couple had stowed away on the presidential jet. There were fears that this would lead to a diplomatic spat between the countries. Both sides denied the allegation, and the South African authorities were in the process of preparing the extradition documentation. The Bushiris claimed that their lives were in danger in South Africa after having received death threats. Questions were raised about how the infamous couple were able to dupe authorities in terms of security protocols. One national newspaper ridiculously claimed that the couple had altered their physical features. The case was still pending at year's end.

The Bushiri saga followed on the back of another diplomatic incident involving businesswoman Bridgette Motsepe Radebe, the wife of ANC stalwart Jeff Radebe, sister of mining magnate Practice Motsepe, and sister-in-law of Cyril Ramaphosa.

The government of Botswana accused Radebe and former president Ian Khama, together with an intelligence officer, Wilhelmina Maswabi, of stealing $ 10 bn from Botswana. According to the charges, Radebe was a co-signatory to two bank accounts holding more than $ 10 bn which had allegedly been stolen from the Botswana authorities to finance terrorism. Radebe had denied all allegations and in August, a South African online media platform reported that she and Khama had been cleared of any wrong-doing. But investigations are still pending because Radebe had hired a global law firm to investigate the matter, which had exonerated her. The matter became more complex when the former public protector Thuli Madonsela was also implicated in the allegations of having dubious links and participating in unlawful transactions. At the press briefing reporting that Radebe, Khama, and Madonsela had been cleared of wrong-doing, Radebe indicated that a defamation case was being considered against the government of Botswana.

Nevertheless, the Botswana government employed the services of AfriForum, a legal organisation based in South Africa, to seek more documentation from the South African government regarding the matter. The issue had now evolved into a political dispute between the two sides, with South African justice department being accused of delay tactics and not acceding to requests. It was also alleged that South Africa had tried to resolve the matter by meeting with officials in Gaborone. Some observers have noted that the situation remains sensitive between the neighbouring countries.

The appointment of Wamkele Mene as the secretary-general of the AfCFTA Secretariat, hosted in Ghana, was a strategic victory for South Africa. There was intense competition between the South African and Nigerian candidates for the position. In the end, Mene, who was South Africa's chief negotiator in the AfCFTA negotiations, prevailed. He assumed his new position in April.

Socioeconomic Developments

The year began with South Africa experiencing some of its worse structural economic constraints: economic growth was recorded at 0.2%, with agriculture being the main drag on economic growth, contracting by 1.4%; formal unemployment reached a historical high of 29%; youth unemployment was the biggest concern, estimated at 53.18%, with those younger than 25 experiencing a rate of 58%; major credit rating agencies like Fitch and Standard and Poor's downgraded South Africa's sovereign debt from 'stable' to 'negative' while the budget deficit widened to 4.5% due to revenue shortfalls; state wages and expenses constituted the highest spending proportion, at over 34% of consolidated expenditure in the 2019/20 budget; bailouts of distressed state-owned enterprises continued; and household debt constituted over 34% of GDP, meaning that more than one-third of families across the country relied on debt as part of their household income.

With the country entering its first coronavirus wave in March, the government had to reprioritise spending in the budget announced in February to assist vulnerable households and communities. Characterised as a bailout package, the measures included the following: the adoption of the Temporary Employer/Employee Relief Scheme (TERS), implemented under the Unemployment Insurance Fund (UIF); debt relief measures for small and medium-sized enterprises negatively affected by the pandemic; the rollout of 'social relief of distress' measures including additional monetary payments for child support beneficiaries; an unemployment grant for those not receiving any form of social assistance; and the disbursement of food parcels to vulnerable households.

As much as the social relief grants were a stop-gap measure to ease the plight of the destitute as well as of an overburdened state, the restrictive measures of the level 5 lockdown exposed the untenable circumstances that South Africa found itself in. First, government did not have the kind of cash injection required to roll out a stimulus package to underwrite the socioeconomic costs of the pandemic. Government found itself caught between a rock and hard place in its attempt to stimulate a flailing economy. Austerity remained an important feature of the government's economic policy, aimed at retaining the dynamics of the neoliberal architecture of a market-led approach and at appeasing international investors.

Second, the disconnect between the macro and the micro dimensions of the economy became overwhelmingly obvious. It was abundantly clear that cottage industries and small businesses operating in sectors like tourism were not able to absorb the costs of the pandemic. Unfortunately, this meant that those with a low skill base became casualties in the unemployment scourge.

Third, by the time the country moved to level 3 lockdown restrictions, the war on the invisible enemy had become a battle of lives versus livelihoods. Food insecurity was rife, with female-headed households the worst affected. This was as a result of businesses and industries collapsing, with formal and informal employment opportunities becoming scarcer.

By the time the second wave hit the country, the state was grappling with an alarming socioeconomic crisis wherein the economy contracted by 7.2%; 2.2 m jobs were shed in the second quarter of 2020; unemployment spiked to its highest levels, at over 32%, in the fourth quarter of 2020; revenue collection from taxes dipped well below expected returns; households were confronted with less disposable income; and poverty and inequality were increasing rapidly.

Gender-based violence intensified. Given the desperate situation the country faced, social development and community-based organisations noted that violence against women and children constituted another pandemic. While the government tried interventions like banning alcohol consumption through limited sales as part of its drive to allow the healthcare sector to have greater capacity to address Covid-19 infections, this did little to alleviate illegal bootlegging sales, which in turn contributed to domestic violence reaching chronic proportions. Trauma cases recorded at hospitals highlighted that acts of GBV had reached new levels of brutality.

In seeking to mitigate the situation, President Ramaphosa noted that there were three bills introduced in parliament that would 'fill the gaps that allow perpetrators of these crimes to evade justice and ... give full effect to the rights of our country's women and children'. The three bills were intended to amend the Criminal Law (Sexual Offences and Related Matters), the Criminal and Related Matters Act, and the Domestic Violence Act. In addition, the adoption of a public register of sex offenders was introduced. But civil society organisations raised concerns that GBV victims faced a worsening crisis of violence, particularly in their inability to access help under the lockdown. The police were criticised for a lack of capacity, and at times apathy, in following proper protocols and assisting victims. In some cases, victims were treated as perpetrators by the police and faced further victimisation rather than being given protection under the law. Criticisms were also levelled against the government for continuing to criminalise sex workers. Advocacy groups highlighted that sex workers needed to be afforded the same protections against abuse as anyone else by law enforcement. The LGBTI community expressed concerns that their rights were being infringed under the constitution and felt that government needed to do more in addressing their plight as a vulnerable group. Both groups also noted that they were excluded from the Covid-19 financial relief measures.

The country continued to grapple with xenophobic attacks, with foreign freight transport drivers being attacked. This led to the local transport workers' union demanding that non-South African drivers be removed from their positions. The stand-off saw local transport groups setting trucks alight and created a tense situation where foreigners feared for their lives. The situation of foreign economic migrants moving between South Africa and other countries in the region became more difficult when the country closed border posts during lockdown. This not only saw migrants stranded on either side of borders but also led to illegal crossing that heightened security issues. The lockdown measures were further exacerbated by the public works minister, Patricia de Lille, announcing the construction of wire fence at the Beitbridge border post with Zimbabwe. At a cost of ZAR 37 m, the fence drew fierce criticisms that South Africa was using the pandemic as a way to deal with illegal Zimbabweans entering the country. The construction of the fence was also caught in an irregular tender fraud scandal and remains a contested issue.

The refugee crisis that emerged in 2019 in the city of Cape Town continued, with asylum seekers claiming that their status in the country remained unresolved. In October, the group organised a protest outside the offices of the UNHCR. They argued that UNHCR should intervene and assist them in leaving the country. They also contended that their situation in the country remained tenuous, since the government had refused to acknowledge claims of xenophobia. The plight of refugees and asylum seekers received more attention when the African Court on Human and Peoples' Rights wrote to President Ramaphosa noting that the government needed to extend pandemic relief measures to such groups. Citing the fact that South Africa is a signatory to the UNHRC codes and protocols, the court emphasised that it was obligatory for the country to do so.

The government also had to consider how to deal with public sector wage negotiations relating to the three-year agreement on inflation-related salary increases for public servants. A stand-off developed over whether government would pay these increases. The government, for its part, noted that due to the unforeseen circumstances of the pandemic, it had to re-evaluate its spending. On the other hand, unions pointed out that the agreement needed to be honoured and reminded government that most public servants were at the coalface of the pandemic. Some unions even demanded risk pay for their members. The government did not relent on the issue, and increases were not paid. This was also in line with government's attempt to find ways to reduce its public sector wage bill. With the three-year agreement coming to an end in March 2021, commentators have warned of potential strikes in the coming year that would add to the socioeconomic woes of the country.

The higher education sector also faced some challenges. Students had to study online due to Covid-19 restrictions but did not have the financial resources to do so. The Department of Higher Education and Training was implored to identify vulnerable students and provide them with laptops and a stipend to cover internet costs. But this soon degenerated into accusations that only some students benefited from such support, and that the scheme was flawed by corruption. The demand was greater than what it was actually possible to deliver.

As the year drew to a close, the socioeconomic landscape was in a debilitated state. The country was placed in an adjusted level 3 lockdown, the volatility of the currency saw fuel price hikes, credit rating agencies pushed South African further into junk status, electricity tariffs increased, and middle-income households started to feel the pinch of the pandemic.

The year under review should not be considered exceptional because of the pandemic. If anything, the pandemic exacerbated existing weaknesses in the structural political, economic, and social conditions of the country. It deepened levels of apathy and distrust towards the ruling elite, and it raised bigger existential questions about whether state institutions were able to provide the necessary social services and protection to improve the lives of ordinary people. The conundrum that South Africa faced in the way its socioeconomic architecture was impacted by the Covid-19 crisis was that most of the challenges experienced by the poor and vulnerable were a result not of the pandemic but rather of the bureaucratic nature of the state and its lack of efficiency.

Zambia

Edalina Rodrigues Sanches

The Patriotic Front (PF) government, headed by President Edgar Lungu, faced a critical year, having to tackle the political and economic impacts of the Covid-19 pandemic. The calendar for the 2021 elections was readjusted so as to meet the constitutional mark of 12 August. Voter registration reached 83% of eligible voters. While voter registration excluded citizens in the diaspora, it extended the right to vote to detainees for the first time. Lungu's eligibility to run for the elections was a controversial issue. The Constitution of Zambia Amendment Bill No. 10 of 2019 failed to pass the second reading in parliament. A series of by-elections were held, resulting in further consolidation of the PF's power. Freedom of expression and assembly and political opposition activities were restricted. Zambia strengthened bilateral ties with Saudi Arabia, Japan, Malawi, and the UK. China remained one of the country's major trade partners and an investor in infrastructural projects. With the Covid-19 shock, the economy contracted by 4–5%, accelerating the debt crisis. Zambia became Africa's first country to default on its debt, in this case Eurobonds worth $ 42.5 m. The IMF held virtual meetings with the country and warned of the need to reduce external borrowing and sustain fiscal adjustment in order to improve macroeconomic performance.

Domestic Politics

Following global concerns over the spread of the *Covid-19 pandemic*, President Lungu announced pre-emptive measures even before the country registered cases. The actions included restrictions on foreign travel (13 March) and the closure of all education institutions (17 March). Further lockdown measures were introduced after the country reported its first two cases of Covid-19 in Lusaka on 18 March, namely the closure of bars, cinemas, casinos, and restaurants, the suspension of international flights (except to and from Kenneth Kaunda International Airport), and the mandatory wearing of masks in public places (from 17 April). Some of these measures were eased a few months later so that the economy could gradually be reopened. From 24 April, places of worship, saloons, barbershops, and some sports activities were allowed to operate subject to compliance with prevention measures. *Churches were divided* on the decision to open places of worship, with some – e.g. the Seventh Day Adventist Church, the Catholic Church, and the Anglicans – continuing their services online. From 21 May, various sectors as well as primary and secondary schools were allowed to reopen, and measures targeting the tourism sector were introduced in June, before the president announced the reopening of all international airports on 25 June. Hakainde Hichilema, the leader of the major opposition party, the United Party for National Development (UPND), commended some of the government measures and urged the nation to rise above partisan politics and work together to fight the pandemic. As of 31 December, the country had a total of 20,725 cases, including 18,660 recoveries, 368 deaths (131 Covid-19 deaths and 257 associated deaths), and 1,677 active cases.

Preparations for the *2021 general elections* were underway. In an interview on Radio Mano, home affairs minister Stephen Kampyongo stated: 'There will be no postponement of the 2021 general elections because of coronavirus simply because the date of our elections is a provision of the republican constitution'. The Electoral Commission of Zambia (ECZ) *realigned the calendar for the 2021 elections* so that elections could be held on 12 August, and moved the start date of voter registration from May to October 2020. Furthermore, it established a new voter registration process to reach 9 m people within 30 days, instead of the 60 days foreseen before the start of the pandemic. There was a landmark decision to extend *voter registration to people in lawful custody*, which represented 16,000 eligible voters. Stakeholders raised concerns about whether the voter registration target would be attainable in such a short period given the prevailing social distancing measures. The ECZ faced further criticism when it announced that *voter registration* would exclude people in the diaspora and decided to more than double the nomination fees for candidates. Various stakeholders, including the Zambia Centre for Inter-Party Dialogue (ZCID) and the UPND, opposed this increase, arguing that it would discourage aspiring candidates from standing. The ECZ responded by reducing nomination fees (in July).

Voter registration started on 9 November and closed on 12 December. The ECZ registered a total of 6,407,752 voters, including 11,359 people in lawful custody. Stakeholders asked the ECZ to extend the process so as to bring the final number closer to the 9 m target. The ECZ subsequently announced a new registration period from 17 to 20 December in all 116 districts across the country. *When voter registration came to an end* on 20 December, a provisional total number of 7,020,749 voters had been registered, representing a record 83% of the projected number of eligible voters.

President Lungu's candidacy for the *2021 general elections* continued to raise controversy. The Law Association of Zambia, constitutional lawyers, opposition parties, and prospective presidential candidates believed that Lungu was not eligible to stand for elections because he had already held office twice. This was in stark contrast with the 2018 constitutional court ruling which stated that Lungu's first presidential tenure – which followed the death of President Michael Sata and lasted one year – could not be considered a full term. President Lungu and several PF cadres considered the court's ruling legitimate.

President Lungu *urged women and youths to participate in the 2021 general elections as candidates* with the declaration: 'We need more women represented in decision-making positions. Zambia is a member of the SADC Protocol and we want to achieve this *50/50 women representation* in decision-making positions; hence all the leadership structures should take note and support women and youths who show interest in standing for these positions.' Hakainde Hichilema announced a *youth empowerment social contract* to ensure that youths take an active role in economic sectors such as mining, tourism, agriculture, and manufacturing through mining licences.

The *Movement for Multiparty Democracy* (MMD), the former ruling party (1991–2011), celebrated its 30th anniversary. The party president, Nevers Mumba, made a speech retracing the party's history and recent challenges and promising a revamped MMD for the 2021 elections. He defended the vision of leadership based on Christian values and cited the election of the Malawi Congress Party in Malawi's recent elections as a lesson for all Zambians. In the National Restoration Party (NAREP), Simataa Simataa was dismissed from the position of party secretary-general in February, a month after he was appointed. NAREP deputy national chairperson Ezra Ngulube claimed that Simataa had failed to reach short-term goals to prepare the party for 2021 elections.

Several by-elections were held but there were numerous complaints of electoral malpractice, as well as clashes between the supporters of the PF and the main opposition parties. Parliamentary by-elections in Chilubi and local government ward by-elections in Lukulu, Mitete, Gwembe, and Kalomo were held on 13 February. Prior to the Chilubi elections, the opposition UPND and National Democratic Congress (NDC) petitioned the high court to postpone elections to 20 February to allow for a level playing field for all political players. However, the election date was not changed and the PF won all seats. In preparation for the 17 September parliamentary by-elections in Lukashya and Mwansabombwe, several political parties joined together for a solidarity march for peaceful elections. The ruling PF once again won the contested seats. The secretary-general of the UPND, Stephen Katuka, criticised the large number of ward by-elections held in the country, accusing the PF of buying UPND councillors. He also spoke out against the cost of elections – money which could otherwise have been invested in education, health, water, and sanitation.

The *Constitution of Zambia Amendment Bill No. 10 of 2019* failed to survive the second reading in parliament on 29 October. The bill needed 111 votes to go through but obtained only 105 votes in favour. The controversial bill was severely criticised on many counts – for proposing to increase the powers of the executive, changing the electoral system and the rules for the nomination of the president, and opening up the possibility of coalition governments led by the candidate receiving the most votes. These and other changes were perceived as attempts by the PF and the incumbent president to further consolidate power.

According to the EIU Democracy Index 2020, *Zambia remained a hybrid regime* with an overall score of 4.86/10 and a regional rank of 15th. The country ranked particularly low in two categories: functioning of government (2.93/10) and political participation (3.89/10). The former captures the withdrawal of civil liberties, attacks on freedom of expression, and the failures of democratic accountability that occurred as a result of the pandemic in 2020. The latter reflects limits on political participation and citizens' engagement.

Opposition parties, regime critics, and activists continued to face intimidation and repression. In September, UPND secretary-general for politics Patrick Mucheleka was detained at Kasama's Milima Prison for undisclosed reasons. In December, four UPND cadres in Ikelenge District were arrested for inciting violence, and Heritage Party (HP) cadres were arrested for unlawful assembly. Transparency International Zambia (TI-Z) and other stakeholders raised concerns about the retraction of *citizens' rights of assembly and expression* and PF cadres' involvement in acts of media intimidation. The government closed Prime Television, a popular television station known for its critical coverage of the government. Media houses that hosted opposition political parties also met with violence from political cadres (e.g. journalists beaten and property destroyed).

The country ranked 117th out of 180 in the TI *Corruption Perceptions Index*, which measures perceived levels of public sector corruption according to experts and businesspeople. Zambia scored 33 on a 100-point scale, 0 being highly corrupt and 100 very clean. In 2019, the country had scored 34/100 and was ranked 113th out of 180. TI-Z noted that several government actors had undermined efforts to fight corruption in the country, and gave the following examples: the 'Minister of Information's comments that corruption was everywhere and should therefore not be a daily song; the arrest and prosecution of the Minister of Health; the scandal at the Ministry of Health involving the questionable award of a $ 17 m contract to Honey Bee Pharmacy; [and] the misuse of the Covid-19 funds'.

Foreign Affairs

Compared with previous years, there were fewer trips during the year due to the mobility restrictions imposed by the Covid-19 outbreak. The country tried to attract external support to tackle the multifaceted effects of the pandemic and also to continue to implement large infrastructural projects. Negotiations for such contacts were conducted mainly by President Lungu, minister of foreign affairs Joseph Malanji, and finance minister Bwalya Ng'andu.

On 30 April, the US, the UK, the AfDB, and the World Bank agreed to provide *financial support to the country to support the fight against the Covid-19 pandemic*. In a statement to the media, Bwalya Ng'andu expressed gratitude for the financial support from the four cooperating partners. In June, Bwalya Ng'andu held a high-level virtual consultative meeting with the World Bank's vice-president for the Africa region, Hafez Ghanem, focusing on development cooperation, public debt, economic reforms, and social sector investments.

On 16 July, Joseph Malanji made an emergency trip to Kigali, *Rwanda*, to confer with President Paul Kagame following public allegations that President Lungu had funded insurgents to topple Kagame. After the meeting, they both stated that bilateral relationships had not been strained and would remain strong.

On 8 August, Malanji held a virtual meeting with UK minister for Africa James Duddridge. Malanji was accompanied by the Ministry of Foreign Affairs permanent secretary for international relations and cooperation, Ambassador Chalwe Lombe. During the meeting, Malanji emphasised the need to *enhance cooperation between Zambia and the* UK by making use of opportunities presented by the Global Britain agenda and the two countries' membership of the Commonwealth and the UN.

On 25–27 August, Zambia held its first ever 'Meet the Farmers' virtual summit, the aim of which was to give farmers an opportunity to exchange knowledge on good agricultural practices and technologies. The meeting attracted regional participation from Uganda, Tanzania, Zimbabwe, Namibia, and South Africa. Agriculture minister Michael Katambo said that the summit was vital, as it would not only increase understanding of modern agricultural practices and technologies to boost productivity but also promote women's participation in the sector.

President Lungu participated in the *UN summit on biodiversity* that was convened by the president of the UNGA on 30 September. Lungu's address urged nations to consider recalibrating their relationship with nature by rebuilding a more environmentally responsible world in the wake of the Covid-19 pandemic. He declared: 'In order to address this serious threat to biodiversity, my government has enacted policy and legislative frameworks to promote biodiversity conservation. Our national Vision 2030 and the 7th National Development Plan (7NDP) have integrated environmental issues. We place emphasis on sectors such as agriculture, forestry, wildlife, and wetlands.'

On 7 November, Joseph Malanji participated in the 8th Session of the *Regional Inter-Ministerial Committee of the International Conference on the Great Lakes Region* (ICGLR), aimed at reviewing the security and political situation in the region. On 20 November, Malanji attended a virtual 8th Ordinary Summit of Heads of State and Government of the ICGLR. On 5 and 6 December, President Lungu attended the AU Heads of State and Government virtual summit on AfCFTA and 'Silencing Guns in Africa'.

Representatives from several countries made visits to Zambia. On 18 February, the chairperson of the Federation Council of the Federal Assembly of the *Russian Federation*, Valentina Matviyenko, addressed the Zambian national assembly, saying that cooperation with Zambia was one of Russia's important priorities. Matviyenko added that Zambia enjoyed a long history of cooperation with the Russian Federation, and that the Soviet Union was the first country to recognise Zambia's independence.

In July, new agreements were signed with *Japan*. Finance minister Bwalya Ng'andu announced that Japan would provide a grant of 436 m kwacha (K) to upgrade two health centres in the Copperbelt (Mushili in Ndola and Chamboli in Kitwe). The project was expected to enhance healthcare provision and human development performance in the targeted locations and their surroundings. Ng'andu highlighted the relevance of this project and its alignment with goals of the 7NDP, as it seeks to provide 'equitable access to essential medical products, vaccines, and technologies of assured quality, safety, efficacy, and cost-effectiveness'.

Following the *Extraordinary China–Africa Summit on Solidarity against Covid-19* held in Beijing on 17 June, the Chinese president Xi Jinping had a telephone conversation with President Lungu, in which they explored avenues for further cooperation.

On 24 September, Malawian president Lazarus Chakwera visited Zambia. President Chakwera called for *enhanced bilateral relations* between the two countries. He also stated: 'I'm looking forward to working with you and the people of this nation despite the problems we face now. Of course we have Covid-19, but Zambia has always been our friend even when we have had disasters in our country. In our region we want economic prosperity, we want industrialisation, we want our livelihoods changed.'

On 1 October, the Ministry of Defence received *personal protective equipment* (PPE) and other infection control supplies worth K 1.5 m. At the request of the Ministry of Defence, the US government, through US Africa Command, secured

PPE and other supplies in support of the Zambian government's inter-ministerial measures to contain the pandemic.

On 8–9 October, UK minister for Africa James Duddridge visited Zambia to strengthen the broad bilateral relationship between the two countries. This was Duddridge's first visit to Zambia and provided an opportunity to *enhance trade links between the UK and Zambia*. Ahead of the meeting, Duddridge stated: 'Zambia has an important role to play in SADC and the southern Africa region and I will be discussing a range of important regional and international trade and security issues with members of the government and other key stakeholders'.

On 18 December, President Lungu received the minister of state for African affairs from *Saudi Arabia*, Ahmed Kattan, and took the opportunity to appeal for FDI from Saudi Arabia into Zambia. During the meeting, Ahmed Kattan invited Lungu to the 2021 Saudi – Africa summit and called for stronger relations between the two countries and the updating of agreements that had been signed on bilateral areas of cooperation within the framework of the Joint Permanent Commission of Cooperation.

The US government nominated David Young as the US deputy ambassador to Zambia. This followed the diplomatic incident which had led to the recall of the US ambassador, Daniel Foote, after his criticism of the Zambian government for the imprisonment of a gay couple. Lazarous Kapambwe was accepted as Zambia's ambassador to the US by President Trump, who stated. 'I welcome Ambassador Kapambwe as a member of the diplomatic corps in Washington and express our government's desire to advance our common agenda and to deepen the strong and abiding friendship between our countries'.

Socioeconomic Developments

Zambia experienced a challenging economic year in line with global trends and due to the impact of lockdown measures to contain the Covid-19 pandemic. The *economy contracted* by 4% to 5% and *government debt* (as a percentage of GDP) escalated to 120%, up from 91% in 2019 (IMF estimates). The country's $ 12 bn debt comprised $ 3.5 bn in Eurobonds, $ 3.5 bn in bilateral debt, $ 2.1 bn in multilateral debt, and $ 2.9 bn owed to other commercial lenders. *China holds a quarter of Zambia's foreign debt* (about $ 3 bn). A Bank of Zambia (BOZ) report stated that the country's fiscal performance in the first semester was 'unfavourable due to high spending on capital projects and external debt service payments, compounded by the *depreciation of the K*'.

Zambia Statistics Agency (ZSA) data charted a *rise in inflation levels* from 12.5% in January to 19.2% in December. Food inflation went from 15.4% to 20.2% and inflation of non-food items (household appliances) from 9.4% to 18.1% in the same period. The Jesuit Centre for Theological Reflection *Basic Needs and Nutrition Basket* stood above K 7,000 throughout the year, reaching K 7,060.80 in June, K 7,126.62 in November, and K 7,404.05 in December. The K 277.43 increase between November and December was attributed to increases in the prices of both food and non-food items. However, food items accounted for 95% of the cost increase.

According to the FAO, *cereal production reached an estimated 3.7 m tonnes*, underpinned by a substantial rise in maize production due to an expansion in the area planted and a recovery in yields. Despite Covid-19, the government continued to support farmers' access to agricultural inputs, primarily through the Fertilizer Input Subsidy Programme (FISP), and proposed removing domestic taxes on tractors to encourage the mechanisation of the agriculture sector.

Zambia *produced a recorded 882,061 tonnes of copper*, which represented a rise of 10.8% from the 796,430 tonnes produced in 2019. Nickel and manganese production increased by 128% and 79%, respectively, during the same period. However, gold and cobalt production fell by 8.5% and 21.8%, respectively, compared with 2019.

ZSA data revealed that Zambia had a trade surplus of K 48.3 bn and that copper was the major trade asset. As of December, Switzerland was the major export destination, accounting for 51.4% of the total export earnings. The other countries in the top five main export destinations (as a percentage of total export earnings) were: China (15.3%), Singapore (11.5%), DRC (8.9%), and Luxembourg (3.0%). These five countries collectively accounted for 90.1% of Zambia's total export earnings in December.

The partnership with China remained relevant for the advance of infrastructural projects. The government engaged China Geo-Engineering Corporation to upgrade the Chambeshi ring road in Mungwi District of Northern Province. ZESCO Limited and Power China signed three contracts worth $ 548 m to develop 600 MW grid-connected solar photovoltaic (PV) power plants to be located in the districts of Chibombo, Chirundu, and Siavonga. A contract worth more than $ 824 m was signed with a subsidiary of China Railway Construction Corporation to upgrade a rail line in southern Zambia over a period of eight years. The railway has a total length of 648.26 km. The country received medical supplies worth $ 38,000 from Huajian Group of China as a donation to help in the fight against Covid-19.

Throughout the year, the government tried to negotiate with multiple countries and entities to better address the debt crisis and the social and macroeconomic impact of the Covid-19 pandemic. From 22 June to 1 July, the IMF had virtual meetings with Zambia to discuss *Covid-19 emergency funding*. After the meeting, the IMF staff team leader, Dhaneshwar Ghura, said that the discussion would continue as the government needed to delineate short- and medium-term policies in the formulation of the revised 2020 budget to restore debt sustainability, revive growth, and reduce poverty.

In October, treasury secretary Fredson Yamba announced that the government had reached a *deal to defer debt repayments* that were due on a loan from the China Development Bank (CDB). In the same month, the *IMF named a new representative for Zambia*, two years after the post had been vacated. The appointment of Preya Sharma, a special assistant to the director of the lender's Africa department, comes after the Zambian government asked Alfredo Baldini to leave in 2018, a move that marked a tense period in Zambia's relations with the IMF.

In November, Zambia became Africa's first pandemic-era sovereign to default *after failing to pay a $ 42.5 m coupon on one of its Eurobonds*. Eurobond holders stated that any relief granted to the country could be used to service debt to Chinese lenders, and demanded more transparency and a credible economic recovery plan. Finance minister Bwalya Ng'andu assured them that the government was committed to an open and transparent dialogue with its creditors, and that the state had no alternative but to build arrears.

On 7 to 9 December, the director of the IMF's African department Abebe Aemro Selassie and Alex Segura-Ubiergo, mission chief for Zambia, visited and held high-level discussions with the Zambian authorities on an economic recovery plan and the request for an IMF-supported programme. Selassie said that the economic recovery plan 'sought to restore macroeconomic stability, attain fiscal and debt sustainability, restore growth, and safeguard social sector spending' and that 'given the deep-rooted challenges faced, policies would need to be calibrated to restore sustainability while protecting the vulnerable and creating more inclusive growth'. Selassie further stressed that 'We look forward to the presentation of the government's home-grown economic strategy, and will be assessing in the coming weeks how the IMF could support the authorities' reform efforts through a possible Fund programme'.

Zimbabwe

Amin Y. Kamete

The year was dominated by the Covid-19 pandemic and its political, social, and economic repercussions. There was turmoil in the main opposition grouping. Also notable were human rights violations and the arrest and prosecution of opposition figures. The Movement for Democratic Change Alliance (MDC-A) continued to consider the presidency of Emmerson Mnangagwa illegitimate. Efforts at re-engagement with the west suffered set-backs. While relations with Africa and other parts of the Global South remained good, there was little improvement in relations with the West or with multilateral institutions. Humanitarian and socioeconomic challenges were worsened by the pandemic. Whereas the opposition and critics blamed the country's problems on corruption, bad governance, and mismanagement, the government and its supporters consistently blamed them on the West's 'illegal' sanctions.

Domestic Politics

The year began quietly, with the main focus being on the *controversial proposed constitutional amendment* gazetted at the end of 2019. The most contentious part of the

Constitution of Zimbabwe Amendment (No. 2) Bill 2019 was the removal of the running mate clause for presidential candidates in favour of giving winners of presidential elections the power to appoint and sack their deputies. Another controversial proposal was the insertion of a clause that would allow presidents to appoint judges. While ZANU-PF championed the amendments, the opposition and civil society vigorously opposed them, arguing that they were meant to consolidate Mnangagwa's grip on power. Some notable criticisms of the amendments were made by the National Constitutional Assembly (NCA), whose leader Lovemore Madhuku was a member of Mnangagwa's Political Actors Dialogue (POLAD). The NCA accused the government of 'arrogance in pursuing unreasonable partisan amendments to the constitution'. Reports on 19 February claimed that Mnangagwa's POLAD partners had threatened to walk out on him if the government did not withdraw the divisive bill. Madhuku, the chairperson of POLAD's governance and legislative agenda subcommittee, said that his committee had recommended that the bill be withdrawn.

The *Covid-19 pandemic* dominated the news. The pandemic had a huge impact on the domestic political scene in terms of governance, freedom, and human rights. On 27 March, Mnangagwa declared a *21-day national lockdown* that began on 30 March. On 16 May, Mnangagwa extended the lockdown indefinitely and indicated that the restrictions would be reviewed fortnightly. Nelson Chamisa, the leader of the MDC-A, said that he supported the government's decision, as Zimbabwe was 'in circumstances of a catastrophe'. However, as the lockdown dragged on and was extended, critics accused the government of using the pandemic as an excuse for repression. The arrest of opposition figures and activists on charges of breaking Covid-19 regulations, coupled with the selective application of the enforcement of restrictions, appeared to vindicate these accusations.

Among those particularly *targeted were unionists, activists, and students*. On 23 June, eight Chinhoyi University of Technology students were arrested for protesting against the clamp-down on human rights activists and police brutality. Takudzwa Ngadziore, the president of the Zimbabwe National Students Union, spent some 40 days in jail during 2020. He was first arrested in February 2020 for organising a protest to free activist Makomborero Haruzivishe. In early September, Ngadziore was rearrested by armed police and charged with participating in a public gathering at Impala Car Rental's head office. The company was accused of having aided in the abduction of Tawanda Muchehiwa, another student activist (see below). Another student leader, Alan Moyo, was arrested on 7 December. He spent the rest of 2020 in jail.

The most notable act that the government was accused of perpetrating under cover of Covid-19 regulations was a supreme court hearing against Chamisa's leadership of the Movement for Democratic Change – Tsvangirai (MDC-T). As the MDC-T was the main partner in the MDC-A – a loose coalition of opposition parties that combined to contest the 2018 election – this case was in fact a challenge to the legitimacy of Chamisa's leadership of the MDC-A. On 31 March, the *supreme court ruled that Chamisa's leadership of the MDC-T was illegitimate*. The court ordered the party to hold an election to replace him within three months. That this was a ruling that was made at night during the lockdown when all 'non-essential services' had been suspended raised eyebrows. Chamisa's MDC-A rejected the ruling, claiming that it was an attempt by the government to usurp the party. Notably, Thokozani Khupe, who was to assume the role of acting president of the main opposition until the election, was a member of POLAD and was seen as being close to Mnangagwa. This was brandished as evidence of ZANU-PF's 'capture' of the judiciary. Suspicion was heightened when Morgan Komichi, the former MDC-A national chairperson, read a prepared statement endorsing the supreme court ruling shortly after it was made. Chamisa's supporters and government critics speculated that Komichi might have known about the ruling before it was delivered. Significantly, Komichi, who insisted he was now the national chairperson, declared, 'All suspensions and dismissals of any party member by the current leadership between February 2018 and today are null and void. The affected members are hereby fully reinstated.'

The controversial ruling precipitated developments that generated *accusations that ZANU-PF had captured the MDC-T* with a view to creating a compliant opposition that did its bidding. Some senior MDC-A figures abandoned Chamisa and joined Khupe's formation. On 1 April, Komichi and Douglas Mwonzora, the former secretary-general of the MDC-T, dumped Chamisa and called on all MDC-A members to support Khupe, the legally recognised leader of the party. The two assumed their former positions in the Khupe-led formation. Former MDC-T vice-president Elias Mudzuri also joined Khupe.

Allegations of capture by ZANU-PF intensified when the *MDC-T began recalling legislators who remained loyal to Chamisa*. As the secretary-general, Mwonzora was instrumental in the recalls. Despite the two formations (MDC-T and MDC-A) having contested the 2018 elections as separate parties, the MDC-T, using the supreme court judgment, claimed that all MDC-A legislators were now MDC-T legislators. On 6 May, four MDC-A legislators, all of them senior MDC-A figures, were recalled on the grounds that they had ceased to represent MDC-T interests. They were Prosper Mutseyami, the chief whip; Chalton Hwende, secretary-general; Thabitha Khumalo, national chairperson; and Senator Lilian Timveos, deputy treasurer. Critics interpreted this as a ZANU-PF plot to destroy the MDC-A. The recalled legislators went to court to have the recalls declared illegal. On 29 May, the high court ruled that the recalls were compliant with the alliance agreement. The court ruled that the agreement that created the MDC-A was valid only for five years. It stated that a group of people who come together under a common name do not become a legal persona, and hence it was improper for the MDC-A to appear before the courts. This effectively meant that the MDC-A was not a legal entity. On 23 June, the MDC-T recalled nine more legislators.

A significant development related to the recalls was *the suspension of by-elections*. On 2 October, Constantino Chiwenga, in his capacity as the health minister, announced an indefinite ban on all by-elections, citing Covid-19 as the reason. The Zimbabwe Electoral Commission (ZEC) had scheduled by-elections for 5 December to fill vacant parliamentary and local government seats. On 7 October, the ZEC confirmed the suspension. Independent commentators said that the suspension affected the independence of the ZEC. Government critics argued that this was a ploy to avoid an embarrassing defeat of the 'captured' MDC-T.

Chamisa's *MDC-A lost its national headquarters*. According to the MDC-A, on 4 June armed soldiers and police assisted the MDC-T in seizing Morgan Richard Tsvangirai House (Harvest House) by facilitating the eviction of MDC-A security guards. Despite the company which owns the building insisting that the MDC-A was the lawful occupant of the property, the MDC-T retained control of the building with the help of security forces who actively prevented the MDC-A from accessing it. Their actions included arresting MDC-A co-vice-presidents Tendai Biti and Lynette Karenyi-Kore on 5 June as they attempted to address a press conference at the building.

The MDC-T extraordinary congress which was supposed to happen within three months was postponed. On 22 July, the MDC-T announced that because of lockdown restrictions, Khupe had indefinitely postponed the congress scheduled for 31 July. The congress finally took place on 27 December. When it was eventually held, the *election of the MDC-T leader* was chaotic and riddled with violence and accusations of rigging. Khupe, who was reportedly assaulted, suspended the election. However, Mwonzora went on to be declared the winner and became the new MDC-T president. Khupe and other losing contestants, including Komichi and Mudzuri, did not concede. The MDC-T ended the year as a deeply divided formation.

The year also saw a *massive crackdown by government*, with civilians and activists reportedly being assaulted, abducted, and tortured. According to HRW, suspected state security agents abducted and tortured over 70 government critics during the year. The state security apparatus 'continued to commit arbitrary arrests, violent assaults, abductions, torture and other abuses against opposition politicians, dissidents and activists'. On 13 May, three MDC-A activists, *legislator Joana Mamombe, Cecilia Chimbiri, and Netsai Marova*, were arrested at a police roadblock in Harare for leading a protest over the government's response to the pandemic and hunger. On the same day, they were allegedly abducted from police custody. On 15 May, they were found abandoned in Bindura. They recounted that during their abduction they were sexually assaulted and tortured. They were hospitalised. No investigation was undertaken into their disappearance and allegations of torture and sexual assault. On 26 May, police charged them with gathering with intent to promote public violence and breach of peace. On 19 June, young activists *Namatai Kwekweza and Vongai Zimudzi* were arrested for protesting against proposed constitutional amendments. Kwekweza was arrested again on 15 July for 'participating in a gathering with intent to promote public violence, breaches of the peace or bigotry'. On 30 July, security agents in Bulawayo raided the home of Mduduzi Mathuthu, a journalist and editor of the online news site Zimlive. Zimlive was the first to expose Covid-19 corruption scandals (see below). When they could not find Mathuthu, the agents arrested his family members, including his nephew, *Tawanda Muchehiwa*. They allegedly tortured Muchehiwa, causing life-threatening injuries.

Another major development related to the arrest of an investigative journalist, *Hopewell Chin'ono*, and the leader of Transform Zimbabwe, *Jacob Ngarivhume*, in July. Chin'ono had been instrumental in exposing corruption scandals implicating people within Mnangagwa's inner circle. His revelations on corruption in the procurement of Covid-19 medical supplies valued at millions of dollars led to the *dismissal of the minister of health and child care, Obadiah Moyo*, and his arrest on corruption charges. He was replaced with Chiwenga, who also retained the vice-presidency. The revelations had been spearheaded by Zimlive.

In July, opposition and civil society groups announced that they would mount protests to force the government to act against rampant public sector corruption and initiate national dialogue to rescue Zimbabwe from crisis. Initiated by Ngarivhume, the idea of the protests was promptly embraced by the opposition, civil society, and independent critics. The government quickly declared the protests illegal and began a massive crackdown. On 20 July, Chin'ono and Ngarivhume were arrested. They spent over 40 days in custody before being granted bail in early September. On 31 July, invoking Covid-19 regulations, heavily armed soldiers and police quashed the protests. They arrested 13 people, among them novelist Tsitsi Dangarembga and MDC-A spokesperson Fadzayi Mahere. Police also sought to arrest *Job Sikhala*, the MDC-A deputy national chairperson, in connection with the protests. He went into hiding and was placed on the police wanted list. He was arrested on 21 August and was incarcerated until he was released on bail on 22 September.

In a move seen as clamping down on freedom of expression, on 15 May the *Cyber Security and Data Protection Bill* was published in the Government Gazette. The bill is intended to consolidate cyber-related offences and provide for data protection. It seeks to 'create a technology-driven business environment and encourage technological development and the lawful use of technology'. Parliament issued a notice announcing that public virtual and physical consultations on the bill would be held between 6 and 10 July. The bill received a lot of criticism. Some commentators contended that it was the government's attempt to protect itself from public criticism and pressure by criminalising dissent on social media platforms. In October, cabinet approved proposed amendments to the Criminal Law (Codification Reform) Act. Among the key provisions of the bill was the criminalisation of protest, cooperation 'with foreign governments', and allegations of abductions. The government said that the proposed law would be modelled on the US's Logan Act.

Though overshadowed by the turmoil in the opposition and the crackdown on dissent, the ZANU-PF *factional wars* persisted. On 4 August, Mnangagwa appointed

Chiwenga as minister of health and child care. The MDC-A criticised the appointment, claiming that Chiwenga was not the right person for the job during the pandemic. There was speculation that the appointment was a symptom of ZANU-PF factional wars. Fractures within ZANU-PF resurfaced on 4 July at a politburo meeting. Isaac Moyo, the director-general of the Central Intelligence Organisation, tabled a report claiming that two members of the committee had been storing posters and placards supporting the ouster of Mnangagwa and praising Chiwenga. Moyo claimed that they had plotted to use the planned 31 July protests as cover for the operation. He reported that the conspiracy was led by politburo member Claveria Chizema and former legislator Tendai Savanhu. There were speculations that the report was prepared at the instigation of Mnangagwa and was targeted at Chiwenga.

On 5 February, ZANU-PF announced that it had *suspended its secretary for youth affairs Pupurai Togarepi, his deputy Lewis Matutu, and the secretary for commissariat Godfrey Tsenengamu* from their party positions for indiscipline. They had addressed a press conference on 3 February, where they fingered top Mnangagwa allies for capturing state institutions and running cartels crippling the economy. A report in the newspaper 'The Standard' on 9 February linked the suspensions to ZANU-PF factional wars. It claimed that Mnangagwa's former advisor Christopher Mutsvangwa had revealed that 'the factional wars were triggered by the fight for control of the country's fuel industry'. While Matutu repented, Tsenengamu refused to back down and was finally expelled from the party on 4 March.

The *illness of Chiwenga* made headlines. In July, it was reported that he had been airlifted to China following the deterioration of his health. Speculation over his whereabouts started after he failed to attend high-profile events, among them two cabinet meetings, a politburo meeting, and a meeting between Mnangagwa and provincial affairs ministers at the state house on 6 July. On 14 July, George Charamba, the presidential spokesperson, confirmed that Chiwenga was in China but could not provide details. In December, it was reported that Chiwenga had gone to China to receive treatment for an undisclosed ailment. The significance of this trip was that it happened after *he had banned 'health tourism'*. On 7 September, he had announced that the government would no longer provide foreign currency to cabinet ministers and senior officials seeking medical treatment outside Zimbabwe.

The government's relationship with the church was strained. On 6 January, the Zimbabwe Council of Churches (ZCC) warned of an uprising if government ignored the social and economic challenges. ZCC secretary-general Reverend Kenneth Mtata warned that the likelihood of an uprising was high if the status quo was maintained. Government reacted angrily, declaring the church's transformational models an incitement to rebellion. On 7 January, the information permanent secretary tweeted that 'dialogue project [sic] is understandable in a democracy until it starts to border on incitement'. In a pastoral letter released on 14 August, the Zimbabwe Catholic Bishops' Conference (ZCBC) accused the government of human rights abuses and cracking down on dissent. The ZCBC said that the country was suffering from 'a multi-layered crisis', including economic collapse, deepening poverty, corruption, and human rights abuses. Reacting to the criticism, the government described the allegations as 'evil' and baseless. Monica Mutsvangwa, the information minister, criticised the ZCBC president, Archbishop Robert Ndlovu, describing the pastoral letter as an 'evil message' intended to incite a 'Rwanda-type genocide'. Her permanent secretary accused the ZCBC of joining groups seeking 'to manufacture crises'.

There were *changes made in the cabinet*. On 21 May, Mnangagwa fired information, publicity, and broadcasting services deputy minister Energy Mutodi. No official reasons were given for the sacking. However, it could be traced to his clashes with senior ZANU-PF colleagues. Mutodi had earlier clashed with Monica Mutsvangwa, claiming that she was abusing state-controlled media. Highlighting ZANU-PF factional wars, Mutodi claimed that his life was in danger. In a tweet, he had indicated that he was 'living in fear of the Chris Mutsvangwa–Moyo [the foreign minister] coalition'. Mutodi also claimed that the three MDC-A female activists who had gone missing and were later found brutalised (see above) had faked their abduction. On 14 August, Mnangagwa sacked Fortune Chasi as minister of energy and power development for alleged misconduct and replaced him with Soda Zhemu. According to the official statement, Chasi was dismissed because his conduct in government business had become incompatible with the president's expectations. On 29 July, Mnangagwa announced the death of agriculture minister Perrance Shiri, the first senior government official to succumb to Covid-19. On 14 August, Mnangagwa appointed Anxious Masuka as agriculture minister.

The Zimbabwe Anti-Corruption Commission (ZACC) continued its *fight against corruption*, but questions continued over its effectiveness and independence. The most high-profile arrest in 2020 was that of health minister Obadiah Moyo. On 19 June, Moyo was arrested over his alleged involvement in the unprocedural contract for medical supplies between the National Pharmaceutical Company of Zimbabwe (NatPharm) and Drax International. The Drax local representative, Delish Nguwaya, who was said to be close to Mnangagwa's family, had been arrested on 13 June and charged over the deal which was later cancelled on the orders of the finance ministry. The alleged corruption was exposed by Zimlive and Chin'ono (see above). Critics interpreted the arrest of Chin'ono and the manhunt for Mathuthu, Zimlive's editor, as persecution for the exposé.

Foreign Affairs

Zimbabwe maintained good relations with most *African and Asian countries* and organisations. Relations with OECD countries and multilateral lenders remained unchanged. Complaints over *'illegal' Western sanctions* by the government and its supporters escalated, as did the dismissal of the opposition and critics as Western puppets. Due to the pandemic, there was a decrease in state visits.

Zimbabwe remained active in the *SADC, the AU, and COMESA*. Unlike the opposition's continued refusal to recognise Mnangagwa's legitimacy, the rest of the world had moved on from the contested 2018 elections. In commemoration of the SADC *anti-sanctions day* in support of the removal of Western sanctions on Zimbabwe, the SADC chairperson, Mozambican president Filipe Nyusi, released a statement expressing solidarity with Zimbabwe, calling on 'all progressive forces to lend diplomatic, political and moral support to [Zimbabwe's] re-engagement efforts'.

Relations with South Africa remained friendly but faced some challenges. In August, *President Cyril Ramaphosa appointed two special envoys to visit Zimbabwe* to assess the political and economic crisis and how South Africa might help. The envoys were Sydney Mufamadi and Baleka Mbete. This came after persistent criticism of South Africa for neglecting the crisis, which had spiralled, with many activists and anti-government protesters being beaten, arrested, and allegedly abducted and tortured in a brutal crackdown. Mafumadi and Mbete arrived in Zimbabwe on 10 August. The visit generated controversy after the envoys were accused of snubbing the MDC-A: they were scheduled to meet MDC-A leaders but the meeting was inexplicably cancelled. The MDC-A accused ZANU-PF of persuading Mafumadi and Mbete to snub the opposition.

At the beginning of September, Ramaphosa announced that he would send *a high-powered African National Congress (ANC) delegation to Zimbabwe*. This was after the ANC's national executive committee (NEC) had resolved to send senior leaders to Harare. This was seen as an acknowledgement that the political and economic situation in Zimbabwe continued to be a threat to South Africa. According to ANC secretary-general Ace Magashule, the delegation would discuss 'challenges faced by South Africa and Zimbabwe, and discuss how it impacts the economic, political and social stability of both countries'. On 9 September, the ANC delegation arrived in Harare, led by Magashule. They met with senior ZANU-PF figures. According to Magashule, they had frank discussions about the political situation in Zimbabwe. The delegation returned to South Africa without holding talks with the opposition. Magashule later said that they would return to Zimbabwe within the following three weeks. This never happened.

There were *challenges in Zimbabwe–South Africa relations*. On 7 August, ZANU-PF reacted angrily to a television interview with Magashule in which he said that the ANC was engaging with ZANU-PF over human rights abuses and repression. Patrick Chinamasa, ZANU-PF's spokesperson, said that Magashule's 'utterances were completely out of order' and denied there was any crisis in Zimbabwe. On 12 September, Chinamasa warned the ANC not to treat Zimbabwe as one of its provinces. He said that the ANC did not have any oversight role in Zimbabwe's internal affairs.

ZIMBABWE

On 16 September, ZANU-PF's director of publicity and information, Tafadzwa Mugwadi, accused the ANC delegation of acting in bad faith and 'forcing' ZANU-PF to meet opposition and civil society groups. He accused South Africa of interfering in Zimbabwe's affairs. Mugwadi was speaking in reaction to a press statement by the ANC in which the party said it would return to Zimbabwe to engage other stakeholders.

Zimbabwe maintained good *relations with China*. In January, China's foreign minister Wang Yi met with Mnangagwa during his visit to Zimbabwe, despite Mnangagwa being on vacation at the time. After the meeting, Mnangagwa said that Zimbabwe–China relations were strengthening. The two countries had earlier differed after Zimbabwe said it had only received $ 3.6 m in aid from China in 2019. China reportedly demanded an explanation, claiming that Zimbabwe had understated the figure by $ 133 m. In June, Zimbabwe supported the Hong Kong national security law at the UN. On 18 April, presidents Xi Jinping and Mnangagwa exchanged congratulatory messages at the 40th anniversary of the establishment of Zimbabwe–China diplomatic relations. On 23 August, an article in 'The Standard' questioned Chinese company Anjin's return to diamond mining in Zimbabwe. The Chinese embassy reacted angrily, accusing the author of falsely claiming that the Chinese government was 'somehow involved in Anjin's business deals and conflicts in the country, which is a distortion and smearing of the Chinese foreign policy towards Zimbabwe'. The Zimbabwe Union of Journalists expressed concern over what it described as an 'undiplomatic and unusual personal attack'.

In April, the Chinese embassy pledged China's help to Zimbabwe *in the fight against the Covid-19 pandemic*. In May, China sent 12 medical experts, and it donated its first batch of medical supplies and equipment to Zimbabwe on 20 April. On 11 June, it donated a second batch of medical supplies. The consignment included 165,000 surgical masks and more than 25,000 pieces of personal protective equipment (PPE). On 21 July, China donated another consignment of medical supplies, including 30,000 testing kits, 220,000 surgical masks, and 40,000 medical gloves.

Relations with Russia continued to be good. On 24 October, Mnangagwa thanked Russia and China for standing by Zimbabwe in its call for the unconditional removal of Western sanctions. On 29 October, Zimbabwe and Russia said that they would intensify joint efforts to improve the legal framework of their relations. They said they were ready to sign several bilateral documents. A joint statement stated that the two countries had signed several MoUs, including on cooperation in platinum and diamond exploration and mining. In December, it was announced that the Zimbabwe–Russia joint venture Great Dyke Investments (GDI) would invest $ 650 m in its platinum project. Afreximbank was the lead financier. GDI is 50% owned by Russia's Vi Holding and 50% by Zimbabwe's Landela Mining Venture. It planned to start mining platinum in 2021.

There was little change in *relations with the EU*. On 17 February, the EU Council restated the EU's continued support for economic and political reforms in Zimbabwe and for formal political dialogue 'as a step towards a more constructive EU–Zimbabwe relationship'. In conclusions that angered Zimbabwe, the EU noted the ongoing 'acute humanitarian crisis in the country' and renewed its 'support for the people of Zimbabwe in various sectors'. Significantly, the council announced a renewal of its arms embargo and targeted asset freeze against Zimbabwe Defence Industries for a further year. This was prompted by the alleged role of the armed and security forces in human rights abuses. The EU suspended restrictive measures against four individuals, including former first lady Grace Mugabe.

On 20 May, a *joint local statement from Heads of Missions* was issued in Harare on the abduction of Mamombe, Chimbiri, and Marova. The signatories included the delegation of the EU, France, Germany, Greece, Italy, the Netherlands, Romania, Sweden, Norway, Switzerland, the UK, and the USA. The statement called for a 'thorough and credible investigation into the abduction and torture'.

There was little change in *relations with the UK*. On 2 September, a report by the Department for International Development (DFID) indicated that the UK's planned budget for Zimbabwe for 2019/20 was £ 86 m. On 20 December, UK ambassador Melanie Robinson accused Mnangagwa of reneging on his promises of political and economic reforms, made when he took over in November 2017. She called on him to implement the reforms. On 31 December, the *Zimbabwe (Sanctions) (EU Exit) Regulations 2019* came into force. Their aim is 'to ensure that certain sanctions measures relating to Zimbabwe continue to operate effectively'. These regulations replaced relevant EU legislation and related UK regulations.

Relations with the US did not improve. On 4 March, President Donald Trump extended sanctions against Zimbabwe by one year, stating that Zimbabwe's policies continued to pose an 'unusual and extraordinary' threat to US foreign policy. On 5 March, Zimbabwe said it was dismayed by the 'baffling' decision. On 11 March, the US 'designated' Anselem Sanyatwe, former commander of the Presidential Guard, and Owen Ncube, the national security minister, for their involvement in human rights abuses, including directing an attack on peaceful demonstrators and political opponents. On 1 June, the government summoned US ambassador Brian Nichols to discuss US national security advisor Robert O'Brien's comments describing Zimbabwe as a 'foreign adversary'. On 5 August, the US imposed financial sanctions on Mnangagwa's ally Kudakwashe Tagwirei and his company, Sakunda Holdings, for alleged corruption.

Relations with multilateral institutions hardly changed. On 9 January, the government announced that it had received $ 10.4 m from the AfDB for the Tax Accountability and Enhancement Project. On February 24, the executive board of the IMF concluded the Article IV consultation. The report noted that Zimbabwe had yet to define the modalities and financing to clear arrears to the World Bank and other multilateral institutions, and to undertake reforms that would facilitate the resolution of arrears with bilateral creditors. Zimbabwe owed $ 7.66 bn to various international financial institutions, including the World Bank, the European Investment Bank, the Paris Club, and the AfDB.

Socioeconomic Developments

Zimbabwe's economic and humanitarian challenges were worsened by the pandemic. *Economic indicators* did not improve. Reserve Bank of Zimbabwe (RBZ) figures showed that the annual CPI for all items was 1,579.1. The annual inflation rate was 557.6%. Monthly inflation reached a peak of 35.5% in July, with the lowest being 3.2% in November. Ministry of Finance estimates put real GDP growth at –4.1%, an improvement on the IMF estimates of –8.3% for 2019. Other figures from the ministry showed that nominal GDP was $ .07 bn; the current account balance excluding transfers was 67.6 bn Zimbabwean dollars (ZWL), compared with ZWL 10.2 bn in 2019. Total international reserves rose to ZWL 1 bn, up from ZWL 0.9 bn in 2019. As of 30 September, Zimbabwe's total public debt stood at ZWL 667.9 bn. The external debt was ZWL 667.9 bn, of which ZWL 516.3 bn was arrears.

Zimbabwe's *performance in several key world rankings* did not change much. The World Bank's Ease of Doing Business report ranked the country 140th out of 190 countries. There are no data for the year for the World Economic Forum's Global Competitiveness Report. In the 2020 Human Development Report, Zimbabwe had an index of 0.571 and was ranked 150th out of 189 countries. The index was up from 0.563, while the rank remained unchanged from the previous year.

The country faced several *humanitarian challenges*. The main drivers were the economic crisis, drought, floods, and the Covid-19 pandemic. According to UNICEF's Humanitarian Response Plan, the number of people in urgent need of humanitarian assistance and protection was seven million, among them 3.2 million children. The Vulnerability Assessment Committee (ZimVAC) estimated that 2.2 million urbanites were 'cereal food insecure'. About 95,000 children under five experienced acute malnutrition. The national global acute malnutrition (GAM) prevalence was 3.6%. Geographically, eight districts recorded a GAM prevalence of over 5%.

The humanitarian situation escalated with *the outbreak of the Covid-19 pandemic* in March. The imposition of the national lockdown brought economic activities to a halt. Particularly badly hit was the informal economy, which generates livelihoods for more than nine in ten of the working population. UNICEF reported that during the first half of 2020, Zimbabwe reported 3,092 cases of Covid-19 across the country. By December, the second wave hit, pushing the number of reported cases to 14,084. The number of deaths recorded rose from 53 in July to 369 in December. There was some suspicion that the government was under-reporting the numbers of both cases and deaths.

On *demographic indicators*, according to estimates, the death rate stood at 7.7 per 1,000 people. Average life expectancy was 61.36 years. The under-five mortality rate was estimated at 54.6 deaths per 1,000 live births. Owing to the pandemic and the closure of borders, the flow of Zimbabweans out of the country declined despite the economic crisis. There were no official estimates for net migration but Macrotrends put the figure at –6.5 per 1,000. The adult literacy rate remained high, at 88.69%.

The Zimbabwe Population-based HIV Impact Assessment (ZIMPHIA) survey put the prevalence of HIV among adults at 12.9%. This translates to about 1.23 m adults living with HIV. HIV prevalence was higher among women (15.3%) than men (10.2%). The number of deaths due to AIDS was estimated at 20,000. The proportion of adults and children living with HIV/AIDS receiving antiretroviral therapy was 86% and 71%, respectively.

Education and health delivery systems continued to experience challenges with staffing, equipment, and funding. The closure of schools as part of the national lockdown in response to the pandemic adversely affected access to education. Schools were closed between March and September. According to UNICEF, by the end of November, 448 pupils had been infected with Covid-19. None had a serious illness and there were no fatalities. Twenty-two teachers tested positive, with one recorded fatality. Both sectors were further compromised by *industrial action and threats of industrial action*, which remained a constant feature throughout the year. When schools opened on 14 January, teachers stayed home, saying that they were 'incapacitated' due to lack of money. On 22 January, doctors agreed to return to work after accepting a funding offer from businessman Strive Masiyiwa, ending a prolonged strike over pay and poor conditions that had paralysed the health sector. On 25 March, doctors and nurses in public hospitals went on strike demanding PPE so that they could safely treat suspected coronavirus patients. In April, doctors took government to court over its failure to provide PPE to frontline doctors. On 19 June, doctors and nurses went on strike demanding salaries in foreign currency. In July, nurses went on strike for the second time over poor wages and the lack of PPE, and in the same month, doctors in state hospitals issued a two-week strike notice demanding to have their salaries paid in US dollars and supplies of PPE. In October, teachers refused to return to schools over poor pay and sanitation.

In February, the Confederation of Zimbabwe Industries projected that the *manufacturing sector capacity utilisation* would drop to 27% if there was no drastic change in the policy environment. The decline was driven by the cost and shortage of raw materials, low local demand, and foreign-currency shortages. According to the RBZ Monthly Economic Review for the period ending September 2020, *total merchandise trade* for the first nine months of 2020 grew by 9.9% from $ 3,155.5 m in 2019 to $ 3,468.6 m in 2020. *Remittances* increased from $ 225.2 m to $ 287.3 Because of the strong export performance, the *trade balance* decreased from a deficit of $ 164.8 m in Q2 2020 to a deficit of $ 131 m in Q3 2020.

On 26 November, finance and economic development minister Mthuli Ncube presented the *2021 national budget* with the theme 'Building Resilience and Sustainable Economic Recovery'. Ncube proposed a ZWL 421 bn budget. Revenue collections for the year were estimated at ZWL 390.8 bn. The budget deficit was expected to be ZWL 30.8 bn, which translated to 1.3% of GDP. GDP growth in 2021 was projected to be 7.4 %, driven by electricity and water (18.8%); agriculture and forestry (11.3%); mining and quarrying (11%); construction (7.2%); finance and insurance (7.2%); transport and communication (7.1%); manufacturing (6.5%); government services (6.2%); and distribution, hotels, and restaurants (5.7%).

Printed in the United States
by Baker & Taylor Publisher Services